Deutschland

1949–1990
DEUTSCHE DEMOKRATISCHE REPUBLIK
BUNDESREPUBLIK DEUTSCHLAND

DÄNEMARK
Sylt
Nordfriesische Inseln
Flensburg
SCHLESWIG-HOLSTEIN
Husum
Kiel
Puttgarden
Fehmarn
Rügen
Ostsee
Helgoland
Nordsee
Neumünster
Stralsund
Rostock
Greifswald
Lübeck
Bad Segeberg
Ostfriesische Inseln
Wismar
MECKLENBURG-VORPOMMERN
HAMBURG
Hamburg
Schwerin
Neubrandenburg
Bremerhaven
Emden
Reinbek
Müritz
BREMEN
Prenzlau
Elsfleth
Westerstede
Oldenburg
Bremen
Lüneburg
die Elbe
LÜNEBURGER HEIDE
Schwedt
die Oder
NIEDERSACHSEN
POLEN
Salzwedel
Wittenberge
BERLIN
Berlin
die Havel
Celle
Stendal
die Weser
Hannover
Wolfsburg
Frankfurt (Oder)
Potsdam
Braunschweig
NIEDERLANDE
Osnabrück
Hildesheim
die Elbe
BRANDENBURG
Hameln
Magdeburg
die Oder
Münster
Bielefeld
HARZ
SACHSEN-ANHALT
Wittenberg
NORDRHEIN-WESTFALEN
Detmold
Halberstadt
Dessau
Cottbus
Gelsenkirchen
Dortmund
Wernigerode
Essen
Bochum
Göttingen
Eisleben
die Saale
Halle
die Spree
die Neiße
Duisburg
die Ruhr
Kassel
Sondershausen
Wurzen
Leipzig
Düsseldorf
Mühlhausen
Meißen
Bautzen
SACHSEN
Dresden
Bergisch-Gladbach
Köln
Eisenach
Weimar
Aachen
Donrath
Erfurt
Jena
Chemnitz
Marburg
Gera
Zwickau
Bonn
der Rhein
THÜRINGEN
WESTERWALD
Giessen
THÜRINGER WALD
Rudolphstadt
ERZGEBIRGE
HESSEN
Fulda
Suhl
Plauen
BELGIEN
EIFEL
Koblenz
die Elbe
RHEINLAND-
Bacharach
Wiesbaden
Frankfurt a. M.
der Main
Bingen
Mainz
Bayreuth
LUXEMBURG
die Mosel
PFALZ
Bamberg
TSCHECHISCHE REPUBLIK
Würzburg
Trier
Worms
Kaiserslautern
Ochsenfurth
Erlangen
Weinheim
BAYERISCHER WALD
SAARLAND
Mannheim
Heidelberg
Nürnberg
Saarbrücken
der Neckar
Rothenburg
BAYERN
die Mosel
Ansbach
Karlsruhe
Regensburg
der Rhein
Stuttgart
Baden-Baden
die Donau
die Isar
Passau
Tübingen
FRANKREICH
SCHWARZWALD
BADEN-WÜRTTEMBERG
Ulm
Augsburg
die Donau
München
der Inn
Freiburg
Bad Krozingen
Starnberger See
Chiemsee
ÖSTERREICH
Tegernsee
Kaufbeuren
Konstanz
BAYERISCHE ALPEN
Berchtesgaden
der Rhein
Bodensee
Garmisch-Partenkirchen
LIECHTENSTEIN
SCHWEIZ
der Inn

0 50 100 150 km
0 50 100 mi

Neue Horizonte

SEVENTH
EDITION

Neue Horizonte

Introductory German

David B. Dollenmayer
Worcester Polytechnic Institute

Thomas S. Hansen
Wellesley College

Australia • Brazil • Japan • Korea • Mexico • Singapore • Spain • United Kingdom • United States

Neue Horizonte: Introductory German, Seventh Edition
David B. Dollenmayer, Thomas S. Hansen

Executive Publisher: Rolando Hernández
Senior Sponsoring Editor: Laurel Miller
Executive Marketing Director: Eileen Bernadette Moran
Senior Development Editor: Judith Bach
Development Editor: Harriet C. Dishman
Project Editor: Harriet C. Dishman
Art and Design Manager: Jill Haber
Cover Design Director: Tony Saizon
Senior Photo Editor: Jennifer Meyer Dare
Senior Composition Buyer: Chuck Dutton
New Title Project Manager: James Lonergan
Marketing Assistant: Lorreen Ruth Pelletier
Cover Image © Age Fotostock/SuperStock

Library of Congress Control Number: 2007942777

ISBN-13: 978-0-618-95479-7

ISBN-10: 0-618-95479-1

Heinle
20 Channel Center Street
Boston, MA 02210
USA

Cengage Learning is a leading provider of customized learning solutions with office locations around the globe, including Singapore, the United Kingdom, Australia, Mexico, Brazil, and Japan. Locate your local office at **international.cengage.com/region**

Cengage Learning products are represented in Canada by Nelson Education, Ltd.

To learn more about Heinle, visit **www.cengage.com/heinle**

Purchase any of our products at your local college store or at our preferred online store **www.ichapters.com**

Printed in China by China Translation & Printing Services Limited
5 6 7 8 9 14 13 12 11

About the Authors

David B. Dollenmayer is Professor of German at the Worcester Polytechnic Institute (Worcester, Massachusetts). He received his B.A. and Ph.D. from Princeton University and was a Fulbright fellow at the University of Munich. He has written on the 20th-century writers Alfred Döblin, Joseph Roth, Christa Wolf, and Ingeborg Bachmann, and is the author of *The Berlin Novels of Alfred Döblin* (Berkeley, CA: University of California Press, 1988) and the translator of works by Michael Kleeberg, Anna Mitgutsch, Perikles Monioudis, and Moses Rosenkranz.

Thomas S. Hansen is Professor of German at Wellesley College (Wellesley, Massachusetts). He received his B.A. from Tufts University, studied six semesters at the University of Tübingen, and received his Ph.D. from Harvard University. His current research focuses on twentieth-century book design. He is the author (with Burton R. Pollin) of *The German Face of Edgar Allan Poe: A Study of Literary References in His Works* (Columbia, SC: Camden House, 1995) and *Classic Book Jackets: The Design Legacy of George Salter* (New York: Princeton Architectural Press, 2005). His website on Salter's book design can be viewed at: http://www.wellesley.edu/German/GeorgeSalter/Documents/home.html

Ellen W. Crocker, author of the Student Activities Manual, is Senior Lecturer in German at the Massachusetts Institute of Technology (Cambridge, Massachusetts). She received her B.A. from Skidmore College and the Magister Artium from the University of Freiburg, Germany. She is co-author (with Claire J. Kramsch) of the workbook/audio CD for conversational management, *Reden, Mitreden, Dazwischenreden* (Boston, MA: Heinle, 1990). Her current research is on the design of digital learning environments based on pedagogical practice. She is co-author (with Kurt E. Fendt) of the hypermedia documentary *Berliner sehen* (Cambridge, MA: M.I.T., 2000), funded by grants from the National Endowment for the Arts and the Consortium for Language Teaching and Learning.

Contents

KAPITEL 15

Kulturelle Vielfalt 408

An Overview of Your Textbook's Main Features

CHAPTER OPENER

Each chapter of ***Neue Horizonte*** sets the stage for learning by opening with a theme-setting photograph, accompanied by communicative and cultural objectives. An overview of chapter material previews the poetry, vocabulary, grammar, reading, and culture in each chapter.

KAPITEL 5

In einer Zeitungsredaktion (*newspaper editorial office*), Frankfurt/Main

Arbeit und Freizeit

Kommunikation
- Asking about prices
- Showing, giving, and telling things to people
- Talking about work and professions

Kultur
- How Germans spend their work and leisure time

In diesem Kapitel
- **Lyrik zum Vorlesen**
  Richard Dehmel, "Der Arbeitsmann"
- **Grammatik**
  1. Dative case
  2. Dative personal pronouns
  3. Word order of nouns and pronouns
  4. Prepositions with the dative case
  5. Verbs with separable prefixes
  6. Verbs with inseparable prefixes
- **Lesestück**
  Drei Deutsche bei der Arbeit
- **Almanach**
  Stellenangebote (*Help Wanted Ads*)

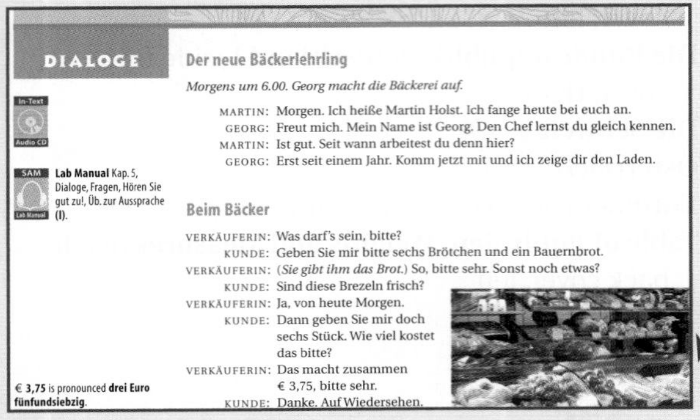

DIALOGE

Der neue Bäckerlehrling

Morgens um 6.00. Georg macht die Bäckerei auf.

MARTIN: Morgen. Ich heiße Martin Holst. Ich fange heute bei euch an.
GEORG: Freut mich. Mein Name ist Georg. Den Chef lernst du gleich kennen.
MARTIN: Ist gut. Seit wann arbeitest du denn hier?
GEORG: Erst seit einem Jahr. Komm jetzt mit und ich zeige dir den Laden.

Lab Manual Kap. 5, Dialoge, Fragen, Hören Sie gut zu!, Üb. zur Aussprache **(I)**.

Beim Bäcker

VERKÄUFERIN: Was darf's sein, bitte?
KUNDE: Geben Sie mir bitte sechs Brötchen und ein Bauernbrot.
VERKÄUFERIN: (*Sie gibt ihm das Brot.*) So, bitte sehr. Sonst noch etwas?
KUNDE: Sind diese Brezeln frisch?
VERKÄUFERIN: Ja, von heute Morgen.
KUNDE: Dann geben Sie mir doch sechs Stück. Wie viel kostet das bitte?
VERKÄUFERIN: Das macht zusammen € 3,75, bitte sehr.
KUNDE: Danke. Auf Wiedersehen.

€ **3,75** is pronounced **drei Euro fünfundsiebzig**.

DIALOGE

The **Dialoge** section introduces new vocabulary and grammar in context, in the form of two or three idiomatic conversations you would encounter in everyday situations. This section supports your communication skills and provides opportunities for you to express yourself in German. The dialogues are recorded on both the In-Text Audio CD and the SAM Audio Program, and English translations are provided in Appendix 4 for your reference.

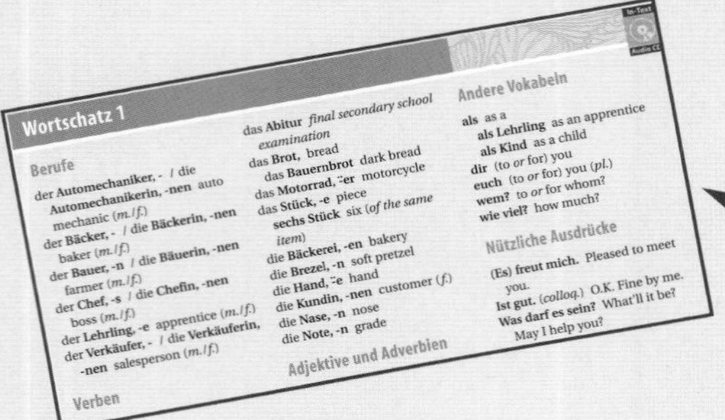

Wortschatz 1

Berufe

der **Automechaniker, -** / die **Automechanikerin, -nen** auto mechanic (*m./f.*)
der **Bäcker, -** / die **Bäckerin, -nen** baker (*m./f.*)
der **Bauer, -n** / die **Bäuerin, -nen** farmer (*m./f.*)
der **Chef, -s** / die **Chefin, -nen** boss (*m./f.*)
der **Lehrling, -e** apprentice (*m./f.*)
der **Verkäufer, -** / die **Verkäuferin, -nen** salesperson (*m./f.*)

das **Abitur** *final secondary school examination*
das **Brot,** bread
das **Bauernbrot** dark bread
das **Motorrad, ¨er** motorcycle
das **Stück, -e** piece
sechs Stück six (*of the same item*)
die **Bäckerei, -en** bakery
die **Brezel, -n** soft pretzel
die **Hand, ¨e** hand
die **Kundin, -nen** customer (*f.*)
die **Nase, -n** nose
die **Note, -n** grade

Verben

Adjektive und Adverbien

Andere Vokabeln

als as a
als Lehrling as an apprentice
als Kind as a child
dir (to *or* for) you
euch (to *or* for) you (*pl.*)
wem? to *or* for whom?
wie viel? how much?

Nützliche Ausdrücke

(Es) freut mich. Pleased to meet you.
Ist gut. (*colloq.*) O.K. Fine by me.
Was darf es sein? What'll it be? May I help you?

WORTSCHATZ 1

Each **Wortschatz** section divides the chapter vocabulary by parts of speech in order to provide you with an easy and convenient guide from which to study. The **Wortschatz** sections are recorded on your In-Text Audio CD Program.

VARIATIONEN

Follow-up activities based on the chapter dialogues encourage you to express your own thoughts, ideas, and experiences, using the German language in more creative ways.

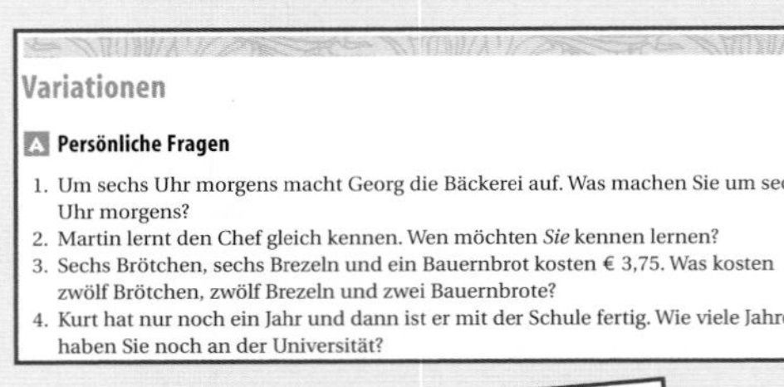

Variationen

A Persönliche Fragen

1. Um sechs Uhr morgens macht Georg die Bäckerei auf. Was machen Sie um sec Uhr morgens?
2. Martin lernt den Chef gleich kennen. Wen möchten *Sie* kennen lernen?
3. Sechs Brötchen, sechs Brezeln und ein Bauernbrot kosten € 3,75. Was kosten zwölf Brötchen, zwölf Brezeln und zwei Bauernbrote?
4. Kurt hat nur noch ein Jahr und dann ist er mit der Schule fertig. Wie viele Jahre haben Sie noch an der Universität?

LYRIK ZUM VORLESEN

Lyrik zum Vorlesen (*Poetry for Reading Aloud*) features authentic poetry, chosen to bring each chapter's theme to life. These poems, recorded on the In-Text Audio CD, offer you an enriching way to practice accurate pronunciation and to discover the beauty of German as a literary language. Marginal notes are provided to assist you with reading comprehension.

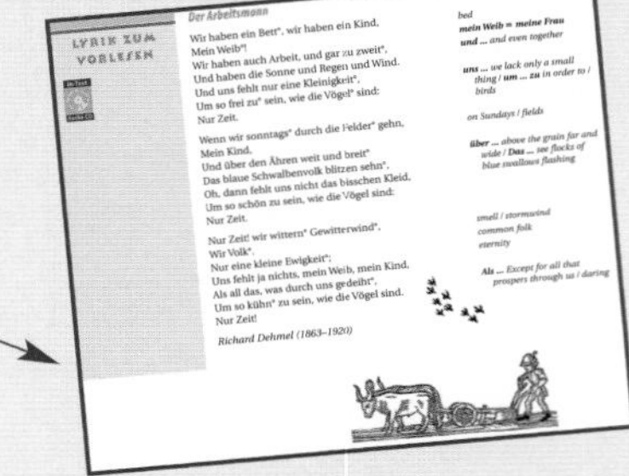

LYRIK ZUM VORLESEN

Der Arbeitsmann

Wir haben ein Bett°, wir haben ein Kind,
Mein Weib°!
Wir haben auch Arbeit, und gar zu zweit°,
Und haben die Sonne und Regen und Wind.
Und uns fehlt nur eine Kleinigkeit°,
Um so frei zu° sein, wie die Vögel° sind:
Nur Zeit.

Wenn wir sonntags° durch die Felder° gehn,
Mein Kind,
Und über den Ähren weit und breit°
Das blaue Schwalbenvolk blitzen sehn°,
Oh, dann fehlt uns nicht das bisschen Kleid,
Um so schön zu sein, wie die Vögel sind:
Nur Zeit.

Nur Zeit! wir wittern° Gewitterwind°,
Wir Volk°.
Nur eine kleine Ewigkeit°;
Uns fehlt ja nichts, mein Weib, mein Kind,
Als all das, was durch uns gedeiht°,
Um so kühn° zu sein, wie die Vögel sind.
Nur Zeit!

Richard Dehmel (1863–1920)

bed
mein Weib = meine Frau
und ... and even together
uns ... we lack only a small thing / **um ... zu** in order to / birds
on Sundays / fields
über ... above the grain far and wide / **Das ...** see flocks of blue swallows flashing
smell / stormwind
common folk
eternity
Als ... Except for all that prospers through us / daring

GRAMMATIK

The Grammar section provides concise yet thorough explanations followed by practice of all main features of German grammar. Activities progress from more guided with simple responses to more open-ended with free communication. New to the Seventh Edition are blue **Definition** boxes that provide thumbnail definitions of basic grammar concepts, such as parts of speech, tenses, etc., as well as *Notes on Usage* boxes.

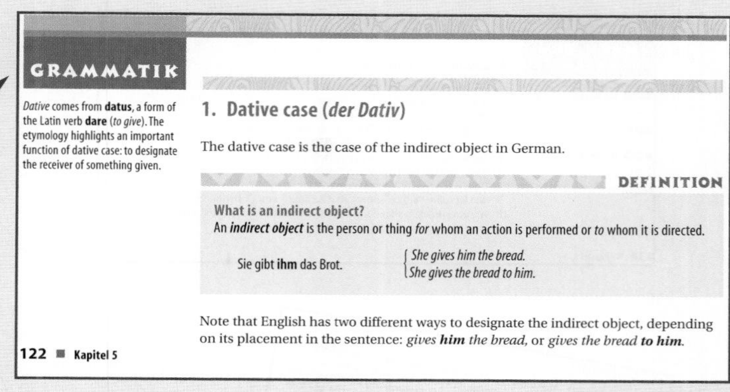

GRAMMATIK

Dative comes from **datus**, a form of the Latin verb **dare** (*to give*). The etymology highlights an important function of dative case: to designate the receiver of something given.

1. Dative case (*der Dativ*)

The dative case is the case of the indirect object in German.

DEFINITION

What is an indirect object?
An ***indirect object*** is the person or thing *for* whom an action is performed or *to* whom it is directed.

Sie gibt **ihm** das Brot. { *She gives him the bread.* / *She gives the bread to him.* }

Note that English has two different ways to designate the indirect object, depending on its placement in the sentence: *gives* ***him*** *the bread*, or *gives the bread* ***to him.***

122 ■ **Kapitel 5**

LESESTÜCK

The **Lesestück** section strengthens your reading skills by offering a selection of cultural readings on a variety of topics. These lively selections, recorded on the In-Text Audio CD, focus on the use of natural language. The reading section consists of the following subsections:

- **Tipps zum Lesen und Lernen** Offers tips for learning and expanding vocabulary, lists of easily recognized cognates, and strategies and activities designed to facilitate reading comprehension.

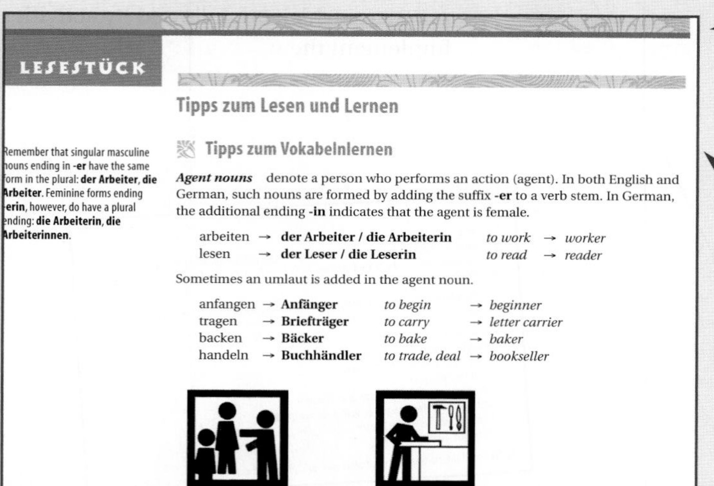

LESESTÜCK

Tipps zum Lesen und Lernen

Remember that singular masculine nouns ending in **-er** have the same form in the plural: **der Arbeiter, die Arbeiter**. Feminine forms ending **-erin**, however, do have a plural ending: **die Arbeiterin, die Arbeiterinnen.**

Tipps zum Vokabelnlernen

Agent nouns denote a person who performs an action (agent). In both English and German, such nouns are formed by adding the suffix **-er** to a verb stem. In German, the additional ending **-in** indicates that the agent is female.

arbeiten	→ **der Arbeiter / die Arbeiterin**	*to work*	→	*worker*
lesen	→ **der Leser / die Leserin**	*to read*	→	*reader*

Sometimes an umlaut is added in the agent noun.

anfangen	→ **Anfänger**	*to begin*	→	*beginner*
tragen	→ **Briefträger**	*to carry*	→	*letter carrier*
backen	→ **Bäcker**	*to bake*	→	*baker*
handeln	→ **Buchhändler**	*to trade, deal*	→	*bookseller*

- **Wortschatz 2** Provides a presentation of vocabulary needed to understand the **Lesestück** and to complete the activities in **Nach dem Lesen.** Like **Wortschatz 1,** this section is recorded on your In-Text Audio CD Program.

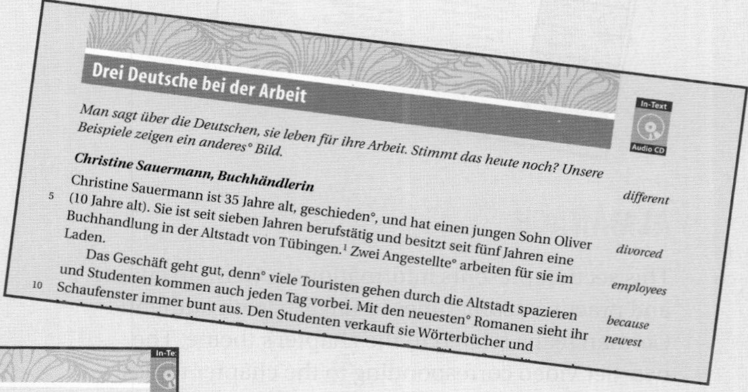

Drei Deutsche bei der Arbeit

In-Text Audio CD

Man sagt über die Deutschen, sie leben für ihre Arbeit. Stimmt das heute noch? Unsere Beispiele zeigen ein anderes° Bild. *different*

Christine Sauermann, Buchhändlerin

Christine Sauermann ist 35 Jahre alt, geschieden°, und hat einen jungen Sohn Oliver (10 Jahre alt). Sie ist seit sieben Jahren berufstätig und besitzt seit fünf Jahren eine Buchhandlung in der Altstadt von Tübingen.[1] Zwei Angestellte° arbeiten für sie im Laden. *divorced* *employees*

Das Geschäft geht gut, denn° viele Touristen gehen durch die Altstadt spazieren und Studenten kommen auch jeden Tag vorbei. Mit den neuesten° Romanen sieht ihr Schaufenster immer bunt aus. Den Studenten verkauft sie Wörterbücher und *because* *newest*

Wortschatz 2

In-Text Audio

Berufe	**Substantive**	
der **Arbeiter, -** / die **Arbeiterin, -nen** worker; industrial worker (*m./f.*)	der **Fußball** soccer	die **Türkei** Turkey
der **Buchhändler, -** / die **Buchhändlerin, -nen** bookseller (*m./f.*)	der **Reiseführer, -** (travel) guidebook	die **Wanderung, -en** hike
der **Graphiker, -** / die **Graphikerin,**	der **Roman, -e** novel	die **Zeitschrift, -en** magazine
	der **Stadtplan, ¨e** city map	die **Lebensmittel** (*pl.*) groceries
	der **Stress** stress	**Die Türkei**, like **die Schweiz**, is always used with the definite article: **Er kommt aus der Türkei.**
	das **Bild, -er** picture; image	**Adjektive und Adverbien**

NACH DEM LESEN

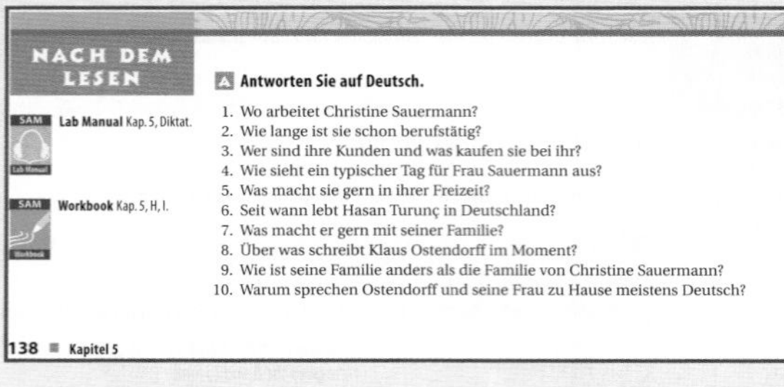
NACH DEM LESEN

SAM Lab Manual Kap. 5, Diktat.

SAM Workbook Kap. 5, H, I.

A Antworten Sie auf Deutsch.

1. Wo arbeitet Christine Sauermann?
2. Wie lange ist sie schon berufstätig?
3. Wer sind ihre Kunden und was kaufen sie bei ihr?
4. Wie sieht ein typischer Tag für Frau Sauermann aus?
5. Was macht sie gern in ihrer Freizeit?
6. Seit wann lebt Hasan Turunç in Deutschland?
7. Was macht er gern mit seiner Familie?
8. Über was schreibt Klaus Ostendorff im Moment?
9. Wie ist seine Familie anders als die Familie von Christine Sauermann?
10. Warum sprechen Ostendorff und seine Frau zu Hause meistens Deutsch?

138 ■ Kapitel 5

The **Nach dem Lesen** section includes personalized questions, role-plays, and post-reading questions that check your comprehension.

- **Info-Austausch** Provides information-gap activities that offer you opportunities to work in pairs with your classmates, exchanging information to complete a set of questions.
- **Vokabeln zum Thema** Contains optional vocabulary related to the theme of the chapter with follow-up activities that emphasize the use of the vocabulary in everyday situations.
- **Schreibtipp** Features suggestions for approaching the writing exercise along with practical tips on standard German writing practices, which are followed by activities to implement them.

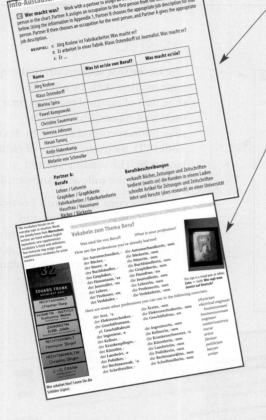

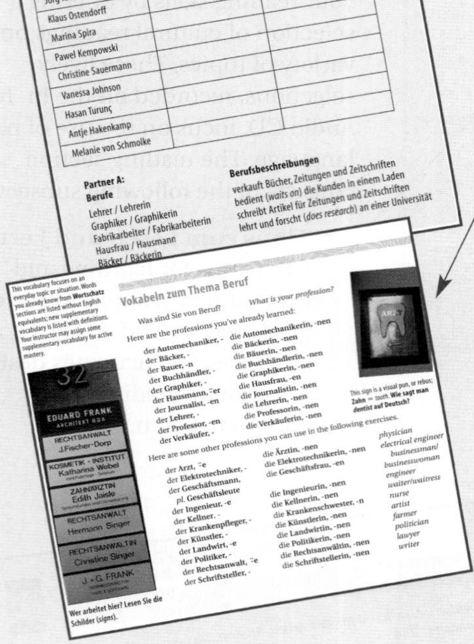
Info-Austausch

C Wer macht was? Work with a partner to assign an occupation and a job description to each person in the chart. Partner A assigns an occupation to the first person from the information given below. Using the information in Appendix 1, Partner B chooses the appropriate job description for that person. Partner B then chooses an occupation for the next person, and Partner A gives the appropriate job description.

BEISPIEL: A: Jörg Krolow ist Fabrikarbeiter. Was macht er?
B: Er arbeitet in einer Fabrik. Klaus Ostendorff ist Journalist. Was macht er?
A: Er ...

Name	Was ist er/sie von Beruf?	Was macht er/sie?
Jörg Krolow		
Klaus Ostendorff		
Marina Spira		
Pawel Kempowski		
Christine Sauermann		
Vanessa Johnson		
Hasan Turunç		
Antje Hakenkamp		
Melanie von Schmolke		

Partner A: Berufe
Lehrer / Lehrerin
Graphiker / Graphikerin
Fabrikarbeiter / Fabrikarbeiterin
Hausfrau / Hausmann
Bäcker / Bäckerin

Berufsbeschreibungen
verkauft Bücher, Zeitungen und Zeitschriften
bedient (*waits on*) die Kunden in einem Laden
schreibt Artikel für Zeitungen und Zeitschriften
lehrt und forscht (*does research*) an einer Universität

This vocabulary focuses on an everyday topic or situation. Words you already know from **Wortschatz** sections are listed without English equivalents; new supplementary vocabulary is listed with definition. Your instructor may assign some supplementary vocabulary for active mastery.

Vokabeln zum Thema Beruf

Was sind Sie von Beruf? *What is your profession?*

Here are the professions you've already learned:

der **Automechaniker, -** die **Automechanikerin, -nen**
der **Bäcker, -** die **Bäckerin, -nen**
der **Bauer, -n** die **Bäuerin, -nen**
der **Buchhändler, -** die **Buchhändlerin, -nen**
der **Graphiker, -** die **Graphikerin, -nen**
der **Hausmann, ⸚er** die **Hausfrau, -en**
der **Journalist, -en** die **Journalistin, -nen**
der **Lehrer, -** die **Lehrerin, -nen**
der **Professor, -en** die **Professorin, -nen**
der **Verkäufer, -** die **Verkäuferin, -nen**

Here are some other professions you can use in the following exercises.

der **Arzt, ⸚e** die **Ärztin, -nen** *physician*
der **Elektrotechniker, -** die **Elektrotechnikerin, -nen** *electrical engineer*
der **Geschäftsmann,** *pl.* **Geschäftsleute** die **Geschäftsfrau, -en** *businessman/businesswoman*
der **Ingenieur, -e** die **Ingenieurin, -nen** *engineer*
der **Kellner, -** die **Kellnerin, -nen** *waiter/waitress*
der **Krankenpfleger, -** die **Krankenschwester, -n** *nurse*
der **Künstler, -** die **Künstlerin, -nen** *artist*
der **Landwirt, -e** die **Landwirtin, -nen** *farmer*
der **Politiker, -** die **Politikerin, -nen** *politician*
der **Rechtsanwalt, ⸚e** die **Rechtsanwältin, -nen** *lawyer*
der **Schriftsteller, -** die **Schriftstellerin, -nen** *writer*

Wer arbeitet hier? Lesen Sie die Schilder (*signs*).

This sign is a visual pun, or rebus: **Zahn** = *tooth*. **Wie sagt man *dentist* auf Deutsch?**

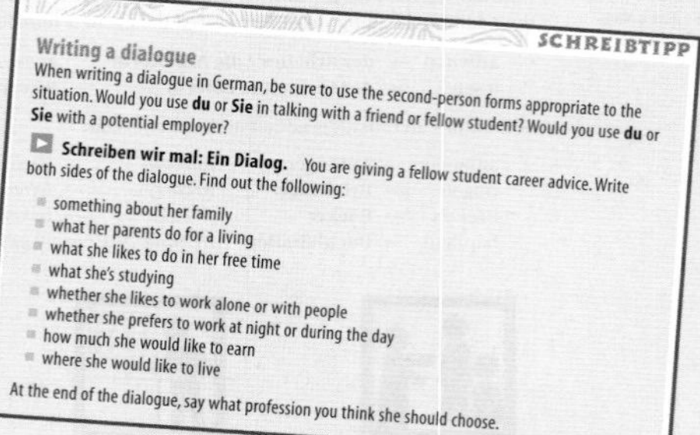
SCHREIBTIPP

Writing a dialogue

When writing a dialogue in German, be sure to use the second-person forms appropriate to the situation. Would you use **du** or **Sie** in talking with a friend or fellow student? Would you use **du** or **Sie** with a potential employer?

D Schreiben wir mal: Ein Dialog. You are giving a fellow student career advice. Write both sides of the dialogue. Find out the following:

- something about her family
- what her parents do for a living
- what she likes to do in her free time
- what she's studying
- whether she likes to work alone or with people
- whether she prefers to work at night or during the day
- how much she would like to earn
- where she would like to live

At the end of the dialogue, say what profession you think she should choose.

ALMANACH

This section presents information on German culture and practices, sometimes in English, with authentic German realia related to the chapter's theme. The two-tier video corresponding to the chapter topics and themes combines situational footage—featuring a diverse cast of German, Turkish-German, Swiss, and Austrian characters—and street interviews that illustrate the use of relevant grammar topics.

ALMANACH

VIDEO

Stellenangebote (*Help Wanted Ads*)

These help-wanted ads from German newspapers range from unskilled labor (**Babysitter/in**) to jobs in highly specialized fields (**Radiologie/Kardiologie**). Note the English business and computer jargon in the technical fields.

Neue Horizonte, Seventh Edition, is a comprehensive first-year German program for college and university students. The goal of ***Neue Horizonte,*** true to its name, is to open up new horizons to German-speaking realities and to guide you, the learner, across the boundaries of your first language into the world of contemporary Germany, Austria, and Switzerland. The text also aims to excite your curiosity about German-speaking cultures and to help you view your own culture through the prism of another.

The main goal of the program is to help you reach a basic level of communicative and interactional competence in German. Such competence includes grammatical, lexical, and discursive knowledge, as well as intercultural awareness. You will learn to use German to understand and produce meaningful utterances and texts, communicate your thoughts and ideas, and interact with other speakers of German.

Neue Horizonte offers a variety of activities that practice the four basic skills of listening, speaking, reading, and writing. You will learn to talk and write in German about yourself, your interests, family, and your life in college or university. In addition, you will encounter many aspects of German culture. ***Neue Horizonte*** includes a variety of texts on family life, school and university studies, and the workplace, as well as on travel and the geography and climate of the German-speaking countries. You will read about city life, history, and the current politics of Germany, Austria, and Switzerland. You will also learn to use different modes of address and registers of politeness, to talk and write in German about past and future occurrences, to express wishes and possibilities, and to recognize and apply differences between the active and the passive voice.

Neue Horizonte prepares you for both intermediate German courses and travel and study in a German-speaking country. Once you are there, you will be able to communicate in many everyday situations and continue to build on what you have learned in this course.

We subscribe to the words of the Austrian philosopher Ludwig Wittgenstein who wrote, "*Die Grenzen meiner Sprache bedeuten die Grenzen meiner Welt*" (The boundaries of my language represent the boundaries of my world). There is no better way to expand those boundaries than to learn another language. With this course in first-year German, we encourage you to cross linguistic, geographical, personal, and symbolic boundaries. Through such acts of determination, each of us begins to achieve an international intellectual identity as we discover new dimensions of the imagination.

Student Components

Student Text

Neue Horizonte consists of an introductory chapter and fifteen regular chapters. Each chapter presents and practices vocabulary (**Dialoge** and **Variationen, Wortschatz 1**), grammar (**Grammatik**), and introduces you to poetry (**Lyrik zum Vorlesen**) and cultural readings (**Lesestücke**). These reading sections feature specific vocabulary (**Leicht zu merken, Wortschatz 2**), reading strategies (**Einstieg in den Text**), and post-reading activities (**Nach dem Lesen**). Each chapter concludes with

Almanach, where information on the cultural theme of the chapter is presented in English and illustrated with photos, maps, and realia.

Einführung (*Introductory chapter*)

From the very first day of the course, you begin talking with your fellow students in German. In this two-day sequence (**Tag 1** and **Tag 2**) you will learn greetings and farewells, as well as basic vocabulary such as the names of classroom objects, the days of the week, and the months of the year. In addition, you will learn how to spell, count to twenty, tell time, talk about the weather, and say where you are from. In other words, after the first two days of this course, you will already have enough basic structures and vocabulary under control to carry on simple conversations.

Reference Section

Neue Horizonte includes four appendices:

- **Appendix 1:** Partner B's portion of the **Info-Austausch** activities.
- **Appendix 2:** A table of the principal parts of the strong and irregular verbs introduced in the book.
- **Appendix 3:** Special Subjunctive and Extended Modifiers.
- **Appendix 4:** English Equivalents of the **Dialoge.**

Both the German-English and the English-German end vocabularies include all the active vocabulary in the **Wortschatz** sections, as well as the optional vocabulary from the **Vokabeln zum Thema** sections and the guessable cognates from **Leicht zu merken**.

For quick reference, the book ends with a comprehensive index of grammatical and communicative topics included in the text.

NEW! *Neue Horizonte* In-Text Audio CD Program

The In-Text Audio CD program includes the **Dialoge** (recorded at normal speed), **Wortschatz 1**, the **Lyrik zum Vorlesen**, **Wortschatz 2,** and the **Lesestücke** for each regular chapter. In addition, the mini-dialogues and basic expressions from the **Einführung** chapter are also recorded.

Student Activities Manual (SAM) and SAM Audio Program

The SAM Audio Program and its coordinated SAM Workbook and Lab Manual are integral parts of ***Neue Horizonte***, Seventh Edition, and are fully integrated with the Student Text.

In order to use the SAM and the SAM Audio Program to their best advantage, you should follow the sequence suggested in the marginal cross-references in your Student Text.

The orange SAM Lab Manual icon directs you to the Lab Manual section of the SAM and the coordinated SAM Audio Program. The SAM Audio Program contains the **Dialoge** from the Student Text with accompanying comprehension checks, pronunciation practice, and self-correcting grammar exercises to help you gain proficiency in listening and speaking as you proceed through each chapter.

The red SAM Workbook icon directs you to a variety of written exercises in the Workbook section of the SAM. These exercises provide graduated practice with the grammar and vocabulary presented in each chapter.

An especially valuable feature of the Workbook are the three **Zusammenfassung und Wiederholung** (*Summary and Review*) sections located after every five chapters, thus after chapters 5, 10, and 15. This section contains condensed grammar summaries and reviews useful expressions. It also includes the self-correcting *Test Your Progress*, which you can use to review the preceding chapters of the textbook.

NEW! *Neue Horizonte* Video

This edition of ***Neue Horizonte*** is accompanied by a new video, which consists of fifteen modules to accompany each chapter of the Student Text. This two-tier video was shot on location in Germany, Austria, and Switzerland and features situational clips with recurring characters, as well as interview segments. The script for these brief, colloquial scenes was written to reinforce and augment the material in the textbook. In each situational clip, a group of young people played by native German-speaking actors using idiomatic language engage in social situations related to the chapter's cultural theme.

Online Study Center

The Online Study Center website includes a variety of resources and practice to be used as you study each chapter or as you review for quizzes and exams. Each chapter contains the following free resources:

- ACE practice tests
- ACE video activities
- Audio flashcards
- Web search activities
- Web links
- In-text audio .mp3 files

Passkey-protected premium content is also included:

- Multimedia eBook
- Interactive practice activities
- Complete video in .mp4 format
- SAM audio program in .mp3 format

NEW! Eduspace (with eBook)

The online multimedia eBook housed in the Eduspace course management system provides you with the entire text online, integrated with links to a wide variety of resources. In addition, all in-text activities are interactive. By clicking on a link at the relevant point in the Student Text, you can immediately practice and reinforce what you have learned. A real-time voice-chat feature allows you to complete pair and group activities. Also included are audio recordings of each chapter's active vocabulary.

eSAM in Quia

This electronic version of the Student Activities Manual contains the same content as the print SAM in an interactive environment that provides immediate feedback on many activities. The audio associated with the Lab Manual portion of the SAM is also integrated at the relevant point.

NEW! Downloadable PDF eBook

This static, downloadable PDF version of the Student Text is well suited for students who use laptops in class and at home, but who do not need the interactive features of the full multimedia version.

We wish to express our special gratitude to our colleagues Susanne Even (*Indiana University at Bloomington*), and Ulrike Brisson (*Worcester Polytechnic Institute*) for countless suggestions for improvement of the text and accompanying programs. Thanks to our editors at Cengage Learning, Judith Bach and Laurel Miller, our tireless development and production editor Harriet C. Dishman, and our proofreaders Susanne van Eyl and Simone Berger for their expertise and unfailing attention to detail. Special thanks to Kurt Fendt, Arthur Jaffe, and Alexander Šimec for providing photographs and realia. We are also in the debt of our colleagues and students at Wellesley College, Worcester Polytechnic Institute, and the Massachusetts Institute of Technology, who have used and improved ***Neue Horizonte*** along with us, as well as to our users, whose comments and criticisms help improve the program from edition to edition.

We wish to thank especially the following colleagues and institutions for their advice and help through several editions of ***Neue Horizonte.***

Prof. emerita Jutta Arend, *College of the Holy Cross and Worcester Polytechnic Institute*

Prof. John Austin, *Georgia State University*

Prof. Maria Beck, *University of North Texas*

Prof. Barbara Bopp, *formerly of University of California at Los Angeles*

Prof. Alfred Cobbs, *Wayne State University*

Deutsche Schule, Washington, D.C.

Prof. Margaret Klopfle Devinny, *Temple University*

Prof. Eugene Dobson, *University of Alabama*

Prof. Monika R. Dressler, *University of Michigan*

Prof. emeritus Wilhelm Eggimann, *Worcester Polytechnic Institute*

Prof. Mine Eren, *Randolph-Macon College*

Prof. Karl-Heinz Finken, *formerly of Wellesley College*

Prof. Andrea Golato, *University of Illinois at Urbana-Champaign*

Prof. Ronald Gougher, *West Chester University, PA*

Prof. emerita Diethild Harrington, *Worcester Polytechnic Institute*

Prof. Charles James, *University of Wisconsin at Madison*

Prof. Dieter Jedan, *Southeast Missouri State University*

Prof. John M. Jeep, *Miami University, OH*

Prof. William Keel, *University of Kansas*

Prof. Harvey Kendall, *formerly of California State University at Long Beach*

Prof. Wighart von Koenigswald, *Universität Bonn*

Prof. Jens Kruse, *Wellesley College*

Prof. John Lalande, *State University of New York, Oswego*

Prof. Jean Leventhal, *formerly of Wellesley College*

Prof. Enno Lohmeyer, *formerly of University of Kansas*

Prof. emeritus James R. McIntyre, *Colby College*
Prof. Hans Mussler, *Idaho State University*
Prof. Thomas Nolden, *Wellesley College*
Prof. Sara Ogger, *formerly of Montclair State University*
Prof. Günther Georg Pfister
Prof. Michael Ressler, *Boston College*
Prof. Sylvia Rieger, *Harvard University*
Prof. Gertraud Rosenbladt, *formerly of Foothill College*
Prof. Dieter Saalmann, *formerly of Wichita State University*
Prof. Annette Steigerwald, *Ohio University*
Prof. Maria Stoffers, *formerly Queensborough Community College*
Prof. Heather I. Sullivan, *Trinity University*
Prof. Carmen Taleghani-Nikazm, *University of Kansas*
Prof. Ute Trevor, *Arbeitskreis DaF in der Schweiz*
Prof. Ann Ulmer, *Carleton College*
Prof. Gretchen Van Galder-Janis, *formerly of Johnson County Community College*
Prof. Elizabeth I. Wade-Sirabian, *formerly of University of Wisconsin at Oshkosh*
Prof. Margaret Ward, *Wellesley College*
Prof. David Weible, *University of Illinois at Chicago*
Prof. Mary Wildner-Bassett, *University of Arizona*
Prof. Christiane Zehl-Romero, *Tufts University*

In addition, we would like to thank the Prof. Sharon M. DiFino, *University of Florida at Gainesville*, who reviewed the manuscript at various stages of its development.

We welcome reactions and suggestions from instructors and students using ***Neue Horizonte***. Please feel free to contact us.

Prof. David B. Dollenmayer
Department of Humanities and Arts
Worcester Polytechnic Institute
Worcester, Massachusetts 01609-2280
E-mail: dbd@wpi.edu

Prof. Thomas S. Hansen
Department of German
Wellesley College
Wellesley, Massachusetts 02481
E-mail: thansen@wellesley.edu

Ellen W. Crocker
Foreign Languages and Literatures
Massachusetts Institute of Technology
Cambridge, MA 02139
E-mail: ecrocker@mit.edu

Bauernhof in Niederösterreich (*Farmyard in Lower Austria*)

Einführung (*Introduction*)

Kommunikation (*Communication*)

- Greeting people and asking their names
- Identifying classroom objects
- Saying good-bye
- Naming the days of the week
- Spelling in German
- Talking about the weather
- Naming the months of the year
- Counting to 20
- Telling time
- Saying where you are from
- **Almanach** (*Almanac*)
  Profile of the Federal Republic of Germany

TAG 1

Tag 1 = *Day 1*

The green in-text audio icon indicates that this material is recorded on your in-text audio CDs.

The shaded boxes in this **Einführung** (*Introduction*) contain useful words and phrases that you should memorize. You will find a complete list of this vocabulary on p. 15.

Guten Tag! *(Hello!)*

German speakers greet each other in various ways. What greeting you use depends on:

a. the time of day:

Guten Morgen!	*Good morning!* (until about 10:00 AM)
Guten Tag!	*Hello!* (literally, *"Good day,"* said after 10:00 AM)
Guten Abend!	*Good evening!* (after 5:00 PM)

b. and how well you know each other and what the social situation is:

Hallo! **Tag!**	*Hi!* (informal greetings)

1 Gruppenarbeit: Guten Tag! *(Group work: Hello!)* When German speakers meet friends and acquaintances, they not only greet each other, but they also shake hands. Greet the students next to you in German. Don't forget to shake hands!

2 Partnerarbeit: Was sagen diese Leute? *(Partner work: What are these people saying?)* With a partner, complete the following dialogues by saying them aloud.

German has no equivalent to English *Ms.* One can avoid the increasingly rare **Fräulein** (*Miss*) by using **Frau** for all women of all ages. In restaurants a waitress is frequently called by saying **Bedienung** (*service*), **bitte!**

Herr = *Mr.*
Frau = *Mrs.* or *Ms.*

The orange SAM Lab Manual icon indicates that this material is recorded in the **SAM Audio Program** and is coordinated with exercises in the **Lab Manual**.

All the dialogues in **Tag 1** are in the **Einführung** chapter of the SAM. Complete introduction to *The Sounds of German* is at the end of the SAM Audio Program for the **Einführung**.

1. ________, Herr Lehmann!
   ________, Frau Schmidt!

2. ________, Brigitte!
   ________, Heinz!

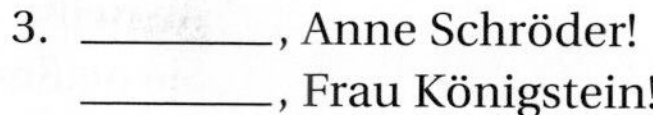

3. ________, Anne Schröder!
   ________, Frau Königstein!

4. ________, Peter!
   ________, Ute!

5. ________, Franz!
   ________, Joseph!

Wie heißt du? *(What's your name?)*

***You:* du *or* Sie?** German has two forms of the pronoun *you.* If you're talking to a relative or good friend, use the familiar form **du**. University students often call each other **du,** even when they're meeting for the first time. If you're talking to an adult whom you don't know well, use the formal **Sie**.

When you meet people for the first time, you want to learn their names. Listen to your instructor, and then repeat the following dialogue.

In-Text Audio CD: These dialogues are on the **Einführung** lesson of the In-Text Audio Program.

SAM Lab Manual: **Lab Manual** These dialogues and variations are in the **Einführung** chapter of the SAM Audio Program.

A:	**Hallo, ich heiße Anna. Wie heißt du?**	*Hello, my name is Anna. What's your name?*
B:	**Hallo, Anna. Ich heiße Thomas.**	*Hello, Anna. My name's Thomas.*
A:	**Freut mich, Thomas!**	*Pleased to meet you, Thomas.*
B:	**Freut mich auch.**	*Pleased to meet you, too.*

If you're meeting an adult who is not a fellow student, the dialogue would go like this.

A: **Ich heiße Schönhuber, und wie heißen Sie?**
B: **Guten Tag, Herr Schönhuber. Ich heiße Meyer.**
A: **Freut mich, Herr Meyer.**
B: **Freut mich auch.**

In-Text Audio CD

SAM Lab Manual

Ich heiße ... = My name is . . .

German verbs have endings that must agree with the subject of the sentence.

ich heiß**e**	*my name is* (literally: *I am called*)
du heiß**t** / Sie heiß**en**	*your name is*
er heiß**t**	*his name is*
sie heiß**t**	*her name is*
Wie heißt du? / **Wie heißen Sie?**	*What's your name?* (literally: *How are you called?*)

3 Partnerarbeit: Wie heißt du? Practice the first dialogue at the bottom of p. 3 with a partner. Substitute your own names for Anna and Thomas and don't forget to switch roles.

4 Gruppenarbeit: Ich heiße ... Now introduce yourself to three or four people in class you don't know, using **du.** Don't forget to shake hands.

Wie heißt du?

Wie heißt er?

Wie heißt sie?

5 Gruppenarbeit: Wie heißt ... ? Your instructor will ask you the names of other students. If you can't remember someone's name, just ask that person, **Wie heißt du?**

Auf Wiedersehen!

Wer ist das? Was ist das? *(Who is that? What is that?)*

In items 1–4, the first word refers to a university classroom (professor and student), while the second word in parentheses refers to a secondary school classroom (teacher and pupil). **Student** in German always means *university student*.

1. der Professor (der Lehrer)
2. die Professorin (die Lehrerin)
3. der Student (der Schüler)
4. die Studentin (die Schülerin)
5. die Tafel
6. der Tisch
7. die Uhr
8. die Wand
9. das Fenster
10. der Stuhl
11. die Tür
12. die Landkarte
13. das Poster
14. die Kreide
15. der Wischer

Note:

- All nouns are capitalized, wherever they occur in the sentence.
- The **-in** suffix denotes a female.

1. das Buch
2. das Heft
3. das Papier
4. der Bleistift
5. der Kugelschreiber
6. der Radiergummi

A:	**Was ist das?**	*What is that?*
B:	**Das ist der Tisch.**	*That's the table.*
	das Buch.	*the book.*
	die Tafel.	*the blackboard.*

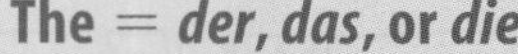

The = *der, das,* or *die*

Every German noun belongs to one of three genders: *masculine, neuter,* or *feminine*. The form of the definite article (**der**, **das**, **die** = *the*) shows the gender of the noun. When you learn a new noun, always learn the article along with it.

masculine	**der** Mann	*the man*
	der Stuhl	*the chair*
neuter	**das** Kind	*the child*
	das Buch	*the book*
feminine	**die** Frau	*the woman*
	die Tafel	*the blackboard*

A:	**Wer ist das?**	*Who is that?*
B:	**Das ist Thomas.**	*That's Thomas.*
	die Professorin.	*the (female) professor.*
	der Professor.	*the (male) professor.*
	die Studentin.	*the (female) student.*
	der Student.	*the (male) student.*

6 Partnerarbeit: Was ist das? Wer ist das? Work together and see how many people and things in the room you can identify.

BEISPIEL: A: Was ist das?
B: Das ist der/das/die ________.

A: Wer ist das?
B: Das ist ________.

Now ask each other where (**wo?**) things are. Respond by pointing to the object and saying it is there (**da**).

BEISPIEL: A: Wo ist die Uhr?
B: Die Uhr ist da. Wo ist das Fenster?
A: Das Fenster ...

QUESTION WORDS

wie?	*how?*
was?	*what?*
wer?	*who?*
wo?	*where?*

Auf Wiedersehen! *(Good-bye!)*

There are several expressions you can use when leaving.

Tschüss is derived from Spanish *adiós*.

In Austria, the informal expression **Servus** means both *Hi* and *So long*. In Switzerland, instead of **Guten Tag**, one says **Grüezi** formally and **Hoi** informally.

Auf Wiedersehen!	*Good-bye!*
Tschüss!	*So long!* (informal, among friends)
Schönes Wochenende!	(*Have a*) *nice weekend!*
Danke, gleichfalls!	*Thanks, same to you!* (*You too!*)
Bis morgen!	*Until tomorrow!*
Bis Montag!	*Until Monday!*

Lab Manual Einführung, The Days of the Week.

Die Wochentage *(Days of the week)*

Heute ist ...	*Today is . . .*
Montag	*Monday*
Dienstag	*Tuesday*
Mittwoch	*Wednesday*
Donnerstag	*Thursday*
Freitag	*Friday*
Samstag (in southern Germany) / **Sonnabend** (in northern Germany)	*Saturday*
Sonntag	*Sunday*

7 Gruppenarbeit: Auf Wiedersehen! At the end of class, turn to your neighbors and say good-bye until next time. Tell your instructor good-bye too.

Lab Manual Einführung, The Alphabet.

Das Alphabet *(The Alphabet)*

The name of almost every letter in German contains the sound ordinarily represented by that letter. You should memorize the German alphabet. Listen to the alphabet on the SAM Audio Program and to your instructor. Besides the regular alphabet, German has four additional symbols you need to learn.

a	ah	**k**	kah	**u**	uh
b	beh	**l**	ell	**v**	fau
c	tseh	**m**	emm	**w**	weh
d	deh	**n**	enn	**x**	iks
e	eh	**o**	oh	**y**	üppsilon
f	eff	**p**	peh	**z**	tsett
g	geh	**q**	kuh	**ß**	ess-tsett
h	hah	**r**	err	**ä**	
i	ih	**s**	ess	**ö**	
j	jott	**t**	teh	**ü**	

Three vowels are modified by a symbol called the **Umlaut: ä, ö, ü**. The letter **ß** represents the unvoiced *s*-sound. It follows long vowels and diphthongs. In Switzerland **ss** is used instead of **ß**.

Guten Morgen, gute Laune.
Bremer Kajenmarkt
jeden Samstag von 10-16 Uhr mit Kinderbetreuung

Lab Manual Einführung, Variations on dialogues in **Tag 2**.

8 Partnerarbeit: Wie schreibt man das? *(How do you spell that?)*

A. Ask each other how you spell your names. Write the last name as your partner spells it, then check to see whether you've written it correctly.

BEISPIEL: A: Wie heißt du?
B: Ich heiße Jay Schneider.
A: Wie schreibt man (*How do you spell*) „Schneider"?
B: Man schreibt das (*You spell it*) S-C-H-N-E-I-D-E-R.

B. Now turn to the classroom objects pictured on p. 5. One partner spells the name of four or five of the objects pictured; the other partner says each word as it is spelled. Then switch roles.

BMW = Bayerische Motorenwerke (*Bavarian Motor Works*), **MP** = Militärpolizei, **ISBN** = Internationale Standardbuchnummer, **EKG** = Elektrokardiogramm, **BASF** = Badische Anilin- und Sodafabrik (*Baden Aniline and Soda Factory*), **EU** = Europäische Union (*European Union*).

9 Gruppenarbeit: Wie sagt man das? *(How do you say that?)* Here are some abbreviations used in both English and German. Take turns saying them in German.

VW	BMW	ISBN	BASF
IBM	MP	EKG	TNT
USA	PVC	CD	EU

10 Gruppenarbeit: Wie spricht man das aus? (*How do you pronounce that?*)

A. Let's move from individual letters to pronouncing entire words in German. Here are some well-known German surnames. Take turns saying them aloud.

Fahrenheit	Kissinger	Nietzsche	Bach
Jung	Freud	Luther	Schönberg
Diesel	Ohm	Zeppelin	Schwarzenegger
Beethoven	Röntgen	Bunsen	Goethe
Hesse	Mozart	Schiffer	Pfeiffer

B. Now here are some words that English has borrowed from German. CAUTION: In English, their pronunciation has been anglicized. Be sure to pronounce them in German and see if you know what the words mean.

Flak = acronym for **Fliegerabwehrkanone** (*anti-aircraft gun*).

Angst	Kindergarten	Schmalz
Ersatz	Kitsch	Strudel
Flak	Leitmotiv	Wanderlust
Gestalt	Poltergeist	Weltanschauung
Gesundheit	Rucksack	Zeitgeist
Hinterland	Schadenfreude	Zwieback

Das Wetter *(The weather)*

The weather is a frequent topic of conversation everywhere.

A: Wie ist das Wetter heute?
B: Es ist **schön** (*beautiful, nice*). (oder [*or*])
Es ist **furchtbar** (*terrible*).

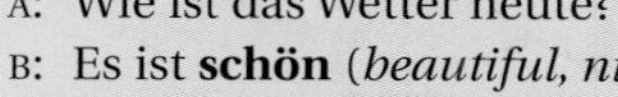

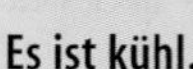
Es ist kühl.

Es ist warm.

Es ist kalt.

Es ist heiß.

Scheint die Sonne heute? ***Is the sun shining today?***

Ja, die Sonne scheint. ***Yes, the sun is shining.***

Nein, es regnet. ***No, it's raining.***

11 Partnerarbeit: Wie ist das Wetter heute? Chat briefly with a partner about today's weather. Use the words and phrases above.

More weather words

Es ist heute wolkig.	*Today it's cloudy.*	**Es regnet.**	*It's raining.*
neblig.	*foggy.*	**Es schneit.**	*It's snowing.*
sonnig.	*sunny.*		
windig.	*windy.*		

12 Partnerarbeit: Wie ist das Wetter in Europa? Below is a typical weather map for Europe. Working with a partner, answer the questions that follow the map.

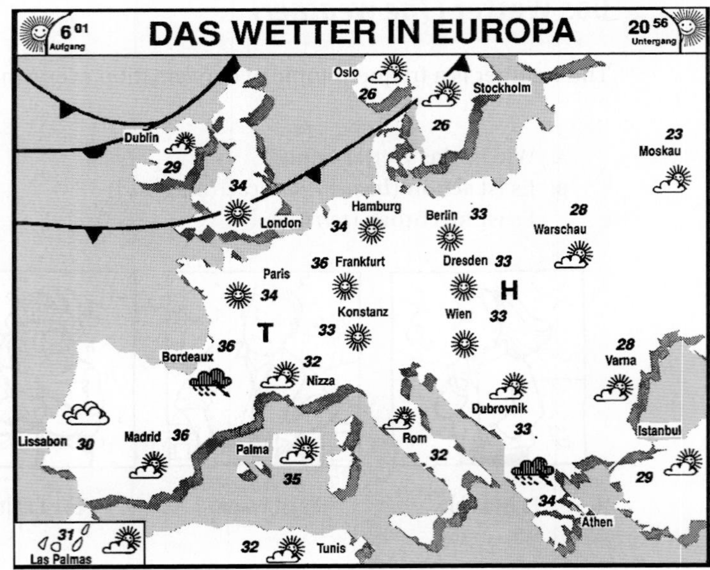

1. Look at the upper left- and right-hand corners of the map. What do **Aufgang** and **Untergang** mean?
2. What season is shown on the map? (**Ist es heiß oder kalt?**)
3. Ask each other about the weather in various cities. (**Wie ist das Wetter in Hamburg?**)

Lab Manual Einführung, The Months.

The stress is on the second syllable in **April** and **August**.

Die Monate (*The months*)

im Januar (*in January*)	im Mai	im September
im Februar	im Juni	im Oktober
im März	im Juli	im November
im April	im August	im Dezember

13 Gruppenarbeit: Im April regnet es. Im Dezember ist es ... Describe the weather typical for the following months.

Wie ist das Wetter im ...

Januar?

August?

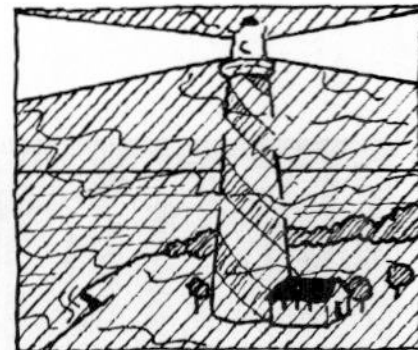

September?

März?

Oktober?

heute?

Die Zahlen (*The numbers*)

Lab Manual Einführung, The Numbers from 0 to 20.

0 null	11 elf
1 eins	12 zwölf
2 zwei	13 dreizehn
3 drei	14 vierzehn
4 vier	15 fünfzehn
5 fünf	16 sechzehn
6 sechs	17 siebzehn
7 sieben	18 achtzehn
8 acht	19 neunzehn
9 neun	20 zwanzig
10 zehn	

QUESTION WORD

wie viele? *how many?*

„Wie ist die Nummer bitte?"

14 Gruppenarbeit: Wie ist die Telefonnummer? (*What is the telephone number?*)

Read these business telephone numbers aloud.

Ristorante Vivarium
Schnampelweg 4 · 64287 Darmstadt · Telefon 06151/47651
Staatliche Schlösser und Gärten
Schloß Schwetzingen
Telefon 06202/81-481
Atelier für Austellungsdesign
ARCHI ME DES
ARCHITEKTUR MEDIEN DESIGN
Urbanstr.116 - 10967 Berlin
Tel 030 / 789 99 0505
www.archi-me-des.de
EIGENER ABSCHLEPPDIENST
K. Walter
VORM. ZINNEKER
1230 WIEN, BREITENFURTERSTR. 213
804 2142
Autokosmetik
KAROSSERIE-FACHWERKSTÄTTE
Einbrenn-und Sonderlackierung
Hotel & Restaurant
Zum Ritter
Elmar Zuspann
Kanalstr. 18–20
36037 Fulda
Tel. 06 61-25 08 00
Fax. 06 61-25 08 01 74
Hotel zum Ritter
Berufskleidung Marx
Silhöfer Straße 10 · 35578 Wetzlar
Telefon 0 64 41 - 4 23 65

These numbers include area codes beginning with 0. When dialing German numbers from outside Germany, omit the zero. For example, to dial the Darmstadt number from the U.S., dial 011 (international operator), 49 (country code), then the area code 6151 (without zero), and then the local number 47651. The numeral 49 is the country code for Germany; it's 43 for Austria and 41 for Switzerland.

Wie spät ist es bitte? (*What time is it, please?*)

„Wie spät ist es?" (Ladenschild [*shop sign*] in Wien)

Lab Manual Einführung, Variations on dialogues.

Es ist drei Uhr.

Es ist Viertel nach sieben.

Es ist Viertel vor zehn.

Es ist ein Uhr. *or* **Es ist eins.**

Es ist elf (Minuten) nach zehn.

Es ist vierzehn vor acht.

The half hour is counted in German in relation to the following full hour, not the preceding hour as in English.

Es ist halb acht.
(literally) *It is halfway to eight; that is, it is 7:30.*

15 Partnerarbeit: Wie spät ist es bitte? Take turns asking each other for the time.

1

2

3

4

5

Persönliche Fragen (*Personal questions*)

QUESTION WORD

woher? *from where?* (origin)

When you meet people, you usually want to find out some basic facts about them, such as where they come from. Listen to the following mini-dialogue and repeat it after your instructor.

Woher kommst du? connotes *Where were you born?*

A: **Woher kommst du?** *Where do you come from?*
B: **Ich komme aus Boston.** *I come from Boston.*

	kommen	***to come***
ich	komme	*I come*
du	kommst	*you come*
Sie	kommen	*you come*
er	kommt	*he comes*
sie	kommt	*she comes*

16 Gruppenarbeit: Woher? Walk around the classroom and find out what cities, states, or foreign countries your classmates are from. Your instructor can help you with the German names of other countries.

BEISPIEL: A: Woher kommst du?
B: Ich komme aus ________.

In-Text Audio CD

Useful classroom expressions

SAM Lab Manual **Lab Manual** Einführung, *Useful Classroom Expressions, The Sounds of German.*

Wie sagt man „the book" auf Deutsch?	*How do you say "the book" in German?*
Man sagt „das Buch".	*You say "das Buch."*
Übersetzen Sie bitte.	*Please translate.*
Wiederholen Sie bitte.	*Please repeat.*
Üben wir!	*Let's practice!*
Machen Sie Nummer drei, bitte.	*Please do number three.*
Alle zusammen, bitte.	*All together, please.*
Sie sprechen zu leise.	*You're speaking too softly.*
Sprechen Sie bitte lauter.	*Please speak more loudly.*
Sie sprechen zu schnell.	*You're speaking too fast.*
Sprechen Sie bitte langsamer.	*Please speak more slowly.*
Wie bitte?	*I beg your pardon? What did you say?*
Antworten Sie bitte auf Deutsch!	*Please answer in German.*
Das ist richtig.	*That's correct.*
Das ist falsch.	*That's incorrect.*
Verstehen Sie das?	*Do you understand that?*

Wortschatz (*Vocabulary*)

The following list contains all the words and expressions from the **Einführung** that you need to know, except the numbers from 1–20 and expressions for telling time.

Greetings

Guten Abend! Good evening!
Guten Morgen! Good morning!
Guten Tag! Hello!
Hallo! / **Tag!** Hi!

Partings

Auf Wiedersehen! Good-bye!
Bis morgen. Until tomorrow.
Schönes Wochenende! Have a nice weekend!
Danke, gleichfalls! Thanks, same to you!
Tschüss! So long!

Days of the week

Montag Monday
Dienstag Tuesday
Mittwoch Wednesday
Donnerstag Thursday
Freitag Friday
Samstag/Sonnabend Saturday
Sonntag Sunday

Question words

was? what?
wer? who?
wie? how?
wie viele? how many?
wo? where?
woher? from where?

Courtesy titles

Frau Mrs., Ms.
Herr Mr.

Personal questions

Wie heißen Sie? / Wie heißt du? What's your name?
Ich heiße ... My name is . . .

Time and place

der Tag day
heute today
morgen tomorrow
da there
Wie spät ist es, bitte? What time is it, please?
Woher kommst du? Where do you come from?

Classroom words

der Lehrer, die Lehrerin (school) teacher
der Professor, die Professorin professor
der Schüler, die Schülerin pupil, student (*pre-college*)
der Student, die Studentin (university) student
der Bleistift pencil
der Kugelschreiber ballpoint pen
der Radiergummi rubber eraser
der Stuhl chair
der Tisch table
der Wischer blackboard eraser
das Buch book
das Fenster window
das Heft notebook
das Papier paper
das Poster poster
die Kreide chalk
die Landkarte map
die Tafel blackboard
die Tür door
die Uhr clock, watch
die Wand wall

Months of the year

Januar
Februar
März
April
Mai
Juni
Juli
August
September
Oktober
November
Dezember

The weather

Wie ist das Wetter heute? How's the weather today?
Es regnet / schneit. It's raining / snowing.
Es ist schön / furchtbar. It's beautiful / terrible.
heiß hot
kalt cold
kühl cool
warm warm
neblig foggy
sonnig sunny
windig windy
wolkig cloudy

Almanach

Profile of the Federal Republic of Germany

Area: 357,000 square kilometers; 138,000 square miles

Population: 82.4 million, or 231 people per square kilometer (597 per square mile)

Currency: der Euro; 1€ = 100 Cent

Major Cities: Berlin (largest city, official capital, pop. 3.4 million) • Hamburg (pop. 1.7 million) • Munich (pop. 1.4 million) • Cologne (pop. 1.02 million) • Frankfurt am Main (pop. 660,000) • Stuttgart (pop. 591,000) • Düsseldorf (pop. 579,000) • Leipzig (pop. 504,000) • Dresden (pop. 490,000)

Religions: Protestant: 33.4% • Catholic: 33.4% • Muslim: 4% • unaffiliated or other: 29.2%

When the Second World War ended in 1945, the victorious Allies divided Germany into four zones of occupation: American, British, French, and Soviet. Their original intention was to denazify and reunite Germany, but in 1949 the ideological tensions of the Cold War led to the creation of two German states. The Federal Republic of Germany (FRG) in the West and the German Democratic Republic (GDR) in the East existed side by side for 41 years. The reunification of 1990 merged one of the most affluent capitalist countries with one of the most prosperous socialist countries from the Eastern bloc.

But the changes brought about by reunification were not all positive. Forty years of state ownership left eastern Germany's industry obsolete and unable to compete in the Western marketplace. Although industries in the former GDR were quickly privatized, this process caused high rates of unemployment in the East. Germans in both East and West still sometimes regard each other with suspicion and resentment, and overcoming those feelings will surely take time.

Today, the unified nation has an area slightly smaller than France. Although the very low birth rate of the Federal Republic is cause for concern (8.25 live births per 1000 inhabitants compared to 14.14 in the USA), the country remains economically one of the strongest members of the European Union (EU).

The FRG today faces new challenges on both a European and a global scale. As one of the most important member states of the EU, Germany has a decisive voice in the development of joint EU defense, agricultural, monetary, and environmental policies. Like its EU partners, Germany struggles to find the right balance between its traditional culture and the diversity brought by immigrants from beyond the borders of the EU. It also needs to find the best way to compete in the global marketplace while retaining the high wages and excellent social services enjoyed by German workers.

Berlin, der Reichstag

KAPITEL

Kapitel = *Chapter*

„Hallo Karin, wie geht's dir?"

Wie geht es dir?

Kommunikation

- Making statements
- Asking yes/no questions
- Asking when, who, where, what, etc.

Kultur (*Culture*)

- Learning about the social implications of German forms of address

In diesem Kapitel (*In this chapter*)

- **Lyrik zum Vorlesen (*Poetry for reading aloud*)**
  Kinderreime, Zungenbrecher
- **Grammatik (*Grammar*)**
  1. Subject pronouns
  2. Verbs: Infinitive and present tense
  3. Nouns: Gender, pronoun agreement, noun plurals
  4. Nominative case
  5. The sentence: German word order
  6. Flavoring particles **(ja)**
- **Lesestück (*Reading*)**
  Wie sagt man *„you"* auf Deutsch?
- **Almanach**
  Where Is German Spoken?

DIALOGE

Dialoge = *Dialogues*

The green in-text audio icon indicates that this material is recorded on your in-text audio CDs.

Lab Manual Kap. (Kapitel) 1, Dialoge, Fragen, Hören Sie gut zu!, Üb. (Übung) zur Aussprache [**ch**].

In Eile

HERR LEHMANN: Guten Morgen, Frau Hauser!
FRAU HAUSER: Morgen, Herr Lehmann. Entschuldigung, aber ich bin in Eile. Ich fliege um elf nach Wien.
HERR LEHMANN: Wann kommen Sie wieder zurück?
FRAU HAUSER: Am Mittwoch bin ich wieder im Büro – also dann, auf Wiedersehen!
HERR LEHMANN: Wiedersehen! Gute Reise!

Die Mensa

KARIN: Tag, Michael!
MICHAEL: Hallo, Karin! Wie ist die Suppe heute?
KARIN: Sie ist ganz gut. Übrigens, arbeitest du viel im Moment?
MICHAEL: Nein, nicht sehr viel. Warum fragst du?
KARIN: Ich gehe heute Abend zu Horst. Du auch?
MICHAEL: Ja, natürlich.
KARIN: Super! Also, tschüss, bis dann.

In colloquial German, **Guten Morgen!**, **Auf Wiedersehen!**, and **Guten Tag!** are often shortened to **Morgen!**, **Wiedersehen!**, and **Tag!**

You can find colloquial English equivalents of the **Dialoge** in Appendix 4.

The expression **Wie geht es Ihnen?** (familiar: **Wie geht es dir?**) means literally "How goes it for you?" The forms **Ihnen** and **dir** (= *to* or *for you*) are pronouns in the dative case. You will learn more about them in **Kapitel 5.**

Typisch für September

FRAU BACHMANN: Guten Tag, Frau Kuhn! Wie geht es Ihnen heute?
FRAU KUHN: Tag, Frau Bachmann! Sehr gut, danke, und Ihnen?
FRAU BACHMANN: Danke, auch gut. Was machen die Kinder heute?
FRAU KUHN: Sie spielen draußen, das Wetter ist ja so schön.
FRAU BACHMANN: Ja, endlich scheint die Sonne. Aber vielleicht regnet es morgen wieder.
FRAU KUHN: Das ist typisch für September.

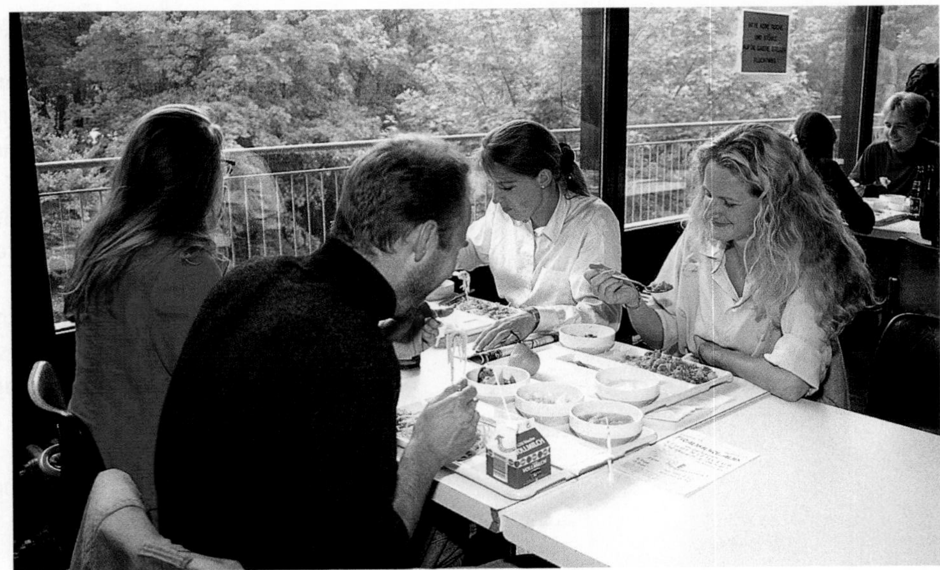

„Wie ist die Suppe heute?"

Wortschatz 1 (*Vocabulary 1*)

Verben (*Verbs*)

arbeiten to work
fliegen to fly
fragen to ask
gehen to go; to walk
kommen to come
machen to make; to do
regnen to rain
scheinen to shine; to seem
sein to be
spielen to play
wohnen to live; to dwell

Nouns are grouped by gender for easier learning. Always learn the article and the plural along with the singular of each noun. Don't just learn **Kind** = *child*, but rather **das Kind, die Kinder**. Noun plurals are presented in a standard abbreviated form. See pp. 27–28 below.

Substantive (*Nouns*)

der **Abend, -e** evening
  heute Abend this evening, tonight
der **Herr, -en** gentleman
  Herr Lehmann Mr. Lehmann
der **Morgen, -** morning
der **September** September
der **Tag, -e** day
das **Büro, -s** office
  im Büro in the office
das **Kind, -er** child
das **Wetter** weather
(das) **Wien** Vienna

City names are neuter in German but are seldom used with the article. The article for cities is given in parentheses in the **Wortschatz**.

die **Frau, -en** woman; wife
  Frau Kuhn Mrs./Ms. Kuhn
die **Mensa** university cafeteria
die **Sonne** sun
die **Straße, -n** street, road
die **Suppe, -n** soup

Adjektive und Adverbien (*Adjectives and adverbs*)

German has no equivalent for the English adverbial ending *-ly*. For example, the German word **natürlich** can mean both *natural* and *naturally.* (Similarly, **gut** means both *good* and *well.*)

auch also, too
da there
dann then
draußen outside
endlich finally
gut good; well
  ganz gut pretty good; pretty well
hier here
natürlich natural(ly); of course
schön beautiful(ly)
sehr very
typisch typical(ly)
vielleicht maybe, perhaps
wieder again

Andere Vokabeln (*Other words*)

aber but
also well
bis until; by
  bis dann until then; by then
danke thanks
für for
in in
ja yes; also (*untranslatable "flavoring particle." See p. 34.*)
nach to (*with cities and countries*)
nein no
nicht not
übrigens by the way
um (*prep.*) at (*with expressions of time*)
und (*conj.*) and
usw. (= **und so weiter**) etc. (= and so forth)
viel (*pron.*) much, a lot

There is a complete list of abbreviations on p. 451.

wann? when?
warum? why?
wie (*conj.*) how; like, as
zu (*prep.*) to (*with people*); (*adv.*) too (*as in* "too much")
zurück back

Nützliche Ausdrücke (*Useful expressions*)

am Mittwoch (Donnerstag usw.) on Wednesday (Thursday, etc.)
Entschuldigung! Pardon me! Excuse me!
Gute Reise! (Have a) good trip!
im Moment at the moment
in Eile in a hurry
Super! Terrific! Great!
Wie geht's? / Wie geht es Ihnen? How's it going? How are you?

Gegensätze (*Opposites*)

Study hint: Learn antonyms (opposites) in pairs. They are all active vocabulary.

gut ≠ schlecht good ≠ bad
hier ≠ da here ≠ there
schön ≠ hässlich beautiful ≠ ugly
der Tag ≠ die Nacht day ≠ night
viel ≠ wenig much, a lot ≠ not much, little

Mit anderen Worten (*In other words*)

wunderschön = sehr schön

Variationen (*Variations*)

A Persönliche Fragen *(Personal questions).* Answer your instructor's questions.

1. Wo wohnen Sie?
2. Wie geht es Ihnen heute?
3. Arbeiten Sie viel im Moment?
4. Was machen Sie heute Abend?

B Partnerarbeit: An welchem Tag? *(Partner work: On which day?)* Ask each other the questions below. Your partner answers with any day of the week.

BEISPIEL: A: Wann kommst du zurück?
B: Am Dienstag.

1. Wann arbeitest du?
2. Wann fliegst du nach Wien?
3. Wann gehst du zu Gisela?
4. Wann kommst du zurück?
5. Wann spielst du Tennis?

C Partnerarbeit: Wann fliegst du? The clock faces show departure times from the Frankfurt airport. Ask each other when you're flying to various places.

BEISPIEL: A: Wann fliegst du nach Zürich?
B: Ich fliege um halb acht.

1. nach Prag

2. nach Moskau

3. nach Kopenhagen

4. nach Madrid

5. nach Toronto

6. nach Singapur

D Vokabeln aktiv: Wie ist die Party? *(How's the party?)*

1. Wie ist die Party? Sie ist ________.
2. Wie ist das Wetter? Es ________.
3. Wie ist die Suppe? Sie ist ________.
4. Wie ist das Büro? Es ist ________.

1.

2.

3.

4.

LYRIK ZUM VORLESEN

Lyrik zum Vorlesen = *Poetry for reading aloud*

In-Text
Audio CD

In each chapter, this section presents some short selections of original German poetry (**Lyrik**), rhymes, or song texts for your enjoyment. Read them aloud. Don't worry about understanding everything. The emphasis here is on the *sound* of German.

Kinderreime°

Children's rhymes

Traditional counting-out rhymes

Eins zwei drei, du bist frei°.
Vier fünf sechs, du bist weg°.
Sieben acht neun, du musst's sein°.

free / *out* / *you are it*

Ich heiße Peter, du heißt Paul.
Ich bin fleißig°, du bist faul°.

hard-working / lazy

Children's alphabet rhyme

A b c d e f und g,
h i j k l m n o p,
q r s t u v w,
x y z und o weh°,
jetzt kann ich das ABC°.

o weh = *oh my*
now I know the ABCs

Zungenbrecher°

Tongue twisters

In Ulm, um Ulm°
und um Ulm herum°.

In Ulm, around Ulm,
and round about Ulm.

Fischers Fritz fischt frische Fische.
Frische Fische fischt Fischers Fritz°.

Fischer's (boy) Fritz fishes fresh fish.
Fresh fish is what Fischer's Fritz fishes.

Ulm lies on the Danube River in the southern German state of Baden-Württemberg. The city's famous Gothic church has the highest spire in the world at 161.6 meters (530 ft.).

GRAMMATIK

Grammatik = *Grammar*

1. Subject pronouns (*Pronomen*)

DEFINITIONEN

What is a pronoun?
A ***pronoun*** is a word such as **er, es,** or **sie** that can be substituted for the name of a person or thing: **Maria ist eine Studentin. *Sie* ist sehr intelligent. Wo ist mein Buch? *Es* ist da.**

What is a subject?
The ***subject*** of a sentence is usually a person or thing performing the action shown by the verb: ***Ich* fliege nach Wien.**

The following German pronouns are used as the subject of a sentence.

	Singular		Plural	
1st person	**ich**	*I*	**wir**	*we*
2nd person	**du** **Sie**	*you* (familiar) *you* (formal)	**ihr** **Sie**	*you* (familiar) *you* (formal)
3rd person	**er** **es** **sie**	*he, it* *it* *she, it*	**sie**	*they*

The three ways to say *you* in German: *du, ihr,* and *Sie*

Use the familiar pronouns **du** (*singular*) and **ihr** (*plural*) when addressing fellow students, children, family members, close friends, animals, and God. Members of certain groups (students, soldiers, athletes, and sometimes colleagues and co-workers) converse among themselves almost exclusively with **du** and **ihr**. People on a first-name basis usually use **du** with each other. In conversation, allow native German speakers to establish which form to use.

Use the formal **Sie** when addressing one or more adults who are not close friends of yours. In writing, always capitalize the pronoun **Sie** when it means *you*. When **sie** means *she* or *they*, it is not capitalized.

The pronoun **ich** is not capitalized unless it is the first word of a sentence.

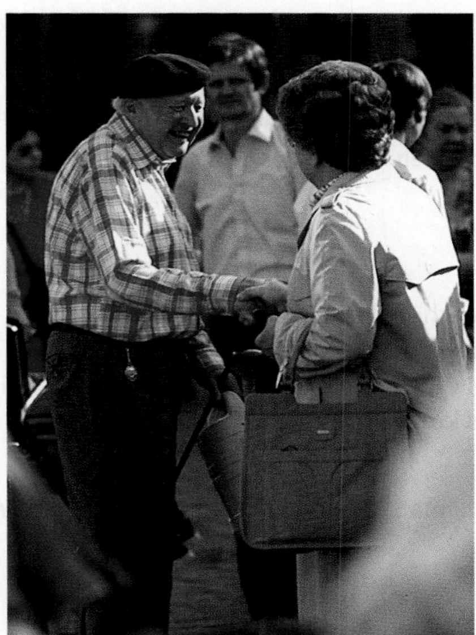

„Tag, Frau Breitenkamp! Wie geht es Ihnen?"

DEFINITION

What is a verb?
A ***verb*** is a word that expresses an action or state of being: **Ich *gehe* zu Horst. Frau Hauser *ist* in Eile.**

2. Verbs (*Verben*): Infinitive and present tense

The infinitive (*der Infinitiv*)

German dictionaries list verbs in the infinitive form. The English infinitive is usually preceded by *to*.

***to** play* ***to** rain*

The German infinitive consists of the verb stem plus the ending **-en** or **-n**.

spiel-	**spielen**	*to play*
wander-	**wandern**	*to hike*

DEFINITION

What is tense?
Tense is a feature of verbs that reflects time levels: past, present, and future: I *ran*, I *run*, I *will run*.

The present tense (*das Präsens*)

A German verb in the present tense has various endings, depending on its subject.

Das Kind spiel**t** draußen.	*The child plays outside.*
Die Kinder spiel**en** draußen.	*The children play outside.*

In order to form the present tense of a German verb, first find the stem by dropping the infinitive ending **-en** or **-n**.

komm- ~~**en**~~

Then add the personal endings.

Stem + ending		Present tense		
ich	komm-**e**	ich	komme	*I come*
du	komm-**st**	du	kommst	*you come* (familiar singular)
er, es, sie	komm-**t**	er, es, sie	kommt	*he, it, she comes*
wir	komm-**en**	wir	kommen	*we come*
ihr	komm-**t**	ihr	kommt	*you come* (familiar plural)
sie, Sie	komm-**en**	sie	kommen	*they come*
		Sie	kommen	*you come* (formal singular and plural)

Lab Manual Kap. 1, Var. (Variation) zu Üb. 1.

Workbook Kap. 1, A.

The verb ending will help you distinguish between **sie** = *she* (**sie kommt**) and **sie**, **Sie** = *they*, *you* (**sie**, **Sie kommen**). The verb ending for third-person plural and the polite *you*-form is always the same. From now on they will be listed together in verb paradigms: **sie**, **Sie kommen**.

1 Übung: Woher kommst du? *(Exercise: Where are you from?)* Say where you and others are from.

BEISPIEL: A: Woher kommst du?
B: Ich komme aus Indiana.

2 Kettenreaktion: Wo wohnst du? *(Chain reaction: Where do you live?)* Say where you live on campus and then ask the next student. If you have an off-campus apartment, say: **Ich wohne privat.**

BEISPIEL: A: Ich wohne in Stone Hall. Wo wohnst du?
B: Ich wohne in ________.

Regular variations in personal endings

Verbs with stems ending in **-d**, **-t**, or a consonant cluster such as **-gn** require an **-e-** before the **du**, **er**, and **ihr** endings to make them pronounceable.

arbeiten *to work*				**regnen** *to rain*
stem: **arbeit-**				stem: **regn-**
ich	arbeite	wir	arbeiten	
du	arbeit**est**	ihr	arbeit**et**	es regn**et**
er, es, sie	arbeit**et**	sie, Sie	arbeiten	

SAM **Lab Manual** Kap. 1, Üb. 3, Var. zur Gruppenarbeit 4.

3 Übung: Wer arbeitet heute? Tell who is working today, using the cued pronoun or name.

BEISPIEL: wir
Wir arbeiten heute.

1. ich
2. Herr Lehmann
3. sie (*they*)
4. du
5. ihr
6. Sie (*you*)
7. wir
8. Michael

4 Gruppenarbeit: Was machst du heute? ***(Group work: What are you doing today?) (4 Personen)*** Ask each other what you're doing today.

A: Was machst du heute, Katrin?
B: Ich fliege nach Wien. Und was machst du heute?
C: Ich ________. Und was machst du heute?

English and German present tense compared

German present tense is equivalent to three English forms:

ich gehe { *I go* / *I am going* / *I do go* }

Present tense with future meaning

In German, the present tense often expresses future meaning, especially when a time phrase in the sentence makes the future meaning clear.

Ich **fliege** um elf nach Wien.	*I'm flying to Vienna at eleven.*
Mittwoch **bin** ich wieder zurück.	*I'll be back Wednesday.*

The verb *sein*: *to be*

Like *to be* in English, the verb **sein** is irregular; its forms must be memorized.

ich	**bin**	*I am*	wir	**sind**	*we are*
du	**bist**	*you are*	ihr	**seid**	*you are*
er, es, sie	**ist**	*he, it, she is*	sie, Sie	**sind**	*they, you are*

SAM Lab Manual

Lab Manual Kap. 1, Var. zu Üb. 5.

Workbook Kap. 1, B.

5 Partnerarbeit: Seid ihr auch so? You can use the following adjectives to describe your personality. Because they all have English cognates, they should be easily understandable. Ask each other questions to find out which of these traits you have in common. Make a list of three or four characteristics you share.

BEISPIEL: A: Ich bin sehr sentimental. Bist du auch sentimental?
B: Ja, ich bin (immer [*always*] / oft / sehr) sentimental. (oder [*or*]) Nein, ich bin (selten / nicht / nie [*never*]) emotional.

aktiv	kreativ
athletisch	modern
clever	naiv
dynamisch	objektiv
elegant	optimistisch
exzentrisch	pessimistisch
intelligent	progressiv
kompetent	sentimental
konservativ	subjektiv

6 Gruppenarbeit. Now go with your partner to another pair of students and ask questions to find out how they describe themselves. Use the words listed in Exercise 5.

BEISPIEL: GRUPPE A: Seid ihr auch sentimental?
GRUPPE B: Nein, wir sind nicht sentimental, wir sind ________. Und ihr?

DEFINITION

What is a noun?
A ***noun*** is a word that denotes a person (**Frau Braun**, **Kind**, **Hermann**), a place (**Wien**), a thing or animal (**Buch**, **Pelikan**), or an idea or quality (**Solidarität**).

3. Nouns (*Substantive*): Noun gender, pronoun agreement, noun plurals

You have learned that German has three genders for nouns, shown by the definite article (**der**, **das**, **die**). When a pronoun replaces a noun (*the chair* = *it*), it must have the same gender.

Wo ist **der** Stuhl?	**Er** ist draußen.	*It's outside.*
Wo ist **das** Buch?	**Es** ist hier.	*It's here.*
Wo ist **die** Tafel?	**Sie** ist da.	*It's there.*

Note that **er**, **es**, and **sie** can all mean *it*. Note also the similarities between the definite article and its corresponding pronoun.

der Stuhl → **er**
da**s** Buch → e**s**
die Tafel → **sie**

Plural forms do not show gender. The definite article **die** is used with all plural nouns, and the pronoun **sie** replaces all plural nouns.

Wo sind die Stühle?
Wo sind die Bücher? } Sie sind hier. *They are here.*
Wo sind die Tafeln?

Lab Manual Kap. 1, Üb. 7; Var. zu Üb. 7.

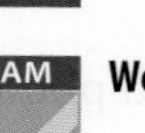
Workbook Kap. 1, C, D.

7 Übung. Answer the questions affirmatively. Use a pronoun.

BEISPIEL: A: Ist Rolf heute in Eile?
B: Ja, er ist heute in Eile.

1. Ist das Buch gut?
2. Ist Frau Schmidt sehr intelligent?
3. Spielen die Kinder draußen?
4. Ist das Wetter typisch für September?
5. Scheint die Sonne heute?
6. Sind Karin und Michael athletisch?
7. Ist die Suppe gut?
8. Ist der Tag schön?

8 Partnerarbeit: Hier oder da? Partner A asks where the things in the left-hand column are. Partner B answers with the correct pronoun, pointing to the object. Reverse roles for the right-hand column.

BEISPIEL: A: Wo ist die Tafel?
B: Sie ist da.

das Buch	der Radiergummi
das Heft	das Fenster
die Tür	der Professor/die Professorin
der Bleistift	der Tisch
die Wand	der Stuhl
die Landkarte	das Poster

 Noun plurals (*der Plural*)

Here are the nouns you learned in the **Einführung** with their plurals:
der Lehrer, - / die Lehrerin, -nen
der Professor, -en / die Professorin, -nen
der Schüler, - / die Schülerin, -nen
der Student, -en / die Studentin, -nen
der Bleistift, -e
das Buch, ¨er
das Fenster, -
das Heft, -e
der Kugelschreiber, -
die Landkarte, -n
das Poster, -
der Stuhl, ¨e
die Tafel, -n
der Tag, -e
der Tisch, -e
die Tür, -en
die Uhr, -en
die Wand, ¨e

The most common plural ending for English nouns is *-s* or *-es*: chair > chair*s*; dish > dish*es*. However, English speakers are also familiar with other ways of forming the plural: man → *men*; mouse → *mice*; child → *children*; sheep → *sheep*.

German has a great variety of plural forms. No single form predominates. Here are examples of all German plural forms.

	Singular	Plural
No change	der Lehrer	die Lehrer
Umlaut added to stem vowel	die Mutter	die M**ü**tter
Add ending **-e**	der Tisch	die Tisch**e**
Umlaut + ending **-e**	der Stuhl	die St**ü**hl**e**
Add ending **-er**	das Kind	die Kind**er**
Umlaut + ending **-er**	das Buch	die B**ü**ch**er**
Add ending **-en**	die Frau	die Frau**en**
Add ending **-n**	die Straße	die Straße**n**
Add ending **-s**	das Büro	die Büro**s**

Dictionaries and vocabulary lists customarily use an abbreviation to indicate the plural. An umlaut above the hyphen indicates that the stem (stressed) vowel is umlauted in the plural.

Dictionary entry	You must learn
der **Lehrer, -**	der **Lehrer**, die **Lehrer**
die **Mutter, -̈**	die **Mutter**, die **Mütter**
der **Tag, -e**	der **Tag**, die **Tage**
der **Stuhl, -̈e**	der **Stuhl**, die **Stühle**

SAM Lab Manual

Lab Manual Kap. 1, Üb. 9, 10.

SAM Workbook

Workbook Kap. 1, E.

Turn to the German-English Vocabulary at end of book for more practice with plurals.

9 Übung. Look at the following nouns and say aloud both the singular and plural forms with their articles.

1. das Kind, -er
2. das Büro, -s
3. der Tisch, -e
4. die Mutter, -̈
5. die Tafel, -n
6. die Straße, -n
7. der Stuhl, -̈e
8. die Frau, -en

10 Übung. Make the subjects plural. Change the verbs accordingly.

BEISPIEL: Der Herr kommt um elf.
Die Herren kommen um elf.

1. Das Büro ist sehr schön.
2. Die Frau fliegt nach Wien.
3. Das Kind kommt heute Abend.
4. Die Straße ist sehr schön.
5. Das Buch ist gut.
6. Der Lehrer arbeitet morgen im Büro.
7. Der Tag ist schön.

Was machen die Kinder heute?

4. Nominative case *(der Nominativ)*

The case of a noun or a pronoun signals its function in the sentence. German has four cases: nominative, accusative, dative, and genitive. The article used with the noun shows its case.

DEFINITION

What is a definite article?

The ***definite article*** in English is *the*. In German, the definite article shows the *gender* (masculine, neuter, or feminine), *number* (singular or plural), and *case* of the noun it is used with. As a result, German has many forms that all correspond to *the* in English.

Der Schüler fragt den Lehrer.	*The pupil asks the teacher.*
Der Lehrer fragt **den** Schüler.	*The teacher asks the pupil.*

Nominative case		*Accusative case*
der Schüler		**den** Schüler
subject	vs.	*direct object*
person asking		*person being asked*

This chapter uses only the nominative case, which is the case for the subject of a sentence and for a predicate nominative (see page 30). The subject pronouns you have learned in this chapter (**ich**, **du**, etc.) are all in the nominative case.

Definite article in the nominative case

You have already learned the definite articles (*the*) in the nominative.

	Singular	Plural
masculine	**der** Mann	**die** Männer
neuter	**das** Kind	**die** Kinder
feminine	**die** Frau	**die** Frauen

Indefinite article in the nominative case

Like the definite article, the indefinite article (*a, an*) also shows the gender, number, and case of the noun it is used with. Here are the indefinite articles in the nominative:

	Singular	Plural
masculine	**ein** Mann	Männer
neuter	**ein** Kind	Kinder
feminine	**eine** Frau	Frauen

NOTE: Masculine and neuter singular indefinite articles are identical in the nominative: **ein** Mann, **ein** Kind. The indefinite article has no plural in German or English.

Ein Kind ist hier. → **Kinder** sind hier. *A **child** is here.* → ***Children** are here.*

11 Übung: Was ist das? What is your instructor pointing to?

BEISPIEL: Was ist das?
Das ist ein Fenster.

Uses of the nominative case

The subject of the sentence is always in the nominative case. Notice that the subject does not have to come at the beginning of the sentence.

Der Herr ist in Eile.	*The gentleman is in a hurry.*
Endlich kommt **die Suppe**.	*The soup is finally coming.*
Morgen fliegt **sie** zurück.	*She's flying back tomorrow.*

A predicate nominative is a noun that refers to the same person or thing as the subject of the sentence. It follows the subject and the linking verb **sein**.

DEFINITION

What is a linking verb?
A ***linking verb*** functions like the equals sign in an equation. **Herr Braun *ist* der Professor**. The most common linking verb in any language is the verb *to be* (**sein**). You will also learn the linking verbs **bleiben** *to remain*; **heißen** *to be called*; and **werden** *to become*. Like **sein**, they are all followed by the predicate nominative.

Das ist **Frau Schmidt**.	*That is Mrs. Schmidt.*
Paul ist **ein Kind**.	*Paul is a child.*

REMEMBER: Always use nominative case after the verb **sein**.

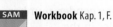

SAM Lab Manual — **Lab Manual** Kap. 1, Var. zu Üb. 12.

12 **Gruppenspiel (*Group game*): Was ist das? Wer ist das?** One student leads the game. The rest are divided into two teams. The leader points to an object or a person in the room and asks who or what it is. Teams answer alternately. The team with the most correct answers wins.

SAM Workbook — **Workbook** Kap. 1, F.

BEISPIEL: Wer ist das? Das ist Peter.
Was ist das? Das ist ein Stuhl.

DEFINITION

What is a sentence?
A ***sentence*** is an utterance containing a noun or pronoun subject and a verb that goes with it.

Making statements is a communicative goal.

5. The sentence (*der Satz*): German word order (*die Wortstellung*)

Statements: Verb-second word order

In English statements, the subject almost always comes immediately before the verb phrase.

subject verb
We **are going** to Richard's tonight.

Other elements may precede the subject-verb combination.

Tonight **we are going** to Richard's.

In German statements, the position of the verb is fixed. *The verb is always the second element.*

1	2	3	4
Wir	**gehen**	heute Abend	zu Richard.

Learn this ironclad rule well. If an element other than the subject begins the sentence, the verb *remains* in second position and the subject then *follows* the verb. Note the difference from English, where the subject always *precedes* the verb.

1	2	3	4
Heute Abend	**gehen**	wir	zu Richard.
Zu Richard	**gehen**	wir	heute Abend.

Time phrases (**heute Abend**) or prepositional phrases (**zu Richard**) count as *one* grammatical element.

NOTE: Initial **ja**, **nein**, **und**, and **aber** do *not* count as first elements.

0	1	2	3
Ja,	wir	gehen	zu Richard.
Aber	wir	gehen	zu Richard.

SAM **Workbook** Kap. 1, G.

13 Übung. Restate the sentences, beginning with the word or phrase in italics.

BEISPIEL: Ich arbeite *übrigens* viel.
Übrigens arbeite ich viel.

1. Die Lehrerin geht *morgen* zu Frau Bachmann.
2. Die Sonne scheint *endlich* wieder.
3. Es regnet *heute*.
4. Das ist *vielleicht* die Straße.
5. Ich arbeite viel *im Moment*.
6. Es regnet *natürlich* viel.

„Es regnet natürlich viel." Straße in Leer, Ostfriesland.

14 Partnerarbeit: Ist es wahrscheinlich? Use the following cues to ask questions. Your partner responds, beginning with an adverb from the right-hand column.

BEISPIEL: fliegen / Berlin?
A: Fliegst du nach Berlin?
B: Vielleicht fliege ich nach Berlin.

Partner A	**Partner B**
gehen / zu Marion?	Natürlich ...
arbeiten / im Moment?	Wahrscheinlich (*probably*) ...
kommen / zurück?	Vielleicht ...
wohnen / hier?	
fliegen / nach Leipzig?	

Questions

There are two main types of questions in German, yes/no questions and information questions.

Asking yes/no questions is a communicative goal.

- Yes/no questions are answered by **ja** or **nein**. In a yes/no question, the verb is always the first element.

Ist Andrea hier?	*Is Andrea here?*
Arbeitet sie in Berlin?	*Does she work in Berlin?*
Kommst du wieder zurück?	*Are you coming back again?*

SAM **Lab Manual** Kap. 1, Üb. 15.

SAM **Workbook** Kap. 1, H, I, J.

15 Übung. Change these statements to yes/no questions.

BEISPIEL: Stefan arbeitet in Stuttgart.
Arbeitet Stefan in Stuttgart?

1. Das ist typisch für September.
2. Ihr geht wieder zu Karin.
3. Es regnet.
4. Herr Hauser fliegt nach Berlin.
5. Frau Kuhn kommt auch.
6. Du arbeitest viel im Moment.
7. Er ist sehr in Eile.
8. Der Herr kommt am Mittwoch zurück.

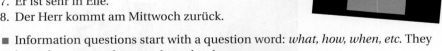

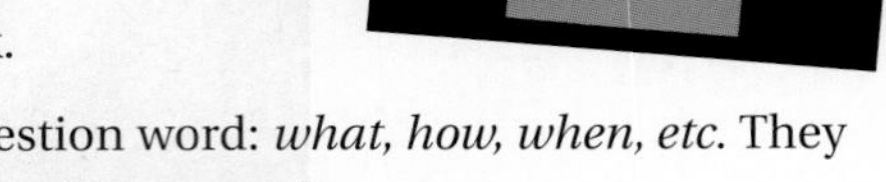

- Information questions start with a question word: *what, how, when, etc.* They have the same verb-second word order as statements.

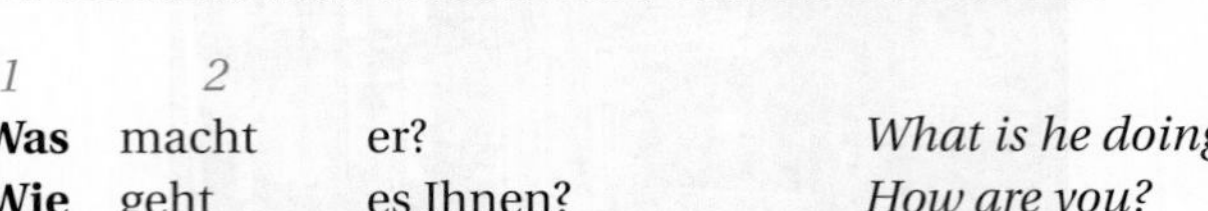

1	*2*		
Was	macht	er?	*What is he doing?*
Wie	geht	es Ihnen?	*How are you?*
Wann	kommen	Sie wieder zurück?	*When are you coming back again?*

Here are some question words.

Asking when, who, where, what, etc. is a communicative goal.

FRAGEWÖRTER

wann	*when*	**Wann** kommt sie zurück?
warum	*why*	**Warum** fragst du?
was	*what*	**Was** macht er?
wer	*who*	**Wer** ist das?
wie	*how*	**Wie** geht es dir?
wo	*where*	**Wo** wohnen Sie?
woher	*from where*	**Woher** kommt ihr?

NOTE: Do not confuse **wer** (*who*) and **wo** (*where*)!

16 Übung. Here are some answers. What were the questions?

BEISPIEL: Das ist der Professor.
Wer ist das?

1. Er fliegt um elf.
2. Die Lehrer sind im Büro.
3. Das ist Frau Bachmann.
4. Das ist die Mensa.
5. Die Suppe ist gut, danke.
6. Sie kommt aus Deutschland.

Info-Austausch (*Information exchange*)

17 Was machen die Kinder heute? Throughout *Neue Horizonte* are activities entitled *Info-Austausch* in which you and a partner will exchange information. In this first one, work together to say what people are doing today. Partner A uses the table below. Partner B uses the corresponding table in Appendix 1.

BEISPIEL: A: Was machen die Kinder heute?
B: Sie spielen draußen. Was macht Karin heute?
A: Sie ________.

Partner A:

die Kinder	
	geht zu Horst
Michael	
	spielt Tennis
Frau Hauser	
	kommt zurück

18 Was machst du? Answer each question, using the English cues in parentheses. Be sure to answer the **du**-questions using **ich,** and **ihr**-questions using **wir**. (**Was machst du? Ich fliege ... Was macht ihr? Wir fliegen ...**).

BEISPIEL: A: Was machst du morgen? (*flying to Vienna*)
B: Ich fliege nach Wien.

1. Was macht ihr heute? (*going to Stefan's*)
2. Was machst du im Moment, Richard? (*working a lot*)
3. Was machst du, Regina? (*playing outside*)
4. Was macht ihr am Mittwoch, Rolf und Helene? (*flying to Hamburg*)

19 Schreiben wir mal. *(Let's write.)* Answer the yes/no questions affirmatively. Use complete sentences.

1. Bist du in Eile?
2. Fliegt der Professor nach New York?
3. Regnet es wieder?
4. Arbeitest du morgen?
5. Ist das Wetter typisch für September?
6. Spielen die Kinder draußen?

Time before place

DEFINITION

What is an adverb?
An ***adverb*** is a word that expresses time, manner, or place and modifies a verb, adjective, or another adverb. Manner describes how something is done: slowly, well, clumsily, etc.

German adverbs such as **heute** and adverbial phrases such as **nach Wien** occur in the sequence *time before place*. The usual sequence in English is exactly the reverse: *place before time*.

	time	*place*		*place*	*time*
Sie fliegt	**morgen**	nach Wien.	*She's flying*	*to Vienna*	***tomorrow.***
Wir gehen	**heute Abend**	zu Horst.	*We're going*	*to Horst's*	***tonight.***

20 Übung: Heute oder morgen? Answer with a complete sentence, using either **heute** or **morgen**.

BEISPIEL: A: Wann gehen Sie zu Stefanie?
B: Ich gehe heute zu Stefanie.

1. Wann fliegt Stefan nach Wien?
2. Wann geht Frau Bachmann zu Frau Kuhn?
3. Wann spielen die Kinder draußen?
4. Wann kommt Herr Lehmann zurück?

6. Flavoring particles (*ja*)

German adds various kinds of emphasis to sentences by using intensifying words known as *flavoring particles*. These can seldom be directly translated into English, but it is important to become familiar with them and understand the intensity, nuance, or "flavor" they add to a sentence.

One flavoring particle frequently used in declarative sentences (i.e., statements) is **ja**. As a flavoring particle, **ja** does not mean *yes*, but rather adds the sense of *after all, really*.

In the third dialogue at the beginning of this chapter, Frau Kuhn says about her children:

Sie spielen draußen, das Wetter ist **ja** so schön. — *They're playing outside—the weather really is so beautiful.*

The flavoring particle **ja** is usually placed immediately after the verb and personal pronouns. Here is how **ja** might be added to some other sentences from the dialogues:

Ich bin **ja** in Eile. — *I'm in a hurry, after all.*
Ich gehe **ja** heute Abend zu Horst. — *I'm going to Horst's tonight, you know.*

LESESTÜCK

Lesestück = *Reading*

These pre-reading exercises help you to acquire the skill to read a text in German. Always work through them carefully before beginning to read the **Lesestück**. The most valuable technique is *re*-reading the German text as many times as possible.

Note the stress shift: **Professor / Professorin.**

Tipps zum Lesen und Lernen (*Tips for reading and studying*)

Tipps zum Vokabelnlernen (*Tips for learning vocabulary*)

The feminine suffix* -*in You've learned that German often has two different nouns to distinguish between a male and a female.

Professor/Professorin
Schüler/Schülerin
Student/Studentin
Lehrer/Lehrerin
Partner/Partnerin

The suffix **-in** always denotes the female, and its plural is always **-innen**.

-in: die Studentin

-innen: die Studentinnen

Partnerarbeit: Wie heißt der Mann, wie heißt die Frau? With a partner, fill in the blanks. Say the words aloud as you write them.

Mann	eine Frau?	zwei Frauen?
1. Amerikaner	*Amerikanerin*	*Amerikanerinnen*
2. Tourist		
3. Lehrer		
4. Professor		
5. Schüler		
6. Student		
7. Partner		

Lab Manual Kap. 1, Üb. zur Betonung.

Leicht zu merken (*Easy to remember*)

German has many words that look so much like their English equivalents that you can easily guess their meanings. Both languages have borrowed many of these words from Latin or French. You will also notice that contemporary German has borrowed a great deal of vocabulary from English, e.g., **E-Mail, Internet**, and **iPod.** When such words occur in the readings, they are previewed in this special section called **Leicht zu merken**. If the German word is stressed on a different syllable than the English, this will be indicated to the right. You should have no trouble guessing the meanings of these cognates:

die **E-Mail, -s**	(*pronounced as in English*)
formell	for<u>mell</u>
der **Tourist, -en**	Tou<u>rist</u>
die **Universität, -en**	Universi<u>tät</u>

Einstieg in den Text (*Getting into the text*)

Here are some tips to help you get the most out of the reading (**Lesestück**) in each chapter.

- Read the title. Ask yourself what it tells you about the following text. For example, the title, *Wie sagt man* ***you*** *auf Deutsch?*, lets you know that the text discusses the various forms of second-person address. You are already familiar with these.
- Read **Wortschatz 2,** the new active vocabulary for the reading, aloud. Try to identify similarities between English and German forms that will help you remember the words; for example, **grüßen** (*greet*), **Schule** (*school*), **Gruppe** (*group*); **freundlich** (*friendly*), **oft** (*often*).
- Now listen to the reading on the In-Text Audio CDs while following the text in your book.

- Read the text once aloud to yourself without referring back to the vocabulary. Do not try to translate as you read. Your purpose is to get a rough idea of content from the key words you recognize in each paragraph. For example, in the first section of the following reading, you will recognize the words **Touristen**, **Deutschland**, and **Amerikaner**. A good working assumption is that the paragraph deals with tourists in Germany.
- Once you have a general idea of the content of each paragraph, read the text at least one more time, again without trying to translate. Your objective this time is to begin to understand the text on the sentence level. The marginal glosses (marked by the raised degree sign °) will help you to understand words and phrases that are not meant for active use.
- Read and try to answer the **Antworten Sie auf Deutsch** and **Richtig oder falsch?** questions that follow the reading. Refer back to the text only if necessary.

Wortschatz 2

In-Text Audio CD

Verben

duzen to address someone with **du**
grüßen to greet, say hello
hören to hear; to listen
meinen to be of the opinion; to think
sagen to say; to tell
schneien to snow
schreiben to write
siezen to address someone with **Sie**
sprechen to speak
studieren to attend a university; to study; to major in (*a subject*)

Substantive

der **Amerikaner, -** American (*m.*)
der **Deutsche, -n** German (man) (*m.*)
der **Schüler, -** primary or secondary school pupil (*m.*)
der **Student, -en** university student (*m.*)
der **Tourist, -en** tourist (*m.*)
(das) **Deutschland** Germany
die **Amerikanerin, -nen** American (*f.*)
die **Deutsche, -n** German (woman) (*f.*)
die **Reise, -n** trip, journey
eine Reise machen to take a trip
die **Schule, -n** school
die **Schülerin, -nen** primary or secondary school pupil (*f.*)
die **Studentin, -nen** university student (*f.*)
die **Touristin, -nen** tourist (*f.*)
die **Woche, -n** week
diese Woche this week

Note the abbreviations *m.* (for *masculine*) or *f.* (for *feminine*) after **Amerikaner**, **Deutsche**, and other nouns. There is a complete list of abbreviations on p. 451, at the beginning of the German-English end vocabulary.

Adjektive und Adverbien

bald soon
freundlich friendly
höflich polite(ly)
müde tired
noch still
oft often
schon already, yet
viele many
wahrscheinlich probably
ziemlich fairly, quite
zusammen together

Andere Vokabeln

bitte please
einander (*pron.*) each other
miteinander with each other
zueinander to each other
man (*indefinite pron.*) one
oder or

Nützliche Ausdrücke

zum Beispiel for example
auf Deutsch in German
Grüß dich! Hello! Hi! (*to someone you address as* **du**; *mainly used in southern Germany*)

Gegensätze

oft ≠ selten often ≠ seldom
zusammen ≠ allein together ≠ alone

Note on **man**: This pronoun is often best translated by *we, you,* or *they*: **Das sagt man oft.** = *They (people) often say that.* See p. 80 for a complete explanation.

Wie sagt man „you" auf Deutsch?

In-Text Audio CD: Listen to the **Lesestück** as you read the text. Practice reading out loud, following the recording.

Touristen in Deutschland sagen oft, die Deutschen sind sehr freundlich und höflich. Das stimmt, aber wahrscheinlich meinen viele Amerikaner auch, die Deutschen sind ziemlich formell. Kollegen° in einer Firma° zum Beispiel siezen einander oft. In einer E-Mail an seine Kollegin Frau Hauser schreibt Herr Lehmann „Sie":

colleagues / company

Hallo Frau Hauser,
ich höre, Sie sind schon aus Wien zurück. War° die Reise angenehm°?

Ich habe eine kleine Bitte°: Können° wir diese Woche miteinander sprechen, zum Beispiel am Donnerstag um 10 oder um 11 Uhr? Was meinen Sie? Sagen Sie mir° bitte, ob das geht°.

was / pleasant
***eine …** a small favor / can*
***Sagen …** Please tell me / **ob …** whether that will work*

Gruß°,
G. Lehmann

greetings

Wie ist es aber in der Schule und an der Universität? Schüler und Studenten duzen einander von Anfang an°. Karin, Michael und Horst studieren[1] zusammen. Sie sagen „du" und „ihr" zueinander:

***von …** from the beginning*

Karin ist schon bei Horst. Michael kommt gerade° aus der Uni-Bibliothek°.

just / university library

HORST: Hallo, Michael!
MICHAEL: Hallo, Horst. Grüß dich, Karin.
KARIN: Grüß dich. Wie ist das Wetter draußen? Schneit es noch?
MICHAEL: Nein, nicht mehr, aber es ist noch ziemlich kalt. Was macht ihr im Moment?
HORST: Wir hören Nachrichten°.
MICHAEL: Geht ihr bald essen°?
KARIN: Ja, natürlich. Du Horst, kommst du auch mit°?
HORST: Nein, ich bin zu° müde.

the news
to eat
along
too

Studenten sagen „du" zueinander.

In **Kapitel 5** you will learn why line 12 reads **in *der* Schule** and **an *der* Universität,** even though **Schule** and **Universität** are feminine nouns.

Understanding the social implications of German forms of address is the cultural goal of this chapter.

[1] Note that **studieren** means to attend college or university and is not used to describe a student's daily activity of studying. Thus, *I'm studying* (i.e., doing homework) *tonight* is translated as **Ich *arbeite* heute Abend,** or **Ich *lerne* heute Abend.**

NACH DEM LESEN

Nach dem Lesen = *After the reading*

Lab Manual Kap. 1, Diktat.

Elizabethan English still used familiar *thou* and formal *you.* Note the following exchange from *Hamlet* (III.iv) in which Gertrude addresses her son informally and he answers formally.

QUEEN: Hamlet, *thou* hast thy father much offended.

HAMLET: Mother, *you* have my father much offended.

A Antworten Sie auf Deutsch. (*Answer in German.*)

1. Was meinen Touristen: Wie sind die Deutschen?
2. Duzen Schüler einander? Siezt Karin Michael?
3. Wie ist das Wetter draußen?

B Richtig oder falsch? (*True or false?*)

1. Studenten siezen einander.
2. Kollegen in einer Firma siezen einander.
3. Die Studenten gehen zusammen essen.

C Partnerarbeit: *Sie* oder *du?*

Fritzi

Frau Haček

Frau Professor Ullmann

Herr Kuhn

Karoline und Dieter Flessner

Niklas Schuhmacher

1. Take turns asking those pictured . . .
   a. what their names are.
   b. whether they're working at the moment.
   c. whether they're tired today.
   d. where they live.
   e. where they work.
2. Partner A plays one of the people pictured above and responds to Partner B, asking the questions above. Then Partner B plays another of these people and answers Partner A's questions.

   BEISPIEL: A: Wo wohnen Sie, Herr Kuhn?
   B: Ich wohne in Wien.
3. Now ask each other three personal questions of your own invention. Use the **du**-form.

Friedrich Schiller (1759–1805) was a great German dramatist, poet, and for ten years a professor of history at the University of Jena.

Schillers Garten in Jena.

D Schreiben wir mal.

1. Write a dialogue using the following cues. You will need to provide verb endings, correct word order, etc.

   ULLI: Tag / Dieter und Jessica! // ihr / arbeiten / morgen?
   DIETER: nein. // warum / du / fragen?
   ULLI: morgen / ich / gehen / zu Hans. // ihr / kommen / auch?
   DIETER: natürlich / wir / kommen

2. Send an e-mail message to another student in your German class. Describe the weather outside and say what you're doing at the moment. Ask how your friend is and what he or she is doing this evening. Don't forget to use the **du-**form. You can start your e-mail with **Hallo** and your friend's name.

SCHREIBTIPP

Writing e-mails in German

Since some e-mail programs cannot write or read umlauted letters, you can indicate that a vowel is umlauted by typing an **e** after it. You can also use **ss** instead of **ß**.

sch**oe**n	=	sch**ö**n
B**ue**ro	=	B**ü**ro
h**ae**sslich	=	h**ä**sslich
drau**ss**en	=	drau**ß**en

E Wie sagt man das auf Deutsch?

1. When are you coming back, Jürgen and Katrin?
2. We are coming back tomorrow.
3. Excuse me, are you in a hurry?
4. Yes, I'm going to Helene's.
5. She says the Germans are friendly.
6. Yes, that's right.
7. How are you, Herr Beck?
8. Fine thanks, and you?
9. The sun is shining again.
10. Good! We'll work outside.

Where Is German Spoken?

German is the official language of the Federal Republic of Germany; Austria; Liechtenstein; and portions of Switzerland, Luxembourg, Belgium, and South Tyrol in northern Italy (until 1919 part of Austria). Linguistic enclaves of German speakers in the USA (notably the Amish in Pennsylvania), Canada, Brazil, Africa (especially in Namibia, once the German colony of South-West Africa), and Australia bring the number of native German speakers to around 95 million. Many eastern Europeans and Japanese study German as a second language.

The following statistics on world languages from the *2007 World Almanac and Book of Facts* represent estimates of the number of native speakers worldwide of various languages. Notice that the German names of almost all languages end in **-sch**.

Chinesisch	950 Millionen
Spanisch	322 Millionen
Englisch	309 Millionen
Arabisch	206 Millionen
Hindi	180 Millionen
Portugiesisch	177 Millionen
Bengale	171 Millionen
Russisch	145 Millionen
Japanisch	122 Millionen
Deutsch	95 Millionen
Französisch	64 Millionen

eine Milliarde = (American) *billion*; **eine Billion** = (American) *trillion*.

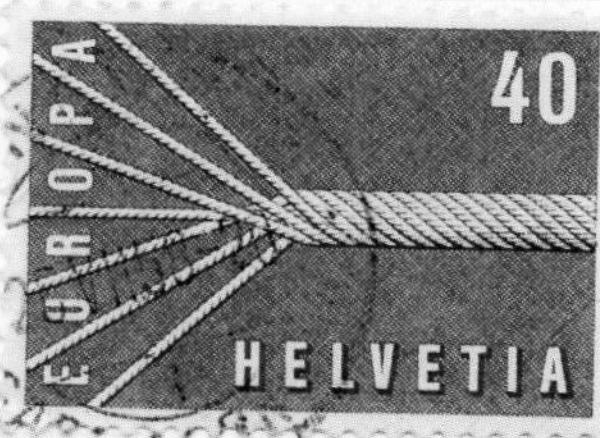

VIDEO

KAPITEL

2

Bruder und Schwester

Familie und Freunde

Kommunikation

- Talking about your family
- Saying what belongs to whom
- Counting above 20

Kultur

- German family life

In diesem Kapitel

- **Lyrik zum Vorlesen**
  Hermann Hesse, "Liebeslied"
- **Grammatik**
  1. Accusative case **(der Akkusativ)**
  2. Verbs with stem-vowel change: **e → i(e)**
  3. The verb **wissen**
  4. Possessive adjectives
  5. Cardinal numbers above 20
- **Lesestück**
  Die Familie heute
- **Almanach**
  Die ganze Familie

DIALOGE

Listen carefully to the In-Text Audio CDs, as well as your instructor, for the difference in the pronunciation of **denn** (short vowel) and **den** (long vowel).

Lab Manual Kap. 2, Dialoge, Fragen, Hören Sie gut zu!, Üb. zur Aussprache [**z,s**].

Pronunciation of **hab'**: **b** becomes unvoiced **p**.

Wer liest die Zeitung?

VATER: Kurt, ich suche meine Zeitung. Weißt du, wo sie ist?
SOHN: Deine Zeitung? Es tut mir Leid, aber ich lese sie im Moment.
VATER: Schon gut. Was liest du denn?
SOHN: Ich lese einen Artikel über unsere Schule.

Ich hab' eine Frage

ANNETTE: Katrin, ich hab' eine Frage. Kennst du den Mann da drüben?
KATRIN: Wen meinst du denn?
ANNETTE: Er spricht mit Stefan. Ich sehe, er kennt dich.
KATRIN: Natürlich kenn' ich ihn – das ist mein Bruder Max!
ANNETTE: Ach stimmt, du hast auch einen Bruder! Ich kenne nur deine Schwester.

Georg sucht ein Zimmer

GEORG: Kennst du viele Leute in München?
STEFAN: Ja, meine Familie wohnt da. Warum?
GEORG: Ich studiere nächstes Semester dort und brauche ein Zimmer.
STEFAN: Unser Haus ist ziemlich groß. Sicher haben meine Eltern ein Zimmer frei.
GEORG: Fantastisch! Vielen Dank!
STEFAN: Bitte, bitte. Nichts zu danken.

NOTES ON USAGE

Unstressed *e* and *denn*

Dropping unstressed *e* In informal conversation, the unstressed ending **-e** in the first-person singular is often dropped.

Katrin, ich **hab'** eine Frage.
Natürlich **kenn'** ich ihn.

The flavoring particle *denn* Probably the most frequently used flavoring particle is **denn**. It adds an element of personal interest to a question. **Denn** is never stressed and usually comes immediately after the verb and personal pronouns.

Was liest du **denn**?
Wen meinst du **denn**?
Wer ist **denn** das?

DIE BANK
FÜR LEUTE
VON HEUTE

Wortschatz 1

Die Familie, -n (*family*)

der **Mann, ¨er** husband; man
die **Frau, -en** wife; woman
die **Eltern** (*pl.*) parents
der **Vater, ¨** father
die **Mutter, ¨** mother
die **Kinder** (*pl.*) children
die **Enkelkinder** (*pl.*) grandchildren
der **Sohn, ¨e** son
der **Bruder, ¨** brother
der **Enkel, -** grandson
die **Tochter, ¨** daughter
die **Schwester, -n** sister
die **Enkelin, -nen** granddaughter

Das Essen (*food*)

der **Käse** cheese
das **Fleisch** meat
das **Gemüse** vegetables
das **Obst** fruit

Verben

brauchen to need
essen (isst) to eat
haben to have
kennen to know, to be acquainted with
lesen (liest) to read
lesen über (+ *acc.*) to read about
meinen to mean
nehmen (nimmt) to take
sehen (sieht) to see
sprechen (spricht) to speak; to talk
sprechen über (+ *acc.*) to talk about
suchen to look for; to seek
wissen (weiß) to know (*a fact*)

Substantive

der **Artikel, -** article
der **Freund, -e** friend
das **Haus, ¨er** house
das **Semester, -** semester
das **Zimmer, -** room
die **Frage, -n** question
die **Zeitung, -en** newspaper
die **Leute** (*pl.*) people

Adjektive und Adverbien

(da) drüben over there
dein (*fam. sing.*) your
dort there
frei free; unoccupied
groß big; tall
mein my
nur only
sicher certain(ly), sure(ly)
unser our

Andere Vokabeln

ach oh, ah
bitte you're welcome
denn *flavoring particle.* *See p. 43.*
mit with
über (+ *acc.*) about
wen? whom?
wessen? whose?

The preposition **über** means *about* with verbs like **sprechen, schreiben, lesen,** etc.

Nützliche Ausdrücke

(Das) stimmt. (That's) right.
Es tut mir Leid. I'm sorry.
Schon gut. Fine. It's okay. No problem.
Fantastisch! Fantastic!
Vielen Dank! Many thanks. Thanks a lot.
nächstes Semester next semester
Nichts zu danken! Don't mention it!

Gegensätze

die Frage, -en ≠ die Antwort, -en
danke ≠ bitte thank you ≠ you're welcome
groß ≠ klein big; tall ≠ little; short

Variationen

A Persönliche Fragen

1. Kurt liest die Zeitung im Moment. Lesen Sie auch eine Zeitung? Oft oder nur selten? Wie heißt sie?
2. Annette hat einen Bruder und eine Schwester. Haben Sie Brüder oder Schwestern? Wie viele? Wie heißen sie?
3. Stefans Haus ist ziemlich groß. Ist Ihr Haus auch groß oder ist es klein? Wie viele Zimmer hat es?
4. Stefan kommt aus München. Woher kommen Sie?

B Partnerarbeit: Wie heißt... ? Help each other recall the names of other students in the class.

A: Wie heißt die Studentin (*oder* der Student) da drüben?
B: Sie/Er heißt ________.

C Partnerarbeit: Wen kennst du hier? Ask your neighbor whom he or she knows in class and how well.

BEISPIELE: A: Wen kennst du hier?
B: Ich kenne ...
A: Kennst du ihn (*oder* sie) gut?
B: Ja, sehr gut. (*oder*: Nein, nicht sehr gut.)

D Partnerarbeit: Was suchst du? Tell what you're looking for. Try to remember the gender of these nouns, then put them into the corresponding column.

Buch	Stuhl	Professor
Bleistift	Kugelschreiber	Professorin
Heft	Landkarte	Zeitung
Uhr		

Ich suche:

meinen (*masculine*)
____
____
____
____

mein (*neuter*)
____
____
____
____

meine (*feminine*)
____
____
____
____

Vielleicht sprechen die Frauen über das Wetter. Was sagen sie zueinander?

Vokabeln zum Thema Familie

Der Stammbaum (*Family tree*)

E Partnerarbeit: Wie heißt...? Work with a partner. Ask each other the names of your family members and create a family tree for your partner.

BEISPIEL: A: Wie heißt deine Großmutter?
B: Sie heißt ______. Wie heißt dein Vater?
A: Er heißt ______.

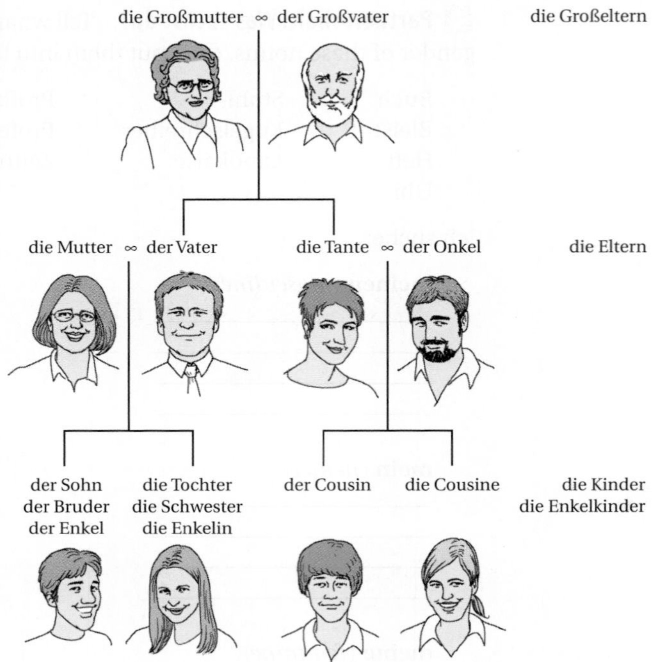

Although he was born in Germany, Hermann Hesse moved to Switzerland before the First World War, partially in protest against growing militarism in his native country. In 1946 Hesse was awarded the Nobel Prize for Literature on the strength of his novels, which include *Siddhartha* (1922) and *Der Steppenwolf* (1927).

Liebeslied	*Love Song*
Wo mag meine Heimat sein?	*Where might my home be?*
Meine Heimat ist klein,	*My home is small,*
Geht von Ort zu Ort,	*Goes from place to place,*
Nimmt mein Herz mit sich fort,	*Takes my heart along with it,*
Gibt mir Weh, gibt mir Ruh;	*Gives me pain, gives me peace;*
Meine Heimat bist du.	*My home is you.*

Hermann Hesse (1877–1962)

GRAMMATIK

1. Accusative case (*der Akkusativ*)

The verb *haben*

Haben (*to have*) is one of the most frequently occurring verbs in German. Note the slightly irregular forms (**du hast, er hat**) in the present tense.

haben *to have*					
stem: **hab-**					
ich	**habe**	*I have*	wir	**haben**	*we have*
du	**hast**	*you have*	ihr	**habt**	*you have*
er, es, sie	**hat**	*he, it, she has*	sie, Sie	**haben**	*they, you have*

Accusative case for the direct object (*das direkte Objekt*)

In **Kapitel 1** you learned the forms and functions of the nominative case. This chapter introduces the accusative case. The direct object of a verb is in the accusative.

The *direct object* is the thing or person acted upon, known, or possessed by the subject.

Subject (nominative)			Direct object (accusative)	
Sie	lesen	→	das Buch.	*They're reading the book.*
Anna	kennt	→	meine Eltern.	*Anna knows my parents.*
Karl	hat	→	einen Bruder.	*Karl has a brother.*

The definite and indefinite articles in the accusative case are identical to the nominative, with the exception of their *masculine singular* forms.

	Nominative			Accusative		
masculine	Hier ist	**der** **ein**	Bleistift.	Ich habe	den einen	Bleistift.
neuter	Hier ist	**das** **ein**	Buch.	Ich habe	**das** **ein**	Buch.
feminine	Hier ist	**die** **eine**	Zeitung.	Ich habe	**die** **eine**	Zeitung.
plural	Hier sind	**die** **meine**	Bücher.	Ich habe	**die** **meine**	Bücher.

The indefinite article **ein** has no plural form. Therefore, this book uses the possessive adjective **mein-** (*my*) to show the plural endings.

Lab Manual Kap. 2, Var. zu Üb. 1, 3, Kettenreaktion 5.

Workbook Kap. 2, A, B.

1 Übung: Wer hat ein Deutschbuch? Your instructor asks who has various things. Say that you have them.

BEISPIEL: Wer hat ein Deutschbuch?
Ich habe ein Deutschbuch.

2 Partnerarbeit: Was hast du dabei? *(What do you have with you?)* Ask each other whether you have the following items with you today. Answer in the affirmative.

BEISPIEL:

A: Hast du einen Bleistift dabei?
B: Ja, ich habe einen Bleistift dabei.
Hast du ... ?

NOTE ON USAGE

Es gibt* + accusative = *there is, there are

The phrase **es gibt** is always followed by accusative case.

In Köln gibt es **einen Dom** (*cathedral*).
Gibt es **eine Universität** in München?
Gibt es **viele Studenten** in Wien?

3 Übung: Was gibt es hier? Say what's in the picture.

BEISPIEL: A: Was gibt es hier?
B: Es gibt einen Tisch.

4 Gruppenarbeit: Was gibt es hier im Klassenzimmer? Now say what's in your classroom.

BEISPIEL: Hier gibt es ______.

5 Kettenreaktion: Was brauchst du? Ask other students what things they need.

BEISPIEL: A: Was brauchst du?
B: Ich brauche den/das/die ______. Und was brauchst du?
C: Ich brauche ...

Accusative personal pronouns

When you substitute a pronoun for a noun direct object, the pronoun must also be in the accusative case:

Kennst du **Stefan**? — *Do you know Stefan?*
Natürlich kenne ich **ihn**! — *Of course I know him!*

Memorize all forms of the accusative personal pronoun.

Singular			Plural		
nominative	**accusative**		**nominative**	**accusative**	
ich	**mich**	*me*	wir	**uns**	*us*
du	**dich**	*you*	ihr	**euch**	*you*
er	**ihn**	*him, it*			
es	**es**	*it*	sie; Sie	**sie; Sie**	*them; you*
sie	**sie**	*her, it*			

6 Übung: Brauchen Sie etwas? Your instructor asks whether you need something. Say that you do need it.

BEISPIEL: A: Brauchen Sie den Stuhl?
B: Ja, ich brauche ihn.

Ruhe = *rest*

FRAGEWORT

The accusative form of the question word **wer** is **wen**:
Wen kennst du in München? — *Whom do you know in Munich?*

7 Partnerarbeit: Wen kennst du hier? Ask each other whom you know in your class. Name as many people as possible.

BEISPIEL: A: Wen kennst du hier?
B: Ich kenne Daniel.
A: Ich kenne ihn auch.
B: Wen kennst *du* hier?

Lab Manual Kap. 2, Var. zu Üb. 6, Partnerarbeit 7.

Workbook Kap. 2, C, D, E.

8 Übung: Kennst du mich? Answer affirmatively.

BEISPIEL: Kennen Sie mich?
Ja, ich kenne Sie.

Kennst du mich?
Ja, ich kenne dich.

2. Verbs with stem-vowel change *e → i(e)*

Some German verbs change their stem vowel in the **du-** and **er-**forms of the present tense.

sprechen *to speak*			
stem: **sprech-** **e → i**			
ich	spreche	wir	sprechen
du	**sprichst**	ihr	sprecht
er, es, sie	**spricht**	sie, Sie	sprechen

Remember that **ie** is simply the way that German spells the **i** sound when it is long.

lesen *to read*				**sehen** *to see*			
stem: **les-**			**e → ie**	stem: **seh-**			
ich	lese	wir	lesen	ich	sehe	wir	sehen
du	**liest**	ihr	lest	du	**siehst**	ihr	seht
er, es, sie	**liest**	sie, Sie	lesen	er, es, sie	**sieht**	sie, Sie	sehen

Stem-vowel changes are indicated in the **Wortschatz** sections by including the **er/es/sie**-form in parentheses following the infinitive: **sehen (sieht)** *to see.*

Two other verbs in this group are **essen (isst)**, *to eat;* and **nehmen (nimmt)**, *to take.* Note that **nehmen** changes some consonants as well as its stem vowel.

essen *to eat*		**nehmen** *to take*	
stem: **ess-**	**e → i**	stem: **nehm-**	
ich	esse	ich	nehme
du	**isst**	du	**nimmst**
er, es, sie	**isst**	er, es, sie	**nimmt**

NOTE ON SPELLING

When verb stems end in **-s, -ß,** or **-z,** the **du**-form ending is simply **-t** rather than **-st**.

Wie **heißt** du?
Was **liest** du denn?
Warum **grüßt** du Frau Kuhn nicht?
Duzt du deinen Lehrer?

Lab Manual Kap. 2, Var. zu Üb. 9.

Workbook Kap. 2, F.

9 Gruppenarbeit (*3 Personen*)

A. Say what you eat, then ask the next person.

BEISPIEL: Ich esse Fleisch, was isst du?

B. Say what you read, then ask the next person.

BEISPIEL: Ich lese den *Spiegel*, was liest du?

C. Say what you see, then ask the next person.

BEISPIEL: Ich sehe eine Frau, was siehst du?

D. Say what languages you speak and then ask the next person.

BEISPIEL: Ich spreche ________, was sprichst du?

Chinesisch	Englisch	Schwedisch	Russisch
Arabisch	Polnisch	Spanisch	Türkisch
Italienisch	Japanisch	Deutsch	Französisch

3. The verb *wissen*

The verb **wissen** (*to know*) is irregular in the present singular. Its forms must be memorized.

wissen *to know*			
stem: **wiss-**			
ich	**weiß**	wir	wissen
du	**weißt**	ihr	wisst
er, es, sie	**weiß**	sie, Sie	wissen

Both the first- and the third-person singular lack endings: **ich weiß**, **er weiß**.

The difference between **wissen** and **kennen** parallels that between French **savoir** and **connaître** and Spanish **saber** and **conocer**. Cf. Scots English *ken: to know* (a person or thing); as in the ballad, "D'ye ken John Peel, with his coat so gay?"

NOTE ON USAGE

German equivalents of *"to know"*

Verbs wissen and kennen Both **wissen** and **kennen** can be translated as to *know,* but **wissen** means to *know a fact* and **kennen** means *to be familiar, acquainted with* and is used, for example, with people, places, and other things you are acquainted with.

Wissen Sie, was ich meine?	*Do you know what I mean?*
Weißt du, wer das ist?	*Do you know what that is?*
Ja, ich **kenne** ihn sehr gut.	*Yes, I know him very well.*
Kennen Sie Berlin, Herr Brandt?	*Do you know Berlin, Mr. Brandt?*
Kennst du den Film?	*Do you know the movie?*
Nein, aber ich **kenne** das Buch.	*No, but I know the book.*

10 ***Wissen* oder *kennen*?** Choose the correct equivalent of the verb to *know.*

A: ________ du den Mann da drüben?
B: Natürlich ________ ich ihn.
A: ________ du, wie er heißt?
B: Ja, er heißt Wolf Breisacher.

SPIEGEL-Leser wissen mehr
DER SPIEGEL

C: Ich ________ München gut.
D: Das ________ ich. Du kommst ja aus München!
C: ________ du Julian Wegener? Er studiert dort.
D: Wirklich? Ich ________ ihn nicht gut, aber ich ________, er wohnt in München.

Workbook Kap. 2, G.

11 Übung: *Wissen oder kennen?*

BEISPIEL: ich / Georg
Ich kenne Georg.

1. er / Michael
2. wir / Berlin
3. Katrin / wo ich wohne
4. ihr / was sie macht
5. ich / Stefan und Annette
6. du / München
7. ich / wer das ist
8. die Schüler / was der Lehrer meint

DEFINITION

What are possessive adjectives?
Possessive adjectives are words such as *my, your, her,* and *their*, that are used with nouns to show possession: ***my** house, **your** friend, **her** eyes, **their** children.* In German: **mein Haus, dein Freund, ihre Augen, ihre Kinder.**

4. Possessive adjectives

Singular		Plural	
personal pronoun	**possessive adjective**	**personal pronoun**	**possessive adjective**
ich	**mein** *my*	wir	**unser** *our*
du	**dein** *your*	ihr	**euer** *your*
er	**sein** *his, its*		
es	**sein** *its*	sie; Sie	**ihr; Ihr** *their; your*
sie	**ihr** *her, its*		

Note that formal **Ihr** (*your*), like formal **Sie** (*you*), is always capitalized.

Learn all forms of the possessive adjectives.

Every possessive adjective must "agree with" its noun. That is, it must have the same case, number, and gender as the noun.

Meine Schwester kommt bald zurück. (nominative singular feminine)
Kennst du **meinen Bruder**? (accusative singular masculine)

This information is shown by the endings attached to the possessive adjectives. As the following table shows, their endings are the same as the endings of **ein**. Possessive adjectives are therefore called **ein**-words.

Endings of *ein*-words				
	masculine	**neuter**	**feminine**	**plural**
nominative	ein	ein	eine	(*no plural*)
	mein	mein	meine	meine
	ihr	ihr	ihre	ihre
	unser	unser	unsere	unsere
	euer	euer	eure	eure
accusative	einen	ein	eine	(*no plural*)
	meinen	mein	meine	meine
	ihren	ihr	ihre	ihre
	unseren	unser	unsere	unsere
	euren	euer	eure	eure

NOTE: The **-er** on **unser** and **euer** is not an ending, but part of the stem. When you add endings to **euer**, drop the **e** before the **-r**.

Das ist **euer** Bruder. Das ist **eure** Schwester.

NOTE: The endings for nominative and accusative possessive adjectives are identical *except in the masculine.*

Masculine nominative	Masculine accusative
Das ist mein Bruder.	Ich sehe meinen Bruder.
Das ist ihr Bruder.	Sie sieht ihr**en** Bruder.
Das ist unser Bruder.	Wir sehen unser**en** Bruder.
Das ist euer Bruder.	Ihr seht eur**en** Bruder.

FRAGEWORT

wessen? *whose?*

Lab Manual Kap. 2, Var. zu Üb. 12.

Workbook Kap. 2, H, I, J, K.

Saying what belongs to whom is a communicative goal.

12 Übung: Wessen Uhr ist das?

A. Your instructor will ask about things that are yours.

BEISPIEL: Was ist das?
Das ist meine Uhr.

B. Partnerarbeit: Now identify a partner's possessions.

BEISPIEL: A: Das ist dein Kugelschreiber.
B: Und das ist ...

C. Now your instructor will ask about things belonging to other people. Notice that with people's first names, you form the possessive by adding **-s,** just as in English, but without the apostrophe: **Marias Heft, Richards Buch.**

BEISPIEL: Ist das Marias Heft?
Ja, das ist ihr Heft.
Ist das Richards Buch?
Ja, das ist sein Buch.

D. Now ask each other what belongs to whom.

BEISPIEL: Wessen Zeitung ist das?
Das ist ihre (seine / meine / ihre) Zeitung.

Das ist mein Bruder.
Und das ist meine Schwester.

Counting above 20 is a communicative goal.

5. Cardinal numbers above 20

The English nursery rhyme "Sing a Song of Sixpence" contains the phrase "four-and-twenty blackbirds." German forms the cardinal numbers above twenty in the same way: 24 = **vierundzwanzig**.

20	zwanzig	30	dreißig
21	einundzwanzig	31	einunddreißig (usw.)
22	zweiundzwanzig	40	vierzig
23	dreiundzwanzig	50	fünfzig
24	vierundzwanzig	60	sechzig
25	fünfundzwanzig	70	siebzig
26	sechsundzwanzig	80	achtzig
27	siebenundzwanzig	90	neunzig
28	achtundzwanzig	100	hundert
29	neunundzwanzig	1 000	tausend

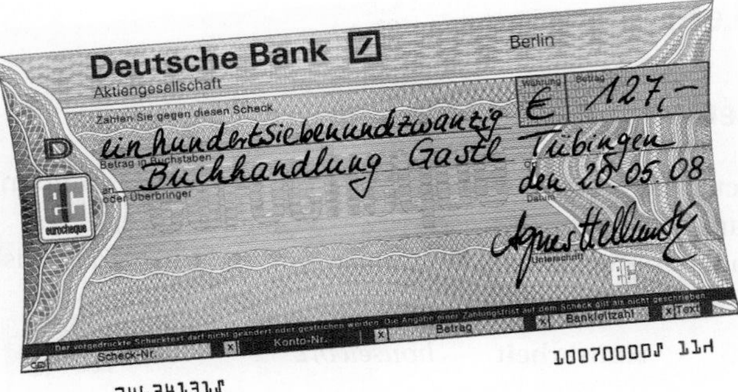

German uses a period or a space where English uses a comma to divide thousands from hundreds, etc., and a comma where English uses a decimal point. The comma is spoken as **Komma**.

German	English
4.982 oder 4 982	4,982
0,5 (null Komma fünf)	0.5 (zero point five)

German numbers above twelve (**zwölf**) are seldom written as words, except on checks. When they *are* written out, each number is one continuous word.
4 982 = viertausendneunhundertzweiundachtzig

Workbook Kap. 2, L.

13 Übung Read these numbers aloud in German. The numbers in the bottom row are years.

The number **1 980** is spoken as **eintausendneunhundertachtzig**.

The year **1980** is spoken as **neunzehnhundertachtzig**.

Two thousand as a year (**2000**) or a number (**2 000**) is spoken **zweitausend**.

26	1066	3 001
69	533	0,22
153	985	3,45
4 772,08	48	71
2002	1991	1800

Die **Ortsmitte** is the center of town, where travelers' information (**i**) is available.

Wie weit ist es nach Garmisch-Partenkirchen?

14 Partnerarbeit: Wie weit ist es nach ... ? *(How far is it to . . . ?)* Take turns asking each other how far it is to the cities and towns listed on the sign.

BEISPIEL: A: Wie weit ist es nach Garmisch-Partenkirchen?
B: Es sind ________ Kilometer.

LESESTÜCK

Lab Manual Kap. 2, Üb. zur Betonung.

Tipps zum Lesen und Lernen

Tipps zum Vokabelnlernen

Compound nouns A characteristic feature of German is its formation of compound nouns from two or more nouns. You should get used to analyzing these words and learn to identify their component parts. You will frequently see similarities to English compound nouns.

Hausfrau *housewife* **Hausarbeit** *housework*

Often a connecting **-(e)s-** or **-(e)n-** is inserted between the components.

das **Eigentum** + die **Wohnung** = die **Eigentumswohnung**
(*property*) (*apartment*) (*condominium*)

der **Bund** (*federation*) + die **Republik** + die **Bundesrepublik**
die **Familie** + die **Diskussion** = die **Familiendiskussion**

The gender of the *last* component noun is *always* the gender of the entire compound.

das **Haus** + die **Frau** = die **Hausfrau**
das **Wort** + der **Schatz** = der **Wortschatz**
(*word*) (*treasure*) (*vocabulary*)

Leicht zu merken

die **Alternative, -n**	Alternative	**relativ**	relativ
der **Konflikt, -e**	Konflikt	**sozial**	sozial
(das) **Nordamerika**		**traditionell**	traditionell
normal	normal		

Einstieg in den Text

- Review the tips for reading on page 36–37 in **Kapitel 1**.
- The following text is entitled "Die Familie heute." This gives you a good idea of what sort of information to expect.

- Before reading, recall the vocabulary you already know that relates to the topic of family, e.g., **Bruder**, **Schwester**, etc.
- Guessing from context will improve your reading skills. The first sentence of a paragraph—the topic sentence—announces the primary topic of what follows. Look at page 58, line 8 of "Die Familie heute." **Die typische Familie** is the topic of this paragraph. Later in the paragraph comes this sentence:

Fast alle Familien besitzen ein Auto und einen Fernseher.

Caution: If you're tempted to think that German **fast** may mean the same as English *fast*, look at its position in the sentence and realize that it's part of the phrase **fast alle Familien**.

The words that are probably immediately comprehensible to you are **alle Familien** and **Auto**. Knowing the topic, you can make an educated guess at the meaning of **fast** and **besitzen**. Such educated guessing, or finding context clues, is very important when reading texts with many unfamiliar words.

Wortschatz 2

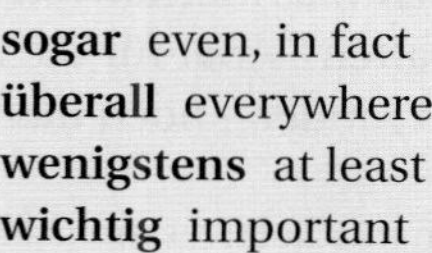

Die Familie

die **Großeltern** (*pl.*) grandparents
der **Großvater, ¨-** grandfather
die **Großmutter, ¨-** grandmother
der **Onkel, -** uncle
die **Tante, -n** aunt
der **Cousin, -s** cousin (*m.*)
die **Cousine, -n** cousin (*f.*)
die **Geschwister** (*pl.*) siblings, brothers and sisters

Verben

bedeuten to mean, signify
besitzen to own
bleiben to stay, remain
finden to find
geben (gibt) to give
kochen to cook

Note the difference between the two verbs corresponding to the meaning *to live*: **leben** (*to be alive*) and **wohnen** (*to dwell*).

leben to live; to be alive
verdienen to earn

Substantive

der **Beruf, -e** profession, vocation
der **Fernseher, -** TV set
das **Auto, -s** car
das **Geld** money
das **Klischee, -s** cliché
das **Problem, -e** problem
die **Arbeit** work
die **Bundesrepublik (Deutschland)** the Federal Republic (of Germany); die **BRD** the FRG
die **Diskussion, -en** discussion
die **Gruppe, -n** group
die **Hausfrau, -en** housewife
die **Rolle, -n** role
die **Stelle, -n** job, position
die **Stimme, -n** voice

Adjektive und Adverbien

anders different
berufstätig employed

Adjectives denoting nationality are *not* capitalized: **amerikanisch** (*American*), **deutsch** (*German*), **kanadisch** (*Canadian*), **schottisch** (*Scottish*).

deutsch German
fast almost
jung young
manchmal sometimes
mehr more
nicht mehr no longer, not any more
noch ein another, an additional
sogar even, in fact
überall everywhere
wenigstens at least
wichtig important

Andere Vokabeln

alle (*pl.*) all; everybody
niemand nobody, no one
zwischen between

Nützliche Ausdrücke

es gibt (+ *acc.*) there is, there are
das sind (*pl. of* **das ist**) those are
zu Hause at home

Gegensätze

jung ≠ alt young ≠ old
niemand ≠ jemand no one ≠ someone
wichtig ≠ unwichtig important ≠ unimportant

Mit anderen Worten

der Job = die Stelle
Kinder sagen:
Vati = Vater
Mutti = Mutter
Oma = Großmutter
Opa = Großvater

Die Familie heute

„Der Vater hat einen Beruf und verdient das Geld, die Mutter ist Hausfrau. Sie bleibt zu Hause, kocht das Essen und versorgt° die Kinder." Die Klischees kennen wir schon. Heute stimmen sie aber nicht mehr, wenigstens nicht für junge[1] Familien in Deutschland. Dort ist die Rollenverteilung° oft anders. Viele Frauen sind berufstätig oder suchen eine Stelle. Tagsüber° ist manchmal niemand zu Hause. Oft machen der Mann und die Frau die Hausarbeit gemeinsam° und in Familiendiskussionen haben die Kinder heute auch eine Stimme°.

Die typische Familie ist relativ klein: Ein oder zwei Kinder, das ist normal. Manchmal wohnen auch die Großeltern mit ihnen zusammen°. Viele Familien in der Bundesrepublik haben ein Haus oder eine Eigentumswohnung°. Fast alle Familien besitzen ein Auto und einen Fernseher. Ihr Lebensstandard° ist sogar oft höher als° in Nordamerika.

Aber das bedeutet nicht, es gibt keine° Probleme. Man findet in Deutschland, wie überall, Konflikte zwischen Eltern und Kindern. Nach dem Schulabschluss° suchen junge Leute manchmal Alternativen wie das Zusammenleben° in Wohngemeinschaften°. Aber für die Mehrheit° bleibt die traditionelle Familie – Mutter, Vater und Kinder – noch die wichtigste° soziale Gruppe.

takes care of
assignment of roles
during the day
jointly
voice
***mit ...** with them*
condominium
*standard of living / **höher als** = higher than /*
no
***Nach ...** after secondary school*
living together/ communal living groups / majority
most important

Learning about German family life is the cultural goal of this chapter.

[1]**junge**: When German adjectives are used before nouns, they have endings, most often **-e** or **-en**. Also: **typische** (line 8), **junge** (line 15), **traditionelle** (line 16), **wichtigste soziale** (line 17). You will learn how to use these endings actively in **Kapitel 9**.

NACH DEM LESEN

Lab Manual Kap. 2, Diktat.

Workbook Kap. 2, M, N, O.

A Antworten Sie auf Deutsch.

1. Was sind die Klischees über die traditionelle Familie?
2. Was suchen heute viele Frauen?
3. Haben Familien in Deutschland viele Kinder?
4. Besitzen alle Familien in Deutschland ein Haus?

B Partnerarbeit: Fragebogen (*Questionnaire*). You are a German sociologist studying family life in various countries. Use the questionnaire below to interview your partner. Be ready to report the information that you collect to the class.

1. **Großeltern**: Leben sie noch? ja / nein
2. **Mutter**: wie alt? ________ berufstätig? ja / nein Beruf? ________
3. **Vater**: wie alt? ________ berufstätig? ja / nein Beruf? ________
4. **Geschwister**: wie viele Brüder? ________ wie alt? ________ wie viele Schwestern? ________ wie alt? ________
5. **Autos**: wie viele? ________
6. **Fernseher**: wie viele? ________
7. Wer kocht das Essen? ________
8. Wer macht die Hausarbeit? ________
9. Wer liest die Zeitung? ________
10. Besitzt Ihre Familie ein Haus? ja / nein

C Familienfotos

1. Here is Sylvie Klein with her family. Sylvie is on the far left, with glasses. Who are the other people in the picture?

   BEISPIEL: Das ist wahrscheinlich ihr ______.

2. Patrick Müller has taken his family on a vacation to the North Sea. Who are the other people in the photo?

Talking about your family is a communicative goal.

3. Bring to class photographs of your own family. Tell the others who's who in your picture.

D Gruppenarbeit. (*3 Personen*) An exchange student from Germany doesn't understand much English yet. Student A plays a reporter asking questions. Student B interprets for the German visitor (student C).

BEISPIEL: A: Where is she from?
B: Woher kommst du denn?
C: Ich komme aus Deutschland.

1. Where does his/her family live?
2. Does it rain there often?
3. What's his/her mother's name?
4. Is he/she employed?
5. Are his/her grandparents alive?
6. Whom does he/she know here?

E Gruppenarbeit. (*3 oder 4 Personen*) How many answers can you give to the following questions?

1. *Was liest du denn?*
   Ich lese ______________.
   ______________.
   ______________.
2. *Wen kennst du?*
   Ich kenne ______________.
   ______________.
   ______________.
3. *Was suchst du?*
   Ich suche ______________.
   ______________.
   ______________.
4. *Was kochst du?*
   Ich koche ______________.
   ______________.
   ______________.
5. *Was brauchst du denn?*
   Ich brauche ______________.
   ______________.
   ______________.
6. *Was siehst du denn?*
   Ich sehe ______________.
   ______________.
   ______________.

F Wie sagt man das auf Deutsch?

1. Her family is quite typical.
2. Their name is Brodersen and they live in Munich.
3. Does her brother work, or is he looking for a job?
4. He's studying in Heidelberg.
5. I'm looking for my newspaper.
6. Fritz has it.
7. He's reading an article.
8. Where are your children, Mr. Asch?
9. They're at home.
10. When are you eating, children?
11. Probably at six.

Ist das eine typische junge Familie? Was meinen Sie?

Eine Postkarte schreiben

- Germans usually put the date at the beginning of a postcard, indicating the day, month, and year they are writing (in that order) separated by periods: 3.10.09 = October 3, 2009.
- If you're writing to a male friend, the greeting will be **Lieber** ... (*Dear* ...); the greeting to a female will be **Liebe** ...
- If you are a male, close your message with **Dein** ...; if a female, close with **Deine** ...

Liebe Nadine, *3.10.09*

kennst du meine Familie? Ich habe drei Geschwister: zwei Brüder und eine Schwester. Unser Vater ist Lehrer und unsere Mutter sucht eine Stelle im Moment. Wir wohnen in Freiburg. Du siehst es hier auf der Postkarte. Es ist sehr schön, nicht wahr?

Dein Max

Feldstr.

14059 Berlin

▶ **Schreiben wir mal.** Write a postcard to a German pen pal telling about your family.

ALMANACH

VIDEO

Die ganze Familie (*The whole family*)

Der Vater, der heißt Daniel,
der kleine Sohn heißt Michael,
die Mutter heißt Regine,
die Tochter heißt Rosine.

Der Bruder, der heißt Kristian,
der Onkel heißt Sebastian,
die Schwester heißt Johanna,
die Tante heißt Susanna.

Der Vetter, der heißt Benjamin,
die Kusine, die heißt Katharin,
die Oma heißt Ottilie –
nun kennst du die Familie!

Vetter = Cousin

Kusine = Cousine

In 2006 these were the most popular names for newborn children according to the **Gesellschaft für deutsche Sprache** (*Society for the German Language*):

Namen für Mädchen	Namen für Jungen
1. Marie	1. Leon
2. Sophie / Sofie	2. Maximilian
3. Maria	3. Alexander
4. Anna, Anne	4. Lukas / Lucas
5. Leonie	5. Paul
6. Lena	6. Luca
7. Emily	7. Tim
8. Johanna	8. Felix
9. Laura	9. David
10. Lea / Leah	10. Elias

Parents do not have absolute freedom in choosing names for their children. A name may be rejected by the government registry office if it does not clearly indicate the child's sex or if it is deemed to „endanger the well-being of the child."

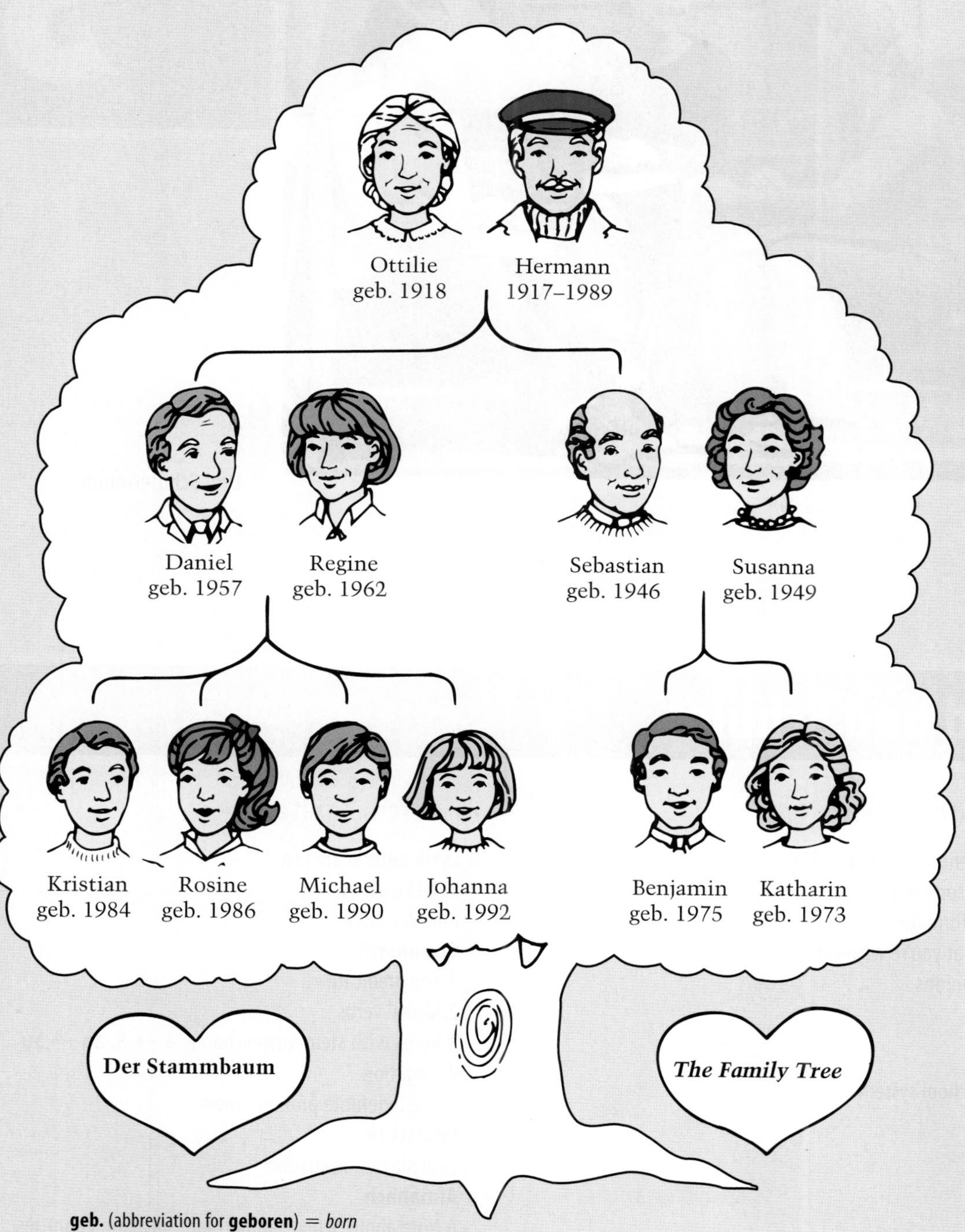

geb. (abbreviation for **geboren**) = *born*

KAPITEL

3

Drei Schülerinnen

Jugend und Schule

Kommunikation

- Negating statements and questions
- Contradicting someone
- Requesting information
- Describing what you're wearing
- Expressing opinions

Kultur

- The German school system

In diesem Kapitel

- **Lyrik zum Vorlesen**
  Rätsel (*riddles*)
  "Bruder Jakob"
- **Grammatik**
  1. The predicate
  2. Modal verbs
  3. Verbs with stem-vowel change **a → ä, au → äu**
  4. Negation
  5. The indefinite pronoun **man**
- **Lesestück**
  Eine Klassendiskussion
- **Almanach**
  A Note about Schools in German-Speaking Countries

DIALOGE

In-Text Audio CD

SAM **Lab Manual** Kap. 3, Dialoge, Fragen, Hören Sie gut zu!, Üb. zur Aussprache **[o/ö]**.

Two cities in Germany are named Frankfurt. They are distinguished by the rivers on which they are situated: Frankfurt am Main (**Frankfurt a. M.** or **Frankfurt/Main**) in the state of Hessen, and Frankfurt an der Oder (**Frankfurt a. d. O.** or **Frankfurt/Oder**) in the state of Brandenburg.

Innsbruck is the capital city of the mountainous Austrian province of Tyrol (German name = **Tirol**). German place names often have topographical significance. The second syllable of **Innsbruck** derives from the German word, **die Brücke** *(the bridge)*. The city was originally a settlement at "the bridge over the Inn River." See map on the inside the front cover of the text.

Du hast es gut!

Renate besucht ihre Freundin Monika in Hinterwalden.

MONIKA: In Frankfurt hast du es gut, Renate!
RENATE: Wieso?
MONIKA: Hier in Hinterwalden ist es immer stinklangweilig.
RENATE: Dann musst du mich bald besuchen. Oder hast du keine Lust?
MONIKA: Doch, ich möchte schon nach Frankfurt, aber ich habe leider kein Geld.
RENATE: Das verstehe ich schon, aber bis Juni kannst du sicher genug verdienen.

Eine Pause

Kurt und Stefan fahren nach Innsbruck.

STEFAN: Wie lange müssen wir noch fahren?
KURT: Nur noch eine Stunde bis Innsbruck.
STEFAN: Können wir jetzt eine Pause machen? Ich möchte ein bisschen laufen.
KURT: Ich auch. Da drüben kann man halten, nicht wahr?
STEFAN: Ja. (*Sie halten.*) Mensch! Der Berg ist wahnsinnig steil!
KURT: Was ist denn los? Bist du nicht fit?
STEFAN: Doch! Das schaff' ich leicht.

Heute gibt's keine Chemiestunde

ANJA: Du Klaus, weißt du's schon?
KLAUS: Was ist denn?
ANJA: Heute gibt's keine Chemiestunde!
KLAUS: Wieso denn?
ANJA: Frau Helmholtz ist erkältet.
KLAUS: Toll, dann müssen wir keine Klassenarbeit schreiben!
ANJA: Richtig! Willst du einen Kaffee trinken?
KLAUS: Gerne, und dann können wir früh nach Hause.

NOTE ON USAGE

The flavoring particle *schon*

Schon is often used as a flavoring particle to strengthen, confirm, or reinforce a statement. It adds the sense of *really, indeed*. In the first dialogue, Monika protests:

Ich möchte **schon** nach Frankfurt, aber ich habe leider kein Geld.	*I really would like to go to Frankfurt, but unfortunately I don't have any money.*

Renate answers:

Das verstehe ich **schon** ...	*I certainly understand that . . .*

Wortschatz 1

Verben

besuchen to visit
erkältet sein to have a cold
fahren (fährt) to drive; to go (*by vehicle*)
halten (hält) to stop (*intrans.*)[1]; to hold
laufen (läuft) to run; to go on foot, walk (*colloq.*)
schaffen to handle, manage; to get done (*colloq.*)
schlafen (schläft) to sleep
tragen (trägt) to carry; to wear
trinken to drink
verstehen to understand

Modalverben (*Modal verbs*)

dürfen (darf) may, to be allowed to
können (kann) can, to be able to
ich möchte I would like to
müssen (muss) must, to have to
sollen (soll) should, to be supposed to
wollen (will) to want to

Berg: cf. English *iceberg*

Substantive

der **Berg, -e** mountain
der **Kaffee** coffee
die **Freundin, -nen** friend (*f.*)
die **Klasse, -n** class; grade
die **Klassenarbeit, -en** written test, in-class examination
die **Minute, -n** minute
die **Pause, -n** break; intermission
eine Pause machen to take a break
die **Stunde, -n** hour; class hour
die **Chemiestunde** chemistry class
die **Deutschstunde** German class

Adjektive und Adverbien

fit in shape
früh early
genug enough
gern(e) gladly
immer always
jetzt now
krank sick
langweilig boring
leicht easy; light (*in weight*)
leider unfortunately
richtig right, correct
steil steep
toll (*colloq.*) great, terrific
wahnsinnig (*colloq. adv.*) extremely, incredibly
wahr true

The final **-e** on **gerne** is optional; **gern** and **gerne** mean the same thing.

Basic meaning of **toll** = *mad, crazy* (**das Tollhaus** = *madhouse*)

Andere Vokabeln

doch yes I *do*, yes I *am*, etc. (*contradictory*, see p. 79)
kein not a, not any, no
nichts nothing
wie lange? how long?
wieso? how come? how's that? what do you mean?
wohin? where to?

Kein has the same endings as **ein**. See p. 78.

Nützliche Ausdrücke

ein bisschen a little; a little bit; a little while
Ich habe keine Lust. I don't want to.
Mensch! Man! Wow!
nach Hause home (*as destination*)
Ich fahre nach Hause. I'm driving home.
nicht (wahr)? isn't it? can't you? doesn't he? etc.
Was ist los? What's the matter? What's going on?

Gegensätze

früh ≠ spät early ≠ late
immer ≠ nie always ≠ never
krank ≠ gesund sick ≠ healthy
langweilig ≠ interessant boring ≠ interesting
leicht ≠ schwer light; easy ≠ heavy; difficult
nichts ≠ etwas nothing ≠ something
richtig ≠ falsch correct ≠ false, incorrect, wrong

Mit anderen Worten

stinklangweilig = sehr, sehr langweilig
wahnsinnig (*colloq.*) **= sehr, sehr**

[1] The abbreviation *intrans.* = intransitive. An intransitive verb cannot take a direct object. When the verb **halten** means *to stop* (**Da drüben kann man halten**), it is intransitive. However, when it means *to hold* (**Er hält den Bleistift in der Hand**), it is transitive.

Variationen

A Persönliche Fragen

1. Wo sind Sie zu Hause?
2. Gibt es da viel zu tun oder ist es langweilig?
3. Haben Sie genug Geld?
4. Sind Sie fit oder nicht?
5. Müssen Sie heute eine Klassenarbeit schreiben?
6. Wollen Sie später einen Kaffee trinken?

B Übung.

Answer your instructor's questions.

1. Kurt möchte ein bisschen laufen. Ich möchte zu Hause bleiben.
   Was möchten Sie denn machen? Ich möchte ________.
2. Kurt und Stefan wollen da drüben halten. Ich will nach Hause laufen.
   Was wollen Sie denn machen? Ich will ________.
3. Klaus und Anja können heute früh nach Hause gehen.
   Was können Sie heute machen? Ich kann ________.

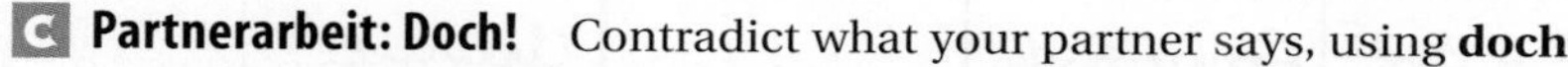

C Partnerarbeit: Doch!

Contradict what your partner says, using **doch**.

BEISPIEL: A: Du bist nicht fit!
B: *Doch,* ich bin fit!

1. Du besuchst mich nicht!
2. Der Tourist kommt nicht aus Amerika!
3. Du verstehst mich nicht!
4. Wir arbeiten heute nicht!
5. Die Schüler gehen nicht früh nach Hause!
6. Robert ist nicht dein Freund!
7. Der Berg ist nicht steil!
8. Es ist nicht spät!

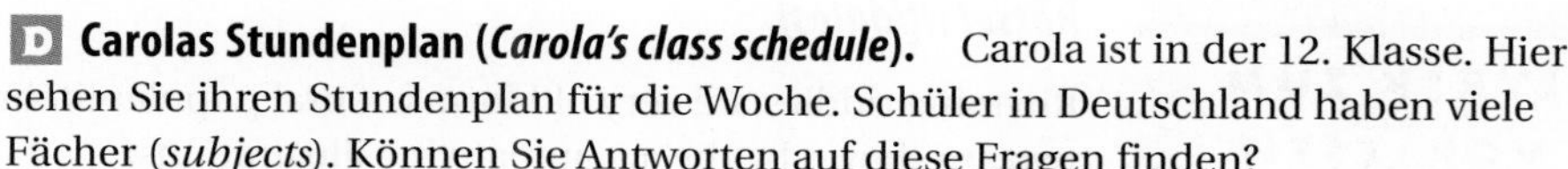

D Carolas Stundenplan (*Carola's class schedule*). Carola ist in der 12. Klasse. Hier sehen Sie ihren Stundenplan für die Woche. Schüler in Deutschland haben viele Fächer (*subjects*). Können Sie Antworten auf diese Fragen finden?

1. Wie viele Fächer hat sie?
2. Welche Fremdsprachen (*which foreign languages*) lernt sie?
3. Wie viele Französischstunden hat sie pro Woche?
4. Welche naturwissenschaftlichen (*natural science*) Fächer hat sie?
5. Was hat sie am Montag und auch am Dienstag?
6. Welche Hausaufgaben (*homework assignments*) muss sie am Mittwochabend machen?
7. Wann spielt sie ihre Violine?
8. Wann kann sie lange schlafen?
9. Wann kann sie früh nach Hause gehen?

Zeit	Montag	Dienstag	Mittwoch	Donnerstag	Freitag
$7^{45} - 8^{30}$	–	–	Französisch	Biologie	–
$8^{35} - 9^{20}$	Englisch	Mathematik	Französisch	Biologie	–
$9^{30} - 10^{15}$	Religion	Politik / Erdkunde	Deutsch	Mathematik	Mathematik
$10^{20} - 11^{05}$	Deutsch	Chemie	Deutsch	Religion	Politik / Erdkunde
$11^{25} - 12^{10}$	Sport	Biologie	Geschichte	Englisch	Englisch
$12^{15} - 13^{00}$	Sport	Biologie	–	Französisch	Geschichte
$13^{00} - 14^{00}$	(Orchester)				
$14^{00} - 14^{45}$	Biologie				
$14^{50} - 15^{35}$	Französisch				
$15^{40} - 16^{25}$	Französisch		Chemie		
$16^{30} - 17^{15}$			Chemie		
$17^{20} - 18^{05}$					

LYRIK ZUM VORLESEN

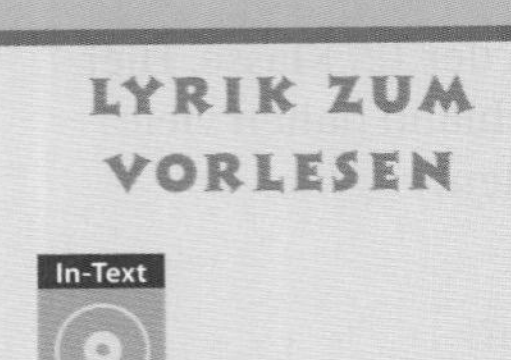

Rätsel (Riddles)

Rhyming riddles are very old forms of oral popular literature. The solutions to these two are shown by the accompanying illustrations.

(der Hummer)

Rot° und gut,
hat Fleisch° und kein Blut°.

red
flesh, meat / blood

(die Schnecke)

Ich gehe alle Tage° aus
Und bleibe doch in meinem Haus.

alle. . . every day

Bruder Jakob

This round for four voices comes originally from France but is sung by children all over the world. In German, *Frère Jacques* is called **Bruder Jakob**.

Bruder Jakob, Bruder Jakob!
Schläfst du noch? Schläfst du noch?
Hörst du nicht die Glocken°?
Hörst du nicht die Glocken?
Ding, ding, dong. Ding, ding, dong.

bells

GRAMMATIK

1. The predicate (*das Prädikat*)

In both German and English, all statements and questions contain a subject (S) and an inflected verb (V).

S V	S V
Ich arbeite viel.	*I work a lot.*
V S	**V S**
Schläfst du?	*Are you sleeping?*

The verb by itself does not always express the entire action or condition in which the subject is involved. For example, consider the simple statement:

Stefan ist jung.

Stefan is the subject and **ist** is the verb. Taken by themselves, however, the words

Stefan ist

are not a meaningful utterance. The verb **sein** must be completed, in this case by the adjective **jung**. **Sein** may also be completed by a noun in the nominative case.

Stefan ist **mein Bruder**.

DEFINITION

What is a complement?
A ***complement*** is a word or words used with the verb to complete the entire verbal idea: **Stefan ist *jung*. Ich trage *Jeans*.**

In both cases, the verb plus its complement make up the entire verbal idea, or predicate. That's why adjectives and nouns that follow the verb **sein** are called *predicate adjectives* and *predicate nominatives*.

Various kinds of words and phrases can complement verbs to form the complete predicate. For instance, in the sentence

Ich trage Jeans. *I'm wearing jeans.*

the verb **trage** is completed by the direct object **Jeans**. In the sentence

Ich möchte laufen. *I would like to run.*

the modal verb **möchte** is completed by the infinitive **laufen**. You will learn about modal verb forms like **möchte** in the following section.

2. Modal verbs (*Modalverben*)

Six verbs in German form a group called *modal verbs*. They do not express an action but rather the subject's *attitude* or *relation* to the action expressed by another verb.

Wir **müssen** noch eine Stunde **fahren**. *We still* ***have to drive*** *for an hour.*

The modal verb **müssen** (*have to*) indicates that it is *necessary* for the subject (**wir**) to perform the action of driving (**fahren**). **Müssen** is the main verb, and the infinitive **fahren** completes the predicate. The German modals are shown below.

Modal verb	*English*	*Express*	
dürfen	*to be allowed to, may*	permission:	*May I . . . ?*
können	*to be able to, can*	ability:	*Can I . . . ?*
müssen	*to have to, must*	necessity:	*Must I . . . ?*
sollen	*to be supposed to, should*	obligation:	*Should I . . . ?*
wollen	*to want to; to intend to*	desire, intention:	*Do I want to . . . ?*
(ich) **möchte**	(*I*) *would like to*	inclination, desire:	*Would I like to . . . ?*

Möchte (*would like to*) is a subjunctive form of the modal verb **mögen** (*to like*), which you will learn in the next chapter.

The modal verbs take no endings in the **ich-** and **er-**forms. Most have a changed stem vowel in the singular.

Lehrer und Schüler

dürfen *to be allowed to*			
ich	**darf**	wir	dürfen
du	**darfst**	ihr	dürft
er, es, sie	**darf**	sie, Sie	dürfen

Darf ich draußen **spielen**? *May I play outside?*

können *to be able to*			
ich	**kann**	wir	können
du	**kannst**	ihr	könnt
er, es, sie	**kann**	sie, Sie	können

Wir **können** da drüben **halten**. *We can stop over there.*

müssen *to have to*			
ich	**muss**	wir	müssen
du	**musst**	ihr	müsst
er, es, sie	**muss**	sie, Sie	müssen

Jetzt **muss** ich leider **gehen**. *Unfortunately, I have to leave now.*

wollen *to want to*			
ich	**will**	wir	wollen
du	**willst**	ihr	wollt
er, es, sie	**will**	sie, Sie	wollen

Willst du jetzt **essen**? *Do you want to eat now?*

Notice that only **sollen** and **möchten** do not have a stem-vowel change in the singular.

sollen *to be supposed to*			
ich	soll	wir	sollen
du	sollst	ihr	sollt
er, es, sie	soll	sie, Sie	sollen

Sollen wir eine Pause **machen**? *Should we take a break?*

möchten *would like to*			
infinitive: **mögen**			
ich	möchte	wir	möchten
du	möchtest	ihr	möchtet
er, es, sie	möchte	sie, Sie	möchten

Ich **möchte** dich **besuchen**. *I would like to visit you.*

In contrast to German, some English modals require a dependent infinitive with *to* (*I want **to read***), while others do not (*I can **read***).

The modal verb is *always* the inflected verb in the sentence. The infinitive, which completes the verbal idea, comes at the end of the sentence. Contrast with English, where the dependent infinitive immediately *follows* the modal verb.

Wir **können** da drüben **halten**.	*We **can stop** over there.*
Das **muss** ich für morgen **lesen**.	*I **have to read** that for tomorrow.*
Marie **soll** ihre Eltern **besuchen**.	*Marie **should visit** her parents.*

NOTE: This two-part predicate is a central structural feature of German.

Lab Manual Kap. 3, Var. zu Üb. 1, 4.

Workbook Kap. 3, A, B, C.

1 Übung: Was will Renate machen? Here are some things people in the dialogues on p. 65 are doing. Use these phrases to answer your instructor's questions.

Monika besuchen	Geld verdienen	früh nach Hause gehen
eine Pause machen	nach Frankfurt fahren	ein bisschen laufen
da drüben halten	Kaffee trinken	

BEISPIEL: Was will Renate machen?
Sie will Monika besuchen.

1. Was möchte Monika machen?
2. Was muss sie bis Juni machen?
3. Was möchte Stefan machen?
4. Wo können die zwei Freunde halten?
5. Was wollen sie dann machen?
6. Was wollen Anja und Klaus trinken?
7. Was können sie heute machen?

2 Gruppenarbeit: Was willst du machen? (*4 Personen*) Ask each other about what you intend to do or be. This list will provide some ideas. What others can you find?

BEISPIEL: A: Was willst du denn machen?
B: Ich will in Deutschland studieren, und du?

eine Familie haben	nach Japan fahren
viel Geld verdienen	Deutschland besuchen
einen guten Job haben	sehr fit bleiben
ein großes Haus besitzen	in Wien studieren

3 Partnerarbeit: Interview. Interview a classmate. Find answers to the following questions. Some possibilities are given in parentheses.

1. Was möchtest du jetzt trinken? (Kaffee, Cola, Wein, Wasser)
2. Was kannst du spielen? Ich kann (Fußball, Tennis, Poker, Pingpong) ...
3. Was musst du heute Abend lernen? Ich muss (Mathematik, Deutsch, Chemie, Soziologie) ...
4. Wen willst du im Sommer besuchen? Ich will (meine Großeltern, meine Cousine, meinen Freund) ...

Omission of the infinitive

German speakers often omit certain clearly implied infinitives from sentences with modal verbs.

- **haben**

Möchten Sie eine Cola?	*Would you like* (*to have*) *a soda?*

- **machen**

Das kann ich leider nicht.	*Unfortunately I can't* (*do that*).

- verbs of motion (**gehen, fahren, fliegen, laufen**) when destination is expressed

Ich muss jetzt nach Hause.	*I have to go home now.*

- **sprechen**, in the following expression:

Kannst du Deutsch?	*Can you speak German?*
Ja, ich kann Deutsch.	*Yes, I can speak German.*
Ich kann auch Dänisch.	*I can also speak Danish.*

4 Übung: Wie sagt man das auf Englisch?

1. Wollen Sie jetzt nach Hause?
2. Er kann das noch nicht.
3. Willst du meinen Bleistift?
4. Mein Vater will das nicht.
5. Sie können schon gut Deutsch.
6. Möchten Sie das Geld?
7. Darf man denn das?
8. Wann wollen Sie nach Amerika?

5 Gruppenarbeit: Mit offenen Büchern. (*3 oder 4 Personen*) Take turns changing each sentence by substituting the new elements provided.

BEISPIEL: Ich möchte morgen nach Berlin. (wollen)
A: Ich will morgen nach Berlin. (Wien)
B: Ich will morgen nach Wien.

1. Ich möchte morgen nach Berlin.
wollen
München
müssen
wir
Kopenhagen
nächstes Semester

2. Wir können da drüben halten.
sollen
eine Pause machen
ich
möchten
arbeiten
zu Hause

3. Im Juni kannst du viel Geld verdienen.
müssen
September
ich
haben
wollen

Wohin (*where to?*) is analogous to the question word **woher**? (*from where?*): **Woher kommst du?** Cf. archaic English usage: *Whence comest thou? Whither goest thou?*

FRAGEWORT

wohin? *where to?*

a = Spanien
b = Korsika
c = Kreta
d = Puerto Rico
e = Griechenland

a

b

d

c

e

6 Partnerarbeit: Wohin willst du im Februar? By the time the semester break comes in mid-February, many German students want to travel where it is warm. Which of these vacation spots (shown above) popular with Germans would you like to visit?

BEISPIEL: A: Wohin willst du im Februar?
B: Ich will nach ________. Wohin willst du?

Können Sie diese Orte (*places*) auf der Landkarte finden? (*See the map on the inside back cover of the text.*)

3. Verbs with stem-vowel change *a → ä, au → äu*

Some verbs change their stem-vowel in the following ways:

fahren *to drive; to go by vehicle*			
stem: **fahr-** shift: **a → ä**			
ich	fahre	wir	fahren
du	**fährst**	ihr	fahrt
er, es, sie	**fährt**	sie, Sie	fahren

halten *to hold; to stop*			
stem: **halt-** shift: **a → ä**			
ich	halte	wir	halten
du	**hältst**	ihr	haltet
er, es, sie	**hält**	sie, Sie	halten

Other verbs in this group are: **schlafen** (**schläft**), *to sleep*; **tragen** (**trägt**), *to carry, wear*.

laufen *to run*			
stem: **lauf-** shift: **au → äu**			
ich	laufe	wir	laufen
du	**läufst**	ihr	lauft
er, es, sie	**läuft**	sie, Sie	laufen

SAM Lab Manual **Lab Manual** Kap. 3, Var. zu Kettenreaktion 7.

SAM Workbook **Workbook** Kap. 3, D.

7 Kettenreaktion. Say how you get home, then ask your classmates how they get home.

BEISPIEL: A: Ich fahre nach Hause. Fährst du nach Hause, oder läufst du?
B: Ich laufe nach Hause. Läufst du nach Hause, oder fährst du?
C: Ich ...

FRAGEWORT

wie lange? *how long?*

8 Kettenreaktion. Wie lange schläfst du?

BEISPIEL: A: Ich schlafe acht Stunden. Wie lange schläfst du?
B: Ich ...

9 Gruppenarbeit: Mit offenen Büchern (*with open books*). Tell one thing that you're wearing, then one thing the person next to you is wearing.

BEISPIEL: Ich trage ______ und er/sie trägt heute ______.

4. Negation

Negating statements and questions is a communicative goal.

For a preview and summary of German negation, see **Zusammenfassung und Wiederholung 1** in the Workbook section of your SAM.

Nicht (not)

Nicht is used to negate a sentence.

Sabrina ist meine Schwester.	*Sabrina is my sister.*
Sabrina ist **nicht** meine Schwester.	*Sabrina is **not** my sister.*

In the preceding example, the position of **nicht** is exactly the same as the position of *not* in English. In most German sentences, however, this will not be the case. Here are guidelines for the position of **nicht**.

In English, *not* almost always immediately follows the inflected verb.

- **Nicht** *follows* the subject, verb, direct object, and all personal pronouns.

Es regnet **nicht**.	*It's not raining.*
Ich kenne deinen Freund **nicht**.	*I don't know your friend.*
Er sagt das **nicht**.	*He doesn't say that.*
Wir besitzen das Auto **nicht**.	*We don't own the car.*
Deine Schwester kennt mich **nicht**.	*Your sister doesn't know me.*

Some examples of definite time are: **jetzt, heute, heute Abend, morgen, am Mittwoch**.

■ **Nicht** *follows* expressions of definite time.

Sie können heute Abend **nicht** kommen.	*They can't come tonight.*
Hans arbeitet jetzt **nicht**.	*Hans isn't working now.*

Lab Manual Kap. 3, Üb. 10, 11.

Workbook Kap. 3, E.

10 Übung. Add **nicht** to negate these sentences.

1. Kurt besucht seinen Bruder.
2. Ich kenne eure Mutter.
3. Frau Schmidt besucht uns morgen.
4. Monika macht das heute Abend.
5. Ich verstehe ihn.
6. Am Donnerstag kochst du.
7. Er liest sein Buch.
8. Mein Großvater schläft.
9. Das schafft er.

■ **Nicht** *precedes* the second part of the predicate. Thus it comes before the following elements:

1. Predicate adjectives

Der Berg ist **steil**.	*The mountain is* ***steep***.
Der Berg ist **nicht** steil.	*The mountain is* ***not*** *steep.*

2. Predicate nominatives

Das ist **Herr Blum**.	*That is* ***Mr. Blum***.
Das ist **nicht** Herr Blum.	*That is* ***not*** *Mr. Blum.*

Some examples of indefinite time are **bald**, **oft**, **selten**, **früh**, and **spät**.

3. Adverbs of manner, indefinite time, and place

Margit und Hans laufen **schnell**.	*Margit and Hans run* ***fast***.
Margit und Hans laufen **nicht** schnell.	*Margit and Hans* ***don't*** *run fast.*
Er besucht mich **oft**.	*He* ***often*** *visits me.*
Er besucht mich **nicht** oft.	*He does**n't** visit me often.*
Sie wohnt **hier**.	*She lives* ***here***.
Sie wohnt **nicht** hier.	*She does* ***not*** *live here.*

4. Prepositional phrases that show destination (**nach Wien, nach Hause**) or location (**in Berlin, zu Hause**)

Sie geht **nach Hause**.	*She's going* ***home***.
Sie geht **nicht** nach Hause.	*She's* ***not*** *going home.*
Er arbeitet **in Berlin**.	*He works* ***in Berlin***.
Er arbeitet **nicht** in Berlin.	*He does**n't** work in Berlin.*

5. Infinitives complementing modal verbs

Er kann mich **sehen**.	*He can* ***see*** *me.*
Er kann mich **nicht** sehen.	*He can'**t** see me.*

11 Übung. Negate these sentences by adding **nicht**.

1. Das Wetter ist schön.
2. Ich kann dich besuchen.
3. Ich möchte Berlin sehen.
4. Der Berg ist steil.
5. Wir wollen halten.
6. Frau Mackensen ist unsere Lehrerin.
7. Ich muss nach Hause gehen.
8. Margit läuft gut.
9. Er kann mich sehen.

12 Partnerarbeit: Unsere neue Professorin. Your class is getting a new instructor. Take turns asking each other questions about her. Answer in the negative.

BEISPIEL: A: Kennt unsere Professorin Berlin?
B: Nein, sie kennt Berlin nicht.

1. Kommt sie aus Dresden?
2. Ist sie unfreundlich?
3. Arbeitet sie heute Abend?
4. Studiert ihr Bruder in Leipzig?
5. Kennst du ihn?
6. Muss sie nach Hause?
7. Fährt sie bald nach Hause?
8. Schläft sie viel?
9. Ist das ihr Auto?
10. Ist sie oft krank?

Kein

Kein (*not a, not any, no*) is the negative form of **ein**. It negates nouns preceded by **ein** or not preceded by any article.

Morgen will ich ein Buch lesen	*I want to read a book tomorrow.*
Morgen will ich **kein** Buch lesen.	*I do **not** want to read a book tomorrow.*
Studenten wohnen hier.	*Students live here.*
Keine Studenten wohnen hier.	***No** students live here.*

Kein is an **ein**-word and takes the same endings as **ein** and the possessive adjectives.

	ein Fernseher.		**einen** Wagen.		**eine** Zeitung.
Das ist	**kein** Fernseher.	Er hat	**keinen** Wagen.	Sie liest	**keine** Zeitung.
	mein Fernseher.		**meinen** Wagen.		**meine** Zeitung.

Nicht and **kein** are mutually exclusive. In any given situation, only one will be correct. If a noun is preceded by the definite article or by a possessive adjective, use **nicht** rather than **kein** to negate it.

Ist das die Professorin?	*Is that the professor?*
Nein, das ist **nicht** die Professorin.	*No, that's not the professor.*
Ist das eure Professorin?	*Is that your professor?*
Nein, das ist **nicht** unsere Professorin.	*No, that's not our professor.*
Ist sie Professorin?	*Is she a professor?*
Nein, sie ist **keine** Professorin.	*No, she's not a professor.*

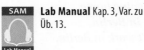

SAM **Lab Manual** Kap. 3, Var. zu Üb. 13.

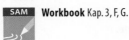

SAM **Workbook** Kap. 3, F, G.

13 Übung. Negate the sentence, using **kein**.

1. Hier gibt es ein Problem.
2. Wir wollen Kaffee trinken.
3. Maria hat heute Geld.
4. Hier wohnen Studenten.
5. Morgen gibt es eine Diskussion.
6. Herr Meyer hat Kinder.

14 Übung. Respond negatively to these questions, using **kein** or **nicht**.

BEISPIELE: A: Hat Barbara einen Freund?
B: Nein, sie hat keinen Freund.

A: Ist das ihr Freund?
B: Nein, das ist nicht ihr Freund.

1. Haben Sie einen Freund in Oslo?
2. Haben Sie Freunde in Washington?

3. Ist das der Professor?
4. Verdient er Geld?
5. Sehen Sie das Haus?
6. Ist das seine Freundin?
7. Suchen Sie das Buch?
8. Suchen Sie ein Buch?

15 Partnerarbeit: Meine Familie. Ask each other about your families. (For family members, see p. 46.)

BEISPIEL: A: Hast du einen Sohn?
B: Nein, ich habe keinen Sohn.

16 Gruppenspiel: Stimmt nicht! (*3 Personen*) Play this game with two other people. One says something obviously false. The others contradict that statement and give the correct information. Then the next player takes a turn.

BEISPIEL: A: Kirsten trägt heute einen Pulli.
B/C: Stimmt nicht! Sie trägt keinen Pulli! Sie trägt ein T-Shirt.

Expecting an affirmative answer: *nicht wahr?*

Nicht wahr? can follow only positive statements.

Nicht wahr? (literally, *not true?*), when added to a positive statement, anticipates confirmation (English: *doesn't she? wasn't he? wasn't it? didn't you?* etc.). In spoken German, you may shorten it to **nicht?**

Heute ist es schön, **nicht wahr?**	*It's beautiful today, isn't it?*
Sie studieren in Freiburg, **nicht?**	*You're studying in Freiburg, aren't you?*
Gisela kennst du, **nicht wahr?**	*You know Gisela, don't you?*

17 Übung: Das ist ein Tisch, nicht wahr? Contradict your instructor if necessary.

BEISPIEL: Das ist ein Tisch, nicht wahr?
Nein, das ist kein Tisch, das ist ein(e) ________.

18 Übung: Wie sagt man das auf Deutsch?

1. You have a car, don't you?
2. You're learning German, aren't you?
3. You'll visit me soon, won't you?
4. He's in good shape, isn't he?
5. We can work today, can't we?
6. You can understand that, can't you?

Contradicting a negative statement or question: *doch*

Contradicting someone is a communicative goal.

To contradict a negative statement or question, use **doch** instead of **ja**.

Ich spreche nicht gut Deutsch.	*I don't speak German well.*
Doch, Sie sprechen sehr gut Deutsch!	*Yes you do, you speak German very well.*
Kennst du Ursula nicht?	*Don't you know Ursula?*
Doch, ich kenne sie sehr gut!	*Sure, I know her very well.*

Lab Manual Kap. 3, Var. zu Üb. 20.

Workbook Kap. 3, H.

Initial **Doch** does not count as the first element in determining word order. See p. 31.

19 Übung: Doch! Contradict these negative statements and questions, beginning your response with a stressed **doch**.

BEISPIEL: Schaffst du das nicht?
Doch, ich schaffe das!

1. Wir wollen nicht halten.
2. Wir haben nicht genug Geld.
3. Hast du keinen Bruder?
4. Es ist nicht sehr spät.
5. Kannst du kein Deutsch?
6. Willst du nicht nach Hause?

20 Übung. Contradict your instructor if necessary.

BEISPIEL: Das ist kein Tisch.
Doch! Natürlich ist das ein Tisch!

5. The indefinite pronoun *man*

The indefinite pronoun **man** refers to people in general rather than to any specific person. Although the English indefinite pronoun *one* may sound formal in everyday speech, **man** does not sound this way in German. It is used in both colloquial and formal language. It is often best translated into English as *people, they, you,* or even *we.*

You can use **man** only as the subject of a sentence, and only with a verb in the third-person singular.

In Deutschland sagt **man** das oft.	***They*** *often say that in Germany.*
Das muss **man** lernen.	***You've*** *got to learn that.*
Das weiß **man** nie.	***One*** *never knows.*

Do not confuse the pronoun **man** with the noun **der Mann** (*the man*).

21 Übung. Match the captions with the pictures.

1. Hier spricht man Deutsch.
2. Der Mann spricht Deutsch.

a. ____________________ b. ____________________

22 Übung. Change the subject to **man**.

1. In Hinterwalden können die Leute nicht genug verdienen.
2. Um elf Uhr machen wir eine Pause.
3. Hoffentlich können wir da drüben halten.
4. Hier können Sie gut essen.
5. Dürfen wir hier schlafen?

23 Übung: Wie sagt man das auf Deutsch? Use **man** as the subject.

1. In America we don't say that.
2. You've got to stop here.
3. One has to do that.
4. People say there are problems here.
5. How do you say that in German?

LESESTÜCK

Tipps zum Lesen und Lernen

Tipp zum Vokabelnlernen

***Masculine nouns ending in** -er* These nouns have the same form in the singular as in the plural.

Singular	Plural
der Lehrer	die Lehrer
der Kugelschreiber	die Kugelschreiber
der Schüler	die Schüler
der Europäer	die Europäer
der Pullover	die Pullover
der Computer	die Computer

Resist the temptation to add an **-s** as in English to form the plural (*two pullovers*). Remember that *very few* German nouns take **-s** in the plural.

Übung. Answer your instructor's questions with the plural form.

1. Wie viele Computer besitzt die Universität?
2. Wie viele Amerikaner sind hier im Zimmer?
3. Wie viele Kugelschreiber besitzen Sie?
4. Wie viele Europäer studieren hier?
5. Wie viele Pullover besitzen Sie?

Leicht zu merken

Lab Manual Kap. 3, Üb. zur Betonung.

international	internatio<u>nal</u>	der **Sport**	
die **Jeans** (*pl.*)		das **System, -e**	Sys<u>tem</u>
optimistisch		das **Schulsystem**	<u>Schul</u>system
pessimistisch		das **Theater**	The<u>a</u>ter

Einstieg in den Text

- The speakers in the following **Klassendiskussion** express opinions about their recent trip. Notice how often they preface opinions with such phrases as **Ich finde**, ... or **Man meint**, ... (*I think . . ., People think . . .*).
- Remember that word order in German is in some ways freer than in English. It is true that the verb must be in second position in statements. In place of the subject, however, an object, an adverb, or some other element can be in first position. You will often find sentences beginning with the direct object.

Das finde ich auch.	*I think so too.*
Das kann ich verstehen.	*I can understand that.*

The clue to understanding such sentences is the personal ending of the verb. Words like **habe** and **finde** are obviously first person and go with the subject pronoun **ich**.

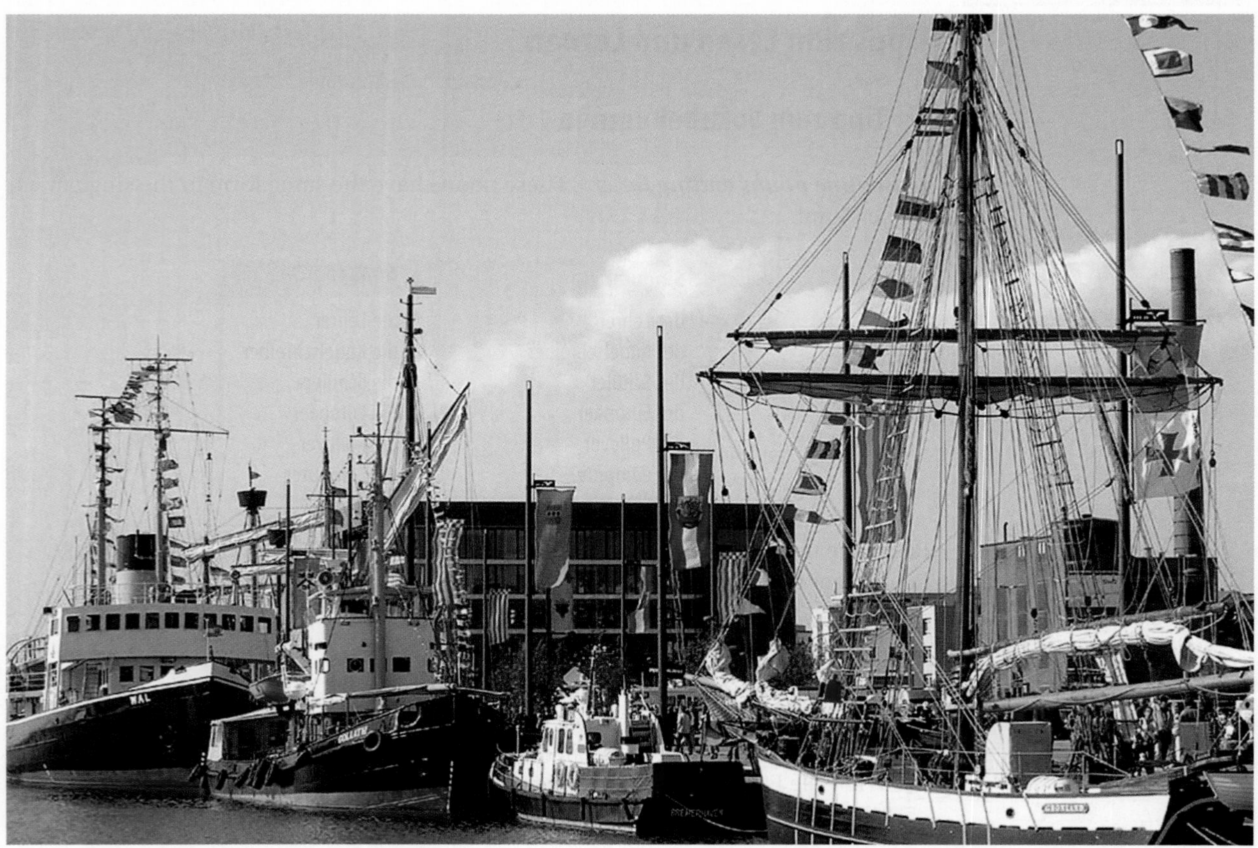

Historische und moderne Schiffe (Bremerhaven)

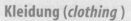

Wortschatz 2

Kleidung (*clothing*)

der **Mantel, ¨** coat
der **Pullover, -** pullover, sweater
also: der **Pulli, -s**
der **Schuh, -e** shoe
der **Turnschuh, -e** sneaker, gym shoe
das **Hemd, -en** shirt
das **Kleid, -er** dress; *pl.* = dresses *or* clothes
die **Hose, -n** trousers, pants
die **Jacke, -n** jacket

Verben

besprechen (bespricht) to discuss
entscheiden to decide
hassen to hate
lachen to laugh
lernen to learn
singen to sing

Substantive

der **Europäer, -** European (*m.*)
(das) **Amerika** America
(das) **Deutsch** German (*language*)
(das) **Englisch** English
(das) **Europa** Europe
das **Gymnasium,** die **Gymnasien** secondary school (*prepares pupils for university*)

Gymnasium derives from a Greek word for the place where athletes trained (**gymnos** = *naked*). The meaning was later generalized to *place of study.*

die **Angst, ¨e** fear
Angst haben to be afraid
die **Europäerin, -nen** European (*f.*)
die **Farbe, -n** color
die **Hausaufgabe, -n** homework assignment
die **Musik** music
die **Sprache, -n** language
die **Fremdsprache** foreign language
die **Umwelt** environment
die **Welt, -en** world
die **Zeit, -en** time
die **Pommes frites** (*pl., pronounced "Pomm fritt"*) French fries

Angst is related to Latin *angustiae* = *a narrow constriction.* English has borrowed **Angst** from German and uses it to mean *anxiety, existential fear.*

Adjektive und Adverbien

ähnlich similar
also thus, for that reason
amerikanisch American
darum therefore, for that reason
dunkel dark
ehrlich honest
eigentlich actually, in fact
fremd strange, foreign
lustig fun; humorous
neu new
schnell fast
so so; like this

Farben

blau blue
braun brown
bunt colorful, multicolored
gelb yellow
grau gray
grün green
rot red
schwarz black
weiß white

Nützliche Ausdrücke

Das finde ich auch. I think so too.
gar nicht not at all
Stimmt schon. That's right.

Gegensätze

dunkel ≠ hell dark ≠ light
hassen ≠ lieben to hate ≠ to love
lachen ≠ weinen to laugh ≠ to cry
neu ≠ alt new ≠ old
schnell ≠ langsam fast ≠ slow
Stimmt schon. ≠ Stimmt nicht. That's right. ≠ That's wrong.

Mit anderen Worten

echt (*colloq.*) = **wirklich**
nagelneu = sehr, sehr neu
uralt = sehr, sehr alt
blitzschnell = sehr, sehr schnell

Eine Klassendiskussion

Learning about German secondary schools is the cultural goal of this chapter.

Last spring, Class 12a from the Kepler Gymnasium in Hannover visited a high school in California. Now they are discussing their impressions of the States with their teacher, Herr Beck; they also plan to write an article for their school newspaper. [2]

HERR BECK: Können wir jetzt unsere Amerikareise besprechen? Rolf, möchtest du etwas sagen? – Ach, er schläft ja wieder. (*Alle lachen.*)

ROLF: Meinen Sie mich? Entschuldigung! Unsere Reise? Sie war° echt lustig.

KIRSTEN: Das finde ich auch. Die Amerikaner sind wahnsinnig freundlich und jetzt weiß ich, die Schüler in Amerika sind eigentlich gar nicht so anders. Dort trägt man ja auch Jeans und Turnschuhe – das ist international. Man hört auch Rockmusik, singt dieselben Schlager° und isst Pommes frites.

HERR BECK: Stimmt schon, aber haben die amerikanischen Schüler auch ähnliche Probleme wie ihr?

ANDREAS: Ach, wissen Sie, alle Schüler hassen Hausaufgaben! (*Alle lachen.*) Nein, aber im Ernst°, wir sind alle manchmal pessimistisch. Man meint, man kann später° keine Arbeit finden, und auch Umweltprobleme gibt es überall. Auch in Amerika haben die Schüler manchmal ein bisschen Angst vor der Zukunft°.

was

Notice the flavoring particle **ja** (lines 5 and 9) conveying the meaning *after all*.

dieselben ... *the same hits*

im ... *seriously*

later

vor ... *of the future*

Klasse 12a bespricht ihre Amerikareise.

[2] Class 12a is one of several parallel 12th-grade classes in the **Gymnasium**. Students stay in the same group for several years and take all their classes together. **Gymnasien** in West Germany used to have 13 grades, but a country-wide reform is under way to make **Klasse 12** the final grade.

HERR BECK: Das kann ich verstehen, muss ich ehrlich sagen. Aber gibt es denn keine Unterschiede° zwischen hier und dort?

differences

KIRSTEN: Doch, natürlich! Dort besuchen° alle Schüler die Highschool, bis sie 18 sind. Wir müssen aber hier mit zehn Jahren entscheiden: Gymnasium, Realschule oder Hauptschule.[3] Die zwei Schulsysteme sind sehr unterschiedlich°.

here: *attend*
= *anders*

CHRISTA: Ich finde, wir müssen hier früher Fremdsprachen lernen. Deutschland hat viele Nachbarländer°, und darum brauchen wir Fremdsprachen. Viele Europäer können z.B. gut Englisch, aber relativ wenige Amerikaner lernen Fremdsprachen. Andererseits° macht man an der Schule[4] in Amerika mehr Sport, Musik und Theater.

neighboring countries
on the other hand

HERR BECK: Jetzt haben wir leider keine Zeit mehr. Aber morgen können wir unseren Artikel über die Reise für die Schülerzeitung schreiben. Auf Wiedersehen bis dann.

---

[3] See **Almanach**, p. 90.
[4] **an der Schule =** *at school.* The article **der** indicates that **Schule** is in the dative case, which is introduced in **Kapitel 5**.

NACH DEM LESEN

SAM **Lab Manual** Kap. 3, Diktat.

SAM **Workbook** Kap. 3, I, J, K.

A Antworten Sie auf Deutsch.

1. Sind die Schüler in Amerika sehr anders oder sind sie ähnlich?
2. Was trägt man zum Beispiel in Amerika und auch in Deutschland?
3. Was isst man auch dort?
4. Was hassen alle Schüler?
5. Warum sind viele Schüler manchmal pessimistisch?
6. Warum müssen die Deutschen Fremdsprachen lernen?
7. Was schreibt die Klasse für ihre Schülerzeitung?

B Unterschiede und Ähnlichkeiten (*differences and similarities*). Which statements apply to schools in Germany, which apply to schools in America, which apply to both (**beide**)?

	Deutschland	**USA**	**beide**
1. Die Schüler hören gern Rockmusik.	______	______	______
2. Man trägt oft Jeans und Turnschuhe.	______	______	______
3. Fremdsprachen sind sehr wichtig.	______	______	______
4. Sport, Musik und Theater sind sehr wichtig.	______	______	______
5. Mit zehn Jahren müssen Schüler die Schule wählen (*choose*).	______	______	______

C Schreiben wir. Auf Seite 84 sehen Sie ein Foto von einer Schulklasse in Deutschland. Schreiben Sie, was man hier sieht und auch was man *nicht* sieht. Schreiben Sie 5–6 Sätze.

BEISPIEL: Hier sieht man eine Schülerin, aber man sieht kein(en) ...

Vokabeln zum Thema Kleidung und Farben

Talking about clothing is a communicative goal.

Was soll ich heute tragen?

Im Lesestück sprechen die Schüler über Kleider in Deutschland und den USA. Hier können Sie mehr Kleidungsvokabular lernen.

You already know some of this vocabulary.

This vocabulary focuses on an everyday topic or situation. Words you already know from **Wortschatz** sections are listed without English equivalents; new supplementary vocabulary is listed with definitions. Your instructor may assign some supplementary vocabulary for active mastery.

die Kleidung (*clothing*)

1. der **Anzug, ¨-e** *suit*
2. die **Bluse, -n** *blouse*
3. die **Brille** (*sing.*) *glasses*
4. der **Handschuh, -e** *glove*
5. das **Hemd, -en**
6. die **Hose, -n**
7. der **Hut, ¨-e** *hat*
8. die **Jacke, -n**
9. das **Kleid, -er**
10. die **Krawatte, -n** *tie*
11. der **Mantel, ¨**
12. der **Pulli, -s**
13. der **Rock, ¨-e** *skirt*
14. der **Schuh, -e**
15. die **Tasche, -n** *pocket; handbag, shoulder bag*
16. das **T-Shirt, -s** *T-shirt*
17. der **Turnschuh, -e**
18. der **Regenschirm, -e** *umbrella*
19. die **Mütze, -n** *cap*

Für Sie geöffnet:
Montags bis Freitags
10 bis 20 Uhr
Samstags: 9.30 bis 16 Uhr
WWW.SPORTHAUS-KAPS.DE

KAPS
SOLMS-OBERBIEL
Telefon 06441/5019-0
Fax 06441/501940

Coole Fashion gibt's bei KAPS

D Gruppenarbeit: Was tragen Sie heute?

BEISPIEL: PROFESSOR: Was tragen Sie heute, Mary?
STUDENTIN: Ich trage ______ und ______.

E Partnerarbeit: Was trägst du heute?

BEISPIEL: A: Was trägst du heute, Mary?
B: Ich trage ______ und ______. Was trägst du?

Info-Austausch

F Was trägst du in diesen Situationen? Work with a partner to say what you would wear in the following situations. The drawing on page 86 will help with clothing vocabulary.

BEISPIEL: A: Es regnet. Was trägst du?
B: Ich trage einen Regenmantel oder einen Regenschirm. Es schneit. Was trägst du?
A: Ich trage ...

Partner A:

Situation	Kleider
Es regnet.	
	einen Mantel und Handschuhe
Es ist sehr windig.	
	ein T-Shirt
Du suchst eine Stelle.	
	Jeans und Turnschuhe

Welche Farbe hat das?

The prefixes **dunkel** and **hell** may be added to the colors you have learned in **Wortschatz 2**.

dunkelblau	*dark blue*
hellgrün	*light green*

Three more colors that may be useful:

rosa	*pink*
lila	*violet, lavender*
orange	*orange*

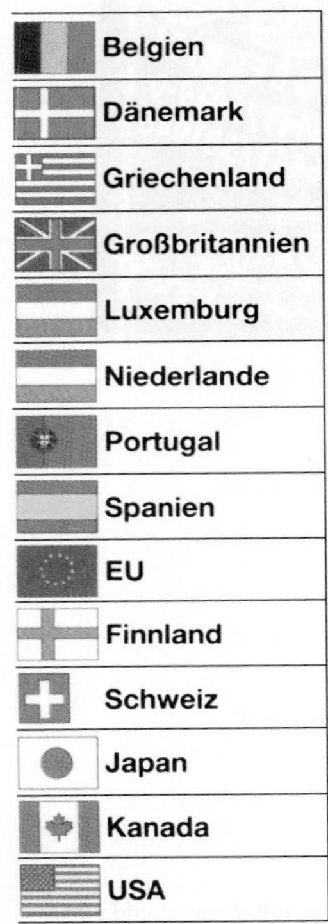

G Übung. Was ist Ihre Lieblingsfarbe (*favorite color*)?

BEISPIEL: Meine Lieblingsfarbe ist rot.

H Übung. Welche Farben haben diese Fahnen (*flags*)?

BEISPIEL: Frankreich: blau, weiß, rot

Deutschland: _____, _____, _____ [*gold*]

Österreich: _____, _____, _____

Schweden: _____, _____

Italien: _____, _____, _____

Irland: _____, _____, _____

I Partnerarbeit. Ask each other about the colors of various things in the classroom and of clothing people are wearing.

BEISPIEL: A: Welche Farben hat die Landkarte?
B: Sie ist _____.

A: Welche Farbe hat Peters Hemd?
B: Sein Hemd ist _____.

Expressing opinions is a communicative goal.

J Gruppenarbeit: Was meinen Sie? (*4 Personen*) Here are some topics of conversation and some adjectives. Using the verbs **meinen** and **finden**, take turns expressing opinions about these topics. Others in the group will agree or disagree.

BEISPIEL: A: Ich finde (meine), die Umwelt ist wichtig.
B: Das finde (meine) ich auch. *oder*
Das finde (meine) ich nicht.

Schulen in Amerika	schön/hässlich
Schulen in Deutschland	wichtig/unwichtig
Rockmusik	interessant/langweilig
klassische Musik	toll
die Umwelt	super
Fremdsprachen	stinklangweilig
Hausaufgaben	wahnsinnig gut

SCHREIBTIPP

Writing with modal verbs

The note you will write in the following exercise contains many modal auxiliary verbs. Remember: when using a modal verb, the second part of the predicate—the infinitive—comes at the end of the sentence.

Vanessa **muss** für die Chemiestunde **lernen**.

Once you've completed your note, check it over for accuracy. Have you used the correct form of the modal verb in each sentence? Are the infinitives properly placed?

J Schreiben wir. Udo is throwing a party, but nobody can come. Finish writing him the following note explaining why. There are some cues to help you.

Lieber Udo,
leider kann niemand zur Party kommen. Monika muss zu Hause bleiben.
Klaus . . .

Klaus / müssen / für morgen / machen / seine Hausaufgaben
Ruth / möchten / fahren / nach Berlin
Peter und Ute / wollen / besuchen / ihre Tante / in Wien
Herr Beck / können / leider / finden / seinen Anzug / nicht
Andreas / dürfen / nicht so spät / kommen / nach Hause
ich / wollen / kommen / aber können nicht

K Wie sagt man das auf Deutsch?

1. Wouldn't you like to stay a bit?
2. Unfortunately, I have to work this evening.
3. What do you have to do?
4. I have to read a book and an article.

5. Don't you have any friends in Hinterwalden?
6. Yes, I do. Unfortunately they're quite boring.
7. Then you have to visit us soon.

8. You want to come to Berlin, don't you?
9. Yes. I can't stay in Hinterwalden.
10. Why not? Aren't there any jobs there?
11. Yes, but not enough. I want to look for a job in Berlin.

ALMANACH

VIDEO

A Note about Schools in German-Speaking Countries

The public school systems in Germany, Austria, and Switzerland all differ from American public schools in the degree to which they track pupils. Relatively early in their schooling, children are steered toward apprenticeships, commercial training, or preparation for university study. In the Federal Republic of Germany, each **Land** (state) has authority over its own school system. In all **Länder**, children attend four years of elementary school (**Grundschule**) together. At the end of the fourth, fifth, or sixth grade (depending on the **Land**), they are then tracked into separate schools. The decision is made on the basis of grades and conferences between teachers and parents.

There are three possibilities: the **Hauptschule**, the **Realschule**, or the **Gymnasium**. The first two are oriented respectively toward trades and business and prepare the pupils for various forms of apprenticeship and job training. The **Gymnasium** is the traditional preparation for university study. After passing their final examination, called **Abitur** in Germany and **Matura** in Austria and Switzerland, pupils may apply to a university.

There has been some experimentation in the Federal Republic with the concept of a **Gesamtschule,** a model that unifies all three types of secondary school. **Gesamtschulen** resemble American high schools, in that important decisions about children's futures need not be made when they are ten, but can wait until they are sixteen. This model, however, has not become widespread.

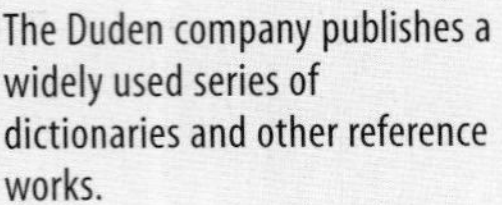

The Duden company publishes a widely used series of dictionaries and other reference works.

KAPITEL

Auf der Ostseeinsel Rügen

Land und Leute

Kommunikation

- Making suggestions and giving commands
- Expressing likes, dislikes, and preferences
- Discussing weather, climate, and landscape

Kultur

- The climate and geography of Germany

In diesem Kapitel

- **Lyrik zum Vorlesen**
  "Die Jahreszeiten"
- **Grammatik**
  1. More uses of the accusative case
  2. Suggestions and commands: The imperative
  3. The verb **werden**
  4. Equivalents of English *to like*
  5. Sentence adverbs
  6. **Gehen** + infinitive
- **Lesestück**
  Deutschland: Geographie und Klima
- **Almanach**
  The Common Origin of German and English

DIALOGE

Lab Manual Kap. 4, Dialoge, Fragen, Hören Sie gut zu!, Üb. zur Aussprache **[r]**.

Am See

FRAU MÜLLER: Wollen Sie noch einmal schwimmen gehen, Frau Brinkmann?
FRAU BRINKMANN: Nein, lieber nicht. Ich bin ein bisschen müde. Und das Wasser ist diesen Sommer so wahnsinnig kalt. Gehen Sie doch ohne mich.
FRAU MÜLLER: Möchten Sie vielleicht lieber Karten spielen?
FRAU BRINKMANN: Ja, gerne!

Kitzbühel is a popular skiing and hiking resort in **Tirol** (in Austria).

Winterurlaub

RICHARD: Möchtest du dieses Jahr im Winter nach Österreich?
EVA: Super! Fahren wir doch im Januar nach Kitzbühel.
RICHARD: Hoffentlich können wir noch ein Hotelzimmer bekommen.
EVA: Ich glaube, es ist noch nicht zu spät.

Das Frühstück originally meant the piece (**das Stück**) of bread eaten early (**früh**) in the morning. **Brötchen** (called **Semmeln** in southern Germany and Austria), crusty rolls baked fresh daily, are the most common breakfast food.

Morgens um halb zehn

ANITA: Also, tschüss! Ich muss jetzt weg.
BEATE: Warte mal! Ohne Frühstück geht's nicht! Iss doch wenigstens ein Brötchen.
ANITA: Leider habe ich keine Zeit mehr. Jeden Montag hab' ich mein Seminar. Es beginnt um zehn, und heute muss ich auch vorher ein Heft kaufen.
BEATE: Nimm doch das Brötchen mit. Später wirst du sicher hungrig.
ANITA: Du hast Recht. Also, bis nachher.

NOTE ON USAGE

noch nicht = *not yet*	Es ist **noch nicht** zu spät.
nicht mehr = *no longer*	Das Wasser ist **nicht mehr** warm.
kein ... mehr = *no more . . .*	Ich habe **keine** Zeit **mehr.**

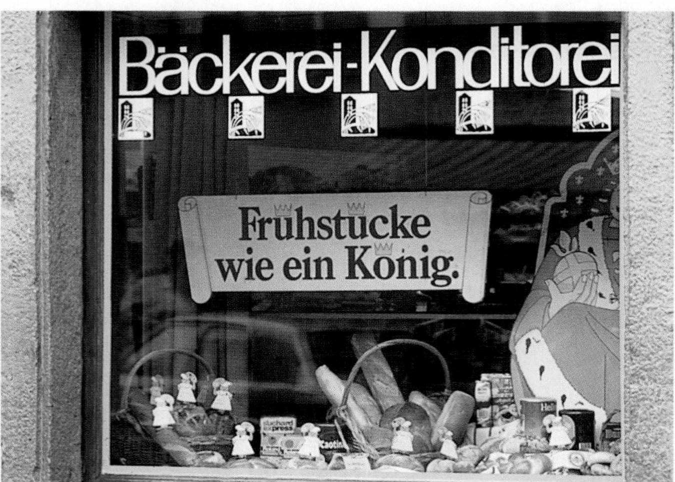

Beim Bäcker kauft man frische Brötchen.

Wortschatz 1

Verben

beginnen to begin
bekommen to receive
frühstücken to eat breakfast
glauben to believe; to think
kaufen to buy
mögen (mag) to like
schwimmen to swim
warten to wait
werden (wird) to become; to get (*in the sense of* "become")

Don't confuse **bekommen** (*to receive*) with **werden** (*to become*).

Substantive

der **See, -n** lake
  am See at the lake
der **Urlaub, -e** vacation (*from a job*)
das **Brötchen, -** roll
das **Frühstück** breakfast
  zum Frühstück for breakfast
das **Hotel, -s** hotel
das **Jahr, -e** year
die **Jahreszeit, -en** season
(das) **Österreich** Austria
das **Seminar, -e** (*university*) seminar

Note stress: **Seminar**

das **Wasser** water
die **Karte, -n** card; ticket; map
Die vier Jahreszeiten
der **Frühling** spring
der **Sommer** summer
der **Herbst** fall
der **Winter** winter
  im Frühling, Sommer, Herbst, Winter in the spring, summer etc.

Adjektive und Adverbien

einmal once
  noch einmal once again, once more
glücklich happy
Gott sei Dank thank goodness
hoffentlich I, (we, etc.) hope . . .
hungrig hungry
lang(e) long; for a long time
lieber (+ *verb*) prefer to, would rather
  Ich spiele lieber Karten. I'd rather play cards.
morgens (*adv.*) in the morning(s)
nachher later on, after that
noch nicht not yet
sauer annoyed, ticked off
selbstverständlich it goes without saying that . . . ; of course
später later
super (*colloq.*) super, great
vorher before that, previously
weg away, gone

Andere Vokabeln

dies- this, these
doch (*flavoring particle with commands; see p. 100*)
jed- each, every
mal (*flavoring particle with commands; see p. 100*)
mit along (with me, us, etc.)

Dies- and **jed-:** These words (*this, every*) always take endings (**dieser, jede**, etc.).

Präpositionen mit Akkusativ

bis until, by
durch through
für for
gegen against
ohne without
um around (the outside of); at (*with times*)

These six prepositions must be followed by the accusative case. See **Grammatik**, p. 96.

Nützliche Ausdrücke

Bis nachher! See you later!
Es geht. It's all right. It's possible. It can be done.
Es geht nicht. Nothing doing. It can't be done.
Lieber nicht. I'd rather not. No thanks. Let's not.
nicht mehr no longer, not any more
  Sie wohnt nicht mehr hier. She doesn't live here any more.
kein ... mehr no more . . . , not a . . . any more
  Ich habe keine Zeit mehr. I have no more time.
  Ich bin kein Kind mehr. I'm not a child any more.
Recht haben to be right
  Du hast Recht. You're right.
Warte mal! Wait a second! Hang on!

Gegensätze

glücklich ≠ unglücklich happy ≠ unhappy
kaufen ≠ verkaufen to buy ≠ to sell
lang ≠ kurz long; for a long time ≠ short; for a short time
vorher ≠ nachher before that ≠ after that

Mit anderen Worten

todmüde = sehr müde
super = fantastisch = prima = sehr gut

Mensch, bin ich todmüde!

Variationen

A Persönliche Fragen

1. Frau Brinkmann und Frau Müller spielen gern Karten. Was machen Sie gern?
2. Spielen Sie gern Karten oder gehen Sie lieber schwimmen?
3. Frau Brinkmann sagt, sie ist ein bisschen müde. Sind Sie heute müde?
4. Wohin wollen Sie im Winter? im Sommer?
5. Essen Sie immer Frühstück oder haben Sie manchmal keine Zeit?
6. Was müssen Sie jeden Montag machen?
7. Wann beginnt die Deutschstunde?
8. Anita muss ein Heft kaufen. Was müssen Sie heute kaufen?

B Gruppenarbeit: Gegensätze. (*mit offenen Büchern*) Contradict each other.

BEISPIEL: A: Fremdsprachen sind unwichtig.
B: Nein, sie sind wichtig.

1. 8.00 Uhr ist zu früh.
2. Dieses Buch ist langweilig.
3. Dieses Zimmer ist schön.
4. Wir kennen jemand in München.
5. Bernd hasst Rockmusik.
6. Du trägst oft Turnschuhe.
7. Sie sind immer müde.
8. Ich esse sehr langsam.

C Partnerarbeit: Wie kann man antworten? For each sentence in the left column choose appropriate responses from the right column.

1. Gehen wir noch einmal schwimmen!	Super!
2. Das Wasser ist zu kalt!	Du hast Recht.
3. Ohne Frühstück geht's nicht.	Stimmt schon.
4. Es gibt keine Hotelzimmer mehr.	Stimmt nicht.
5. Spielen wir zusammen Karten!	Das finde ich auch.
6. Das schaffst du leicht.	Gar nicht!
7. Bist du hungrig?	Es tut mir Leid.
8. Ein Hotelzimmer mit Frühstück kostet 125 Euro!	Was ist denn los?
9. Du kommst wieder zu spät.	Um Gottes Willen!
10. Mensch, bin ich müde.	Nichts zu danken.
	Mensch!
	Fantastisch!
	Doch!
	Prima!
	Gerne!

Vokabeln zum Thema Frühstück

D Gruppenarbeit: Was isst und trinkst du gern zum Frühstück? (*2–3 Personen*) Tell each other what you like to eat for breakfast or what you never eat for breakfast.

Articles are not included because they are not needed for this exercise. Most nouns with their articles will be introduced later as active vocabulary.

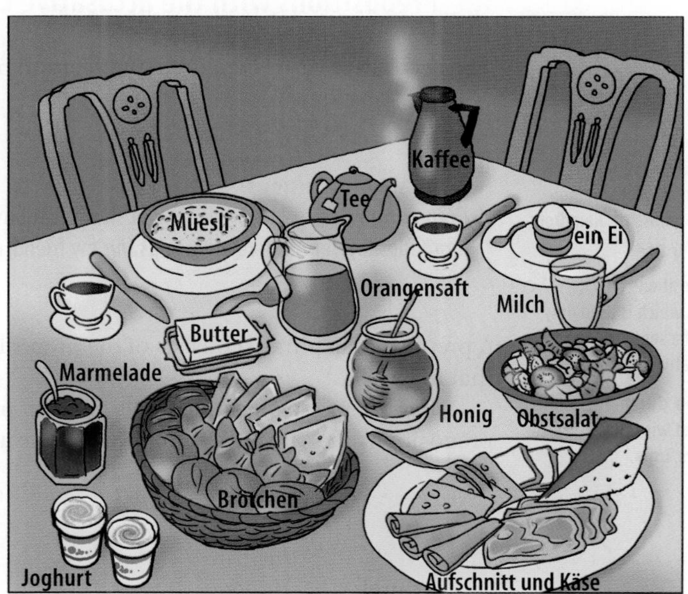

Ich esse (trinke) gern ________ zum Frühstück, und du? *oder*
Ich esse (trinke) nie ________ zum Frühstück, und du?

Viele deutsche Kinder lernen dieses traditionelle Gedicht (*poem*) über die Jahreszeiten.

Die Jahreszeiten

Es war° eine Mutter, — *there was*
Die hatte° vier Kinder: — *who had*
Den Frühling, den Sommer,
Den Herbst und den Winter.
Der Frühling bringt Blumen°, — *flowers*
Der Sommer bringt Klee°, — *clover*
Der Herbst, der° bringt Trauben°, — *it / grapes*
Der Winter bringt Schnee°. — *snow*

GRAMMATIK

1. More uses of the accusative case

In addition to being the case of the direct object, the accusative is also used with some prepositions and time phrases.

 Prepositions with the accusative case (*Präpositionen mit Akkusativ*)

The accusative case is required after certain prepositions.

A good mnemonic device for the prepositions with accusative: sing them to the first phrase of "Raindrops Keep Falling on My Head."

No German prepositions take nominative case, which is used only for the subject of a sentence and for predicate nominatives (see p. 30).

In spoken German, **durch**, **für**, and **um** often contract with the article **das**: **durchs**, **fürs**, **ums**.

DEFINITION

What are prepositions?
Prepositions are a class of words that show relationships of space (*through* the mountains), time (*until* Tuesday), or other relationships (*for* my friend, *without* any money)

A prepositional phrase consists of the preposition and the noun or pronoun object that follows it.

The case of the object depends on what preposition it follows. Here is the list of prepositions that are always followed by the accusative case. Memorize this list.

bis	*until*	Wir warten **bis Dienstag**.
	by	Ich muss es **bis morgen** lesen.
durch	*through*	Er fährt **durch die Berge**.
für	*for*	Sie arbeitet **für ihren Vater**.
gegen	*against*	Was hast du **gegen mich**?
ohne	*without*	Wir gehen **ohne dich**.
um	*around* (the outside of)	Das Auto fährt **um das Hotel**.
	at (with times)	Karl kommt **um drei**.

Lab Manual Kap. 4, Var. zu Üb. 2.

Workbook Kap. 4, A, B.

1 Übung: Für wen?

1. Sie suchen eine Karte. Für wen suchen Sie sie?
   Ich suche sie für mein-________.
2. Sie machen heute das Frühstück. Für wen machen Sie es?
   Ich mache es für mein-________.

2 Übung: Ich mache das allein. Your instructor asks if you do things with other people in your class. Using pronouns, say that you do everything without them.

1. Spielen Sie mit Richard Karten? Nein, ohne ________.
2. Arbeiten Sie morgen mit Ingrid zusammen? Nein, leider ohne ________.
3. Gehen Sie mit Robert und Susan schwimmen?
4. Frühstücken Sie am Mittwoch mit Patrick?

3 Übung: Wohin fährt Monika? Monika is going to drive through various locations. Tell where she's driving. Use complete sentences.

BEISPIEL: Sie fährt durch ________. Dann fährt sie durch ________.

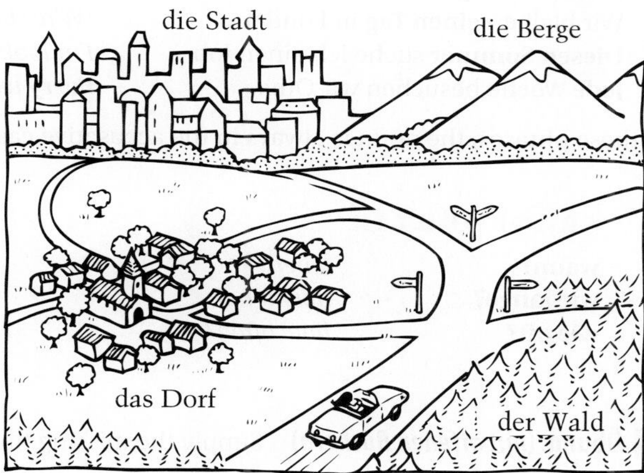

4 Übung: Wann beginnt das? Using the TV guide below, answer your instructor's questions about when shows begin. Note that official time-telling in German uses the 24-hour clock instead of AM and PM. Thus, 2:45 PM is **vierzehn Uhr fünfundvierzig** (**14.45 Uhr**).

BEISPIEL: Wann beginnt die Tagesschau?
Sie beginnt um 15.00 Uhr.

21. April SAMSTAG

ARD

15.00 **Tagesschau**	**18.10** **Brisant**	**22.40** **Sportschau live: Boxen** Weltmeisterschafts-Qualifikation Super-Mittelgewicht: Markus Beyer - Manuel Lopez	
15.05 **Die Lümmel von der ersten Bank** D Spielfilm v. 1967	**18.47** **Dr. Sommerfeld - Neues vom Bülowbogen**	**00.45** **Tagesschau**	
16.30 **Europamagazin**	**19.51** **Lottozahlen**	**00.55** **Rocky** US Spielfilm v. 1976	
17.00 **Tagesschau**	**20.00** **Tagesschau**	**02.50** **Tagesschau**	
17.03 **ARD-Ratgeber: Bauen & Wohnen**	**20.15** **Das Frühlingsfest der Volksmusik**	**02.55** **Opfer seiner Wut** US Spielfilm v. 1993	
17.30 **Sportschau** u.a. Fußball-Bundesliga	**22.15** **Tagesthemen - mit Sport**		
18.00 **Tagesschau**	**22.35** **Das Wort zum Sonntag**		

PRO 7

14.35	**Friends**
15.05	**Die Simpsons**
15.35	**Sabrina - Total verhext**
16.05	**Charmed - Zauberhafte Hexen**
17.00	**Roswell**
18.00	**Lovestories**
19.00	**Talk, Talk, Talk**
19.30	**Max**
19.55	**Nachrichten / Sport / Wetter**
20.15	**Die Nervensäge**

5 Übung: Wie sagt man das auf Deutsch?

1. Are you for me or against me?
2. I'd like to take a trip around the world.
3. I hope I can do it without my parents.
4. She's looking for a card for her grandfather.
5. We want to drive through the mountains.

Time phrases in the accusative case

Some time phrases include a preposition:

Sie kommt **um** 3 Uhr.	*She's coming **at** three o'clock.*
Ich warte **bis** morgen.	*I'll wait **until** tomorrow.*

Other time phrases have no preposition:

Remember that expressions of time (**dieses Jahr**) precede expressions of place or destination (**in Deutschland**).

Note that the German equivalent of ***for** a day* is simply **einen Tag** without a preposition.

Ich studiere **dieses Jahr** in Deutschland.	*I'm studying in Germany **this year**.*
Jeden Montag hat sie ein Seminar.	***Every Monday** she has a seminar.*
Wir bleiben **einen Tag** in London.	*We're staying in London **for a day**.*
Diesen Sommer suche ich einen Job.	*I'm looking for a job **this summer**.*
Jede Woche besuchen wir Oma.	***Every week** we visit Grandma.*

In these phrases, the noun is always in the accusative case.

FRAGEWÖRTER

wann?	*when?*
wie lange?	*how long?*
wie oft?	*how often?*

SAM Workbook **Workbook** Kap. 4, C.

6 Übung. (*mit offenen Büchern*) Supply the missing time phrases cued in English.

1. Wie oft schlafen Sie bis 8 Uhr?
   Ich schlafe ________ bis 8 Uhr. (*every day*)
2. Wann besuchen Sie Ihre Eltern?
   Ich besuche sie ________. (*this Wednesday*)
3. Wie lange bleiben Sie in Tübingen?
   Ich bleibe ________ dort. (*a year*)
4. Wann arbeitest du denn mit Karl zusammen?
   Wahrscheinlich arbeite ich ________ mit ihm zusammen. (*this week*)
5. Wie lange wartet ihr noch?
   Wir warten noch ________ vor der Bäckerei. (*for an hour*)
6. Hoffentlich kannst du lange bei uns bleiben.
   Nein, leider kann ich nur ________ bei euch sein. (*one day*)
7. Wann ist das Wetter bei euch besonders schön?
   Das Wetter ist ________ mild und sonnig. (*every October*)
8. Wann kann ich Sie besuchen, Herr Wahrig?
   ________ um 9 Uhr bin ich frei. (*every Tuesday*)

7 Partnerarbeit: Was machst du dieses Wochenende (*weekend*)? Ask each other the following questions.

1. Was machst du dieses Wochenende?
   Dieses Wochenende ________.
2. Was musst du jede Woche machen?
   Jede Woche muss ich ________.
3. Wohin fährst du diesen Sommer?
   Diesen Sommer ________.
4. Was isst du jeden Morgen zum Frühstück?
   Jeden Morgen ________.
5. Wie lange dauert (*lasts*) die Deutschstunde? das Semester? ________.

2. Suggestions and commands: The imperative (*der Imperativ*)

Making suggestions and giving commands are communicative goals.

The imperative form of German verbs is used either to make suggestions ("Let's go swimming") or to give commands ("Wait!").

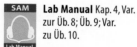

"Let's do something": The *wir*-imperative

Fahren wir nach Österreich.	***Let's go to*** *Austria.*
Spielen wir Karten.	***Let's play*** *cards.*

The **wir**-imperative has the same word order as a yes/no question, but at the end of the sentence, the voice drops instead of rising. Compare these intonation curves:

Gehen wir nach Hause? **Gehen wir nach Hause!**

SAM **Lab Manual** Kap. 4, Var. zur Üb. 8; Üb. 9; Var. zu Üb. 10.

SAM **Workbook** Kap. 4, D.

8 Gruppenarbeit: Ja, machen wir das! Here are some activities you could do today. Take turns suggesting them to each other.

BEISPIEL: schwimmen gehen
A: Gehen wir heute schwimmen!
B: Ja, machen wir das! *oder* Nein, lieber nicht.

jetzt frühstücken	eine Reise machen
Karten spielen	eine Pause machen
eine Zeitung kaufen	nach Hause laufen
zu Hause arbeiten	das Auto verkaufen

Now suggest other things to do today.

"Do something": The *Sie*-imperative

In the first dialogue on page 92, Frau Brinkmann uses the **Sie**-imperative: ***Gehen Sie* doch ohne mich.**

Fahren Sie nach Österreich.	***Go*** *to Austria.*
Bitte **besuchen Sie** mich im Mai.	*Please **visit** me in May.*

The **Sie**-imperative has the same word order as a yes/no question, but has falling intonation.

NOTE ON USAGE

Flavoring particles *doch* and *mal*

Doch (Why don't you . . . ?) You can soften a command to a suggestion by adding the unstressed flavoring particle **doch**.

Gehen Sie nach Hause!	*Go home!*
Gehen Sie **doch** nach Hause.	*Why don't you go home?*

Mal You can make a command more peremptory by adding the unstressed flavoring particle **mal**.

Warte!	*Wait!*
Warte **mal**!	*Wait a second!*
Hören Sie **mal**!	*Just listen here!*

Bitte also turns an imperative into a polite request: **Gehen Sie *bitte* nach Hause.**

Note on punctuation: German uses an exclamation mark to add emphasis to commands.

9 Übung: Machen Sie das doch! Encourage your instructor to go ahead and do something.

BEISPIEL: Ich möchte eine Reise machen.
Machen Sie doch eine Reise!

1. Ich möchte Brötchen kaufen.
2. Ich möchte eine Pause machen.
3. Ich möchte nach Hause gehen.
4. Ich möchte Tennis spielen.
5. Ich möchte Frau Klein besuchen.
6. Ich möchte mein Auto verkaufen.

10 Übung: Machen Sie das nicht! What should your instructor *not* do?

BEISPIEL: Was soll ich nicht kaufen?
Kaufen Sie keinen Sportwagen!

Was soll ich nicht essen?
Was soll ich nicht trinken?
Wen soll ich nicht besuchen?
Wohin soll ich nicht reisen?

11 Übung: Wie sagt man das auf Deutsch? (*mit offenen Büchern*) Use the **Sie**- or **wir**-imperative.

1. Let's go swimming.
2. Buy a notebook.
3. Let's discuss our trip.
4. Learn a foreign language.
5. Please speak slowly.
6. Don't sleep now.
7. Let's walk a little bit.
8. Don't wear that.

KOMM IN DIE BERGE
. . . mach Ferien im Schnee!

Imperative forms for *du*

To give commands or make suggestions to someone you address with **du**, use the **du**-imperative. The **du**-imperative for most verbs is simply the verb stem without an ending.

Geh ohne mich.	***Go*** *without me.*
Frag mich nicht.	*Don't* ***ask*** *me.*
Fahr schnell nach Hause!	***Drive*** *home quickly!*
Sei nicht so langweilig.	*Don't* ***be*** *so boring.*

Note: The pronoun **du** is *not* used with the **du**-imperative!

Verb stems ending in **-d** or **-t** usually add an **-e** to the stem.

Arbeite nicht so viel.	*Don't work so hard.*
Warte doch!	*Wait!*

SAM Lab Manual **Lab Manual** Kap. 4, Var. zu Üb. 12, Var. zu Partnerarbeit 13.

12 Übung: Ja, tu das doch! Your instructor plays the part of your friend Beate. Tell her to go ahead and do the things she asks about.

Halt! Warte auf mich!

BEISPIEL: A: Soll ich da drüben halten?
B: Ja, halte doch da drüben.

1. Soll ich Englisch lernen?
2. Soll ich Karten spielen?
3. Soll ich schnell laufen?
4. Soll ich hier warten?
5. Soll ich Brötchen kaufen?
6. Soll ich etwas singen?
7. Soll ich schwimmen gehen?
8. Soll ich eine Jacke tragen?

13 Partnerarbeit: Nein, lieber nicht. Now tell your partner *not* to do the things listed in **Übung 12**. This time, do *not* use **doch**.

BEISPIEL: A: Soll ich da drüben halten?
B: Nein, halte nicht da drüben.

14 Partnerarbeit: Sei doch (nicht) . . . ! Give your partner some ideas for self-improvement. Take turns telling each other how you should be (or not be).

BEISPIEL: Sei doch ehrlich!
Sei doch nicht sauer!

langweilig
müde
glücklich
sauer
unglücklich
freundlich
höflich
fit
ehrlich

Du-imperative of stem-changing verbs

If a verb changes its stem vowel from **e** to **i(e)**, the *changed* stem is used for the **du**-imperative.

Verb	Statement	*du*-imperative
lesen	Du **liest** das für morgen.	**Lies** das für morgen.
geben	Du **gibst** Peter das Buch.	**Gib** Peter das Buch.
essen	Du **isst** ein Brötchen.	**Iss** ein Brötchen.
nehmen	Du **nimmst** dieses Buch **mit**.	**Nimm** dieses Buch **mit**.
sprechen	Du **sprichst** mit Gina.	**Sprich** mit Gina.

15 Partnerarbeit: Lies doch die Zeitung! Give each other some advice about what you should read, eat, and take along with you today.

1. Was soll ich denn heute lesen?
2. Was soll ich denn essen?
3. Was soll ich heute mitnehmen?

16 Partnerarbeit: Nein, das darfst du nicht! Ask your partner permission to do something. Your partner tells you to do something else. The list will help you get started. Then try inventing some of your own exchanges.

BEISPIEL: zu Hause bleiben? (draußen spielen)
A: Darf ich zu Hause bleiben?
B: Nein, spiel doch draußen!

nach Hause fahren? (zu Fuß gehen [= *to go on foot*])
Tennis spielen? (deine Hausaufgaben machen)
jetzt Pizza essen? (bis heute Abend warten)

Imperative forms for *ihr*

REMINDER: **Sie**- and **wir**-imperatives include the pronoun; **ihr**- and **du**-imperatives do not.

To give commands or make suggestions to two or more people whom you address with **ihr**, use the **ihr**-imperative. The **ihr**-imperative is identical to the present-tense **ihr**-form but without the pronoun.

Present tense	*ihr*-imperative
Ihr **bleibt** hier.	**Bleibt** hier.
Ihr **singt** zu laut.	**Singt** nicht so laut.
Ihr **seid** freundlich.	**Seid** freundlich.

SAM Lab Manual **Lab Manual** Kap. 4, Üb. 17

17 Übung: Sollen wir das machen?

A. Your instructor plays one of a group of children and asks what they all should do.

BEISPIEL: Sollen wir bald nach Hause kommen?
Ja, kommt doch bald nach Hause.

1. Sollen wir Karten spielen?
2. Sollen wir das Buch lesen?
3. Sollen wir nach Hause laufen?
4. Sollen wir die Brötchen essen?

B. Now tell them what not to do.

BEISPIEL: Sollen wir nach Hause kommen?
Nein, kommt nicht nach Hause.

18 Partnerarbeit: Macht das bitte für uns!

A. Machen Sie zusammen eine Liste: Was können andere Studenten für Sie machen? Seien Sie kreativ!

BEISPIEL: Sie können für uns ...
die Bücher tragen
die Hausaufgaben schreiben
usw.

B. Sie und Ihr Partner sagen jetzt zu zwei anderen Studenten, sie sollen etwas für Sie machen. Die anderen antworten **ja** oder **nein.**

BEISPIEL:
A + B: Jennifer und Brian, tragt bitte die Bücher für uns.
C + D: Ja, O.K., das machen wir gern für euch. *oder*
Nein, das wollen wir nicht machen.

Wie bitte? Was sollen wir essen?

Imperative of *sein*

The verb **sein** is irregular in the **Sie**- and **wir**-imperatives (the **du**- and **ihr**-forms are regular).

Seien Sie bitte freundlich, Herr Kaiser.	*Please be friendly, Mr. Kaiser.*
Seien wir freundlich.	*Let's be friendly.*
Seid freundlich, Kinder.	*Be friendly, children.*
Sei freundlich, Rolf.	*Be friendly, Rolf.*

19 Übung: Sei doch ... !

SAM Lab Manual **Lab Manual** Kap. 4, Var. zu Üb. 19.

A. Tell the following people to be honest.

BEISPIEL: Richard
Sei doch ehrlich, Richard!

SAM Workbook **Workbook** Kap. 4, D.

1. Kinder
2. Herr Bachmann
3. wir
4. Barbara

B. Now tell them not to be so boring.

BEISPIEL: Herr Stolze
Seien Sie doch nicht so langweilig, Herr Stolze!

1. Ute
2. Frau Klein
3. Thomas und Beate
4. wir

20 Übung: Wie sagt man das auf Deutsch? (*mit offenen Büchern*)

1. Be honest.
2. Wear a coat.
3. Read the article.
4. Give Anita your notebook.
5. Ask me later.
6. Wait here.
7. Work together.
8. Don't be pessimistic.

3. The verb *werden*

The only German verbs that are irregular in the present tense are **werden**, **sein**, **haben**, **wissen**, and the modal verbs. You have now learned them all.

Werden (*to become*) is a high-frequency verb; it is irregular in the present-tense **du**- and **er**-forms.

werden *to become*			
ich	werde	wir	werden
du	**wirst**	ihr	werdet
er, es, sie	**wird**	sie, Sie	werden

The basic English equivalent of **werden** is *to become, get*.

Es **wird** kalt.	*It's getting cold.*
Ihre Kinder **werden** groß.	*Your children are getting big.*
Meine Schwester will Professorin **werden**.	*My sister wants to become a professor.*
Am Montag **werde** ich endlich 21.	*I'm finally turning 21 on Monday.*

21 Übung: Wer wird müde? Say who is getting tired.

BEISPIEL: Barbara
Barbara wird müde.

1. wir
2. die Kinder
3. meine Mutter
4. ihr
5. du
6. ich

22 Übung: Wie sagt man das auf Englisch?

1. Morgen wird es heiß.
2. Wann wirst du denn zwanzig?
3. Draußen wird es warm.
4. Das Buch wird endlich interessant.
5. Meine zwei Freunde wollen Lehrer werden.

4. Equivalents of English *to like*

Expressing likes, dislikes, and preferences is a communicative goal.

Gern is etymologically related to English *yearn*.

Verb + *gern(e)* = *to like to do something*

Ich **laufe gern**.	*I like to walk.*
Sie **geht gern** schwimmen.	*She likes to swim.*
Hören Sie **gerne** Musik?	*Do you like to listen to music?*

Gern(e) generally comes immediately after the subject and verb. The negation of **gern** is **nicht gern**.

Ich schwimme **nicht gern**.	*I don't like to swim.*

Lab Manual Kap. 4, Var. zu Partnerarbeit 23.

23 Partnerarbeit: Ich höre gern Musik. Take turns saying what you like to eat (**essen**), read (**lesen**), play (**spielen**), and listen to (**hören**). Here are some suggestions.

BEISPIEL: Ich höre gern Rockmusik. Und du?

Jazz	Fußball	Frühstück
Pizza	Brötchen	Volksmusik
Mozart	Zeitungen	Bücher
Tennis	Tischtennis	Lyrik (*poetry*)

24 Kettenreaktion: Was machen Sie gern? Was machen Sie lieber? Take turns talking with your classmates about what you like to do. Follow the model.

A: Ich spiele gern Tennis.
B: Sie spielt gern Tennis, aber ich lese lieber Bücher.
C: Er liest gern Bücher, aber ich _____ lieber _____.
usw.

Mögen = *to like someone or something*

Ich **mag** dich sehr.	*I like you very much.*
Ich **mag** dich **nicht**.	*I don't like you at all.*

Mögen is a modal verb. Its present-tense forms are:

mögen *to like (something)*			
ich	**mag**	wir	mögen
du	**magst**	ihr	mögt
er, es, sie	**mag**	sie, Sie	mögen

Use **mögen** or **gern** + *verb* to say what you like to eat: **Ich mag die Suppe heute** and **Brötchen esse ich gern.**

Unlike the other modals, it is usually used without an infinitive.

Ich **mag** Maria.	*I like Maria.*
Mögen Sie die Suppe nicht?	*Don't you like the soup?*

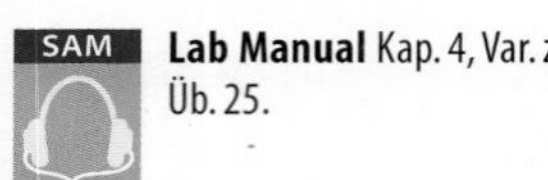
Lab Manual Kap. 4, Var. zu Üb. 25.

25 Übung. Tell who likes Frau Brandt. Use the appropriate form of **mögen**.

BEISPIEL: die Schüler
Die Schüler mögen Frau Brandt.

1. du
2. wir
3. Franz
4. meine Eltern
5. ich
6. ihr

26 Übung: Was mögen Sie? Wen mögen Sie? Say which things and people you like or dislike. Here are some ideas. Add some of your own.

meine Freunde	die Uni
das Mensaessen	meine Arbeit
den Winter	meine Geschwister
Hausaufgaben	Fremdsprachen

Möchte = would like to

Ich **möchte** Innsbruck besuchen. — *I would like to visit Innsbruck.*
Ich **möchte** einen Kaffee (haben). — *I would like (to have) a coffee.*

Möchte expresses a wish for something, while a *verb* + **gern** makes a general statement about your likes or dislikes.

Ich **möchte** Karten spielen. — *I would like to play cards.*
Ich **spiele gern** Karten. — *I like to play cards.*

27 Gruppenarbeit Say what you like and don't like about university life. Also say what you like and don't like to do. Your instructor will write your responses on the board.

BEISPIEL: A: Ich mag dieses Zimmer sehr.
B: Ich spiele gern Tennis.

28 Übung: Wie sagt man das auf Deutsch?

1. I like the soup.
2. I like to eat soup.
3. I would like the soup.
4. They would like to study in Germany.
5. Karl doesn't like to wait.
6. Do you like Professor Lange?
7. Our children like to play outside.
8. We would like to drive home.
9. I don't like that.
10. I like her.

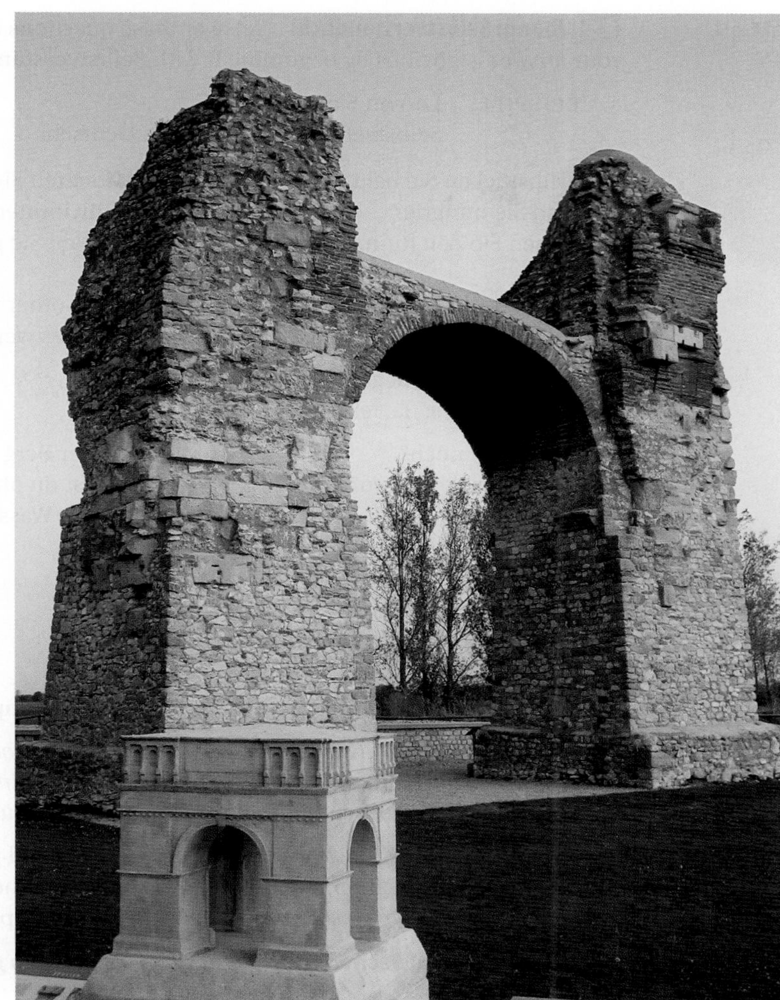

Römisches Tor [*gate*] und Rekonstruktion (Carnuntum an der Donau, östlich von Wien)

DEFINITION

What do adverbs usually modify?
Adverbs usually modify a verb (She ran *quickly*), an adjective (It was *miserably* hot), or another adverb (The child was *often* extremely quiet), and, in German, often answer the question **wie**.

5. Sentence adverbs

Sentence adverbs modify entire sentences and express the speaker's attitude toward the content of the whole.

Natürlich bin ich morgens müde.	***Of course*** *I'm tired in the morning.*
Du hast **sicher** genug Geld.	*You* ***surely*** *have enough money.*
Leider habe ich keine Zeit mehr.	***Unfortunately*** *I have no more time.*
Gott sei Dank ist es nicht mehr so heiß.	***Thank goodness*** *it's not so hot any more.*
Du kannst mich **hoffentlich** verstehen.	***I hope*** *you can understand me.*
Selbstverständlich mag ich Pizza.	***Of course*** *I like pizza.*
Übrigens habe ich kein Geld mehr.	***By the way,*** *I don't have any more money.*

Lab Manual Kap. 4, Var. zu Üb. 29.

Workbook Kap. 4, E.

29 Übung: Selbstverständlich! Answer these questions emphatically. Show that your answer is obvious by beginning it with **Selbstverständlich ...** or **Natürlich ...**

BEISPIEL: Lernen Sie Deutsch?
Selbstverständlich lerne ich Deutsch!

1. Frühstücken Sie bald?
2. Sind Sie hungrig?
3. Haben Sie Zeit für mich?
4. Möchten Sie nach Österreich?
5. Schwimmen Sie gern?
6. Spielen Sie gern Karten?

30 Partnerarbeit: Leider! Take turns asking each other these questions. Show that you regret having to answer yes by beginning your answer with **Ja, leider ...**

BEISPIEL: A: Regnet es noch?
B: Ja, leider regnet es noch.

1. Schneit es noch?
2. Hast du viele Fragen?
3. Bist du sehr müde?
4. Ist der Berg sehr steil?
5. Gehst du ohne mich?
6. Ist das Wasser zu kalt?

6. *Gehen* + infinitive

The verb **gehen** is often used with an infinitive as its complement.

Sie **geht** oft **schwimmen**. — *She often goes swimming.*
Gehen wir noch einmal **schwimmen**! — *Let's go swimming again!*
Ich **gehe** mit Dieter **schwimmen**. — *I'm going swimming with Dieter.*

The complementary infinitive **schwimmen** is the second part of the predicate and comes at the end of the sentence. Note what happens when the entire verbal idea **schwimmen gehen** (*to go swimming*) is used as the complement of a modal verb:

Wir wollen heute **schwimmen gehen**. — *We want to go swimming today.*

Info-Austausch

31 Dann sollst du schlafen gehen! Work with a partner. One partner states a desire or need. The other says what to do about it. Partner B's information is in Appendix 1.

BEISPIEL: A: Ich bin so müde!
B: Dann sollst du doch schlafen gehen. Ich bin so hungrig.
A: Dann sollst du doch ...

Partner A:

Ich bin so müde.	
	essen gehen
Ich bin nicht fit genug.	
	arbeiten gehen

32 Partnerarbeit: Ich möchte heute schwimmen gehen! Tell each other what you would like to go do today, then report to the class what your partner wants to go do.

LESESTÜCK

Tipps zum Lesen und Lernen

Tipps zum Vokabelnlernen

Compass points Note that all four compass points are masculine.

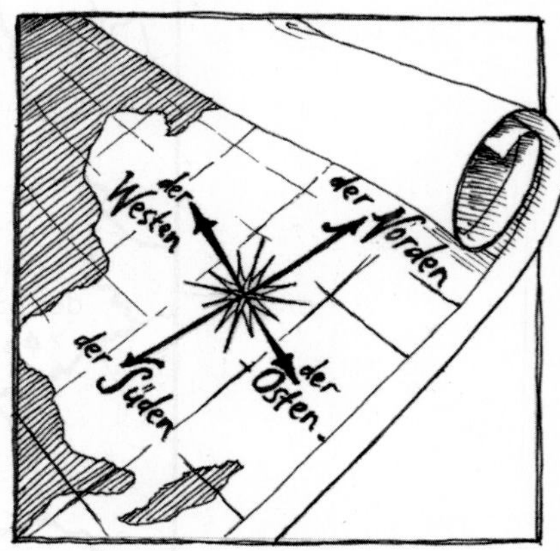

Other masculine nouns Remember that names of the days of the week, seasons, and the months are also masculine.

der Montag (am Montag), der Dienstag (am Dienstag) usw.
der Frühling (im Frühling), der Sommer (im Sommer) usw.
der Januar (im Januar), der Februar (im Februar) usw.

Haupt is derived from Latin *caput* (head).

Haupt This prefix is attached to nouns and adds the meaning *main, chief, primary, principal,* or *most important.*

die **Haupt**regionen	*the principal regions*
die **Haupt**frage	*the main question*
die **Haupt**stadt	*the capital city*
die **Haupt**rolle	*the leading role*
die **Haupt**straße	*the main street*

Lab Manual Kap. 4, Üb. zur Betonung.

Leicht zu merken

die **Alpen**	
barbarisch	
die **Geographie**	Geographie
geographisch	
die **Kolonie, -n**	Kolonie
der **Kontrast, -e**	Kontrast
die **Kultur, -en**	Kultur
mild	
die **Region**	Region
der **Rhein**	
wild	
zirka	

Kolonie: Both this word and the city name Cologne (German **Köln**) are derived from Latin *colonia*. The Roman emperor Claudius named the city *Colonia Agrippinensis* in A.D. 50 after his wife, Agrippina. Its strategic position on the Rhine made it the capital of the Roman colony of *Germania Inferior*.

Remember to pronounce cognates like **mild** and **wild** according to the rules of German pronunciation.

Rivers in German generally take the article **die**. Exceptions are **der Rhein, der Main, der Inn, der Lech, der Neckar**, and foreign rivers (**der Nil, der Mississippi**), except those ending in **-a** or **-e** (**die Themse, die Rhone**).

Einstieg in den Text

The reading in this chapter builds on familiar vocabulary about the weather (**das Wetter**) and discusses climate and geography (**Klima und Geographie**).

Study this map of Germany and try to guess the meanings of the new words.

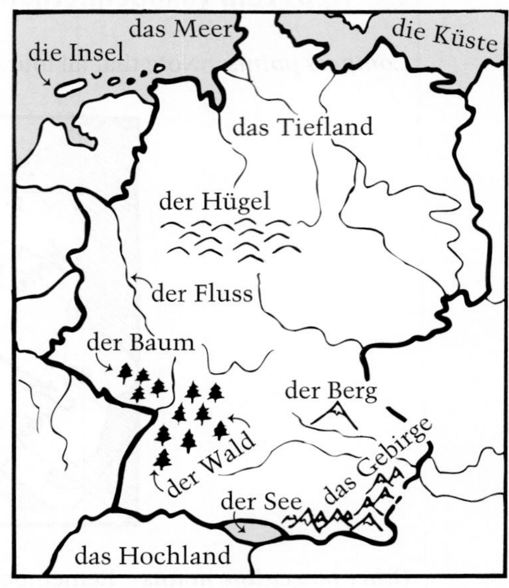

Wortschatz 2

Geographie und Landschaft

der **Baum, ¨-e** tree
der **Fluss, ¨-e** river
der **Hügel, -** hill
der **Wald, ¨-er** forest

The obvious cognates in points of the compass and seasons (**der Herbst** → English *harvest*) recall common Germanic designations for time and space.

der **Norden** the North
der **Osten** the East
der **Süden** the South
der **Westen** the West
im Süden (**im Norden usw.**) in the South (in the North, etc.)
das **Land, ¨-er** land; country
das **Meer, -e** ocean
das **Tal, ¨-er** valley
die **Landschaft, -en** landscape
die **Stadt, ¨-e** city

Verben

beschreiben to describe
fließen to flow
liegen to lie; to be situated
wandern to hike; to wander

Substantive

der **Fuß, ¨-e** foot
der **Schnee** snow
der **Wein, -e** wine
das **Bier, -e** beer
(das) **Italien** Italy
das **Klima** climate
das **Leben** life
das **Lied, -er** song
das **Volkslied, -er** folk song
das **Märchen, -** fairy tale
die **Schweiz** Switzerland

Adjektive und Adverbien

flach flat
hoch high
immer noch / noch immer still (*intensification of* **noch**)
modern modern
nass wet, damp
schrecklich terrible
trocken dry

Andere Vokabeln

von from

Nützlicher Ausdruck

zu Fuß gehen to go on foot

Gegensätze

modern ≠ altmodisch modern ≠ old-fashioned
nass ≠ trocken wet ≠ dry

Deutschland: Geographie und Klima

Für die alten Römer° war° das Leben in der Kolonie Germania nicht sehr schön. Der Historiker° Tacitus (zirka 55 bis 115 n. Chr.°) beschreibt das Land als° kalt und neblig. Über die Germanen° schreibt er: „Sie sind ohne Kultur, haben keine Städte und leben im Wald. Sie sind wild und barbarisch, wie ihr Land."

Das moderne Deutschland liegt in Mitteleuropa und die „wilden Germanen" wohnen heute zum größten Teil° in der Stadt.[1] Es gibt keinen Urwald° mehr, aber der Wald ist immer noch typisch und wichtig für die Landschaft in Deutschland, Österreich und der Schweiz. Am Sonntag wandert man gern zu Fuß durch die Wälder und die Kinder hören auch heute noch gern Märchen wie „Hänsel und Gretel" oder „Schneewittchen".[2] In solchen° Märchen und auch in deutschen Volksliedern spielt der Wald eine große Rolle.

Auch das Klima in Deutschland ist Gott sei Dank nicht so schrecklich, wie° Tacitus meint. Selbstverständlich ist es nicht so warm und sonnig wie in Italien, aber das deutsche Klima ist eigentlich ziemlich mild. In den Flusstälern wird es zum Beispiel im Winter nicht sehr kalt. Die großen Flüsse – der Rhein, die Weser, die Elbe und die Oder – fließen durch das Land von Süden nach Norden. Nur die Donau° fließt von Westen nach Osten. Am Rhein und an der° Donau trinkt man gern Wein; die Römer brachten° den Weinbau° nach Deutschland. Die Deutschen trinken also nicht nur Bier.

Romans / was
historian / **nach Christus** *= A.D. / as / Germanic peoples*
zum ... *for the most part / primeval forest*
such
so ... wie *= as . . . as*
the Danube River
am *and* **an der** *= on the*
brought / viniculture

The word **Wein** is not of Germanic origin but was introduced by the Romans (Latin *vinum*) along with viniculture. The word **Bier** comes from Latin *bibere* (*to drink*). The Germanic word for beer is preserved in English *ale*, which was brewed without hops. The medieval cloister breweries first added hops to the beverage.

Familienwanderung im Regen

[1] **Die Germanen** were the ancient tribes that the Romans called collectively *germani*. The word **Deutsch** comes from Old High German **diot** (*people*). The French applied the name of one tribe, the *alemanni*, to the whole people: *les Allemands*.

[2] *Snow White*. Other fairy tales are **Dornröschen** (*Sleeping Beauty*), **Rotkäppchen** (*Little Red Riding Hood*), **Aschenputtel** (*Cinderella*), and **Der Froschkönig** (*The Frog Prince*).

Weinberge (*vineyards*) und Burgruine (*castle ruin*) Landshut an der Mosel (Bernkastel-Kues)

Learning about the climate and geography of Germany is the cultural goal of this chapter.

Es gibt in Deutschland drei geographische Hauptregionen. Im Norden ist das Land flach und fruchtbar° und ohne viele Bäume. Hier beeinflusst° das Meer – die Nordsee und die Ostsee – Landschaft und Klima. Diese Region nennt man° das Norddeutsche Tiefland°. In der Mitte des Landes° gibt es aber viele Hügel und kleine Berge. Diese Region heißt das Mittelgebirge°. Im Süden liegt das Hochgebirge° – die Alpen. Hier gibt es natürlich viel Schnee im Winter, denn° die Berge sind sehr hoch. Deutschlands höchster° Berg ist die Zugspitze (2 963 m). Man sieht also, in Deutschland gibt es viele Kontraste: Stadt und Land, Wald und Feld°, Berge und Meer.

fertile / influences
***nennt ...** one calls / North German lowlands*
***In ...** In the middle of the country / central mountains / high mountains / because highest / field*

NACH DEM LESEN

Lab Manual Kap. 4, Diktat.

Workbook Kap. 4, F, G, H.

A Antworten Sie auf Deutsch.

1. Wie beschreibt Tacitus die Kolonie Germania?
2. Was ist noch immer typisch für die Landschaft in Deutschland?
3. Was macht man gern am Sonntag?
4. Wie ist das Klima in Deutschland?
5. Ist es so warm und sonnig wie in Italien?
6. Wo trinkt man viel Wein?
7. Wie ist das Land im Norden?
8. Wo gibt es viel Schnee im Winter?
9. Wie heißen die drei geographischen Hauptregionen?

B Partnerarbeit: Märchen. Take turns reading aloud these descriptions of well-known **Märchen**. Then match the descriptions with the silhouettes below. Use context to help you guess unknown vocabulary.

1. Vier Freunde – ein Esel, ein Hund, eine Katze und ein Hahn – sind alt und können nicht mehr arbeiten. Also gehen sie zusammen nach Bremen. Dort wollen sie Straßenmusikanten werden und so ihr Brot verdienen.
2. Eine Frau isst Rapunzeln (*lamb's lettuce, a leafy salad vegetable*) aus dem Garten ihrer Nachbarin. Diese Nachbarin ist aber eine Hexe. Die Hexe nimmt die erstgeborene Tochter der Frau und schließt sie in einen Turm.
3. Ein kleines Mädchen bringt ihrer kranken Großmutter Kuchen und Wein. Sie muss durch einen Wald, aber im Wald wartet ein Wolf. Der Wolf frisst die Großmutter und das Mädchen auf.
4. Eine Familie ist sehr arm und hat nicht genug zu essen. Die Stiefmutter zwingt den Vater, seine Kinder im Wald zu lassen. Bruder und Schwester finden dort ein kleines Haus aus Brot, Kuchen und Zucker. Dort wohnt aber eine böse Hexe und sie will die Kinder essen.

Scherenschnitte (*silhouettes*) von Dora Polster, 1911

C Partnerarbeit: Tacitus modern – Gespräch (*conversation*) mit einem römischen Historiker. Tacitus has returned to modern Germany. Work in pairs. Correct his outdated impressions by completing the following dialogue, then perform it for your classmates.

TACITUS: Ihr Germanen seid alle furchtbar barbarisch.
REAKTION: Das stimmt gar nicht mehr! Wir sind heute ______
TACITUS: Euer Klima ist schrecklich, immer kalt und neblig.
REAKTION: ______.
TACITUS: Ihr lebt ja alle im Wald wie die wilden Tiere (*animals*).
REAKTION: ______.
TACITUS: Ihr trinkt nur Bier und keinen Wein. Das finde ich barbarisch.
REAKTION: ______.

Vokabeln zum Thema Klima, Wetter und Landschaft

Discussing weather, climate, and landscape is a communicative goal.

You already know some of these words from the introductory chapter (see pages 9–11). Review them before doing the activity.

This vocabulary focuses on an everyday topic or situation. Words you already know from the **Wortschatz** sections are listed without English equivalents; new supplementary vocabulary is listed with definitions. Your instructor may assign some supplementary vocabulary for active mastery.

Klima und Wetter

die **Luft** *air*
der **Nebel** *fog, mist*
  neblig
der **Regen** *rain*
  regnerisch *rainy*
  Es regnet.
der **Schnee**
  Es schneit.
die **Sonne**
  sonnig
der **Wind** *wind*
  windig
die **Wolke** *cloud*
  wolkig
kalt ≠ heiß
warm ≠ kühl
nass ≠ trocken
mild

Landschaft

der **Baum, ¨-e**
der **Berg, -e**
  bergig *mountainous*
der **Hügel, -**
  hügelig *hilly*
der **Wald, ¨-er**
das **Meer, -e**
das **Tal, ¨-er**

D Gruppenarbeit: Sprechen wir über Klima und Landschaft. Beschreiben Sie die Landschaft in diesen Fotos.

1.

2.

3.

E Partnerarbeit: Landschaft und Klima, wo ich wohne. Find out where your partner comes from and ask about the climate and geography there.

BEISPIEL: Woher kommst du denn?
Wie ist das Klima dort im Sommer?
Kannst du die Landschaft beschreiben?

F Partnerarbeit: Städte in Deutschland. Work with a partner and the map of Germany on the inside front cover. Fill in the missing information in the grid below by asking your partner questions.

BEISPIEL: A: Wo liegt München?
B: Es liegt im Süden. Wie heißt das Bundesland?
A: Es heißt Bayern.

Stadt	Wo in Deutschland? Im Norden, Süden, Osten, Westen? In der Mitte (*center*)?	Bundesland
Kiel		
Frankfurt am Main		
Dresden		
Köln		
München		
Leipzig		
Stuttgart		
Erfurt		

SCHREIBTIPP

Free writing in German

This is the first time you will write a short essay in German.

- Expect your writing in German to be on a much simpler level than in English.
- Do not first think of what you want to say in English and then try to translate it into German. This never results in good writing.
- Try to formulate your thoughts in German from the outset, using structures and vocabulary you have learned. In the following essay, for instance, you will have to confine yourself to the present tense.
- Begin by reviewing vocabulary you have recently learned and see how you can incorporate it into your essay.

Schreiben wir mal: Fantasiefrage – Tacitus modern. Write in the voice of the Roman historian Tacitus. You have updated your impressions of ancient *Germania* to reflect modern **Deutschland**. Write half a page on the country, telling what people in Germany still (**noch**) do or no longer (**nicht mehr**) do. What plays a role in modern life? How do you like the cities, the wine, etc.? (Do not confuse the ancient **Germanen** with **die Deutschen** of today.)

NOTE ON SPELLING

You can create special characters using Microsoft Word for either Windows or Macintosh using one of these methods.

Method 1

	Windows	**Macintosh**
ä, ö, ü	(CTRL + [shift] + colon) + a, o, *or* u	(OPTION + u) + a, o, *or* u
Ä, Ö, Ü	(CTRL + [shift] + colon) + [shift] + a, o, *or* u	(OPTION + u) + [shift] + a, o, *or* u
ß	(CTRL + [shift] + &) + s	OPTION + s

Method 2

Alternatively, you can use the following number pad combinations on any computer, as long as "NumLock" is on:

ä = ALT + 132
ö = ALT + 148
ü = ALT + 129
Ä = ALT + 142
Ö = ALT + 153
Ü = ALT + 154
ß = ALT + 225
€ (Euro symbol) = ALT + 0128

G Wie sagt man das auf Deutsch?

1. The sun is shining and the water is warm. Let's go swimming.
2. I don't want to go swimming yet. Go without me.
3. But I don't like to swim alone.
4. Do you like the winter, Stefan?
5. No, I don't like it any more.
6. I don't like to walk through the snow.
7. Wait here, Sabrina and Harald.
8. We don't want to wait.
9. I hope that you still have money.
10. Unfortunately, I don't have any more money.
11. Can you do something for me?
12. Of course, but I have to go home at three o'clock.

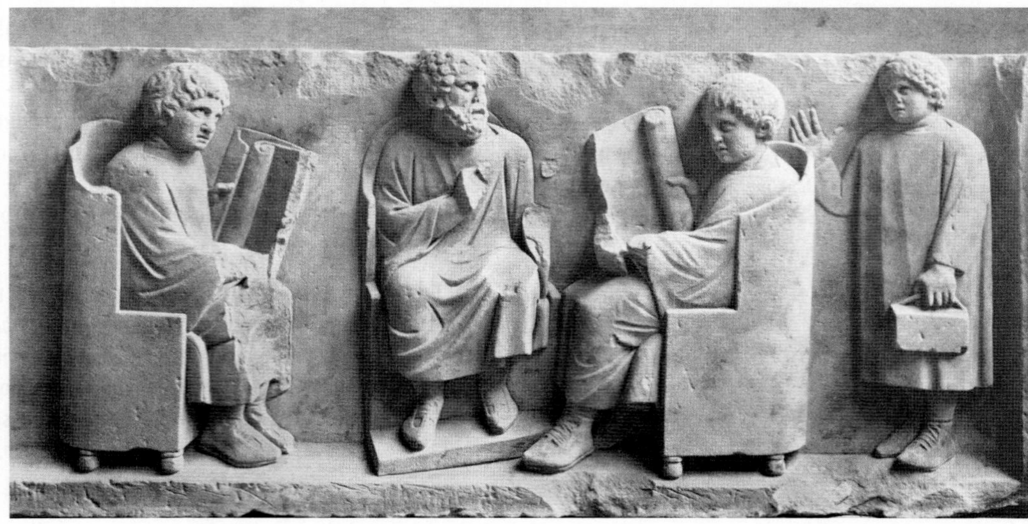

Schulstunde in *Germania* (römisches Relief aus Neumagen an der Mosel)

ALMANACH

The Common Origin of German and English

Although Tacitus thought the Germanic tribes had "always been there," in fact, they originated in the region of southern Scandinavia and the North Sea around the second millennium B.C. As the Roman Empire began to collapse in the fourth century A.D., the Germanic peoples migrated south, a movement that continued for nearly two hundred years. The **Germani** (as they were called by the Romans) displaced the Celts from the heart of the European continent, pushing them as far west as Ireland. The Romans temporarily halted Germanic expansion southward by establishing their own northern frontier, a series of fortifications called the **limes**, literally the "limits" or boundaries of their empire. Remains of the **limes** can be seen in Germany today. Contemporary dialects and regional differences within the German-speaking countries have their origins in the various Germanic tribes of the early Middle Ages.

Thanks to the migration of the Germanic Angles and Saxons to the British Isles in the fifth century A.D. the Germanic language that was to evolve into modern English was introduced there. German and English thus share a common origin. Some other languages included in the Germanic family are Yiddish, Dutch, Flemish, Norwegian, Swedish, Danish, and Icelandic. You will easily recognize cognates (words that have the same etymological root) in English and German, although different meanings may have developed. These words can be readily identified by some regularly occurring consonant shifts. Try guessing the English equivalents for the following words:

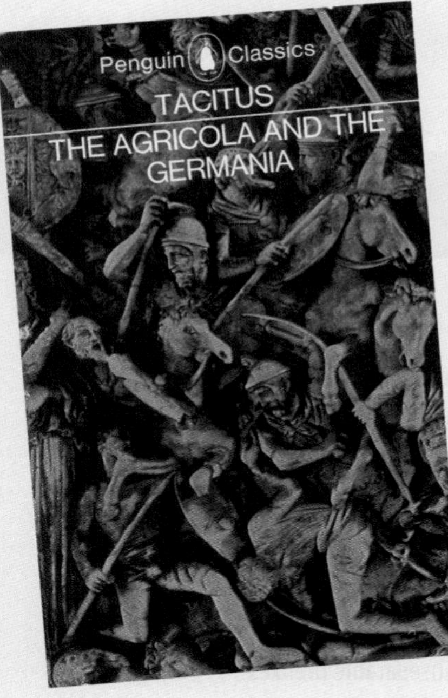

German	English	Related words
z	**t**	zehn = *ten*
		Herz =
ss	**t**	Wasser =
		groß =
pf	**p**	Pflanze =
ff	**p** or **pp**	Schiff =
		Pfeffer und Salz =
ch	**k**	machen =
		Milch =
t	**d**	Tag =
		Tür =
d	**th**	du =
		drei =
		Pfad =

Hochdeutsch (*High German*) is the official, standardized language of the German-speaking countries. It is the language of the media, the law, and education, and is based on written German (**Schriftdeutsch**). Educated native speakers are bi-dialectal, knowing their local dialect and High German, which they may speak with a regional accent.

VIDEO

KAPITEL

In einer Zeitungsredaktion (*newspaper editorial office*), Frankfurt/Main

Arbeit und Freizeit

Kommunikation

- Asking about prices
- Showing, giving, and telling things to people
- Talking about work and professions

Kultur

- How Germans spend their work and leisure time

In diesem Kapitel

- **Lyrik zum Vorlesen**
  Richard Dehmel, "Der Arbeitsmann"
- **Grammatik**
  1. Dative case
  2. Dative personal pronouns
  3. Word order of nouns and pronouns
  4. Prepositions with the dative case
  5. Verbs with separable prefixes
  6. Verbs with inseparable prefixes
- **Lesestück**
  Drei Deutsche bei der Arbeit
- **Almanach**
  Stellenangebote (*Help Wanted Ads*)

DIALOGE

Der neue Bäckerlehrling

Morgens um 6.00. Georg macht die Bäckerei auf.

MARTIN: Morgen. Ich heiße Martin Holst. Ich fange heute bei euch an.
GEORG: Freut mich. Mein Name ist Georg. Den Chef lernst du gleich kennen.
MARTIN: Ist gut. Seit wann arbeitest du denn hier?
GEORG: Erst seit einem Jahr. Komm jetzt mit und ich zeige dir den Laden.

Lab Manual Kap. 5, Dialoge, Fragen, Hören Sie gut zu!, Üb. zur Aussprache **(I)**.

Beim Bäcker

VERKÄUFERIN: Was darf's sein, bitte?
KUNDE: Geben Sie mir bitte sechs Brötchen und ein Bauernbrot.
VERKÄUFERIN: (*Sie gibt ihm das Brot.*) So, bitte sehr. Sonst noch etwas?
KUNDE: Sind diese Brezeln frisch?
VERKÄUFERIN: Ja, von heute Morgen.
KUNDE: Dann geben Sie mir doch sechs Stück. Wie viel kostet das bitte?
VERKÄUFERIN: Das macht zusammen € 3,75, bitte sehr.
KUNDE: Danke. Auf Wiedersehen.
VERKÄUFERIN: Wiedersehen.

€ 3,75 is pronounced **drei Euro fünfundsiebzig**.

Lehrling = *apprentice-in-training*, colloquially called **Azubi** (acronym for the official term, **Auszubildender** = *person to be trained*). The nouns **Lehrling** and **Azubi,** both masculine, apply to both males and females. In the German-speaking countries, there is an extensive system of apprenticeships in jobs not requiring higher education. Whether young people want to go into retail sales or to become skilled craftsmen, those not going on to university divide their week between classes in trade school and apprenticeships in business and industry.

Schule oder Beruf?

VATER: Warum willst du denn jetzt die Schule verlassen? Deine Noten sind ja ganz gut und du hast nur noch ein Jahr.
KURT: Aber das Abitur brauch' ich nicht. Ich will ja Automechaniker werden.
VATER: Sei nicht so dumm! Als Lehrling verdienst du schlecht.
KURT: Aber ich hab' die Nase einfach voll. Ich möchte lieber mit den Händen arbeiten.
VATER: Quatsch! Du schaffst das Abitur und ich schenke dir ein Motorrad. Einverstanden?
KURT: Hmmm.

NOTE ON USAGE

Seit wann?

English uses the perfect tense (*have worked* or *have been working*) for a situation beginning in the past but still continuing. German uses present (**arbeitest**).

Seit wann **arbeitest** du hier?	*How long **have** you **been working** here?* *How long **have** you **worked** here?*

Wortschatz 1

Berufe

der **Automechaniker, -** / die **Automechanikerin, -nen** auto mechanic (*m./f.*)
der **Bäcker, -** / die **Bäckerin, -nen** baker (*m./f.*)
der **Bauer, -n** / die **Bäuerin, -nen** farmer (*m./f.*)
der **Chef, -s** / die **Chefin, -nen** boss (*m./f.*)
der **Lehrling, -e** apprentice (*m./f.*)
der **Verkäufer, -** / die **Verkäuferin, -nen** salesperson (*m./f.*)

Verben

See p. 130 for an explanation of the raised dot in **an·fangen** and in other verbs.

an·fangen (fängt an) to begin, start
an·kommen to arrive
an·rufen to call up
auf·hören (mit etwas) to cease, stop (doing something)
auf·machen to open
auf·stehen to stand up; to get up; get out of bed
kennen lernen to get to know; to meet
kosten to cost
mit·kommen to come along
schenken to give (*as a gift*)
stehen to stand
verlassen (verlässt) (*trans.*) to leave (*a person or place*)
zeigen to show

Substantive

der **Euro, -s** euro (€)
der **Kunde, -n** customer (*m.*)
der **Laden, ¨** shop, store
der **Name, -n** name
das **Abitur** *final secondary school examination*
das **Brot,** bread
das **Bauernbrot** dark bread
das **Motorrad, ¨er** motorcycle
das **Stück, -e** piece
sechs Stück six (*of the same item*)
die **Bäckerei, -en** bakery
die **Brezel, -n** soft pretzel
die **Hand, ¨e** hand
die **Kundin, -nen** customer (*f.*)
die **Nase, -n** nose
die **Note, -n** grade

Adjektive und Adverbien

dumm dumb
einfach simple, easy
erst not until; only
fertig (mit) done, finished (with); ready
frisch fresh
gleich right away, immediately
heute Morgen this morning
voll full

Präpositionen mit Dativ

These eight prepositions are followed by the dative case. See **Grammatik**, section 1.

aus out of; from
außer except for; besides, in addition to
bei at; at the home of
bei euch with you, at your place (*i.e., where you work or live*)
mit with
nach after; to (*a city or country*)
seit since (*temporal*)
von from; of; by
zu to

Andere Vokabeln

als as a
als Lehrling as an apprentice
als Kind as a child
dir (to *or* for) you
euch (to *or* for) you (*pl.*)
wem? to *or* for whom?
wie viel? how much?

Nützliche Ausdrücke

(Es) freut mich. Pleased to meet you.
Ist gut. (*colloq.*) O.K. Fine by me.
Was darf es sein? What'll it be? May I help you?
Bitte sehr. Here it is. There you are.
Sonst noch etwas? Will there be anything else?
Das macht zusammen ... All together that comes to . . .
Ich habe die Nase voll. I'm fed up. I've had it up to here.
Quatsch! Nonsense!
Einverstanden. Agreed. It's a deal. O.K.

Gegensätze

an·fangen ≠ auf·hören to start ≠ to stop
auf·machen ≠ zu·machen to open ≠ to close
dumm ≠ klug dumb ≠ smart, bright
einfach ≠ schwierig simple ≠ difficult
voll ≠ leer full ≠ empty

Mit anderen Worten

das Abi = das Abitur (*Schülerslang*)
blöd = dumm

Variationen

A Persönliche Fragen

1. Um sechs Uhr morgens macht Georg die Bäckerei auf. Was machen Sie um sechs Uhr morgens?
2. Martin lernt den Chef gleich kennen. Wen möchten *Sie* kennen lernen?
3. Sechs Brötchen, sechs Brezeln und ein Bauernbrot kosten € 3,75. Was kosten zwölf Brötchen, zwölf Brezeln und zwei Bauernbrote?
4. Kurt hat nur noch ein Jahr und dann ist er mit der Schule fertig. Wie viele Jahre haben Sie noch an der Universität?
5. Kurt sagt, das Abitur braucht er nicht. Was brauchen *Sie* nicht?
6. Kurt arbeitet gern mit den Händen. Arbeiten Sie auch gern mit den Händen?
7. Der Vater schenkt Kurt ein Motorrad. Was schenkt Ihnen Ihr Vater? Er schenkt mir ________.

Asking about prices is a communicative goal.

B Partnerarbeit: Hoffentlich habe ich genug Geld.

Das neue Semester beginnt bald. Sie müssen viel kaufen, aber Sie haben nur € 150. Was wollen Sie denn kaufen? (Partner A spielt den Verkäufer oder die Verkäuferin, Partner B spielt die Kundin oder den Kunden.)

A: Guten Tag. Was darf's denn sein, bitte?
B: Zeigen Sie mir bitte ________.
A: Bitte sehr.
B: Was kostet denn ________?
A: Das kostet ________.
B: Ich möchte gern ________, ________ und ________ kaufen.
A: Das macht zusammen € ________, bitte sehr.

C Gruppenarbeit: Mit anderen Worten.

The class forms two teams. The instructor says a sentence, and the first team to think of a more colorful or colloquial way to say the same thing gets a point.

BEISPIEL: Heute ist es *sehr, sehr* kalt.
Heute ist es *wahnsinnig* kalt.

1. Der Film ist *sehr langweilig.*
2. Ich schenke meiner *Großmutter* ein Foto von mir.
3. Roberts VW ist *sehr* alt.
4. Die Autos fahren *sehr schnell* durch die Stadt.
5. Heute bin ich *sehr, sehr müde.*
6. Die Berge in Österreich sind *sehr schön.*

LYRIK ZUM VORLESEN

Der Arbeitsmann

Wir haben ein Bett°, wir haben ein Kind,
Mein Weib°!
Wir haben auch Arbeit, und gar zu zweit°,
Und haben die Sonne und Regen und Wind.
Und uns fehlt nur eine Kleinigkeit°,
Um so frei zu° sein, wie die Vögel° sind:
Nur Zeit.

Wenn wir sonntags° durch die Felder° gehn,
Mein Kind,
Und über den Ähren weit und breit°
Das blaue Schwalbenvolk blitzen sehn°,
Oh, dann fehlt uns nicht das bisschen Kleid,
Um so schön zu sein, wie die Vögel sind:
Nur Zeit.

Nur Zeit! wir wittern° Gewitterwind°,
Wir Volk°.
Nur eine kleine Ewigkeit°;
Uns fehlt ja nichts, mein Weib, mein Kind,
Als all das, was durch uns gedeiht°,
Um so kühn° zu sein, wie die Vögel sind.
Nur Zeit!

Richard Dehmel (1863–1920)

bed
mein Weib = meine Frau
***und ...** and even together*
***uns ...** we lack only a small thing* / ***um ... zu** in order to* / *birds*
on Sundays / *fields*
***über ...** above the grain far and wide* / ***Das ...** see flocks of blue swallows flashing*
smell / *stormwind*
common folk
eternity
***Als ...** Except for all that prospers through us* / *daring*

GRAMMATIK

Dative comes from **datus**, a form of the Latin verb **dare** (*to give*). The etymology highlights an important function of dative case: to designate the receiver of something given.

1. Dative case (*der Dativ*)

The dative case is the case of the indirect object in German.

DEFINITION

What is an indirect object?
An ***indirect object*** is the person or thing *for* whom an action is performed or *to* whom it is directed.

Sie gibt **ihm** das Brot. { *She gives him the bread.* / *She gives the bread to him.* }

Note that English has two different ways to designate the indirect object, depending on its placement in the sentence: *gives **him** the bread,* or *gives the bread **to him**.*

Die Arbeit in der Bäckerei fängt früh an.

1 Übung. Identify the direct object and the indirect object in the following English sentences.

1. We owe him a debt of gratitude.
2. I bought my father a necktie.
3. Tell me what you think.
4. We're cooking spaghetti for the kids.
5. Peel me a grape.
6. To whom did you say that?

The indirect object in German (*das indirekte Objekt*)

Here are some verbs you already know that can take a dative and an accusative object in the same sentence: **sagen (Sag mir etwas); geben (Ich gebe dir 2 Euro); kochen; tragen; schreiben; singen; kaufen; verkaufen; beschreiben; schenken; zeigen.**

The forms of the dative case are different from the two cases you already know, nominative and accusative. For example:

dir, Ihnen	*to you, for you*
der Lehrerin	*to the (female) teacher, for the teacher*
seinem Sohn	*to his son, for his son*

Note that German does *not* use a preposition to show the indirect object. It is signalled by the dative case alone.

Showing, giving, and telling things to people are communicative goals.

Ich kaufe **dir** einen Laptop.	*I'll buy **you** a laptop.* *I'll buy a laptop **for you**.*
Sag **der Lehrerin** guten Morgen.	*Tell **the teacher** good morning.* *Say good morning **to the teacher**.*
Er gibt **seinem Sohn** das Geld.	*He's giving **his son** the money.* *He's giving the money **to his son**.*

The German case system allows great flexibility in word order. The following sentences all say basically the same thing, with some minor shifts in emphasis.

Sie gibt **ihrer Tochter das Geld**.
Sie gibt **das Geld ihrer Tochter**.
Das Geld gibt sie **ihrer Tochter**.
Ihrer Tochter gibt sie **das Geld**.

In order to find your way through such sentences, you need to learn the forms of the dative case—essentially three new endings for articles and possessive adjectives.

Dative endings

The chart below shows the three dative endings (**-em** for both masculine and neuter, **-er** for feminine, and **-en** for plural). The nominative and accusative articles are included for comparison.

Note that **-em** is the dative ending for both masculine and neuter nouns.

Dative case				
	masculine	**neuter**	**feminine**	**plural**
nominative **accusative**	der Vater den Vater	das Kind	die Frau	die Leute
dative	-em	-em	-er	-en -n
	dem Vater	**dem** Kind	**der** Frau	**den** Leute**n**
	dies**em** Vater	dies**em** Kind	dies**er** Frau	dies**en** Leute**n**
	ein**em** Vater	ein**em** Kind	ein**er** Frau	kein**en** Leute**n**
	unser**em** Vater	dein**em** Kind	sein**er** Frau	mein**en** Leute**n**

Note: *All nouns* in the dative plural add an **-n** to the noun itself (**den** Leute**n**, **den** Hände**n**), except those nouns already ending in **-n** (**den** Frauen) and those ending in **-s** (**den** Hotel**s**).

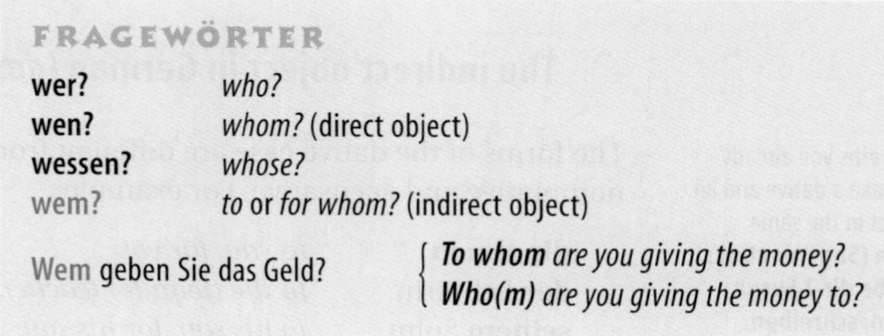
FRAGEWÖRTER

wer? *who?*
wen? *whom?* (direct object)
wessen? *whose?*
wem? *to or for whom?* (indirect object)

Wem geben Sie das Geld? *To* **whom** *are you giving the money?* / **Who(m)** *are you giving the money to?*

Lab Manual Kap. 5, Var. zu Üb. 2

To review family vocabulary, see pp. 46, 62.

2 Übung: Wem soll sie es geben?

A. Silke kann ihr Brötchen nicht essen. Wem soll sie es geben?

BEISPIEL: die Lehrerin
Sie soll es der Lehrerin geben.

Feminine nouns

1. ihre Freundin
2. ihre Schwester
3. die Professorin
4. die Chefin

B. Hasan hat ein neues Auto. Wem will er es zeigen?

BEISPIEL: das Kind
Er will es dem Kind zeigen.

Neuter and masculine nouns

1. sein Freund
2. der Lehrer
3. sein Vater
4. der Automechaniker

C. Pawel geht einkaufen (*shopping*). Wem soll er etwas kaufen?

BEISPIEL: die Kinder
Er soll den Kindern etwas kaufen.

Nouns in the plural

1. diese Leute
2. die Studenten
3. seine Freunde
4. seine Eltern

Das gebe ich dir, aber was gibst du mir?

3 Kettenreaktion: Wem schenkst du den Pulli? Sie kaufen einen schönen Pulli für jemand in Ihrer Familie. Wem schenken Sie ihn?

BEISPIEL: A: Wem schenkst *du* den Pulli?
B: Meiner Schwester. Wem schenkst *du* den Pulli?
C: Mein-________. Wem ... ?

4 Übung: Wie sagt man das auf Deutsch? Benutzen Sie (*Use*) den **du**-Imperativ.

BEISPIEL: Buy the child a book.
Kauf dem Kind ein Buch.

1. Buy your sister a book.
2. Give my parents the money.
3. Describe the problem to the mechanic.
4. Write your mother a card.
5. Cook the food for your friends.
6. Show my friend the city.

2. Dative personal pronouns

This table of dative personal pronouns includes the nominative and accusative forms for comparison.

English has only one pronoun form for both direct and indirect objects: *I know **him/her**. I'm giving **him/her** a car.* Ich kenne **ihn/sie**. Ich schenke **ihm/ihr** ein Auto. Only **uns** and **euch** are identical in the accusative and dative.

Singular				Plural			
nom.	***acc.***	***dat.***		***nom.***	***acc.***	***dat.***	
ich	mich	**mir**	*to/for me*	wir	uns	**uns**	*to/for us*
du	dich	**dir**	*to/for you*	ihr	euch	**euch**	*to/for you*
er	ihn	**ihm**	*to/for him*	sie	sie	**ihnen**	*to/for them*
es	es	**ihm**	*to/for it*	Sie	Sie	**Ihnen**	*to/for you*
sie	sie	**ihr**	*to/for her*				

Note the similarities between the third-person dative pronouns and the dative endings of articles.

ihm → **dem** Mann
ihr → **der** Frau
ihnen → **den** Freunden

Lab Manual Kap. 5, Var. zu Üb. 5.

Workbook Kap. 5, A, B, C.

5 Übung: Kaufen wir Brot. Sie wollen Brot kaufen. Ihre Professorin möchte wissen, **wem** Sie es kaufen.

BEISPIEL: Wem kaufen Sie das Brot? (*points to another student*)
Ich kaufe es *ihm*/*ihr*.

6 Gruppenarbeit: Was zeigst du mir? (*4–5 Personen*) Use a verb from the list below to ask other students what they are going to do for you. Other students use a noun from the list to answer. After asking each person in the group, a new questioner starts over with a different verb.

BEISPIEL: A: Was kaufst du mir, Joanne?
B: Ich kaufe dir einen Fernseher.
A: Vielen Dank! Was ________ du mir, Steve?

Verbs	**Nouns**		
beschreiben	Artikel	Fotos	Reise nach Berlin
geben	Auto	Frühstück	Stadt
kaufen	Brezel	Geld	Suppe
kochen	Brot	Hemd	Tasche
schenken	Brötchen	Mantel	Uhr
verkaufen	Buch	Motorrad	Zeitung
zeigen	Fernseher		

3. Word order of nouns and pronouns

MERIAN zeigt Ihnen die Welt.

Verbs like **geben**, **schenken**, **sagen**, and **zeigen** often have two objects. The indirect object in the dative usually comes first, followed by the direct object in the accusative.

Ich zeige **meiner Freundin den Laden.** — *I'm showing my girlfriend the shop.*

However, if one of the objects is a pronoun, it comes first, as in English.

Ich zeige **ihr den Laden**. — *I'm showing her the shop.*
Ich zeige **ihn meiner Freundin**. — *I'm showing it to my girlfriend.*

If both objects are pronouns, the accusative comes first—again, as in English.

Ich zeige **ihn ihr**. — *I'm showing it to her.*

Personal pronouns that are not in the first position come *immediately after the verb.*

Ich gebe **ihm** mein Buch. — *I'll give **him** my book.*
Ich gebe **es** meinem Bruder. — *I'll give **it** to my brother.*
Kann **uns** dein Opa anrufen? — *Can your grandpa phone **us**?*

Note the 3rd example: the direct-object pronoun **uns** even precedes the noun subject (**dein Opa**).

Personal pronouns following the verb come in the order *nominative, accusative, dative*. Again, this is just like English word order: *subject pronoun, direct-object pronoun, indirect-object pronoun.*

Ich gebe **es Ihnen** heute. — *I'll give **it to you** today.*
Heute gebe **ich es Ihnen**. — *Today **I'll** give **it to you**.*

Lab Manual Kap. 5, Var. zu Üb. 7.

Workbook Kap. 5, D.

7 Übung: Wem schenken Sie das Buch? You've bought copies of your favorite novel as presents. Your instructor will ask to whom you're giving them. Answer the questions affirmatively, using pronouns.

BEISPIEL: Wem schenken Sie das Buch? Schenken Sie es Ihrer Mutter?
Ja, ich schenke es ihr.

Wem schenken Sie das Buch? Schenken Sie es ...

1. Ihrem Vater?
2. den Kindern?
3. Ihrem Freund?
4. Ihrer Cousine?
5. mir?
6. uns?

Remember that **nicht** follows all personal pronouns (see p. 76): **Ich gebe *sie dir* nicht.**

As with the list of accusative prepositions (p. 96), learn this list until you can repeat it in your sleep. Mnemonic: you can sing this list to the tune of the *Blue Danube Waltz*.

For more on **seit**, see *Note on Usage*, p. 119.

8 Partnerarbeit: Gibst du mir etwas? Take turns asking each other for things. Respond as in the example.

BEISPIEL: A: Gibst du mir deine Uhr?
B: Ja, ich gebe sie dir. / Nein, ich gebe sie dir nicht.

4. Prepositions with the dative case (*Präpositionen mit Dativ*)

The dative case is also used for the object of the following prepositions.

aus	*out of* *from* (native country, city, or region)	Sie sieht **aus dem Fenster.** Ich komme **aus Toronto.**	*She's looking out of the window.* *I'm from Toronto.*
außer	*except for* *besides, in addition to*	**Außer ihm** sind wir alle hier. **Außer ihm** wohnt auch sein Bruder hier.	*We're all here except for him.* *Besides him, his brother lives here too.*
bei	*in the home of* *at*	Ich wohne **bei meiner Tante.** Er ist **bei der Arbeit.**	*I live at my aunt's.* *He's at work.*
mit	*with*	Ich arbeite **mit den Händen.**	*I work with my hands.*
nach	*after* *to* (with country and city names)	**Nach der Arbeit** bin ich manchmal müde. Wir fahren **nach England.**	*After work I'm sometimes tired.* *We're going to England.*
seit	*since* (referring to time)	**Seit dem Tag** mag ich ihn nicht mehr.	*Since that day I haven't liked him.*
von	*from* *of* *by*	Das Buch habe ich **von meiner Mutter.** Er ist ein Freund **von mir.** Das ist ein Buch **von Hermann Hesse.**	*I got that book from my mother.* *He's a friend of mine.* *That's a book by Hermann Hesse.*
zu	*to* (people and some locations)	Ich gehe **zur Schule** und dann **zu meinen Freunden.**	*I'm going to school and then to my friends' house.*

Contractions

The following contractions are standard.

bei dem	→	**beim**	Brezeln kaufe ich immer **beim** Bäcker.
von dem	→	**vom**	Ich komme gerade **vom** Chef.
zu dem	→	**zum**	Ich muss schnell **zum** Professor.
zu der	→	**zur**	Ich gehe jetzt **zur** Schule.

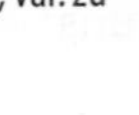

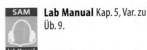

SAM **Lab Manual** Kap. 5, Var. zu Üb. 9.

SAM **Workbook** Kap. 5, E.

9 Übung: Bei wem wohnen Sie? Sie sind alle Studenten in Tübingen. Sie wohnen aber nicht im Studentenwohnheim (*dormitory*). Sagen Sie Ihrem Professor oder Ihrer Professorin, bei wem Sie wohnen.

BEISPIEL: Bei wem wohnen Sie?
Bei meinem Freund.

Tante	Freundin	Bruder	Großeltern
Familie	Vater	Freund	Frau König

Er arbeitet in Frankfurt,
sein Geld arbeitet international.
Bei seiner Bank.

10 Kettenreaktion: Zu wem gehst *du*? Say whom you are going to see, then ask another student.

BEISPIEL: Zu wem gehen Sie?
A: Ich gehe zu meiner Familie. Zu wem gehst *du*?
B: Ich gehe zum Bäcker. Zu wem ... ?

Automechaniker	Bäckerin	Freund
Professorin	Automechanikerin	Chefin
Professor	Eltern	Familie
Chef	Freundin	Bäcker

11 Übung: Mit wem gehen Sie schwimmen? Sie gehen mit Freunden aus der Deutschstunde schwimmen. Sagen Sie, mit wem Sie schwimmen gehen.

BEISPIEL: PROFESSOR/IN: Mit wem gehen Sie schwimmen?
STUDENT/IN: (*points to one or more other students in the class*) Mit ihr/ihm/ihnen/Ihnen.

12 Übung. Fill in the blanks with the correct dative ending or dative personal pronoun.

1. Ich wohne seit ein-________ Monat bei mein-________ Tante in Tübingen.
2. Mit ________ (*her*) gehe ich fast jeden Tag einkaufen.
3. Sie bekommt oft Briefe von ihr-________ Freunden und ihr-________ Bruder.
4. Sie schreibt ________ (*them*) oft Postkarten mit Fotos von d-________ Stadt.
5. Nach d-________ Seminar gehe ich mit mein-________ Freunden Fußball spielen.

5. Verbs with separable prefixes

The meanings of many English verbs are changed or modified by the addition of another word.

to find → *to find out*
to look → *to look up*
to burn → *to burn down*
to hang → *to hang around*

Likewise, the meanings of many German verbs are modified—or even changed completely—by the addition of a prefix.

stehen	*to stand*	→	**auf**stehen	*to stand up; get out of bed*
kommen	*to come*	→	**mit**kommen	*to come along*
hören	*to hear*	→	**auf**hören	*to cease, stop*
fangen	*to catch*	→	**an**fangen	*to begin*

Similarly:

ankommen	*to arrive*
anrufen	*to call up*
aufmachen	*to open*
kennen lernen	*to get to know, meet*
zurückkommen	*to come back*

Note that although **kennen lernen** is written as two words, the first element, **kennen** functions like a separable prefix.

In these verbs, the primary stress falls on the prefix (**an**kommen, **auf**hören).

In the present tense and the imperative, the prefix is *separated* from the verb and placed at the end of the sentence or clause.

Ich **stehe** morgen sehr früh **auf**.	*I'm getting up very early tomorrow.*
Wann **stehst** du **auf**?	*When are you getting up?*
Stehen Sie bitte **auf**!	*Please get up!*
Steht ihr denn bald **auf**?	*Are you getting up soon?*

Note that the prefix is *not* separated in the infinitive form of the verb, as when the separable-prefix verb is the complement of a modal verb.

Without a modal	**With a modal**
Er **fängt** morgen **an**.	Er soll morgen **anfangen**.
Sie **kommt** bald **zurück**.	Sie möchte bald **zurückkommen**.

NOTE: Separable prefixes are indicated in the **Wortschatz** sections by a raised dot between prefix and root verb: **an·fangen**. This symbol is used throughout the textbook whenever new separable-prefix verbs are introduced. Note that the dot is *not* part of the word and should not be written in normal usage.

"The Germans have an inhuman way of cutting up their verbs. Now a verb has a hard enough time of it in this world when it's all together. It's downright inhuman to split it up. But that's just what those Germans do. They take part of a verb and put it down here, like a stake, and they take the other part of it and put it away over yonder like another stake, and between these two limits they just shovel in German."

Mark Twain

from: *The Disappearance of Literature* (1900)

SAM **Lab Manual** Kap. 5, Var. zu Üb. 13, 14.

SAM **Workbook** Kap. 5, F, G.

13 Übung. Ihre Professorin sagt, Sie sollen etwas machen. Antworten Sie, Sie können es nicht machen.

BEISPIEL: Fangen Sie doch heute an.
Ich kann heute nicht anfangen.

1. Hören Sie doch auf.
2. Kommen Sie doch mit.
3. Machen Sie das Fenster auf.
4. Rufen Sie doch Ihre Mutter an.
5. Stehen Sie bitte auf.
6. Kommen Sie bitte heute zurück.

14 Übung. Ihr Professor sagt, Sie müssen etwas machen. Sie antworten, Sie sind einverstanden.

BEISPIEL: Sie müssen um sieben aufstehen.
Einverstanden, ich stehe um sieben auf.

1. Sie müssen jetzt anfangen.
2. Sie müssen früh aufstehen.
3. Sie müssen um acht aufmachen.
4. Sie müssen Helena anrufen.
5. Sie müssen aufhören.
6. Sie müssen gleich mitkommen.

15 Partnerarbeit: Mach das bitte für mich.

A. Aufmachen. Partner A asks partner B to open (**aufmachen**) various things, and B agrees.

BEISPIEL: A: Mach doch ________ auf.
B: Gut, ich mache ________ auf.

Buch	Tür
Fenster	Rucksack
Laden	Zeitung
Tasche	

B. Anrufen. Partner B tells A to call up (**anrufen**) various relatives and friends. Partner A doesn't want to.

BEISPIEL: B: Ruf doch dein-________ an.
A: Aber ich will mein-________ nicht anrufen.

Onkel	Tante	Freundin	Lehrer
Bruder	Schwester	Großeltern	Professorin
Mutter	Vater	Geschwister	

C. Um 7 Uhr. Partner A wants to know when B is going to do various things. Partner B answers with the time.

BEISPIEL: A: Wann kommst du denn zurück?
B: Ich komme um 7 zurück.

ankommen	mit deiner Arbeit aufhören
zurückkommen	morgen aufstehen
anfangen (fängst ... an)	den Chef kennen lernen

16 Schreiben wir mal: Der Arbeitstag. Gerd hat einen neuen Job. Er schreibt seinen Eltern und beschreibt ihnen einen typischen Arbeitstag. *(Use the cues to reconstruct his letter.)*

Liebe Mutti, lieber Vati!

aufstehen / morgens / 7.00
Arbeit / anfangen / 8.30
ich / arbeiten / mit / mein Freund Kurt / zusammen
Laden / zumachen / 6.00
nach / Arbeit / ich / gehen / Bier / trinken
nach / Essen / anrufen / meine Freundin
abends / ich / sein / todmüde

Euer Gerd

6. Verbs with inseparable prefixes

There are also German verbs with *inseparable* prefixes. These prefixes *never* separate from the root verb. You can tell them from separable prefixes in these ways:

- They are *never* stressed: **be<u>deu</u>ten, ver<u>die</u>nen**.
- The prefixes have no independent meaning. (Separable prefixes usually resemble other parts of speech, such as prepositions [**mit**kommen] or adverbs [**zurück**kommen]).

The inseparable prefixes are: **be-**, **emp-**, **ent-**, **er-**, **ge-**, **ver-**, and **zer-**. Here are the verbs with inseparable prefixes that you have already learned:

bedeuten	**besitzen**	**verdienen**
beginnen	**besprechen**	**verlassen**
bekommen	**besuchen**	**verstehen**
beschreiben	**entscheiden**	

17 Übung. Say these verb pairs aloud to practice the difference between stressed separable prefixes and unstressed inseparable prefixes. Then complete the following sentences with the appropriate verb.

Inseparable	**Separable**
verstehen	**auf**stehen
beschreiben	**auf**schreiben (*to write down*)
gehören (*to belong to*)	**auf**hören
bekommen	**mit**kommen
erfahren (*to find out*)	**ab**fahren (*to depart*)

1. Ich ________ dich nicht. (*understand*)
   Ich ________ um 7 Uhr ________. (*get up*)
2. ________ Sie es bitte! (*describe*)
   ________ Sie es bitte ________! (*write down*)
3. Harald ________ heute einen Laptop. (*is getting*)
   Bernd ________ heute ________. (*is coming along*)
4. Das Motorrad ________ dem Chef. (*belongs to*)
   ________ endlich mit deiner Arbeit ________! (*stop*)

LESESTÜCK

Tipps zum Lesen und Lernen

Remember that singular masculine nouns ending in **-er** have the same form in the plural: **der Arbeiter, die Arbeiter**. Feminine forms ending **-erin**, however, do have a plural ending: **die Arbeiterin, die Arbeiterinnen**.

Tipps zum Vokabelnlernen

Agent nouns denote a person who performs an action (agent). In both English and German, such nouns are formed by adding the suffix **-er** to a verb stem. In German, the additional ending **-in** indicates that the agent is female.

arbeiten →	**der Arbeiter / die Arbeiterin**	*to work*	→	*worker*
lesen →	**der Leser / die Leserin**	*to read*	→	*reader*

Sometimes an umlaut is added in the agent noun.

anfangen →	**Anfänger**	*to begin*	→	*beginner*
tragen →	**Briefträger**	*to carry*	→	*letter carrier*
backen →	**Bäcker**	*to bake*	→	*baker*
handeln →	**Buchhändler**	*to trade, deal*	→	*bookseller*

Mit Menschen zu tun haben

Handwerklich arbeiten

Im Labor arbeiten

Am Schreibtisch arbeiten

A Übung. Was machen diese Leute?

1. Die Frauen arbeiten in der Fabrik. Sie sind ________.

2. Die Studenten wandern gern am Sonntag. Sie sind ________.

3. Die Kinder spielen Klavier. Sie sind ________.

4. Robert und Luise lesen Zeitung und trinken Kaffee. Sie sind ________ und ________.

Adverbs of time German adds an **-s** to the names of the days or parts of the day to form adverbs showing regular or habitual occurrence.

morgens	*in the mornings, every morning*
nachmittags	*in the afternoons, every afternoon*
abends	*in the evenings, every evening*
nachts	*at night, every night*
montags	*Mondays, every Monday*
dienstags	*Tuesdays, every Tuesday*
usw.	*etc.*

NOTE: Because these words are *adverbs,* not nouns, they are not capitalized.

B Partnerarbeit: Was machst du morgens? Use the adverbs on page 136 to ask each other what you do at different times and on different days. Write down your answers and report to the class.

BEISPIEL: A: Was machst du denn samstags?
B: Samstags kann ich bis 9 Uhr schlafen, dann ________.

Briefträgerin in Bielefeld (Nordrhein-Westfalen)

Lab Manual Kap. 5, Üb. zur Betonung.

 Leicht zu merken

die **Boutique, -n**	
das **Café, -s**	
der **Computer, -**	
campen	(pronounced **kämpen**)
der **Journalist, -en**	Journalist
(das) **Kanada**	
der **Korrespondent, -en**	Korrespondent
das **Marketing**	
der **Partner, -**	
perfekt	perfekt
realistisch	
der **Supermarkt**	
die **USA** *(pl.)*	

Einstieg in den Text

The title *Drei Deutsche bei der Arbeit* lets you know that the reading will focus on three individuals and their work. What sorts of things would you expect to learn about people's personal and professional lives from such a reading? You can apply to this text the familiar question words that you have been using to ask about each other's lives.

Before reading the whole text, skim the third portrait and see if you can quickly find answers to the following questions:

Wie heißt dieser Mann?
Wie alt ist er?
Was macht er?
Wo wohnt er?
Wer sind die anderen *(other)* Menschen in seiner Familie?

Let these questions guide your reading for information as you work through the entire text.

Wortschatz 2

In-Text Audio CD

Berufe

der **Arbeiter, -** / die **Arbeiterin, -nen** worker; industrial worker (*m./f.*)
der **Buchhändler, -** / die **Buchhändlerin, -nen** bookseller (*m./f.*)
der **Graphiker, -** / die **Graphikerin, -nen** graphic artist (*m./f.*)
der **Kollege, -n** / die **Kollegin, -nen** colleague, co-worker (*m./f.*)

Verben

ab·holen to pick up, fetch, get
aus·sehen (sieht aus) to appear, look (happy, tired, fit, etc.)
  Du siehst schrecklich aus. You look terrible.
berichten to report
ein·kaufen to shop for; to go shopping
fern·sehen (sieht fern) to watch TV
reisen to travel
schließen to close

schließen: *synonym* = **zumachen**

sitzen to sit
spazieren gehen to go for a walk
sterben (stirbt) to die
vergessen (vergisst) to forget
verlieren to lose
vorbei·kommen to come by, drop by

Substantive

der **Fußball** soccer
der **Reiseführer, -** (travel) guidebook
der **Roman, -e** novel
der **Stadtplan, ¨-e** city map
der **Stress** stress
das **Bild, -er** picture; image
das **Dorf, ¨-er** village
das **Geschäft, -e** business; store
das **Mittagessen** midday meal, lunch
das **Schaufenster, -** store window
das **Wochenende, -n** weekend
  am Wochenende on the weekend
das **Wort** word (*2 plural forms*:
  die Worte = words in a context;
  die Wörter = words in a list, as in a dictionary)
das **Wörterbuch, ¨-er** dictionary
die **Altstadt, ¨-e** old city center
die **Buchhandlung, -en** bookstore
die **Firma, Firmen** company, firm
die **Freizeit** free time
die **Muttersprache, -n** native language
die **Postkarte, -n** postcard
die **Türkei** Turkey
die **Wanderung, -en** hike
die **Zeitschrift, -en** magazine
die **Lebensmittel** (*pl.*) groceries

Die Türkei, like **die Schweiz**, is always used with the definite article: **Er kommt aus der Türkei.**

Adjektive und Adverbien

abends (in the) evenings
aktuell current, topical
besonders especially
fleißig industrious, hard-working
meistens mostly, usually
türkisch Turkish
witzig witty, amusing
zufrieden pleased, satisfied

Andere Vokabeln

ein paar a couple (of), a few

Gegensätze

fleißig ≠ faul hard-working ≠ lazy

Mit anderen Worten

stressig (*colloq.*) = **mit viel Stress**

BUCHHANDL
Bei uns dürfen Sie Ihre Internet-Bestellung sogar selbst abholen.
Libri.de

Drei Deutsche bei der Arbeit

Man sagt über die Deutschen, sie leben für ihre Arbeit. Stimmt das heute noch? Unsere Beispiele zeigen ein anderes° Bild.

different

Christine Sauermann, Buchhändlerin

Christine Sauermann ist 35 Jahre alt, geschieden°, und hat einen jungen Sohn Oliver (10 Jahre alt). Sie ist seit sieben Jahren berufstätig und besitzt seit fünf Jahren eine Buchhandlung in der Altstadt von Tübingen.[1] Zwei Angestellte° arbeiten für sie im Laden.

divorced
employees

Das Geschäft geht gut, denn° viele Touristen gehen durch die Altstadt spazieren und Studenten kommen auch jeden Tag vorbei. Mit den neuesten° Romanen sieht ihr Schaufenster immer bunt aus. Den Studenten verkauft sie Wörterbücher und Nachschlagewerke°, aber die Touristen kaufen meistens Reiseführer, Stadtpläne und Postkarten von der Stadt.

because
newest
reference works

Morgens macht sie um 9 Uhr auf und abends um 6 Uhr zu. Von 1 Uhr bis 3 Uhr macht sie Mittagspause°. Sie schließt den Laden, holt Oliver von der Schule ab und geht mit ihm nach Hause. Dort kocht sie das Mittagessen und kauft später dann noch Lebensmittel im Supermarkt ein.[2]

midday break

Außer sonntags arbeitet Christine Sauermann jeden Tag sehr fleißig in ihrem Laden. In ihrer Freizeit möchte sie also Erholung° vom Stress. Darum macht sie gern Wanderungen mit ihrem Sohn zusammen. Diesen Sommer zum Beispiel gehen sie zusammen in Schottland° campen.

relaxation
Scotland

Hasan Turunç (42 Jahre alt), Computergraphiker

Hasan Turunç lebt seit 1971 in Dortmund.[3] Mit 10 Jahren kam° er mit seiner Familie aus Anatolien[4] nach Deutschland. Seit 1980 arbeitet er als Computergraphiker in einer großen Marketing-Firma. Mit seinem Beruf ist er sehr zufrieden und die Arbeit ist gut bezahlt°. Seine Frau Zehra arbeitet halbtags° als Verkäuferin in einer Boutique, solange° die Kinder noch klein sind. Nach der Arbeit spielt Hasan gern Fußball mit seinen Söhnen oder sieht mit der Familie fern. Am Wochenende sitzt er oft ein paar Stunden mit Freunden im Café zusammen.

came
***gut** ... well paid / half days*
while

Hasan ist noch türkischer Staatsbürger°, aber er wird so gut bezahlt wie° seine deutschen Kollegen. Im Büro arbeiten sie gut zusammen, denn er ist witzig und spricht fast perfekt Deutsch. Seine Kinder sind natürlich völlig zweisprachig°.

*citizen / **wird** ... is as well paid as*
***völlig** ... completely bilingual*

Die Tochter Saliha ist 2000 geboren und hat die doppelte Staatsbürgerschaft[5]. Aber mit 23 Jahren muss sie entscheiden: Will sie deutsche oder türkische Staatsbürgerin sein?

Learning about how Germans spend their work and leisure time is the cultural goal of this chapter.

---

[1] Most German cities and towns have an **Altstadt** in their centers, which may date from the Middle Ages. These are often pedestrian zones. **Tübingen** is a university town on the Neckar River about twenty miles south of Stuttgart. The university was founded in 1477.

[2] Many small shops and businesses close from 1:00 to 2:30 or 3:00 PM, but this practice is less common nowadays in large cities. The noon meal is traditionally the main meal of the day.

[3] **Dortmund:** An industrial city in North Rhine-Westphalia. See map on the inside front cover.

[4] **Anatolien:** Anatolia, the eastern part of Turkey.

[5] **doppelte Staatsbürgerschaft** = *dual citizenship.* Children born in Germany to foreign residents after January 1, 2000, are eligible for German citizenship if at least one parent has lived in Germany legally for at least eight years. By the age of 23, they must choose which citizenship they want to hold.

Wie die meisten° Deutschen hat Hasan fünf Wochen Urlaub im Jahr. In den Schulferien° fliegt die Familie fast immer in die Türkei. Dort besucht er seine Mutter und seine Geschwister in Anatolien. Seine Kinder spielen gern mit ihren türkischen Cousinen und verlieren so den Kontakt mit der türkischen Kultur nicht.

most
school vacations

Klaus Ostendorff (53 Jahre alt), Journalist

Klaus Ostendorff ist Korrespondent bei der Deutschen Presseagentur° in Nordamerika. Seit fünfzehn Jahren berichtet er über die USA und Kanada für Zeitungen und Zeitschriften in Deutschland. Seine Artikel geben den Lesern ein realistisches Bild von beiden° Ländern.

Im Moment schreibt Ostendorff einen Artikel über das Waldsterben° in Nordamerika. Dieses Problem ist in Deutschland besonders aktuell: Auch in Europa bedroht° der saure° Regen die Wälder.

Ostendorff lebt mit seiner Frau Martina und ihren drei Kindern in Washington. Die Kinder sollen ihre Muttersprache nicht vergessen und darum spricht die Familie zu Hause meistens Deutsch. Die Kinder besuchen das deutsche Gymnasium in Washington und reisen im Sommer nach Deutschland. Dort macht die ganze° Familie Urlaub in einem Dorf in den Bayerischen° Alpen.

wire service
both
death of the forests
threatens / acid
whole
Bavarian

Note the **ihr**-imperative on this sticker.

NACH DEM LESEN

Lab Manual Kap. 5, Diktat.

Workbook Kap. 5, H, I.

A Antworten Sie auf Deutsch.

1. Wo arbeitet Christine Sauermann?
2. Wie lange ist sie schon berufstätig?
3. Wer sind ihre Kunden und was kaufen sie bei ihr?
4. Wie sieht ein typischer Tag für Frau Sauermann aus?
5. Was macht sie gern in ihrer Freizeit?
6. Seit wann lebt Hasan Turunç in Deutschland?
7. Was macht er gern mit seiner Familie?
8. Über was schreibt Klaus Ostendorff im Moment?
9. Wie ist seine Familie anders als die Familie von Christine Sauermann?
10. Warum sprechen Ostendorff und seine Frau zu Hause meistens Deutsch?

B Vokabelspiel: Nein, das stimmt nicht! (*mit offenen Büchern*) Take turns contradicting each other.

BEISPIEL: Dieses Auto ist *neu!*
Nein, das stimmt nicht. Dieses Auto ist *alt!*

1. Wir holen die Kinder *früh* ab.
2. Hamburg liegt in *Süddeutschland.*
3. Jetzt *fangen* wir *an.*
4. Der Lehrling *schließt* den Laden.
5. Der Chef möchte *etwas* sagen.
6. Wir essen *viel.*
7. Ich glaube, *jemand* wohnt da drüben.
8. Meine Nase ist *hässlich.*
9. Diese Jacke ist *altmodisch.*
10. Diese Übung ist *schwer.*

Info-Austausch

C Wer macht was? Work with a partner to assign an occupation and a job description to each person in the chart. Partner A assigns an occupation to the first person from the information given below. Using the information in Appendix 1, Partner B chooses the appropriate job description for that person. Partner B then chooses an occupation for the next person, and Partner A gives the appropriate job description.

BEISPIEL: A: Jörg Krolow ist Fabrikarbeiter. Was macht er?
B: Er arbeitet in einer Fabrik. Klaus Ostendorff ist Journalist. Was macht er?
A: Er ...

Name	Was ist er/sie von Beruf?	Was macht er/sie?
Jörg Krolow		
Klaus Ostendorff		
Marina Spira		
Pawel Kempowski		
Christine Sauermann		
Vanessa Johnson		
Hasan Turunç		
Antje Hakenkamp		
Melanie von Schmolke		

Partner A:

Berufe
Lehrer / Lehrerin
Graphiker / Graphikerin
Fabrikarbeiter / Fabrikarbeiterin
Hausfrau / Hausmann
Bäcker / Bäckerin

Berufsbeschreibungen
verkauft Bücher, Zeitungen und Zeitschriften
bedient (*waits on*) die Kunden in einem Laden
schreibt Artikel für Zeitungen und Zeitschriften
lehrt und forscht (*does research*) an einer Universität

D **Die Deutsche Schule Washington.** Klaus Ostendorffs Kinder besuchen die Deutsche Schule Washington. Hier sehen Sie die Fächer (*subjects*) für Klasse 11. Suchen Sie Antworten auf diese Fragen.

All students must choose a **Wahlpflichtfach** (*required elective*) from group 1 and at least one from group 2. Additional electives may be chosen from group 2, but not exceeding 42 hours per week.

1. Welche (*which*) Fremdsprachen müssen die Schüler in Klasse 11 lernen?
2. Welches Fach lernt man auf Englisch?
3. Wie viele Stunden pro Woche haben die Schüler Sport? Deutsch? Englisch? Informatik?
4. Wie viele Stunden hat man maximal in Klasse 11?

Pflichtfächer = *required courses*
Wochenstunden = *hours per week*

2. Fremdsprache = *second foreign language*

Sozialkunde = *social studies*

Naturwissenschaft = *natural science*

Vortragsreihe = *lecture series*

Kunst = *art*

Informatik = *computer science*

Pflichtfächer	Wochenstunden	Summe
Deutsch	4	
Englisch	5	
2. Fremdsprache (Französisch oder Latein)	3	
Sozialkunde	3	
US-History	3	
Mathematik	4	
1. Naturwissenschaft	2	
2. Naturwissenschaft	2	
Sport	2	
Vortragsreihe	1	
		29
Wahlpflichtfächer 1		
Kunst oder Musik	2	
		31
Wahlpflichtfächer 2		
3. Naturwissenschaft	2	
Informatik	2	
Spanisch	4	
Latein	3	
	Mindestzahl für alle Schüler:	***33***
	Maximale Stundenzahl in Klasse 11:	***42***

This vocabulary focuses on an everyday topic or situation. Words you already know from **Wortschatz** sections are listed without English equivalents; new supplementary vocabulary is listed with definitions. Your instructor may assign some supplementary vocabulary for active mastery.

Vokabeln zum Thema Beruf

Was sind Sie von Beruf? *What is your profession?*

Here are the professions you've already learned:

der **Automechaniker,** -	die **Automechanikerin, -nen**
der **Bäcker,** -	die **Bäckerin, -nen**
der **Bauer, -n**	die **Bäuerin, -nen**
der **Buchhändler,** -	die **Buchhändlerin, -nen**
der **Graphiker,** -	die **Graphikerin, -nen**
der **Hausmann, ¨er**	die **Hausfrau, -en**
der **Journalist, -en**	die **Journalistin, -nen**
der **Lehrer,** -	die **Lehrerin, -nen**
der **Professor, -en**	die **Professorin, -nen**
der **Verkäufer,** -	die **Verkäuferin, -nen**

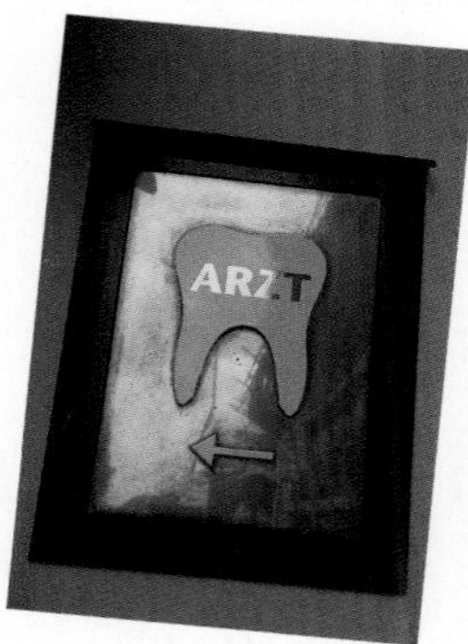

This sign is a visual pun, or rebus; **Zahn** = *tooth*. **Wie sagt man *dentist* auf Deutsch?**

Here are some other professions you can use in the following exercises.

der **Arzt, ¨e**	die **Ärztin, -nen**	*physician*
der **Elektrotechniker,** -	die **Elektrotechnikerin, -nen**	*electrical engineer*
der **Geschäftsmann,** *pl.* **Geschäftsleute**	die **Geschäftsfrau, -en**	*businessman/ businesswoman*
der **Ingenieur, -e**	die **Ingenieurin, -nen**	*engineer*
der **Kellner,** -	die **Kellnerin, -nen**	*waiter/waitress*
der **Krankenpfleger,** -	die **Krankenschwester, -n**	*nurse*
der **Künstler,** -	die **Künstlerin, -nen**	*artist*
der **Landwirt, -e**	die **Landwirtin, -nen**	*farmer*
der **Politiker,** -	die **Politikerin, -nen**	*politician*
der **Rechtsanwalt, ¨e**	die **Rechtsanwältin, -nen**	*lawyer*
der **Schriftsteller,** -	die **Schriftstellerin, -nen**	*writer*

Wer arbeitet hier? Lesen Sie die Schilder (*signs*).

E Was wissen Sie über diese Berufe?

1. Wer muss für seinen Beruf an der Universität studieren?
2. Wer macht eine Lehre (*apprenticeship*)?
3. Wer verdient gut? Wer verdient relativ schlecht?
4. Wer hat viel Freizeit? Wer hat nicht viel Freizeit?
5. Wer hat flexible Arbeitszeiten?
6. Wer arbeitet oft nachts / morgens / abends?
7. Wer arbeitet draußen?
8. Wer braucht vielleicht einen Computer bei der Arbeit?
9. Wer arbeitet meistens allein, wer mit anderen Menschen zusammen?

NOTE ON USAGE

Stating profession or nationality

German does not use an indefinite article before the noun.

Ich will Automechaniker werden.	*I want to become **an** auto mechanic.*
Frau Gerhard ist Amerikanerin.	*Ms. Gerhard is **an** American.*

Talking about work and professions is a communicative goal.

F Gruppendiskussion: Was willst du werden, und warum? (*4 Personen*)

First tell each other what you want to do after your studies. Then ask questions about each other's career plans.

BEISPIEL:
A: Was willst du werden?
B: Ich möchte Lehrer werden.
C: Verdienen Lehrer genug Geld?
D: Sind deine Eltern Lehrer?
A: Wo möchtest du denn arbeiten? usw.

G Partnerarbeit mit dem Almanach: Suchen wir eine Stelle.

Sie und Ihr Partner suchen Stellen. Im Almanach (S. 144) sind einige Stellenangebote (*job offers, help wanted ads*) aus deutschen Zeitungen. Besprechen Sie sie zusammen. Was möchten Sie gern machen? Was möchten Sie lieber nicht machen?

SCHREIBTIPP

Writing a dialogue

When writing a dialogue in German, be sure to use the second-person forms appropriate to the situation. Would you use **du** or **Sie** in talking with a friend or fellow student? Would you use **du** or **Sie** with a potential employer?

Schreiben wir mal: Ein Dialog. You are giving a fellow student career advice. Write both sides of the dialogue. Find out the following:

- something about her family
- what her parents do for a living
- what she likes to do in her free time
- what she's studying
- whether she likes to work alone or with people
- whether she prefers to work at night or during the day
- how much she would like to earn
- where she would like to live

At the end of the dialogue, say what profession you think she should choose.

H Wie sagt man das auf Deutsch?

1. When are you getting up tomorrow?
2. At six. I have to leave the house early.
3. Why? What are you doing?
4. I'm driving with my girlfriend to Munich.
5. Have a good trip!

6. What are you doing on the weekend?
7. I don't know yet. Why do you ask?
8. Can you come by? A student from Germany is visiting me.
9. Gladly. I'd like to meet him.
10. I want to show him the city tomorrow.
11. Good. I'll come by at ten.
12. Please don't forget that.

sowas = **so etwas** (= *that kind of thing*)

With this chapter you have completed the first third of ***Neue Horizonte.*** For a concise review of the grammar and idiomatic phrases in chapters 1–5, you may consult the **Zusammenfassung und Wiederholung 1** (*Summary and Review 1*) in the Workbook section of your SAM. The review section is followed by a self-correcting test.

ALMANACH

Stellenangebote *(Help Wanted Ads)*

These help-wanted ads from German newspapers range from unskilled labor (**Babysitter/in**) to jobs in highly specialized fields (**Radiologie/Kardiologie**). Note the English business and computer jargon in the technical fields.

VIDEO

Verfügen Sie über gute Englischkenntnisse?
Haben Sie Spaß am Umgang mit 4-10jährigen Kindern ?
Dann werden Sie **in Ihrer Stadt** selbständige/r oder freiberufliche/r

Englischdozent/in
für Kinder und/oder Senioren
(haupt- oder nebenberuflich)

Wir sind Deutschlands führende Sprachschule für Englisch für Kinder und Senioren mit bundesweit mehr als 230 Vertretungen. Wir bieten intensive Schulungen, überdurchschnittliche Verdienstmöglichkeiten und hervorragende Arbeitsbedingungen

Our World® ENGLISCH FÜR JUNG UND ALT

Für erste Informationen sprechen Sie bitte mit
Diana Stäbler - 07161-986757
www.our-world-sprachen.de

Koch/Köchin
– motorisiert –

Wir suchen Sie für unsere Betriebsküche von Montag bis Freitag. Sie sind zwischen 30-55 Jahre jung, verfügen über die notwendigen Erfahrungen, haben Freude an der Arbeit mit einem motivierten Team und suchen die Möglichk...

Studienplätze frei !

Polizeikommissarin oder **Polizeikommiss...**
... eine Chance auch für Nichtdeutsche

Hessische Polizeischule - Z 1 -
Schönbergstraße 100 65199 Wiesbaden
☎ 0611-9460-163 🖷 0611-9460-166
www.polizeischule-hessen.de

Suche
freundliche Verkäuferin
stundenweise, Teil- oder Vollzeit
(mögl. aus der näheren Umgebung)
Metzgerei Thomas Riehl
Rügnerstr.27, 64319 Pfungstadt
Tel. 06157 / 2708

BABYSITTER/IN gesucht,
die ab und zu unsere drei Kinder nachmittags für einige Stunden in DA-Mitte betreut, (14,- DM pro Stunde).

Wir su. liebevolle und zuverlässige
Kinderfrau

Sekretär/in mit guten Englischkenntnissen gesucht.
Wir freuen uns auf Ihren Anruf!

Übungsleiter/in
oder Interessierte gesucht für
Eltern-Kind-Turnen
(mittwochs 15-17 Uhr)
beim **SKV Rot-Weiss Darmstadt**

Wer baut uns eine Webseite u. brin... uns ins Internet? ☎ 06151/976916...

Medizinbranche:
Radiologie / Kardiologie
Digitale Bildsysteme
Internationale Kunden - Englisch -
Abwechslungsreich und spannend
Sicherer Arbeitsplatz

VEPRO COMPETENCE IN IMAGING www.vepro.com

PC-Netzwerk Spezialist
Installation - Training - Support

VEPRO - ein dynamisches Unternehmen mit 20-jähriger Erfahrung in Entwicklung, Vertrieb und Support von digitalen Bildmanagementlösungen in einem schnell wachsenden Markt. Wir installieren, schulen und betreuen - auch international - Kliniken. radiologische und kardiologische Praxen.
Und dafür **benötigen wir Sie - den Profi** - der mit Erfahrung, analytischem Denkvermögen und Umgangsgeschick, sowohl kleinere als auch größere Installationen mit Umsicht durchführt. Unsere Anlagen werden im Hause vorgefertigt und haben ihren Qualitätscheck bereits überstanden. Sie nehmen die Anlagen vor Ort in Betrieb, schulen den Kunden und übernehmen die Betreuung von unserer Firmenzentrale in Pfungstadt via Telefon oder Remote-Support. Dabei können Sie wählen, ob Sie lediglich national oder auch international eingesetzt werden möchten. Wenn Sie vorgenannte Voraussetzungen erfüllen, sind wir gerne bereit Ihnen alles weitere beizubringen.
Interessiert ? Dann senden Sie bitte Ihre aussagefähigen Bewerbungsunterlagen an:

VEPRO GmbH • An der Tuchbleiche 26 • D - 64319 Pfungstadt • Fax: 06157 800666 • mail@vepro.com

KAPITEL

6

An der Freien Universität, Berlin

An der Universität

Kommunikation

- Talking about events in the past
- Writing an extended e-mail in German

Kultur

- German student life and the university system

In diesem Kapitel

- **Lyrik zum Vorlesen**
  Johann Wolfgang von Goethe, "Wanderers Nachtlied"
- **Grammatik**
  1. Simple past tense of **sein**
  2. Perfect tense
  3. Two-way prepositions
  4. Masculine N-nouns
- **Lesestück**
  Eine E-Mail aus Freiburg
- **Almanach**
  Universities in the German-Speaking Countries

DIALOGE

Karin sucht ein Zimmer

STEFAN: Hast du endlich ein Zimmer gefunden?
KARIN: Nee, ich suche noch. Leider habe ich keinen Platz im Studentenwohnheim bekommen.
STEFAN: Du! Gestern ist bei uns in der WG die Helga ausgezogen. Also, jetzt ist ein Zimmer frei und wir suchen einen Mitbewohner. Willst du zu uns?
KARIN: Super! Meinst du, das ist möglich?
STEFAN: Selbstverständlich, kein Problem!

Lab Manual Kap. 6, Dialoge, Fragen, Hören Sie gut zu!, Üb. zur Aussprache (**b**, **d**, **g**/**p**, **t**, **k**).

Dormitory space is scarce in Germany. Students frequently live together in apartments called **Wohngemeinschaften** (abbreviated **WG**).

Hard copies of course catalogues must be purchased from local bookstores, but catalogues are also available online.

Am Semesteranfang

CLARA: Wo warst du denn so lange?
EVA: In der Bibliothek und später in der Buchhandlung.
CLARA: Hast du mir ein Vorlesungsverzeichnis mitgebracht?
EVA: Ja, ich hab's auf den Schreibtisch gelegt.
CLARA: Ach ja, da liegt es unter der Zeitung. Wie viel hat's denn gekostet?
EVA: Drei Euro, aber ich schenk's dir.
CLARA: Das ist echt nett von dir! Vielen Dank!
EVA: Nichts zu danken.

Students in Europe calculate time spent at the university in semesters rather than years.

Konstanz is a city on Lake Constance (**der Bodensee**) with a university founded in 1966.

An der Uni in Tübingen

PETRA: Hast du den Peter schon kennen gelernt?
KLAUS: Ist das der Austauschstudent aus Kanada?
PETRA: Ja. Er kann fantastisch Deutsch, nicht?
KLAUS: Ich glaube, er hat schon zwei Semester in Konstanz studiert.
PETRA: Ach, darum!

NOTE ON USAGE

Definite article with names

In informal colloquial speech, Germans often use the definite article with proper names. The dialogues contain two examples of this.

Gestern ist bei uns in der WG **die** Helga ausgezogen.	*Yesterday Helga moved out of our apartment.*
Hast du **den** Peter schon kennen gelernt?	*Have you met Peter yet?*

Wortschatz 1

An der Universität

der **Austauschstudent, -en, -en**[1] exchange student (*m.*)
der **Mitbewohner, -** roommate (*m.*)
das **Studentenwohnheim, -e** student dormitory
das **Vorlesungsverzeichnis, -se** university course catalogue
die **Austauschstudentin, -nen** exchange student (*f.*)
die **Bibliothek, -en** library
die **Mitbewohnerin, -nen** roommate (*f.*)
die **Universität, -en** university
  an der Universität at the university
die **Vorlesung, -en** university lecture

Verben

aus·ziehen, ist ausgezogen[2] to move out
bringen, hat gebracht[2] to bring
legen to lay, put down
mit·bringen, hat mitgebracht to bring along, take along
ziehen, hat gezogen[2] to pull

Substantive

der **Anfang, -̈e** beginning
  am Anfang in the beginning, at the beginning
der **Mensch, -en, -en**[1] person, human being
der **Platz, -̈e** place; space; city square
der **Schreibtisch, -e** desk
das **Bett, -en** bed
(das) **Kanada** Canada
die **Wohngemeinschaft, -en** communal living group

Adjektive und Adverbien

gestern yesterday
möglich possible
nett nice
so lange for such a long time
wirklich real; really

Präpositionen mit Dativ oder Akkusativ

an to, toward; at, alongside of
auf onto; on, upon, on top of
hinter behind
in into, to; in
neben beside, next to
über over, across; above
unter under; beneath
vor in front of
zwischen between

Gegensätze

am Anfang ≠ am Ende at the beginning ≠ at the end
ausziehen ≠ einziehen to move out ≠ to move in
möglich ≠ unmöglich possible ≠ impossible

Mit anderen Worten

die **Uni, -s** (*colloq.*) = **Universität**
die **WG, -s** (*colloq.*) = **Wohngemeinschaft**
nee (*colloq.*) = **nein**

[1] For an explanation of the second ending, see **Grammatik**, p. 163.
[2] For an explanation of the forms **ist ausgezogen**, **hat gebracht**, and **hat gezogen**, see **Grammatik**, pp. 151–158.

Variationen

A Persönliche Fragen

1. Wo wohnen Sie: im Studentenwohnheim, bei einer Familie, in einer WG oder zu Hause bei Ihren Eltern?
2. Stefan wohnt in einer WG. Kennen Sie Studenten in WGs? Was ist dort anders als im Studentenwohnheim?
3. Eva kauft ein Vorlesungsverzeichnis. Was müssen Sie am Semesteranfang kaufen?
4. Eva schenkt Clara das Vorlesungsverzeichnis. Was schenken Sie Ihrem Mitbewohner oder Ihrer Mitbewohnerin?
5. An der Uni in Tübingen gibt es viele Austauschstudenten. Gibt es auch an Ihrer Uni Austauschstudenten? Woher kommen sie?

B Übung: Das möchte ich auch. Your instructor tells you something he has done. Say you would like to do that too.

BEISPIEL: Ich habe in Berlin gewohnt.
Ich möchte auch in Berlin wohnen.

1. Ich habe einen Sportwagen gekauft.
2. Ich habe um acht Uhr gefrühstückt.
3. Ich habe Karten gespielt.
4. Ich habe Russisch gelernt.
5. Ich habe eine Reise gemacht.

C Übung: Was meinen Sie? Antworten Sie mit dem Gegensatz.

BEISPIEL: Finden Sie den Film *gut*?
Nein, ich finde ihn *schlecht*.

1. Soll man *spät* aufstehen?
2. Ist dieses Klassenzimmer zu *groß*?
3. Sind Fremdsprachen *unwichtig*?
4. Ist Deutsch *schwer*?
5. Soll man *immer* in Eile sein?
6. Spricht der Professor zu *langsam*?
7. Soll man *allein* arbeiten?
8. Sind die Studenten hier meistens *faul*?

Use a search engine to find the homepage of the Universität Freiburg. Find the **Vorlesungsverzeichnis** and see if you can find a German course that corresponds to one you're taking now.

Vokabeln zum Thema Studentenzimmer

Singular is **das Möbelstück.**

Die Möbel *(pl.) furniture*

Dieses Zimmer ist **möbliert** (*furnished*).

1. der Boden, ¨
2. der Teppich, -e
3. die Lampe, -n
4. der Wecker, -
5. die CD, -s
6. das Bett, -en
7. das Poster, -
8. der Spiegel, -
9. das Bücherregal, -e
10. das Radio, -s
11. der CD-Spieler, -
12. die Decke, -n
13. der Kleiderschrank, ¨e
14. der Computer, -
15. der Schlüssel, -
16. das Handy, -s

D Gruppenarbeit: Beschreiben wir dieses Zimmer. Wie finden Sie dieses Zimmer? Ist es typisch für die Studentenzimmer bei Ihnen? Kann man hier gut wohnen? Wie sieht *Ihr* Zimmer aus? Was gibt es zum Beispiel *nicht* bei Ihnen?

Lyrik zum Vorlesen

Many composers have set this text to music. One of the most famous settings is Franz Schubert's Opus 96, No. 3 (D 768).

This brief poem from 1780 is perhaps the most famous in the German language. Goethe first wrote it on the wall of a forest hut where he was spending the night. The simplicity of its three main images (mountains, trees, and birds) and the evocative language of stillness make this a profound statement of the relationship between man and nature.

Wanderers Nachtlied

Über allen Gipfeln°	*mountain peaks*
Ist Ruh°,	*peace*
In allen Wipfeln°	*tree tops*
Spürest° du	*feel*
kaum° einen Hauch°;	*hardly / breath*
Die Vögelein° schweigen° im Walde.	*little birds / are silent*
Warte nur, balde°	***balde = bald***
Ruhest° du auch.	*rest*

Johann Wolfgang von Goethe (1749–1832)

Grammatik

Talking about events in the past is a communicative goal.

1. Simple past tense of *sein* (*das Imperfekt, das Präteritum*)

You have been using the present tense to talk about events in the present and future:

Lena **ist** nicht zu Hause.	*Lena is not at home.*
Ich **bin** morgen in Berlin.	*I'll be in Berlin tomorrow.*

German also has a one-word form called the *simple past tense* to talk about events in the past:

Lena **war** nicht zu Hause.	*Lena was not at home.*
Ich **war** gestern in Berlin.	*I was in Berlin yesterday.*

Because the simple past of the verb **sein** is used so frequently, you should learn its forms now. (You will learn how to form the simple past tense of other verbs in **Kapitel 10**.)

sein *to be*					
ich	**war**	*I was*	wir	**waren**	*we were*
du	**warst**	*you were*	ihr	**wart**	*you were*
er, es, sie	**war**	*he, it, she was*	sie, Sie	**waren**	*they, you were*

Lab Manual Kap. 6, Var. zu Üb. 1.

Workbook Kap. 6, A.

1 Übung: Wo waren sie? Tell each other where people were last summer. Turn to the map at the back of the book and report on their vacation travels.

BEISPIEL: Wo war Eva?
Sie war in Belgien.

1. Wo war Clara?
2. Wo war Franz?
3. Wo warst du?
4. Wo waren die Studenten?
5. Wo war ich?
6. Wo wart ihr?
7. Wo waren wir?
8. Wo waren Sie?

2. Perfect tense (*das Perfekt*)

With most verbs, spoken German uses the *perfect tense* to talk about events in the past. The perfect tense is a compound tense consisting of an *auxiliary* ("helping") *verb* (**haben** or **sein**) and a form of the main verb called the *past participle*.

DEFINITION

What is a compound tense?

A ***compound tense*** is made up of two words: Er **hat** die Zeitung **gelesen**. The examples below show that while spoken German uses the perfect tense for events in the past, English uses the simple past (one-word form) for the same purpose.

Sie **sind** gestern nach Berlin **geflogen**.	*They **flew** to Berlin yesterday.*
Ich **habe** die Zeitung um sieben **gelesen**.	***I read** the newspaper at seven.*

Sie sind geflogen is the equivalent of four English past-tense forms:

Sie sind geflogen. {
They flew.
They have flown.
They were flying.
They did fly.

In the perfect tense in German, the auxiliary verb is conjugated to agree with the subject of the sentence. The past participle is a fixed form that never changes. It is placed at the end of the clause or sentence.

Ich **habe** endlich ein Zimmer **gefunden**.	*I have finally found a room.*
Gestern **ist** die Helga **ausgezogen**.	*Yesterday Helga moved out.*

Conjugation with *haben*

Most German verbs use **haben** as their auxiliary verb. Here is a sample conjugation:

aux. *part.*	
Ich **habe** das Buch **gekauft**.	*I bought the book.* (OR: *I have bought the book.*)
Du **hast** es **gekauft**.	*You bought it.*
Sie **hat** es **gekauft**.	*She bought it.*
Wir **haben** es **gekauft**.	*We bought it.*
Ihr **habt** es **gekauft**.	*You bought it.*
Sie **haben** es **gekauft**.	*They bought it.*

Past participles of weak verbs (*schwache Verben*)

REMINDER: Drop **-en** or **-n** from the infinitive to get the verb stem. Stems ending in **-d** or **-t** add **-et**: **arbeit-** (stem), **ge**arbeit**et** (past participle).

There are two basic classes of verbs in German: the *weak* verbs and the *strong* verbs. They are distinguished by the way they form their past participles.

The weak verbs form their past participle by adding the unstressed prefix **ge-** and the ending **-t** or **-et** to the verb stem. Here are some examples of weak verbs you have already learned.

Infinitive	Stem	Auxiliary + past participle
arbeiten	arbeit-	hat **gearbeitet**
haben	hab-	hat **gehabt**
kaufen	kauf-	hat **gekauft**
kosten	kost-	hat **gekostet**
legen	leg-	hat **gelegt**
meinen	mein-	hat **gemeint**

SAM **Lab Manual** Kap. 6, Var. zu Üb. 2, 5, 9, 10, 12, 13, 14.

SAM **Workbook** Kap. 6, B–F.

2 Übung: Warum warst du gestern nicht da? Petra gave a birthday party yesterday. Use the cues to say why you didn't come.

BEISPIEL: keine Zeit
Ich habe keine Zeit gehabt.

1. keine Freizeit
2. kein Auto
3. kein Geschenk (*present*)
4. kein Geld
5. keine Lust

3 Übung: Was haben Sie gekauft und was hat das gekostet? You went on a shopping spree yesterday. Your instructor will ask you which of the things listed below you bought and what they cost.

1. einen Laptop (€ 949)
2. eine Digital-Kamera (€ 379)
3. ein Vorlesungsverzeichnis (€ 3)
4. eine Espressomaschine (€ 85)

BEISPIEL: A: Was haben Sie gestern gekauft?
B: Ich habe ein-_______ gekauft.
A: Was hat das denn gekostet?
B: Das hat _______ Euro gekostet.

4,1 Mega-Pixel
Schnapp den Rabatt Sie sparen 220.-
JENOPTIK Digitalkamera
JD 4100 z3 4,1 Mega-Pixel
• hochwertige Digitalkamera mit 3-fach optischem Zoom + 2-fach digital Zoom,
• Objektiv 8–24 mm (vergleichbar Kleinbild 38–114 mm),
• Serienbildfunktion, LCD-Farbmonitor auf der Gehäuse-Rückseite,
• inkl. 16 MB Compact Flash Karte, Tasche und umfangreichem Zubehör
ehem. Preisempfehlung des Herstellers
€599.-
jetzt € 379.-
NUR SOLANGE GLOBUS VORRAT REICHT!
2 JAHRE GLOBUS-GARANTIE

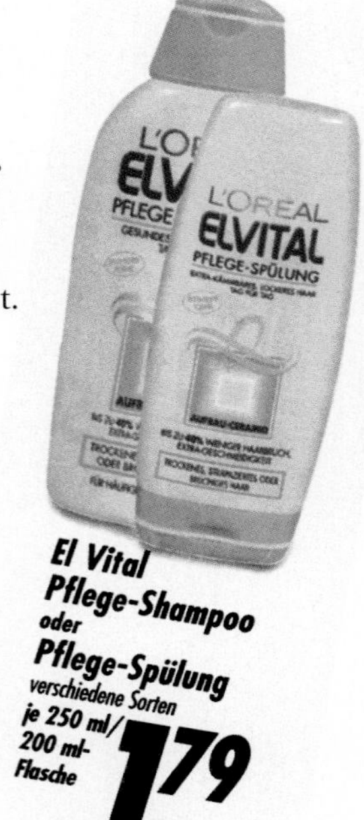

L'OREAL ELVITAL
PFLEGE-SPÜLUNG
El Vital Pflege-Shampoo oder Pflege-Spülung
verschiedene Sorten
je 250 ml/ 200 ml-Flasche
€ 1.79
100 ml ab € 0.72

Past participles of verbs ending in *-ieren*

Verbs ending in **-ieren** are *always* weak verbs. They do *not* add the prefix **ge-** to the past participle, but only add a **-t** to the stem.

studieren → studier- → hat **studiert**

Er hat in Freiburg **studiert**.
He studied in Freiburg.

4 Partnerarbeit: Austauschstudenten. Tell your partner where the exchange students come from and where they studied.

BEISPIEL: A: Nicole kommt aus Frankreich und sie hat in Leipzig studiert.
B: Yukiko . . . .

Name	**Heimat (*homeland*)**	**Universitätsstadt**
Nicole	Frankreich	Leipzig
Yukiko	Japan	Tübingen
Pedro	Spanien	Zürich
Cathleen	Irland	Wien
Matthew	Kanada	Berlin
Pawel	Polen	Frankfurt an der Oder

Past participles of strong verbs (*starke Verben*)

Beginning in **Wortschatz 1** of this chapter, the past participle (and present-stem vowel change, when applicable) of each new strong verb is given following the infinitive.

Strong verbs form their past participle by adding the prefix **ge-** and the suffix **-n** or **-en** to the verb stem. Many strong verb participles also have changes in their stem vowels. Some verbs change consonants in the stem as well. For this reason, *the past participle of each strong verb must be memorized.* Here are some examples:

Strong verbs in English also form their past tense by changing their root vowels and sometimes adding *-n: give, gave, has given; see, saw, has seen; stand, stood, has stood; drink, drank, has drunk; sit, sat, has sat.*

Infinitive	**Auxiliary + past participle**
geben	hat **gegeben**
sehen	hat **gesehen**
stehen	hat **gestanden**
trinken	hat **getrunken**
sitzen	hat **gesessen**

5 Übung: Was haben Sie gesehen? Was haben Sie gestern gesehen? Sagen Sie es der Gruppe.

BEISPIEL: Sagen Sie uns, was Sie gestern gesehen haben.
Ich habe ________, ________ und ________ gesehen.

NATIONALE FORSCHUNGS-
UND GEDENKSTÄTTEN DER KLASSISCHEN
DEUTSCHEN LITERATUR IN WEIMAR

GOETHEHAUS
GOETHEMUSEUM

209198

EINTRITTSKARTE 5,00

6 Kettenreaktion: Was hast du getrunken? You and your friends were thirsty yesterday. Say what you drank and then ask the next person.

BEISPIEL: A: Gestern habe ich ________ getrunken.
Was hast du getrunken?
B: Ich habe ________ getrunken.

Conjugation with *sein*

Some verbs use **sein** rather than **haben** as the auxiliary in the perfect tense.

Gestern **ist** die Helga ausgezogen. *Helga moved out yesterday.*

To use **sein** as an auxiliary, a verb must fulfill two conditions:

1. It must be *intransitive* (that is, it *cannot* take a direct object), and
2. It must indicate *change of location or condition.*

Here are some examples of verbs with **sein** as their auxiliary.

For the forms **ausgezogen** and **aufgestanden**, see p. 156.

Infinitive	Auxiliary + past participle	
ausziehen	**ist ausgezogen**	*change of location*
fliegen	**ist geflogen**	
gehen	**ist gegangen**	
wandern	**ist gewandert**	
reisen	**ist gereist**	
aufstehen	**ist aufgestanden**	*change of condition*
sterben	**ist gestorben**	
werden	**ist geworden**	

As you can see, verbs with **sein** may be either weak (ist **gereist**) or strong (ist **geflogen**).

Two frequently used verbs are exceptions to the second rule: **sein** itself and **bleiben**. In the perfect tense, these verbs use **sein** as their auxiliary, even though they don't show change of location or condition.

Wo **bist** du so lange **gewesen**? *Where have you been for so long?*
Wir **sind** bei unseren Freunden **geblieben**. *We stayed with our friends.*

7 Kettenreaktion: Wohin bist du gereist? Alle haben sicher Reisen gemacht. Wohin sind *Sie* einmal gereist?

BEISPIEL: A: Ich bin nach Mexiko gereist. Wohin bist du gereist?
B: Ich bin nach ________ gereist. (usw.)

8 Übung: Was ist sie geworden? You've all lost touch with your old school friend, Karoline. Tell your instructor what you think she became.

BEISPIEL: Was glauben *Sie* ?
Ich glaube, sie ist Ärztin geworden.

There are about 200 strong or irregular verbs in German, many of low frequency. In ***Neue Horizonte*** you will learn about 70 frequently used ones. The strong verb forms are the result of a linguistic development in the Germanic languages that was completed hundreds of years ago. New verbs coined in German today are always regular weak verbs, often borrowed from English: **interviewen (hat interviewt), formatieren (hat formatiert).**

Table of strong verbs

The following table contains all the strong verbs that you have learned so far.[3] Review your knowledge of the infinitives and stem-vowel changes in the present tense.

Infinitive	Stem-vowel change in present tense[4]	Auxiliary + past participle	English
anfangen	fängt an	**hat angefangen**	*to begin*
anrufen		**hat angerufen**	*to call up*
beginnen		**hat begonnen**	*to begin*
besitzen		**hat besessen**	*to possess*
bleiben		**ist geblieben**	*to stay*
entscheiden		**hat entschieden**	*to decide*
essen	isst	**hat gegessen**	*to eat*
fahren	fährt	**ist gefahren**	*to drive*
finden		**hat gefunden**	*to find*
fliegen		**ist geflogen**	*to fly*
fließen		**ist geflossen**	*to flow*
geben	gibt	**hat gegeben**	*to give*
gehen		**ist gegangen**	*to go*
halten	hält	**hat gehalten**	*to hold; to stop*
heißen		**hat geheißen**	*to be called*
kommen		**ist gekommen**	*to come*
laufen	läuft	**ist gelaufen**	*to run*
lesen	liest	**hat gelesen**	*to read*
liegen		**hat gelegen**	*to lie*
nehmen	nimmt	**hat genommen**	*to take*
scheinen		**hat geschienen**	*to shine; to seem*
schlafen	schläft	**hat geschlafen**	*to sleep*
schließen		**hat geschlossen**	*to close*
schreiben		**hat geschrieben**	*to write*
schwimmen		**ist geschwommen**	*to swim*
sehen	sieht	**hat gesehen**	*to see*
sein	ist	**ist gewesen**	*to be*
singen		**hat gesungen**	*to sing*
sitzen		**hat gesessen**	*to sit*
sprechen	spricht	**hat gesprochen**	*to speak*
stehen		**hat gestanden**	*to stand*
sterben	stirbt	**ist gestorben**	*to die*
tragen	trägt	**hat getragen**	*to carry; to wear*
trinken		**hat getrunken**	*to drink*
vergessen	vergisst	**hat vergessen**	*to forget*
verlassen	verlässt	**hat verlassen**	*to leave (trans.)*
verlieren		**hat verloren**	*to lose*
werden	wird	**ist geworden**	*to become*
ziehen		**hat gezogen**	*to pull*

---

[3] Except for **anfangen**, **anrufen**, **besitzen**, **entscheiden**, **vergessen**, and **verlassen**, this list includes only the basic verb (e.g., **stehen** but not **aufstehen** or **verstehen**). See pp. 156–157 for the formation of past participles of verbs with separable and inseparable prefixes.

[4] Note that verbs with a present-tense stem-vowel change in the **du**- and **er**-forms (see pp. 50 and 75) are all strong verbs. However, not all strong verbs have this stem-vowel change.

Talking about events in the past is a communicative goal.

9 Partnerarbeit: Was hast du gestern gemacht? Fragen Sie einander, was Sie gestern gemacht haben.

BEISPIEL: A: Was hast du gestern getragen?
B: Ich habe einen Pullover getragen.

1. Was hast du gestern getragen?
2. Was hast du gestern gelesen?
3. Was hast du gestern gegessen?
4. Was hast du gestern getrunken?
5. Mit wem hast du gestern gesprochen?
6. Wohin bist du gestern gegangen?
7. Wen hast du gestern gesehen?
8. Was hast du gestern verloren?
9. Was hast du gestern vergessen?
10. Was hast du gestern gesungen?

10 Übung: Heute und gestern. Sie hören etwas über heute. Sie sagen, auch gestern ist es so gewesen.

BEISPIEL: A: Heute scheint die Sonne.
B: Auch gestern hat die Sonne geschienen.

1. Heute liegt die Zeitung da.
2. Heute singt er zu laut.
3. Heute nimmt Vater das Auto.
4. Heute schließe ich den Laden.
5. Heute steht Markus draußen.
6. Heute Abend wird es kalt.
7. Heute findet sie die Vorlesung gut.
8. Heute schlafen wir bis acht.
9. Heute läuft Christian durch den Wald.
10. Heute kommt ihr um neun Uhr.
11. Heute geb' ich meinem Kind ein Brötchen.
12. Heute hält das Auto hier.

To review separable prefixes, see p. 129.

Past participles of separable-prefix verbs

Verbs with separable (stressed) prefixes form their past participles by inserting **-ge-** *between* the prefix and the verb stem.

anfangen → hat **angefangen**
aufmachen → hat **aufgemacht**

Das Konzert hat um acht Uhr **angefangen**.	*The concert began at eight o'clock.*
Wann bist du denn **aufgestanden**?	*When did you get up?*
Wer hat den Laden **aufgemacht**?	*Who opened the store?*

11 Übung: Ich habe das schon gemacht! Ihr Professor sagt Ihnen, Sie sollen etwas machen. Sagen Sie, Sie haben es schon gemacht.

BEISPIEL: Machen Sie doch die Tür auf.
Ich habe sie schon aufgemacht.

1. Fangen Sie doch an.
2. Hören Sie doch auf.
3. Stehen Sie doch auf.
4. Kaufen Sie doch ein.
5. Machen Sie doch die Tür zu.
6. Rufen Sie doch Robert an.

Past participles of inseparable-prefix verbs

To review inseparable prefixes, see p. 132.

Verbs with inseparable (unstressed) prefixes do *not* add the prefix **ge-** in the past participle.

berichten → hat **berichtet**
verstehen → hat **verstanden**

Sie hat uns über Amerika **berichtet**.	*She reported to us about America.*
Das habe ich nicht **verstanden**.	*I didn't understand that.*

12 Übung: Ich habe das schon gemacht! Ihre Professorin sagt Ihnen, Sie sollen etwas machen. Sagen Sie, Sie haben es schon gemacht.

BEISPIEL: Beginnen Sie bitte.
Ich habe schon begonnen.

1. Beschreiben Sie die Landschaft.
2. Vergessen Sie das.
3. Besuchen Sie Ihre Großeltern.
4. Berichten Sie über Ihre Reise.
5. Besprechen Sie das Problem.
6. Verlassen Sie das Zimmer.
7. Verlieren Sie den Schlüssel (*key*) nicht.
8. Verkaufen Sie mir das Auto.

Perfect tense of mixed verbs

A handful of German verbs have the weak participle form **ge—t** but also change their stem. They are called "mixed verbs." The ones you have learned so far are:

bringen	hat **gebracht**
mitbringen	hat **mitgebracht**
kennen	hat **gekannt**
wissen	hat **gewusst**

13 Partnerarbeit: Das habe ich schon gewusst! Take turns telling each other things. Respond either that you did or did not know that already.

BEISPIEL: A: Mark kommt aus Kanada.
B: Das habe ich schon gewusst! (*oder*)
Wirklich? Das habe ich nicht gewusst.

Schon gehört? . . .
Nee, hab' ich nicht gewusst.

14 Kettenreaktion: Was hast du heute mitgebracht? Say what you've brought with you to class today, then ask what the next student has brought.

BEISPIEL: A: Ich habe heute einen Bleistift mitgebracht. Was hast du mitgebracht?
B: Ich habe ein-________ mitgebracht.

15 Gruppenarbeit: Was hat Maria letzte Woche gemacht? Maria studiert Philosophie an der Uni in Tübingen. Sie ist sehr gut organisiert. Das sieht man an ihrem Terminkalender für letzte Woche. Wo war sie letzte Woche und was hat sie gemacht?

BEISPIEL: Am Montag hat sie mit Thomas im Café Völter Kaffee getrunken.

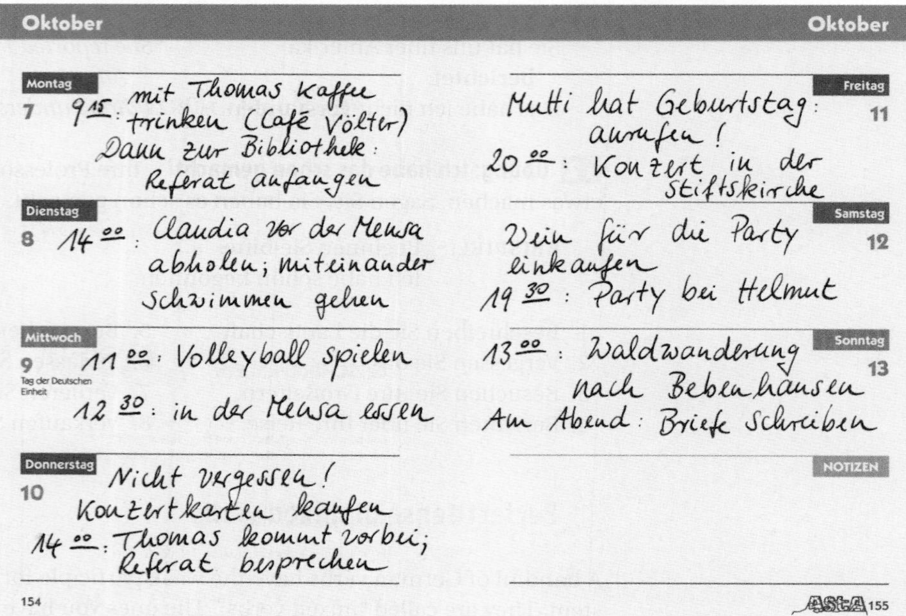

Ein Referat is an oral report or a research paper.

16 Gruppenarbeit: Was haben Sie letzte Woche gemacht? *(3 oder 4 Personen)* Jetzt machen Sie *Ihren* Terminkalender auf. Was haben *Sie* letzte Woche gemacht?

17 Was habe ich letzte Woche gemacht? Now that you have described both Maria's activities and your own, write a paragraph describing what you did last week.

NOTE ON USAGE

Modal verbs in the perfect tense

Instead of using a past participle, modal verbs form the perfect tense with a structure called a *double infinitive.*

Ich habe Tanja **anrufen müssen**.	*I had to call Tanja.*
Wir haben nach Hause gehen wollen.	*We wanted to go home.*

3. Two-way prepositions (*Wechselpräpositionen*)

Review accusative prepositions, p. 96, and dative prepositions, p. 127. Memorize the list of two-way prepositions that follows.

You have learned that some prepositions are always followed by the accusative case, others by the dative case. A third group, called the *two-way prepositions,* all show spatial relationships in their basic meanings. They are followed by the *accusative* case when

Some two-way prepositions can also show nonspatial relationships, e.g., **über** + *accusative* = *about*: **Wir haben *über* unsere Amerikareise gesprochen.**

they signal *destination*, and by the *dative* when they signal *location*. In the example sentences in the table below, notice how the verb determines location or destination. Verbs like **stehen** and **sein** show location (*dative*); verbs like **fahren** and **gehen** show destination (*accusative*).

Preposition	Destination (accusative): answers *wohin?*	Location (dative): answers *wo?*
an	*to, toward* Ich gehe **ans Fenster.** *I'm going to/toward the window.*	*at, alongside of* Ich stehe **am Fenster.** *I'm standing at the window.*
auf	*on, onto* Wohin legt Inge das Buch? Sie legt es **auf den Tisch.** *She's putting it on the table.*	*on, on top of* Wo liegt das Buch? Es liegt **auf dem Tisch.** *It's lying on the table.*
hinter	*behind* Das Kind läuft **hinter das Haus.** *The child is running behind the house.*	*behind* Das Kind spielt **hinter dem Haus.** *The child is playing behind the house.*
in	*into, in* Wo gehen die Studenten hin? Sie gehen **in die Mensa.** *They're going (in)to the cafeteria.*	*in* Wo sind die Studenten? Sie sind **in der Mensa.** *They're in the cafeteria.*
neben	*beside, next to* Leg dein Buch **neben die Zeitung.** *Put your book next to the newspaper.*	*beside, next to* Dein Buch liegt **neben der Zeitung.** *Your book is next to the newspaper.*
über	*over, across* Wir fliegen **über das Meer.** *We're flying across the ocean.*	*over, above* Die Sonne scheint **über dem Meer.** *The sun is shining over the ocean.*
unter	*under* Die Katze läuft **unter das Bett.** *The cat runs under the bed.*	*under, beneath* Die Katze schläft **unter dem Bett.** *The cat sleeps under the bed.*
vor	*in front of* Der Bus fährt **vor das Hotel.** *The bus is driving up in front of the hotel.*	*in front of* Der Bus hält **vor dem Hotel.** *The bus is stopping in front of the hotel.*
zwischen	*between* Er läuft **zwischen die Bäume.** *He's running between the trees.*	*between* Er steht **zwischen den Bäumen.** *He's standing between the trees.*

NOTE: The prepositions **an** and **in** are regularly contracted with the articles **das** and **dem** in the following way:

an das → **ans**   in das → **ins**
an dem → **am**   in dem → **im**

FRAGEWÖRTER

The question words **wohin** and **woher** can be separated in the following way:

Wohin gehst du? *oder* **Wo** gehst du **hin?**
Woher kommen Sie? *oder* **Wo** kommen Sie **her?**

Lab Manual Kap. 6, Var. zu Üb. 22.

Workbook Kap. 6, G–J.

18 Übung: *Wo oder wohin?* Ihre Professorin fragt Sie, **wo** einige (*some*) Leute sind, oder **wohin** sie gehen. Antworten Sie mit **In der Mensa** oder **In die Mensa**.

1. Wo ist Karin?
2. Wo geht ihr jetzt hin?
3. Wo habt ihr gestern gegessen?
4. Wo sind Horst und Petra?
5. Wo hast du Wolf gesehen?
6. Wohin läuft Peter so schnell?

19 Partnerarbeit: *Wo oder wohin?* (*mit offenen Büchern*) Ask each other questions about where things are lying or where they are being placed. Answer with **Auf dem Tisch** or **Auf den Tisch** as appropriate.

1. Wo liegt meine Zeitung?
2. Wohin soll ich das Geld legen?
3. Wohin hast du das Buch gelegt?
4. Wo liegen die Karten für heute Abend?
5. Wo liegt denn das Vorlesungsverzeichnis?

20 Übung: Wo war Martina heute? Martina war heute viel unterwegs. Sagen Sie, wo sie war.

BEISPIEL: Sie war in der Stadt.

gehen
halten
sein
warten
lesen
arbeiten
liegen
fahren
laufen
wohnen

21 Gruppenarbeit. (*mit offenen Büchern*) Take turns replacing the verbs in the sentences below with new verbs from the list on the left. Change the case of the prepositional object according to whether the verb you use shows destination or location. Choose three or four new verbs for each sentence.

1. Wir fahren in die Stadt.
2. Jutta steht hinter dem Haus.
3. Das Kind läuft unter den Tisch.
4. Hans steht am Fenster.
5. Wir sind im Zimmer.
6. Ich lese im Bett.

More about the prepositions *an* and *auf*

The prepositions **an** and **auf** do not correspond exactly to any English prepositions.

- **an** generally signals motion *toward* or location *at* a border, edge, or vertical surface.

Gehen Sie bitte **an die Tafel**.	*Please go to the blackboard.*
Wir fahren **ans Meer**.	*We're driving to the ocean.*
Sie steht **am Tisch**.	*She's standing at the table.*

- **auf** generally signals motion *onto* or location *upon* a horizontal surface.

Leg das Buch **auf den Tisch**.	*Put (or lay) the book on the table.*
Das Buch liegt **auf dem Tisch**.	*The book is (lying) on the table.*

22 Übung: Wo ist Hans? Wohin geht er? Sagen Sie, wohin Hans geht oder wo er steht.

23 Übung: *an* oder *auf*? Complete each sentence with **an** or **auf** and the appropriate article.

A. Wohin? Antworten Sie mit Präposition + Artikel im Akkusativ.

1. Karl geht ________ Tafel.
2. Legen Sie Ihren Mantel ________ Stuhl.
3. Marga fährt im Sommer ________ Meer.
4. Ich habe die Zeitung ________ Schreibtisch gelegt.

B. Wo? Antworten Sie mit Präposition + Artikel im Dativ.

5. Das Kind steht ________ Stuhl.
6. Karl wartet ________ Tür.
7. Das Haus liegt ________ Meer.
8. Das Essen ist schon ________ Tisch.

24 Übung: Wo im Klassenzimmer? Answer the questions about where the people and things are located in the classroom shown below. Then describe the locations of other people and objects.

BEISPIEL: Wo sitzt Herr Schröder?
Er sitzt auf dem Tisch (vor Marie usw.).

1. Wo sitzt Marie?
2. Wo steht Jutta?
3. Wo steht Karl?
4. Wo steht Gertrud?
5. Wo sitzt der Lehrer?
6. Wo steht Emil?
7. Wo liegt die Zeitung?
8. Wo sind diese Leute?

25 Gruppenarbeit. Jetzt beschreiben Sie *Ihr* Klassenzimmer. Wo stehen oder sitzen die Menschen?

26 Gruppenarbeit. Look on below at a different picture of the same classroom. Now everyone is moving around and doing things. Tell where they are going and what they are doing. Describe any other actions you can.

1. Wohin legt Gertrud ihr Buch?
2. Wo geht Karl hin?
3. Wohin legt der Lehrer das Buch?
4. Wo geht Emil hin?
5. Wo geht Anna hin?

4. Masculine N-nouns

A few masculine nouns take the ending **-en** or **-n** in all cases except the nominative singular. They are called *N-nouns.*

	Singular	Plural
nominative	der Student	die Student**en**
accusative	den Student**en**	die Student**en**
dative	dem Student**en**	den Student**en**

Nominative: Dieser Student kennt München sehr gut.
Accusative: Kennst du diesen Student**en**?
Dative: Ich habe diesem Student**en** einen Stadtplan verkauft.

A good rule-of-thumb is that a noun that is masculine, refers to a person or animal, and has the plural ending **-en** or **-n** is an N-noun. Here are the N-nouns you have already learned. The first ending is for all cases in the singular *except* nominative; the second ending is for all cases in the plural. From now on, the presence of this additional ending will signal that the noun is an *N-noun.*

When **Herr** is used as a title (*Mr.*), it also must have the N-noun singular ending: **Das ist Herr Weiß;** *but* **Kennen Sie Herrn Weiß?**

der **Bauer, -n, -n**	*farmer*
der **Herr, -n, -en**	*gentleman; Mr.*
der **Journalist, -en, -en**	*journalist*
der **Kollege, -n, -n**	*colleague, co-worker*
der **Kunde, -n, -n**	*customer*
der **Mensch, -en, -en**	*person, human being*
der **Student, -en, -en**	*student*
der **Tourist, -en, -en**	*tourist*

Lab Manual Kap. 6, Var. zu Üb. 27.

Workbook Kap. 6, K, L.

27 Partnerarbeit: Wer ist das? Ich kenne ihn nicht. Partner A asks who one of these men is; partner B answers. Partner A says he/she doesn't know this person. Switch roles for the next man.

BEISPIEL: A: Wer ist das?
B: Das ist ein Bauer.
A: Ich kenne diesen ________ nicht.
B: Wer ist das? (usw.)

LESESTÜCK

Tipps zum Lesen und Lernen

Lab Manual Kap. 6, Üb. zur Betonung.

 Leicht zu merken

automatisch	
der **Film, -e**	
finanzieren	finanzieren
das **Foto, -s**	
das **Konzert, -e**	Konzert
die **Party, -s**	
die **Philosophie**	Philosophie
praktisch	
privat	privat
das **Programm, -e**	Programm
der **Protest, -e**	Protest

 Einstieg in den Text

Eine E-Mail lesen The following e-mail from Claudia, a German student, in response to a message from her American friend, Michael, who is coming to Germany as an exchange student. Such informal communication between friends is more loosely structured and associative than formal prose. It tends to be midway between spoken and written style. In Claudia's letter, for instance, you'll find conversational phrases and slang (e.g., "Ich kann dir eine Menge erzählen" or "Da staunst du wohl, oder?").

Claudia writes first about what she's studying, then tells a bit about student life in Freiburg and compares it to America. Finally, she describes the difficulty of finding a

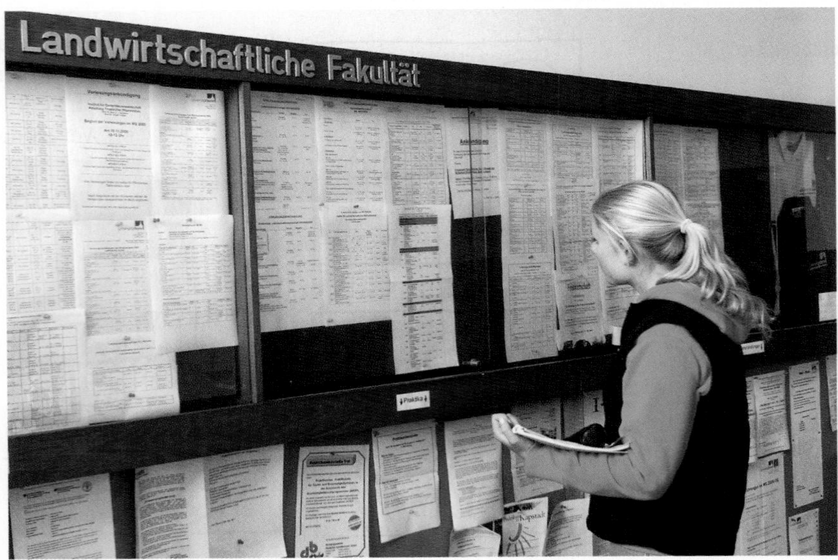

Studentin am Schwarzen Brett ihrer Fakultät

place to live and talks about the rich cultural life in Freiburg. It is clear that she is responding to what Michael has written her. She refers to his e-mail with the following phrases:

"deine Mail ist gestern angekommen, . . ." (line 9)

"Du schreibst, ... " (lines 9–10)

Claudia also asks him some questions:

"Wie ist es denn bei dir? Bekommst du ... ?" (line 41)

How might Michael respond in his next letter to her?

Wortschatz 2

Verben

aus·geben, hat ausgegeben to spend (*money*)
beantworten to answer (*a question or a letter*)
Ich kann deine Frage nicht beantworten. I can't answer your question.
belegen to take (*a university course*)
bezahlen to pay for
enttäuschen to disappoint
erzählen to tell, recount
feiern to celebrate; to party
schicken to send
staunen to be amazed, surprised

Substantive

der **Ausweis, -e** ID card
der **Studentenausweis** student ID
der **Brief, -e** letter
der **Krieg, -e** war
der **Staatsbürger, -** citizen
der **Termin, -e** appointment
das **Ende, -n** end
das **Glück** happiness; luck
Glück haben to be lucky
das **Haar, -e** hair
das **Hauptfach, ¨er** major field (*of study*)
das **Kino, -s** movie theater
ins Kino gehen to go to the movies
das **Nebenfach, ¨er** minor field (*of study*)

Glück haben means *to be lucky*, but **glücklich sein** means *to be happy*.

das **Referat, -e** oral report; written research paper
das **Stipendium, Stipendien** scholarship, stipend
das **Studium** (university) studies
das **Tempo** pace, tempo
die **Geschichte, -n** story; history
die **Klausur, -en** written test
die **Kneipe, -n** tavern, bar
die **Wohnung, -en** apartment
die **Ferien** (*pl.*) (school or university) vacation
die **Semesterferien** semester break

Der Urlaub is a vacation from a job. **Die Ferien** (always plural) is the term for school and university vacations.

Adjektive und Adverbien

billig inexpensive, cheap
gerade just, at this moment
je ever
kostenlos free of charge
lieb dear, nice, sweet
Das ist lieb von dir! That's sweet of you!
schlimm bad
sofort immediately, right away
sonst otherwise, apart from that
verantwortlich (für) responsible (for)
wohl probably

Andere Vokabeln

alles (*sing.*) everything
einige some
selber *or* **selbst** by oneself (myself, yourself, ourselves, etc.)

Remember: **alle** (*pl.*) = *everybody*.

Nützliche Ausdrücke

das heißt that means, in other words
d.h. i.e. (= that is)
Herzlich willkommen! Welcome! Nice to see you!
letzte Woche last week

Gegensätze

billig ≠ teuer cheap ≠ expensive
Glück haben ≠ Pech haben to be lucky ≠ to be unlucky
je ≠ nie ever ≠ never
der Krieg ≠ der Frieden war ≠ peace

Mit anderen Worten

die **Bude, -n** (*Studentenslang*) = **das Studentenzimmer** (rented room, not in a **Studentenwohnheim**)
eine Katastrophe = eine schlimme Situation
klasse = super, prima
die **Mail** = die **E-Mail**
eine Menge (*colloq.*) = **viel**

Eine E-Mail aus Freiburg[5]

In-Text Audio CD

Learning about German student life and the university system is the cultural goal of this chapter.

Claudia Martens hat gerade eine E-Mail von ihrem amerikanischen Freund Michael Hayward bekommen. Claudia war ein Jahr in Amerika als Austauschschülerin an Michaels Schule in Atlanta. Sie schickt ihm sofort eine Antwort.

Von: Claudia Martens
An: mxh5793@aol.com
Datum: 20.02.08
Thema: Gruß aus Freiburg!

Hallo Michael,
deine Mail ist gestern angekommen und ich möchte sie sofort beantworten. Du schreibst, du willst zwei Semester an der Uni in Freiburg Geschichte studieren. Das finde ich super! Ich studiere auch Geschichte, aber nur im Nebenfach. Mein Hauptfach ist eigentlich Philosophie. Letztes° Semester habe ich ein sehr interessantes Seminar über den Ersten Weltkrieg belegen müssen. Es war wirklich klasse! Vielleicht können wir im Herbst zusammen in die Vorlesung über Bismarck und die Gründerzeit[6] gehen.

Last

Habe ich dir je über unser Universitätssystem und das Studentenleben bei uns berichtet? Die Semesterferien[7] haben gerade begonnen, also habe ich endlich ein bisschen Freizeit und kann dir eine Menge erzählen. Im Allgemeinen° ist das Tempo bei uns etwas langsamer und das Studium weniger° stressig als bei euch. Wir schreiben nicht so viele Klausuren und Referate und man ist als Student mehr für sich selbst° verantwortlich. Das heißt zum Beispiel, du kannst abends zu Hause sitzen und Bücher wälzen° oder mit Freunden in die Kneipe gehen. Erst am Semesterende musst du für das Seminar ein Referat schreiben; dann bekommst du einen Schein°. Bei einer Vorlesung gibt es weder Referate noch° Klausuren! Da staunst du wohl, oder°?

***Im …** in general*
weniger = nicht so
***für …** for oneself*
***Bücher …** hit the books*
*certificate of course credit / **weder … noch** = neither … nor / **oder? = nicht wahr?***

Wie du vielleicht schon weißt, sind unsere Unis staatlich°; das bedeutet, sie sind für uns Studenten fast kostenlos. Seit ein paar Jahren gibt es bei uns Studiengebühren°. Sie sind nicht so hoch wie° in den USA, aber es gibt viele Proteste dagegen°. Ansonsten° muss man praktisch nur für Wohnung, Essen, Bücher und Kleidung Geld ausgeben. Außerdem° bekommen viele Studenten auch das so genannte° Bafög.[8] Wie finanzierst du eigentlich dein Jahr in Deutschland? Mit einem Stipendium, oder musst du alles selber bezahlen?

state-run
tuition fees
***so … wie** = as … as / against them / Otherwise*
In addition / so-called

Jedenfalls° ist das Essen in der Mensa immer billig und relativ gut, aber mit dem Wohnen ist es echt eine Katastrophe. Es gibt nicht genug Studentenwohnheime für alle

In any case

---

[5] **Freiburg**: City in Baden-Württemberg between the Black Forest and the Rhine. The Albert-Ludwigs-Universität was founded in 1457.

[6] **Otto von Bismarck** (1815–1898): German statesman and Prussian Chancellor, under whose leadership the German states were united into the German Empire in 1871. **Gründerzeit**: the "Founders Era" refers to the period of 1871–1900, when many German businesses were established.

[7] The German academic year has a **Wintersemester** that begins in mid-October and ends in mid-February. The **Sommersemester** begins in late April and ends in mid-July. The **Semesterferien** come between the two semesters.

[8] Inexpensive government loans for university students in Germany are mandated by the Federal Education Support Law, or **Bundesausbildungsförderungsgesetz (Bafög).** This acronym has entered the university vocabulary.

Wo möchte dieser Student wohnen? Kann man ihn anrufen?

Studenten und private Buden sind wahnsinnig teuer geworden. Die Wohnungsnot° ist besonders schlimm: In den Jahren nach der Wiedervereinigung° sind viele Deutsche aus der ehemaligen° DDR und Aussiedler aus Osteuropa in den Westen gekommen.[9] Übrigens habe ich letztes Semester einigen Schulkindern aus zwei Aussiedlerfamilien Nachhilfestunden° in Deutsch gegeben, denn° diese neuen Staatsbürger können oft nur wenig Deutsch.

housing shortage
reunification
former
tutoring / because

Wie ist es denn bei dir? Bekommst du durch das Austauschprogramm automatisch einen Platz im Studentenwohnheim? Wenn nicht°, dann hast du Glück: Du kannst zu uns in die WG! Wir haben nämlich° nächstes Semester ein Zimmer frei und du bist herzlich willkommen. Michael, du bist immer so gern ins Kino und Konzert gegangen. Ich bin sicher, die Filme und Konzerte hier werden dich nicht enttäuschen°. Mit deinem Studentenausweis bekommst du im Theater, Kino und Museum immer eine Ermäßigung°.

Wenn … *If not*
you see
werden … *will not disappoint you / discount*

Das ist aber eine lange Mail geworden! Jetzt habe ich einen Termin beim Arzt und muss nachher für eine Party einkaufen. Wir feiern nämlich heute Abend das Semesterende. Also, genug für heute, aber ich schreibe dir bald wieder. Viele herzliche Grüße an dich und deine Familie.

Deine Claudia

P.S. Im Internet kannst du sicher einen interaktiven Stadtplan von Freiburg finden. Übrigens habe ich ein neues Foto von mir angehängt°. Kennst du mich noch mit kurzen Haaren? Lustig, nicht?

attached

mit kurzen Haaren: The plural form is most common: **Jetzt hat sie kurze Haare.**

„Kennst du mich noch mit kurzen Haaren?"

---

[9] Citizens of the former German Democratic Republic and the **Aussiedler** (*emigrants who are ethnic Germans from other eastern European countries*) have a constitutional right to German citizenship.

NACH DEM LESEN

SAM Lab Manual **Lab Manual** Kap. 6, Diktat.

SAM Workbook **Workbook** Kap. 6, Üb. M.

A Antworten Sie auf Deutsch.

1. Wo hat Claudia Michael kennen gelernt?
2. Was will Michael in Freiburg studieren?
3. Wie ist das Tempo im Studentenleben in Freiburg?
4. Warum kostet das Studium in Deutschland nicht sehr viel?
5. Warum sind Studentenzimmer manchmal wahnsinnig teuer?
6. Was hat Claudia letztes Semester in ihrer Freizeit gemacht?
7. Wo kann Michael in Freiburg wohnen?
8. Was hat ihm Claudia außer einem Brief geschickt?
9. Was war für Michael neu auf dem Foto von Claudia?

Vokabeln zum Thema Studium

This vocabulary focuses on an everyday topic or situation. Words you already know from **Wortschatz** sections are listed without English equivalents; new supplementary vocabulary is listed with definitions. Your instructor may assign some supplementary vocabulary for active mastery.

Einige Wörter kennen Sie schon.

studieren an (+ *dat.*)	*to study at*
Ich studiere an der FU. (= **Freien Universität, Berlin**).	
die **Bibliothek, -en**	
das **Fach, ¨er**	*area of study, subject*
das **Hauptfach**, das **Nebenfach**	
die **Klausur, -en**	
das **Labor, -s**	*lab*
das **Referat, -e**	
ein Referat halten	*to give an oral report*
ein Referat schreiben	*to write a paper*
das **Semester, -**	
das **Sommersemester**	*spring term* (*usually April to July*)
das **Wintersemester**	*fall term* (*usually October to February*)
das **Seminar, -e**	
die **Vorlesung, -en**	
die **Wissenschaft, -en**	*science; scholarship; field of knowledge*

Note stress: **La<u>bor</u>**.

Einige Studienfächer

Note that most academic disciplines are feminine.

Additional vocabulary: **Völkerkunde** *or* **Anthropologie**, **Theologie**, **Amerikanistik** (*American studies*). **Hoch- und Tiefbau** (*civil engineering*), **Architektur**. In student slang, **WiWi** = **Wirtschaftswissenschaft** (*economics*). In Austria and Switzerland, **Jura** = **Jus**.

die **Anglistik**	Angl<u>is</u>tik	*English studies*
die **Betriebswirtschaft**		*management, business*
die **Biologie**	Biolog<u>ie</u>	*biology*
die **Chemie**	Che<u>mie</u>	*chemistry*
die **Elektrotechnik**		*electrical engineering*
die **Germanistik**	Germa<u>nis</u>tik	*German studies*
die **Geschichte**		*history*
die **Informatik**	Infor<u>ma</u>tik	*computer science*
Jura (*used without article*)		*law*
die **Kunstgeschichte**		*art history*
die **Linguistik**	Lingu<u>is</u>tik	*linguistics*
der **Maschinenbau**		*mechanical engineering*

die **Mathematik**	Mathematik	*mathematics*
die **Medizin**	Medizin	*medicine*
die **Musikwissenschaft**		*musicology*
die **Pädagogik**	Pädagogik	*education*
die **Philosophie**	Philosophie	*philosophy*
die **Physik**	Physik	*physics*
die **Politikwissenschaft**		*political science*
die **Psychologie**	Psychologie	*psychology*
die **Soziologie**	Soziologie	*sociology*
die **Wirtschaftswissenschaft**		*economics*

B **Gruppenarbeit: Was studierst du denn?**

1. Welche (*which*) Studienfächer in der Liste kann man auch an Ihrer Universität oder an Ihrem College studieren? Gibt es Studienfächer bei Ihnen, die nicht in der Liste sind?
2. Was ist Ihr Hauptfach und was belegen Sie dieses Semester?

BEISPIEL: Mein Hauptfach ist ______. Dieses Semester belege ich Deutsch, ______, ______ und ______. Was studierst denn du?

Info-Austausch

C **Welches Fach ist das?** Arbeiten Sie mit Ihrem Partner zusammen. Finden Sie die richtige Beschreibung (*description*) von jedem Hauptfach.

BEISPIEL: A: Man studiert Philosophie. Was macht man an der Uni?
B: Man studiert und analysiert große Denker wie Kant und Wittgenstein.
B: Man studiert Organismen: Tiere (*animals*) und Pflanzen (*plants*). Welches (*which*) Fach ist das?
A: Das ist Biologie.

Partner B's information is found in Appendix 1. Partner B has the descriptions of Partner A's **Hauptfächer**, and vice versa.

Partner A:

Im Hauptfach studiert man ...	Das macht man an der Uni.
Philosophie	Man studiert Lerntheorien und will später in der Schule lehren.
Germanistik	Man liest und schreibt über die Vergangenheit (*past*) und interpretiert sie.
Informatik	Man studiert die Theorien von Newton und Einstein.
Biologie	Man vergleicht (*compares*) politische Systeme.

D **Partnerarbeit: Interview.** Interview each other in more detail about your studies. Take notes if necessary, and be prepared to report to the whole class. Ask each other questions such as the following:

1. Was machst du lieber: Referate schreiben oder Referate halten? Wie oft musst du das machen?
2. Arbeitest du oft in der Bibliothek oder mehr im Labor?
3. Was willst du nach dem Studium machen?
4. Brauchst du Deutsch für dein Studium oder für deinen Beruf?
5. Wie finanzierst du das Studium? Bekommst du ein Stipendium?
6. Wohnst du im Studentenwohnheim oder privat?

Writing a letter in German is a communicative goal.

Einen Brief schreiben

In **Kapitel 2** you learned how to write a simple postcard in German (see page 61). When writing an informal letter, Germans often include the place before the date. Also notice that if you are writing to two friends, one male and one female, you must repeat the saluation with the correct adjective ending. (One cannot write **Liebe Sabine und Markus**; one must write **Liebe Sabine, lieber Markus.**) You should be able to read the handwritten letter below, despite some differences between English and German handwriting. Note especially that the letters **u** and **n** can often look very similar in German.

Place and date: day / month / year

Salutation: **-e** with a female name, **-er** with a male name

Jena, den 20.05.08

Liebe Sabine, lieber Markus!

Hallo! Wie geht's euch denn? Gestern sind wir hier angekommen und haben schon eure Cousine Gertrud besucht. Sie und ihre Freunde sind wahnsinnig nett und haben uns sehr viel von Jena gezeigt.

Morgen fahren wir nach Berlin und sind dann Freitag wieder zu Hause.

Bis dann

Standard closing = *many cordial greetings*

Viele herzliche Grüße von

Tanja und Fabian

Schreiben wir mal: „Liebe Claudia, ...“ Claudias E-Mail an Michael Hayward haben Sie schon gelesen. In dieser Mail hat sie ihm das Studentenleben in Freiburg beschrieben. Jetzt spielen Sie die Rolle von Michael Hayward und schreiben eine Antwort an Claudia. Beantworten Sie ihre Fragen und schreiben Sie über das Studentenleben bei Ihnen. Haben Sie andere Fragen an Claudia über Freiburg und das Studium dort?

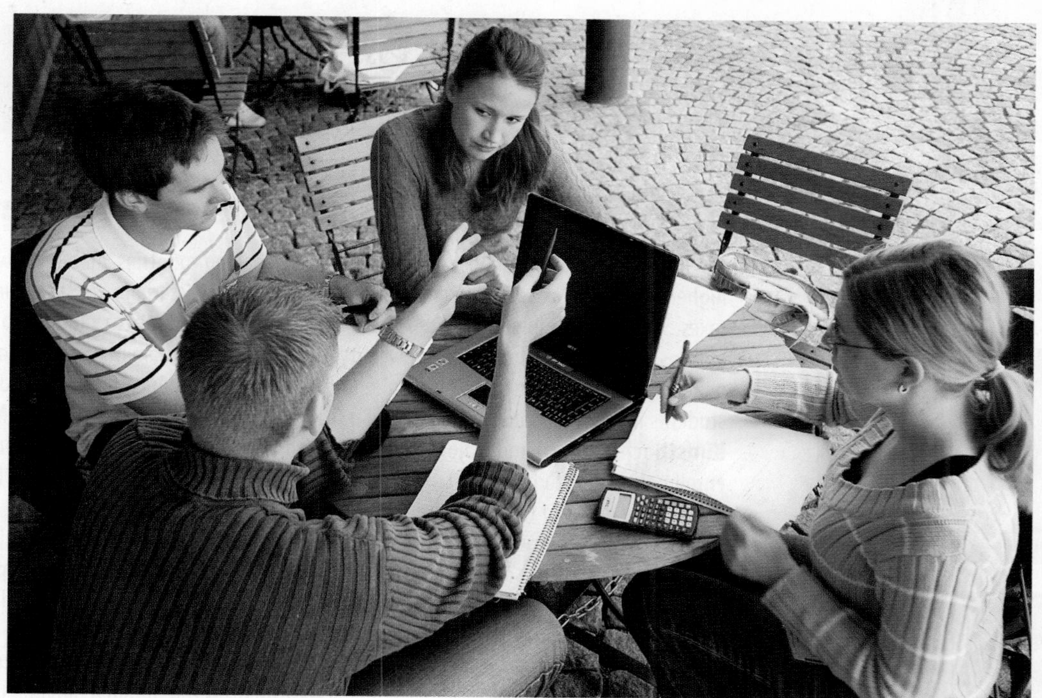

„Arbeiten wir zusammen am Referat."

E Wie sagt man das auf Deutsch?

1. I've brought you the novel for your seminar.
2. Thanks a lot. Did it cost much?
3. No, it was cheap. Shall I put it on your desk?

4. The lecture began at ten o'clock.
5. Unfortunately, I arrived too late.
6. I stood behind my friends and didn't hear anything.

7. What did you study in Dresden?
8. History was my major but I also studied German.

9. Tonight we're going to the movies together.
10. I hope you haven't forgotten your student I.D.
11. No, it's in my pocket.
12. Good, let's go! We have to be there before eight o'clock.

VIDEO

Universities in the German-Speaking Countries

The university system is similar in all the German-speaking countries. All but a few institutions of higher learning (**Hochschulen**) in Austria, Germany, and Switzerland are state-run and financed by taxes. Successful completion of the **Abitur** examination (called **Matura** in Austria and Switzerland) entitles a student to enroll in any university in the country. German universities do not have the general education or distribution requirements common at American colleges and universities; students begin their studies in a particular major. Some specialized schools (e.g., **Musikhochschulen**, **Kunsthochschulen**) and majors in high demand (e.g., medicine and management) have restricted enrollments, and students' **Abitur** grades determine whether and how long they have to wait for a place in the major of their choice.

Educational reforms in the 1960s and 70s led both to an increase in the number of students and more diversity in their socio-economic backgrounds. In 1950, for example, only 6 percent of German pupils completed the **Abitur**, and they were mostly the children of the upper middle class and had parents who also had a university education. Today, the percentage of students in any given year who go on to university varies from about 16 percent in Switzerland to about 30 percent in Germany. Moreover, students who have not attended a **Gymnasium** can obtain a diploma that allows them to study at **Fachhochschulen**, which emphasize applied knowledge rather than theory. For example, one can study electrical engineering but not physics at a **Fachhochschule**, while hotel management is offered at some **Fachhochschulen**, not at universities.

Foto: dpa

The biggest contrast to the United States is the fact that students pay little or no tuition. In recent years, individual **Länder** have begun to charge modest tuition fees (**Studiengebühren**) to help finance the universities. At the most, this amounts to €500 tuition per semester, but there have been large protests against such fees. (See p. 173.)

The European Union has worked to make university programs in all its member countries compatible with each other. Many EU students complete at least part of their education in other countries.

Studiengebühren: Was die Bundesländer planen

Schleswig-Holstein:
Gebühren geplant; Höhe und Termin noch offen
Mecklenburg-Vorpommern:
derzeit keine Gebühren geplant
Hamburg:
500 Euro pro Semester ab Sommer 2007
Bremen:
500 Euro Langzeitgebühren pro Semester ab WS 2006/2007
Berlin:
derzeit keine Gebühren geplant
Niedersachsen:
500 Euro pro Semester ab WS 2006/2007
Brandenburg:
derzeit keine Gebühren geplant
Sachsen-Anhalt:
Erststudium kostenfrei, schon jetzt 500 Euro Langzeitgebühren pro Semester
Nordrhein-Westfalen:
bis zu 500 Euro pro Semester ab WS 2006/2007
Sachsen:
Erststudium kostenfrei; bis 450 Euro pro Semester für ein Zweitstudium
Thüringen:
Erststudium kostenfrei, schon jetzt 500 Euro Langzeitgebühren pro Semester
Hessen:
schon jetzt 500 bis 900 Euro Langzeitgebühren pro Semester; regulär 500 Euro/Semester ab WS 2007/2008 geplant
Rheinland-Pfalz:
Erststudium kostenfrei, Zweitstudium und Langzeitgebühren: 650 Euro pro Semester
Saarland:
300-500 Euro pro Semester ab WS 2007/2008
Bayern:
100 bis 500 Euro pro Semester ab Sommer 2007
Baden-Württemberg:
500 Euro pro Semester ab Sommer 2007
Studiengebühren ab WS 2006/2007
Einführung von Studiengebühren geplant
Derzeit keine Gebühren geplant

KAPITEL

7

Radfahrer am Abend

Auf Reisen

Kommunikation

- Expressing opinions, preferences, and polite requests
- Telling time with the 24-hour clock
- Making travel plans and talking about traveling
- Talking on the telephone

Kultur

- Traveling in Europe

In diesem Kapitel

- **Lyrik zum Vorlesen**
  Wilhelm Müller, "Wanderschaft"
- **Grammatik**
  1. **Der**-words and **ein**-words
  2. Coordinating conjunctions
  3. Verbs with dative objects
  4. Personal dative
  5. Using **würden** + infinitive
  6. Verbs with two-way prepositions
  7. Official time-telling
- **Lesestück**
  Unterwegs mit Fahrrad, Auto und der Bahn
- **Almanach**
  Jugendherbergen

DIALOGE

Lab Manual Kap. 7, Dialoge, Fragen, Hören Sie gut zu!, Üb. zur Aussprache **[u/ü]**.

11.27 Uhr is spoken **elf Uhr siebenundzwanzig.**

die Flasche: English cognate: *flask*

der Straßenatlas: Most drivers carry a bound road atlas of Europe rather than folding maps.

Am Bahnhof

Ein Student sieht eine alte Dame mit viel Gepäck und will ihr helfen.

STUDENT: Darf ich Ihnen helfen?
TOURISTIN: Ja, bitte! Würden Sie mir den Koffer tragen?
STUDENT: Gerne. Wohin müssen Sie denn?
TOURISTIN: Gleis dreizehn. Mein Zug fährt um 11.27 Uhr ab.

Vor der Urlaubsreise

MARION: Suchst du die Thermosflasche?
THORSTEN: Nein, nicht die Thermosflasche, sondern den Straßenatlas. Ich glaube, ich habe ihn auf den Tisch gelegt.
MARION: Ja, hier liegt er unter meiner Jacke.
THORSTEN: Häng die Jacke doch auf, dann haben wir mehr Platz. Wir müssen unsere Reise nach Venedig planen.
MARION: Vergessen wir nicht, unsere Tickets stecken in der Tasche.

Am Telefon

Marion und Thorsten waren drei Wochen mit dem Wagen unterwegs. Jetzt sind sie wieder zu Hause und Marion ruft ihren Vater am Nachmittag an. Es klingelt lange, aber endlich kommt Herr Krogmann ans Telefon.

HERR KROGMANN: Krogmann.
MARION: Hallo Papa! Hier ist Marion. Warum hast du nicht gleich geantwortet?
HERR KROGMANN: Ach, Marion, seid ihr wieder zurück? Ich habe auf dem Sofa gelegen und bin eingeschlafen.
MARION: Oh, tut mir Leid, Papa, ich habe dich geweckt.
HERR KROGMANN: Macht nichts. Ich habe sowieso aufstehen wollen. Wie war denn eure Reise?
MARION: Alles war wunderbar.

Am Bahnhof

Wortschatz 1

Auf Reisen

ab·fahren (fährt ab), ist abgefahren to depart, leave (*by vehicle*)
an·kommen, ist angekommen to arrive
reservieren to reserve
der **Bahnhof, ⸚e** train station
der **Koffer, -** suitcase
der **Straßenatlas** road atlas
der **Wagen, -** car, automobile
der **Zug, ⸚e** train
das **Gepäck** luggage
das **Gleis, -e** (railroad) track

Verben

danken (+ *dat.*) to thank
ein·schlafen (schläft ein), ist eingeschlafen to fall asleep
gefallen (gefällt), hat gefallen (+ *dat.*) to please, appeal to
Das Buch gefällt mir. I like the book.
gehören (+ *dat.*) to belong to (a person)
hängen, hat gehängt (*trans.*) to hang
auf·hängen to hang up
hängen, hat gehangen (*intrans.*) to be hanging
helfen (hilft), hat geholfen (+ *dat.*) to help
klingeln to ring
planen to plan
setzen to set (down), put
stecken to put (into), insert; to be (inside of)
stellen to put, place
tun, hat getan to do
wecken (*trans.*) to wake (someone) up
Weck mich bitte um sieben.
würden (+ *infinitive*) would (do something)

Substantive

der **Nachmittag, -e** afternoon
am Nachmittag in the afternoon
das **Telefon, -e** telephone
(das) **Venedig** Venice
die **Flasche, -n** bottle
die **Thermosflasche** thermos bottle

Adjektive und Adverbien

sowieso anyway
unterwegs on the way; en route; on the go
wunderbar wonderful

Andere Vokabeln

sondern but rather, but . . . instead
welch- which

Nützliche Ausdrücke

Es tut mir Leid. I'm sorry.
Das macht nichts. That doesn't matter.
Das ist (mir) egal. It doesn't matter (to me). I don't care.
Das macht (mir) Spaß. That's fun (for me).
Wie viel Uhr ist es? = Wie spät ist es?

Often shortened in spoken German: **Tut mir Leid. Macht nichts. Mir egal.**

Gegensätze

auf·stehen ≠ ins Bett gehen to get up ≠ to go to bed
ein·schlafen ≠ auf·wachen to fall asleep ≠ to wake up

Mit anderen Worten

Das ist mir Wurscht. (*colloq.*) = **Das ist mir egal.**

Variationen

A Persönliche Fragen

With means of transportation **mit** = *by*: **Die Touristin fährt mit dem Zug.**

1. Fahren Sie oft mit dem Zug? Wohin sind Sie denn gefahren?
2. Fahren Sie gern mit dem Zug oder lieber mit dem Wagen?
3. Die Touristin muss zu ihrem Zug. Wohin müssen Sie heute?
4. Thorsten und Marion brauchen einen Straßenatlas für ihre Reise. Was brauchen Sie für eine Reise?
5. Thorsten plant eine Reise nach Venedig. Planen Sie eine Reise in den Ferien? Wohin?
6. Schlafen Sie gern nachmittags wie Herr Krogmann?
7. Herr Krogmann schläft auf dem Sofa. Wo schlafen Sie lieber am Nachmittag, auf dem Sofa oder auf dem Bett?

Review high-frequency idiomatic phrases like these in each **Zusammenfassung und Wiederholung** section in the Workbook section of the SAM. They are important for authentic conversational German.

B Reaktionen. Respond to the statements and questions on the left with an appropriate phrase from the right.

1. Ich kann den Koffer nicht tragen.
2. Würden Sie mir bitte helfen?
3. Hast du das nicht gewusst?
4. Wo fährt denn Ihr Zug ab?
5. Waren die Hausaufgaben besonders schwer?
6. Wie war die Reise?
7. Wohin hast du den Atlas gelegt?
8. Wo liegt denn der Stadtplan?
9. Gehen wir zusammen einkaufen?
10. Was ist denn los?
11. Wann seid ihr angekommen?
12. Wann fährt unser Zug ab?

Einverstanden!
Sofort.
Doch!
Oh, das tut mir Leid!
Das macht nichts!
Gerne!
Heute Morgen.
Auf dem Tisch.
Gar nichts.
Auf das Sofa.
Das finde ich auch.
Bitte sehr.
Auf Gleis zehn.
Nee, gar nicht.
Wunderbar!

C Übung: Im Reisebüro (*at the travel agency*). Im Reisebüro fragt man, ob Sie etwas machen wollen. Antworten Sie, Sie würden das gerne tun.

BEISPIEL: A: Wollen Sie ein Hotelzimmer reservieren?
B: Ja, ich würde gern ein Hotelzimmer reservieren.

1. Wollen Sie Ihren Mantel aufhängen?
2. Wollen Sie morgen abfahren?
3. Wollen Sie morgen Abend in Venedig ankommen?
4. Wollen Sie im Zug schlafen?
5. Wollen Sie mir Ihr Gepäck geben?
6. Wollen Sie Ihre Familie anrufen?

D Partnerarbeit: Am Telefon. Situation: Barbara Hinrich phones her father to tell him when she's coming home tonight. He asks where she is and whether she's eating at home tonight. She says she's going out to eat with friends and then to a movie. Her father says he'll see her later. They say good-bye (on the telephone it's **Auf Wiederhören**). Complete this conversation with your partner.

VATER: Hinrich.
BARBARA: Hallo ________! Hier ist ________.
VATER: Ach hallo ________! Wo ________?
BARBARA: ________.
VATER: Wirklich? ________?
BARBARA: ________.
VATER: Also, ________. Auf Wiederhören, bis ________!
BARBARA: ________!

Freude für Tante Erna: Die ganze Familie ruft an.

Lyrik zum Vorlesen

In-Text Audio CD

Set to music by Franz Schubert, this poem is the first song in his cycle "Die schöne Müllerin," op. 5, no. 1 (D 795).

German Romantic literature uses nature images to evoke themes of yearning for the unknown, for wandering, and for love. The Romantic poets were obsessed with the illusory world of appearances expressed in moonlit nights, fog, and the forest. In the early 19th century **das Wandern** described the life of an itinerant journeyman. These were artisans who journeyed from town to town, gaining experience with different master craftsmen.

Wilhelm Müller's poem cycle *Die schöne Müllerin* (1820) is unified by the theme of the love of the journeyman for the miller's daughter. In this poem the youth is moved to **Wanderlust** by the mill itself with its rushing water and turning wheels. He ends by asking the miller and his wife for permission to depart.

Wanderschaft°

journeying

Das Wandern ist des Müllers Lust°,
Das Wandern!
Das muss ein schlechter Müller sein,
Dem niemals fiel das Wandern ein°,
Das Wandern.

des ... *the miller's desire*
Dem ... *Who has never thought of wandering*

Vom Wasser haben wir's gelernt,
Vom Wasser!
Das hat nicht Rast° bei Tag und Nacht,
Ist stets° auf Wanderschaft bedacht°,
Das Wasser.

rest
stets = immer */ intent*

Das sehn wir auch den Rädern ab°,
Den Rädern!
Die gar nicht gerne stille stehn
Und sich mein Tag nicht müde drehn°,
Die Räder.

sehn ... *see also from the wheels*
Und ... *never tire of turning*

Die Steine selbst°, so schwer sie sind,
Die Steine!
Sie tanzen mit den muntern Reihn°
Und wollen gar noch schneller sein,
Die Steine!

Steine ... *Even the stones*
cheerful dances

O Wandern, Wandern, meine Lust,
O Wandern!
Herr Meister und Frau Meisterin,
Lasst mich in Frieden weiterziehn°
Und wandern!

Lasst ... *Let me go in peace*

Wilhelm Müller (1794–1827)

GRAMMATIK

1. *Der*-words and *ein*-words

You know that the definite and indefinite articles **der** and **ein** and similar words such as **dies-**, **jed-**, **mein**, **kein**, and **alle** are followed by nouns. Because of slight differences in their endings, such words are divided into two groups: the **der**-words and the **ein**-words.

der-words		*ein*-words		
der, das, die	*the*	**ein**	*a, an*	
dies-	*this, these*	**kein**	*no, not a*	
jed-	*each, every*	**mein**	*my*	possessive adjectives
welch-	*which*	**dein**	*your*	possessive adjectives
all-	*all*	**sein**	*his, its*	possessive adjectives
		ihr	*her, its*	possessive adjectives
		unser	*our*	possessive adjectives
		euer	*your*	possessive adjectives
		ihr	*their*	possessive adjectives
		Ihr	*your*	

Since the endings of the definite article (**der**, **das**, **die**) are slightly irregular, **dieser** is used here to review the **der**-word endings in the three cases you know so far.

der-word endings	masculine	neuter	feminine	plural
nom.	dieser Stuhl	dieses Buch	diese Uhr	diese Bücher
acc.	diesen Stuhl	dieses Buch	diese Uhr	diese Bücher
dat.	diesem Stuhl	diesem Buch	dieser Uhr	diesen Büchern

The **ein**-words have the same endings as **der**-words *except in three cases* where they have *no* endings, as highlighted in the following table.

ein-word endings	masculine	neuter	feminine	plural
nom.	mein Stuhl	mein Buch	meine Uhr	meine Bücher
acc.	meinen Stuhl	mein Buch	meine Uhr	meine Bücher
dat.	meinem Stuhl	meinem Buch	meiner Uhr	meinen Büchern

Die Bahn DB

1 Übung. Ihre Professorin stellt eine Frage und Sie antworten.

BEISPIEL: Welcher Stuhl ist alt?
Dieser Stuhl ist alt.

1. Welche Schuhe sind neu?
2. Welcher Student sitzt am Fenster?
3. Welche Studentin hat ihr Buch vergessen?
4. Welcher Student heißt ________?
5. Welches Fenster ist schmutzig (*dirty*)?
6. Welcher Student trägt ein neues T-Shirt?
7. Welche Studentin ist heute spät aufgestanden?
8. Welches Buch finden Sie gut?

SAM **Lab Manual** Kap. 7, Üb. 2.

SAM **Workbook** Kap. 7, A.

2 Übung. Respond to each statement as in the model.

BEISPIEL: Dieser Berg ist steil.
Ja, aber nicht jeder Berg ist steil.

1. Dieser Koffer ist schwer.
2. Dieses Studentenwohnheim ist neu.
3. Dieser Zug fährt bald ab.
4. Dieses Telefon klingelt zu laut.
5. Diese Thermosflasche ist teuer.
6. Dieser Tourist kann Deutsch.
7. Diese Vorlesung ist langweilig.

3 Partnerarbeit: Dieses Buch ist mein Buch. Take turns saying what belongs to you.

BEISPIEL: A: Dieses Buch ist mein Buch.
B: Diese Hose ist meine Hose.

Now look around at other people in the room and ask what belongs to whom.

BEISPIEL: A: Welche Jacke ist seine Jacke?
B: Diese Jacke ist seine Jacke.
A: Welches Heft ist ihr Heft? usw.

2. Coordinating conjunctions (*koordinierende Konjunktionen*)

DEFINITIONEN

What are conjunctions?
Conjunctions are words such as *and*, *or*, *but*, and *because* that join together words, phrases, or clauses in various ways.

What is a clause?
A ***clause*** is a unit containing a subject and an inflected verb. A simple sentence consists of one clause; a compound sentence has two or more clauses.

Coordinating conjunctions join clauses that could each stand alone as a simple sentence. The coordinating conjunction joins them into a compound sentence.

Christa ist achtzehn. Ihr Bruder ist sechzehn.
Christa ist achtzehn **und** ihr Bruder ist sechzehn.

Kannst du das Fenster aufmachen? Soll ich es machen?
Kannst du das Fenster aufmachen **oder** soll ich es machen?

The most common coordinating conjunctions in German are:

Do not confuse the conjunction **denn** with the flavoring particle used with questions: **Wo warst du denn so lange?**

und	*and*
oder	*or*
aber	*but, however*
sondern	*but rather, instead*
denn	*for, because*

Remember this iron-clad rule: The verb is always in second position in German statements. A coordinating conjunction, however, is *not* counted as being in first position. Therefore, the word order of the second clause is *not* affected by the conjunction.

0 1 2
Ute kommt nicht zu Fuß, **sondern** sie fährt mit dem Auto.

0 1 2
Ich kann dich erst am Abend anrufen, **denn** ich bin bis sieben in der Bibliothek.

0 1 2
Klaus muss bis drei arbeiten, **aber** dann kann er nach Hause.

Coordinating conjunctions are also used to connect words and phrases.

Ich habe einen Bruder **und** eine Schwester.
Möchtest du Wein **oder** Bier?
Dieser Laden ist gut, **aber** sehr teuer.
Barbara ist nicht hier, **sondern** in Italien.

Note on punctuation: *Always* place a comma before **aber**, **sondern**, and **denn**.

Lab Manual Kap. 7, Var. zu Partnerarbeit 4, Üb. 5.

Workbook Kap. 7, B, C.

4 Partnerarbeit. Use **und**, **aber**, **oder**, or **denn** to join each sentence from column A to one from column B. Try to find the most logical pairings. Compare results with other students.

A		B
Meine Eltern kommen morgen.		Ich möchte sie dort besuchen.
Bist du krank?	*und*	Willst du in einer WG wohnen?
Gisela studiert in Freiburg.		Ich zeige ihnen meine Wohnung.
Ich bringe das Buch mit.		Mein Bruder wohnt auf dem Land.
Ich wohne in der Stadt.		Du sollst es lesen.
Ich bin jetzt in Eile.		Sie hat ihn nicht beantwortet.
Willst du in der Mensa essen?		Mein Zug fährt gleich ab.
Willst du allein wohnen?		Wollen wir bei mir etwas kochen?
Ich habe Sabine einen Brief geschrieben.		Geht es dir gut?

Aber versus *sondern*

Aber and **sondern** are both translated with English *but*. Both express a contrast, but they are *not* interchangeable. **Sondern** *must* be used when *but* means *but . . . instead, but rather*.

Er bleibt zu Hause, **aber** sie geht einkaufen.	*He's staying home, but she's going shopping.*
Er bleibt nicht zu Hause, **sondern** geht einkaufen.	*He's not staying home,* ***but*** *is going shopping* ***instead****.*

Sondern *always* follows a *negative* statement and connects *mutually exclusive alternatives*. Note that the clause following **sondern** often leaves out elements it has in common with the first clause. Such deletion is called *ellipsis*.

Er bleibt nicht zu Hause, sondern [er] geht einkaufen.
Das ist kein Wein, sondern [das ist] Wasser.
Käthe hat es nicht getan, sondern die Kinder [haben es getan].

5 Übung: *Aber* oder *sondern*? Combine each pair of simple sentences into a compound sentence, using **aber** or **sondern** as appropriate. Use ellipsis where possible.

1. Sie fliegt nach Italien. Ihr Mann fährt mit dem Zug.
2. Sie hasst mich nicht. Sie liebt mich.
3. Es ist noch nicht sieben Uhr. Er ist schon zu Hause.
4. Ich fahre nicht mit dem Auto. Ich gehe zu Fuß.
5. Du sollst mich nicht um acht Uhr wecken. Du sollst mich um sieben wecken.
6. Bernd mag dieses Bier nicht. Lutz trinkt es gern.

Word order: nicht *X*, sondern *Y*

Notice how the position of **nicht** shifts when it is followed by **sondern**.

Ich kaufe den Mantel nicht.
but:
Ich kaufe **nicht den Mantel**, sondern die Jacke.

Johanna arbeitet heute nicht.
but:
Johanna arbeitet **nicht heute**, sondern morgen.

6 Übung: Nein, nicht x, sondern y. Answer these questions negatively, using **sondern**.

BEISPIEL: Wollen Sie *um sieben* frühstücken?
Nein, ich will nicht um sieben frühstücken, sondern um zehn.

1. Suchen Sie *die Thermosflasche*?
2. Gehen Sie *am Mittwoch* ins Kino?
3. Gehen Sie *mit Ursula* in die Stadt?
4. Gehen Sie mit Ursula in *die Stadt?*
5. Wollen Sie mir *die Fotos* zeigen?
6. Waren Sie *gestern* in der Bibliothek?

3. Verbs with dative objects (*Verben mit Dativobjekt*)

Review dative endings for **der**-words, p. 179, and dative forms of the personal pronouns, p. 125.

A few German verbs require an object in the dative case rather than the accusative. Two of these are **helfen** and **antworten**.

Ich sehe den Mann.	*I see the man.*
but:	
Ich helfe **dem** Mann.	*I'm helping the man.*
Du fragst die Frau.	*You ask the woman.*
but:	
Du antwortest **der** Frau.	*You answer the woman.*

This chapter introduces the following verbs with dative objects:

antworten	*to answer* (someone)
danken	*to thank*
gefallen	*to please*
gehören	*to belong to*
glauben	*to believe* (someone)
helfen	*to help*

The dative object is usually a person.

Marie dankt **ihrem Lehrer**.	*Marie thanks her teacher.*
Wem gehört dieser Wagen?	*Who owns this car?* (Literally: *To whom does this car belong?*)
Diese Stadt gefällt **mir**.	*I like this city.* (Literally: *This city is pleasing **to me**.*)

Note that **gefallen** is another way of saying that you like something. However, since its literal meaning is *to please* (*someone*), the subject and object are the reverse of English. Remember that the verb must agree in number with the subject.

SAM **Lab Manual** Kap. 7, Var. zu Üb. 7.

SAM **Workbook** Kap. 7, D, E.

Die Vorlesungen gefallen **mir**. Literally: *The lectures please me.*

***I** like the **lectures**.*

7 Übung: Was gefällt Ihnen hier? Was gefällt Ihnen an dieser Uni oder diesem College? Hier sind einige Möglichkeiten (*possibilities*).

die Deutschstunde	mein Zimmer
das Essen in der Mensa	das Klima
meine Mitbewohner	die Professoren
die Vorlesungen	die anderen (*other*) Studenten

BEISPIEL: Mir gefällt das Klima.

8 Übung: Wem haben Sie einmal geholfen? Im ersten Dialog auf Seite 175 („Am Bahnhof") hilft ein Student einer Touristin mit ihrem Koffer. Sagen Sie, wem Sie einmal geholfen haben.

BEISPIEL: Ich habe einmal meiner Mutter geholfen.

9 Übung: Wem gehört das Buch? Say what belongs to whom.

BEISPIEL: A: Wem gehört dieses Buch?
B: Es gehört mir. Es ist mein Buch.

4. Personal dative

The dative case is also used to indicate a person's involvement in or reaction to a situation. This *personal dative* is often translated by English *to* or *for*.

Wie geht es **dir**?	*How are you?* (Literally: *How is it going **for you**?*)
Wie geht es **deiner Mutter**?	*How is **your mother**?*
Es ist **mir** kalt.	*I'm cold.*
Diese Farbe ist **mir** zu dunkel.	*This color is too dark **for me**.*
Das ist **mir** egal.	*It's all the same **to me**.*
Das macht **mir** Spaß.	*That's fun **for me**.*

When personal dative is omitted, a statement is more absolute. Contrast **Es ist zu dunkel** with **Es ist mir zu dunkel**.

The personal dative may often be omitted without changing the basic meaning of the sentence.

Ist es kalt?	Wie geht es?
Die Farbe ist zu dunkel.	Das macht Spaß.

It may *not* be omitted in the following idiom:

Das tut mir Leid. *I'm sorry about that.*

SAM **Lab Manual** Kap. 7, Var. zu Üb. 10.

SAM **Workbook** Kap. 7, F.

auch nicht = *not . . . either*

10 Übung: Ist es Ihnen zu kalt? Your instructor asks how you feel about something. Give your opinion, then ask your neighbor for an opinion.

BEISPIEL: Ist es Ihnen hier zu kalt?
A: Mir ist es nicht zu kalt. Und dir?
B: Mir ist es auch nicht zu kalt.

1. Ist es Ihnen zu dunkel hier?
2. Ist Ihnen dieses Zimmer zu heiß?
3. Ist Ihnen ein BMW zu teuer?
4. Ist Ihnen dieser Stuhl zu hart (*hard*)?
5. Macht Ihnen Deutsch Spaß?
6. Ist Ihnen der Winter hier zu kalt?

11 Partnerarbeit: Reaktionen. Make at least three statements (invented or real) about how things are going for you, what you're doing at the moment, etc. Your partner must decide whether to respond with indifference, sympathy, or enthusiasm. Then switch roles.

BEISPIEL: A: Ich muss morgen eine Klausur schreiben.
B: Oh, das tut mir Leid. (*oder*) Das ist mir egal.

B: Am Dienstag fahren wir nach Venedig.
A: Das finde ich toll!

5. Using *würden* + infinitive

Expressing opinions, preferences, and polite requests is a communicative goal.

To express opinions, preferences, and polite requests, **würden** is used with an infinitive.

Ich **würde** das nicht **machen**.	*I wouldn't do that.*
Was **würdest** du gerne **tun**?	*What would you like to do?*
Würden Sie mir den Koffer **tragen**?	*Would you carry my suitcase?*

Würden is the German equivalent of English *would*. It functions like a modal verb, with a dependent infinitive in final position.

würden *would*			
ich	**würde** sagen, ...	wir	**würden** sagen, ...
du	**würdest** sagen, ...	ihr	**würdet** sagen, ...
er, sie	**würde** sagen, ...	sie, Sie	**würden** sagen, ...

12 Gruppenarbeit: Würden Sie bitte . . . ? Ask your instructor to do a favor for you. Some possibilities are listed below.

BEISPIEL: Würden Sie bitte das Fenster schließen?

mir den Koffer tragen	für uns ein Foto machen
mir eine Brezel kaufen	Lebensmittel einkaufen
das Mittagessen kochen	Ihre Arbeit beschreiben
mir den Bahnhof zeigen	mir den Straßenatlas geben

13 Kettenreaktion: Ich würde gern . . . Was würden Sie dieses Wochenende gerne machen? Sagen Sie es und dann fragen Sie weiter.

BEISPIEL: A: Dieses Wochenende würde ich gern ______. Und du?
B: Ich würde gern ______.

Expressing preferences is a communicative goal.

14 Partnerarbeit: Was würdest du lieber machen? Here are some choices you might make when traveling. Ask each other which you would rather do. State a preference and give a reason.

BEISPIEL:

sprechen
Ihre Muttersprache? eine Fremdsprache?
Ich würde lieber eine Fremdsprache sprechen, denn das macht mehr Spaß.

übernachten (*stay overnight*)
im Hotel? in einer Jugendherberge (*youth hostel*)?

reisen
mit dem Wagen? mit dem Zug?

mitbringen
einen Rucksack? einen Koffer?

Mit dem Fahrrad (*bicycle*) kann man billig reisen und auch fit bleiben. Wo ist Thüringen? Was bedeutet Fernradwanderwege?

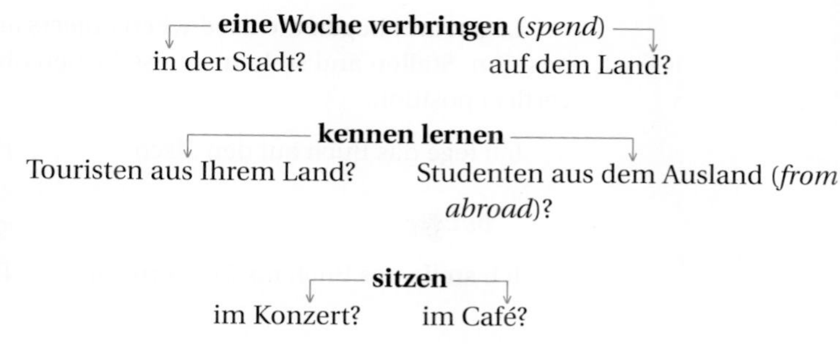

6. Verbs with two-way prepositions

There is an important group of verb pairs used with the two-way prepositions. One verb shows destination and always takes the accusative case. The other shows location and always takes the dative case.

Review two-way prepositions on pp. 158–159.

Destination (accusative)	Location (dative)
weak transitive verbs	**strong intransitive verbs**
legen, hat gelegt *to lay (down), put* Ich lege das Buch **auf den Schreibtisch.** *I'm putting the book on the desk.*	**liegen, hat gelegen** *to lie, be lying* Das Buch liegt **auf dem Schreibtisch**. *The book is (lying) on the desk.*
setzen, hat gesetzt *to set (down), put* Sie setzt das Kind **auf den Stuhl**. *She's putting the child on the chair.*	**sitzen, hat gesessen** *to sit, be sitting* Das Kind sitzt **auf dem Stuhl**. *The child is (sitting) on the chair.*
stellen, hat gestellt *to place (down), put* Ich stelle die Flasche **auf den Tisch**. *I'll put the bottle on the table.*	**stehen, hat gestanden** *to stand, be standing* Die Flasche steht **auf dem Tisch**. *The bottle is (standing) on the table.*
hängen, hat gehängt *to hang up* Er hat die Karte **an die Wand** gehängt. *He hung the map on the wall.*	**hängen, hat gehangen** *to be hanging* Die Karte hat **an der Wand** gehangen. *The map hung on the wall.*

The weak verb **stecken** is both transitive and intransitive.

Ich habe das Geld **in meine Tasche** gesteckt. *I put the money into my pocket.*	Das Geld steckt **in meiner Tasche**. *The money's in my pocket.*

Note that **hängen** has one infinitive form but a weak participle (**gehängt**) and a strong participle (**gehangen**).

Legen and **liegen** are used when objects are *laid down* or are *lying* in a horizontal position. **Stellen** and **stehen** are used when objects are *stood up* or are *standing* in a vertical position.

Ich **lege** das Buch auf den Tisch. — *I'm putting the book (down flat) on the table.*

but:

Ich **stelle** das Buch ins Bücherregal. — *I'm putting the book (upright) in the bookcase.*

Workbook Kap. 7, G, H.

15 Übung: Bei Frau Schneider zu Hause. Frau Schneider is working around the house. Describe what she is doing in the left-hand pictures, then the results of her efforts in the right-hand pictures.

16 Gruppenarbeit: Was mache ich jetzt? The class is divided into two groups. The instructor does various things, and each team in turn tries to describe the action. A correct answer scores a point. If your team answers incorrectly, the other team has a chance to describe the same action.

BEISPIEL: A: Was mache ich jetzt?
B: Sie stellen die Flasche auf den Stuhl.

Telling time with the 24-hour clock is a communicative goal.

7. Official time-telling

Wann kann man Dr. Niederstadt donnerstags in der Praxis besuchen?

Brokerage 24
21.45 ist in Deutschland Schlafenszeit, in New York Börsenzeit, bei uns immer noch Orderzeit.

You already know how to tell time in German (see page 13). For official time-telling, however, there is another system. One gives the full hour and the number of minutes past it. In addition, rather than AM or PM, the twenty-four hour clock is used. This is the way the time is given in the media, in train schedules, on announcements of events, etc. Subtract 12 to get the PM time as expressed in English.

Written	Spoken	English
1.40 Uhr	ein Uhr vierzig	*1:40 AM*
7.55 Uhr	7 Uhr 55	*7:55 AM*
13.25 Uhr	13 Uhr 25	*1:25 PM*
20.00 Uhr	zwanzig Uhr	*8:00 PM*

Midnight can be both **0 Uhr** and **24.00 Uhr**. However, one minute past midnight is **0.01** (**null Uhr eins**).

LIEBE IST… EIN STÄDTETRIP NACH PARIS!

SCHON AB € 29,- INKL. SITZPLATZRESERVIERUNG BRINGT SIE DAS SPARSCHIENE-TICKET NACH PARIS.

EN 262		EN 263
20:34	Wien Westbahnhof	08:30
23:57	Salzburg Hbf.	04:44
10:27	Paris Est	17:16

Lab Manual Kap. 7, Üb. 17.

Workbook Kap. 7, I.

17 Übung: Wie viel Uhr ist es? Sagen Sie die Uhrzeit auf Deutsch.

BEISPIEL: 11:20 PM
Es ist 23.20 Uhr (dreiundzwanzig Uhr zwanzig).

1. 1:55 PM
2. 6:02 PM
3. 11:31 AM
4. 9:47 PM
5. 10:52 PM
6. 2:25 AM

Info-Austausch

18 Wann kommt der Zug an? Arbeiten Sie mit einem Partner zusammen und ergänzen Sie (*complete*) die Informationen in dem Zugfahrplan am Hauptbahnhof Mannheim.

BEISPIEL: A: Wann kommt der Zug Nummer 6342 in Mannheim an?
B: Um 14.22 Uhr. Wann fährt der Zug Nummer 2203 nach Innsbruck in Mannheim ab?

Partner A:

Ankunft (*arrivals*) **und Abfahrt** (*departures*)					
Zug-Nr.	**ab**[1]	**an**[1]	**Zug-Nr.**	**ab**	**an**
6342	Hamburg	Mannheim	1338	Mannheim	Zürich
	9.33 Uhr				8.12 Uhr
7422	München	Mannheim	2472	Mannheim	Nürnberg
		13.10 Uhr			9.33 Uhr
1387	Frankfurt/Main	Mannheim	6606	Mannheim	Straßburg
	11.20 Uhr			7.55 Uhr	
7703	Wien	Mannheim	2203	Mannheim	Innsbruck
	10.10 Uhr			10.12 Uhr	
9311	Berlin	Mannheim	3679	Mannheim	Prag
		19.16 Uhr		13.23 Uhr	

The train schedule for Partner B is found in Appendix 1.

[1] **ab** = place and time of departure; **an** = place and time of arrival.

LESESTÜCK

Tipps zum Lesen und Lernen

Tipps zum Vokabelnlernen

Translating English *to spend* The reading passage in this chapter mentions spending both time and money. Note the different verbs that German uses to distinguish between these two kinds of spending.

Zeit: verbringen

Wir ***verbringen*** unsere Ferien in den Alpen.	*We're spending our vacation in the Alps.*
Sie hat den Nachmittag zu Hause ***verbracht***.	*She spent the afternoon at home.*

Sparen (*to save*) is used with both time *and* money.

Geld: ausgeben

Wie viel muss man für ein Zimmer **ausgeben**?	*How much do you have to spend for a room?*
Wir haben sehr viel Geld **ausgegeben**.	*We spent a lot of money.*

Note the verbal noun in Wilhelm Müller's poem on p. 178: ***Das Wandern* ist des Müllers Lust.**

Verbal nouns Any German infinitive may act as a noun. It is then capitalized and is always neuter.

reisen → **das Reisen** (*traveling*)

Das Reisen ist heutzutage leicht.	*Traveling is easy nowadays.*

These verbal nouns correspond to English gerunds (the form ending in *-ing*); some have additional, more specific meanings. For instance, **das Essen** means *eating* but also *food* and *meal*. Here are some other examples:

das **Fliegen**	*flying*
das **Lernen**	*learning, studying*
das **Leben**	*living; life*
das **Sein**	*being; existence*
das **Wissen**	*knowing; knowledge*

Lab Manual Kap. 7, Üb. zur Betonung.

Leicht zu merken

der **Horizont, -e**	Horizont
das **Instrument, -e**	Instrument
die **Kamera, -s**	
der **Kontakt, -e**	Kontakt
packen	
spontan	
die **Tour, -en**	
die **Wanderlust**	

Einstieg in den Text

In "Unterwegs mit Fahrrad, Auto und der Bahn," three young people describe their experiences traveling in Europe. First read over Wortschatz 2 to preview new vocabulary. Then, to gain a first impression of the text, simply skim it; do not read it word for word. Look for familiar travel-related vocabulary and keep an eye out for context clues. As you skim, you will find obvious cognates, such as **Instrument**.

After skimming the text, go back and read it through once completely. Use the following questions as a guide to highlight some main ideas. See whether you can answer them after a first reading.

Wie kann man durch Europa reisen?
Warum reisen diese Menschen gern?
Wie kann man beim Reisen Geld sparen?
Wo kann man unterwegs Menschen kennen lernen?
Wo kann man auf der Reise übernachten?

Im Flugzeug am Fensterplatz

Wortschatz 2

Unterwegs (*on the go; en route*)

ein·steigen, ist eingestiegen to get in (*to a vehicle*)
aus·steigen, ist ausgestiegen to get out (*of a vehicle*)
Rad fahren (fährt Rad), ist Rad gefahren to bicycle
übernachten to spend the night
der **Führerschein, -e** driver's license
  den Führerschein machen to get one's driver's license
der **Rucksäcke, ¨-e** rucksack, backpack
das **Ausland** (*sing.*) foreign countries
  im Ausland abroad (*location*)
  ins Ausland abroad (*destination*)
das **Benzin** gasoline
das **Fahrrad, ¨-er** bicycle
  das **Rad, ¨-er** wheel; bike (*slang*)
das **Flugzeug, -e** airplane
die **Autobahn, -en** expressway, high-speed highway
die **Bahn** railroad; railroad system
die **Fahrkarte, -n** ticket (*for means of transportation*)
die **Jugendherberge, -n** youth hostel

Verben

genießen, hat genossen to enjoy
hoffen to hope
quatschen (*colloq.*) to talk nonsense; to chat
sparen to save (*money or time*)
verbringen, hat verbracht (+ *time phrase*) to spend (*time*)

Substantive

der **Geburtstag, -e** birthday
  Wann hast du Geburtstag? When is your birthday?
der **Platz, ¨-e** seat
das **Ding, -e** thing
das **Foto, -s** photograph
  ein Foto machen to take a picture
(das) **Frankreich** France
(das) **München** Munich
die **Freiheit, -en** freedom
die **Tasche, -n** pocket; hand *or* shoulder bag

The word **Frankreich** recalls the original empire of the Franks (**die Franken**), a Germanic tribe that settled mainly west of the Rhine. The greatest Frankish king was Charlemagne (**Karl der Große**), 747–814 A.D.

Adjektive und Adverbien

bequem comfortable
gut gelaunt in a good mood
herrlich great, terrific, marvelous
italienisch Italian
pünktlich punctual, on time
so so
sympathisch friendly, congenial, likeable
unbekannt unknown
verliebt in (+ *acc.*) in love with
  Sie ist in ihn verliebt. She's in love with him.
verrückt crazy, insane

Andere Wörter

nicht nur ... sondern auch not only . . . but also
viele (*pron.*) many people

Gegensätze

bekannt ≠ unbekannt known; well-known ≠ unknown
bequem ≠ unbequem comfortable ≠ uncomfortable
gut gelaunt ≠ schlecht gelaunt in a good mood ≠ in a bad mood
sympathisch ≠ unsympathisch likeable; friendly ≠ unlikeable; unfriendly

Radfahrerin im Altmühltal, Bayern

Unterwegs mit Fahrrad, Auto und der Bahn

Mit dem Sommer kommt wieder die Wanderlust. Dann packt man den Koffer oder den Rucksack und macht eine Reise. Viele fahren mit dem eigenen° Wagen oder mit dem Flugzeug, aber junge Leute mit wenig Geld in der Tasche können nicht immer so viel ausgeben. Sie fahren lieber mit der Bahn oder machen Radtouren. Ein paar erzählen hier von ihren Reiseerfahrungen°.

own
Learning about traveling in Europe is the cultural goal of this chapter.
travel experiences

Adrienne, 18, Azubi° aus Kaisersaschern

= Lehrling

„Radfahren erweitert° den Horizont. Ich habe oft mit meinem Freund Markus in Deutschland und auch im Ausland Radtouren unternommen°. Das Radfahren macht uns echt Spaß und hält° uns fit. Uns gefallen besonders die kleinen unbekannten Dörfer und Täler. Man kann sie einfach nicht genießen, wenn° man mit 160[2] auf der Autobahn vorbeisaust°!

broadens
taken
keeps
when
roars by

Letzten Sommer waren wir zwei Wochen in Italien unterwegs und haben überall Glück gehabt: Das Wetter war herrlich, die Menschen waren sympathisch und wir haben auch eine Menge Geld gespart. Ich glaube, wir waren unterwegs fast immer gut gelaunt. Wir sind von Venedig nach Florenz[3] gefahren und haben immer in Jugendherbergen übernachtet. In einer Gaststätte° auf dem Land haben wir eine nette italienische Familie kennen gelernt. Sie haben ein bisschen Deutsch verstehen können und wir haben sogar drei Tage bei ihnen verbracht. Mit meiner Kamera habe ich ein paar schöne Fotos von den Kindern gemacht. Ich hoffe, wir können in Kontakt bleiben und vielleicht besuchen sie uns nächstes Jahr. Ja, im Zug oder im Auto lernt man die Menschen einfach nicht so gut kennen."

= kleines Restaurant

Thomas, 19, Abiturient° aus München

pupil in the last year of Gymnasium

„Die Deutschen waren schon immer in ihre Autos verliebt. Letztes Jahr habe ich den Führerschein gemacht und zum Geburtstag haben mir meine Eltern einen Gebrauchtwagen° geschenkt. Ein amerikanischer Freund hat mir erzählt, in den USA darf man schon mit 16° Auto fahren. Da bin ich aber neidisch°, denn bei uns darf man das erst mit 18 Jahren. Die Versicherung° und Benzin muss ich natürlich selber bezahlen, aber das ist kein großes Problem, und die Bewegungsfreiheit° gefällt mir sehr.

used car
mit ... *at age 16 / envious*
insurance
freedom of movement

In München fahre ich natürlich meistens mit der Straßenbahn und der S-Bahn°, denn in der Stadt findet man keinen Parkplatz. Aber am Wochenende kann ich jetzt mit Freunden spontan in die Berge zum Skifahren oder Klettern° fahren. Nach dem Abitur planen wir eine große Tour über° Südfrankreich an die Costa del Sol".[4]

Straßenbahn ... *streetcar and urban rail system*
rock climbing
via

Herbert, 29, Assistenzarzt° aus Jena[5]

resident (physician)

„Als Student bin ich manchmal per Autostopp gereist°, aber heute würde ich das nicht mehr machen. Die Unsicherheit° ist mir zu stressig und ich habe nicht mehr so viel Freizeit. Das Reisen mit der Bahn gefällt mir, denn es ist sehr praktisch und bequem. Man geht einfach zum Bahnhof, kauft eine Fahrkarte und steigt in den Zug ein. Und meistens kommt man pünktlich an.

per ... *hitchhiked*
uncertainty

---

[2] 160 = **160 km/h (Stundenkilometer)**.
[3] **Florenz**: Florence, city in Tuscany famous as a center of Italian Renaissance culture.
[4] **Costa del Sol:** Popular Mediterranean resort area on the southeastern coast of Spain.
[5] **Jena**: University town on the Saale River

Im Zug quatsche ich gern ein bisschen mit den Mitreisenden° über viele Dinge. Letztes Wochenende bin ich zum Beispiel nach Berlin gefahren. Neben mir hat ein Musikstudent aus Leipzig gesessen. Er ist in Wittenberg[6] ausgestiegen und ich habe ihm mit seinem Gepäck geholfen. Er hatte° nicht nur einen Rucksack und einen Koffer mit, sondern auch eine Bassgeige°. Für sein Instrument hat er einen zweiten° Platz reservieren müssen. Verrückt, nicht?"

fellow passengers

had

double bass / second

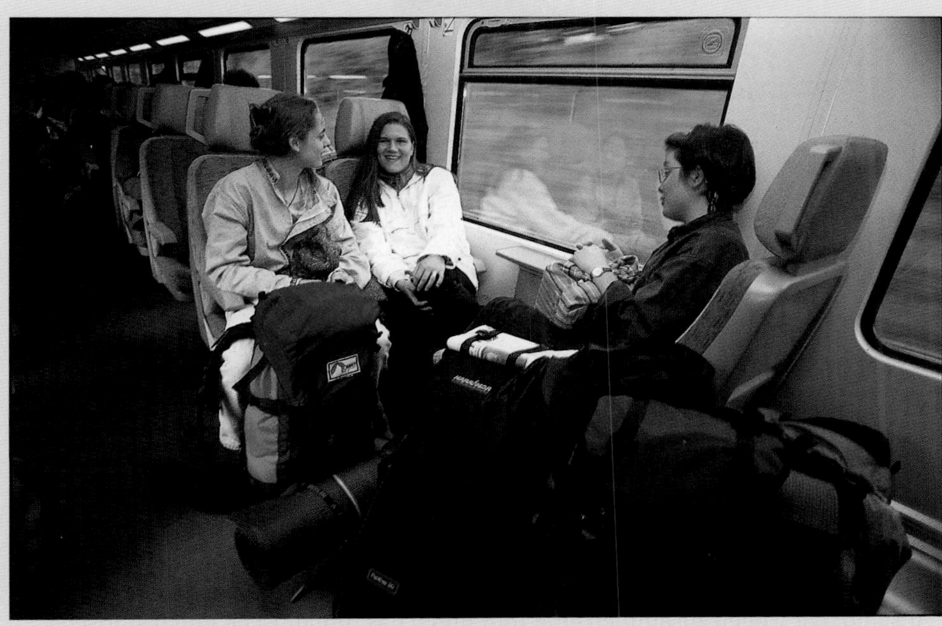

Unterwegs mit der Bahn

[6] The composer Johann Sebastian Bach (1685–1750) spent the greater part of his life in **Leipzig** (in the state of Saxony). The church reformer Martin Luther (1483–1546) is buried in **Wittenberg** (in the state of Saxony-Anhalt).

NACH DEM LESEN

SAM  **Lab Manual** Kap. 7, Diktat.

SAM  **Workbook** Kap. 7, J.

A Antworten Sie auf Deutsch.

1. Mit welchen Verkehrsmitteln (*means of transportation*) kann man reisen?
2. Wohin ist Adrienne mit dem Rad gefahren?
3. Hat es ihr Spaß gemacht? Warum?
4. Wen hat sie in Italien kennen gelernt?
5. Wo kann man billig übernachten?
6. In welchem Alter (*at what age*) macht man in Deutschland den Führerschein?
7. Ein Auto kann teuer sein. Muss Thomas alles selber (*himself*) bezahlen?
8. Wohin fährt Thomas nach dem Abitur?
9. Warum würde Herbert heute nicht mehr per Autostopp fahren?
10. Warum fährt er gern mit dem Zug?
11. Wen hat er im Zug kennen gelernt? Warum hat er das komisch gefunden?

Urlaub auf dem Bauernhof
Ferien auf dem Lande

Seite 140 Marlene Jensen, Steinbergkirche
Einzelhof, ruhig und schön gelegen, Spielplatz, Tischtennis, Fahrräder, 7 km zur Ostsee, BAB-Abfahrt Tarp, Bahnstation Sörup.

B Gruppenarbeit: Eine Radtour durch das Neckartal. ***(3–4 Personen)*** Der Allgemeine Deutsche Fahrrad-Club (ADFC) organisiert viele Radtouren in Deutschland und im Ausland. Wir wollen zusammen eine Tour durch das romantische und historische Neckartal planen, aber wir brauchen einige Infos (*facts*) aus der Broschüre (auf Seite 197) vom ADFC.

1. Wie lang ist die Tour? (________ km)
2. Wo beginnt sie?
3. Wo endet sie?
4. Wo in Deutschland ist das Neckartal? im Nordosten?
5. Durch welche Großstadt würden wir fahren?
6. Welche zwei Kulturstädte würden wir sehen?
7. Die Broschüre beschreibt ein Pauschalangebot (*package tour*) mit Übernachtung und Frühstück (ÜF). Wie viele Tage dauert diese Tour?
8. Was kostet sie pro Person in Euro? (€ ________)

DER NECKARTAL RADWEG

Bahnhof Schwenningen

Neckarquelle im Stadtpark Möglingshöhe

AUF EINEN BLICK

teilweise hügelig

Anreise: Villingen, Rottweil, Stuttgart, Heidelberg
Länge: 375 km
Beginn: Villingen-Schwenningen
Ziel: Heidelberg
Charakter: Die Route entlang des Neckar erschließt dem Radler gegensätzliche und sehenswerte Landschaften, kombiniert mit Kulturstädten wie Tübingen und Heidelberg oder der Metropole Stuttgart. Ausbauzustand und das nur gelegentliche Vorhandensein von Steigungen machen die Route für jeden befahrbar.
Wegweisung: grünes Fahrrad mit rot-gestreiftem Vorderrad und Routennamen auf weißem Grund

Karten- und Literaturtipps:
Radtourenbuch „Neckar-Radweg", 1:50.000, Esterbauer-Verlag; Radwanderkarte „Neckartal-Radweg", Bielefelder Verlagsanstalt; Radwanderkarte „Neckartal-Radweg", Stöppel Verlag; Fahrradführer „Am Strom entlang", Moby Dick Verlag

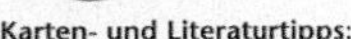

weitere Infos:
Arbeitsgemeinschaft Neckartal-Radweg
Verkehrsamt Villingen-Schwenningen
Bahnhof Schwenningen,
78054 Villingen-Schwenningen
Tel. + 49 (0) 77 20/81 02 77
Fax + 49 (0) 77 20/81 02 79
e-mail: neckartalradweg@t-online.de

PAUSCHALANGEBOTE:

8x ÜF, Infopaket, Gepäcktransfer, DZ

p.P. ab 822,- DM / 420,28 €

Tel.: +49/(0) 77 20/81 02 77

54

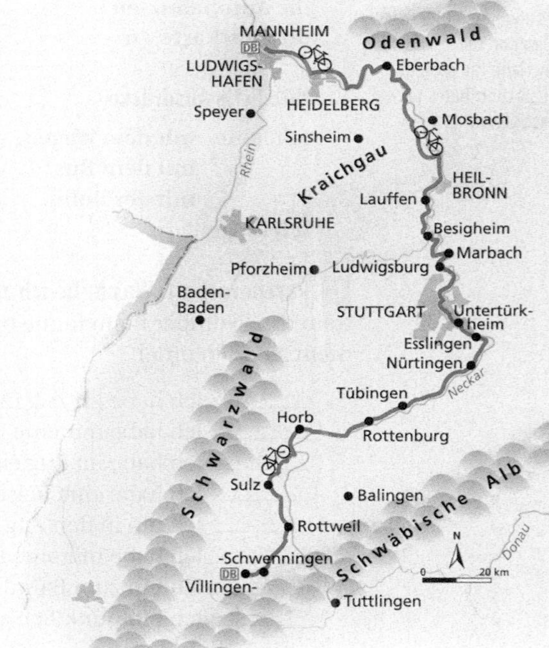

This vocabulary focuses on an everday topic or situation. Words you already know from **Wortschatz** sections are listed without English equivalents; new supplementary vocabulary is listed with definitions. Your instructor may assign some supplementary vocabulary for active mastery.

Vokabeln zum Thema Reisen und Verkehr (*travel and traffic*)

Some of these words are already familiar.

Verben

ab·fahren ≠ an·kommen
ein·steigen ≠ aus·steigen
um·steigen — *to transfer, change (buses, trains, etc.)*

Substantive

der **Bahnhof, ¨-e**
der **Bus, -se** — *bus*
der **Flughafen, ¨** — *airport*
der **Verkehr** — *traffic*
der **Wagen, -**
der **Zug, ¨-e**
das **Auto, -s**
das **Flugzeug, -e**
das **Ticket, -s** — *ticket*
die **Autobahn, -en**
die **Fahrkarte, -n**

Das Ticket is used mainly for airline tickets and international train travel. In a train, however, the conductor will say **Fahrkarten, bitte** (*Tickets, please*).

Debate continues about whether to impose a speed limit on the **Autobahn**. Many claim the present lack of a speed limit contributes to Germany's high accident rate.

Nützliche Ausdrücke

Ich fahre **mit dem Wagen**. — *. . . by car.*
mit dem Bus. — *. . . by bus.*
mit der Bahn. — *. . . by train.*
Ich fliege.

C Partnerarbeit: Was habe ich zuerst gemacht? Here are eight statements about a train trip. Number them in the order that the events most likely happened. Then read them aloud in order.

_______ Ich habe im Zug mit der Frau neben mir gequatscht.
_______ Ich habe mir eine Fahrkarte gekauft.
_______ Ich habe im Zug einen guten Roman gelesen.
_______ Ich habe eine Reise ins Ausland machen wollen.
_______ Ich bin in den Zug eingestiegen.
_______ Ich habe mir eine Landkarte gekauft.
_______ Ich bin zum Bahnhof gegangen.
_______ Ich bin pünktlich angekommen.

Making travel plans and talking about traveling is a communicative goal.

D Gruppenarbeit: Planen wir unsere Reise. (*4 Personen*) Planen Sie eine Reise nach Europa. Besprechen Sie diese Fragen zusammen. Benutzen Sie die Landkarte.

Welche Länder wollen wir besuchen?
Wie lange wollen wir bleiben?
Wie wollen wir durch Europa reisen? Mit der Bahn? Mit dem Rad? Mit dem Auto?
Wo wollen wir übernachten? In einer Jugendherberge? Im Hotel?
Was wollen wir mitnehmen? Machen wir eine Liste.
Haben wir etwas vergessen?

Jetzt berichtet jede Gruppe über ihre Pläne.

Talking on the telephone is a communicative goal.

E Partnerarbeit: Am Telefon. Choose one of the following situations and invent a telephone conversation. Since long distance rates are expensive, be brief and convey as much information as efficiently as you can.

1. Phone a friend to report about your vacation abroad.
2. Phone home to say you have arrived somewhere.
3. Phone your roommate to say you've forgotten something.
4. Find out whether a youth hostel or hotel has room for you.

SCHREIBTIPP

More on free writing

In **Kapitel 4** (p. 115) you were given some tips on free writing in German. Now that you have learned how to use the perfect tense, you can write about your own experiences in the past. In the first option below you are asked to recount a trip you have taken.

- Write only in German, not in English.
- Make preliminary notes about your memories of the trip, using "telegram style" instead of complete sentences, e.g., **2006 nach Kalifornien; mit Familie; im Meer geschwommen**.
- Look up vocabulary in an English-German dictionary only when absolutely necessary.
- Adverbs of time you already know will give your account a clear beginning, middle, and end: **Am Anfang ... und dann ... nachher ... endlich**.

Schreiben wir mal.

1. Sie haben sicher schon einmal eine interessante Reise gemacht. Schreiben Sie eine Seite über diese Reise.
2. Schreiben Sie das Gespräch (*conversation*) im Zug zwischen Herbert und dem Musikstudenten aus Leipzig. (Siehe S. 194–195.)

F Wie sagt man das auf Deutsch?

1. Did you take a trip this year?
2. Yes, we went to Italy.
3. How did you like it? (*use* **gefallen**)
4. Very much. We especially enjoyed Venice.
5. Does this suitcase belong to you?
6. Not to me, but to my brother.
7. Where should I put it?
8. Would you please put it under the table?
9. How's your husband?
10. It's his birthday today.
11. Unfortunately he's sick and has to spend the day in bed.
12. Oh, I'm sorry about that.

ALMANACH

VIDEO

Jugendherbergen

There are about 550 **Jugendherbergen** in Germany, 40 in Austria, 58 in Switzerland, and 10 in Luxembourg. They are meeting places for young travelers from all over the world. In addition to providing inexpensive food and lodging, they offer a variety of courses and organized trips.

Membership in the AYH (American Youth Hostels) entitles the cardholder to privileges in hostels all over the world. Membership costs as of 2007: under 18 years of age, free; 18–54, $28.00; 55 and over, $18.00. To apply for membership, write to:

American Youth Hostels, Inc.
733 15th St. NW, Suite 840
Washington, D.C. 20005
(202) 783-6161
FAX: (202) 783-6171

You can find Web addresses for youth hostel organizations in the United States and the German-speaking countries on the ***Neue Horizonte*** Website.

Here are some excerpts from the Youth Hostel handbook for Germany.

Tübingen 32 A2

Name:	JH Tübingen
Adresse:	Gartenstr. 22/2 72074 Tübingen Tel. 07071/23002; Fax 25061 email: jh-tübingen@t-online.de
Herbergseltern:	Ingrid und Gerhard Barth
Träger:	LVB Baden-Württemberg
Raumangebot:	161 Betten, 5 Tagesräume, 19 Betreuerzimmer
Kat.IV Preis:	Jun. Ü/F 28,00 DM Jun. Ü/F 14,32 € Sen. Ü/F 33,00 DM Sen. Ü/F 16,87 €
Sport & Freizeit:	Motorradfreizeiten mit Sichherheitstraining, Bootsverleih am Neckar
Geschlossen:	zeitweise im Winter, bitte voranmelden
Sonstiges:	grundsätzlich Halbpension und Vollpension gegen Aufpreis möglich
Nächste JH:	Erpfingen-Sonnenbühl, 30 km Esslingen, 40 km

T

Lage und Anreise: Am Rande des Stadtkerns, direkt am Neckar.
Bahnhof 1 km. Ab Europaplatz mit Bus Linie 11 bis Haltestelle "Jugendherberge".
Auto: B 27 oder A 81.

592

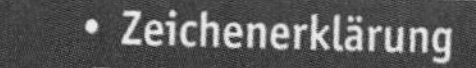

• Zeichenerklärung •
• Explanation of Signs •
• Explication des Symboles •
• Explicacion de los Simbolos •

Für Familien geeignet
Suitable for families
Convient aux familles
Hay habitaciones familiares

Für Seminare geeignet
Suitable for training courses
Convient aux stages d´instruction
Hay habitaciores para seminarios

Für Rollstuhlfahrer geeignet*
Suitable for wheelchair users
Convient aux fauteuils roulants
Instalaciones adecuadas para usuarios con sillas de ruedas

Musikinstrumente vorhanden/für Musikgruppen geeignet
musical instruments in the youth hostel/
suitable for music groups
instruments de musique à l'auberge/
convient aux groupes de musique
instrumentos de música en el albergue/
preparado para grupos de música

Sportmöglichkeiten im/am Haus
Sports available at or near the hostel
Sports à ou près de l´auberge
Instalaciones deportivas en o cerca del albergue

Wintersport
Ski hostel
Centre de ski
Zona de esquí

* Für Rollstuhlfahrer stehen geeignete Zimmer und Sanitäreinrichtungen zur Verfügung. Die Anzahl der Zimmer reicht nicht immer für Gruppen aus. Bitte in der Jugendherberge anfragen.

EZ	Einzelzimmer
DZ	Doppelzimmer
FZ	Familienzimmer
LZ	Leiterzimmer
TR	Tagesraum

Die angegebenen Preise verstehen sich, sofern nichts anderes angegeben, inklusive Frühstück.

KAPITEL

8

Berlin, Kreuzberg

Das Leben in der Stadt

Kommunikation

- Talking about food
- Ordering in a restaurant
- Discussing city life
- Asking for directions

Kultur

- Life in German cities

In diesem Kapitel

- **Lyrik zum Vorlesen**
  Ernst Stadler, "Kleine Stadt"
- **Grammatik**
  1. Subordinate clauses and subordinating conjunctions
  2. Infinitive constructions with **zu**
  3. Genitive case
  4. Prepositions with the genitive case
  5. Nouns of measure, weight, and number
  6. Equivalents of English *to*
- **Lesestück**
  Aspekte der Großstadt
- **Almanach**
  Mit dem Bus durch Berlin

DIALOGE

Lab Manual Kap. 8, Dialoge, Fragen, Hören Sie gut zu!, Üb. zur Aussprache [**e/er**].

Hat es Ihnen geschmeckt? (*How was everything?*) means literally *Did it taste good to you?*

Remember: € **13,50** is spoken **dreizehn Euro fünfzig**. Note on tipping (**Trinkgeld** = *tip*): Many restaurants automatically add 15% for service to the bill. When paying, however, it is customary to round up the bill.

It is customary in German-speaking countries to eat a hot meal at noon and a simple supper of cold cuts, bread, cheese, and salad in the evening.

Im Restaurant: Zahlen bitte!

GAST: Zahlen bitte!
KELLNERIN: Augenblick, bitte! ... (*Sie kommt an den Tisch.*) So, hat es Ihnen geschmeckt?
GAST: Ausgezeichnet!
KELLNERIN: Möchten Sie noch etwas bestellen?
GAST: Nein, danke, ich möchte zahlen, bitte.
KELLNERIN: Sie haben Schnitzel, Pommes frites, einen Salat und ein Bier gehabt, nicht wahr?
GAST: Ja, und auch eine Tasse Kaffee.
KELLNERIN: Das macht zusammen € 13,50, bitte sehr.
GAST: (*Gibt ihr 20 Euro*) 14 Euro.
KELLNERIN: Danke sehr, und sechs Euro zurück.

Was brauchen wir noch?

DORA: Heute Morgen habe ich Max zum Abendessen eingeladen. Weißt du, ob er kommt?
FRANZ: Ja, aber er hat mir gesagt, dass er erst um halb sieben kommen kann. Wie viel Uhr ist es jetzt?
DORA: Halb sechs. Also muss ich noch schnell um die Ecke, um ein paar Sachen einzukaufen. Was brauchen wir noch?
FRANZ: Ein Kilo Kartoffeln, 200 Gramm Leberwurst, Käse, eine Flasche Rotwein und Obst zum Nachtisch.
DORA: Ist das alles?
FRANZ: Ich glaube schon.

EINE FRAGE DES GELDES

Ein Stadtbummel

Marianne besucht ihren Freund Helmut in Köln. Er hat ihr das Stadtzentrum noch nicht gezeigt, weil es geregnet hat.

Du is used here as an attention-getter, equivalent to *hey, look*.

HELMUT: Du, der Regen hat endlich aufgehört! Hast du jetzt Lust etwas zu unternehmen?
MARIANNE: Ja gerne! Jetzt können wir unseren Stadtbummel machen, aber können wir zuerst etwas essen? Ich hab' so einen Hunger!
HELMUT: Selbstverständlich! In der Nähe des Doms gibt es ein Lokal, wo wir griechisch essen können.
MARIANNE: Hmm, das klingt lecker!
HELMUT: Nachher können wir dann den Dom besuchen und von da ist es nicht mehr weit zum Kunstmuseum.

Wortschatz 1

In-Text Audio CD

Essen und Trinken

der **Durst** thirst
Durst haben to be thirsty
der **Hunger** hunger
Hunger haben to be hungry
der **Nachtisch** dessert
zum Nachtisch for dessert
der **Salat, -e** salad; lettuce
das **Abendessen** supper, dinner, evening meal
zum Abendessen for supper
das **Lokal, -e** neighborhood restaurant or tavern
das **Restaurant, -s** restaurant
das **Schnitzel, -** cutlet, chop
die **Kartoffel, -n** potato
die **Wurst, ¨-e** sausage
die **Leberwurst** liverwurst

Verben

bestellen to order
ein·laden (lädt ein), hat eingeladen to invite
klingen, hat geklungen to sound
schmecken to taste; to taste good
Wie schmeckt es dir? How does it taste? How do you like it?
unternehmen (unternimmt), hat unternommen to do, start *(an activity)*, undertake
Hast du Lust etwas zu unternehmen? Do you want to do something?
zahlen to pay

Note that **unternehmen** has an inseparable prefix**: Er unternimmt eine Reise nach Istanbul.**

Substantive

der **Abend, -e** evening
am Abend in the evening
der **Augenblick, -e** moment
(Einen) Augenblick, bitte! Just a moment, please.
der **Bummel, -** stroll, walk
einen Stadtbummel machen to take a stroll through town
der **Dom, -e** cathedral

Dom comes from Latin *domus dei* (*house of God*).

der **Gast, ¨-e** guest; patron
der **Kellner, -** waiter
der **Liter** liter
der **Regen** rain
das **Gebäude, -** building
das **Glas, ¨-er** glass
das **Gramm** gram
das **Kilogramm** (*or* das **Kilo**) kilogram
(das) **Köln** Cologne
das **Museum, Museen** museum
das **Stadtzentrum** city center
die **Ecke, -n** corner
an der Ecke at the corner
um die Ecke around the corner
die **Kellnerin, -nen** waitress
die **Kunst, ¨-e** art
die **Sache, -n** thing; item
die **Tasse, -n** cup

die Kunst comes from verb **können**, showing the connection between art and ability. The meaning is preserved in **die Kochkunst, der Lebenskünstler**.

Adjektive und Adverbien

ausgezeichnet excellent
griechisch Greek
lecker tasty, delicious
weit far; far away
zuerst first, at first

Andere Vokabeln

dass (*sub. conj.*) that
noch etwas something else, anything more
ob (*sub. conj.*) whether, if
um ... zu in order to

Nützliche Ausdrücke

Guten Appetit! *Bon appétit!* Enjoy your meal!
griechisch (italienisch, französisch usw.) essen to eat Greek (Italian, French, etc.) food
Ich glaube schon. I think so.
in der Nähe (+ *gen.*) near, nearby
Lust haben (etwas zu tun) to want to (do something)
Zahlen bitte! (May I have the) check please!

Gegensätze

Ich glaube schon. ≠ Ich glaube nicht. I think so. ≠ I don't think so.
weit ≠ nah(e) far ≠ near
zuerst ≠ zuletzt at first ≠ finally, last of all

Mit anderen Worten

der Kram (*colloq.*) = **die Sachen; alte Sachen**

SEIT 1390
HISTORISCHES
Hotel-Restaurant
Goldener Adler
GOETHE-STUBE • BATZENHÄUSL
Besitzer • Familie Cammerlander
Direktion • Familie Cammerlander
6020 INNSBRUCK
Herzog Friedrich Str. 6.
Tel. ++43 / 512 / 57 11 11 - 0

Variationen

A Persönliche Fragen

1. Haben Sie heute gefrühstückt? Was haben Sie denn gegessen und getrunken? Hat's Ihnen geschmeckt?
2. Kennen Sie ein Lokal, wo man sehr gut essen kann? Wie heißt es?
3. Essen Sie gern griechisch? italienisch? französisch? deutsch?
4. Trinken Sie viel Kaffee? Was trinken Sie sonst?
5. Was essen Sie gern zum Nachtisch: Eiscreme? Joghurt? Obst?
6. Laden Sie oft Freunde zum Abendessen ein?
7. Kaufen Sie im Supermarkt ein? Wie oft?
8. Marianne hat Lust einen Stadtbummel zu machen. Haben Sie Lust heute etwas zu machen? Was denn?
9. Gehen Sie gern ins Kunstmuseum? Welche Künstler (*artists*) mögen Sie?

B Übung: Raten Sie mal! (*Take a guess!*) Marianne und Helmut wollen einen Stadtbummel machen. Das heißt, sie haben ein bisschen Freizeit und können langsam durch die Stadt gehen. Um einen Bummel zu machen braucht man also Zeit. Raten Sie mal, was diese Wörter bedeuten:

1. Sie machen einen **Schaufensterbummel**.
2. Ich hab' ein bisschen Geld in der Tasche. Machen wir doch einen **Einkaufsbummel**.
3. Der Zug hat an jedem kleinen Bahnhof gehalten. Ich fahre nie wieder mit diesem **Bummelzug**!
4. Fritz studiert seit 13 Semestern an der Uni und ist immer noch nicht fertig. Er ist ein **Bummelstudent**!
5. Die Arbeiter arbeiten immer noch, aber sehr langsam. Sie machen einen **Bummelstreik**.

C Partnerarbeit: Schmeckt es dir? Fragen Sie Ihren Partner, was er gern isst und trinkt.

Talking about food is a communicative goal.

BEISPIEL: A: Isst du gern Tomatensuppe?
B: Nein, das schmeckt mir nicht. (*oder*)
Ja, das schmeckt mir.

Käse	Kartoffeln	Kaffee	Wiener Schnitzel
Bier	Pommes frites	Brot	griechisches Essen
Pizza	Leberwurst	Salat	Wein

Unser SB-Wurst-Angebot:
Pfälzer Leberwurst
400-g-Packung
€1,78

Käse des Monats:

Echter Käse aus Holland
holländischer Schnittkäse, 30% Fett i.Tr., 100 g €1,99

Granny Smith Äpfel
Chile, Kl. I, neuerntig
1 kg
€1,53

Obstabteilung!

Griech. Victoria-Trauben
Hkl. I
1 kg
€1,49

Südafrik. Outspan-Orangen
Hkl. I
7er Netz
€2,00

Vokabeln zum Thema

Am Tisch

1. die **Serviette, -n**
2. die **Gabel, -n**
3. der **Teller, -**
4. das **Messer, -**
5. der **Löffel, -**
6. das **Glas, ¨er**
7. die **Speisekarte, -n**
8. die **Flasche, -n**
9. das **Salz**
10. der **Pfeffer**

D Partnerarbeit: Am Cafétisch. Work together and fill in the blanks with words from the drawing on this page.

Der Tisch ist für zwei Personen gedeckt (*set*). Sie wissen noch nicht, was Sie essen wollen. Sie müssen zuerst ________ lesen.

A: Ich habe Durst und bestelle mir eine ________ Mineralwasser. Das trinke ich aus ________.

B: Ich habe Hunger und bestelle mir Spaghetti bolognese und einen Salat. Ich lege mir die ________ auf meinen Schoß (*lap*).

A: Das klingt lecker. Aber ich bestelle mir ein Schnitzel. Das esse ich mit ________ und ________.

B: Zum Nachtisch bestellen wir Eiscreme. Die essen wir mit ________. Dann sind wir fertig und der Kellner nimmt unsere ________ weg.

E Übung: Beim Frühstück

a. Was essen Sie mit dem Löffel beim Frühstück? Was essen Sie mit Messer und Gabel?
b. Was trinken Sie aus der Tasse? aus dem Glas? aus der Flasche?

LYRIK ZUM VORLESEN

Ernst Stadler

Ernst Stadler (1883–1914) was born in the Alsatian town of Colmar, now in France, but then part of the German Empire. After studying in Strassburg, Munich, and Oxford (where he was a Rhodes Scholar), he was appointed assistant professor at the University of Toronto but was unable to go to Canada when the First World War broke out. He was killed at the Battle of Ypres.

Stadler belonged to a generation of poets and painters known as the Expressionists. Their works often explore themes of urban life and the horrors of modern war. The following excerpt from his poem "Kleine Stadt" (1914) depicts a small town in transition from an agricultural to an industrial economy.

Kleine Stadt

Die vielen kleinen Gassen°, die die
langgestreckte° Hauptstraße überqueren°,
Laufen alle ins Grüne°. Überall fängt Land an.
Überall strömt Himmel ein° und Geruch° von
Bäumen und der starke Duft° der Äcker°.
.....
Am Abend, wenn die Fabriken schließen,
ist die große Straße mit Menschen gefüllt°.
Sie gehen langsam oder bleiben
mitten auf° der Gasse stehn.
Sie sind geschwärzt° von Arbeit und
Maschinenruß°. Aber ihre Augen tragen
noch Scholle°, zähe Kraft des Bodens°
und das feierliche Licht der Felder°.

= ***Straßen***
= ***lang*** / *cross*
ins Grüne = in die Natur
strömt... *sky floods in / smell*
fragrance / fields
filled
mitten... *in the middle of*
blackened
soot
earth / ***zähe...*** *resilient strength of the soil /* ***feierliche...*** *solemn light of the fields*

GRAMMATIK

1. Subordinate clauses and subordinating conjunctions (*Nebensätze und subordinierende Konjunktionen*)

DEFINITION

What is a subordinate clause?

A ***subordinate clause*** has a subject and a verb, but is *not* an independent sentence.

main clause	subordinate clause
I know	*that they still remember me.*

When it answers a question, a subordinate clause can stand alone.
A: **Wie lange müssen wir warten?**
B: **Bis der Regen aufhört.**

The subordinate clause "that they still remember me" is not a complete sentence, but depends on—or is subordinate to—the main clause "I know." Subordinate clauses are introduced by subordinating conjunctions such as "that" in the example above.

The most common subordinating conjunctions in German are:

Causal meaning of *since*: *Since* it's raining, let's stay inside (**Da es regnet ...**); temporal meaning of *since*: I've lived here *since* November (**seit November**).

bis	*until*
da	*since* (causal, not temporal)
dass	*that*
ob	*whether, if* (when it means *whether*)
weil	*because*
wenn	*if*

Verb-last word order in the subordinate clause

Review the coordinating conjunctions **und**, **oder**, etc. on p. 181, which do *not* change word order in the second clause.

A subordinate clause is always set off by a comma preceding the subordinating conjunction.

You have learned that coordinating conjunctions do not affect word order. By contrast, subordinating conjunctions *move the inflected verb to the end of the subordinate clause.*

Wir **essen** um halb sieben.

Ich glaube, **dass** wir um halb sieben **essen**.
I think that we're eating at 6:30.

Brauchen wir noch etwas?

Weißt du, **ob** wir noch etwas **brauchen**?
Do you know whether we need anything else?

Ich **habe** gerade gegessen.

Ich habe keinen Hunger, **weil** ich gerade gegessen **habe**.
I'm not hungry because I've just eaten.

Ich **habe** Zeit.

Ich helfe dir, **wenn** ich Zeit **habe**.
I'll help you if I have time.

Lab Manual Kap. 8, Üb. 1, 2, 7; Var. zu Üb. 3, 5, 8.

Workbook Kap. 8, A–D.

1 Übung: Ich weiß, dass ...

Sie planen miteinander ein Abendessen. Ihre Professorin sagt Ihnen etwas. Sagen Sie, dass Sie das wissen.

BEISPIEL: Die Äpfel sind teuer.
Ich weiß, dass sie teuer sind.

1. Wir essen um sieben.
2. Wir brauchen Rotwein.
3. Der Käse schmeckt gut.
4. Die Kinder wollen essen.
5. Tante Marie kommt zum Abendessen.
6. Wir haben keinen Salat.
7. Wir brauchen etwas zum Nachtisch.
8. Tante Marie trinkt keinen Kaffee.

Reichelt
Vanille
Reichelt
Eiscreme
verschiedene Sorten,
jeder 1000-ml-Becher
2,04

2 Übung: Ich weiß nicht, ob ... Ihr Professor ist neu in dieser Stadt. Er hat viele Fragen, aber Sie wohnen auch nicht lange hier und können ihm keine Antworten geben.

BEISPIEL: Ist dieses Restaurant teuer?
Ich weiß nicht, ob es teuer ist.

1. Gibt es hier einen Automechaniker?
2. Ist dieses Hotel gut?
3. Ist die Uni weit von hier?
4. Gibt es eine Buchhandlung in der Nähe?
5. Kann man den Dom besuchen?
6. Kann man hier einen Stadtplan kaufen?

3 Partnerarbeit: Warum lernst du Deutsch? Ask each other why you do the things listed below. Give your reason, then ask the next question.

BEISPIEL: A: Warum lernst du Deutsch?
B: Ich lerne Deutsch, *weil* es interessant ist. Warum ... ?

Deutsch lernen
zur Buchhandlung gehen
jetzt essen
viel Kaffee trinken
Rad fahren
einen Rucksack tragen
bis 9.00 schlafen
draußen sitzen
keine Leberwurst essen
früh aufstehen

Conditional sentences: If *X* is true, then *Y* is true

"If you can speak German, you'll get more out of your trip." In this sentence, the clause beginning with "if" states a condition, and the second clause states the result. "**Wenn du Deutsch kannst, hast du mehr von deiner Reise.**" In the German equivalent, the conditional clause begins with **wenn** and the verb must be at the end. The result clause may begin with an optional **dann** which does not affect word order. Here's another example:

condition *result*

Wenn ich Zeit habe, helfe ich dir.

Wenn ich Zeit habe, **dann** helfe ich dir.

In der Fußgängerzone (Oldenburg, Niedersachsen)

4 Übung: Wenn ..., dann ...

A. Complete these sentences by supplying a result clause.

1. Wenn wir Hunger haben, dann ...
2. Wenn du griechisch essen willst, dann ...
3. Wenn du mich morgen einlädst, dann ...

B. Now supply the conditional clause.

1. Wenn ... , dann können wir etwas unternehmen.
2. Wenn ... , dann kannst du einen Nachtisch bestellen.
3. Wenn ... , dann müssen wir noch schnell einkaufen.

Question words as subordinating conjunctions

All the question words (**wann**, **warum**, **was**, **wer**, etc.) act as subordinating conjunctions when they follow such phrases as **Weißt du, ... ?** and **Kannst du mir sagen, ... ?**

Question:	Was brauchen wir zum Abendessen?
Indirect question:	Weißt du, was wir zum Abendessen brauchen? *Do you know what we need for supper?*
Question:	Wer ist das?
Indirect question:	Ich kann Ihnen nicht sagen, wer das ist. *I can't tell you who that is.*

5 Übung: Eine Bahnreise nach Skandinavien. Eine Studentengruppe möchte in den Semesterferien eine Bahnreise nach Skandinavien machen, aber Sie wissen nichts über die Reise, denn Sie fahren nicht mit. Also können Sie keine Fragen über die Reise beantworten (*answer*).

BEISPIEL: Wer plant die Reise?
Ich weiß nicht, wer die Reise plant.

1. Wohin fährt die Gruppe?
2. Wo wollen sie übernachten?
3. Warum fahren sie mit der Bahn?
4. Welche Städte besuchen sie?
5. Was wollen sie dort sehen?
6. Wen wollen sie besuchen?
7. Wann kommen sie zurück?

...für meine Familie tu' ich alles.
Aber was passiert, wenn mir was passiert?

Verbs with separable prefixes in subordinate clauses

In a subordinate clause, a separable-prefix verb moves to the end of the clause and the prefix is attached to it:

Dort **kaufe** ich immer ein.

Weißt du, warum ich ______ immer dort ein**kaufe**?

6 Partnerarbeit: Wie lange müssen wir warten? Sie warten zusammen vor der Mensa. Sagen Sie einander, bis wann Sie warten müssen. (*Use the cues below.*)

BEISPIEL: Wie lange müssen wir noch warten? (der Bus / ankommen)
Wir müssen warten, bis der Bus ankommt.

1. der Regen / aufhören
2. Max / uns abholen
3. unsere Freunde / ankommen
4. die Vorlesung / anfangen
5. die Buchhandlung / aufmachen

7 Übung: Ich habe eine Frage. Ihre Professorin stellt Fragen. Sie berichten den anderen Studenten, was die Professorin wissen möchte.

BEISPIELE: A: Ich habe eine Frage: Wann stehen Sie auf?
B: Sie möchte wissen, wann ich aufstehe.
A: Kommt Bernd vorbei?
C: Sie möchte wissen, ob Bernd vorbeikommt.

1. Wann fängt das Semester an?
2. Kommt Ingrid vorbei?
3. Warum geht Regine weg?
4. Bringt Maria die Kinder mit?
5. Hört die Musik bald auf?
6. Mit wem geht Hans spazieren?
7. Wo steigt man in die Straßenbahn ein?
8. Wo steigen wir aus?
9. Wer macht das Fenster zu?
10. Laden Sie Max zum Abendessen ein?

Order of clauses in the sentence

Subordinate clauses may either follow or precede the main clause.

1 2
Ich spreche langsam, da ich nicht viel Deutsch gelernt habe.

1 2
Da ich nicht viel Deutsch gelernt habe, spreche ich langsam.

When the subordinate clause comes first, the *entire* subordinate clause is considered the first element in the sentence. The verb of the main clause therefore follows it immediately in second position.

Subordinate clause	Main clause
Wenn ich Zeit **habe**,	**gehe** ich ins Museum.
Ob er sympathisch **ist**,	**weiß** ich nicht.

8 Übung. Ihr Professor hat Fragen, aber Sie wissen die Antworten nicht.

BEISPIEL: Wie ist das Wetter?
Wie das Wetter ist, weiß ich nicht.

1. Wer ist das?
2. Wem gehört das?
3. Wohin fährt er?
4. Was kostet das?
5. Wie heißt sie?
6. Warum ist er müde?
7. Wessen Koffer ist das?
8. Wen kennt sie?

9 Übung: Ich mache heute keinen Stadtbummel. You've decided not to take a stroll through town today. Use the cues below to explain why.

BEISPIEL: Es regnet noch.
Da es noch regnet, mache ich keinen Stadtbummel.

1. Ich habe keine Zeit.
2. Das Wetter ist schlecht.
3. Ich brauche nichts in der Stadt.
4. Ich gehe nicht gern allein.
5. Ich bin heute spät aufgestanden.
6. Ich habe zu viel Arbeit.

Süßigkeiten (*candy*) im Schaufenster (Wien)

2. Infinitive constructions with *zu* (*der Infinitivsatz*)

When used in a sentence, the German infinitive is frequently preceded by **zu**. For the most part, this construction parallels the use of the English infinitive with *to*:

Was gibt's hier **zu sehen**?	*What's there to see here?*
Hast du Zeit diesen Brief **zu lesen**?	*Do you have time to read this letter?*

Note especially the second sentence above. In German, the infinitive with **zu** comes at the end of its phrase. In English, the infinitive with *to* comes at the beginning of its phrase.

When a separable-prefix verb is used, the **zu** is inserted between the prefix and the stem infinitive.

ab**zu**fahren spazieren **zu** gehen

Ich hoffe bald **abzufahren**.	*I hope to leave soon.*
Hast du Lust mit mir **spazieren zu gehen**?	*Would you like to go for a walk with me?*

Here are some cases in which the infinitive with **zu** is used:

- as a complement of verbs like **anfangen**, **aufhören**, **beginnen**, **helfen**, **hoffen**, **lernen**, **planen**, **scheinen**, and **vergessen**.

Ich fange an **einen Brief zu schreiben**.	*I'm starting to write a letter.*
Sie hofft **Geschichte zu studieren**.	*She's hoping to study history.*
Ich habe vergessen **dir von meiner Reise zu erzählen**.	*I forgot to tell you about my trip.*

- as a complement of constructions like **Lust haben**, **Zeit haben**, and **Spaß machen**.

Hast du Lust **einen Stadtbummel zu machen**?	*Do you want to take a walk through town?*
Ich habe keine Zeit **einkaufen zu gehen**.	*I have no time to go shopping.*

- as a complement of many adjectives such as **dumm**, **einfach**, **schön**, and **wichtig**.

Es ist sehr wichtig **das zu verstehen**.	*It's very important to understand that.*
Es ist schön **dich wiederzusehen**.	*It's nice to see you again.*

Man ist nie zu alt eine Fremdsprache zu lernen!

10 Partnerarbeit: Wie findest du das? On the left are some adjectives you can use to describe your attitude toward the activities listed on the right. Take turns telling each other what you think.

BEISPIEL: Ich finde es wunderschön schwimmen zu gehen.

altmodisch	einen Stadtbummel zu unternehmen
barbarisch	Deutsch zu lernen
bequem	schwimmen zu gehen
blöd	Hausaufgaben zu machen
einfach	meine Eltern anzurufen
fantastisch	um 6 Uhr aufzustehen
furchtbar	mit dir zu frühstücken
gut	Romane zu lesen
interessant	ins Museum zu gehen
klug	Geld zu sparen
leicht	im Sommer zu arbeiten
nett	Freunde einzuladen
schwierig	Kaffee zu trinken
stinklangweilig	ein Zimmer zu finden

11 Kettenreaktion: Was hast du vergessen? Sie haben alle vergessen etwas zu tun. Sagen Sie, was Sie vergessen haben, dann fragen Sie den nächsten Studenten.

BEISPIEL: A: Ich habe vergessen meine Hausaufgaben zu schreiben. Was hast du vergessen?
B: Ich habe vergessen ...

Diese Liste gibt Ihnen einige Möglichkeiten (*possibilities*):

to invite my friends	to shop
to order tickets	to buy potatoes
to order dessert	to show you my photographs

Lab Manual Kap. 8, Var. zu Üb. 12, 13; Üb. 16.

Workbook Kap. 8, E, F.

12 Übung: Es macht mir Spaß ... Sagen Sie Ihrer Professorin, was Ihnen Spaß macht.

BEISPIELE: Es macht mir Spaß am Telefon zu quatschen.
Es macht mir Spaß spazieren zu gehen.

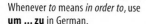

Infinitives with *um ... zu* and *ohne ... zu*

Whenever *to* means *in order to*, use **um ... zu** in German.

- **um ... zu** = *in order to*

Ich muss in die Stadt, **um Lebensmittel einzukaufen**.	*I have to go to town (in order) to buy groceries.*
Ich fahre nach Deutschland, **um Deutsch zu lernen**.	*I'm going to Germany in order to learn German.*

- **ohne ... zu** = *without . . . -ing*

Sie ist abgefahren, **ohne mich zu besuchen**.	*She left without visiting me.*
Ich habe das Buch gelesen, **ohne es zu verstehen**.	*I read the book without understanding it.*

Rikscha-Taxistand vor dem Kölner Dom

13 Schreiben wir mal. Rewrite each sentence, changing the **weil**-clause to an **um ... zu** phrase. Don't forget to eliminate the modal verb and its subject.

BEISPIEL: Ich gehe in die Stadt, weil ich einkaufen will.
Ich gehe in die Stadt *um einzukaufen.*

1. Ich gehe ins Lokal, weil ich etwas essen will.
2. Sie sitzt am Fenster, weil sie die Straße sehen möchte.
3. Studenten essen in der Mensa, weil sie Geld sparen wollen.
4. Manchmal fährt man ins Ausland, weil man mehr lernen möchte.

14 Gruppenarbeit: Warum tust du das? Ask each other why you do certain things. Answer with an **um ... zu** phrase.

BEISPIEL: A: Warum gehst du in die Altstadt?
B: Um einen Schaufensterbummel zu machen.

1. Warum gehst du ins Wasser?
2. Warum lernst du Deutsch?
3. Warum macht man oft Radtouren?
4. Warum bringt man eine Kamera mit, wenn man reist?
5. Warum fährt man im Winter in die Alpen?
6. Warum rufst du deine Freunde an?
7. Warum arbeitest du diesen Sommer?
8. Warum gehst du ins Museum?

15 Partnerarbeit: Warum machst du das gern? Find out two things your partner likes to do, and why. Answers may use either **weil** or **um ... zu**. Report your finding to the class.

BEISPIEL: A: Was machst du denn gern?
B: Ich gehe gern in die Stadt.
A: Warum?
B: Um ins Kino zu gehen. (*oder*)
Weil ich gern ins Kino gehe.

16 Übung. Combine these sentences, changing the second one to an **ohne ... zu** phrase.

> BEISPIEL: Er hat den Koffer genommen. Er hat mich nicht gefragt.
> Er hat den Koffer genommen, ohne mich zu fragen.

1. Sie sind abgefahren. Sie haben nicht Auf Wiedersehen gesagt.
2. Ich arbeite in einem Geschäft. Ich kenne den Chef nicht.
3. Karin hat ein Zimmer gefunden. Sie hat nicht lange gesucht.
4. Geh nicht spazieren. Du trägst keinen Mantel.
5. Geh nicht weg. Du hast kein Frühstück gegessen.
6. Sie können nicht ins Konzert. Sie haben keine Karten gekauft.

3. Genitive case (*der Genitiv*)

With the genitive you have learned all four cases in German.

Genitive case expresses possession (***John's** books*) or a close relationship between two nouns (*the color **of your eyes***). Here are some examples of genitive phrases:

der Wagen **meiner Mutter**	***my mother's** car*
die Freunde **der Kinder**	***the children's** friends*
das Haus **meines Bruders**	***my brother's** house*
das Ende **des Tages**	*the end **of the day***
der Name **des Kindes**	***the child's** name*
in der Nähe **des Bahnhofs**	*in the vicinity **of the train station***
Egons Freundin	***Egon's** girlfriend*

As you can see, the genitive generally *follows* the noun it modifies, whereas in English, the possessive *precedes* the noun: **das Haus meines Bruders** (*my brother's house*). Proper names, however, usually *precede* the nouns they modify, as in English, but without an apostrophe: **Egons Freundin** (*Egon's girlfriend*), **Muttis Wagen** (*Mom's car*).

Genitive endings

There are only two genitive endings for the limiting words: **-es** for masculine and neuter and **-er** for feminine and plural.
Note the following:

- For masculine and neuter nouns, in addition to the genitive ending on the limiting word, *the noun itself has the genitive ending* **-s** (in der Nähe de**s** Bahnhof**s**). The ending for monosyllabic nouns is usually **-es** (das Auto mein**es** Mann**es**).
- Masculine N-nouns are exceptions because they add the same **-en** or **-n** as in the accusative and dative. Wissen Sie die Adresse **dieses Studenten**?

Genitive case				
	masculine	**neuter**	**feminine**	**plural**
nominative **accusative**	der Mann den Mann	das Kind	die Frau	die Leute
dative	dem Mann	dem Kind	der Frau	den Leuten
genitive	-es -(e)s **des** Mannes **eines** Mannes **meines** Mannes **dieses** Mannes	-es -(e)s **des** Kindes **eines** Kindes **eures** Kindes **jedes** Kindes	-er **der** Frau **einer** Frau **Ihrer** Frau **welcher** Frau	-er **der** Leute **keiner** Leute **unserer** Leute **dieser** Leute

Lab Manual Kap. 8, Üb. 17; Var. zu Üb. 18.

SAM Workbook

Workbook Kap. 8, G.

17 Übung. Change these noun phrases from nominative to genitive.

BEISPIEL: der Zug
des Zuges

1. ein Arzt
2. mein Freund
3. unser Vater
4. die Lehrerin
5. das Kind
6. die Leute
7. jede Uni
8. deine Mutter
9. der Student
10. dieser Herr
11. das Essen
12. diese Zimmer

RUNDGANG
durch Schillers Gartenhaus
Ein Museum der Friedrich-Schiller-Universität Jena

NOTE ON USAGE

The preposition *von* + dative

German uses **von** + *dative* where English uses ***of*** + *possessive.*

a friend of my brother's	**ein Freund von meinem Bruder**
a cousin of mine	**eine Cousine von mir**
Is Max a friend of yours?	**Ist Max ein Freund von dir?**

18 Übung: Wie sagt man das auf Deutsch?

BEISPIEL: your girlfriend's sister
die Schwester deiner Freundin

1. the walls of my room
2. the end of the week
3. Karl's major
4. the children's pictures
5. the history of the war
6. his brother's house
7. her sister's boyfriend
8. the cities of Switzerland
9. a student's letter
10. the rooms of the house
11. Maria's students
12. the cities of Europe
13. the windows of this room
14. your mother's car
15. the history of these countries
16. Grandpa's clock
17. a friend of yours
18. a student of mine

19 Partnerarbeit: Wessen ... ist das? Pictured below are Ute's family and some things that belong to them. Take turns asking what belongs to whom.

BEISPIEL: A: Wessen Buch ist das?
B: Das ist das Buch ihrer Schwester.

4. Prepositions with the genitive case (*Präpositionen mit Genitiv*)

You've already memorized the accusative, dative, and two-way prepositions on pp. 96, 127, and 159. Remember that no prepositions take the nominative case.

A few German prepositions take the genitive case.

statt or **anstatt**	*instead of*	Schreib eine Karte **statt eines Briefes**.
trotz	*in spite of, despite*	**Trotz des Wetters** sind wir ans Meer gefahren.
während	*during*	**Während der Woche** fährt er oft in die Stadt.
wegen	*because of, on account of*	**Wegen meiner Arbeit** kann ich nicht mitkommen.

NOTE: **Statt** and **anstatt** are interchangeable and equally correct.

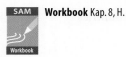

Workbook Kap. 8, H.

20 Übung. Form prepositional phrases with the elements provided and give English equivalents. Then make a complete sentence for each phrase.

BEISPIEL: während / Sommer
während des Sommers (*during the summer*)
Während des Sommers habe ich gearbeitet.

1. trotz / Wetter
2. während / Ferien
3. statt / Stadtplan
4. wegen / mein / Mutter
5. wegen / mein / Studium
6. trotz / Arbeit
7. während / Tag
8. anstatt / Hotel

21 Übung: Warum tun Sie das? Ihre Professorin möchte wissen, warum Sie etwas tun. Sagen Sie es ihr. Die Liste von Gründen (*reasons*) hilft Ihnen.

BEISPIEL: Warum arbeiten Sie so viel?
Wegen meines Studiums.

Studium	Eltern	Wetter
Klausur	Schnee	Klima
Arbeit	Regen	Stress

1. Warum bleiben Sie heute zu Hause?
2. Warum wollen Sie im Süden wohnen?
3. Warum dürfen Sie heute Abend nicht mitkommen?
4. Warum brauchen Sie Ferien?
5. Warum brauchen Sie manchmal Aspirin?
6. Warum wollen Sie heute draußen sitzen?

22 Übung: Wann machen Sie das? Ihr Professor fragt, wann Sie etwas machen. Die Liste der Zeitangaben (*time phrases*) hilft Ihnen mit der Antwort.

BEISPIEL: Wann haben Sie Zeit eine Reise zu machen?
Während der Ferien. / Im Sommer. / usw.

am	**im**	**während**
Morgen	Frühling	Woche
Abend	Herbst	Ferien
Wochenende	Winter	Vorlesung
Montag (usw.)	Januar (usw.)	Konzert

You can also use phrases such as **nach meiner Vorlesung** and **vor dem Frühstück**.

1. Wann gehen Sie zur Deutschstunde?
2. Wann haben Sie Zeit einzukaufen?
3. Wann schreiben Sie Briefe?
4. Wann schlafen Sie gern?
5. Wann haben Sie Lust ins Ausland zu fahren?
6. Wann haben Sie keine Zeit ins Kino zu gehen?

5. Nouns of measure, weight, and number

See the **Table of Equivalent Weights and Measures** on the inside back cover of the book.

German noun phrases indicating measure and weight do not use a preposition. Equivalent English phrases use *of.*

ein Glas Bier	*a glass **of** beer*
eine Tasse Kaffee	*a cup **of** coffee*
ein Liter Milch	*a liter **of** milk*
eine Portion Pommes frites	*an order **of** French fries*

Masculine and neuter nouns of measure *remain in the singular*, even following numerals greater than one.

drei **Glas** Bier	*three glasses of beer*
zwei **Kilo** Kartoffeln	*two kilos of potatoes*
vier **Stück** Brot	*four pieces of bread*

Feminine nouns of measure, however, *do* use plural forms.

zwei Tass**en** Kaffee	*two cups of coffee*
drei Flasch**en** Wein	*three bottles of wine*

15-08-08 #0000

GAST/TISCH # 161
2 PAELLA VAL. *20.45
1 SCHNITZEL PA *7.16
1 KINDERTELLER *4.60
1 FL WASSER *1.79
1 FL LIMO *1.79
1 MÄRZEN 0.5 *1.43
1 WEIZEN *1.79
1 MÄRZEN 0.3 *0.92
BROT *1.02
BAR *40.95
ENTH.MWST14% *5.67

BESTEN DANK
COSTA DEL SOL

Ordering in a restaurant is a communicative goal.

23 Übung: Im Lokal. Sie reisen mit einer Studentengruppe durch Deutschland und essen in einem Lokal. Die anderen in der Gruppe können kein Deutsch. Sie müssen der Kellnerin sagen, was sie bestellen wollen.

BEISPIEL: *I'd like a cup of coffee.*
Bringen Sie uns bitte eine Tasse Kaffee.

I'd like . . .

1. *a glass of wine and two cups of coffee.*
2. *three glasses of water and two glasses of beer.*
3. *a bottle of wine and two orders of French fries.*
4. *three glasses of beer, two glasses of wine, and a cup of coffee.*

A **Konditorei** is a bakery-café serving pastries and sometimes light fare such as cold cuts and egg dishes.

Vokabeln zum Thema

In der Konditorei

Auf der Speisekarte der Konditorei finden Sie:

die **Butter**	*butter*
das **Ei, -er**	*egg*
das **Eis**	*ice cream*
das **Kännchen, -**	*small (coffee or tea) pot*
der **Kuchen, -**	*cake*
die **Milch**	*milk*
die **Portion, -en**	*serving of, order of*
der **Saft, ¨e**	*juice*
die **Sahne**	*cream*
der **Schinken**	*ham*
der **Tee**	*tea*

24 Gruppenarbeit: In der Konditorei. ***(3 oder 4 Personen)*** Sie sitzen zusammen in der Café-Konditorei Reidel und bestellen etwas zu essen und zu trinken. Jemand in der Gruppe spielt den Kellner oder die Kellnerin. Die anderen bestellen von der Speisekarte.

❖ *Café-Konditorei Reidel*

Warme Getränke

Tasse Kaffee	1,20
Kännchen Kaffee	2,35
Tasse Mocca	2,25
Kännchen Mocca	2,80
Tasse Kaffee Hag	1,25
Kännchen Kaffee Hag	2,45
Tasse Kakao mit Sahne	1,25
Kännchen Kakao mit Sahne	2,50
Glas Tee mit Milch oder Zitrone	1,20
Glas Tee mit Rum	2,30
Glas Pfefferminztee	1,20
Glas Grog von Rum 4 cl	2,60
Glas Glühwein 0,2l	2,30
Glas heiße Zitrone	1,35

Eis und Eisgetränke

Portion gemischtes Eis	1,65
Portion gemischtes Eis mit Sahne	2,00
Früchte-Eisbecher „Florida"	3,35
Eis-Schokolade	2,10

Kalte Getränke

Flasche Mineralwasser	1,10
Flasche Coca Cola	1,10
Flasche Orangeade	1,10
Pokal Apfelsaft	1,25
Glas Orangensaft	1,50
Glas Tomatensaft	1,50
Glas Zitrone natur	1,35

Frühstück

Kleines Gedeck 1 Kännchen Kaffee, Tee od. Schokolade, 2 Brötchen, Butter, Konfitüre	3,10
Großes Gedeck 1 Kännchen Kaffee, Tee od. Schokolade, 2 Brötchen, Butter, Konfitüre, 1 gek. Ei, 1 Scheibe Schinken od. Käse	4,05

Ergänzung zum Frühstück

1 gekochtes Ei	0,75
1 Portion Konfitüre	0,45
1 Portion Butter	0,45
1 Scheibe Käse	0,90
1 Scheibe Schinken	1,00
1 Brötchen oder 1 Scheibe Brot	0,35

Kaffee Hag is decaffeinated coffee; **Glühwein** is hot mulled wine; **Zitrone natur** is fresh lemonade; **Konfitüre = Marmelade**.

6. Equivalents of English *to*

The all-purpose English preposition indicating destination is *to*: We're going *to Germany, to the ocean, to the train station, to the movies, to Grandma's*. German has several equivalents for English *to*, depending on the destination.

SAM Workbook **Workbook** Kap. 8, I.

- Use **nach** with cities, states, and most countries.

  Wir fahren **nach Wien**.
  nach Kalifornien.
  nach Deutschland.
  nach Europa.

  and in the idiom: **nach Hause**.

Remember also that **an** + *accusative* signals motion toward a border, edge, or vertical surface: **Ich gehe ans Fenster/an die Tafel/an die Tür. Wir fahren ans Meer/an den See.** (Review p. 159.)

- Use **zu** with people and some locations.

  Ich gehe **zu meinen Freunden**.
  zu meiner Großmutter.
  zum Arzt.
  zum Bahnhof.
  zur Buchhandlung.
  zur Post (*to the post office*).

- Use **in** with countries whose names are feminine or plural, and with some locations.

  Ich fahre **in die Schweiz**.
  in die Bundesrepublik.
  in die USA.

  Wir gehen **ins Kino**.
  ins Bett.
  ins Konzert.
  ins Museum.
  ins Restaurant/ins Lokal.
  ins Theater.
  in die Stadt (*downtown*).
  in die Kirche (*to church*).
  in die Mensa.

Here is a rough rule-of-thumb for deciding whether to use **zu** or **in** with a destination within a city: **in** is usually used with destinations where one will spend a relatively long time (**ins Kino**, **in die Kirche**, **ins Bett**); **zu** is usually used with destinations involving a briefer visit (**zum Bahnhof**, **zur Post**).

25 Übung: Wohin gehen Sie? Antworten Sie auf Deutsch.

BEISPIEL: Wohin gehen Sie, wenn Sie einkaufen wollen?
Ich gehe in die Stadt.

Wohin gehen Sie, wenn Sie ... ?

1. krank sind
2. mit der Bahn reisen
3. müde sind
4. Musik hören wollen
5. ein Buch kaufen wollen
6. Ihre Familie besuchen wollen
7. Hunger haben
8. einen Film sehen wollen
9. einen Brief schicken wollen
10. Kunst sehen wollen

Wo gehen wir hin?
Essen & Trinken · Freizeit & Unterhaltung

LESESTÜCK

Tipps zum Lesen und Lernen

Tipp zum Vokabelnlernen

***Compounds with** -stadt* The topic of this chapter is **die Stadt**. Compound nouns with **Stadt** define various kinds of cities. You have already encountered, for example, **die Altstadt**, *the old city* (or the medieval core of modern German cities), and **die Hauptstadt**, *the capital city*. A city center can also be called **die Innenstadt** or **das Zentrum**. In the following reading, other kinds of cities are mentioned: **Großstadt**, **Kleinstadt**, **Hafenstadt** (*port city*), **Heimatstadt** (*hometown*), and **Residenzstadt** (*seat of a monarch's court*).

Übung. Try to describe in German the following kinds of cities.

BEISPIEL: Industriestadt
Eine Stadt mit viel Industrie. (*oder*)
Eine Stadt, wo es viel Industrie gibt.

1. Touristenstadt
2. Universitätsstadt
3. Kulturstadt
4. Weltstadt
5. Ferienstadt
6. Millionenstadt

Leicht zu merken

Lab Manual Kap. 8, Üb. zur Betonung.

The meaning of **die Residenz** is restricted in German to a royal palace.

der **Architekt, -en, -en** (*m.*)	Architekt
der **Aspekt, -e**	Aspekt
die **Dynastie, -n**	Dynastie
(das) **Großbritannien**	
hektisch	
historisch	
das **Kulturzentrum**	Kulturzentrum
ökonomisch	
die **Residenz**	Residenz
die **Restauration, -en**	Restauration
die **Ruine, -n**	Ruine
der/die **Sozialarbeiter/in**	Sozialarbeiter
symbolisch	
die **Tradition, -en**	Tradition

Einstieg in den Text

Discussing city life is a communicative goal.

In the following reading, entitled **Aspekte der Großstadt**, an American exchange student in Hamburg and a German family from Dresden tell about themselves and their experiences living in large cities. Before reading it, think about your own experiences in or impressions of cities. Write a few sentences in German about what you like or dislike about big cities.

Das Stadtleben	
Das gefällt mir:	**Das gefällt mir nicht:**

Wortschatz 2

Verben

auf·wachsen (wächst auf), ist aufgewachsen to grow up
bauen to build
führen to lead
nennen, hat genannt to name
zerstören to destroy

Substantive

der **Alltag** everyday life
der **Eindruck, ¨-e** impression
der **Hafen, ¨** port, harbor
der **Künstler, -** artist (*m.*)
das **Jahrhundert, -e** century
das **Kreuz, -e** cross
(das) **Sachsen** Saxony
das **Schloss, ¨-er** palace
die **Arbeitslosigkeit** unemployment
die **Aufgabe, -n** task
die **Brücke, -n** bridge
die **Fabrik, -en** factory
die **Gelegenheit, -en** opportunity
die **Großstadt, ¨-e** large city (*over 100,000 inhabitants*)
die **Heimatstadt, ¨-e** hometown; native city
die **Kirche, -n** church
die **Kleinstadt, ¨-e** small city, town (*population 5,000 to 20,000*)
die **Künstlerin, -nen** artist (*f.*)
die **Sehenswürdigkeit, -en** place of interest, sight, attraction

Adjektive und Adverbien

arbeitslos unemployed
geradeaus straight ahead
im Jahr(e) 2008 in 2008

Im Jahr(e): Like the final **-e** in **nach Hause**, this **-e** is an old dative ending.

links to *or* on the left
rechts to *or* on the right
stark strong
trotzdem in spite of that, nevertheless

Nützliche Ausdrücke

auf dem Land in the country (i.e., rural area)
aufs Land to the country
im Gegenteil on the contrary

Gegensätze

führen ≠ folgen to lead ≠ to follow (+ *dat.*)
stark ≠ schwach strong ≠ weak

Mit anderen Worten

riesengroß = sehr, sehr groß

Aspekte der Großstadt

Die meisten° Deutschen leben in Städten mit über 80 000 Einwohnern. Welche Vorteile und Nachteile° gibt es, wenn man in einer Großstadt wohnt?

most

***Vorteile ...** advantages and disadvantages*

Eindrücke eines Amerikaners

Mark Walker, Austauschstudent in Hamburg:[1] Da ich aus einer Kleinstadt in Colorado komme, schien° mir Hamburg zuerst riesengroß. Es war mir schwer zu verstehen, wie die Deutschen so dicht zusammengedrängt° leben können.

seemed

***dicht ...** crowded together*

Aber das heißt nicht, dass Hamburg mir nicht gefällt. Im Gegenteil! Ich finde es fantastisch, dass man in der Stadt so viel unternehmen kann. Wenn ich Lust habe, kann ich jeden Tag ins Konzert, ins Kino oder ins Museum gehen. Hamburg ist die zweitgrößte° Stadt der Bundesrepublik. Weil es eine Hafenstadt ist, gibt es seit Jahrhunderten Verbindungen° mit dem Ausland.

second largest

ties

Wenn das Stadtleben mir zu viel wird, dann ist es sehr leicht mein Fahrrad zu nehmen, in die Bahn zu steigen und aufs Land zu fahren. In der Lüneburger Heide[2] südlich von° Hamburg kann man schöne Radtouren machen. Dieser Kontrast zwischen Stadt und Land scheint mir typisch für Deutschland. Das Land ist den Einwohnern° der Städte sehr wichtig als Erholung° vom Stress des Alltags.

south of

inhabitants / relaxation

Learning about life in German cities is the cultural goal of this chapter.

Familie Oberosler aus Dresden[3]

Anke Oberosler, 26, Fremdenführerin° in Dresden: Also, da ich in Dresden aufgewachsen bin, kenne ich die Stadt wie meine eigene° Tasche. Sie ist die Hauptstadt von Sachsen und hat eine lange Tradition als Kulturzentrum. Die

tourist guide

own

Blumenstand auf dem Markt (Pasing being München)

---

[1] **Hamburg**: A deep-water port on the Elbe River, population ca. 2 million.

[2] **Die Lüneburger Heide** (*heath*) is an extensive nature preserve on the North German plain between Hamburg and Hannover.

[3] **Dresden** (population ca. 500,000) on the Elbe River is the capital of the federal state of Saxony (**Sachsen**). Under the 18th-century Saxon kings it reached its zenith as a center of art and culture. It is renowned for its beautiful public buildings and art treasures.

Blick (*view*) auf Dresden mit der Frauenkirche links (Bernardo Bellotto [Canaletto], 1747)

Das zerstörte Dresden, 1945

wunderbaren Kirchen, Schlösser und Museen aus dem 18. und 19. Jahrhundert und die Lage° an der Elbe machen Dresden zu einer der schönsten° Städte Deutschlands. Als Fremdenführerin habe ich jeden Tag die Gelegenheit, Besuchern die Sehenswürdigkeiten der Stadt zu zeigen.

location / most beautiful

Vielleicht wissen Sie schon, dass die Wettiner – die königliche Dynastie in Sachsen – berühmte Kunstsammler° waren. August der Starke (1670–1733) hat hervorragende° Künstler und Architekten nach Dresden gebracht, um seine Residenz so prachtvoll wie möglich° zu machen. Wegen der Schönheit der Stadt hat man Dresden oft „Elbflorenz“[4] genannt.

art collectors
outstanding
so … as magnificent as possible

Aber fast am Ende des Krieges haben Luftangriffe° der Briten° und Amerikaner die Innenstadt mit einem Feuersturm° zerstört. Tausende von Menschen[5] sind ums Leben gekommen° und fast alle historischen Gebäude der Innenstadt waren

air raids / British
firestorm
ums … = gestorben

---

[4] “Florence on the Elbe”

[5] Historians do not agree about the number of civilians killed in the Dresden air raids of February 13–14, 1945. Estimates range from 35,000 to over 100,000.

abgebrannt°. Heute ist es unsere Aufgabe, aus dieser Katastrophe etwas Positives° zu machen. Mein Vater kann Ihnen von der Restaurationsarbeit berichten.

Clemens Oberosler, 52; Steinmetz°: Wie mein Vater bin ich auch Steinmetz und habe jahrelang° am Wiederaufbau° meiner Heimatstadt gearbeitet, besonders an der Restauration der Frauenkirche.[6] Die Restaurationsarbeit wurde im Jahr 2005 endlich beendet°. Das neue Kreuz für die Kuppel° hat uns eine Gruppe aus Großbritannien geschenkt. Das war für mich eine schöne Geste der Versöhnung°. Wir bauen neue Gebäude aus den Ruinen und gleichzeitig° neue Brücken zwischen Menschen.

Beate Oberosler, 49, Sozialarbeiterin: Ich arbeite mit arbeitslosen Jugendlichen°. Bei uns in Ostdeutschland gibt es immer noch mehr Arbeitslosigkeit als im Westen. Nach der Wiedervereinigung° hat man viele Betriebe° geschlossen, weil sie nicht konkurrenzfähig° waren. In der DDR[7] hat es Arbeit für alle gegeben und darum hat diese neue Arbeitslosigkeit bei vielen Jugendlichen zu Bitterkeit° geführt. Einige suchen dann Lösungen° bei den Rechtsradikalen°.

Ich bin trotzdem optimistisch, weil Firmen wie VW und Siemens bei uns neue Fabriken bauen und neue Arbeitsplätze schaffen°. Ich hoffe, dass die ökonomischen Unterschiede° zwischen Ost- und Westdeutschland allmählich° kleiner werden.

burned down / ***etwas ...*** *something positive*
stonemason
for years / reconstruction
wurde ... beendet = *was completed / cupola*
Geste ... *gesture of reconciliation / simultaneously*
= ***junge Leute***
reunification / factories
competitive
bitterness
solutions / right-wing radicals
neue ... *create new jobs*
differences / gradually

Seals of the five federal states created from the former German Democratic Republic; from left to right: Mecklenburg-Vorpommern, Sachsen-Anhalt, Thüringen, Sachsen, and Brandenburg

[6] **Frauenkirche**: The Church of Our Lady, completed in 1743, is architecturally one of the most important Protestant churches in Germany. Contributions toward the work of restoration were received from all over the world.

[7] **DDR** = **Deutsche Demokratische Republik**, the former East German socialist state that became part of the Federal Republic of Germany in 1990.

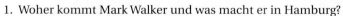

NACH DEM LESEN

SAM **Lab Manual** Kap. 8, Diktat.

SAM **Workbook** Kap. 8, J–L.

A Antworten Sie auf Deutsch.

1. Woher kommt Mark Walker und was macht er in Hamburg?
2. Wie gefällt ihm das Stadtleben?
3. Was können die Einwohner (*inhabitants*) der Stadt unternehmen, wenn ihnen der Stress des Alltags zu hektisch wird?
4. Wo liegt Dresden? In welchem Bundesland? An welchem Fluss?
5. Kennen Sie noch eine Stadt an diesem Fluss?
6. Was ist Anke Oberosler von Beruf? Und ihre Eltern?
7. Welche Sehenswürdigkeiten gibt es in Dresden?
8. Was ist am Ende des Krieges in Dresden passiert (*happened*)?
9. Herr Oberosler hat an der Restaurierung einer Kirche aus dem achtzehnten Jahrhundert mitgearbeitet. Wie heißt sie?
10. Welche Probleme sieht die Sozialarbeiterin Beate Oberosler heute in Dresden?

B **Wie ist es bei Ihnen zu Hause?** Sie haben über zwei deutsche Städte gelesen. Jetzt beschreiben Sie einem deutschen Freund den Ort, wo Sie wohnen. Geben Sie z.B. Informationen über diese Themen:

Größe (*size*)
Lage und Umgebung (*location and surroundings*)
Industrie
Kultur (Museen, Konzerte, Kinos usw.)
Geschäfte
Hochschulen

BEISPIEL: Boston ist eine Großstadt mit vielen Unis und Colleges. Es ist eine Hafenstadt und historisch sehr interessant. Usw.

Vokabeln zum Thema Stadt

This vocabulary focuses on an everday topic or situation. Words you already know from **Wortschatz** sections are listed without English equivalents; new supplementary vocabulary is listed with definitions. Your instructor may assign some supplementary vocabulary for active mastery.

Gebäude und Orte (*Buildings and places*)

die **Apotheke, -n** — *pharmacy*
die **Brücke, -n**
das **Café, -s**
die **Fußgängerzone, -n** — *pedestrian zone*
die **Haltestelle, -n** — *streetcar or bus stop*
das **Kaufhaus, ¨er** — *department store*
die **Kirche, -n**
die **Konditorei, -en**
die **Post** — *post office*
das **Rathaus, ¨er** — *city hall*

neu
City map
aktueller Cityplan
Der
"kleene"
Berliner
Cityplan
mit vielen Sehenswürdigkeiten
Fuchs-Verlag

Verkehrsmittel (***Means of transportation***)

der **Bus, -se**
das **Taxi, -s** — *taxicab*
die **Straßenbahn** — *streetcar*
die **U-Bahn** — *subway*

U-Bahn is short for **Untergrundbahn**.

Fragen wir nach dem Weg. (***Let's ask for directions.***)

Entschuldigung, wie komme ich **zur Post**?
... **zum Bahnhof**?
Das ist gleich in der Nähe.
Das ist nicht weit von hier.
Gehen Sie über die Straße und dann **geradeaus.**
... **nach links.**
... **nach rechts.**
... **um die Ecke.**

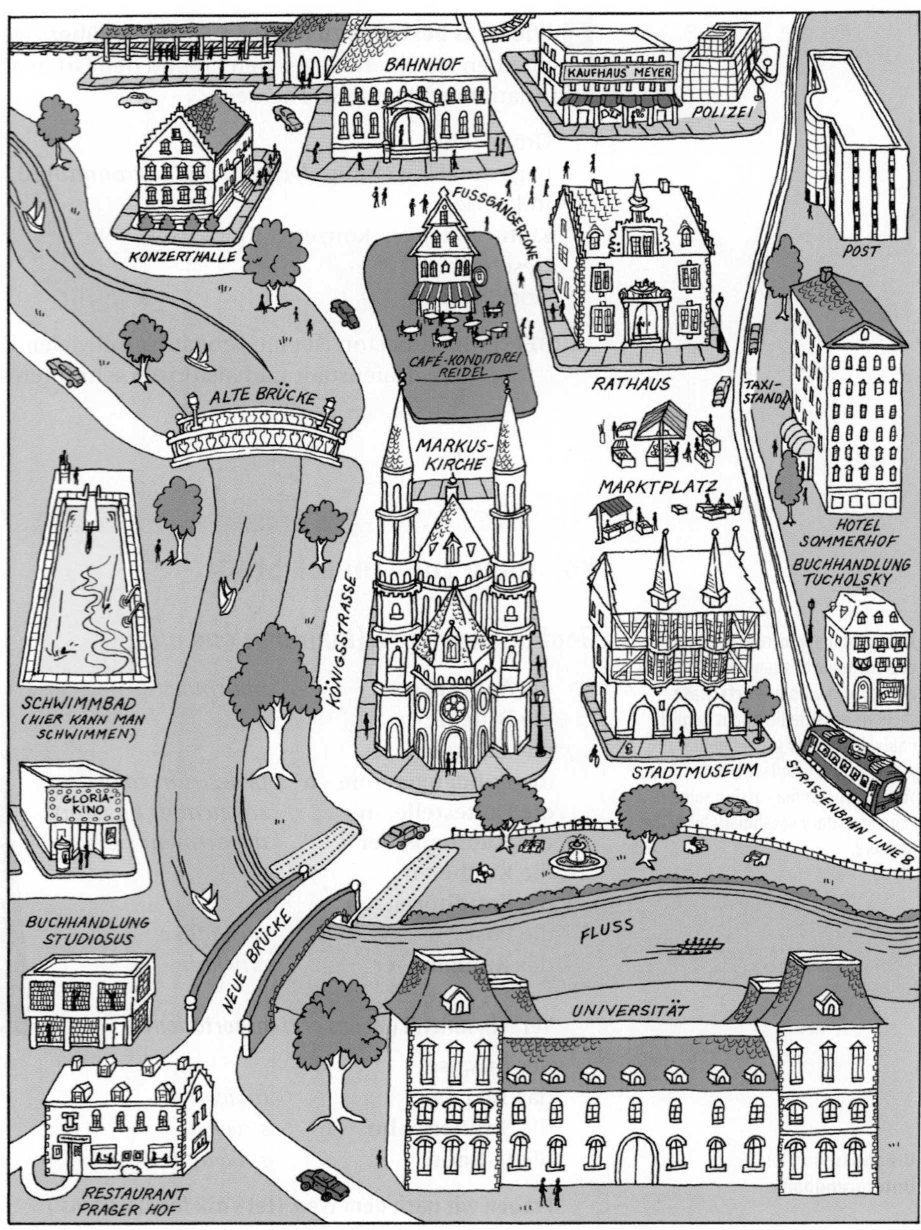

Asking directions is a communicative goal.

C Partnerarbeit: Wie komme ich zu ... ? Partner A ist fremd in dieser Stadt und benutzt den Stadtplan, um nach dem Weg zu fragen. Partner B ist hier zu Hause und sagt Partner A den Weg durch die Stadt. Dann tauschen (*exchange*) Sie die Rollen.

1. Sie stehen vor der Post und wollen zum Marktplatz.
2. Sie sind im Museum und müssen zum Hotel zurück, um zu Mittag zu essen.
3. Sie sind in der Fußgängerzone und haben Hunger. Sie brauchen Hilfe (*help*), um ein Restaurant zu finden.

D **Gruppendiskussion: Was machen wir denn morgen?** Mit einer Studentengruppe machen Sie eine Reise durch Deutschland. Heute Abend sind Sie in einer Großstadt angekommen und übernachten im Hotel Sommerhof (siehe Stadtplan). Besprechen Sie, was Sie morgen unternehmen wollen.

Wohin wollen wir gehen?
Was gibt es dort zu tun oder zu sehen?
Wo wollen wir essen?
Was machen wir denn am Abend?
Wie kommen wir hin (*get there*)? Zu Fuß, mit einem Taxi oder mit der Straßenbahn?

SCHREIBTIPP

Brainstorming ideas for a topic

This essay topic requires you to conceptualize an ideal city based on your experiences. Before you start writing, it's often helpful to brainstorm ideas about the topic. For instance, if the topic is City Life, then you might write down, "many things to do, lots of friends, too hectic, too much noise," etc.

When you're writing in a foreign language, let the relevant vocabulary you already know guide your brainstorming. For instance, **Stadtleben: Kulturleben gefällt mir, manchmal zu hektisch, man kann viel unternehmen**, usw. Resort to an English-German dictionary as little as possible.

▶ **Schreiben wir mal: Die ideale Stadt.** Sie sind Städteplaner/in von Beruf und kennen viele Städte. Einige haben Ihnen sicher gefallen, einige nicht. Jetzt dürfen Sie die ideale Stadt planen. Beschreiben Sie diese Stadt. Was würde sie haben, was würde sie nicht haben? Warum?

In the **Schreiben wir mal** activity and in exercise E, avoid using adjectives attributively (before nouns). Attributive adjectives need endings, which are taught in **Kapitel 9.**

E **Ein Brief nach Hause.** Sie kennen schon die Stadt auf Seite 228. Sie haben den Tag dort verbracht. Jetzt sitzen Sie am Abend im Hotel und schreiben einen Brief nach Hause. Beschreiben Sie Ihrer Familie, wie der Tag war und was Sie unternommen haben. Was sind Ihre Eindrücke von der Stadt und von den Menschen?

F **Wie sagt man das auf Deutsch?**

1. Can you please tell me where the cathedral is?
2. It isn't far from here. If you go around the corner, you'll see it.
3. Thanks very much.

4. What do you do when city life gets too stressful for you?
5. Sometimes I go to the country and go for a walk.

6. Do I still have time to go shopping?
7. Yes, of course. If we can go right away, I'll come along.
8. My brother's girlfriend has a birthday tomorrow and I want to buy her something.

9. During the week I don't have time to go to the museum.
10. Therefore I'd like to stay here until it closes.

ALMANACH

VIDEO

Mit dem Bus durch Berlin

Most German cities have superb public transportation systems that make it easy to get around. Berlin, for instance, has a comprehensive system of subways, buses, streetcars, and commuter trains. These pages from a brochure give information about touring the city with the double-decker buses of the **BVG** (Berlin's public transportation authority). The map of bus line 100 (**die Hunderter Linie**) through the heart of Berlin (**Berlin Mitte**) and the accompanying photos show points of interest along the route. These include the Brandenburg Gate (**das Brandenburger Tor**) and Museum Island (**die Museumsinsel**).

8 Brandenburger Tor

Wahrzeichen für die Stadt Berlin und seit dem Mauerfall auch Symbol für die Einheit Deutschlands. 1788-91 wurde das Brandenburger Tor von Langhans nach antikem Vorbild erbaut. 1793 wurde Schadows Quadriga mit der Siegesgöttin aufgestellt.

9 Staatsoper Unter den Linden

Die Lindenoper feierte 1992 ihr 250-jähriges Jubiläum. Mendelssohn-Bartholdy, Furtwängler und Richard Strauss feierten hier große künstlerische Triumphe. Der 1742 eingeweihte Knobelsdorf-Bau ist ein Zeugnis des norddeutschen Rokoko.

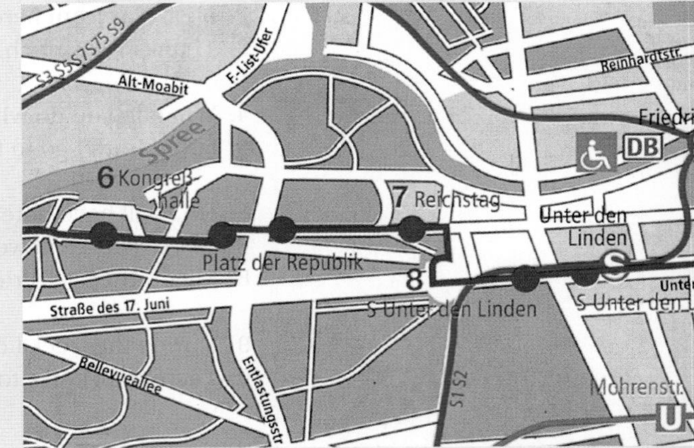

Berliner Dom

11

Im Stil der Neorenaissance wurde die Hofkirche der Hohenzollern in den Jahren 1893 bis 1905 erbaut. Im Krieg stark zerstört, wurde der größte Kirchenbau Berlins 1993 nach 18jähriger Renovierung wiedereröffnet. Hörenswert sind die Konzerte auf der historischen Orgel des Doms.

Museumsinsel

10

Zwischen dem Alten Museum und dem Bodemuseum erstreckt sich auf einer Insel zwischen Spree und Kupfergraben einer der weltweit bedeutendsten Museumskomplexe. Unter anderem befindet sich hier auch das Pergamonmuseum. Attraktionen sind der beeindruckende Pergamon-Altar und das berühmte Markttor von Milet. Nehmen Sie sich Zeit für einen Spaziergang in einer Welt von Kunst und Geschichte.

KAPITEL

9

Windräder und Kühe (Norddeutschland)

Unsere Umwelt

Kommunikation

- Discussing the environment and recycling
- Using adjectives to describe things
- Giving the date
- Talking about sports

Kultur

- German and global environmental issues

In diesem Kapitel

- **Lyrik zum Vorlesen**
  Heinrich Heine, "Ich weiß nicht, was soll es bedeuten" ("Die Loreley")
- **Grammatik**
  1. Attributive adjectives and adjective endings
  2. Word order of adverbs: Time/manner/place
  3. Ordinal numbers and dates
- **Lesestück**
  Unsere Umwelt in Gefahr
- **Almanach**
  Seid ihr schlaue Umweltfüchse?

DIALOGE

In-Text Audio CD

Haus also = *apartment house, building*
Note the accusative ending on the N-noun **Herrn** (see p. 163).

SAM **Lab Manual** Kap. 9, Dialoge, Fragen, Hören Sie gut zu!

Recycling in unserem Wohnhaus

Frau Berg trifft Herrn Reh auf der Treppe.

FRAU BERG: Um Gottes Willen! Wohin mit dem riesengroßen Sack?
HERR REH: In den Keller. Die neuen Container sind da. Jetzt können wir Altglas und Altpapier hier im Haus sammeln.
FRAU BERG: Na, endlich! Jetzt brauche ich meinen Müll nicht mehr zum Recycling zu schleppen.
HERR REH: Glücklicherweise ist das auch nicht mehr nötig. Wenn wir alle mitmachen, dann ist das ein großer Fortschritt.

Ein umweltfreundliches Geburtstagsgeschenk

DANIEL: Hallo Frank! Das ist aber ein schönes Fahrrad! Woher hast du es denn?
FRANK: Marianne hat's mir zum Geburtstag geschenkt, weil wir unseren Zweitwagen verkauft haben.
DANIEL: Wieso denn?
FRANK: Er war sowieso kaputt, und da wir in die Stadt umgezogen sind, kann ich jetzt mit dem Rad zur Arbeit fahren.
DANIEL: Da sparst du aber viel Geld.
FRANK: Ja, und ich habe auch ein gutes Gefühl, weil ich etwas gegen die Luftverschmutzung tue.

Treibst du gern Sport?

JUNGE: Sag mal, treibst du gern Sport?
MÄDCHEN: Klar. Ich verbringe das ganze Wochenende auf dem Tennisplatz. Spielst du auch Tennis?
JUNGE: Ja, das ist mein Lieblingssport, aber ich bin kein guter Spieler.
MÄDCHEN: Da kann ich dir einen wunderbaren Tennislehrer empfehlen.

NOTES ON USAGE

Adverb *da* and flavoring particle *aber*

The adverb *da* At the beginning of a clause, the adverb **da** often means *then, in that case, under those circumstances, for that reason.*

Da sparst du aber viel Geld.
Da kann ich dir einen wunderbaren Tennislehrer empfehlen.

The flavoring particle *aber* As a flavoring particle, **aber** is often used to intensify a statement. It adds the sense of *really, indeed.*

Da sparst du **aber** viel Geld. — *Then you'll **really** save a lot of money.*

The particle **aber** can also add a note of surprise or admiration.

Mensch, das ist **aber** teuer! — *Wow, that's **really** expensive!*
Du siehst **aber** schön aus! — *You **really** look great!*

Wortschatz 1

In-Text Audio CD

Verben

empfehlen (empfiehlt), hat empfohlen to recommend
mit·machen to participate, cooperate
sammeln to collect
schleppen (*colloq.*) to drag, lug (along), haul
treffen (trifft), hat getroffen to meet
treiben, hat getrieben to drive, force, propel
  Sport treiben to play sports
um·ziehen, ist umgezogen to move, change residence

Substantive

der **Container, -** large trash container
der **Fortschritt, -e** progress
der **Geburtstag, -e** birthday
  zum Geburtstag for (your/her/my/etc.) birthday
der **Junge, -n, -n** boy
der **Keller, -** cellar, basement
der **Müll** trash, refuse
der **Sack, ⸚e** sack
der **Sport** sport
der **Tennisplatz, ⸚e** tennis court
der **Zweitwagen, -** second car
das **Gefühl, -e** feeling
das **Geschenk, -e** present
das **Mädchen, -** girl
das **Papier, -e** paper
das **Recycling** recycling; recycling center
das **Tennis** tennis
das **Wohnhaus, ⸚er** apartment building
die **Luft** air
die **Treppe** staircase, stairs
  auf der Treppe on the stairs
die **Verschmutzung** pollution
  die **Luftverschmutzung** air pollution

Adjektive und Adverbien

da then, in that case
ganz whole, entire
  das ganze Wochenende all weekend, the whole weekend
glücklicherweise fortunately
kaputt (*colloq.*) broken, kaput; exhausted
klar clear; (*colloq.*) sure, of course
nötig necessary
schmutzig dirty
sportlich athletic
umweltfreundlich environmentally safe, nonpolluting
zweit- second

Andere Vokabeln

Lieblings- (*noun prefix*) favorite
  Lieblingssport favorite sport
was für ... ? what kind of . . . ?

Nützliche Ausdrücke

Na endlich! at last! high time!
Um Gottes Willen! For heaven's sake! Oh my gosh!

Gegensätze

nötig ≠ unnötig necessary ≠ unnecessary
schmutzig ≠ sauber dirty ≠ clean

Mit anderen Worten

dreckig (*colloq.*) = **schmutzig**

The word **kaputt** comes from a French card-playing term, *être capot* = "to lose all the tricks at cards; to be wiped out."

Note that **zweit-** must have an adjective ending. See pp. 246–247. It can also be a prefix, as in **Zweitwagen**.

Thema der Woche
DO
Umweltschutz
e·on
Neue Energie

Variationen

A Persönliche Fragen

1. Ist man in Ihrem Studentenwohnheim umweltfreundlich? Was macht man da für die Umwelt?
2. Auch als Hobby kann man Dinge sammeln, z. B. Briefmarken (*stamps*), Münzen (*coins*) oder CDs. Sammeln Sie etwas?
3. Frau Berg hat früher ihren Müll zum Recycling geschleppt. Was müssen Sie jeden Tag mitschleppen (z. B. in Ihrem Rucksack)?
4. Zum Geburtstag hat Frank ein neues Fahrrad bekommen. Was würden Sie gern zum Geburtstag bekommen?
5. Besitzt Ihre Familie einen Zweitwagen? Wenn ja, warum brauchen Sie zwei Wagen?
6. Fährt jemand in Ihrer Familie mit dem Rad zur Arbeit? Wenn nicht, warum nicht?
7. Meinen Sie, dass die Luftverschmutzung hier ein Problem ist? Wie ist die Luft bei Ihnen zu Hause?
8. Treiben Sie Sport? Wie oft in der Woche?
9. Was ist Ihr Lieblingssport? Lieblingsfilm? Lieblingsbuch? Und Ihre Lieblingsstadt?

B Kettenreaktion: Warum brauchst du denn Geld? Sagen Sie, warum Sie Geld brauchen. Dann fragen Sie weiter.

BEISPIEL: A: Ich brauche Geld, um einen Pulli zu kaufen. Rebecca, warum brauchst du denn Geld?
B: Ich ...

Neue Mode: Alte Häuser

Review colors on p. 88.

C Übung: Welche Farbe hat das? Sagen Sie, welche Farbe diese Dinge haben.

BEISPIEL: Welche Farbe hat Georgs Hemd?
Es ist rot.

Welche Farbe hat/haben ...

der Wald?
der Kaffee?
das Meer?
die Wände dieses Zimmers?
die Bluse dieser Studentin?
der Wein?
das Hemd dieses Jungen?
diese Landkarte?
die Bäume im Sommer? im Herbst?
Ihr Pulli?

Vokabeln zum Thema Sport

Talking about sports is a communicative goal.

„Wer Sport treibt, bleibt fit" hört man oft. Was meinen Sie? Treiben Sie Sport, um fit und gesund zu bleiben, oder nur, weil es Ihnen Spaß macht? Hier sind einige Piktogramme von den Olympischen Spielen.

laufen
der **Läufer**
die **Läuferin**

schwimmen
der **Schwimmer**
die **Schwimmerin**

Ski fahren
der **Skifahrer**
die **Skifahrerin**

(Eis)hockey spielen
der **Hockeyspieler**
die **Hockeyspielerin**

Volleyball spielen
der **Volleyballspieler**
die **Volleyballspielerin**

Fußball spielen
der **Fußballspieler**
die **Fußballspielerin**

Rad fahren
der **Radfahrer**
die **Radfahrerin**

D Gruppenarbeit: Treibst du gern Sport? (*2 oder 3 Personen*) Take turns asking each other the following questions about what sports you like to play.

BEISPIEL: A: Treibst du gern Sport?
B: Ja, ich schwimme gern. Und du?

1. Treibst du gern Sport?
2. Warum gefällt dir dieser Sport?
3. Treibst du an der Uni Sport?
4. Hast du auch in der Schule Sport getrieben?

Lyrik zum Vorlesen

Heinrich Heine

The cliff called the **Loreley** is on the Rhine River at its deepest spot. Heinrich Heine's famous poem, "Ich weiß nicht, was soll es bedeuten" (1823), is a retelling of a Romantic legend invented by his contemporary, Clemens Brentano (1778–1842). It recounts the tale of a siren who lures boatmen to their deaths at this place. Set to music by the composer Friedrich Silcher in 1837, it achieved the status of a folk song.

Ich weiß nicht, was soll es bedeuten (Die Loreley)

Ich weiß nicht, was soll es bedeuten,	
dass ich so traurig° bin;	*sad*
ein Märchen aus alten Zeiten,	
das kommt mir nicht aus dem Sinn°.	***das ... Sinn = das kann ich nicht vergessen***
Die Luft ist kühl und es dunkelt°,	***es dunkelt = es wird dunkel***
und ruhig° fließt der Rhein;	*peacefully*
der Gipfel° des Berges funkelt°	*mountain top / glistens*
im Abendsonnenschein.	
Die schönste Jungfrau° sitzet°	*most beautiful maiden /* ***sitzet = sitzt***
dort oben° wunderbar,	*high above*
ihr goldenes Geschmeide° blitzet°,	*jewelry / sparkles*
sie kämmt° ihr goldenes Haar.	*combs*
Sie kämmt es mit goldenem Kamme°,	*comb*
und singt ein Lied dabei°;	*while doing so*
das hat eine wundersame°,	***= wunderbare***
gewaltige° Melodei.	*powerful*

Den Schiffer° im kleinen Schiffe°	*sailor / boat*
ergreift es° mit wildem Weh°;	***ergreift ...** is gripped / longing*
er schaut° nicht die Felsenriffe°,	*= **sieht** / submerged rock*
er schaut nur hinauf in die Höh°.	***hinauf ...** up to the heights*

Ich glaube, die Wellen° verschlingen°	*waves / swallow*
am Ende Schiffer und Kahn°;	*boat*
und das hat mit ihrem Singen	
die Loreley getan.	

Heinrich Heine (1797–1856)

GRAMMATIK

1. Attributive adjectives and adjective endings (*Adjektivendungen*)

Predicate adjectives versus attributive adjectives

Adjectives are used in two different ways:

- **Following linking verbs.** After the verbs **sein**, **werden**, **bleiben**, and **scheinen** they are called PREDICATE ADJECTIVES because they constitute the second part of the predicate.

Dein Rucksack ist **groß**.	*Your backpack is **big**.*
Meine Großeltern werden **alt**.	*My grandparents are getting **old**.*
Das Wetter bleibt **schön**.	*The weather will stay **beautiful**.*

Predicate adjectives in German have *no endings*.

- **Preceding nouns.** Preceding a noun, adjectives are called *attributive adjectives*.

dein **großer** Rucksack	*your **big** backpack*
meine **alten** Großeltern	*my **old** grandparents*
schönes Wetter	***beautiful** weather*

German attributive adjectives *always* have endings.

The noun phrase

Attributive adjectives occur in noun phrases. A noun phrase consists of some combination of three types of words: *limiting words, attributive adjectives*, and *nouns*. Limiting words are the **der**-words and **ein**-words you already know.

der-words	*ein*-words	
der, das, die	ein	
dieser	kein	
jeder	mein	possessive adjectives (mein, dein, sein, ihr, unser, euer, ihr)
welcher	dein	
alle	sein	
	ihr	
	unser	
	euer	
	ihr	

DEFINITION

Why are *der*-words and *ein*-words called "limiting words"?
These words are called ***limiting words*** because they *limit* the noun in some way rather than describing it: ***dieses*** **Fahrrad** (***this*** *bicycle, not that one*), ***meine*** **Großeltern** (***my*** *grandparents, not* ***yours***).

Here are some examples of noun phrases. Note that the noun phrase does not necessarily contain both a limiting word and an attributive adjective.

Limiting word +	Attributive adjective +	Noun	
das	**neue**	Fahrrad	*the new bicycle*
jede		Woche	*every week*
alle	**deutschen**	Studenten	*all German students*
	heißer	Kaffee	*hot coffee*
meine	**kleine**	Schwester	*my little sister*

Remember that these endings show the case, number, and gender of the noun.

German adjective endings have acquired the reputation of being a formidable obstacle for the learner. However, the system is conceptually quite simple and just requires practice until it becomes automatic in spoken German. To be able to use attributive adjectives, you need to know only two sets of endings, the *primary endings* and the *secondary endings*, and three rules for their use. Good news: the primary endings are simply the endings of the **der**-words, which you already know.

Primary endings				
	masculine	**neuter**	**feminine**	**plural**
nominative	-er	-es	-e	-e
accusative	-en	-es	-e	-e
dative	-em	-em	-er	-en
genitive	-es	-es	-er	-er

There are only two secondary endings, **-e** and **-en,** distributed as follows:

Secondary endings				
	masculine	**neuter**	**feminine**	**plural**
nominative	-e	-e	-e	-en
accusative	-en	-e	-e	-en
dative	-en	-en	-en	-en
genitive	-en	-en	-en	-en

Note that the **-en** occurs *in all forms of the plural* as well as *in all forms of the dative and genitive cases.*

EIN NEUES DENKEN FÜR EINE NEUE ZEIT

Rules for the use of adjective endings

Rule #1: With a few exceptions, each noun phrase contains a primary ending. If the limiting word has a primary ending, the following attributive adjective(s) have the secondary ending.

Limiting word with primary ending	+	Attributive adjective with secondary ending	+	Noun	
dies**es**		schön**e**		Bild	*this beautiful picture*
mit mein**er**		gut**en**		Freundin	*with my good friend*

Rule #2: If the noun phrase has no limiting word or has an **ein**-word without an ending, then the attributive adjective, if there is one, takes the primary ending.[1]

Note that the noun phrase **dein Bruder** contains no attributive adjective and thus no primary ending. When an attributive adjective is added, it has the primary ending: **dein kleiner Bruder**.

No limiting word, or *ein*-word without ending	+	Attributive adjective with primary ending	+	Noun	
dein		—		Bruder	*your brother*
		alte		Häuser	*old houses*
		heißer		Kaffee	*hot coffee*
ein		altes		Haus	*an old house*

VORSICHT!
BISSIGER
HUND

[1]There is one exception to Rule # 2: In the masculine and neuter genitive singular, the attributive adjective not preceded by a limiting word takes the *secondary ending* **-en** rather than the primary ending.

trotz tief**en** Schnee**s**	*in spite of deep snow*
wegen schlecht**en** Wetter**s**	*because of bad weather*

Such phrases are quite rare. Moreover, note that the primary ending *is* present on the noun itself.

The following examples contrast noun phrases with and without limiting words. Note how the primary ending shifts from the limiting word to the adjective.

dies**e** neu**en** Tennisplätze → neu**e** Tennisplätze
mit mein**em** amerikanisch**en** Geld → mit amerikanisch**em** Geld
welch**es** deutsch**e** Bier → deutsch**es** Bier

Rule #3: Attributive adjectives in succession have the same ending.

ein groß**es** alt**es** Haus *a large old house*
groß**e** alt**e** Häuser *large old houses*
gut**er** deutsch**er** Wein *good German wine*

Pay special attention to the three instances in which **ein**-words have no endings. They are the *only* instances in which **ein**-word endings differ from **der**-word endings.

Masculine nominative	**Neuter nominative and accusative**
ein alt**er** Mann	ein klein**es** Kind
but	*but*
d**er** alt**e** Mann	dies**es** klein**e** Kind

Adjectives whose basic forms end in unstressed **-er** (**teuer**) or **-el** (**dunkel**) drop the **-e-** when they take endings.

Die Theaterkarten waren **teuer**. Das waren aber **teure** Karten!
Ist diese Farbe zu **dunkel**? Ich mag **dunkle** Farben.

IN SUMMARY:
The first table below shows the complete declension of an adjective following a **der**-word; the second, following an **ein**-word. The highlighted forms in the second table show the only instances in which the **ein**-word endings differ from the **der**-word endings. The third table shows adjective endings in noun phrases without limiting words.

Adjective endings following a *der*-word				
	masculine	**neuter**	**feminine**	**plural**
nom.	dies**er** jung**e** Mann	dies**es** jung**e** Kind	dies**e** jung**e** Frau	dies**e** jung**en** Leute
acc.	dies**en** jung**en** Mann	dies**es** jung**e** Kind	dies**e** jung**e** Frau	dies**e** jung**en** Leute
dat.	dies**em** jung**en** Mann	dies**em** jung**en** Kind	dies**er** jung**en** Frau	dies**en** jung**en** Leuten
gen.	dies**es** jung**en** Mannes	dies**es** jung**en** Kindes	dies**er** jung**en** Frau	dies**er** jung**en** Leute

Adjective endings following an *ein*-word				
	masculine	**neuter**	**feminine**	**plural**
nom.	ein jung**er** Mann	ein jung**es** Kind	ein**e** jung**e** Frau	mein**e** jung**en** Leute
acc.	ein**en** jung**en** Mann	ein jung**es** Kind	ein**e** jung**e** Frau	mein**e** jung**en** Leute
dat.	ein**em** jung**en** Mann	ein**em** jung**en** Kind	ein**er** jung**en** Frau	mein**en** jung**en** Leuten
gen.	ein**es** jung**en** Mannes	ein**es** jung**en** Kindes	ein**er** jung**en** Frau	mein**er** jung**en** Leute

Adjective endings without a limiting word				
	masculine	**neuter**	**feminine**	**plural**
nom.	kalt**er** Wein	kalt**es** Wasser	kalt**e** Milch	kalt**e** Suppen
acc.	kalt**en** Wein	kalt**es** Wasser	kalt**e** Milch	kalt**e** Suppen
dat.	kalt**em** Wein	kalt**em** Wasser	kalt**er** Milch	kalt**en** Suppen
gen.	kalt**en** Weines	kalt**en** Wassers	kalt**er** Milch	kalt**er** Suppen

Unser königliches Bier.
REX PILS
Weisse Flotte Potsdam - wir haben es für Sie an Bord!

Lab Manual Kap. 9, Var. zu Üb. 1, 2, 6, 8.

Workbook Kap. 9, A–H.

Using adjectives to describe things is a communicative goal.

1 Übung: Welcher Tisch ist das? (*mit offenen Büchern*) Below is a list of some people and classroom objects arranged by gender, as well as a list of adjectives that you can use to describe them. Your instructor will ask you about them. Describe them with adjectives as in the example.

BEISPIEL: Welches Bild ist das?
Das ist das neue Bild.

Masculine	**Neuter**	**Feminine**	**Plural**	**Adjectives**
Bleistift	Bild	Gruppe	Bücher	alt
Junge	Buch	Hose	Jeans	billig
Kugelschreiber	Fenster	Jacke	Schuhe	blau, rot, grün usw.
Mantel	Foto	Kamera	Studenten	bunt
Pulli	Glas	Landkarte		fleißig
Radiergummi	Heft	Studentin		freundlich
Stadtplan	Hemd	Tafel		groß
Student	Kleid	Tasche		herrlich
Stuhl	Mädchen	Tür		höflich
	Papier	Uhr		kaputt
	Poster	Zeitschrift		kurz
	Wörterbuch	Zeitung		langweilig
				lustig
				neu
				schrecklich
				toll
				typisch
				wunderbar

2 **Gruppenarbeit: Beschreiben wir das Klassenzimmer.**

BEISPIEL: Dort hängt ein großes Bild an der Wand.
Dort steht ein kleiner Tisch.

Was sehen Sie sonst? Benutzen Sie (*use*) Adjektive!

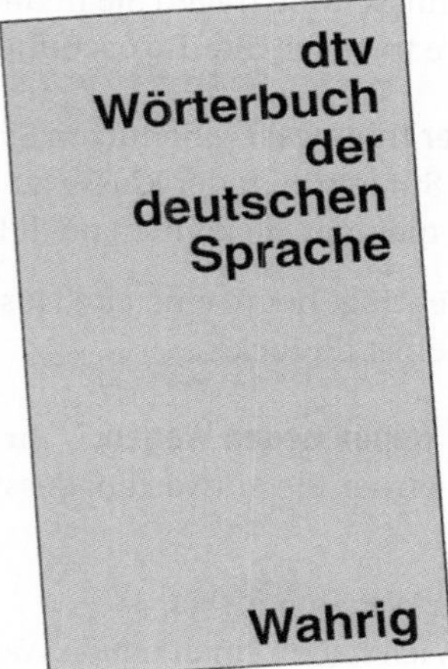

3 **Übung: Sehen Sie den Tisch?** Your instructor asks whether you see certain objects or people. You're not sure which ones are meant, so you ask for more information.

BEISPIEL: Sehen Sie den Schreibtisch?
Meinen Sie den *neuen* Schreibtisch?

Was für can also introduce exclamations: **Was für ein schöner Wagen!** (*What a beautiful car!*)

FRAGEWORT

Was für ... ? *What kind of . . . ?*

Was für ein Mensch ist sie?	*What sort of person is she?*
Was für einen Wagen hast du?	*What kind of car do you have?*
Mit **was für** Menschen lebst du zusammen?	*What kind of people do you live with?*

4 **Übung: Was für ein Buch ist das?** Jetzt fragt Ihr Professor zum Beispiel, was für ein Buch das ist. Sie beschreiben das Buch.

BEISPIEL: Was für ein Buch ist das?
Das ist ein interessantes Buch.

5 **Partnerarbeit: Nicht wahr?** Respond to each other's impressions. One partner asks, the other responds, then switch roles.

BEISPIEL: A: Das Haus ist schön, nicht wahr?
B: Ja, das ist ein schönes Haus. (*oder*)
Nein, das ist kein schönes Haus.

1. Die Kneipe ist alt, nicht?
2. Der Junge ist lustig, nicht wahr?
3. Das Hotel ist teuer, nicht wahr?
4. Der Automechaniker ist gut, nicht?
5. Das Kind ist müde, nicht wahr?
6. Die Buchhandlung ist fantastisch, nicht?
7. Das Bett ist bequem, nicht?
8. Der Tag ist warm, nicht?

Now create your own sentences on the same pattern.

6 Übung: Was für ein Buch brauchen Sie? Jetzt möchte Ihre Professorin wissen, was für Sachen Sie brauchen, tragen usw. Sagen Sie es ihr.

BEISPIELE: Was für ein Buch brauchen Sie?
Ich brauche ein neues Buch.

Was für Schuhe tragen Sie heute?
Heute trage ich alte Turnschuhe.

7 Gruppenarbeit: Wer trägt was? Benutzen Sie Adjektive, um die Kleider eines Studenten oder einer Studentin in der Klasse zu beschreiben. Die anderen müssen raten (*guess*), wen Sie meinen. Sie können auch Ihre eigenen Kleider beschreiben.

BEISPIEL: A: Wer trägt heute eine alte Hose und ein hässliches Hemd?
B: Meinst du Rick?

8 Übung: Wir haben keinen neuen Wagen. Ihr Professor fragt Sie nach (*about*) etwas. Sie antworten, dass Sie es nicht haben.

BEISPIEL: Ist Ihr Wagen neu?
Nein, ich habe keinen neuen Wagen.

1. Ist Ihr Fahrrad neu?
2. Sind diese Bücher langweilig?
3. Ist der Tennislehrer wunderbar?
4. Ist der Kaffee heiß?
5. Ist die Wurst frisch?
6. Sind Ihre Freunde lustig?
7. Sind diese Kleider schmutzig?
8. Ist Ihr Zimmer groß?
9. Ist Ihr Mantel neu?

9 Übung: Was machen Sie lieber? Der Professor fragt Sie, was Sie lieber machen.

BEISPIEL: Dieser Zug fährt langsam, aber dieser fährt schnell.
Mit welchem Zug fahren Sie lieber?
Ich fahre lieber mit dem langsamen Zug.

1. Dieser Kaffee ist heiß, aber dieser ist kalt. Welchen trinken Sie lieber?
2. Dieses Hemd ist rot und dieses ist gelb. Welches gefällt Ihnen besser?
3. Diese Kartoffeln sind groß, aber diese sind klein. Welche nehmen Sie?
4. Dieser See ist warm, aber dieser ist kühl. In welchem würden Sie lieber schwimmen?
5. Diese Stadt ist schön, aber diese ist hässlich. In welcher würden Sie lieber wohnen?
6. Dieses Zimmer ist hell, aber dieses ist dunkel. Welches gefällt Ihnen?
7. Dieses Hotel ist alt, aber dieses ist neu. In welchem würden Sie lieber übernachten?
8. Diese Brezeln sind frisch, aber diese sind alt. Welche würden Sie lieber essen?

Braunkohletagebau (*lignite strip mine*), Grevenbroich (Nordrhein-Westfalen)

10 Schreiben wir mal: Ich habe ein interessantes Bild gefunden. Suchen Sie in einem Bilderbuch oder einer Zeitschrift ein interessantes Bild oder Foto. Beschreiben Sie es. Benutzen Sie viele Adjektive! Sie können Ihre Beschreibung in der Deutschstunde vorlesen (*read aloud*).

BEISPIEL: Ich habe dieses schöne Bild in einem alten Buch gefunden. Hier sieht man viele Häuser in einem kleinen Dorf. In der Mitte des Bildes steht eine alte Kirche und vor dieser schönen Kirche geht ein alter Mann mit einem kleinen Kind spazieren. Hinter dem Dorf sieht man auch einen dunklen Wald usw.

2. Word order of adverbs: Time/manner/place

Place can be either location (**zu Hause**) or destination (**nach Kopenhagen**).

You learned in **Kapitel 1** that adverb sequence in German is *time* before *place*.

	time	*place*
Ich fahre	**morgen**	**nach Kopenhagen**.
Wir bleiben	**heute**	**zu Hause**.

If an adverb or adverbial phrase of *manner* (answering the questions **wie?** or **mit wem?**) is also present, the sequence is *time—manner—place*.

	time	*manner*	*place*
Ich fahre	morgen	**mit der Bahn**	nach Kopenhagen.
Sie bleibt	heute	**allein**	zu Hause.

A good mnemonic device is that adverbs answer the following questions in alphabetical order:

wann? (morgen) **wie?** (mit der Bahn) **wo (hin)?** (nach Kopenhagen)

SAM Workbook Kap. 9, I.

11 Gruppenarbeit: Wie? Mit wem? Create your own answers to these questions. Follow the example sentences.

1. Wie können wir morgen nach Berlin fahren?
   Wie viele Möglichkeiten gibt es für eine Reise nach Berlin?

   BEISPIEL: Wir können morgen *mit der Bahn* nach Berlin fahren.

2. Mit wem gehen Sie abends ins Kino?

   BEISPIEL: Ich gehe abends *mit meinem Freund* ins Kino.

12 Schreiben wir mal. Combine elements of your choice from the following lists to write ten sentences that describe activities. Create both statements and questions and use both present and perfect tense.

Wann?	**Wie?**	**Wo(hin)?**	**Verben**
im Oktober	mit meinen Freunden	ins Ausland	reisen
letzten Dienstag	allein	im Bett	liegen
morgen	mit dem Zug	in der Bibliothek	lesen
gestern	mit dem Auto	ins Kino	übernachten
2008	ziemlich schnell	in die Bibliothek	gehen
heute	gerne	in der Jugendherberge	essen
am Mittwoch	fleißig	im Tennisklub	joggen
nächsten Monat	zusammen	an der Uni	Sport treiben
dieses Semester	ohne mich	in der Mensa	Tennis spielen
letztes Jahr	glücklicherweise	nach Österreich	sein

BEISPIELE: Am Mittwoch esse ich mit meinen Freunden in der Mensa.
Wann habt ihr zusammen in der Jugendherberge übernachtet?

3. Ordinal numbers and dates (*Ordinalzahlen; das Datum*)

The ordinal numbers (*first, second, third,* etc.) are adjectives and in German take the usual adjective endings.

German numbers up to **neunzehn** add **-t-** to the cardinal number and then the appropriate adjective ending. Note the three irregular forms in boldface.

der, das, die	**erste**	*1st*	elfte	*11th*
	zweite	*2nd*	zwölfte	*12th*
	dritte	*3rd*	dreizehnte	*13th*
	vierte	*4th*	vierzehnte	*14th*
	fünfte	*5th*	fünfzehnte	*15th*
	sechste	*6th*	sechzehnte	*16th*
	siebte	*7th*	siebzehnte	*17th*
	achte	*8th*	achtzehnte	*18th*
	neunte	*9th*	neunzehnte	*19th*
	zehnte	*10th*		

The numbers **zwanzig** and above add **-st-** and the adjective ending to the cardinal number.

der, das, die	zwanzigste	*20th*
	einundzwanzigste	*21st*
	zweiundzwanzigste	*22nd*
	dreiundzwanzigste	*23rd*
	usw.	
	dreißigste	*30th*
	vierzigste	*40th*
	hundertste	*100th*
	tausendste	*1000th*

In German, an ordinal number is seldom written out in letters. It is usually indicated by a period after the numeral.

The ordinal numbers are capitalized here (**die Erste, der Zweite**) because they are being used as nouns. See **Kapitel 11**, pp. 301–302.

der **10**. November = der zehnte November

13 Kettenreaktion: Ich bin die Erste. Ich bin der Zweite. Count off using ordinal numbers. Males say **der** ..., females say **die** ...

Giving the date is a communicative goal.

Dates in German

In German, the full date is given in the order: day, month, year.

den 01.02.2009 *February 1, 2009*

Here is how to say on what date something occurs or occurred:

Das war **am zehnten** August.	*That was on the tenth of August.*
Wir fliegen **am Achtzehnten**.	*We're flying on the eighteenth.*

To tell in what year something happened, English uses a phrase with *in*: *in 2008*. The German equivalent is **im Jahre 2008** or simply **2008** (no **in**): **Ich bin 1990 geboren. Im Jahre 2005 war ich mit meiner Familie in Berlin.**

Here is how to ask for and give the date:

Den Wievielten haben wir heute? *or* **Der Wievielte** ist heute?	*What's the date today?* (literally: *"The 'how manyeth' do we have today / is today?"*)
Heute haben wir **den Dreizehnten.** *or* Heute ist **der Dreizehnte.**	*Today is the thirteenth.*

SAM **Lab Manual** Kap. 9, Üb. 14, 15.

SAM **Workbook** Kap. 9, J, K.

14 Übung: Der Wievielte ist heute? Tell your instructor what date it is, using the cues below.

A. Der Wievielte ist heute?
Heute ist der ...
3. August
9. Februar
1. Mai
20. Juli
2. Januar
8. April

B. Den Wievielten haben wir heute?
Heute haben wir den ...
5. März
13. Juni
19. November
11. September
7. Dezember
28. Oktober

15 Übung: Wann kommt Frank? Tell your instructor when Frank is coming, using the cues below.

Er kommt am ...
4. Januar
30. September
5. April
25. Juli
31. Oktober
20. Februar
24. März

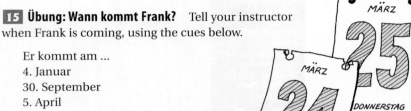

16 Partnerarbeit: Wann gehen wir ins Konzert? Auf Seite 249 sehen Sie einen Spielplan aus Berlin. Es spielen hauptsächlich Jugendorchester aus der ganzen Welt in einem Sommerfestival der klassischen Musik. Suchen Sie mit Ihrem Partner diese Informationen auf dem Plan.

1. Aus welchen Ländern kommen die Orchester? Finden Sie mindestens (*at least*) sechs Länder.
2. An welchem Tag spielt das Danubia Youth Symphony Orchestra? (Sagen Sie das Datum.) (Am ...)
3. Welches Orchester spielt am 4.8.?
4. Wann kann man ein Werk von Richard Strauss hören? (Am ... und am ...) Und von Beethoven? (Am ...) Von Prokofjew? (Am ...)
5. Wo kann man Konzerte im Freien (= *draußen*) hören?
6. Um wie viel Uhr beginnt das Konzert auf dem Gendarmenmarkt am 12.7.? (Um ...)

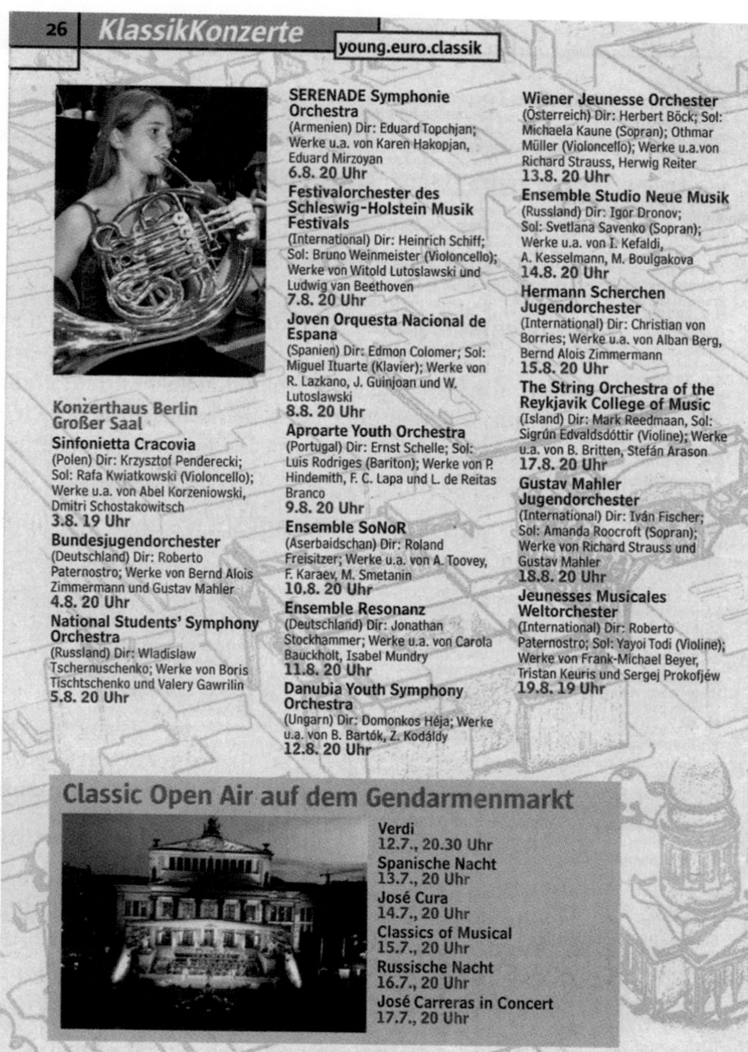

26 KlassikKonzerte young.euro.classik

Konzerthaus Berlin
Großer Saal

Sinfonietta Cracovia
(Polen) Dir: Krzysztof Penderecki; Sol: Rafa Kwiatkowski (Violoncello); Werke u.a. von Abel Korzeniowski, Dmitri Schostakowitsch
3.8. 19 Uhr

Bundesjugendorchester
(Deutschland) Dir: Roberto Paternostro; Werke von Bernd Alois Zimmermann und Gustav Mahler
4.8. 20 Uhr

National Students' Symphony Orchestra
(Russland) Dir: Wladislaw Tschernuschenko; Werke von Boris Tischtschenko und Valery Gawrilin
5.8. 20 Uhr

SERENADE Symphonie Orchestra
(Armenien) Dir: Eduard Topchjan; Werke u.a. von Karen Hakopjan, Eduard Mirzoyan
6.8. 20 Uhr

Festivalorchester des Schleswig-Holstein Musik Festivals
(International) Dir: Heinrich Schiff; Sol: Bruno Weinmeister (Violoncello); Werke von Witold Lutoslawski und Ludwig van Beethoven
7.8. 20 Uhr

Joven Orquesta Nacional de Espana
(Spanien) Dir: Edmon Colomer; Sol: Miguel Ituarte (Klavier); Werke von R. Lazkano, J. Guinjoan und W. Lutoslawski
8.8. 20 Uhr

Aproarte Youth Orchestra
(Portugal) Dir: Ernst Schelle; Sol: Luis Rodriges (Bariton); Werke von P. Hindemith, F. C. Lapa und L. de Reitas Branco
9.8. 20 Uhr

Ensemble SoNoR
(Aserbaidschan) Dir: Roland Freisitzer; Werke u.a. von A. Toovey, F. Karaev, M. Smetanin
10.8. 20 Uhr

Ensemble Resonanz
(Deutschland) Dir: Jonathan Stockhammer; Werke u.a. von Carola Bauckholt, Isabel Mundry
11.8. 20 Uhr

Danubia Youth Symphony Orchestra
(Ungarn) Dir: Domonkos Héja; Werke u.a. von B. Bartók, Z. Kodály
12.8. 20 Uhr

Wiener Jeunesse Orchester
(Österreich) Dir: Herbert Böck; Sol: Michaela Kaune (Sopran); Othmar Müller (Violoncello); Werke u.a.von Richard Strauss, Herwig Reiter
13.8. 20 Uhr

Ensemble Studio Neue Musik
(Russland) Dir: Igor Dronov; Sol: Svetlana Savenko (Sopran); Werke u.a. von I. Kefaldi, A. Kesselmann, M. Boulgakova
14.8. 20 Uhr

Hermann Scherchen Jugendorchester
(International) Dir: Christian von Borries; Werke u.a. von Alban Berg, Bernd Alois Zimmermann
15.8. 20 Uhr

The String Orchestra of the Reykjavik College of Music
(Island) Dir: Mark Reedmaan, Sol: Sigrún Edvaldsdóttir (Violine); Werke u.a. von B. Britten, Stefán Arason
17.8. 20 Uhr

Gustav Mahler Jugendorchester
(International) Dir: Iván Fischer; Sol: Amanda Roocroft (Sopran); Werke von Richard Strauss und Gustav Mahler
18.8. 20 Uhr

Jeunesses Musicales Weltorchester
(International) Dir: Roberto Paternostro; Sol: Yayoi Todi (Violine); Werke von Frank-Michael Beyer, Tristan Keuris und Sergej Prokofjéw
19.8. 19 Uhr

Classic Open Air auf dem Gendarmenmarkt

Verdi
12.7., 20.30 Uhr
Spanische Nacht
13.7., 20 Uhr
José Cura
14.7., 20 Uhr
Classics of Musical
15.7., 20 Uhr
Russische Nacht
16.7., 20 Uhr
José Carreras in Concert
17.7., 20 Uhr

17 Adjektive im Kontext. Rewrite this narrative, filling in each blank with an appropriate adjective. Don't forget to add the endings where they are needed.

Heute ist der ________ Mai und es ist ein ________ Tag. Ich bin mit meiner ________ Freundin Laura im ________ Wald spazieren gegangen. Die Sonne war ________ und im Wald war es sehr ________. Wir haben unser Mittagessen mitgebracht und um ein Uhr waren wir schon hungrig. Aber wir haben vergessen eine Flasche Wein mitzubringen. Glücklicherweise hat es im Wald ein ________ Restaurant gegeben, und bald haben wir es gefunden. Dort haben wir also eine ________ Flasche Wein gekauft. Die Kellnerin war eine sehr ________ Frau. Mit ihr haben wir über das ________ Wetter gesprochen. Sie hat auch ein ________ Kind gehabt und wir haben ein bisschen mit diesem ________ Mädchen gespielt. Später haben wir meinen ________ Freund Hannes getroffen. Er hat uns seinen ________ Wagen gezeigt. Am Ende dieses ________ Tages sind wir dann mit der Straßenbahn in die ________ Stadt zurückgefahren.

LESESTÜCK

Tipps zum Lesen und Lernen

Tipps zum Vokabelnlernen

Identifying noun gender Now that you have acquired a German vocabulary of several hundred words, you can begin to recognize some patterns in the gender and formation of nouns. You have already learned that agent nouns ending in **-er** are always masculine (**der Lehrer**) and that the ending **-in** always designates a female (**die Lehrerin**).

The gender of many nouns is determined by a suffix. Here are some of the most common noun suffixes.

- Nouns with the following suffixes are *always feminine* and *always* have the plural ending **-en**:

-ung, -heit, -keit, -schaft, -ion, -tät

- The suffix **-ung** forms nouns from verb stems.

lösen (*to solve*) → **die Lösung** (*solution*)
zerstören (*to destroy*) → **die Zerstörung** (*destruction*)
verschmutzen (*to pollute*) → **die Verschmutzung** (*pollution*)

- The suffixes **-heit** and **-keit** form nouns from adjective stems and from other nouns.

frei →	**die Freiheit**	(*freedom*)
freundlich →	**die Freundlichkeit**	(*friendliness*)
gesund →	**die Gesundheit**	(*health*)
Mensch →	**die Menschheit**	(*humanity*)
sicher →	**die Sicherheit**	(*security, safety; certainty*)

- The suffix **-schaft** forms collective and more abstract nouns from concrete nouns.

Studenten →	**die Studentenschaft**	(*student body*)
Land →	**die Landschaft, -en**	(*landscape*)
Freund →	**die Freundschaft, -en**	(*friendship*)

- Words with the suffixes **-ion** and **-tät** are borrowed from French or Latin. Most have English cognates.

die Diskussion, -en **die Universität, -en**
die Generation, -en **die Elektrizität**

Internationales Immobilienbüro
in München sucht
flexible Sekretärin
für sämtliche Bürotätigkeiten bei
bester Bezahlung.
office@tarumhall.com

- The suffixes **-chen** and **-lein** form diminutives. The stem vowel of the noun is umlauted wherever possible, and the noun automatically becomes *neuter*. The plural and singular forms are always identical.

die Karte →	**das Kärtchen, -**	(*little card*)
das Stück →	**das Stückchen, -**	(*little piece*)
das Brot →	**das Brötchen, -**	
die Magd (archaic: *maid*) →	**das Mädchen, -**	
die Frau →	**das Fräulein, -**	(*Miss; young woman*)
das Buch →	**das Büchlein, -**	(*little book*)

Übung: Raten Sie mal! (*Take a guess!*) Was bedeuten diese Wörter?

1. die Möglichkeit
2. die Wanderung
3. die Ähnlichkeit
4. die Mehrheit
5. die Meinung
6. die Lehrerschaft
7. die Wohnung
8. die Schönheit
9. die Dummheit
10. die Studentenschaft
11. die Radikalität
12. die Gesundheit
13. die Schwierigkeit
14. das Brüderlein
15. das Liedchen
16. das Städtchen
17. das Würstchen
18. das Häuschen
19. die Kindheit
20. die Menschheit

Lab Manual Kap. 9, Üb. zur Betonung.

Leicht zu merken

aktiv	aktiv
akut	
das **Atom, -e**	Atom
die **Basis**	
die **Elektrizität**	Elektrizität
die **Energie**	Energie
enorm	
die **Industrie, -n**	Industrie
die **Konsequenz, -en**	Konsequenz
der **Lebensstandard**	
die **Natur**	Natur
das **Ökosystem**	Ökosystem
das **Plastik**	
politisch	
produzieren	produzieren
das **Prozent** (%)	
radikal	radikal
sortieren	sortieren
sowjetisch	sowjetisch
der **Supertanker, -**	

**Die Wälder sterben-
nach den Wäldern
sterben die Menschen.**

Einstieg in den Text

The following text discusses environmental issues of global concern. They are particularly crucial in densely populated Europe.

Look over **Wortschatz 2**, then read the following hypotheses about the environment. Do you agree or disagree with them? Compare your responses to the opinions expressed in the reading.

	Das stimmt.	Das stimmt nicht.
1. Wir sind heute immer noch sehr abhängig von (*dependent upon*) der Natur.	☐	☐
2. Die Schwerindustrie ist für die Umweltverschmutzung verantwortlich.	☐	☐
3. Die Atomenergie ist eine gute Alternative zum Öl.	☐	☐
4. Der Durchschnittsbürger (*average citizen*) kann im Alltag viel gegen die Umweltverschmutzung tun.	☐	☐
5. Die Politiker müssen viel mehr für die Umwelt tun.	☐	☐

You have now learned all four cases in German, you understand the stucture of dependent clauses and infinitive phrases, and you have learned how to use attributive adjectives. Consequently, you can now understand fairly complex and sophisticated German. You will notice that in the second half of ***Neue Horizonte***, the **Lesestücke** are more challenging. Here is a sentence from lines 29–31:

> Aber nicht nur die umweltbewusste Jugend, sondern auch Deutsche aus allen Altersgruppen sind heute bereit ihr Leben zu ändern, um Meere, Wälder, Tiere und Pflanzen zu retten.

Although much of the vocabulary in this sentence is new, try to identify the following elements and write them down without looking up words.

1. the lengthy compound subject in first position
2. the two elements being contrasted by **nicht nur ... sondern auch**
3. the verb of the main clause in second position
4. the predicate adjective used with the verb
5. the infinitive phrase at the end of the main clause
6. the **um ... zu** phrase that ends the sentence

Now try translating the entire sentence into English. The glosses will help you.

Storks (**der Storch, ¨e**) are an endangered species; they nest in Europe and winter in North Africa. Europeans put wagon wheels on high roofs as nesting platforms for storks, which are traditionally believed to bring good luck.

MEHR LEBENSRAUM
FÜR DEN WEISS-STORCH

Wortschatz 2

In-Text Audio CD

Verben

benutzen to use
lösen to solve
retten to rescue, save
verschmutzen to pollute; to dirty
verschwenden to waste
werfen (wirft), hat geworfen to throw
  weg·werfen to throw away, discard

Substantive

der **Fisch, -e** fish
der **Politiker, -** politician (*m.*)
der **Preis, -e** price
der **Unfall, ¨e** accident
der **Vogel, ¨** bird
das **Beispiel, -e** example
das **Kraftwerk, -e** power plant
  das **Atomkraftwerk** atomic power plant
das **Öl** oil
das **Tier, -e** animal
die **Chance, -n** chance
die **Dose, -n** (tin) can
die **Gefahr, -en** danger
die **Gesellschaft, -en** society
die **Gesundheit** health
die **Jugend** (*sing.*) youth; young people
die **Kraft, ¨e** power, strength
die **Lösung, -en** solution
die **Menschheit** mankind, human race
die **Partei, -en** political party
die **Pflanze, -n** plant
die **Politik** politics; policy
die **Politikerin, -nen** politician (*f.*)
die **Technik** technology
die **Ware, -n** product
die **Zukunft** the future

Adjektive und Adverbien

bereit prepared, ready
eigen- own
ernst serious
erstaunlich astounding
gefährlich dangerous
gesund healthy
hoch (*predicate adj.*),
  hoh- (*attributive adj.*) high
  Das Gebäude ist **hoch**. *aber* Das ist ein **hohes** Gebäude.
jährlich annually
sauer sour; acidic
  der saure Regen acid rain
ungefähr approximately

Andere Vokabeln

mancher, -es, -e many a (*in plural* = some)
  manche Pflanzen some plants
obwohl (*sub. conj.*) although
solcher, -es, -e such, such a

Gegensätze

die **Gesundheit** ≠ die **Krankheit** health ≠ sickness
hoch ≠ **niedrig** high ≠ low
sauer ≠ **süß** sour ≠ sweet

BITTE VERLASSEN SIE DIESEN PLANETEN SO, WIE SIE IHN VORZUFINDEN WÜNSCHEN!

PVC = Polyvinylchlorid

Gesunder Wald in den Alpen

Learning about German and global environmental issues is the cultural goal of this chapter.

Unsere Umwelt in Gefahr

Das Problem: Der Mensch gegen die Natur?

Wir leben heute in Europa und Nordamerika in einer hoch industrialisierten° Welt. Wir lieben unseren Luxus° und brauchen die Technik, denn sie ist die Basis unseres hohen Lebensstandards. Aber der Preis für diesen erstaunlichen Fortschritt ist sehr hoch. Manchmal vergessen wir, dass wir immer noch von der Natur abhängig° sind.

Um unsere Lebensweise° möglich zu machen, brauchen wir enorm viel Energie. Obwohl die Nordamerikaner und Westeuropäer nur zirka 15% der Weltbevölkerung° sind, verbrauchen° sie zirka 65% aller produzierten Energie. Spätestens° seit der Katastrophe im sowjetischen Atomkraftwerk in Tschernobyl am 26. April 1986 weiß man aber, wie gefährlich diese Energiequelle° für unser Ökosystem sein kann. Ein zweites Beispiel ist die Exxon-Valdez-Katastrophe vom Jahre 1989; das Öl aus diesem verunglückten° Supertanker hat das Meer verschmutzt und Fische und Vögel weit und breit° in Gefahr gebracht. Die schlimmen Folgen° von solchen Unfällen können jahrelang fortdauern°. Leider sind aber alle unsere Hauptenergiequellen (Öl, Kohle°, Atomkraft) schädlich° für die Natur und für unsere Gesundheit.

Aber nicht nur die Schwerindustrie muss für die Umwelt verantwortlich sein, sondern auch jeder einzelne° Mensch. Wir fahren zu viel Auto, wir essen zu viel in Fastfood-Restaurants, wir benutzen zu viele Spraydosen° und produzieren zu viel

hoch ... *highly industrialized*
luxury
von ... *dependent on nature*
way of life
world population
consume / at the latest
energy source
grounded
weit... *far and wide / consequences /* ***jahrelang ...*** *persist for years / coal / harmful*
individual
aerosol cans

Waldsterben

Müll. Die Konsequenzen sind: der saure Regen, Müllhalden° voll von unnötigen Plastikverpackungen° und die Zerstörung der Ozonschicht°. Das Problem ist im dicht besiedelten° Deutschland besonders akut. Dort wirft jeder Bürger jährlich ungefähr 300 bis 400 kg Müll weg! Man möchte wirklich fragen: Sind wir Menschen denn die Feinde° der Natur?

trash dumps
plastic packaging / ozone layer / ***dicht besiedelt*** *= densely populated*
enemies

Die Lösung: aktiv umweltfreundlich sein!

Besonders die junge Generation in Deutschland zeigt für diese ernsten Probleme starkes Engagement°. Manche finden bei den Grünen eine Alternative zu der Umweltpolitik der anderen Parteien.[2] Für viele zeigen Wind- und Sonnenenergie anstatt Atomkraft den Weg in die Zukunft. Auch in ihrem eigenen Leben suchen sie Alternativen zu der Wegwerfgesellschaft. Aber nicht nur die umweltbewusste° Jugend, sondern auch Deutsche aus allen Altersgruppen° sind heute bereit ihr Leben zu ändern°, um Meere, Wälder, Tiere und Pflanzen zu retten.[3]

commitment
environmentally conscious
age groups
change

Wie kann man denn ein umweltfreundliches Leben führen? Man kann z. B. mehr Rad fahren oder zu Fuß gehen und weniger° Auto fahren. Man sollte° nur Waren ohne unnötige Verpackung kaufen und den Hausmüll sortieren und zum Recycling bringen. Man kann auch so wenig Wasser und Elektrizität wie° möglich verschwenden. Diese Vorschläge° für den Alltag sind nur ein Anfang. Man muss natürlich auch von den Politikern mehr Umweltbewusstsein° fordern°. Die Menschheit hat nicht mehr viel Zeit. Nur wenn alle Länder politisch zusammenarbeiten, haben wir noch eine Chance unsere Umwelt zu retten.

less / should
so ... wie *= as ... as*
suggestions
environmental awareness / demand

---

[2] **Die Grünen** (*the Greens*) began as an environmental and anti-nuclear party and was the junior partner in coalition with the SPD (Social Democratic Party) from 1998 to 2006. All the major German parties now take environmental issues seriously in their platforms.

[3] In 1990 the Federal Republic became the first nation to ban the production and use of ozone-depleting chlorofluorocarbons.

NACH DEM LESEN

SAM **Lab Manual** Kap. 9, Diktat.

SAM **Workbook** Kap. 9, L–N.

Discussing ecology and recycling is a communicative goal.

A Antworten Sie auf Deutsch.

1. Von welchen Umweltkatastrophen haben Sie schon gehört?
2. Wann war die Katastrophe in Tschernobyl?
3. Wie können Umweltkatastrophen für die Natur gefährlich sein?
4. Wer soll denn für die Umwelt verantwortlich sein?
5. Nennen Sie unsere Hauptenergiequellen.
6. Kennen Sie alternative Energiequellen?
7. Wie kann unser modernes Alltagsleben für die Umwelt gefährlich sein?
8. Wie können wir ein umweltfreundliches Leben führen?

B Gruppenarbeit: Unsere Wegwerfgesellschaft? (*4 oder 5 Personen*) Jeden Tag benutzen wir viele Sachen. Aber wir verschwenden auch eine Menge, besonders Dinge aus Plastik. Machen Sie eine Liste von solchen Dingen aus Ihrem Alltag. Was haben Sie in den letzten Tagen wegwerfen müssen? Warum?

Liste: „Das haben wir in letzter Zeit weggeworfen."

C Gruppenarbeit: Es gibt eine Alternative! Hier sind einige Beispiele der Umweltverschmutzung. Können Sie Alternativen geben?

BEISPIEL: Einen Plastiklöffel wirft man meistens weg.
Alternative: Aber ich muss nicht mit Plastiklöffeln essen.

1. Meine Familie wirft jede Woche viele Flaschen weg.
2. Sonntags fahre ich gern im eigenen Auto aufs Land.
3. Im Supermarkt sind die Lebensmittel alle in Plastik verpackt.
4. Manchmal werfen Menschen Papier auf die Straße.
5. Wenn mein Kugelschreiber keine Tinte (*ink*) mehr hat, werfe ich ihn weg.
6. In unserem Studentenwohnheim gibt es keine Recyclingcontainer.

D Übung. Construct sentences from the elements provided. Be prepared to translate your sentences into English.

1. mein / umweltfreundlich / Mitbewohner / tragen / Müll / in / Keller
2. alle / neu / Einwohner / unser- (*gen.*) / Studentenwohnheim- / mitmachen
3. das / riesengroß / Zimmer / ist / sonnig / und / ich / haben / mein / eigen / Schreibtisch
4. um / ein / lang, / gesund / Leben / haben, / sollen / jed- / Mensch / aktiv / bleiben
5. bei / dies- / schön / Wetter / wir / wollen / zusammen / zum / neu / Tennisplatz / gehen
6. ich / haben / ein / gut / Gefühl, / wenn / ich / mein- / schmutzig / alt / Dosen / zum / Recycling / schleppen

SCHREIBTIPP

Using adjectives in descriptions

- Before you begin writing, think about the place or person you are describing and make a list of adjectives appropriate to your subject. If you were going to write about a place on the ocean, you might list **sonnig**, **warm**, **flach**, **blau**, etc. Consult an English-German dictionary for adjectives you don't find in ***Neue Horizonte***.
- Try to use your adjectives attributively, i.e., instead of writing **Das Meer ist blau**, write **Das blaue Meer ist wunderschön**.
- Once you've written your first draft, review each noun phrase. Have you used the correct adjective endings?

Schreiben wir mal. Schreiben Sie eine Seite über eines dieser Themen (*themes*).

1. Sie kennen sicher eine Landschaft oder einen Ort (*place*), wo die Natur besonders schön ist. Beschreiben Sie diesen Ort und sagen Sie, warum Sie ihn schön finden. Benutzen Sie Adjektive!

   BEISPIEL: Hinter unserem Haus gibt es einen kleinen Wald mit schönen, hohen Bäumen.
   Dort habe ich als Kind ...

2. Beschreiben Sie einen wichtigen Menschen in Ihrem Leben.

E Klassendiskussion: Was meinen Sie?

1. Kann man fit bleiben, ohne Sport zu treiben?
2. In Deutschland gibt es viele Sportklubs, aber nur wenige (*few*) Universitätsmannschaften (*university teams*). Finden Sie es gut, dass es solche Mannschaften an amerikanischen Unis gibt? Warum?

F Wie sagt man das auf Deutsch?

1. What's the date today?
2. It's April 5th. Why do you ask?
3. My old friend Markus has a birthday today, and I haven't called him up yet.

4. Can you recommend a good restaurant to me?
5. Do you like to eat French food?
6. Of course. Do you know a good French restaurant?
7. Yes. My favorite restaurant is in the old part of town (**Altstadt**).

8. Are you throwing these old bottles away, Frau Schuhmacher?
9. Yes, I don't have time to carry them to the cellar.
10. May I have them? I'm collecting bottles to earn money.

ALMANACH

Seid ihr schlaue Umweltfüchse?

Der „Bund für Umwelt und Naturschutz Deutschland" ist eine Lobby von umweltfreundlichen Menschen. In einer Broschüre geben sie Tipps zum Schutz (*protection*) der Umwelt.

Umweltfüchse wissen, ...

- dass Wasser ein Lebensmittel ist.
- dass jeder Deutsche pro Tag zirka 150 Liter Trinkwasser benutzt.

Schlaue Umweltfüchse ...

- werfen keine Medikamente in die Toilette, sondern bringen sie zur Sammelstelle für Giftmüll.
- duschen lieber, als ein Vollbad zu nehmen, weil sie beim Duschen nur 50 bis 100 Liter Wasser benutzen, statt 200 Liter beim Baden.

Umweltfüchse wissen, ...

- dass die Bundesrepublik jedes Jahr einen Müllberg produziert, der so groß wie die Zugspitze ist.
- dass nur 11 Prozent dieses Mülls echter Müll sind. 89 Prozent wären recyclebar.

Schlaue Umweltfüchse ...

- kaufen Recyclingprodukte, z. B. Umweltschutzpapier.
- sortieren ihren Müll und bringen Glasflaschen, Metall und Papier zu Containern oder direkt zum Recycling.

Hier kann man Glas recyceln (Darmstadt).

Wäsche an der Leine in der Nähe von Herford (Niedersachsen). Warum ist das besonders umweltfreundlich?

KAPITEL

10

Frankfurt am Main

Deutschland im 20. Jahrhundert

Kommunikation

- Narrating events in the past
- Telling how long ago something happened
- Telling how long something lasted

Kultur

- The Weimar Republic (1919–1933)

In diesem Kapitel

- **Lyrik zum Vorlesen**
  Bertolt Brecht, "Mein junger Sohn fragt mich"
- **Grammatik**
  1. Simple past tense
  2. Equivalents of *when*: **als, wenn, wann**
  3. Past perfect tense
  4. More time expressions
- **Lesestück**
  Eine Ausstellung historischer Plakate aus der Weimarer Republik
- **Almanach**
  German Politics and the European Union

DIALOGE

Lab Manual Kap. 10, Dialoge, Fragen, Hören Sie gut zu!

Damals

Zwei Senioren sitzen nachmittags auf einer Bank.

HERR ZIEGLER: Wie lange wohnen Sie schon hier, Frau Planck?
FRAU PLANCK: Seit letztem Jahr. Vorher habe ich in Mainz gewohnt.
HERR ZIEGLER: Tatsächlich? Das wusste ich ja gar nicht. Als ich ein Kind war, habe ich immer den ganzen Sommer dort bei meinen Großeltern verbracht.
FRAU PLANCK: Ja, damals vor dem Krieg war die Stadt natürlich ganz anders.

Das ärgert mich!

The tag question ... **oder**? (here = *Did you?*) can follow either positive or negative statements. **Nicht wahr?** (p. 79) follows positive statements only.

JÜRGEN: Heinz, was ist denn los? Du siehst so besorgt aus.
HEINZ: Ach, Barbara hat mir vor zwei Tagen ihren neuen iPod geliehen ...
JÜRGEN: Na und? Du hast ihn doch nicht verloren, oder?
HEINZ: Keine Ahnung. Ich hatte ihn in meinem Rucksack, aber vor zehn Minuten konnte ich ihn dann plötzlich nicht mehr finden.
JÜRGEN: So ein Mist! Meinst du, jemand hat ihn dir geklaut?
HEINZ: Nee, ich glaube nicht, denn mein Geldbeutel fehlt nicht ... Mensch, das ärgert mich!

Schlimme Zeiten

Als Hausaufgabe muss Steffi (14 Jahre alt) ihre Oma interviewen.

STEFFI: Oma, für die Schule sollen wir unsere Großeltern über die Kriegszeit interviewen.
OMA: Nun, was willst du denn wissen, Steffi?
STEFFI: Also ... wann bist du eigentlich geboren?
OMA: 1935. Als der Krieg anfing, war ich noch ein kleines Mädchen.
STEFFI: Erzähl mir bitte, wie es euch damals ging.
OMA: Gott sei Dank lebten wir auf dem Land und zuerst ging es uns relativ gut, obwohl wir nicht reich waren.
STEFFI: Was ist dann passiert?
OMA: Das dauerte nur bis 1943. Dann ist mein Bruder in Russland gefallen und ein Jahr später starb meine Mutter.

Remember: English *in 1935* = **1935** (no *in*) or **im Jahre 1935**.

Note the restricted meaning of **fallen** in this context: *to die in combat*. Proverb: **Generale siegen, Soldaten fallen** (**siegen** = *to be victorious*).

NOTE ON USAGE

Flavoring particle *doch*

In **Kapitel 4**, you learned that **doch** can soften a command to a suggestion. In a statement, **doch** adds emphasis in the sense of *surely, really*. In the second dialogue, Jürgen fears the worst and says to Heinz:

Du hast ihn **doch** nicht verloren, oder? (*Surely*) *you haven't lost it, have you?*

Wortschatz 1

Verben

ärgern to annoy
dauern to last; to take (time)
fallen (fällt), fiel, ist gefallen to fall; to die in battle
fehlen to be missing; to be absent
interviewen, hat interviewt to interview
leihen, lieh, hat geliehen to lend, loan; to borrow
passieren, passierte, ist passiert to happen
stehlen (stiehlt), stahl, hat gestohlen to steal

Substantive

der **Geldbeutel, -** wallet, change purse
der **Monat, -e** month
der **Senior, -en, -en** senior citizen
die **Bank, ¨-e** bench

Adjektive und Adverbien

besorgt worried, concerned
damals at that time, back then
letzt- last
plötzlich sudden(ly)
reich rich
tatsächlich actually, really

Andere Vokabeln

als (*sub. conj.*) when, as
doch (*flavoring particle, see p. 261*)
nachdem (*sub. conj.*) after
nun now; well; well now

Nützliche Ausdrücke

(Ich habe) keine Ahnung. (I have) no idea.
den ganzen Sommer (Tag, Nachmittag usw.) all summer (day, afternoon, etc.)
Na und? And so? So what?
So ein Mist! (*crude, colloq.*) What a drag! What a lot of bull!
Wann sind Sie geboren? When were you born?

Gegensätze

besorgt ≠ unbesorgt concerned ≠ carefree
reich ≠ arm rich ≠ poor

Mit anderen Worten

klauen (*colloq.*) = **stehlen**
nerven (*colloq.*) = **ärgern**

Variationen

A Persönliche Fragen

1. Heinz sieht besorgt aus, weil er etwas verloren hat. Haben Sie je etwas verloren? Was denn?
2. Was machen Sie, wenn Sie etwas nicht finden können?
3. Würden Sie jemand Ihren iPod leihen? Warum oder warum nicht?
4. Wissen Sie, wann und wo Ihre Eltern geboren sind? Ihre Großeltern?
5. Wie lange wohnen Sie schon in dieser Stadt?
6. Herr Ziegler hat als Kind seine Sommerferien bei seinen Großeltern verbracht. Wo haben Sie als Kind die Sommerferien verbracht?

B **Partnerarbeit: Fundbüro (*Lost and Found*).** Sie gehen zum Fundbüro, weil Sie etwas verloren haben. Unten ist eine Liste von Dingen im Fundbüro. Sagen Sie, was Sie verloren haben. Dann beschreiben Sie es.

BEISPIEL: A: Was haben Sie verloren?
B: Ich habe meine Kamera verloren.
A: Können Sie sie beschreiben?
B: Es war eine ______ Kamera.

Fahrrad	Pulli
Jacke	Turnschuhe
Koffer	Geldbeutel
Tasche	Reisetasche
Wörterbuch	Sonnenbrille

Fahrrad

Sonnen-
brillen
und Sport-Sonnenbrillen für Damen und Herren

C **Übung: Was ist passiert?** Gestern war sehr viel los. Sagen Sie, was passiert ist.

BEISPIEL: Können Sie uns sagen, was gestern passiert ist?
Ja, gestern ...

D **Übung: Den ganzen Tag.** How long did you do certain things? Answer that you did them all morning, all day, all week, all semester, and so on.

BEISPIEL: Wie lange sind Sie in Europa gewesen?
Ich war *den ganzen Sommer* da.

1. Wie lange haben Sie gestern Tennis gespielt?
2. Wie lange waren Sie in der Bibliothek?
3. Wie lange waren Sie mit Ihren Freunden zusammen?
4. Wie lange sind Sie im Bett geblieben?
5. Wie lange haben Sie an Ihrem Referat gearbeitet?

E **Kettenreaktion: Ich suche ... (*mit offenen Büchern*)** Wählen Sie ein Adjektiv und ein Substantiv und sagen Sie dann, was Sie suchen. Der nächste Student sagt, er hat das nicht. Dann geht's weiter.

BEISPIEL: A: Ich suche deutsche Zeitungen.
B: Leider habe ich keine deutschen Zeitungen. *Ich* suche ...

Adjektive		**Substantive**	
amerikanisch	bunt	Romane	Fahrräder
kurz	frisch	Menschen	Alternativen
bekannt	freundlich	Pullis	Politiker
gesund	kostenlos	Geschenke	Restaurants
toll	leer	Brötchen	Arbeiter
deutsch	nagelneu	Rucksäcke	Gebäude
lang	riesengroß	Flaschen	Kleider
ehrlich	sportlich	Bücher	Wälder
reich	umweltfreundlich	Professoren	Poster
interessant		Ideen	

LYRIK ZUM VORLESEN

Bertolt Brecht, whose best-known work is **Die Dreigroschenoper** (*Three-Penny Opera,* 1928, with music by Kurt Weill), fled Germany in 1933 to settle first in France, then in Scandinavia. This poem, written in Finland during World War II, is the sixth of the short cycle *1940*. It reflects events of that year.

›Der Klassiker der Vernunft‹
Bertolt Brecht
Große kommentierte Berliner und
Frankfurter Ausgabe in 30 Bänden
Suhrkamp

Mein junger Sohn fragt mich

Mein junger Sohn fragt mich: Soll ich
Mathematik lernen?
Wozu°, möchte ich sagen. Dass zwei
Stück Brot mehr ist als eines
Das wirst du auch so merken°.
Mein junger Sohn fragt mich: Soll
ich Französisch lernen?
Wozu, möchte ich sagen. Dieses Reich
geht unter°. Und
Reibe° du nur mit der Hand den Bauch°
und stöhne°
Und man wird dich schon verstehen.
Mein junger Sohn fragt mich: Soll
ich Geschichte lernen?
Wozu, möchte ich sagen. Lerne du
deinen Kopf in die Erde stecken°
Da wirst du vielleicht übrigbleiben°.

Ja, lerne Mathematik, sage ich
Lerne Französisch, lerne Geschichte!

Bertolt Brecht (1898–1956)

what for?
***Das ...** You'll notice that anyway*
***Reich ...** empire will collapse*
rub / belly
groan
***deinen ...** to stick your head in the sand*
***wirst übrigbleiben** = will survive*

GRAMMATIK

Narrating events in the past is a communicative goal.

Like the German present tense (see **Kapitel 1**, p. 24), the German past tense lacks progressive and emphatic forms (English: *was living, did live*).

You learned the simple past tense of **sein** in grammar section 1 of **Kapitel 6**.

1. Simple past tense *(das Präteritum)*

Written German uses the *simple past tense* (also called the *preterite*) to narrate events in the past. Most novels and stories are written in the simple past. In spoken German, however, the *perfect tense* is used to relate past events. Exceptions are **sein**, **haben**, and the modal verbs, which are used most frequently in the simple past in both conversation and writing.

Weak verbs and strong verbs form the simple past tense in different ways. About 90 percent of German verbs are weak, but the strong verbs introduced in ***Neue Horizonte*** occur very frequently.

Simple past of weak verbs

The marker for the simple past of weak verbs is **-te**. Weak verbs form the simple past by adding the following endings to the verb stem:

First- and third-person singular forms are identical: **ich wohnte**, **er wohnte**.

wohnen *to live*					
stem: **wohn-**					
ich	wohn-**te**	*I lived*	wir	wohn-**ten**	*we lived*
du	wohn-**test**	*you lived*	ihr	wohn-**tet**	*you lived*
er, es, sie	wohn-**te**	*he, it, she lived*	sie, Sie	wohn-**ten**	*they, you lived*

Verbs whose stems end in **-d** or **-t** add **-e-** between the stem and these endings:

arbeiten *to work*					
stem: **arbeit-**					
ich	arbeit-**ete**	*I worked*	wir	arbeit-**eten**	*we worked*
du	arbeit-**etest**	*you worked*	ihr	arbeit-**etet**	*you worked*
er, es, sie	arbeit-**ete**	*he, it, she worked*	sie, Sie	arbeit-**eten**	*they, you worked*

SAM Lab Manual — **Lab Manual** Kap. 10, Var. zu Üb. 1, 2, 4, 5, 7.

For weak verbs, the only form you need to know to generate all other possible forms is the infinitive: **wohnen**, **wohnte**, **hat gewohnt**; **arbeiten**, **arbeitete**, **hat gearbeitet**.

SAM Workbook — **Workbook** Kap. 10, A–E.

In narratives German uses the simple past rather than the perfect.

1 Übung: Doras Einkaufstag. Here is a present-tense narrative of Dora's day in town. Retell it in the simple past tense.

Dora **braucht** Lebensmittel. Sie **wartet** bis zehn Uhr, dann **kauft** sie in einer kleinen Bäckerei ein. Sie **bezahlt** ihre Brötchen und **dankt** der Verkäuferin. Draußen **schneit** es und sie **hört** Musik auf der Straße. Sie **sucht** ein Restaurant. Also **fragt** sie zwei Studenten. Die Studenten **zeigen** ihr ein gutes Restaurant gleich in der Nähe. Dort **bestellt** sie etwas zu essen und eine Tasse Kaffee. Es **schmeckt** ihr sehr gut, aber die Menschen am nächsten Tisch **quatschen** zu laut und das **nervt** sie ein bisschen.

Simple past of strong verbs

Strong verbs do *not* have the tense marker **-te**. Instead, the verb stem changes. This changed stem is called the *simple past stem*, e.g., nehmen, **nahm**, hat genommen. This new stem takes the following personal endings in the simple past tense:

nehmen *to take*					
simple past stem: **nahm-**					
ich	nahm	*I took*	wir	nahm-**en**	*we took*
du	nahm-**st**	*you took*	ihr	nahm-**t**	*you took*
er, es, sie	nahm	*he, it, she took*	sie, Sie	nahm-**en**	*they, you took*

Note that the **ich**- and the **er**, **es**, **sie**-forms of strong verbs have *no* endings in the simple past: **ich nahm**, **sie nahm**.

„Ich kam,
ich sah,
ich siegte."

Julius Cäsar

Principal parts of strong verbs

Not all strong verbs have a stem-vowel change in the **du**- and **er**-forms of the present tense (e.g., **ich sehe, du siehst, er sieht**), but all verbs having this change are strong.

The simple past stem is one of the *principal parts* of a strong German verb. The principal parts (**Stammformen**) are the three (or sometimes four) forms you must know in order to generate all other forms of a strong verb. You have now learned all of them.

infinitive	*3rd-person sing. present*	*simple past stem*	*auxiliary + past participle*
nehmen	**(nimmt)**	**nahm**	**hat genommen**

The table below lists the principal parts of all the strong verbs you have learned so far. As an aid to memorization, they have been arranged into groups according to the way their stem vowels change in the past tenses. Memorize their simple past stems and review your knowledge of the other principal parts. Verbs formed by adding prefixes to these stems are not included in the table, e.g., **abfahren**, **aufstehen**, **beschreiben**, **verstehen**.

Principal Parts of Strong Verbs				
Infinitive	**3rd p. sing. pres.**	**Simple past**	**Perfect**	**English**
anfangen	fängt an	**fing an**	hat angefangen	*to begin*
fallen	fällt	**fiel**	ist gefallen	*to fall; to die in battle*
halten	hält	**hielt**	hat gehalten	*to hold; to stop*
schlafen	schläft	**schlief**	hat geschlafen	*to sleep*
verlassen	verlässt	**verließ**	hat verlassen	*to leave*

These are the 51 strong verbs introduced so far. The new simple past tense forms are boldfaced. Give yourself plenty of time to learn these and practice them aloud with a friend.

Infinitive	3rd p. sing. pres.	Simple past	Perfect	English
aufwachsen	wächst auf	**wuchs auf**	ist aufgewachsen	*to grow up*
einladen	lädt ein	**lud ein**	hat eingeladen	*to invite*
fahren	fährt	**fuhr**	ist gefahren	*to drive*
tragen	trägt	**trug**	hat getragen	*to carry; to wear*
essen	isst	**aß**	hat gegessen	*to eat*
geben	gibt	**gab**	hat gegeben	*to give*
lesen	liest	**las**	hat gelesen	*to read*
sehen	sieht	**sah**	hat gesehen	*to see*
vergessen	vergisst	**vergaß**	hat vergessen	*to forget*
empfehlen	empfiehlt	**empfahl**	hat empfohlen	*to recommend*
helfen	hilft	**half**	hat geholfen	*to help*
nehmen	nimmt	**nahm**	hat genommen	*to take*
sprechen	spricht	**sprach**	hat gesprochen	*to speak*
stehlen	stiehlt	**stahl**	hat gestohlen	*to steal*
sterben	stirbt	**starb**	ist gestorben	*to die*
treffen	trifft	**traf**	hat getroffen	*to meet*
werfen	wirft	**warf**	hat geworfen	*to throw*
bleiben		**blieb**	ist geblieben	*to stay*
entscheiden		**entschied**	hat entschieden	*to decide*
leihen		**lieh**	hat geliehen	*to lend*
scheinen		**schien**	hat geschienen	*to shine; to seem*
schreiben		**schrieb**	hat geschrieben	*to write*
treiben		**trieb**	hat getrieben	*to drive, propel*
finden		**fand**	hat gefunden	*to find*
klingen		**klang**	hat geklungen	*to sound*
singen		**sang**	hat gesungen	*to sing*
trinken		**trank**	hat getrunken	*to drink*
beginnen		**begann**	hat begonnen	*to begin*
schwimmen		**schwamm**	ist geschwommen	*to swim*
liegen		**lag**	hat gelegen	*to lie*
sitzen		**saß**	hat gesessen	*to sit*
fliegen		**flog**	ist geflogen	*to fly*
fließen		**floss**	ist geflossen	*to flow*
genießen		**genoss**	hat genossen	*to enjoy*
schließen		**schloss**	hat geschlossen	*to close*
verlieren		**verlor**	hat verloren	*to lose*
ziehen		**zog**	hat gezogen	*to pull*
anrufen		**rief an**	hat angerufen	*to call up*
gehen		**ging**	ist gegangen	*to go*
hängen		**hing**	hat gehangen	*to be hanging*
heißen		**hieß**	hat geheißen	*to be called*
kommen		**kam**	ist gekommen	*to come*
laufen	läuft	**lief**	ist gelaufen	*to run*
sein	ist	**war**	ist gewesen	*to be*
stehen		**stand**	hat gestanden	*to stand*
tun		**tat**	hat getan	*to do*

2 Übung: Auf der Terrasse eines Cafés. Here is a present-tense narrative about two old friends. Retell it in the simple past tense.

Herr Ziegler und Frau Planck **sitzen** draußen am Cafétisch und **sprechen** miteinander. Beide **tragen** leichte, helle Kleidung, denn es **ist** sommerlich warm. Die Sonne **scheint** und sie **genießen** das herrliche Wetter. Sie **lesen** die Speisekarte zusammen. Herr Ziegler **trinkt** eine Tasse Kaffee und **isst** ein Stück Kuchen (*cake*), aber Frau Planck **nimmt** nur eine Tasse Tee. Die Tochter von Herrn Ziegler **kommt** später vorbei und **lädt** die zwei Senioren zum Abendessen am Samstag ein. Sie **bleiben** noch ein paar Minuten am Tisch, dann **stehen** sie auf, **geben** der Kellnerin ein Trinkgeld (*tip*) und **gehen** zusammen im Park spazieren.

3 Übung: Ein Brief. Complete this letter by filling in the verbs in the simple past tense. Some of the verbs are strong and some are weak.

Liebe Martina,

weißt du, was dem armen Ulrich vorgestern passiert ist? Er hat mich gestern angerufen und ________ (erzählen) es mir. Er ________ (kennen lernen) im Park eine sympathische junge Studentin ______. Sie ______ (aussehen) ganz elegant und reich ________. Zusammen ________ (sitzen) sie auf einer Bank und ________ (sprechen) über das Studium. Ulrich ________ (tragen) eine Jacke, aber weil es sehr heiß war, ________ (legen) er sie auf die Bank. Alles ________ (scheinen) gut zu gehen und Ulrich ________ (einladen) sie in ein Konzert ________. Sie ________ (sagen) ja und ________ (geben) ihm ihre Adresse und Telefonnummer. Nach ungefähr einer Stunde _____ (stehen) die Studentin auf und ________ (gehen) in die Bibliothek zurück. Am Abend ________ (kommen) er nach Hause und ________ (suchen) seinen Hausschlüssel in der Tasche seiner Jacke. Aber dort ________ (finden) er keinen Schlüssel und auch sein Geld ________ (sein) weg. Er ________ (rufen) die Nummer der Studentin an, aber sie ________ (wohnen) gar nicht da. So ein Mist, nicht?

Jetzt muss ich gehen. Viele Grüße,

deine Annelies

Simple past of modal verbs

English has no past tense for modal verbs like *must* and *may*. Instead, English uses *had to* and *was allowed to*. The German system is much more regular.

The modal verbs form their simple past with the **-te** marker, like the weak verbs. But those modals that have an umlaut in the infinitive *drop* it in the past tense.

müssen, musste					
ich	muss**te**	*I had to*	wir	muss**ten**	*we had to*
du	muss**test**	*you had to*	ihr	muss**tet**	*you had to*
er, es, sie	muss**te**	*he, it, she had to*	sie, Sie	muss**ten**	*they, you had to*

Similarly:

dürfen	ich **durfte**	*I was allowed to*
können	ich **konnte**	*I was able to*
mögen	ich **mochte**	*I liked*
sollen	ich **sollte**	*I was supposed to*
wollen	ich **wollte**	*I wanted to*

Note that **mögen** drops the umlaut and also has a consonant change in the simple past.

4 Übung

1. Sagen Sie, was Sie gestern machen mussten.

   BEISPIEL: Ich musste gestern zwei Bücher lesen.

2. Jetzt sagen Sie, was Sie und Ihre Freunde gestern machen wollten.

   BEISPIEL: Wir wollten gestern Ski fahren gehen.

3. Was durften Sie als Kind nicht machen?

   BEISPIEL: Ich durfte nie allein schwimmen gehen.

Simple past of mixed verbs

The mixed verbs (see p. 157) use the **-te** marker for the simple past but attach it to the *changed* stem, which you have already learned for the past participles:

Remember that **wissen** is irregular in the present-tense singular: ich **weiß**, du **weißt**, er **weiß**.

wissen, wusste, hat gewusst					
ich	wuss**te**	*I knew*	wir	wuss**ten**	*we knew*
du	wuss**test**	*you knew*	ihr	wuss**tet**	*you knew*
er, es, sie	wuss**te**	*he, it, she knew*	sie, Sie	wuss**ten**	*they, you knew*

SIMILARLY:

bringen, **brachte**, hat gebracht
kennen, **kannte**, hat gekannt
nennen, **nannte**, hat genannt

Simple past of *haben* and *werden*

Only **haben** and **werden** are irregular in the simple past tense.

haben, hatte, hat gehabt					
ich	hatte	*I had*	wir	hatten	*we had*
du	hattest	*you had*	ihr	hattet	*you had*
er, es, sie	hatte	*he, it, she had*	sie, Sie	hatten	*they, you had*

werden, wurde, ist geworden					
ich	wurde	*I became*	wir	wurden	*we became*
du	wurdest	*you became*	ihr	wurdet	*you became*
er, es, sie	wurde	*he, it, she became*	sie, Sie	wurden	*they, you became*

5 Übung. Retell the following short narrative in the simple past.

Andreas **kennt** Mainz sehr gut, weil seine Großeltern dort **wohnen**. Als er 11 Jahre alt **wird**, **darf** er allein mit dem Zug nach Mainz fahren. Er **verbringt** jeden Sommer dort. Die Großeltern **wissen** alles über die Stadt, denn sie **leben** seit Jahren in Mainz. Er **bringt** ihnen immer ein Geschenk mit und das **haben** sie gern.

Use of the simple past tense

In English there is a difference in *meaning* between past tense and perfect tense. Compare these sentences:

I saw Marion in the restaurant.
I have seen Marion in the restaurant.

I saw Marion refers to a unique event in the past, while *I have seen Marion* implies that Marion has been in the restaurant on several occasions and may be there again.

In German, there is *no* difference in meaning between simple past and perfect tense. They both simply convey that the action is in the past:

Ich **sah** Marion im Restaurant. Ich **habe** Marion im Restaurant **gesehen.**	*I saw Marion in the restaurant.*

The difference between German simple past and perfect tenses is mainly in the situations in which they are used. As you have already learned, the perfect tense is used in conversation to refer to events in the past. The simple past tense is used in conversation *only* with frequently occurring verbs such as **sein**, **haben**, and the modal verbs.

A: Wo **warst** du denn gestern? Ich habe auf dich gewartet.	*Where were you yesterday? I waited for you.*
B: Ich **hatte** kein Geld mehr und **musste** nach Hause.	*I didn't have any more money and had to go home.*

The primary use of simple past tense is in *written* German (in letters, newspaper reports, short stories, novels, etc.) to narrate a series of events in the past. Here, for example, is the beginning of the fairy tale "Hänsel und Gretel":

Es war einmal ... is the formulaic beginning for German fairy tales.

Es **war** einmal ein armer Holzhacker. Er **wohnte** mit seinen zwei Kindern vor einem Wald. Sie **hießen** Hänsel und Gretel. Sie **hatten** wenig zu essen und ihre Stiefmutter **wollte** sie los werden.

Once upon a time there was a poor woodcutter. He lived at the edge of a forest with his two children. Their names were Hansel and Gretel. They had little to eat and their stepmother wanted to get rid of them.

6 Gruppenarbeit: Schreiben wir eine Geschichte zusammen. ***(4–5 Personen)*** Unten finden Sie eine Wortliste. Benutzen Sie diese Verben, um zusammen eine kurze Geschichte zu schreiben. Sie brauchen einen Sekretär oder eine Sekretärin. Er oder sie soll die Geschichte aufschreiben (*write down*). Der erste Satz der Geschichte ist: „Vor vielen Jahren lebte ein armer Student in einem alten Gebäude in der Altstadt." Student A wählt ein Verb von der Liste und sagt den zweiten Satz. Studentin B sagt einen dritten Satz usw. Sie dürfen natürlich auch andere Verben benutzen und sollen auch viele Adjektive benutzen.

A useful phrase when composing your stories: **eines Tages** = *one day*.

aufstehen	aufmachen	aussehen	beginnen
benutzen	besitzen	bleiben	einkaufen
essen	dauern	frühstücken	heißen
hoffen	kochen	bekommen	liegen
machen	nehmen	schlafen	trinken
sitzen	spazieren gehen	klauen	lernen
verdienen	verlieren	sagen	zahlen
anrufen	helfen	sterben	übernachten

Lesen Sie einander Ihre Geschichten vor. (**vorlesen** = *to read aloud*)

Simple past after the conjunction *als*

Clauses introduced by the subordinating conjunction **als** (*when* or *as* referring to a point or stretch of time in the past) require the simple past tense.

Remember that the inflected verb comes at the end of a subordinate clause.

Hans hat uns oft besucht, **als** er in New York **wohnte**.	*Hans often visited us when he lived in New York.*
Als ich meinen Geldbeutel **suchte**, konnte ich ihn nicht finden.	*When I looked for my wallet I couldn't find it.*

7 Partnerarbeit: Wie geht's weiter? Take turns completing the following sentences with an **als**-clause.

1. Jürgen konnte seinen Schlüssel nicht finden, als ...
2. Herr Ziegler hat jeden Sommer seine Großeltern besucht, als ...
3. Es ging der Großmutter nicht gut, als ...
4. Ute lief schnell ins Haus, als ...
5. Alle Schüler lachten, als ...
6. Das Telefon klingelte, als ...
7. Meine Freunde kamen vorbei, als ...

Now restate the sentences, beginning with your **als**-clause.

BEISPIEL: *Als* Jürgen nach Hause kam, konnte er seinen Schlüssel nicht finden.

2. Equivalents of "when": *als, wenn, wann*

Three German subordinating conjunctions may be translated by English *when*, but they are not interchangeable:

- **als** = *when* (in the past); *as*
  Als refers to an event or state *in the past* and requires the simple past tense.

Als wir in Wien waren, haben wir Andreas besucht.	*When we were in Vienna, we visited Andreas.*

- **wenn** = *when/if*; *whenever*
  Wenn means *when* in reference to an event *in the present or future*. Since it can also mean *if*, clauses with **wenn** can be ambiguous.

Wenn wir in Wien sind, besuchen wir Andreas.	*When (If) we're in Vienna, we'll visit Andreas.*

Wenn also means *whenever* in reference to repeated action in the past or present. To avoid confusion between *whenever* and *if*, add the adverb **immer** if you mean *whenever*.

Wenn Hans nach Wien kommt, geht er **immer** ins Kaffeehaus.	*Whenever Hans comes to Vienna, he always goes to a coffeehouse.*

Note carefully the difference in meaning between **als** and **wenn** used with simple past tense.

Als sie das sagte, wurde er rot.	*When she said that, he turned red.*
Wenn sie das sagte, wurde er immer rot.	*Whenever she said that, he always turned red.*

Rule of thumb: For cases in which English *when* = *at what time*, use German **wann**. If *when* = *if* or *whenever*, use **wenn**.

- **wann** = *when, at what time*
  Wann is always a question word, used both in direct questions and in indirect questions:

Wann ist das passiert?	*When did that happen?*
Ich weiß nicht, **wann** das passiert ist.	*I don't know when that happened.*

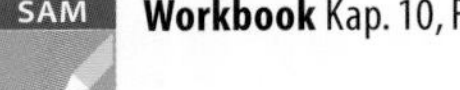

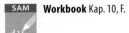

Workbook Kap. 10, F.

8 Übung: *Als, wenn* oder *wann*? (*mit offenen Büchern*)

1. Mutti, ________ darf ich spielen?
   ________ du das Altglas in den Keller getragen hast.
2. ________ fängt das Konzert an?
   Ich weiß nicht, ________ es anfängt.
   Karl kann es uns sagen, ________ er zurückkommt.
   Wir haben viele Konzerte gehört, ________ wir Berlin besuchten.
   Das möchte ich auch tun, ________ ich nächstes Jahr in Berlin bin.
3. ________ ich gestern an der Uni war, habe ich Angelika getroffen. Sie hat gesagt, sie kommt heute Abend mit.
   Gut! ________ Angelika mitkommt, macht es mehr Spaß.
   Sag mir bitte noch einmal, ________ die Party beginnt.

9 Partnerarbeit: Wie sagt man das auf Deutsch? Sagen Sie diese Dialoge auf Deutsch.

1. A: When did you meet Claudia?
   B: I met her when I was studying in Vienna. Whenever I'm there, I always write her a postcard.
   A: I don't know when I'll go to Vienna again.
2. A: When I was in Europe, I went to Prague.
   B: When I go to Europe, I'll do that too.
   A: When are you going to Europe?
   B: When I have enough money.

10 Partnerarbeit: Als meine Großeltern jung waren. Interviewen Sie einander über die Jugend Ihrer Großeltern. Füllen Sie den Fragebogen aus (*fill out the questionnaire*).

1. Wo sind deine Großeltern geboren? ______
2. Wo lebten sie als Kinder? ______
3. Kamen sie aus großen Familien? ______
4. Wo und wie lernten sie einander kennen? ______
5. Wie war ihre Kindheit und Jugend anders als heute? ______

Alte Ansichtskarte (*postcard*) von dem Reichstag in Berlin. Erbaut 1884–94 vom Architekten Paul Wallot im Renaissancestil.

3. Past perfect tense (*das Plusquamperfekt*)

The past perfect tense is used for an event in the past that preceded another event in the past.

Als Hans aufstand, **hatte** Ulla schon **gefrühstückt**.	*When Hans got up, Ulla **had** already **eaten breakfast**.*

The form of the past perfect tense is parallel to that of the perfect tense, but the auxiliary verb (**haben** or **sein**) is in the past tense instead of the present (**haben** → **hatte**, **sein** → **war**).

ich	**hatte gegessen**	*I had eaten*
du	**hattest gegessen**	*you had eaten*
er	**hatte gegessen**	*he had eaten*
wir	**hatten gegessen**	*we had eaten*
ihr	**hattet gegessen**	*you had eaten*
sie	**hatten gegessen**	*they had eaten*
ich	**war aufgestanden**	*I had gotten up*
du	**warst aufgestanden**	*you had gotten up*
sie	**war aufgestanden**	*she had gotten up*
wir	**waren aufgestanden**	*we had gotten up*
ihr	**wart aufgestanden**	*you had gotten up*
sie	**waren aufgestanden**	*they had gotten up*

Look at the following timetable of morning events at Hans and Ulla's house, then at how they are combined in the sentences that follow.

8.00 Uhr: Ulla hat gefrühstückt.

9.00 Uhr: Hans ist aufgestanden.

10.00 Uhr: Ulla ist zur Uni gegangen.

11.00 Uhr: Hans hat gefrühstückt.

Event 1 (8.00 Uhr)	**Event 2 (9.00 Uhr)**
Ulla **hatte** schon **gefrühstückt,**	als Hans aufstand.
Ulla had already eaten breakfast,	*when Hans got up.*

The order of the clauses may of course be reversed:

Event 2 (9.00 Uhr)	**Event 1 (8.00 Uhr)**
Als Hans aufstand,	**hatte** Ulla schon **gefrühstückt.**
When Hans got up,	*Ulla had already eaten breakfast.*

Distinguish between the preposition **nach** (+ noun in the dative) and the conjunction **nachdem** (+ clause with the verb in final position). Both are translated *after*. **Nach der Deutschstunde** ... (*after German class*); **Nachdem wir das Essen bestellt hatten** ... (*After we had ordered the meal* ...).

The subordinating conjunction **nachdem** (*after*) is often used with the past perfect tense.

Nachdem Ulla gefrühstückt hatte, ging sie zur Uni. — *After Ulla had eaten breakfast, she went to the university.*

Lab Manual Kap. 10, Var. zu Üb. 12.

Workbook Kap. 10, G.

11 **Übung: Als Ulla nach Hause kam.** Sie spielen die Rolle von Hans. Sie sind heute vor Ulla nach Hause gekommen und hatten genug Zeit, eine Menge zu machen. Sagen Sie, was Sie schon gemacht hatten, als Ulla um 23.00 Uhr endlich nach Hause kam.

BEISPIEL: Lebensmittel eingekauft
Als Ulla nach Hause kam, hatte ich schon Lebensmittel eingekauft.

1. nach Hause gekommen
2. Kartoffeln gekocht
3. alles sauber gemacht
4. die Kinder abgeholt
5. einkaufen gegangen
6. den Kindern das Essen gegeben
7. die Zeitung gelesen
8. ein Glas Wein getrunken
9. die Kinder ins Bett gebracht
10. ein paar Briefe geschrieben
11. meine Cousine angerufen
12. ins Bett gegangen

4. More time expressions

The preposition *vor* + dative = *"ago"*

Telling how long ago something happened is a communicative goal.

The preposition **vor** is used with various time expressions in the dative case to mean *ago*.

vor fünf Minuten *five minutes ago*
vor einer Stunde *an hour ago*
vor drei Tagen *three days ago*
vor vielen Wochen *many weeks ago*
vor einem Monat *a month ago*
vor hundert Jahren *a hundred years ago*

12 **Übung: Wann war das?** Sagen Sie auf Deutsch, wann Sie einen Freund angerufen haben.

BEISPIEL: Wann haben Sie ihn angerufen?
(*two days ago*): Vor zwei Tagen.

1. a minute ago
2. an hour ago
3. three years ago
4. five months ago
5. ten days ago
6. a couple of weeks ago

„Vor 60 Jahren hast du mich
hier ins Kino eingeladen.
Nächstes Jahr
lade ich dich ein."

13 **Partnerarbeit: Wann hast du zuletzt ... gemacht?** Ask each other when you last did these things.

BEISPIEL: A: Wann hast du zuletzt deine Großeltern besucht?
B: Ich habe sie vor drei Monaten besucht.

deine Oma besuchen
Geld ausgeben
einen Stadtbummel machen
einen langen Roman lesen
fernsehen
Sport treiben
Musik hören
in ein neues Haus umziehen
etwas für die Umwelt tun
einen Brief bekommen

Duration ending in the past

Telling how long something lasted is a communicative goal.

German and English differ in the way they show an action ending in the past versus an action continuing into the present. English makes this distinction by using different verb tenses:

*We **lived** in Berlin for three years.*	*Past tense* for a state ending in the past (i.e., we don't live there any more).
*We **have lived** in Berlin for three years.*	*Perfect tense* for a state continuing at the moment of speaking (i.e., we're *still* living there).

In German, however, both the SIMPLE PAST and the PERFECT TENSE are used for a state ending in the past.

Wir **wohnten** drei Jahre in Berlin.
Wir **haben** drei Jahre in Berlin **gewohnt**. } *We **lived** in Berlin for three years.*

Duration beginning in the past but continuing in the present

For a state beginning in the past but continuing at the moment of speaking, German uses PRESENT TENSE and one of these adverbial phrases:

schon (+ accusative) → **schon drei Jahre**
seit (+ dative) → **seit drei Jahren**

Wir **wohnen** ***schon drei Jahre*** in Berlin.
Wir **wohnen** ***seit drei Jahren*** in Berlin. } *We **have lived** in Berlin **for three years**.*

Note carefully the difference between verb tenses in the two languages!

NOTE ON USAGE

"For a long time"

Notice the different ways to express *for a long time*.

Ich hoffe, du kannst **lange** bleiben.	*I hope you can stay **for a long time.*** (continuing into the future)
Ich wohne **schon lange** hier. Ich wohne **seit langem** hier. }	*I've lived here **for a long time.*** (continuing from the past)

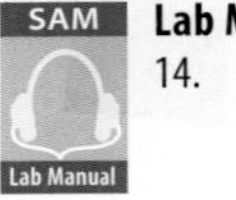

Lab Manual Kap. 10, Üb. 14.

SAM **Workbook** Kap. 10, H.

14 Übung: Wie lange schon? Ihre Professorin möchte wissen, wie lange Sie etwas schon machen. Sagen Sie, Sie machen es schon zwei Jahre.

BEISPIEL: Wie lange arbeiten Sie schon hier?
Ich arbeite schon zwei Jahre hier.

A. Antworten Sie mit **schon**.

1. Wie lange studieren Sie schon hier?
2. Wie lange lernen Sie schon Deutsch?
3. Wie lange treiben Sie schon Sport?
4. Wie lange wohnen Sie schon im Studentenwohnheim?
5. Wie lange fahren Sie schon Rad?

B. Antworten Sie mit **seit**.

6. Seit wann kennen Sie mich?
7. Seit wann haben Sie kurze Haare?
8. Seit wann studieren Sie hier?
9. Seit wann haben Sie den Führerschein?
10. Seit wann spielen Sie ein Musikinstrument?

15 Partnerarbeit: Wie sagt man das auf Deutsch? Übersetzen Sie diese Sätze.

1. We've known him for a year.
2. She's lived here for two weeks.
3. He's been lending me money for a long time.
4. Barbara has already been here five days.
5. She has studied in Halle for two semesters.
6. For ten years there's been an excellent restaurant here.
7. Michael has been interviewing her for three hours.
8. He's been annoying me for two days.

16 Partnerarbeit: Wie lange machst du das schon? Fragen Sie einander, wie lange oder seit wann Sie etwas machen. Unten (*below*) sind einige Ideen, aber Sie können auch Ihre eigenen Fragen stellen.

1. Wie lange studierst du schon hier?
2. Seit wann lernst du Fremdsprachen?
3. Wie lange lernst du schon Deutsch?
4. Seit wann gibt es diese Uni?
5. Wie lange kannst du schon Auto fahren?
6. Seit wann arbeitest du mit dem Computer?
7. Wie lange sind wir heute schon in der Deutschstunde?

LESESTÜCK

Tipps zum Lesen und Lernen

Tipps zum Vokabelnlernen

Other examples: **Nihilismus, Kapitalismus, Protektionismus, Sozialismus, Anarchismus, Modernismus, Expressionismus, Futurismus, Terrorismus**.

Nouns ending in -ismus The following reading mentions several concepts such as National Socialism, Communism, and anti-Semitism. English words ending in *-ism* denote a system of belief, a doctrine, or a characteristic. Their German equivalents end in the suffix **-ismus**. These words are all masculine in German and the stress is always on the penultimate syllable (**Opti<u>mis</u>mus**).

der Antisemitismus	der Idealismus	der Optimismus
der Extremismus	der Kommunismus	der Pessimismus

This is the origin of words like *hamburger*, *wiener*, *frankfurter*, *Budweiser*, and *pilsner* (from *Budweis* and *Pilsen*, German names for the Czech towns **České Budejovice** and **Plzeň**).

City names as adjectives The reading also mentions the *Weimar* Republic, the *Versailles* Treaty, and the *New York* Stock Exchange. When the names of cities are used as adjectives in German, they are capitalized and simply add the ending **-er** in all cases: **die Weimarer Republik**, **der Versailler Vertrag**, **die New Yorker Börse**.

Die neue Reichstagskuppel (*dome*) von Sir Norman Foster (1999). (Siehe die alte Kuppel auf Seite 273.)

Lab Manual Kap. 10, Üb. zur Betonung.

Leicht zu merken

die **Demokratie, -n**	Demokratie	**katastrophal**	katastrophal
demokratisch		**manipulieren**	manipulieren
der **Direktor, -en**		die **Methode, -n**	Methode
die **Epoche, -n**	Epoche	die **Monarchie, -n**	Monarchie
extrem		die **Opposition, -en**	Opposition
die **Form, -en**		die **Republik, -en**	Republik
ideologisch		die **Situation, -en**	Situation
illegal	illegal	**terroristisch**	terroristisch
die **Inflation**	Inflation		

Einstieg in den Text

In the following reading, you will encounter quite a bit of factual historical information about an important period in modern German history, the Weimar Republic. Much of the information may be new to you, but you already know enough German to be able to understand complex prose.

When reading the text through for the first time, keep the following basic information questions in mind as a guide:

Was war die Weimarer Republik?
Wann war diese historische Epoche?
Wer hat damals eine Rolle gespielt?
Warum war diese Zeit so wichtig?

Before reading, also examine the illustrations that accompany and are referred to in the reading. These convey an impression of the content of the reading and will help you to understand the issues discussed.

Was für Plakate sind das?
Aus welcher Zeit kommen sie?
Was zeigen die Bilder?
Welche Wörter oder Namen können Sie schon verstehen?

Wortschatz 2

In-Text Audio CD

Verben

erklären to explain
steigen, stieg, ist gestiegen to climb
stören to disturb
unterbrechen (unterbricht), unterbrach, hat unterbrochen to interrupt
versuchen to try, attempt
wachsen (wächst), wuchs, ist gewachsen to grow
wählen to choose; to vote; to elect
zählen to count

Substantive

der **Arm, -e** arm
der **Schriftsteller, -** writer (*m.*)
der **Staat, -en** state
der **Wähler, -** voter
das **Plakat, -e** poster
das **Reich, -e** empire, realm
das **Volk, ¨-er** people, nation, folk
die **Ausstellung, -en** exhibition
die **Bedeutung, -en** meaning, significance
die **Dame, -n** lady
die **Idee, -n** idea
die **Schriftstellerin, -nen** writer (*f.*)
die **Wahl, -en** choice; election

German equivalents for *people*: **das Volk** (a people defined by a common language and culture: **das deutsche Volk**); **Menschen** (people in general: **die Menschen in dieser Stadt**); **Leute** (more restricted grouping: **die Leute hier im Zimmer**).

Idea: **die Idee** is the most general equivalent: **Das ist eine gute Idee. Ahnung** means *inkling*: **Ich habe keine Ahnung.**

Adjektive und Adverbien

ausländisch foreign
hart hard; tough; harsh
unruhig restless, uneasy, troubled

Andere Vokabel

bevor (*sub. conj.*) before

Nützliche Ausdrücke

zu Ende sein to end, be finished, be over
1918 war der Krieg zu Ende. The war ended in 1918.
eine Frage stellen to ask a question

Fragen takes a direct object of person (**Ich habe ihn gefragt**).

Gegensätze

unruhig ≠ ruhig restless ≠ calm, peaceful

Eine Ausstellung historischer Plakate aus der Weimarer Republik

In-Text Audio CD

Im Hessischen Landesmuseum° gab es vor einigen Jahren eine Ausstellung politischer Plakate aus der Weimarer Republik (1919–1933). Der Museumsdirektor führte eine Gruppe ausländischer Studenten durch die Ausstellung.

Hessian State Museum

Plakat is the term for *informational posters*, **Poster** for *decorative posters* (performers, vacation spots, etc.).

Learning about the Weimar Republic is the cultural goal of this chapter.

„Meine Damen und Herren, herzlich willkommen im Landesmuseum! Bevor wir in die Ausstellung gehen, möchte ich Ihnen ein paar Worte über die Geschichte der Weimarer Republik sagen. Vielleicht ist Ihnen diese Epoche schon bekannt, aber wenn Ihnen etwas nicht klar ist, können Sie immer Fragen stellen – das stört mich gar nicht.

Was war das eigentlich, die Weimarer Republik? So nennen wir den deutschen Staat in der Zeit zwischen dem Ende des Ersten Weltkrieges 1918 und dem Anfang des Dritten Reiches[1] im Januar 1933. Es war Deutschlands erster Versuch° eine

attempt

[1] **Das Dritte Reich**: The Nazis' own name for their regime (1933–1945). The first empire was the Holy Roman Empire (962–1806). The second empire (**das Deutsche Reich**, 1871–1918) collapsed at the end of the First World War.

demokratische Staatsform zu entwickeln°. Unsere Plakate zeigen die extremen ideologischen Gegensätze° dieser Epoche. Aber sie zeigen auch, wie man gegensätzliche° Ideen oft mit ähnlichen Bildern darstellen° kann."

Hier unterbrach ein Student mit einer Frage: „Entschuldigung, aber können Sie uns erklären, warum es die ‚Weimarer' Republik hieß? War Berlin nicht damals die Hauptstadt Deutschlands?"

„Sicher. Berlin blieb auch die Hauptstadt, aber die Politiker kamen 1919 in der Stadt Weimar zusammen, um die neue demokratische Verfassung zu beschließen°. In Berlin war die politische Situation damals sehr unruhig und außerdem° hatte Weimar wichtige symbolische Bedeutung als die Stadt, wo die großen Schriftsteller Goethe und Schiller[2] früher gelebt und gearbeitet hatten.

Die ersten Jahre der Republik waren eine Zeit der Arbeitslosigkeit und der hohen Inflation. Deutschland hatte den Ersten Weltkrieg verloren und die Monarchie war zu Ende.[3] Unter dem harten Versailler Friedensvertrag musste der neue demokratische Staat 20 Milliarden° Goldmark an die Siegermächte° (besonders an Frankreich) zahlen. Unser erstes Plakat, aus der Zeit vor 1925, zeigt den deutschen Reichsadler° durch den Versailler Vertrag gefesselt°.

Als die New Yorker Börse° 1929 stürzte°, wurde die Wirtschaftskrise° in den Industrieländern Europas katastrophal. Man zählte im Februar 1930 schon mehr als° 3,5 Millionen arbeitslose Menschen in Deutschland.

Diese Wirtschaftskrise brachte die junge deutsche Demokratie in Gefahr, denn schon 1932 waren sieben Millionen Menschen arbeitslos. Es gab damals mehr als dreißig politische Parteien und besonders die antidemokratischen konnten schnell wachsen. Auf diesem zweiten Plakat sieht man, wie die ‚starke Hand' der katholischen Zentrumspartei[4] die extremen Parteien erwürgt°.

develop
polarities /
contradictory / represent
***Verfassung ...** ratify the constitution / moreover*
billion / victors
imperial eagle
fettered
*stock market / crashed / economic crisis / **mehr als** = more than*
strangles

[2] Johann Wolfgang von Goethe (1749–1832); Friedrich von Schiller (1759–1805).
[3] Kaiser Wilhelm II (1859–1941) abdicated in November 1918 and went into exile in the Netherlands. The Treaty of Versailles officially ended the First World War in 1919.
[4] The conservative Center Party, consisting mainly of Catholic voters.

The symbols on the snakes from left to right identify the following parties: the Social Democrats (SPD), the Nazis (NSDAP), and the Communists (KPD). The fourth snake behind the others probably represents the right-wing German National People's Party (DNVP).

In den Wahlen nach 1930 stieg aber die Macht der Nationalsozialistischen Deutschen Arbeiterpartei (NSDAP) – der Nazis –, bis sie die stärkste° im Reichstag[5] wurde. Ihr Führer Adolf Hitler benutzte den Antisemitismus und Antikommunismus, um die Ängste des Volkes zu manipulieren. Ein Plakat der Nazis zeigt den symbolischen ‚starken Mann', der° Deutschland retten soll. Die Opposition sehen Sie noch auf diesem Plakat von 1931, wo starke Arme versuchen, das Hakenkreuz° der Nazis zu zerreißen°."

Eine Studentin stellte eine Frage: „Ist denn Hitler nicht illegal an die Macht gekommen°?"

„Eigentlich nicht", antwortete der Museumsdirektor. „Nachdem die Wähler den Nazis die meisten Stimmen° gegeben hatten, musste man Hitler zum Reichskanzler ernennen°. Erst als er Kanzler geworden war, konnte er mit terroristischen Methoden die Republik in eine Diktatur verwandeln°. Deutschland ist also tatsächlich ein gutes Beispiel für die Zerstörung einer schwachen Demokratie durch wirtschaftliche Not° und politischen Extremismus."

strongest
who
swastika
rip apart
***an ...** came to power*
(here) *votes*
***zum ...** appoint chancellor*
***in ...** transform into a dictatorship*
***wirtschaftliche Not** = economic hardship*

[5] The name of the German Parliament until 1945, now called **der Bundestag**. The parliament building in Berlin is still called the **Reichstag**.

SPD poster for the Reichstag election of May 1924 ("The Answer to the Hitler Trial")

After the failed Nazi putsch in Munich in November 1923, Hitler received a light prison sentence of five years and his National Socialist Party was officially banned. The SPD made a weak showing in the election, while both the Communists and the radical Right gained strength.

NACH DEM LESEN

Lab Manual Kap. 10, Diktat.

Workbook Kap. 10, Üb. H–K.

A Antworten Sie auf Deutsch.

1. Warum besuchte die Studentengruppe das Museum?
2. Aus welcher Zeit waren die Plakate dieser Ausstellung?
3. Wer führte die Gruppe durch die Ausstellung?
4. Was für Plakate haben die Studenten im Museum gesehen?
5. Warum hieß der deutsche Staat damals die „Weimarer" Republik?
6. Wie war die Situation in Deutschland nach dem Ersten Weltkrieg? Beschreiben Sie die Probleme.
7. Warum war die junge Demokratie in Gefahr?
8. Wann wurde Hitler Reichskanzler?
9. Wie ist er an die Macht gekommen?

B Gruppendiskussion: Bilder erzählen Geschichte. Im Lesestück finden Sie fünf politische Plakate aus der Weimarer Republik. Besprechen Sie diese historischen Bilder.

1. Lesen Sie den Text auf dem Plakat vor.
2. Beschreiben Sie das Bild so ausführlich (*completely*) wie möglich.
3. Interpretieren Sie die Bilder: Was symbolisiert z. B. der Adler auf dem ersten Plakat? die Hand auf dem zweiten? die Kette auf dem letzten? usw.

„Notgeld" (*emergency money*), frühe 20er Jahre (*early 1920s*), aus der Inflationszeit in Deutschland und Österreich. Zu dieser Zeit durfte jede Stadt ihr eigenes Geld drucken (*print*).

Vokabeln zum Thema Politik

This vocabulary focuses on an everyday topic or situation. Words you already know from **Wortschatz** sections are listed without English equivalents; new supplementary vocabulary is listed with definitions. Your instructor may assign some supplementary vocabulary for active mastery.

In dem Lesestück haben Sie nicht nur etwas über Geschichte, sondern auch etwas über Politik gelernt. Was hat denn diese politische Diskussion mit unserem Leben zu tun? Wir sind alle politische Menschen und die Politik spielt eine Rolle in unserem Alltag, ob wir es wollen oder nicht.

Spielen wir jetzt ein bisschen mit der Sprache und den Bildern der Politik. Zuerst einige Wörter (viele sind Ihnen schon bekannt):

Politik also means *policy*: **Außenpolitik** (*foreign policy*), **Energiepolitik**, **Umweltpolitik** usw.

Regierung = *government in power, administration*

die **Freiheit**	der **Staat, -en**
der **Frieden**	die **Umwelt**
der **Krieg, -e**	das **Volk, ¨er**
die **Politik**	die **Wahl, -en**
der **Politiker/die Politikerin**	**wählen**
die **Regierung, -en**	der **Wähler, -**

C Gruppenarbeit: Wir sind politisch aktiv. (*in kleinen Gruppen*) Gründen Sie (*found*) eine neue politische Partei.

Der Name unserer Partei: _____
Unser Parteiprogramm:
Wir sind für _____, _____ usw.
Wir sind gegen _____, _____ usw.
Wir sehen viele Probleme in der modernen Welt: _____
Unsere Lösungen sind: _____
Unsere Parole (*slogan*) für die Wahlen: _____

D Gruppenarbeit: politische Symbole. Ihre politische Partei braucht auch ein Symbol für ihr Wahlplakat. Wie Sie gerade gelesen haben, waren Tiere wichtige Symbole auf den Plakaten in der Weimarer Republik. Wählen Sie ein Tier als Symbol Ihrer Partei und machen Sie ein Wahlplakat.

der **Adler, -**	*eagle*
der **Bär, -en, -en**	*bear*
der **Elefant, -en, -en**	*elephant*
der **Esel, -**	*donkey*
der **Fuchs, ¨e**	*fox*
der **Löwe, -n, -n**	*lion*
die **Schlange, -n**	*snake*
die **Taube, -n**	*dove*

E Gruppenarbeit: Wahlkampagne (*election campaign*). Jetzt zeigen Sie den anderen Studenten Ihr Wahlplakat. Erklären Sie, warum man Ihre Partei wählen soll. Die „Wähler“ können natürlich Fragen stellen oder kritisieren.

Unser Plakat zeigt ...
Wählt unsere Partei, weil ...

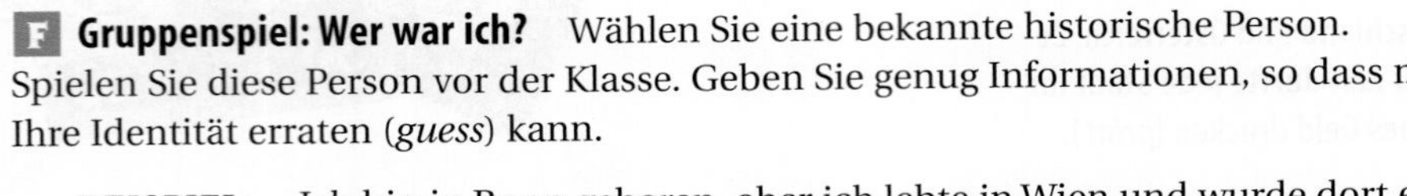

F Gruppenspiel: Wer war ich? Wählen Sie eine bekannte historische Person. Spielen Sie diese Person vor der Klasse. Geben Sie genug Informationen, so dass man Ihre Identität erraten (*guess*) kann.

BEISPIEL: Ich bin in Bonn geboren, aber ich lebte in Wien und wurde dort ein großer Komponist. Meine neunte Symphonie ist besonders bekannt. Wer war ich?

G Übung. Create sentences with a verb from column 1, an indirect object from column 2, and a direct object from column 3. Don't forget to change adjective endings where necessary.

BEISPIEL: Ich habe meinem lieben Onkel einen langen Brief geschrieben.

1	2	3
geben	mein lieber Onkel	ein langer Brief
schenken	die nette Austauschstudentin	das neue Restaurant
kaufen	die kleinen Kinder	unsere schöne Altstadt
zeigen	unsere neuen Freunde	unser großer Straßenatlas
erzählen	meine Großeltern	ein Geburtstagsgeschenk
schreiben	das sympathische Mädchen	neue Turnschuhe
beschreiben	mein sportlicher Freund	ein neuer iPod
empfehlen	die ausländischen Touristen	das alte Märchen
leihen	meine gute Freundin	dieser neue Roman

H Museumsbesuch. Write a friend a note about your visit to the poster exhibition. Use the simple past and the past perfect tenses.

1. nachdem / ich / essen (*past perfect tense*) // ich / treffen / mein / Freunde / vor / Museum
2. dort / es / geben / interessant / Ausstellung / von / politisch / Plakate
3. wir / wollen / sehen / Ausstellung // um ... zu / lernen / über / modern / Geschichte
4. wir / unterbrechen / der Museumsdirektor // um ... zu / Fragen / stellen
5. Plakate / zeigen / die / viel / Partei / während / dies- / Zeit
6. nachdem / wir / verbringen / ganz / Nachmittag / dort (*past perfect tense*) // gehen / miteinander / in / Café

SCHREIBTIPP

Using simple past tense to write about the past

- Simple past tense is used primarily in written German to narrate events that occured in the past.
- If you choose to write about the first topic below, you will use simple past when mentioning events during the Weimar Republic, but present tense when drawing conclusions for the present (e.g., "Die Wirtschaftskrise der Weimarer Republik **brachte** die Demokratie in Gefahr. Heute **kann** eine schwache Wirtschaft auch gefährlich sein").
- If you choose to write a story (topic 3 below), write entirely in the simple past (or past perfect) except for dialogue (e.g., "Vor vielen Jahren **lebte** ein armer Student in einem alten Gebäude in der Altstadt. Jeden Tag **aß** er sein Mittagsessen allein. Aber eines Tages **fragte** ihn eine Freundin: ‚**Willst** du nicht mit uns in der Mensa essen?' ")

▶ **Schreiben wir mal.** Wählen Sie 1, 2 oder 3 und schreiben Sie eine Seite über dieses Thema.

1. Was können wir aus der Geschichte der Weimarer Republik lernen?
2. Warum ist es wichtig für Politiker, die Geschichte ihres Landes zu kennen?
3. Take a story you composed orally with your classmates in exercise 6 on p. 271 and polish it as a written assignment.

I Wie sagt man das auf Deutsch?

1. How long have you lived in this house?
2. We've been here for two years. We like it a lot.
3. When we worked in Rostock, we only had a small apartment.

4. You look worried. Did something happen to you?
5. I think that somebody stole my new backpack.
6. I had it beside me in the restaurant and suddenly it was gone.
7. I hope you had your ID and your wallet in your pocket.

8. When were you in Heidelberg?
9. Two years ago, when I was an exchange student in Germany.
10. I tried all year to find an old friend of my parents, but he had died.

With this chapter you have completed the second third of ***Neue Horizonte***. For a concise review of the grammar and idiomatic phrases in chapters 6–10, you may consult **Zusammenfassung und Wiederholung 2** (*Summary and Review 2*) in the Workbook section of the SAM. The review is followed by a self-correcting test.

ALMANACH

VIDEO

German Politics and the European Union

On December 2, 1990, with the addition of the five new **Länder** (*states*) from the former German Democratic Republic, a united Germany held its first free elections in 58 years. The last had been in November 1932, just before Hitler's seizure of dictatorial powers. In order to prevent the profusion of small parties that had weakened the **Reichstag** during the Weimar Republic, the framers of the post-war **Grundgesetz** (*Basic Law* or constitution of the Federal Republic of Germany) in 1949 added a requirement that a party must receive at least 5% of the popular vote to be represented in the **Bundestag** (*Federal Parliament*). This provision has effectively excluded small extremist parties of both the Right and the Left.

Stimmzettel
für die Wahl zum Deutschen Bundestag
im Wahlkreis 134 Herford - Minden-Lübbecke II
am 18. September 2005

Sie haben 2 Stimmen

hier 1 Stimme
für die Wahl
eines/einer Wahlkreisabgeordneten

hier 1 Stimme
für die Wahl
einer Landesliste (Partei)
- maßgebende Stimme für die Verteilung der Sitze insgesamt auf die einzelnen Parteien -

Erststimme

1	**Spanier,** Wolfgang Schulleiter Kottenbrink 65 32052 Herford	**SPD** Sozialdemokratische Partei Deutschlands	◯
2	**Dr. Göhner,** Reinhard Rechtsanwalt Elsestr. 23 32278 Kirchlengern	**CDU** Christlich Demokratische Union Deutschlands	◯
3	**Schäffler,** Frank Dipl.-Betriebswirt Holland 29 32052 Herford	**FDP** Freie Demokratische Partei	◯
4	**Holstiege,** Angela Margareta Lehrerin Turnerstr. 22 32257 Bünde	**GRÜNE** BÜNDNIS 90 / DIE GRÜNEN	◯
5	**Höger-Neuling,** Inge Dipl.-Betriebswirtin Hermannstr. 42 32052 Herford	**Die Linke.** Die Linkspartei.	◯
8	**Koch,** Michael Verkäufer Heidestr. 20a 32257 Bünde	**NPD** Nationaldemokratische Partei Deutschlands	◯

Zweitstimme

◯	**SPD**	**Sozialdemokratische Partei Deutschlands** Franz Müntefering, Dr. Angelica Schwall-Düren, Eike Hovermann, Ursula (Ulla) Schmidt, Dr. Barbara Hendricks	1
◯	**CDU**	**Christlich Demokratische Union Deutschlands** Dr. Norbert Lammert, Wolfgang Bosbach, Ilse Falk, Ronald Pofalla, Dr. Norbert Röttgen	2
◯	**FDP**	**Freie Demokratische Partei** Dr. Guido Westerwelle, Gisela Piltz, Jörg van Essen, Dr. Werner Hoyer, Gudrun Kopp	3
◯	**GRÜNE**	**BÜNDNIS 90 / DIE GRÜNEN** Bärbel Höhn, Dr. Reinhard Loske, Britta Haßelmann, Volker Beck, Kerstin Müller	4
◯	**Die Linke.**	**Die Linkspartei.** Oskar Lafontaine, Ursula (Ulla) Lötzer, Inge Höger-Neuling, Paul Georg Schäfer, Ursula Jelpke	5
◯	**REP**	**DIE REPUBLIKANER** Ursula Winkelsett, Ralf Goertz, Dr. Jürgen Heydrich, Frank Maul, Arnd Schubeus	6
◯	**Die Tierschutzpartei**	**Mensch Umwelt Tierschutz** Jürgen Foß, Frank Bresonik, Dr. Ingeborg Gräßer, Michael Möllmann, Martin Klaßen	7
◯	**NPD**	**Nationaldemokratische Partei Deutschlands** Dr. Gerhard Frey, Udo Voigt, Stephan Haase, Max Branghofer, Claus Gerd Cremer	8
◯	**FAMILIE**	**FAMILIEN-PARTEI DEUTSCHLANDS** Peter Wülfing, Sieglinde Nowak, Maria Hartmann, Jessica Burgmann, Bernhard Suek	9

The **CDU** (**Christlich-Demokratische Union**), with its Bavarian sister party the **CSU** (**Christlich-Soziale Union**), form the conservative end of the German political spectrum and have consistently received 45–50% of the popular vote. The **SPD** (**Sozialdemokratische Partei Deutschlands**) is the oldest party in the **Bundestag**, with a history stretching back to the beginnings of socialism in the 19th century. Today's SPD is dedicated to the welfare state and protecting the work force from the shocks of globalization. It traditionally receives 35–45% of the popular vote from industrial workers, students, and young professionals.

Two smaller parties have had an influence out of proportion to their size because the larger parties have often needed them as coalition partners to achieve a majority in the **Bundestag**: the economically liberal **FDP** (**Freie Demokratische Partei**) and the environmental and anti-nuclear party **Die Grünen**. The newest party in the German political spectum, called simply **Die Linke** (*the Left*), is comprised of former East German Communists and Socialists and former left-wing Social Democrats.

Since the end of World War II, the central concern of German foreign policy has been to insure Germany's integration into a peaceful Europe. The rabid nationalism that led to two disastrous wars in the first half of the 20th century was replaced by a firm commitment to European unity. France and Germany, archenemies since the 19th century, formed a coal and steel cooperative in 1950 that gradually grew into today's European Union. The 1992 Treaty of Maastricht committed the Union's 15 member nations to a central banking system and a common currency (the Euro) and to increased political coordination, especially in the areas of foreign policy and security.

Germans have been divided in their attitude toward their Eastern European neighbors, but since the early 1970s, the major parties of both the Right and the Left have recognized the need for increasing contact and dialogue with the East. Since the break-up of the Soviet Union in the late 1980s, most of its former satellite states in Europe have become members of both the European Union and NATO, e.g., Bulgaria, the Czech Republic, Hungary, Poland, and Romania. Because of Germany's history of division between West and East, its central location, and its strong economy, it will continue to play a leading role in the unification of Europe. With its significant Turkish minority, for instance, Germany is an important participant in the ongoing debate about Turkish membership in the European Union.

Wahlplakat in München

KAPITEL 11

Brandenburger Tor und Berliner Mauer im Jahre 1989

Deutschland nach der Mauer

Kommunikation

- Designating nationalities and saying where people are from
- Identifying the parts of the body
- Describing morning routines

Kultur

- Germany's role in Europe today

In diesem Kapitel

- **Lyrik zum Vorlesen**
  Hoffmann von Fallersleben, "Das Lied der Deutschen"
- **Grammatik**
  1. Reflexive verbs and pronouns
  2. Dative pronouns with clothing and parts of the body
  3. Adjectives and pronouns of indefinite number
  4. Adjectival nouns
  5. More on **bei**
  6. Designating decades: The 90s, etc.
- **Lesestück**
  Deutschland im europäischen Haus
- **Almanach**
  Zeittafel zur deutschen Geschichte, 1939 bis heute

DIALOGE

aus den USA: Note dative plural.

Lab Manual Kap. 11, Dialoge, Fragen, Hören Sie gut zu!

Das Brandenburger Tor: The Brandenburg Gate is a triumphal arch completed in 1795 and topped by the **Quadriga**, a chariot pulled by four horses and driven by the goddess of victory. From 1961 to 1989 the Berlin Wall ran just west of it (see photo, p. 288).

More information on unification is found in the **Lesestück** in this chapter. See also the map of Germany on the inside front cover.

Am Brandenburger Tor

Helen aus den USA war 1989 in Berlin. Jetzt ist sie wieder dort, um ihre Bekannte Anke zu besuchen. Zusammen stehen sie am Brandenburger Tor.

ANKE: Weißt du noch, wie es am 9. November 1989 hier an der Mauer aussah?
HELEN: Als die DDR die Grenze öffnete? Das vergess' ich nie!
ANKE: Die Menschen haben sich so gefreut, sogar die Polizeibeamten waren freundlich!
HELEN: Ja, der Unterschied ist unglaublich! Heute sieht man nichts als neue Architektur und gar nichts mehr von der Mauer.
ANKE: Doch, ein Stück der Mauer existiert noch als Denkmal. Aber stell dir vor: Für Schulkinder heute ist das alles jetzt Geschichte.
HELEN: Ja, Berlin ist inzwischen wieder eine große europäische Hauptstadt geworden.

Ein Unfall: Stefan bricht sich das Bein

23.00 Uhr. Stefans Vater liegt schon im Bett. Seine Mutter spricht am Telefon. Plötzlich läuft sie ins Schlafzimmer.

MUTTER: Markus, zieh dich schnell an und komm mit! Etwas Schlimmes ist passiert!
VATER: Was ist denn los?
MUTTER: Stefan hat sich beim Radfahren verletzt! Ich fürchte, er hat sich das Bein gebrochen.
VATER: Um Gottes Willen! Beeilen wir uns!

Anna besucht Stefan im Krankenhaus

ANNA: Wie geht's dir denn, du Armer?
STEFAN: Hallo, Anna! Schön, dass du gekommen bist.
ANNA: Fühlst du dich heute besser oder tut dir das Bein noch weh?
STEFAN: Ach, glücklicherweise ist es nicht so schlimm. Ich kann mich schon selber waschen, aber ich darf noch nicht aufstehen.
ANNA: Schade! Schau mal, ich habe dir Schokolade und Blumen mitgebracht.
STEFAN: Oh, die sind hübsch! Danke, das ist aber lieb von dir!
ANNA: Nichts zu danken! Gute Besserung!

NOTE ON USAGE

The definite article as pronoun

The definite article can replace the personal pronoun in colloquial spoken German to add greater emphasis. The definite article used in this way usually comes at the beginning of the sentence.

Die (= sie) sind hübsch! ***Those** are pretty.*

Wortschatz 1

Körperteile (*parts of the body*)

der **Finger, -** finger
der **Kopf, -¨e** head
der **Mund, -¨er** mouth
der **Zahn, -¨e** tooth
das **Auge, -n** eye
das **Bein, -e** leg
das **Gesicht, -er** face
das **Ohr, -en** ear

You already know **der Arm, der Fuß, das Haar, die Hand, die Nase.**

Verben

sich[1] etwas an·sehen (sieht an), sah an, hat angesehen to take a look at something
sich an·ziehen, zog an, hat angezogen to get dressed
sich beeilen to hurry
brechen (bricht), brach, hat gebrochen to break
sich erkälten to catch a cold
existieren to exist
sich freuen to be happy
sich fühlen to feel (*intrans.*)
fürchten to fear
sich etwas leisten können to be able to afford something
Das kann ich mir nicht leisten. I can't afford that.
öffnen to open
schauen to look
schneiden, schnitt, hat geschnitten to cut
sich setzen to sit down
sich verletzen to injure oneself, get hurt
sich verspäten to be late
sich etwas vor·stellen to imagine something
waschen (wäscht), wusch, hat gewaschen to wash
weh·tun, tat weh, hat wehgetan (+ *dat. of person*) to hurt
Das tut (mir) weh. That hurts (me).

Compare: **Das tut mir weh** (*That hurts me*) with **Es tut mir Leid** (*I'm sorry*).

Substantive

der **Arzt, -¨e** doctor (*m.*)
der **Beamte, -n** (*adj. noun*) official; civil servant (*m.*)
der/die[2] **Bekannte, -n** (*adj. noun*) acquaintance, friend
der **Unterschied, -e** difference
der/die **Verwandte, -n** (*adj. noun*) relative
das **Denkmal, -¨er** monument, memorial
das **Krankenhaus, -¨er** hospital
das **Schlafzimmer, -** bedroom
das **Tor, -e** gate
die **Ärztin, -nen** doctor (*f.*)
die **Beamtin, -nen** official; civil servant (*f.*)
die **Begeisterung** enthusiasm
die **Blume, -n** flower
die **Deutsche Demokratische Republik (DDR)** German Democratic Republic (GDR)
die **Grenze, -n** border
die **Hauptstadt, -¨e** capital city
die **Mauer, -n** (*freestanding or outside*) wall
die **Polizei** (*sing. only*) police
die **Schokolade** chocolate

Contrast **die Mauer** (*freestanding wall*) with **die Wand** (*interior wall*). The two words tell the cultural story of Roman innovations in building techniques. A **Mauer** (from the Latin *murus*) was made of stone and capable of having windows (= **Fenster,** from Latin *fenestra*), whereas the Germanic **Wand** is related to the verb **winden** (*to wind*) and described a wall of woven twigs.

Adjektive und Adverbien

ander- other, different
europäisch European
genau exact, precise
hübsch pretty, handsome
inzwischen meanwhile, in the meantime
mehrere several, a few
unglaublich unbelievable
wenige few

Andere Vokabel

sich (*third-person reflexive pronoun; see p. 293*)

Nützliche Ausdrücke

Gute Besserung! Get well soon!
schade too bad
Das ist schade! That's a shame! Too bad! What a pity!
Schau mal. Look. Look here.
Weißt du noch? Do you remember?

Gegensätze

sich an·ziehen ≠ sich aus·ziehen to get dressed ≠ to get undressed

Mit anderen Worten

schnell machen (*colloq.*) = **sich beeilen**

[1] **Sich** is a reflexive pronoun. This will be explained on pp. 293–294.
[2] Inclusion of both masculine and feminine articles indicates that this is an adjectival noun. See pp. 301–302.

Variationen

A Persönliche Fragen

1. Helen besucht ihre Bekannte in Berlin. Haben Sie Bekannte oder Verwandte im Ausland? Wo leben sie? Haben Sie sie schon einmal besucht?
2. Helen sagt, sie vergisst den 9. November 1989 nie. Gibt es einen Tag, den Sie nie vergessen können? Was ist an diesem Tag passiert?
3. Stefan hatte einen Unfall beim Radfahren. Haben Sie je einen Unfall gehabt? Mit dem Rad oder dem Auto? Wie geht es Ihnen inzwischen?
4. Er hat sich verletzt. Ist Ihnen so was je passiert? Wenn ja, wie?
5. Sind Sie je im Krankenhaus gewesen? Warum? Haben Ihnen Ihre Freunde etwas mitgebracht? Was denn?
6. Anna bringt Stefan Schokolade und Blumen mit. Was bringen Sie mir, wenn ich im Krankenhaus bin?

B Übung: Ich habe etwas Interessantes gemacht! Choose from the list of adjectives below to characterize something you have done. Then say what it was you did.

BEISPIEL: Ich habe einmal etwas Blödes gemacht.
Ich habe mein Deutschbuch vergessen.

blöd	toll	wahnsinnig	intelligent
interessant	gefährlich	neu	furchtbar
wunderbar	schwierig	langweilig	schlimm

C Partnerarbeit: Wie geht's denn weiter? Take these two lines from the second dialogue and compose your own continuation. Then perform it for the class.

A: Zieh dich schnell an und komm mit!
B: Was ist denn los?
A: ________.
B: ________. etc.

LYRIK ZUM VORLESEN

August Heinrich Hoffmann von Fallersleben. Porträt von Carl Georg Christian Schumacher (1819).

The famous "Lied der Deutschen," also known as the "Deutschlandlied," is one of the most nationalistic—and controversial—political songs ever composed. Although the first stanza is commonly associated with German militarism, the author was, ironically, an opponent of repressive government and a fervent proponent of German unification. His anti-authoritarian sentiments cost him his post as professor at the University of Breslau. The text proclaims abstract concepts ("unity, law, freedom") and calls for a unification of all German-speaking territories into one state. The Romantic dreams of unity were appropriate for Hoffmann von Fallersleben's generation, which had survived the ravages of the Napoleonic Wars and was frustrated by the division of Germany into many small states.

Hoffmann von Fallersleben wrote the text in 1841 to a popular tune by Franz Joseph Haydn in praise of the Austrian Emperor, "Gott erhalte Franz den Kaiser" (*God*

Preserve Kaiser Franz, [1797]). Haydn also used this melody in his magnificent *Kaiserquartett* (op. 76, no. 3, 2nd movement). The song did not become the German national anthem until 1922, when it was chosen by the young Weimar Republic. In 1945 it was banned by the allied military government. In 1952, when no satisfactory substitute could be found, the third stanza alone became the national anthem of the Federal Republic of Germany. Fearing that the nationalist sentiments of this text could be misused by modern extremists, the German government has banned the singing of the first stanza in public.

Das Lied der Deutschen

Deutschland, Deutschland über alles,
Über alles in der Welt,
Wenn es stets° zu Schutz und Trutze° — **= immer / *Schutz ...*** *defense and defiance*
Brüderlich zusammenhält;
Von der Maas bis an die Memel,
Von der Etsch bis an den Belt:
Deutschland, Deutschland über alles,
Über alles in der Welt!

die Maas = *the Meuse River* (Belgium); **die Memel** = *the Nemunas River* (Lithuania); **die Etsch** = *the Adige River* (South Tirol, Italy); **der Belt** = *strait between two Danish islands in the Baltic Sea.*

Deutsche Frauen, deutsche Treue°, — *loyalty*
Deutscher Wein und deutscher Sang° — *song*
Sollen in der Welt erhalten° — *preserve*
Ihren alten, schönen Klang°, — *sound*
Uns zu edler Tat begeistern° — ***Uns ...*** *Inspire us to noble deeds*
Unser ganzes Leben lang:
Deutsche Frauen, deutsche Treue,
Deutscher Wein und deutscher Sang!

Einigkeit° und Recht° und Freiheit — *unity / justice*
Für das deutsche Vaterland!
Danach lasst uns alle streben° — ***lasst ...*** *let us strive*
Brüderlich mit Herz und Hand!
Einigkeit und Recht und Freiheit
Sind des Glückes Unterpfand°: — ***des ...*** *guarantees of happiness*
Blüh° im Glanze° dieses Glückes, — *flourish / glow*
Blühe, deutsches Vaterland!

August Heinrich Hoffmann von Fallersleben (1798–1874)

GRAMMATIK

1. Reflexive verbs and pronouns (*Reflexivverben und Reflexivpronomen*)

In most cases, the subject and the object are two different people or things.

subj.	*obj.*	
Ich habe **ihn** verletzt.		*I injured **him**.*

Sometimes, however, the subject and object are the same.

subj. *obj.*
Ich habe **mich** verletzt. *I hurt **myself**.*

The verb is then called *reflexive* and the object is called a *reflexive pronoun*. English reflexive pronouns end in *-self* or *-selves*, e.g., *myself, himself, herself, themselves*. German has both accusative and dative reflexive pronouns. German reflexive pronouns in the first and second person are identical to the accusative and dative personal pronouns, which you already know (**mich, mir, dich, dir**, etc.). However, the reflexive pronoun in the third person and the formal second person is new: **sich**.

Note on spelling: **sich** is not capitalized even when used with the polite **Sie**: **Fühlen Sie *sich* heute besser?**

Reflexive pronouns

	accusative	dative		accusative	dative
ich	mich	mir	**wir**	uns	uns
du	dich	dir	**ihr**	euch	euch
er, es, sie	sich	sich	**sie, Sie**	sich	sich

In the plural, the reflexive pronouns often denote reciprocity and are equivalent to the English *each other*.

Wir treffen **uns** morgen.	*We'll meet **each other** tomorrow.*
Kennt ihr **euch**?	*Do you know **each other**?*
Sie kennen **sich** seit langem.	*They've known **each other** for a long time.*
Wir verstehen **uns** gut.	*We understand **each other** well.*

NOTE ON USAGE

The pronoun *einander* (each other)

Plural reflexive pronouns used reciprocally may be replaced by the reciprocal pronoun **einander** (*each other*).

Kennt ihr **euch**? = Kennt ihr **einander**?

Remember that **einander** can also combine with prepositions.

gegeneinander	*against each other*
miteinander	*with each other*
zueinander	*to each other*

SAM **Lab Manual** Kap. 11, Var. zu Üb. 1, 5, 8, 10.

SAM **Workbook** Kap. 11, A–E.

1 Partnerarbeit: Wir verstehen uns. Use each of the verbs and verb phrases below in the following routine.

BEISPIEL:
A: Verstehst du mich?
B: Ja, ich verstehe dich. Verstehst du mich?
A: Ja, ich verstehe dich auch.
A & B: Wir verstehen uns! (Wir verstehen einander!)

1. verstehen
2. sehen
3. brauchen
4. kennen
5. morgen treffen
6. am Wochenende besuchen

Verbs with accusative reflexive pronouns

Any transitive verb can be used reflexively.

DEFINITION

What are transitive and intransitive verbs?

A ***transitive verb*** is a verb that takes a direct object (e.g., **sehen**, **tragen**, **verletzen**).

Ich trage meine Jacke.

An ***intransitive verb*** cannot take a direct object (e.g., **sein**, **werden**, **schlafen**).

Ich schlafe bis sieben.

Here is a sample conjugation using **sich verletzen**.

Ich habe **mich** verletzt.	*I hurt **myself**.*
Du hast **dich** verletzt.	*You hurt **yourself**.*
Sie hat **sich** verletzt.	*She hurt **herself**.*
Wir haben **uns** verletzt.	*We hurt **ourselves**.*
Ihr habt **euch** verletzt.	*You hurt **yourselves**.*
Sie haben **sich** verletzt.	*They hurt **themselves**.* (*You hurt **yourself / yourselves**.*)

2 Kettenreaktion: Wer hat sich verletzt? Die ganze Klasse war im Bus, als der Busfahrer einen kleinen Unfall hatte. Fragen Sie einander, wer sich verletzt hat.

BEISPIEL: A: Ich habe mich nicht verletzt. Hast du dich verletzt?
B: Ja, ich habe mich verletzt. Hast du ...

NOTE ON USAGE

Intensifiers *selber* and *selbst*

The words **selber** and **selbst** are often used to intensify or emphasize a reflexive pronoun.

Soll ich das Kind waschen?	*Should I wash the child?*
Nein, sie kann sich **selber** waschen.	*No, she can wash herself.*

3 Übung: Er kennt nur sich selbst. Answer these questions by saying that the person knows, sees, etc. only himself or herself.

BEISPIEL: Wen kennt er denn?
Er kennt nur sich selbst.

1. Wen sieht sie denn?
2. Wen versteht er denn?
3. Wen haben Sie geärgert?
4. Wen brauche ich denn?
5. Wen lieben Sie denn?

Proverb: **Liebe dich selbst, so hast du keine Rivalen.**

German reflexive verbs that are not reflexive in English

Many reflexive verbs in German are not reflexive in English. Their English equivalents often use *get*. Here are some examples:

Sie wäscht **sich**.	*She's getting washed.*
Er zog **sich** an.	*He got dressed.*
Bitte, setzen Sie **sich**.	*Please sit down.* (literally: *Please seat yourself* or *yourselves.*)

4 Übung: Bitte setzen Sie sich! Your instructor will tell you to stand up or sit down. Then say what you have done.

BEISPIEL: Bitte stehen Sie auf!
(*Jemand steht auf.*) Ich bin aufgestanden.
Bitte setzen Sie sich.
(*Er/Sie setzt sich.*) Ich habe mich gesetzt.

Verbs requiring the accusative reflexive

Verbs like **anziehen** and **waschen** can be used either reflexively (**ich wasche mich**) or nonreflexively (**ich wasche den Wagen**). Some German verbs, however, must *always* be used with an accusative reflexive pronoun. Their English equivalents are *not* reflexive.

sich beeilen	*to hurry*
sich erkälten	*to catch cold*
sich freuen	*to be happy*
sich fühlen	*to feel*
sich verspäten	*to be late*

5 Gruppenarbeit: Wann freust du dich besonders? (*3 oder 4 Personen*) Sagen Sie, wann sie sich besonders freuen. Die Bilder geben Ihnen einige Ideen, aber Sie dürfen auch frei antworten.

BEISPIEL: A: Ich freue mich, wenn die Sonne scheint. Wann freust du dich?
B: Ich freue mich, wenn ...

6 Gruppenarbeit: Warum musst du dich beeilen? Jetzt sind Sie alle in Eile. Sagen Sie einander warum. Die Bilder geben Ihnen einige Ideen.

BEISPIEL: A: Ich muss mich beeilen, weil ich zur Uni muss. Warum musst du dich beeilen?
B: Ich muss mich beeilen, weil ...

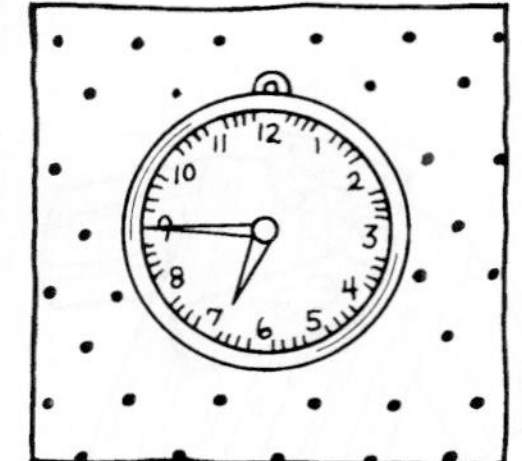

7 **Übung: Warum hast du dich verspätet?** Jeder verspätet sich manchmal. Erzählen Sie der Klasse, warum Sie sich verspätet haben. Unten sind einige Möglichkeiten, aber Sie dürfen auch frei antworten.

BEISPIEL: Ich habe mich verspätet, weil ______.

krank sein	Fahrrad kaputt
spät aufstehen	die Deutschstunde vergessen
sich verletzen	die Uhr verlieren
einen Unfall haben	einen Freund im Krankenhaus besuchen

Verbs with dative reflexive pronouns

When people do things for themselves, then the indirect object is a *dative* reflexive pronoun.

Note: Except for **mir** and **dir**, the dative reflexive pronouns are identical in form to the accusative reflexive pronouns.

Ich kaufe **mir** Blumen.	*I'm buying **myself** flowers. (I'm buying flowers **for myself**.)*
Du kaufst **dir** Blumen. / Sie kaufen **sich** Blumen.	*You're buying **yourself** flowers.*
Er kauft **sich** Blumen.	*He's buying **himself** flowers.*
Wir kaufen **uns** Blumen.	*We're buying **ourselves** flowers.*
Ihr kauft **euch** Blumen. / Sie kaufen **sich** Blumen.	*You're buying **yourselves** flowers.*
Sie kaufen **sich** Blumen.	*They're buying **themselves** flowers.*

The dative reflexive pronoun may be omitted without changing the basic meaning of the sentence.

Ich kaufe mir eine Jacke.	*I'm buying myself a jacket.*
Ich kaufe eine Jacke.	*I'm buying a jacket.*

8 **Übung: Einkaufsbummel.** Jetzt gehen wir zusammen einkaufen. Jeder hat € 350 und darf sich etwas kaufen. Erzählen Sie den anderen, was Sie sich kaufen. Die Bilder geben Ihnen einige Ideen, aber Sie dürfen sich auch andere Sachen kaufen.

BEISPIEL: A: Was kaufen Sie sich, Robert?
B: Ich kaufe mir ein neues Hemd und eine Zeitung.

Verbs requiring the dative reflexive

Some German verbs are *always* used with dative reflexive pronouns. They all require a *direct object* in the accusative as well. Their English equivalents are *not* reflexive.

German: dative reflexive	English: not reflexive
sich etwas ansehen	*to take a look at, look over*
Ich wollte **mir** den Wagen ansehen.	*I wanted to take a look at the car.*
sich etwas leisten können	*to be able to afford*
Kannst du **dir** ein neues Fahrrad leisten?	*Can you afford a new bicycle?*
sich etwas vorstellen	*to imagine*
Das kann ich **mir** nicht vorstellen.	*I can't imagine that.*

Since the pronoun **sich** is both accusative and dative, how can you tell which case to use with a particular reflexive verb? A **Wortschatz** entry in this book that contains the pronoun **etwas** indicates that the reflexive pronoun is dative. If you look up **ansehen**, for example, you find **sich etwas ansehen**. This tells you that **etwas** is accusative and **sich** is dative.

A parallel English structure is *to cook oneself something* (**sich etwas kochen**). *I'm cooking myself* (ind. obj.) *an egg* (dir. obj.). = **Ich koche mir ein Ei.**

sich (*dative*) **etwas** (*accusative*) ansehen

Ich möchte **mir** das **Auto** ansehen.

9 Kettenreaktion: Die armen Studenten. Wie alle Studenten haben Sie nie genug Geld. Sagen Sie, was Sie sich nicht leisten können, und dann fragen Sie weiter.

BEISPIEL: A: Ich kann mir keine Europareise leisten. Was kannst du dir nicht leisten?
B: Ich kann mir ...
C: Ich ...

10 Partnerarbeit: Was wollen wir uns heute Nachmittag ansehen? Sehen Sie sich den Stadtplan auf Seite 228 an. Sie verbringen den Nachmittag miteinander in dieser Stadt. Sagen Sie einander, was Sie sich ansehen möchten.

BEISPIEL: A: Ich möchte mir die Markuskirche und ________ ansehen. Und du?
B: Ich möchte mir lieber ________ ansehen.

2. Dative pronouns with clothing and parts of the body

German does not usually use possessive adjectives with parts of the body or with articles of clothing when they are being put on or taken off. It uses the personal dative instead.

Note that plural **die Haare** is more common than singular: **Sie hat dunkle Haare.**

Die Mutter wäscht **dem Kind** die Hände.	*The mother washes **the child's** hands.*
Meine Freundin schneidet **mir** die Haare.	*My girlfriend cuts **my** hair.*
Sie zog **ihm** den Mantel an.	*She put the coat on **him**.*

If you are performing the action on yourself, the dative pronoun is of course *reflexive*.

Ich habe **mir** die Hände gewaschen.	*I washed **my** hands.*
Sie zog **sich** den Mantel an.	*She put on **her** coat.*
Ich schneide **mir** selber die Haare.	*I cut **my** hair myself.*
Stefan hat **sich** das Bein gebrochen.	*Stefan broke **his** leg.*
Warum hast du **dir** die Jacke angezogen?	*Why did you put on **your** jacket?*

Identifying the parts of the body is a communicative goal.

11 Übung: Körperteile. Identify the parts of the body in the picture below.

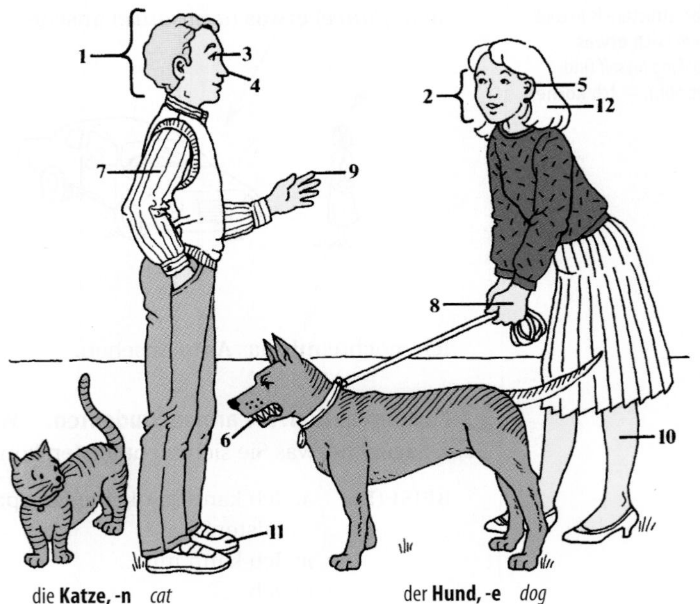

die **Katze, -n** *cat* der **Hund, -e** *dog*

Rätsel (Riddle)

Was ist das? Hat Arme, aber keine Hände, läuft und hat doch keine Füße.

Lab Manual Kap. 11, Var. zu Üb. 11.

12 Übung: Wo tut es Ihnen weh? Stefan tut das Bein noch ein bisschen weh. Sagen Sie Ihrer Professorin, wo es Ihnen wehtut.

BEISPIEL: A: Wo tut's Ihnen denn weh?
B: Mir tut der Kopf weh.

Describing morning routines is a communicative goal.

Ich ziehe **mich** an. = *I'm getting dressed.*

Ich ziehe **mir** ein Hemd an. = *I'm putting on a shirt.*

13 Übung. Sagen Sie Ihrem Professor, **wann** Sie sich heute angezogen haben, und dann, **was** Sie sich angezogen haben.

BEISPIEL: A: Um wie viel Uhr haben Sie sich heute angezogen?
B: Ich habe mich um halb acht angezogen.
A: Was haben Sie sich angezogen?
B: Ich habe mir ________, ________ und ________ angezogen.

14 Übung: Die Morgenroutine. Welcher Satz gehört zu welchem Bild?

Er kämmt sich die Haare.	Er rasiert sich.	Sie schminkt sich.
Sie badet sich.	Sie putzt sich die Zähne.	Er duscht sich.

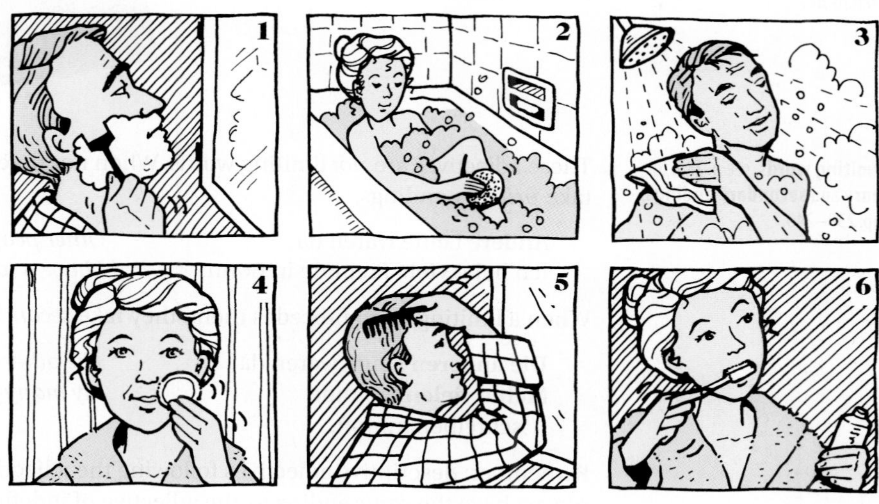

15 Schreiben wir mal: Gute Besserung! Schreiben Sie diese Anekdote als Dialog zwischen Dr. Büchner und seinem Patienten Herrn Lenz. Der arme Herr Lenz liegt im Krankenhaus.

Write as a series of natural exchanges, beginning like this:

DR. BÜCHNER: **Guten Morgen, Herr Lenz!**

HERR LENZ: **Morgen, Herr Doktor.**

DR. BÜCHNER: **Es tut mir Leid, dass ich mich verspätet habe ...**

Dr. Büchner läuft morgens um 10.00 Uhr ins Krankenzimmer und sagt Herrn Lenz, es tut ihm Leid, dass er sich verspätet hat. Herr Lenz grüßt ihn und sagt, es macht gar nichts. Dr. Büchner würde gern wissen, wie es Herrn Lenz geht und ob er sich besser fühlt. Herr Lenz antwortet, dass es ihm nicht so gut geht und dass er noch sehr krank ist. Der Arzt fragt, wo es ihm noch wehtut. Herr Lenz antwortet, dass es ihm überall wehtut. Dr. Büchner möchte wissen, ob ihm etwas im Krankenhaus nicht gefällt und ob er sonst noch etwas braucht. Der Patient antwortet, dass ihm das Essen im Krankenhaus nicht schmeckt und dass er das Fernsehen langweilig findet und einige neue Romane haben möchte. Dr. Büchner lacht und sagt, dass er sich schon vorstellen kann, wie langweilig es ist, so lange im Bett liegen zu müssen. Es freut ihn auch zu sehen, dass Herr Lenz so viel besser aussieht. Er soll sich anziehen, denn er darf heute nach Hause.

3. Adjectives and pronouns of indefinite number

You already know these adjectives, which are used with plural nouns to indicate indefinite amounts.

The greeting on this card is also a standard phrase used at the end of a letter to close friends or relatives. What would the English equivalent be?

wenige	*few*
einige	*some*
mehrere	*several*
andere	*other(s)*
viele	*many*

For **limiting words**, see p. 239; for **primary** and **secondary endings**, see pp. 239–240.

These adjectives are *not* limiting words. When not preceded by a limiting word, they take *primary* endings.

Andere Leute waren da.	*Other people were there.*
Ich habe **viele** Freunde in Bonn.	*I have a lot of friends in Bonn.*

When a limiting word precedes them, they take *secondary* endings.

Die anderen Leute waren da.	*The other people were there.*
Meine vielen Freunde schreiben mir oft.	*My many friends often write to me.*

Remember: descriptive adjectives following the adjective of indefinite number will *always* have the *same* ending as the adjective of indefinite number.

Ander**e** jung**e** Leute waren da.	*Other young people were there.*
Die ander**en** jung**en** Leute waren da.	*The other young people were there.*

16 Gruppenarbeit: Viele oder wenige? Choose a word from each column and state your opinion about a group of people. Begin with **Ich würde sagen, ...**

BEISPIEL: Ich würde sagen, viele sportliche Frauen sind gesund.

A	B	C	D
viele	jung	Menschen	Sport treiben
wenige	sportlich	Amerikaner	gesund sein
	reich	Professoren	Müll recyceln
	arm	Studenten	glücklich sein
	stark	Frauen	Deutsch sprechen
	sympathisch	Männer	gut verdienen
	verrückt	Eltern	sich erkälten
	kreativ		sich beeilen

Lab Manual Kap. 11, Var. zu Üb. 17.

Workbook Kap. 11, F.

17 Übung. Supply the correct adjective endings.

1. Ich möchte mir einig_______ schön_______ Postkarten ansehen.
2. Sie hat schon mehrer_______ deutsch_______ Bücher gelesen.
3. Viel_______ jung_______ amerikanisch_______ Schüler verstehen das nicht.
4. Haben Sie auch die ander_______ neu_______ Arbeiter kennen gelernt?
5. Ich habe mit viel_______ interessant_______ Menschen gesprochen.
6. Deine viel_______ neu_______ Ideen gefallen mir sehr.
7. Das sind die Probleme der ander_______ jung_______ Journalisten.
8. Ich habe einig_______ interessant_______ Denkmäler in Berlin gesehen.

Indefinite pronouns

viele	=	*many people*
wenige	=	*few people*
einige	=	*some people*
andere	=	*other people, others*

When these words are not followed by nouns (as in **viele Häuser**), they function as indefinite pronouns referring to human beings.

Viele sagen das.	*Many (people) say that.*
Einige gehen ins Kino, **andere** ins Theater.	*Some (people) are going to the movies, others to the theater.*

18 Übung: Einige und andere. Not everyone in your class likes doing the same things. Answer the following questions by saying that *some* of you (**einige**) like doing one thing, *others* (**andere**) prefer something else.

BEISPIEL: A: Gehen Sie gern ins Kino?
B: *Einige* gehen gern ins Kino.
C: *Andere* gehen lieber _______.

1. Spielen Sie gern Tennis?
2. Sprechen Sie gern über Politik?
3. Essen Sie gern Wurst?
4. Fahren Sie gern Ski?
5. Lesen Sie gern Zeitung?
6. Arbeiten Sie gern in der Bibliothek?
7. Trinken Sie gern Kaffee zum Frühstück?
8. Sitzen Sie gern vor dem Fernseher?

4. Adjectival nouns

Referring to people

In English, adjectives such as *sick, rich,* and *famous* occasionally function as nouns that refer *collectively* to a group of people.

*Florence Nightingale cared for **the sick**.*
*Lifestyles of **the rich and famous**.*

Adjectival nouns are more frequent in German. Moreover, they can refer to individuals, not just to collective groups as in English. Masculine adjectival nouns designate men, feminine ones designate women, while plural adjectival nouns are not gender specific.

Colloquial **mein Alter/meine Alte** can mean *my father/my mother.*

der Alte die Alte die Alten

Like all nouns in German, adjectival nouns are capitalized, but they *receive adjective endings* as though they were followed by the nouns **Mann**, **Frau**, or **Menschen**. The following examples include these nouns in brackets to make the structure clear. *Note the adjective endings!* As in any noun phrase, these endings will change depending on whether or not a limiting word is present.

Die Alte [Frau] lag im Bett.	*The old woman was lying in bed.*
Kennst du **den Großen** [Mann] da?	*Do you know that tall man there?*
Er wollte **den Armen** [Menschen] helfen.	*He wanted to help the poor.*

In principle, any adjective can be used as an adjectival noun. Here are some high-frequency ones you should learn:

Only the masculine form **der Beamte** is an adjectival noun. The feminine form is **die Beamtin**.

der/die Deutsche is the *only* noun of nationality that is adjectival.

der/die **Alte, -n**	*old man/woman*
der/die **Arme, -n**	*poor man/woman*
der **Beamte, -n**	*official, civil servant*
der/die **Bekannte, -n**	*acquaintance, friend*
der/die **Deutsche, -n**	*German (man/woman)*
der/die **Grüne, -n**	*member of the Greens (the environmental political party)*
der/die **Kleine, -n**	*little boy/girl* or *short man/woman*
der/die **Kranke, -n**	*sick man/woman*
der/die **Verwandte, -n** (from **verwandt** = *related*)	*relative*

This advertisement for childrens' chairs contains adjectival nouns in nominative and genitive plural. Can you translate, "**damit (= so dass) die Kleinen am Tisch der Großen sitzen können**"?

Immer auf der richtigen Höhe – damit die Kleinen am Tisch der Großen sitzen können.
Fürs vierte Jahr
Fürs erste Jahr

Lab Manual Kap. 11, Üb. 19.

Workbook Kap. 11, G.

19 Übung. Complete each sentence with the appropriate form of **mein Bekannter** (*my acquaintance, friend* [m.]).

BEISPIEL: Das ist ________.
Das ist mein Bekannter.

1. Heute zum Mittagessen treffe ich ________.
2. Ich gehe oft mit ________ Volleyball spielen.
3. Das ist die Frau ________.
4. ________ heißt Robert.

Now use a form of **meine Bekannten** (*my friends*).

5. Das sind ________.
6. Kennen Sie ________?
7. Helfen Sie bitte ________!
8. Das sind die Kinder ________.

Now use a form of **die Deutsche** (*the German* [f.]).

9. Wie heißt denn ________?
10. Meinst du ________?
11. Ich reise mit ________ nach Italien.
12. Ist das der Rucksack ________?

Now use a form of **unser Verwandter** (*our relative* [m.]).

13. Helmut ist ________.
14. Kennst du ________?
15. Du sollst mit ________ sprechen.
16. Die Tochter ________ besucht uns morgen.

Neuter adjectival nouns referring to qualities

Compare the adjective endings in **etwas Modernes** (*something modern*) and **das Moderne** (*what is modern; modern things*).

Neuter adjectival nouns designate qualities (e.g., *something good, nothing new*). They occur only in the singular, most frequently after the indefinite pronouns **etwas, nichts, viel,** and **wenig.** Note that after these words, the adjectival noun has the *primary* neuter ending **-es.**

etwas Herrliches	*something marvelous*
nichts Neues	*nothing new*
viel Gutes	*much that is good*
wenig Interessantes	*little of interest*

Neuter adjectival nouns can also occur after the definite article **das**. In this case, they are abstract nouns signaling the *quality* designated by the adjective. There are several English equivalents for this.

Das Moderne gefällt mir. *I like modern things.*
I like what is modern.

Sie sucht immer **das Gute**. *She's always seeking the good.*
She's always seeking what's good.

Der Eimer = ***trash bin*****. Was bedeutet „Kleines"?**

Info-Austausch

Partner B's information is found in Appendix 1.

20 Weihnachtsgeschenke (*Christmas presents*). Sie und Ihr Partner schenken einander viele Sachen zu Weihnachen. Fragen Sie, was Sie einander schenken.

BEISPIEL: A: Schenkst du mir etwas Neues?
B: Ja, ich schenke dir eine tolle neue CD. Schenkst du mir etwas Warmes?
A: Ja, ich schenke dir einen neuen Pulli.

Partner A:

	Schokolade
umweltfreundlich	
	ein Stückchen von der Berliner Mauer
teuer	
	ein Bernhardiner (*St. Bernard dog*)
grün	
	ein neuer Pulli
neu	

SAM **Workbook** Kap. 11, H, I.

21 Schreiben wir mal. Complete the three mini-dialogues with appropriate nouns formed from adjectives. Choose from the following list:

gut	schön	verwandt	bekannt
deutsch	einfach	altmodisch	interessant
neu	kalt	toll	modern
besonder-	schlimm	herrlich	

The first sentence in item 2 requires a designation of nationality (without article, see pp. 142, 307).

1. A: Hast du etwas ________ zu berichten?
   B: Ja, in der Stadt habe ich heute etwas ganz ________ gesehen!
   A: Wirklich? In unserer langweiligen Stadt? Das ist schon etwas ________!
2. A: Kennst du Steffi Hartmann? Sie ist ________ und ist gerade aus Stuttgart angekommen.
   B: Wie nett dich kennen zu lernen, Steffi! Eine alte ________ von mir aus der Schulzeit heißt Hartmann und wohnt auch in Stuttgart.
   C: Ja, dann ist sie vielleicht sogar eine ________ von mir. Unsere Familie ist ziemlich groß.
3. A: Das ________ bei uns im Sommer ist nicht nur das Wetter, sondern auch die hohen Berge und die schöne Natur.
   B: Super. Für mich ist das etwas ________. Ich bin in der Großstadt zu Hause.
   A: Aber in unserem kleinen Dorf auf dem Lande ist das Leben manchmal noch wie im 19. Jahrhundert. Da gibt es wenig ________ zu tun.
   B: Das ist mir ja egal! So was gibt's in der Großstadt! Ich bin zu euch gekommen um das ________ zu sehen.

22 Rollenspiel: Schade, dass du im Krankenhaus bist! (*3 Personen*) Lesen Sie zusammen diese Situation und dann spielen Sie sie miteinander:

Ein Student spielt einen Verletzten. Er hat einen Unfall gehabt und liegt jetzt im Krankenhaus. Die anderen zwei sind alte Bekannte und besuchen ihn dort. Sie haben noch nichts Genaues über den Unfall gehört. (Sie wissen z. B. nicht, wie er sich verletzt hat.) Sie stellen ihm Fragen. Sie haben ihm natürlich auch Geschenke mitgebracht.

5. More on *bei*

You already know that **bei** has the spatial meanings *in the home of* **(Ich wohne *bei* meiner Tante)** or *at* **(Er war gestern *beim* Arzt). Bei** is also used to set a scene. It then has the meanings *during, while . . . ing* (an activity). In this meaning, **bei** is often used with verbal nouns (p. 191).

Er hat sich **beim Radfahren** verletzt.	*He injured himself while riding his bicycle.*
Liest du oft **beim Essen?**	*Do you often read while eating?*

Lab Manual Kap. 11, Var. zu Üb. 23.

23 Übung: Wann passiert das? Sagen Sie, wann etwas passiert oder nicht passiert. Benutzen Sie **bei** in Ihrer Antwort.

BEISPIEL: Ich falle nie, wenn ich Ski fahre (*go skiing*).
Ich falle nie beim Skifahren.

1. Mein Mitbewohner stört mich, wenn ich lese.
2. Wir treffen uns oft, wenn wir Rad fahren.
3. Höfliche Kinder singen nicht, wenn sie essen.
4. Wenn wir spazieren gehen, können wir miteinander sprechen.
5. Ich höre gern Musik, wenn ich Auto fahre.
6. Wenn ich arbeite, ziehe ich mir die Schuhe aus.

The two elements of the verbs **Ski fahren** (*to ski*) and **Rad fahren** (*to bike*) are written separately. When they become verbal nouns, they are written together: **das Skifahren** (*skiing*), **das Radfahren** (*biking*). Similarly, mountain climbing is **das Bergsteigen**.

24 Übung. Antworten Sie mit **bei**.

BEISPIEL: Wie hat er sich denn verletzt? (*while bicycling*)
Beim Radfahren.

1. Wie haben Sie sich erkältet? (*while swimming*)
2. Wo sind Sie morgens um zehn? (*at work*)
3. Wann lernt man viele Menschen kennen? (*while traveling*)
4. Wann sprechen Sie nicht viel? (*when driving a car*)
5. Wo ist denn Ihre Frau? (*at the doctor's*)
6. Wie hast du so viel Geld verloren? (*playing cards*)

6. Designating decades: The 90s, etc.

These examples show how German designates decades (**das Jahrzehnt, -e**).

die 20er (zwanziger) Jahre	*the 20s (twenties)*
aus den 60er Jahren	*from the 60s*
in den 90er Jahren	*in the 90s*

Note that the cardinal number adds the ending **-er**. No other adjective ending is used, regardless of case.

25 Übung: Historische Briefmarken (*historical stamps*). Aus welchen Jahrzehnten kommen diese Briefmarken?

LESESTÜCK

Tipps zum Lesen und Lernen

Tipps zum Vokabellernen

Designating nationalities and saying where people are from are communicative goals.

Country names; nouns and adjectives of nationality The only designation of nationality that is an adjectival noun is **der/die Deutsche**. Some other nouns of nationality have a masculine form ending in **-er** and a feminine in **-erin**. You already know some of these:

Country	Male native	Female native	Adjective
Amerika	der Amerikaner	die Amerikanerin	amerikanisch
England	der Engländer	die Engländerin	englisch
Italien	der Italiener	die Italienerin	italienisch
Kanada	der Kanadier	die Kanadierin	kanadisch
Österreich	der Österreicher	die Österreicherin	österreichisch
die Schweiz	der Schweizer	die Schweizerin	schweizerisch

Other nouns of nationality are N-nouns in the masculine that add **-in** (and sometimes an umlaut) in the feminine.

Country	Male native	Female native	Adjective
China	der Chinese, -n, -n	die Chinesin	chinesisch
Frankreich	der Franzose, -n, -n	die Französin	französisch
Russland	der Russe, -n, -n	die Russin	russisch

Remember that when stating a person's nationality, Germans do *not* use the indefinite article.

Sind Sie Deutsche? — *Are you a German?*
Nein, ich bin Französin. — *No, I'm French.*

A Gruppenarbeit: Woher kommst du? Sie sind auf einer internationalen Studententagung (*convention*). Sie bekommen vom Professor ein Stück Papier. Auf dem Papier steht der Name Ihrer Heimat (*native country*). Jetzt fragen Sie einander, woher Sie kommen.

BEISPIEL: A: Woher kommst du denn?
B: Ich komme aus England.
A: Ach, du bist Engländerin!

Lab Manual Kap. 11, Üb. zur Betonung.

Leicht zu merken

die **Demokratisierung**	
die **Demonstration, -en**	Demonstrati<u>on</u>
die **Europäische Union (EU)**	Uni<u>on</u>
der **Fall**	
die **Integration**	Integrati<u>on</u>
investieren	inves<u>tie</u>ren

der **Kapitalismus**	Kapitalismus
der **Kommunismus**	Kommunismus
der **Manager, -**	
die **Million, -en**	Million
modernisieren	modernisieren
Osteuropa	
die **Reform, -en**	
reformieren	reformieren
repressiv	repressiv
die **Revolution, -en**	Revolution
(das) **Rumänien**	
separat	separat
die **Sowjetunion**	Sowjetunion
stabil	stabil
das **Symbol, -e**	Symbol
zentral	zentral
die **Zone, -n**	

Einstieg in den Text

Word features such as prefixes and suffixes can help you build on your existing vocabulary and recognize new words in context.

***The negating prefix** un-* The prefix **un-** attached to a noun or adjective forms the antonym of that word. Guess the meanings of these words from the **Lesestück**:

> die **Unsicherheit** (line 4)
> **ungelöste Probleme** (line 35)

***The suffix* -los** The suffix **-(s)los** is attached to nouns and forms adjectives and adverbs, e.g., **arbeitslos**. It is the equivalent of the English suffix *-less*. Guess the meanings of these words from the **Lesestück**:

> **gewaltlos** (from **Gewalt**: *force, violence*), line 27
> **hoffnungslos** (from **Hoffnung**: *hope*), line 37

Past participles as adjectives Past participles of verbs are often used as attributive adjectives. They take regular adjective endings.

bauen → gebaut-	*to build → built*
Das ist das neu **gebaute** Studentenwohnheim.	*That's the newly built dormitory.*

The reading contains the following participles used as adjectives:

besiegen *to defeat*	→	**besiegt-** (line 8)
entnazifizieren *to denazify*	→	**entnazifiziert-** (line 9)
lösen *to solve*	→	**ungelöst-** (line 35)

B Übung. Wie heißt das Adjektiv (mit Endung!)? Und wie heißt der neue Satz auf Englisch?

BEISPIEL: Jemand hat diese Waren gestohlen.
Die Polizei hat die *gestohlenen* Waren gefunden.
The police found the stolen goods.

1. Ich habe Altpapier gesammelt und jetzt schleppe ich das ________ Altpapier zum Recycling.
2. Eine Fabrik hat diesen Fluss verschmutzt und jetzt darf man in dem ________ Wasser nicht schwimmen.
3. Der Krieg hat viele deutsche Städte zerstört. Jetzt hat Deutschland seine ________ Städte wieder aufgebaut.
4. Wir hatten eine schöne Reise nach Schottland geplant, aber leider konnten wir uns die ________ Reise nicht leisten.
5. Ich habe meiner Mutter ein schönes Zimmer reserviert, aber das ________ Zimmer war ihr zu klein.

Wortschatz 2

In-Text Audio CD

Verben

ändern to change (*trans.*)
Sie hat ihr Leben geändert. She changed her life.
sich ändern to change (*intrans.*)
Ihr Leben hat sich geändert. Her life changed.
auf·geben (gibt auf), gab auf, hat aufgegeben to give up
aus·wandern ist ausgewandert to emigrate
rufen, rief, hat gerufen to call, shout
vereinen to unite
verschwinden, verschwand, ist verschwunden to disappear

Substantive

der **Hass** hatred
der **Nachbar, -n, -n** neighbor
der **Schlüssel, -** key
der **Spiegel, -** mirror
der **Teil, -e** part
der **Tod** death
das **Mitglied, -er** member
das **Ziel, -e** goal
die **Heimat** homeland; native country
die **Macht, ¨-e** power, might
die **Nachbarin, -nen** neighbor (*f.*)
die **Regierung, -en** government in power, administration
die **Wirtschaft** economy

Adjektive und Adverbien

beid- both
berühmt famous
heutig today's, of today
offen open
tief deep
tot dead
verschieden various, different
wirtschaftlich economic

Compare **verschieden** (*various, different*) and **ander-** (*other, different*): **Ich kenne viele verschiedene Lieder** (*I know many different songs*) vs. **Ich kenne andere Lieder als du** (*I know different songs than you*).

Gegensätze

auswandern ≠ einwandern to emigrate ≠ to immigrate
der Hass ≠ die Liebe hatred ≠ love
offen ≠ geschlossen open ≠ closed
der Tod ≠ das Leben death ≠ life
die Zukunft ≠ die Vergangenheit future ≠ past

Understanding Germany's role in Europe today is the cultural goal of this chapter.

Berlin, Potsdamer Platz

Deutschland im europäischen Haus

Im Jahre 1989 ging mit dem Fall der Berliner Mauer eine Epoche der europäischen Geschichte zu Ende: Die Nachkriegszeit war endlich vorbei°. Besonders für die Länder Osteuropas sind die Jahre seit 1989 eine Zeit der neuen Hoffnungen, aber auch der Unsicherheit. Deutschland ist mit seiner zentralen Lage° zwischen Ost und West und seiner starken Wirtschaft ein Schlüssel zum neuen „europäischen Haus".[3]

over
location

Historischer Hintergrund°: 1945 bis 1989

background

1945 teilten die vier Alliierten° – Amerika, Großbritannien, Frankreich und die Sowjetunion – das besiegte° Hitlerreich in vier Zonen auf°, mit dem Ziel einen neuen entnazifizierten° Staat zu bilden°. Aber bald änderte sich das politische Klima. Es begann der so genannte° Kalte Krieg zwischen dem Kommunismus im Osten und dem Kapitalismus im Westen. Anstatt eines vereinten Landes gründete° man 1949 die Bundesrepublik Deutschland (BRD) und die Deutsche Demokratische Republik (DDR), zwei separate und sehr verschiedene Staaten.

Allies
*defeated / **teilten ... auf** = divided / denazified / form*
so-called
founded

Bis 1961 blieb die Grenze zwischen Ost- und Westberlin offen. So konnten zirka 2,7 Millionen Menschen aus der DDR in den Westen auswandern,[4] um dem repressiven kommunistischen Staat zu entfliehen° und ein besseres Leben zu suchen. Die DDR verblutete°. Um diesen langsamen Tod zu verhindern°, baute die

flee
was bleeding to death / to prevent

---

[3] The phrase "European House" was coined by the former Soviet President Mikhail Gorbachev, leader of the Soviet Union from 1985 to 1991.

[4] Although Berlin was located in the middle of the Soviet Occupation Zone, it too was divided among the Allies because of its importance as the capital. Air and highway corridors linked it to the West.

DDR-Wagen kurz vor der Wiedervereinigung. Was bedeutet „BRDDR"?

ostdeutsche Regierung 1961 eine Mauer mitten durch° Berlin. Die Berliner Mauer, das berühmte Symbol des Kalten Krieges, existierte 28 Jahre, bis die zwei Supermächte USA und die Sowjetunion endlich ihre Feindschaft° aufgaben.

***mitten ...** through the middle of*
enmity

November 1989: Die Grenze öffnet sich

In den 80er Jahren begann eine Liberalisierung in der Sowjetunion, die° Reformbewegungen auch in anderen osteuropäischen Ländern einleitete°. Im Sommer 1989 gab es in vielen Städten der DDR riesengroße friedliche° Demonstrationen gegen die kommunistische Regierung. „Wir sind das Volk", riefen die Demonstranten°, und dann: „Wir sind *ein* Volk." Diese Demonstrationen leiteten die erste gewaltlose Revolution der deutschen Geschichte ein. Die Regierung musste die Grenze öffnen. Im März 1990 gab es die ersten freien Wahlen in der DDR und im Oktober die Vereinigung° der beiden Teile Deutschlands.

which
initiated
peaceful
demonstrators
unification

Deutschland im neuen Europa

Als Wirtschaftsmacht und größtes° Mitglied der Europäischen Union[5] spielt das heutige Deutschland eine wichtige Rolle als Brücke zwischen Ost und West. Deutschland ist selber ein Spiegel der großen Unterschiede in Europa. Wie sieht denn die Zukunft des europäischen Hauses aus?

biggest

Es gibt natürlich noch ungelöste Probleme. Die Umwelt in Osteuropa war durch die Industrie viel mehr beschädigt° als° im Westen. Auch waren die meisten° Fabriken im Osten hoffnungslos veraltet° und konnten mit der westeuropäischen Industrie nicht mehr konkurrieren°. Man musste sie entweder schließen oder° sehr viel investieren, um sie zu modernisieren. Das brachte im Osten mehr Arbeitslosigkeit und Ressentiments° gegen die neuen Manager aus dem Westen.

damaged / than / most
***hoffnungslos ...** hopelessly antiquated / compete /* ***entweder ... oder** = either . . . or*
resentment

[5] The European Union is a political and economic alliance of European nations.

Die Wirtschaft in Osteuropa war nach der Auflösung° der Sowjetunion so schwach, dass viele Menschen ihre Heimat verließen und nach Deutschland auswanderten. Aber in den 90er Jahren ist das Leben in vielen osteuropäischen Ländern besser geworden, so dass die Zahl der Zuwanderer° nach Deutschland immer kleiner° wurde.[6]

Die Demokratisierung und Integration Osteuropas mit dem Westen sind nicht mehr aufzuhalten°. Osteuropäische Länder wie Ungarn, Polen und die Tschechische Republik° sind jetzt Mitgliedstaaten der EU. Zwischen den neuen EU-Nachbarn im Osten und den reichen Demokratien im Westen steht die politisch stabile und wirtschaftlich starke Bundesrepublik.

dissolution

immigrants

***immer...** smaller and smaller*

***sind...** can no longer be stopped / **Ungarn...** Hungary, Poland, and the Czech Republic*

[6] In 2005, Germany accepted 96,000 immigrants. Other factors contributing to the decline in immigration were more restrictive asylum laws, the end of the wars in the former Yugoslavia, and an economic slow-down in Germany itself.

NACH DEM LESEN

SAM

Lab Manual Kap. 11, Diktat.

SAM

Workbook Kap. 11, Üb. J, K.

A Antworten Sie auf Deutsch.

1. Wer hat zuerst von einem „europäischen Haus" gesprochen? Was bedeutet das?
2. Warum ist Deutschlands Rolle so wichtig im neuen Europa?
3. Wie kam es zu zwei deutschen Staaten?
4. Warum waren die beiden deutschen Staaten so verschieden?
5. Warum hat die Regierung der DDR die Mauer gebaut?
6. Wie hat die friedliche Revolution in der DDR begonnen?
7. Wann hat die DDR-Regierung die Grenze ganz geöffnet?
8. Welche osteuropäischen Staaten sind EU-Mitglieder geworden?

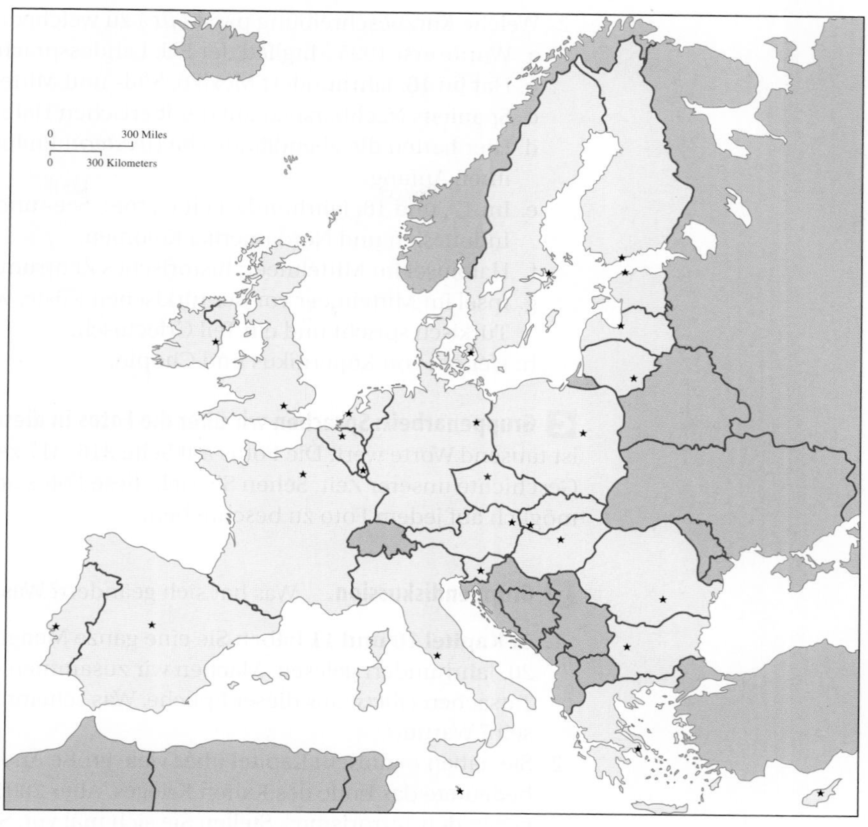

B Partnerarbeit: EU-Quiz.

1. Arbeiten Sie mit einem Partner und tragen Sie die Namen der EU-Mitgliedstaaten und ihrer Hauptstädte auf die Karte ein. (**eintragen**: *to enter*)

Mitgliedstaaten

Belgien
Dänemark
Deutschland
Finnland
Frankreich
Griechenland
Großbritannien
Irland
Ungarn
Slowenien
Polen
Litauen
Slowakei

Italien
Luxemburg
Niederlande
Österreich
Portugal
Schweden
Spanien
Malta
Estland
Zypern
Tschechische Republik
Lettland

Hauptstädte

Athen
Berlin
Brüssel
den Haag
Dublin
Helsinki
Kopenhagen
Lissabon
Warschau
Bratislava
Budapest
Ljubljana
Riga

London
Luxemburg
Madrid
Paris
Rom
Stockholm
Wien
Valletta
Nicosia
Prag
Tallin
Vilnius

2. Welche Kurzbeschreibung passt (*fits*) zu welchem Land?
   a. Wurde erst 1995 Mitglied der EU. Landessprache: Deutsch.
   b. Hat im 16. Jahrhundert Mexiko, Süd- und Mittelamerika kolonisiert.
   c. Spaniens Nachbarstaat auf der iberischen Halbinsel.
   d. Hier hatten die abendländische (*western*) Philosophie und die Demokratie ihren Anfang.
   e. Im 17. und 18. Jahrhundert eine große See- und Handelsmacht; hatte in Afrika, Indonesien und Nordamerika Kolonien.
   f. Halbinsel im Mittelmeer; historisches Zentrum eines alten Weltreichs.
   g. Insel im Mittelmeer vor der türkischen Küste, wo ein Teil der Bewohner Türkisch spricht und ein Teil Griechisch.
   h. Heimat von Kopernikus und Chopin.

C Gruppenarbeit: Sprechen wir über die Fotos in diesem Kapitel. Man sagt, ein Bild ist tausend Worte wert. Die Fotos auf Seite 316–317 zeigen die menschliche Seite der Geschichte unserer Zeit. Sehen Sie sich diese Fotos an und versuchen Sie so viel wie möglich auf jedem Foto zu beschreiben.

D Gruppendiskussion. Was hat sich geändert? Was muss sich noch ändern?

1. In **Kapitel 10 und 11** haben Sie eine ganze Menge über deutsche Geschichte im 20. Jahrhundert gelesen. Machen wir zusammen eine kurze Liste von einigen Tatsachen (*facts*) aus dieser Epoche. Was scheint Ihnen besonders wichtig zu sein? Warum?
2. Sie haben in diesem Kapitel über viele große Änderungen gelesen. Das Jahr 1989 bedeutete das Ende des Kalten Krieges. Aber 2001 begann ein neuer „Krieg" gegen den Terrorismus. Stellen Sie sich mal vor, Sie sind politische Berater (*advisors*). Was sind Ihre Prioritäten? Was soll sich in der Welt ändern?

E Die Berliner Mauer und das vereinigte Deutschland. Machen Sie ganze Sätze. Vergessen Sie die Endungen nicht! (// = Komma)

1. (*perfect tense*) wegen / dies- / Situation / auswandern / viel- / Menschen
2. (*first clause: past perfect tense*) nachdem / man / Mauer / bauen // (*second clause: simple past tense*) können / wenig- / Menschen / nach Westen / reisen
3. (*simple past tense*) Mauer / müssen / 28 Jahre / existieren // bis / politisch / Situation / sich ändern
4. (*present tense*) nach / Vereinigung / beid- (*genitive*) / deutsch- / Staaten / aussehen / Zukunft / anders
5. (*present tense*) all- / Menschen / sich freuen // wenn / Völker / Europa (*genitive*) / in Frieden / miteinander / leben / können

Angela Merkel, erste Bundeskanzlerin der BRD.

Enhancing your writing through variation

Below you are asked to write about your morning routine. In describing a series of actions, the temptation is to give every sentence the same structure, e.g., **Ich stehe auf. Ich wasche mich. Ich ...** To make your prose more interesting and informative, vary sentence structure and add transition words and time phrases, e.g., **Ich stehe fast immer um 7 Uhr auf. Zuerst ... Und dann ... Um 8 Uhr ... Aber am Wochenende ...**

Schreiben wir mal: Meine Morgenroutine. Beschreiben Sie Ihre Morgenroutine. Hier sind einige nützliche Verben:

- frühstücken
- den Rucksack packen
- aufstehen
- zur Uni gehen
- sich rasieren (*shave*) oder sich schminken (*put on makeup*)
- sich die Zähne putzen
- eine zweite Tasse Kaffee trinken
- sich anziehen
- sich duschen (*shower*) oder sich baden (*take a bath*)
- sich die Haare kämmen (*comb one's hair*)

F Wie sagt man das auf Deutsch?

1. When did your relatives immigrate to America?
2. Some emigrated from Germany sixty years ago.
3. Others arrived at the beginning of the 19th century.

4. Ute told me that you got hurt.
5. Yes, I broke my arm last week.
6. How did that happen?
7. I had an accident with my new bicycle.

8. Hurry up or we'll be late!
9. I still have to wash and get dressed.
10. Thank goodness we can afford a taxi.
11. Have the children already eaten?
12. Yes, and they've washed and are already in bed.

Deutsche Fußballfans während der Weltmeisterschaft 2006

ALMANACH

VIDEO

Zeittafel zur deutschen Geschichte, 1939 bis heute

1939 Deutscher Einmarsch in Polen; Anfang des Zweiten Weltkriegs.

1945 9. Mai Kapitulation Deutschlands. Der Zweite Weltkrieg ist zu Ende in Europa.

1946 Erste demokratische Kommunalwahlen seit 1933.

1947 Marshall-Plan bringt den Westzonen ökonomische Hilfe. Der Wiederaufbau beginnt.

1948 Währungsreform im Westen. Berlin-Blockade durch die Sowjets, Berliner Luftbrücke.

1949 Gründung der BRD und der DDR, Deutschland in zwei Staaten geteilt.

1953 Protestdemonstrationen in Ostberlin gegen zu hohe Arbeitsnormen.

1955 BRD wird Mitglied der NATO, DDR wird Mitglied des Warschauer Paktes.

1961 Bau der Mauer zwischen Ost- und West-Berlin.

1963 Besuch des US-Präsidenten John F. Kennedy an der Mauer.

70er Jahre Willy Brandts Ostpolitik. Normalisierung der Beziehungen zwischen BRD und DDR.

1987
750-Jahr-Feier in beiden Teilen der Stadt Berlin.

1989 Spätsommer Tägliche Flucht vieler DDR-Bürger über Ungarn. Erich Honecker tritt zurück. Millionen demonstrieren in Ostberlin, Leipzig und anderen Städten.
9. November Die Regierung öffnet die Grenzen.

1990 März Erste demokratische Wahlen in der DDR.
Juli Währungsunion der beiden deutschen Staaten.
Oktober Deutsche Vereinigung.
Dezember Erste gesamtdeutsche demokratische Wahlen seit 1932.

1991 Berlin wird wieder die Hauptstadt Deutschlands.

1994 Die letzten alliierten Truppen verlassen Berlin.

1995 Österreich wird Mitglied der Europäischen Union.

1999 Im Kosovo nehmen deutsche Truppen zum ersten Mal seit dem Zweiten Weltkrieg an einer Militäraktion im Ausland teil.

2002 Der Euro wird die offizielle Währung aller EU-Länder außer Großbritannien und Dänemark. Deutschland schickt Bundeswehrsoldaten nach Afghanistan.

2005 Angela Merkel wird die erste Bundeskanzlerin.

KAPITEL

12

Der Mainzer Dom

Erinnerungen

Kommunikation

- Comparing things
- Saying how often things happen
- Talking about memories

Kultur

- Reading an authentic German literary text

In diesem Kapitel

- **Lyrik zum Vorlesen**
  Joseph von Eichendorff, "Heimweh"
- **Grammatik**
  1. Comparison of adjectives and adverbs
  2. Relative pronouns and relative clauses
  3. The verb **lassen**
  4. Time phrases with **Mal**
  5. Parts of the day
- **Lesestück**
  Anna Seghers, "Zwei Denkmäler"
- **Almanach**
  Denkmäler

DIALOGE

Lab Manual Kap. 12, Dialoge, Fragen, Hören Sie gut zu!

Idiotensicher

HANS-PETER: Du, Karin, hast du das Buch mit, das ich dir geliehen habe?
KARIN: Ach, tut mir Leid. Ich hab's wieder zu Hause gelassen. Ich arbeite noch an meinem Referat.
HANS-PETER: Ist ja egal. Du darfst es ruhig noch behalten. Hast du noch viel zu tun?
KARIN: Nein, ich bin fast fertig. Ich benutze zum ersten Mal meinen neuen Laptop. Die Software ist echt idiotensicher.

Klatsch

PETRA: Wer war denn der Typ, mit dem Rita gestern weggegangen ist?
LUKAS: Der Mann, der so komisch angezogen war?
PETRA: Genau, den meine ich.
LUKAS: Das war der Rudi. Stell dir vor, sie hat sich mit ihm verlobt!
PETRA: Wenigstens sah er intelligenter aus als ihr letzter Freund.

Vor der Haustür

Frau Schwarzer, die neulich ins Haus eingezogen ist, redet nach der Arbeit mit ihrem Nachbarn Herrn Beck.

FRAU SCHWARZER: Ach Herr Beck, ich wollte Sie etwas fragen: Wo kann ich hier in der Gegend meinen VW reparieren lassen?
HERR BECK: Da empfehle ich Ihnen den Herrn Haslinger in der nächsten Querstraße. Er ist hier der beste Mechaniker, aber leider nicht der billigste.
FRAU SCHWARZER: Hmm ... Im Augenblick bin ich etwas knapp bei Kasse. Ich glaub', ich mache es diesmal lieber selber.
HERR BECK: Na, viel Spaß ... Also, dann wünsche ich Ihnen einen schönen Abend noch.
FRAU SCHWARZER: Danke, gleichfalls!

Notice endings on N-nouns in dative and accusative: **ihrem Nachbarn** and **Herrn Haslinger**.

Guten Abend is a greeting. (**Ich wünsche Ihnen einen**) **schönen Abend noch** is said when parting.

NOTES ON USAGE

The words *es* and *etwas*

In spoken German, the pronoun **es** is often contracted to **'s**.

Ich **hab's** wieder zu Hause gelassen.

Note three different meanings of **etwas**:

Ich wollte Sie **etwas** fragen.	*something*
Ich bin **etwas** knapp bei Kasse.	*somewhat, a little*
Hast du **etwas** Geld?	*some*

Wortschatz 1

In-Text Audio CD

Verben

behalten (behält), behielt, hat behalten to keep, retain
erinnern an (+ *acc.*) to remind of
sich erinnern an (+ *acc.*) to remember
lassen (lässt), ließ, hat gelassen to leave (something or someone); leave behind; to let, allow; to cause to be done
reden to talk, speak
reparieren to repair
sich verloben mit to become engaged to
weg·gehen, ging weg, ist weggegangen to go away, leave
wünschen to wish

Substantive

der **Augenblick, -e** moment
im Augenblick at the moment
der **Besuch, -e** visit
der **Laptop, -s** laptop computer
der **Klatsch** gossip
der **Typ, -en** (*slang*) guy

der Typ: Used colloquially for males (**ein sympathischer Typ**). It is used for both male and female in the expression: **Er/Sie ist nicht mein Typ.**

das **Mal, -e** time (*in the sense of "occurrence"*)
jedes Mal every time
zum ersten Mal for the first time
die **Erinnerung, -en** memory
die **Gegend, -en** area, region
die **Nacht, ¨-e** night
in der Nacht at night
Gute Nacht. Good night.
die **Querstraße, -n** cross street
die **Software** software

Adjektive und Adverbien

diesmal this time
etwas somewhat, a little
idiotensicher foolproof
intelligent intelligent
knapp scarce, in short supply
knapp bei Kasse short of money
komisch peculiar, odd; funny
nächst- nearest; next
neulich recently
ruhig (*as sentence adverb*) feel free to, go ahead and
Du kannst ruhig hier bleiben. Feel free to stay here.

Remember the basic meaning of **ruhig**: peaceful, calm. Cf. cartoon on p. 70.

übermorgen the day after tomorrow
vorgestern the day before yesterday

Andere Vokabeln

als (*with adj. or adv. in comparative degree*) than
intelligenter als more intelligent than
na well . . .

Nützliche Ausdrücke

(Einen) Augenblick, bitte! Just a moment, please!
Danke, gleichfalls. Thanks, you too. Same to you.
Viel Spaß! Have fun!

Gegensätze

sich erinnern ≠ vergessen to remember ≠ to forget

PROVERB: **Reden ist Silber, Schweigen ist Gold.**

reden ≠ schweigen, schwieg, hat geschwiegen to speak ≠ to be silent
reparieren ≠ kaputt machen to repair ≠ to break
weggehen ≠ zurückkommen to go away ≠ to come back
die Nacht ≠ der Tag night ≠ day

Variationen

A Persönliche Fragen

1. Würden Sie Ihren Freunden Bücher leihen oder nicht? Wie ist es mit CDs, Ihrem Laptop oder mit Kleidern?
2. Was haben Sie heute zu Hause gelassen?
3. Lukas sagt, dass Rudi komisch angezogen war. Ziehen Sie sich manchmal komisch an? Was tragen Sie dann?
4. Wie alt soll man sein, bevor man sich verlobt? Was meinen Sie?
5. Besitzen Sie einen Wagen? Was für einen?
6. Können Sie Ihr Auto selber reparieren?

B Übung: Was braucht man? Um ihr Referat zu schreiben, braucht Karin Bücher, einen Laptop und vielleicht auch ein Wörterbuch. Was braucht man, um ...

einen Brief zu schreiben?
das Frühstück zu machen?
eine Urlaubsreise zu machen?
eine Fremdsprache zu lernen?
einkaufen zu gehen?
eine Radtour zu machen?
eine Bergwanderung zu machen?

C Übung: Das Beste in der Gegend. Herr Beck weiß, wer der beste Mechaniker in der Gegend ist. Wissen Sie, wo man das Beste in der Gegend findet? Wo ist hier in unserer Gegend zum Beispiel ...

das beste griechische Restaurant?
das beste französische Restaurant?
das beste Kleidergeschäft?
das beste Hotel?
die beste Kneipe?
die beste Pizzeria?
das beste Sportgeschäft?
der beste Supermarkt?

Spätnachmittag in einem alten Schloss in Böhmen (*Bohemia*)

The sentence adverb **ruhig** goes immediately after the inflected verb and all personal pronouns.

D Partnerarbeit: Das darfst du ruhig machen. Sie brauchen etwas (z. B., einen Kuli). Ihr Partner sagt, Sie dürfen ruhig seinen Kuli benutzen.

BEISPIEL: A: Ich brauche einen Kuli.
B: Du kannst *ruhig* meinen Kuli benutzen.

Here are some examples of things you might need: **Laptop, Auto, Wörterbuch, Spiegel, Fahrrad, Handy.**

LYRIK ZUM VORLESEN

In-Text Audio CD

Joseph von Eichendorff was one of the foremost poets of the Romantic movement in Germany. Reverence for nature, longing for one's beloved, and nostalgia for one's homeland are all typical themes for the Romantics. The poem "Heimweh" (*Homesickness*) is from Eichendorff's story ***Aus dem Leben eines Taugenichts*** (*From the Life of a Good-for-Nothing*), in which the hero, in Italy, yearns for Germany and his beloved.

Heimweh

Wer in die Fremde° will wandern — = ***ins Ausland***
Der muss mit der Liebsten° gehn, — *beloved*
Es jubeln° und lassen die andern — *rejoice*
Den Fremden alleine stehn.

Was wisset ihr, dunkele Wipfel° — *treetops*
Von der alten, schönen Zeit?
Ach, die Heimat hinter den Gipfeln°, — *peaks*
Wie liegt sie von hier so weit!

Am liebsten° betracht° ich die Sterne°, — *most of all / contemplate / stars*
Die schienen, wie° ich ging zu ihr, — = ***als***
Die Nachtigall° hör ich so gerne, — *nightingale*
Sie sang vor der Liebsten Tür.

Der Morgen, das ist meine Freude°! — *joy*
Da steig ich in stiller° Stund' — *quiet*
Auf den höchsten° Berg in die Weite°, — *highest / distance*
Grüß dich, Deutschland, aus
Herzens Grund°! — ***aus...*** *from the bottom of my heart*

Joseph von Eichendorff (1788–1857)

Zeichnung (*drawing*) von Ludwig Richter (19. Jahrhundert)

GRAMMATIK

1. Comparison of adjectives and adverbs

DEFINITION

What does comparison mean?
Comparison here means adding endings onto adjectives and adverbs to indicate their degree of intensity, e.g., *hot, hotter, hottest*.

Comparing things is a communicative goal.

When adjectives or adverbs are used in comparisons, they can occur in three stages or degrees.

- Positive degree (*basic form*)

genauso interessant wie = *just as interesting as*
genauso schnell wie = *just as fast as*

Ich finde, Chemie ist **genauso interessant wie** Physik.	*I think that chemistry is **just as interesting as** physics.*
Susanne **läuft genauso schnell wie** ich.	*Susanne runs just **as fast as** I do.*

- Comparative degree (*marker:* **-er**)

interessanter als = *more interesting than*
schneller als = *faster than*

Ich finde Philosophie **interessanter als** Psychologie.	*I think philosophy is **more interesting than** psychology.*
Susanne läuft **schneller als** Jörg.	*Susanne runs **faster than** Jörg.*

- Superlative degree of attributive adjectives (*marker:* **-(e)st**)

das interessanteste Fach = *the most interesting subject*
die schnellste Läuferin = *the fastest runner*

Ich finde Linguistik **das interessanteste Fach.**	*I think linguistics is **the most interesting subject.***
Susanne ist **die schnellste Läuferin** in unserer Schule.	*Susanne is **the fastest runner** in our school.*

- Superlative of adverbs and predicate adjectives (*marker*: **am _______ -(e)sten**)

am interessantesten = *most interesting*
am schnellsten = *fastest*

Von allen Fächern finde ich Linguistik **am interessantesten**.	*Of all subjects I find linguistics the **most interesting**.*
Susanne läuft **am schnellsten**.	*Susanne runs **fastest**.*

Reklame (*advertisement*) für den Schnellzug vom Wiener Flughafen in das Stadtzentrum (= die City)

fly the train
Der schnellste Weg in die City.

Formation of comparative degree (*der Komparativ*)

- To form the comparative degree of any adjective or adverb, add the marker **-er** to the basic form.

SPELLING NOTE: Adjectives ending in **-el** and **-er** drop the **-e-** in the comparative:
dunkel → dunkler
teuer → teurer

Basic form	+	*-er*	=	Comparative degree
schnell-		-er		**schneller**
dunkel-		-er		**dunkler**
interessant-		-er		**interessanter**

English adjectives longer than two syllables form their comparative with *more*: *interesting* → *more interesting*. In German, simply add **-er** to make the comparative, no matter how long the adjective is: **interessant → interessanter**.

- Attributive adjectives add the regular adjective endings *after* the comparative **-er**-ending.

Basic form	+	*-er-*	+	Adjective ending
schnell-		-er-		-en
interessant-		-er-		-es

Wir fuhren mit dem **schnelleren** Zug. — *We took the faster train.*
Ich lese ein **interessanteres** Buch. — *I'm reading a more interesting book.*

- **Als** = *than* (when used with the comparative).

Das Buch ist interessanter **als** der Artikel. — *The book is more interesting than the article.*

Lab Manual Kap. 12, Üb. 1 and Var. zu Üb. 3, 4, 6, 7, 9–12.

Workbook Kap. 12, A–F.

1 Übung. Everyone is praising Jörg, but you respond that you are *more* everything than he is.

BEISPIEL: A: Jörg ist interessant.
B: Aber ich bin interessanter als er.

1. Jörg ist hübsch.
2. Er ist ruhig.
3. Er läuft schnell.
4. Er ist ehrlich.
5. Jörg ist fleißig.
6. Er ist freundlich.
7. Er steht früh auf.
8. Er ist sportlich.

2 Übung: Vergleichen wir! (*Let's compare!*)

Compare each pair of things below with each other, using the verb phrase given.

BEISPIEL: Ein Auto fährt schneller als ein Fahrrad.

schnell fahren

langsam sein

gut (besser) schmecken

modern sein

reich sein

3 Übung: Im Kaufhaus. Sie sind Verkäufer oder Verkäuferin im Kaufhaus (*department store*). Ihr Professor spielt einen Kunden. Nichts scheint ihm zu gefallen. Sie versuchen ihm etwas Schöneres, Billigeres usw. zu zeigen.

BEISPIEL: Dieses Hemd ist mir nicht dunkel genug.
Hier haben wir dunklere Hemden.

1. Diese Blumen sind mir nicht schön genug.
2. Diese Brötchen sind mir nicht frisch genug.
3. Diese Schuhe sind mir nicht elegant genug.
4. Diese Bücher sind mir nicht billig genug.
5. Diese Fahrräder sind mir nicht leicht genug.
6. Diese Computer sind mir nicht schnell genug.

Wer hilft mir, meine Ziele zu verwirklichen?
LEHRER
...mehr als nur ein Job!

Formation of the superlative (*der Superlativ*)

The superlative is formed in the following ways:

Adverbs All adverbs form their superlative using the following pattern:

am ________ -(e)sten
am schnellsten = *most quickly*

Susanne läuft **am schnellsten**. *Susanne runs **fastest**.*
Hans hat **am schönsten** gesungen. *Hans sang **most beautifully**.*

Note on spelling: An extra **-e-** is added when the basic form ends in **-d**, **-t**, **-s**, **-ß**, or **-z**: **am mildesten, am heißesten.**

German has no superlative marker like English *most.* No matter how long an adverb is, simply add **-(e)sten**: **am interessantesten** = *most interestingly.*

Attributive adjectives With attributive adjectives, add the regular adjective endings after the superlative **-(e)st-**, for example:

Basic form	+	*-(e)st-*	+	Adjective ending
interessant-		-est-		-e
schnell-		-st-		-en

Das **interessanteste** Bild hängt im Museum. *The **most interesting** picture is in the museum.*
Wir fuhren mit dem **schnellsten** Zug. *We took the **fastest** train.*

The superlative makes logical sense only with the *definite* article, never with the *indefinite* article: **der tiefste See** (*the deepest lake*, but not *"a" deepest lake*).

When the superlative adjective is used as an adjectival noun, it is capitalized: **der/die Interessanteste** = *the most interesting person;* **das Neueste** = *the newest (or latest) thing.*

Predicate Adjectives Predicate adjectives in the superlative may occur either in the **am ________-(e)sten** pattern or with the definite article and regular adjective endings.

Albert ist **am interessantesten.**	*Albert is **most interesting.***
Albert ist **der Interessanteste.**	*Albert is **the most interesting person.***
Diese Bücher sind **die interessantesten.**	*These books are **the most interesting (ones).***

4 Übung: Ich mache das am besten! A visitor is praising the whole class. You then praise yourself in the superlative.

BEISPIEL: A: Sie laufen alle schnell.
B: Aber ich laufe am schnellsten.

1. Sie sind alle freundlich.
2. Sie sind alle sehr fleißig.
3. Sie singen alle sehr schön.
4. Sie sind alle elegant angezogen.
5. Sie sind alle sehr sportlich.
6. Sie denken alle sehr kreativ.

5 Gruppenarbeit: Ich bin der/die ________-ste! Here are some adjectives you can use to describe yourself. Choose the one that you think you exemplify the best of anyone in the class. (Don't take this too seriously!) Then say, **Ich bin der/die ________-(e)ste.**

BEISPIEL: Ich bin der/die Schönste hier!

aktiv	elegant	hungrig
altmodisch	faul	modern
blöd	fleißig	radikal
clever	höflich	wahnsinnig

6 Übung: Im Laden. Spielen Sie wieder den Verkäufer oder die Verkäuferin. Ihre Professorin ist eine Kundin. Sagen Sie ihr, Sie haben das Neueste, Billigste usw.

BEISPIEL: Ich suche billige Weine.
Hier sind unsere *billigsten* Weine.

1. Ich suche neue Schuhe.
2. Ich suche schöne Bilder.
3. Ich suche interessante Bücher.
4. Ich suche moderne Stühle.
5. Ich suche ein leichtes Fahrrad.
6. Ich suche elegante Kleider.

Hier sehen Sie einen der größten Kohlendioxidfresser der Welt.

Umlaut in comparative and superlative

Some comparative and superlative adjectives have two possible forms: **roter/röter, nasser/nässer, gesunder/gesünder**. **Gesund** is the only two-syllable adjective where umlaut is possible.

Many one-syllable adjectives and adverbs whose stem vowels are **a**, **o**, or **u** (but *not* **au**) are umlauted in the comparative and superlative degrees. Here is a list of adjectives and adverbs you already know. Some occur in easy-to-remember pairs of opposites.

	Positive	Comparative	Superlative
old	alt	älter	am ältesten
young	jung	jünger	am jüngsten
dumb	dumm	dümmer	am dümmsten
smart	klug	klüger	am klügsten
cold	kalt	kälter	am kältesten
warm	warm	wärmer	am wärmsten
short	kurz	kürzer	am kürzesten
long	lang	länger	am längsten
strong	stark	stärker	am stärksten
weak	schwach	schwächer	am schwächsten
sick	krank	kränker	am kränksten
healthy	gesund	gesünder	am gesündesten
poor	arm	ärmer	am ärmsten
hard, harsh	hart	härter	am härtesten
often	oft	öfter	am öftesten
red	rot	röter	am rötesten
black	schwarz	schwärzer	am schwärzesten

7 Gruppenarbeit: kalt / kälter / am kältesten. The first student reads a sentence, and the next two respond with the comparative and superlative.

BEISPIEL: A: Meine Wohnung ist kalt.
B: Meine Wohnung ist noch kälter.
C: Aber meine Wohnung ist am kältesten.

1. Mein Bruder ist stark.
2. Mein Auto ist alt.
3. Mein Referat ist lang.
4. Mein Freund ist krank.
5. Meine Schwester ist jung.
6. Mein Zimmer ist warm.
7. Mein Besuch war kurz.
8. Mein Beruf ist hart.

8 Gruppenarbeit: Vergleichen wir. (*Let's compare.*) Sechs oder sieben Studenten stehen vor der Klasse. Zuerst sagen sie auf Deutsch, wann sie geboren sind. Dann beantwortet die Klasse diese Fragen.

1. Wer ist der/die Älteste?
2. Wer ist der/die Jüngste?
3. Wer ist der/die Größte?
4. Wer ist der/die Kleinste?
5. Wer hat die längsten/kürzesten Haare?
6. Wer ist heute am schönsten angezogen?

Eine Firma wie Alice nennt man auf gut Neudeutsch einen *Internet-Provider*. Was will diese Werbung verkaufen?

Irregular comparatives and superlatives

Some of the most frequently used adjectives and adverbs in German have irregular forms in the comparative and superlative.

NOTE: The irregularity of **groß** is that it adds **-t** (**größt-**) rather than **-est** to the stem.

Positive	Comparative	Superlative	
groß	größer	am größten	*big/bigger/biggest*
gut	besser	am besten	*good, well/better/best*
hoch, hoh-	höher	am höchsten	*high/higher/highest*
nahe	näher	am nächsten	*near/nearer/nearest; next*
viel	mehr	am meisten	*much, many/more/most*
gern	lieber	am liebsten	*like to/prefer to/most of all like to*

- The three degrees of **gern** are used to say how much you like to do things.

Ich gehe **gern** ins Kino.	*I like to go to the movies.*
Ich gehe **lieber** ins Theater.	*I'd rather* (or) *I prefer to go to the theater.*
Ich gehe **am liebsten** ins Konzert.	*Most of all, I like to go to concerts.*

Wenig, the antonym of **viel**, functions in the same way.
Ich esse *wenig* Brot.
Ich habe *wenige* Freunde.
Ich habe *weniger* Freunde als du.

- **Viel** means *much* or *a lot of* and it has *no adjective endings.* **Viele** means *many* and *does* have regular plural endings.

Ich esse **viel** Brot.	*I eat a lot of bread.*
Ich habe **viele** Freunde.	*I have many friends.*

- The comparative degree **mehr** *never* has adjective endings.

Du hast **mehr** Freunde als ich.	*You have more friends than I.*

- The superlative degree **meist-** *does* take endings; in addition, it is used with the definite article, in contrast to English *most.*

Die meisten Studenten essen in der Mensa.	***Most** students eat in the cafeteria.*

9 **Übung: gut, besser, am besten.** Rank the items according to the criteria below.

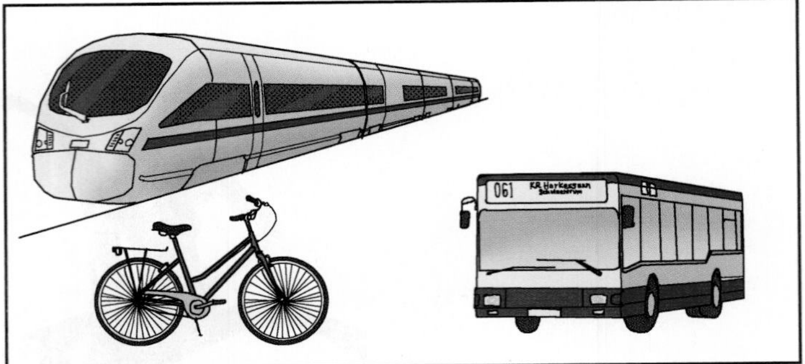

BEISPIEL: schnell fahren
Ein Fahrrad fährt schnell, ein Bus fährt schneller und ein Zug fährt am schnellsten.

gut schmecken

hoch sein

nahe sein

viel wissen

10 Übung: Was sind Ihre Präferenzen? Rank your preferences, as in the example.

BEISPIEL: trinken Tee, Kaffee, Milch
Ich trinke gern Milch. Ich trinke lieber Kaffee. Aber am liebsten trinke ich Tee.

1. lesen	Zeitungen, Gedichte, Romane
2. hören	Rockmusik, Jazz, klassische Musik
3. wohnen	in der Stadt, auf dem Land, am Meer
4. spielen	Fußball, Tennis, Volleyball
5. bekommen	Briefe, Geschenke, gute Noten
6. essen	Pommes frites, Sauerkraut, Bauernbrot
7. schreiben	Briefe, Referate, Postkarten

Comparisons

genauso ... wie = *just as . . . as*
nicht so ... wie = *not as . . . as*

Heute ist es **genauso kalt wie** gestern. Aber es ist **kälter als** vorgestern.	*Today is **just as cold as** yesterday. But it's **colder than** the day before yesterday.*
Stuttgart ist **nicht so groß wie** Berlin. Aber es ist **größer als** Tübingen.	*Stuttgart is **not as large as** Berlin. But it's **bigger than** Tübingen.*

immer ______ **-er** (shows progressive change)

Das Kind wird **immer größer**. Sie liest **immer mehr** Bücher.	*The child's getting **bigger and bigger**. She's reading **more and more** books.*

11 Gruppenarbeit: Damals und jetzt. Vergleichen wir damals und jetzt. Jeder sagt, wie es früher war und wie sich alles immer mehr ändert.

BEISPIELE: A: Früher hatte man mehr Zeit, heute ist man immer mehr in Eile.
B: Früher war das Lebenstempo langsamer, jetzt wird es immer schneller.
C: Früher kostete das Studium ...

12 Schreiben wir mal. Find similarities and differences in two pictures that you have drawn, photographed, or found in books or magazines. Compare them in German.

BEISPIELE: Diese Bäume sind höher als diese hier, aber dieser Berg ist genauso hoch wie der andere.
Diese Mutter sieht nicht so jung aus wie diese hier, aber dieses Kind ist genauso alt wie das Kind da. Das dritte Kind ist das älteste.

13 Gruppenarbeit: Weltrekorde. Jeder von Ihnen stellt den anderen eine Frage über einen Weltrekord. Die anderen müssen die Antwort erraten (*guess*).

BEISPIEL: Wie heißt der höchste Berg der Welt?
Wer ist die beste Tennisspielerin der Welt?

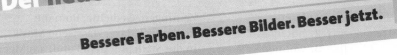

Der neue KODAK FARBWELT Film ist da.

Bessere Farben. Bessere Bilder. Besser jetzt.

www.kodak.de

2. Relative pronouns and relative clauses (*Relativpronomen und Relativsätze*)

A relative clause is a subordinate clause that modifies or further clarifies a noun. Relative clauses are introduced by relative pronouns. Compare the following sentences:

Das ist das **neue** Buch. *That's the **new** book.*

	rel. pron.	
Das ist das Buch,	***das***	**du mir geliehen hast**.
That's the book	***that***	*you lent me.*

The relative clause **das du mir geliehen hast**, like the descriptive adjective **neue**, modifies **Buch** by telling *which* book is being talked about.

In English, the relative pronouns are *that, which, who, whom,* and *whose.* In German, the relative pronoun is almost identical to the definite article. Study this table and note the forms in bold that are *different* from the definite article.

Compare declension of definite article on p. 216.

Relative pronouns

	Masculine	Neuter	Feminine	Plural
nominative	der	das	die	die
accusative	den	das	die	die
dative	dem	dem	der	**denen**
genitive	**dessen**	**dessen**	**deren**	**deren**

Relative pronouns refer (or "relate") back to a noun (called the *antecedent*) in the main clause. Here are some examples. Note how the antecedent and the relative pronoun always denote the same person or thing.

antecedent — *masc. sing. nom.*

1. Das ist **der Typ**. **Er** war im Kino.

   Das ist der Typ, **der** im Kino war.

   rel. pron.

   *That's the guy **who** was at the movies.*

fem. sing. dat.

antecedent

2. Kennst du **die Frau**? Ich arbeite mit **ihr**.

   Kennst du die Frau, mit **der** ich arbeite?

   rel. pron.

   *Do you know the woman [**whom**] I work with?*

masc. sing. gen.

antecedent

3. Das ist **der Autor**. Die Romane **des Autors** sind berühmt.

   Das ist der Autor, **dessen** Romane berühmt sind.

   rel. pron.

   *That's the author **whose** novels are famous.*

acc. plural

antecedent

4. Hast du **die Bücher**? Ich habe **sie** dir geliehen.

   Hast du die Bücher, **die** ich dir geliehen habe?

   rel. pron.

   *Do you have the books [**that**] I lent you?*

Rules for relative clauses

1. The relative pronoun is *never* omitted in German, as it often is in English (examples 2 and 4 above).
2. The gender and number of the relative pronoun are *always* the same as those of its antecedent.
3. The case of a relative pronoun is determined by its function in the relative clause.

   fem. sing. nom. *fem. sing. dat.*

   Das ist **die Frau**, mit **der** ich arbeite.
4. When the relative pronoun is the object of a preposition, the preposition *always precedes* it in the relative clause (example 2, above). In English the preposition often comes at the end of the relative clause (e.g., *the woman I work **with***). This is *never* the case in German (**die Frau, *mit* der ich arbeite).**
5. The relative clause is always a SUBORDINATE CLAUSE with verb-last word order. The relative clause is *always* set off from the rest of the sentence by commas.
6. The relative clause is usually placed immediately after its antecedent.

   Das Buch, das du mir geliehen hast, hat mir geholfen. — ***The book that** you lent me helped me.*

SAM **Lab Manual** Kap. 12, Üb. 14, and Var. zu Üb. 17, 21, 22.

SAM **Workbook** Kap. 12, G–K.

14 Kettenreaktion. A liest den ersten Satz auf Deutsch vor. B gibt eine englische Übersetzung und liest dann den nächsten Satz vor usw.

1. Das ist der Mann, der hier wohnt.
2. Das ist der Mann, den ich kenne.
3. Das ist der Mann, dem wir helfen.
4. Das ist der Mann, dessen Frau ich kenne.

5. Das ist das Fahrrad, das sehr leicht ist.
6. Das ist das Fahrrad, das sie gekauft hat.
7. Das ist das Fahrrad, mit dem ich zur Arbeit fahre.
8. Das ist das Fahrrad, dessen Farbe mir gefällt.

9. Das ist die Frau, die Deutsch kann.
10. Das ist die Frau, die wir brauchen.
11. Das ist die Frau, der wir Geld geben.
12. Das ist die Frau, deren Romane ich kenne.

13. Das sind die Leute, die mich kennen.
14. Das sind die Leute, die ich kenne.
15. Das sind die Leute, denen wir helfen.
16. Das sind die Leute, deren Kinder wir kennen.

15 Übung. Lesen Sie jeden Satz mit dem richtigen Relativpronomen vor.

In Europa ist nur die Wolga in Russland länger als die Donau (2.850 km). Die Zugspitze (2.692 m) ist der höchste Berg Deutschlands.

1. Die Donau ist ein Fluss, ________ durch Österreich fließt. (*that*)
2. Der Berg, ________ man am Horizont sieht, ist die Zugspitze. (*that*)
3. Kennst du den Herrn, ________ dieser Wagen gehört? (*to whom*)
4. Der Professor, ________ Bücher dort liegen, kommt gleich zurück. (*whose*)
5. Das ist ein Schaufenster, ________ immer bunt aussieht. (*that*)
6. Mir schmeckt jedes Abendessen, ________ du kochst. (*that*)
7. Das Kind, ________ ich geholfen habe, ist wieder gesund. (*whom*)
8. Sie kommt aus einem Land, ________ Regierung undemokratisch ist. (*whose*)
9. Die Studentin, ________ neben mir saß, war im zweiten Semester. (*who*)
10. Beschreiben Sie mir die Rolle, ________ ich spielen soll. (*that*)
11. Christa, ________ der Computer gehört, leiht ihn dir gerne. (*to whom*)
12. Die Touristengruppe, ________ Gepäck dort steht, ist aus England. (*whose*)
13. Wer sind die Leute, ________ dort vor der Mensa stehen? (*who*)
14. Da sind ein paar Studenten, ________ du kennen lernen sollst. (*whom*)
15. Es gibt viele Menschen, ________ dieser Arzt geholfen hat. (*whom*)
16. Sind das die Kinder, ________ Hund gestorben ist? (*whose*)

Johannes Brahms (1833–1897), einer der berühmtesten Komponisten des 19. Jahrhunderts. Brahms, der in Hamburg geboren war, verbrachte den größten Teil seines Lebens in Wien, wo er auch begraben ist.

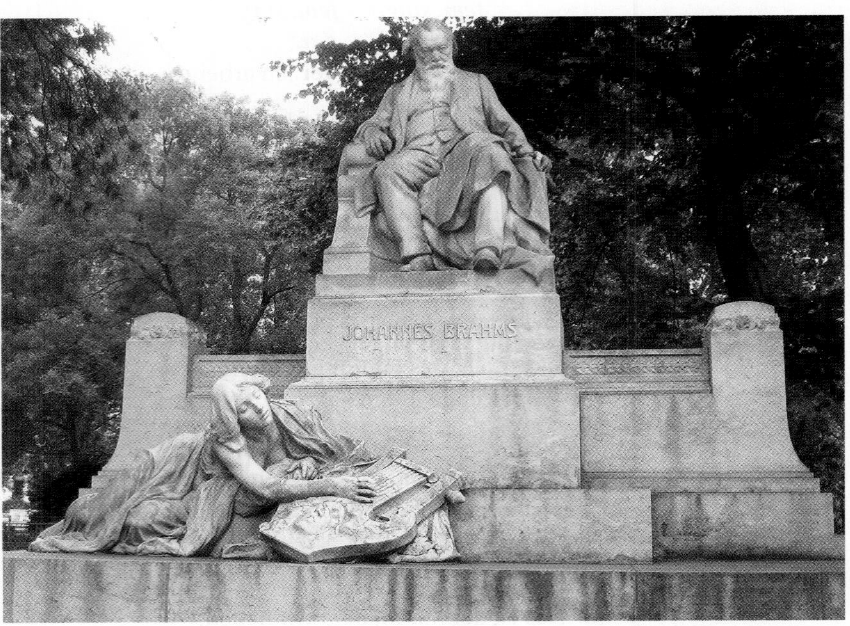

Brahms-Denkmal in Wien (erbaut 1908)

16 Spiel: Ratet mal, wen ich meine! Choose another student in the room to describe, but don't tell anyone who it is. When your turn comes, say **Ich kenne eine Studentin, die ...** or **Ich kenne einen Studenten, der ...** and then add some description. The others must guess whom you mean.

BEISPIEL: Ich kenne eine Studentin, die heute eine gelbe Hose trägt.

17 Partnerarbeit. Complete the question with a relative clause. Exchange roles for the next sentence.

BEISPIEL: A: Ich arbeite für eine internationale Firma.
B: Wie heißt die Firma, für ... ?
Wie heißt die Firma, für die du arbeitest?

1. A: Ich bin durch eine schöne Stadt gefahren.
   B: Wie heißt die Stadt, durch ...
2. A: Ich habe in einem eleganten Hotel übernachtet.
   B: Wo war das Hotel, ...
3. A: Ich habe mit einigen Ausländern geredet.
   B: Woher kommen die Ausländer, ...
4. A: Der Austauschstudent kommt aus einer Großstadt.
   B: Wie heißt denn die Stadt, ...
5. A: Ich wohnte bei einer netten Familie.
   B: Wie groß war die Familie, ...
6. A: Ich habe hinter der großen Kirche geparkt.
   B: Wo steht denn die Kirche, ...

18 Übung. Machen Sie aus den zwei Sätzen *einen* Satz. Machen Sie aus dem zweiten Satz einen Relativsatz.

These sentences are paired as conversational exchanges. The relative clauses in items 4, 10, and 13 begin with prepositions. In items 11 and 14, the relative pronoun is in the genitive case.

BEISPIEL: Ich kenne die Frau. (Du meinst sie.)
Ich kenne die Frau, die du meinst.

1. Suchst du die Schokolade? (Sie war hier.)
2. Nein, ich habe selber Schokolade. (Ich habe sie mitgebracht.)
3. Ist das die Geschichte? (Horst hat sie erzählt.)
4. Ja, er erzählt Geschichten. (Man muss über seine Geschichten lachen.)
5. Das ist ein Buch. (Ingrid hat es schon letztes Jahr gelesen.)
6. Meinst du das Buch? (Es ist jetzt sehr bekannt.)
7. Ist das der Mann? (Sie haben ihm geholfen.)
8. Nein, ich habe einem anderen Mann geholfen. (Er war nicht so jung.)
9. Kennst du die Studenten? (Sie wohnen in der Altstadt.)
10. Ja, das sind die Studenten. (Mit ihnen esse ich zusammen in der Mensa.)
11. Wie heißt der Junge? (Sein Vater ist Professor.)
12. Er hat einen komischen Namen. (Ich habe ihn vergessen.)
13. Ist die Frau berufstätig? (Du wohnst bei ihr.)
14. Ja, sie ist eine Frau. (Ihre Kinder wohnen nicht mehr zu Hause.)

19 Partnerarbeit: Ist das ein neuer Mantel? Fragen Sie einander, ob Ihre Kleider und andere Sachen neu sind. Antworten Sie, dass Sie alles letztes Jahr gekauft haben. Benutzen Sie einen Relativsatz in Ihrer Antwort.

BEISPIEL: A: Ist das ein neuer Mantel?
B: Nein, das ist ein Mantel, *den* ich letztes Jahr gekauft habe.

20 Schreiben wir mal. Antworten Sie mit Ihren eigenen Worten. Benutzen Sie in Ihrer Antwort einen Relativsatz (*relative clause*).

BEISPIEL: Mit was für Menschen verbringen Sie gern Ihre Freizeit?
Ich verbringe gern meine Freizeit mit Menschen, mit denen ich Sport treiben kann.

1. Was für Bücher würden Sie gern lesen?
2. Mit was für Menschen leben Sie gern zusammen?
3. Aus was für einer Familie kommen Sie?
4. Was für Städte gefallen Ihnen besonders gut?
5. In was für einem Gebäude wohnen Sie?
6. Mit was für Menschen verbringen Sie gern Ihre Freizeit?

ACHT MINIS, DIE SPASS HABEN.

The relative pronoun *was*

A relative clause following the pronoun antecedents **das**, **etwas**, **nichts**, **viel**, **wenig**, and **alles** begins with the relative pronoun **was**. Note again that English often leaves out the relative pronoun, whereas German requires it.

Stimmt **das**, **was** er uns erzählte?	*Is what he told us right?* (literally: *Is that right what he told us?*)
Gibt es noch **etwas**, **was** Sie brauchen?	*Is there something else [that] you need?*
Nein, Sie haben **nichts**, **was** ich brauche.	*No, you have nothing [that] I need.*
Alles, **was** er sagt, ist falsch.	*Everything [that] he says is wrong.*

Was must also begin a relative clause whose antecedent is a neuter adjectival noun (see p. 303):

Was war **das Interessante**, **was** du mir zeigen wolltest?	*What was the interesting thing [that] you wanted to show me?*
Ist das **das Beste**, **was** Sie haben?	*Is that the best [that] you have?*

Was also begins a relative clause whose antecedent is an entire clause (English uses *which*):

Rita hat sich verlobt, was ich nicht verstehen kann.	*Rita got engaged, which I can't understand.*

21 Gruppenarbeit: Etwas, was mir gefällt. / Etwas, was mich ärgert. Jeder Student erzählt oder berichtet etwas. Die anderen sagen, ob es ihnen gefällt oder ob es sie ärgert.

BEISPIEL: Die Umwelt ist sehr verschmutzt.
Das ist etwas, was mich ärgert!

1. Nächstes Jahr wird das Studium teurer.
2. Ich möchte euch Geld schenken.
3. Deine Mitbewohnerin spielt abends laute Rapmusik.
4. Heute Abend gibt es Pizza zum Abendessen.
5. Bald haben wir Ferien.
6. Morgen kommen deine Verwandten zu Besuch.

Jetzt machen Sie Ihre eigenen Aussagen (*statements*).

Informationen, die Sie nicht über Ihr Telefon bekommen
Frankfurter Allgemeine

22 Partnerarbeit: Was war das Tollste, was du je gemacht hast? Below are cues for asking each other questions such as, "What's the greatest thing you've ever done?" Take turns asking each other the questions.

BEISPIEL: toll / machen
A: Was war das Tollste, was du je gemacht hast?
B: Ich habe in der Schweiz Winterurlaub gemacht.

1. schwierig / machen
2. schön / sehen
3. gefährlich / machen
4. dumm / sagen
5. erstaunlich / hören
6. gut / essen
7. interessant / lesen
8. toll / bekommen

3. The verb *lassen*

The verb **lassen** has several meanings in German.

- *to leave (something or someone), leave behind*

Lassen Sie uns bitte allein.	*Please leave us alone.*
Hast du deinen Mantel im Restaurant **gelassen**?	*Did you leave your coat in the restaurant?*

Lab Manual Kap. 12, Var. zu Üb. 23, 26.

Workbook Kap. 12, L, M.

23 Übung: Warum ist das nicht hier? Sagen Sie, wo Sie diese Menschen oder Dinge gelassen haben. Rechts gibt es einige Möglichkeiten, aber Sie können auch frei antworten.

BEISPIEL: Warum haben Sie heute keine Jacke?
Ich habe sie zu Hause gelassen.

1. Warum sind Ihre Kinder nicht hier?	in der Schweiz
2. Warum tragen Sie heute keine Brille (*glasses*)?	im Rucksack
3. Warum haben Sie Ihr Referat nicht mit?	bei der Großmutter
4. Warum haben sie Ihren Ausweis nicht mit?	auf dem Bett
5. Warum haben Sie Ihren Wagen nicht mit?	zu Hause
6. Warum ist Ihre Tochter nicht hier?	in der Manteltasche

24 Partnerarbeit: Wo hast du das gelassen? Hat Ihre Partnerin heute etwas nicht mitgebracht? Fragen Sie sie, wo sie es gelassen hat.

BEISPIEL: A: Wo hast du heute deine grüne Jacke gelassen?
B: Ich habe sie im Zimmer gelassen.

- *to allow (to), to let:* **lassen** + *infinitive*

Lasst mich bitte mitkommen. — *Please let me come along.*
Lass mich doch fahren! — *Let me drive.*

25 Übung: Oma, lass mich für dich kochen! You're visiting your grandmother who hasn't been feeling well. Offer to do things for her, for example:

zum Supermarkt fahren
einkaufen gehen
das Altglas recyceln
die Betten machen
aufräumen
die Wohnung putzen

- *to have or order something done:* **lassen** + *infinitive*

In the following sentences **lassen** shows that the subject is not performing an action, but rather having it done by someone else.

Sie **lässt** ihren Wagen **reparieren**. — *She's having her car fixed.*

The accusative case shows who performs the action:

Sie lässt **den Mechaniker** ihren Wagen reparieren. — *She's having the mechanic fix her car.*

A dative reflexive pronoun shows explicitly that one is having something done for one's own benefit.

Ich lasse **mir** ein Haus bauen. — *I'm having a house built (for myself).*

When **lassen** is used with a dependent infinitive, it takes the double infinitive construction in the perfect tense. The structure is parallel to that of the modal verbs (see page 158).

double infinitive
Die Beamtin hat mich nicht **reden lassen**.
The official didn't let me speak.

double infinitive
Ich habe den Wagen **reparieren lassen.**
I had my car repaired.

26 Übung: Er hat es machen lassen. Manchmal will man etwas nicht selber machen, sondern man will es lieber machen lassen. Was haben diese Leute machen lassen?

BEISPIEL: Hat Fritz das Mittagessen selber gekocht?
Nein, er hat es kochen lassen.

1. Hat Herr von Hippel sein Haus selber gebaut?
2. Hat Frau Beck ihren Wagen selber repariert?
3. Hat Oma ihren Koffer selbst getragen?
4. Hat deine Freundin sich die Haare selber geschnitten?
5. Hat Frau Schwarzer den Brief selbst abgeschickt (*sent off*)?
6. Hat Günter das Referat selbst geschrieben?
7. Hat Robert seine Schuhe selber geputzt (*cleaned*)?

Info-Austausch

Partner B's information is found in Appendix 1.

27 Du kannst das selber machen. Arbeiten Sie mit einem Partner/einer Partnerin zusammen. Sagen Sie, er/sie soll etwas machen lassen, oder sagen Sie, er/sie soll es selber tun.

BEISPIEL: A: Mein Handy ist kaputt.
B: Du sollst es reparieren lassen. Ich möchte Kaffee trinken.
A: Du kannst ihn selber kochen.

Partner A:

Mein Handy ist kaputt.	
	selber kochen
Meine Haare sind jetzt zu lang.	
	das Mittagessen selber machen
Ich will mein Referat nicht selber tippen (*type*).	
	selber einkaufen gehen
Mein Auto ist schmutzig.	

NOTES ON USAGE

German equivalents of *to leave*

The equivalent you choose for the English verb *to leave* depends on whether it means *to go away* (intransitive) or *to leave something behind* (transitive), and also on what or whom you are leaving.

- Intransitive: **gehen**, **weggehen**; **abfahren** (= *leave by vehicle*)

Ich muss jetzt **gehen**.	*I have to leave now.*
Er **ging weg**, ohne etwas zu sagen.	*He left without saying anything.*
Um elf **fuhr** sie mit dem Zug **ab**.	*She left by train at eleven.*

- Transitive: **lassen** (= *leave something somewhere*); **verlassen** (= *leave a person or place*)

Ich habe meine Tasche zu Hause **gelassen.**	*I left my bag at home.*
Viele wollten ihre Heimat nicht **verlassen.**	*Many did not want to leave their homeland.*

28 Übung: Wie sagt man das auf Deutsch?

1. Jörg left the house at seven.
2. Jörg left at seven.
3. Jörg's train left at seven.
4. Jörg left his book in the Mensa.
5. Jörg, please leave the room.
6. Jörg left his car in front of the hotel.
7. Jörg wants to leave school.
8. Jörg left his dog outside.

Leider mussten wir den Hund draußen lassen.

4. Time phrases with *Mal*

The English word *time* has two German equivalents, **die Zeit** and **das Mal**.

- **Zeit** denotes time in general.

Ich brauche mehr **Zeit**.	*I need more time.*

- **Mal** denotes an occurrence.

Das erste **Mal** habe ich das Buch nicht verstanden.	*I didn't understand the book the first time.*
Wie viele **Male** hast du es gelesen?	*How many times did you read it?*

Wie viele Male = Wie oft

Learn the following idioms with **Mal**.

das erste Mal	*the first time*	**diesmal**	*this time*
zum ersten Mal	*for the first time*	**jedes Mal**	*every time*
zum zweiten Mal	*for the second time*	**das nächste Mal**	(*the*) *next time*
zum letzten Mal	*for the last time*		

NOTE ON USAGE

Saying how often things happen is a communicative goal.

The suffix *-mal*

Note that **-mal** added as a suffix to a cardinal number forms an adverb indicating repetition.

einmal	*once*
zweimal	*twice*
zwanzigmal	*twenty times*
hundertmal	*a hundred times*
zigmal	*umpteen times*

Workbook Kap. 12, N.

29 Gruppenarbeit: Wie oft haben Sie das schon gemacht? Fragen Sie einander, wie oft Sie etwas schon gemacht haben.

BEISPIEL: A: Wie oft hast du schon dein Lieblingsbuch gelesen?
B: Ich habe es schon viermal gelesen.

1. Wie oft hast du schon deinen Wagen reparieren lassen?
2. Wie oft bist du dieses Jahr schon nach Hause gefahren?
3. Wie oft bist du dieses Semester schon ins Kino gegangen?
4. Wie oft hast du dieses Semester schon Referate schreiben müssen?
5. Wie oft hast du dieses Semester schon deinen besten Freund angerufen?
6. Wie oft bist du schon am Wochenende weggefahren?

30 Übung: Wie sagt man das auf Deutsch?

1. I need a little more time.
   Unfortunately, we don't have any more time.
2. I'm trying it for the first time.
   The next time it's easier.
3. I need time and money.
   You say that every time.

31 Übung: Was haben Sie an der Uni zum ersten Mal erlebt? Wenn man studiert, erlebt (*experiences*) und lernt man viel Neues. Sagen Sie, was Sie hier an der Uni oder am College zum ersten Mal getan, erlebt, gelernt, gesehen, angefangen oder versucht haben.

BEISPIEL: A: Ich habe zum ersten Mal etwas über Astronomie gelernt.
B: Ich habe zum ersten Mal über Politik diskutiert.

5. Parts of the day

German divides up the day in the following way:

PROVERB: **Morgenstund' hat Gold im Mund.** (*The early bird catches the worm.*)

gestern	früh *oder* Morgen Nachmittag Abend	*yesterday*	*morning* *afternoon* *evening*
heute	früh *oder* Morgen Nachmittag Abend	*this*	*morning* *afternoon* *evening*
morgen	früh Nachmittag Abend	*tomorrow*	*morning* *afternoon* *evening*

In addition, recall:

SAM Workbook

Workbook Kap. 12, O.

32 Gruppenarbeit: Gestern, heute und morgen. Fragen Sie einander, wann Sie verschiedene Dinge zum letzten Mal gemacht haben.

BEISPIEL: A: Wann hast du zum letzten Mal Kaffee getrunken?
B: Gestern Abend. (*oder*) Heute früh.

1. Wann hast du zum letzten Mal mit deinem besten Freund geredet?
2. Wann bist du zum letzten Mal einkaufen gegangen?
3. Wann hast du zum letzten Mal Hausaufgaben gemacht?
4. Wann bist du zum letzten Mal ins Kino gegangen?
5. Wann hast du zum letzten Mal telefoniert?

Jetzt fragen Sie, wann Sie verschiedene Dinge das nächste Mal machen.

6. Wann besuchst du das nächste Mal deine Eltern?
7. Wann gehst du das nächste Mal ins Konzert?
8. Wann gehst du das nächste Mal ins Museum?
9. Wann fährst du das nächste Mal Rad?
10. Wann triffst du das nächste Mal deine Freunde?

LESESTÜCK

Lab Manual Kap. 12, Üb. zur Betonung.

Tipps zum Lesen und Lernen

Tipps zum Vokabellernen

***The prefix** irgend-* With question words like **wo**, **wie**, and **wann**, the prefix **irgend-** creates indefinite adverbs, as does the English word *some* in *somewhere, somehow, sometime,* etc.

Similarly: **irgendwer** (= **irgendjemand**), **irgendwas** (= **irgendetwas**), **irgendwohin**, **irgendwoher**.

irgendwo	*somewhere (or other)*
irgendwie	*somehow (or other)*
irgendwann	*sometime (or other)*

Hast du meine Zeitung **irgendwo** gesehen?	*Have you seen my newspaper anywhere?*
Kommen Sie **irgendwann** vorbei?	*Will you come by sometime?*
Meinen Schlüssel habe ich **irgendwie** verloren.	*Somehow or other I've lost my key.*

Im Lesetext für dieses Kapitel schreibt Anna Seghers:

Der Dom hat die Luftangriffe ... **irgendwie** überstanden.	*The cathedral survived the air raids somehow or other.*

Einstieg in den Text

Like the poems in **Lyrik zum Vorlesen**, the following reading, *Zwei Denkmäler* by Anna Seghers, was written not for students learning German, but for an audience of German speakers. Nonetheless, you have now learned enough German to read an authentic text with a little help from marginal glosses.

Zwei Denkmäler is an essay about a story that Seghers began but never finished and could not "get out of her head" (**Das geht mir heute nicht aus dem Kopf**). She focuses on two monuments (**Denkmäler**)—one of grand cultural significance, the other of individual suffering.

Now that you have learned how relative clauses work in German, you will notice how frequent they are in expository prose like *Zwei Denkmäler.* During your first reading of the text, be on the lookout for the eight relative clauses it contains. On a separate piece of paper, list each antecedent and relative clause. Here is the first one:

1. ... eine Erzählung, die der Krieg unterbrochen hat. (. . . *a story that the war interrupted.*)
2. ________
3. ________

etc.

Wortschatz 2

In-Text Audio CD

Verben

holen to fetch, get
vergleichen, verglich, hat verglichen to compare
wiedersehen (sieht wieder), sah wieder, hat wiedergesehen to see again, meet again

REMEMBER: **auf Wiedersehen** = *good-bye*. On the telephone one says **auf Wiederhören**.

Substantive

der **Stein, -e** stone
das **Schiff, -e** ship
die **Erde** earth
die **Erzählung, -en** story, narrative
die **Freude, -n** joy
die **Größe, -n** size; greatness
die **Milch** milk

Adjektive und Adverbien

einzig- single, only
fern distant, far away
grausam terrible, gruesome; cruel
jüdisch Jewish

Nützliche Ausdrücke

Das geht mir nicht aus dem Kopf. = **Das kann ich nicht vergessen.**
werden aus to become of
Was ist aus ihnen geworden? What has become of them?

Kurfürst Johann Friedrich von Sachsen (1503–1554), gründete die Universität Jena im Jahre 1548.

Zwei Denkmäler

Anna Seghers

Anna Seghers is the pseudonym of Netty Reiling, who was born in Mainz in 1900. She studied art history and sinology. Because of her membership in the Communist Party, she was forced to flee Germany in 1933. She sought asylum in France and Mexico. Much of her writing in exile reflects the turbulent existence of a refugee and committed antifascist. In 1947 she moved to the German Democratic Republic, where she died in 1983.

The opening sentence of Seghers's essay establishes the historical context of an exile from Hitler's Germany, writing during World War II about the horrors of World War I. The writer addresses loss on many levels: of human life during wartime, of a literary manuscript, and of the memory of one woman's sacrifice. She suggests, however, that in the story she wanted to write, Frau Eppstein's daughter would have preserved that memory.

In der Emigration° begann ich eine Erzählung, die der Krieg unterbrochen hat. Ihr Anfang ist mir noch in Erinnerung geblieben. Nicht Wort für Wort, aber dem Sinn nach°. Was mich damals erregt° hat, geht mir auch heute nicht aus dem Kopf. Ich erinnere mich an eine Erinnerung.

here: in exile

***dem ...** the sense of it / excited*

In meiner Heimat, in Mainz am Rhein, gab es zwei Denkmäler, die ich niemals° vergessen konnte, in Freude und Angst, auf Schiffen, in fernen Städten. Eins° ist der Dom. Wie ich als Schulkind zu meinem Erstaunen° sah, ist er auf Pfeilern° gebaut, die tief in die Erde hineingehen° – damals kam es mir vor°, beinahe° so hoch wie der Dom hochragt°. Ihre Risse sind auszementiert worden°, sagte man, in vergangener° Zeit, da, wo das Grundwasser Unheil stiftete°. Ich weiß nicht, ob das stimmt, was uns ein Lehrer erzählte: Die romanischen[1] und gotischen[2] Pfeiler seien haltbarer° als die jüngeren.

*= **nie***

one of them

astonishment / pillars

*go into / **kam ...** it seemed to me / = **fast** / looms up / **Risse ...** cracks have been patched / past / **Grundwasser ...** groundwater caused damage / **seien ...** were more durable*

Dieser Dom über der Rheinebene° wäre mir in all seiner Macht und Größe geblieben°, wenn ich ihn auch nie wieder gesehen hätte°. Aber ebensowenig° kann ich ein anderes Denkmal in meiner Heimatstadt vergessen. Es bestand nur aus° einem einzigen flachen Stein, den man in das Pflaster° einer Straße gesetzt hat. Hieß die Straße Bonifaziusstraße? Hieß sie Frauenlobstraße? Das weiß ich nicht mehr. Ich weiß nur, dass der Stein zum Gedächtnis° einer Frau eingefügt wurde°, die im Ersten Weltkrieg durch Bombensplitter umkam°, als sie Milch für ihr Kind holen wollte. Wenn ich mich recht erinnere, war sie die Frau des jüdischen Weinhändlers° Eppstein. Menschenfresserisch°, grausam war der Erste Weltkrieg, man begann aber erst an seinem Ende mit Luftangriffen° auf Städte und Menschen. Darum hat man zum Gedächtnis der Frau den Stein eingesetzt, flach wie das Pflaster, und ihren Namen eingraviert°.

*Rhine plain / **wäre geblieben** = would have remained / **wenn** ... even if I had never seen it again / no less / consisted of only / pavement / in memory of / had been set in / **durch** ... was killed by shrapnel / wine merchant / cannibalistic*

air raids

engraved

Der Dom hat die Luftangriffe des Zweiten Weltkriegs irgendwie überstanden°, wie auch° die Stadt zerstört worden ist°. Er ragt° über Fluss und Ebene. Ob der kleine flache Gedenkstein° noch da ist, das weiß ich nicht. Bei meinen Besuchen habe ich ihn nicht mehr gefunden.

survived

*= **obwohl** / **zerstört ...** was destroyed / looms / commemorative stone*

---

[1] **romanisch:** Romanesque style (mid-11th to mid-12th century), characterized by round arches and vaults.

[2] **gotisch:** Gothic style (mid-12th to mid-16th century), characterized by pointed arches and vaults.

Berlin um 1900

Reading an authentic German literary text is the cultural goal of this chapter.

In der Erzählung, die ich vor dem Zweiten Weltkrieg zu schreiben begann und im Krieg verlor, ist die Rede von° dem Kind, dem die Mutter Milch holen wollte, aber nicht heimbringen° konnte. Ich hatte die Absicht°, in dem Buch zu erzählen, was aus diesem Mädchen geworden ist.

ist ... *the story is about* / = ***nach Hause bringen*** / *intention*

NACH DEM LESEN

Lab Manual Kap. 12, Diktat.

A Antworten Sie auf Deutsch.

1. Was hat Anna Seghers' Erzählung unterbrochen?
2. Welche Stadt war Anna Seghers' Heimatstadt?
3. Was konnte sie nie vergessen?
4. Über welche Denkmäler schreibt sie?
5. Vergleichen Sie diese zwei Denkmäler.
6. An wen sollte der Stein erinnern?
7. Hat Anna Seghers den Stein wiedergefunden?
8. Wann begann sie die Erzählung zu schreiben?
9. Was wollte sie erzählen?

B Gruppendiskussion: Wo haben Sie als Kind gelebt? Leben Sie noch in der Stadt, wo Sie geboren sind, oder sind Sie umgezogen? Gefällt es Ihnen besser, wo Sie jetzt wohnen? Besuchen Sie manchmal Ihren Geburtsort? Was wollen Sie dort sehen? Was hat sich dort geändert?

Johann Gutenberg (born and died in Mainz, c. 1400–1468), was chosen Man of the Millennium by an international panel of scholars because of the vast importance of his invention of movable type.

Creative writing in German

The second writing assignment below asks you to expand on Anna Seghers' essay by inventing either the beginning or the end of the story about Frau Eppstein and her daughter. This would be the story that Seghers planned but never wrote. You are thus being asked to invent characters only suggested by Seghers. Keep the following things in mind while writing:

- If you write the beginning of the story, you will focus on the mother. Imagine her distress in this extreme situation.
- If you write the end of the story, imagine what happened to the daughter in subsequent years and how the experience of losing her mother at an early age affected her life.
- Narrate in the simple past tense.
- Consult a good English-German dictionary for vocabulary you need.
- Confine yourself to familiar grammatical structures.
- Try using some new structures you learned in this chapter, such as relative clauses and adjectives in the comparative or superlative degree.

Talking about memories is a communicative goal.

Schreiben wir mal.

1. Schreiben Sie über eine wichtige Erinnerung aus Ihrer Kindheit. Gibt es z. B. einen besonderen Menschen, an den Sie sich erinnern? Oder einen Lieblingsort oder ein Gebäude, wo Sie gewohnt haben oder Zeit verbracht haben? Warum geht es Ihnen nicht aus dem Kopf?
2. Anna Seghers hat eine Erzählung über das Mädchen begonnen, dessen Mutter im Ersten Weltkrieg Milch holen wollte, aber sie hat diese Erzählung nie zu Ende geschrieben. Wie würden Sie diese Geschichte erzählen? Schreiben Sie entweder den Anfang oder das Ende der Erzählung aus der Perspektive der Tochter.
   a. Wie würde die Geschichte anfangen?
   b. Schreiben Sie das Ende der Geschichte. Was ist aus dem Mädchen geworden?

C Wie sagt man das auf Deutsch?

1. Can you repair your car yourself?
2. No, I never learned that. I always have it repaired.
3. A German I know is the best mechanic in the city.

4. Are German trains really more punctual than American trains?
5. Yes, but French trains are the fastest.

6. Have you heard the newest gossip?
7. Not yet. What's going on?
8. Rita went away with the richest guy in the office.
9. She left poor Rudi, who was always short of cash.

VIDEO

Denkmäler

Jedes Volk baut sich Denkmäler, die an wichtige historische Personen und Ereignisse (*events*) in seiner Geschichte erinnern. Unten sehen Sie Fotos von Denkmälern aus den deutschsprachigen Ländern. Sind Ihnen einige dieser Menschen und Ereignisse schon bekannt? Kennen Sie Denkmäler in Ihrer Heimat?

Kaiser Wilhelm-Gedächtniskirche (Berlin)

1891–1895 als Kaiser Wilhelm-Kirche gebaut. Im November 1943 durch Bomben zerstört. Zur Erinnerung an den Krieg als Ruine stehen gelassen.

Wilhelm Tell-Denkmal (Altdorf, Kanton Uri)

Der legendäre Schweizer Patriot aus dem 13. Jahrhundert.

Stolpersteine (Köln)

Die Kölner Stolpersteine (*"stumbling blocks"*) erinnern an Kölner Juden (*Jews*), die im Holocaust gestorben sind.

Martin Luther-Denkmal (Wittenberg)

An der Universität in Wittenberg war Luther (1483–1546) Student und Professor.

KAPITEL

13

Blick auf Zürich und den Zürcher See

Die Schweiz

Kommunikation

- Talking about the future
- Introducing yourself and others
- Telling people you'd like them to do something

Kultur

- The culture and history of Switzerland

In diesem Kapitel

- **Lyrik zum Vorlesen**
  Eugen Gomringer, "nachwort"
- **Grammatik**
  1. Verbs with prepositional complements
  2. Pronouns as objects of prepositions: **da-** and **wo-** compounds
  3. Future tense
  4. Directional prefixes: **hin-** and **her-**
  5. Wanting *X* to do *Y*
- **Lesestück**
  Zwei Schweizer stellen ihre Heimat vor
- **Almanach**
  Profile of Switzerland

DIALOGE

Lab Manual Kap. 13, Dialoge, Fragen, Hören Sie gut zu!

Ski is pronounced (and alternatively spelled) **Schi**. Note the colloquial contraction **vorm = vor dem**.

Skifahren in der Schweiz

Kurz vor dem Semesterende sprechen zwei Studentinnen über ihre Ferienpläne.

BRIGITTE: Ich freue mich sehr auf die Semesterferien!
JOHANNA: Hast du vor wieder Ski zu fahren?
BRIGITTE: Ja, ich werde zwei Wochen in der Schweiz verbringen. Morgen früh flieg' ich nach Zürich.
JOHANNA: Tatsächlich! Da bin ich ja ganz baff! Früher hast du doch immer Angst vorm Fliegen gehabt!
BRIGITTE: Stimmt, aber ich habe mich einfach daran gewöhnt.

Probleme in der WG: Im Wohnzimmer ist es unordentlich

Nina liest in ihrem Zimmer. Ute und Lutz klopfen an die Tür.

NINA: Herein! (*Sie gehen hinein.*) Morgen! Was gibt's Neues?
LUTZ: Hallo, Nina. Können wir schnell etwas mit dir besprechen?
NINA: Na klar. Was ist denn?
UTE: Hör mal zu: Wirst du deine Sachen im Wohnzimmer endlich aufräumen?
NINA: Oh, tut mir Leid! Das mach' ich gleich. Seid mir nicht böse – ich musste mich heute Morgen wahnsinnig beeilen.
LUTZ: Ja, das sagst du immer. Jetzt haben wir aber die Nase voll.
UTE: In der WG müssen doch alle mitmachen.
NINA: Ihr habt Recht. Von jetzt an werde ich mich mehr darum kümmern.

Am Informationsschalter in Basel

In Europe, signs with a lower-case **i** lead to information offices or booths. Here one finds maps, brochures, hotel and theater bookings, and other useful tips.

TOURIST: Entschuldigung. Darf ich Sie um Auskunft bitten?
BEAMTIN: Gerne. Wie kann ich Ihnen helfen?
TOURIST: Ich bin nur einen Tag in Basel und kenne mich hier nicht aus. Was können Sie mir empfehlen?
BEAMTIN: Es kommt darauf an, was Sie sehen wollen. Das Historische Museum lohnt sich besonders. Wenn Sie sich für das Mittelalter interessieren, dürfen Sie die neue Ausstellung nicht verpassen.
TOURIST: Das interessiert mich aber sehr. Wie komme ich denn dahin?
BEAMTIN: Gehen Sie hier hinaus und direkt vor dem Bahnhof ist die Haltestelle. Dort müssen Sie in die Straßenbahnlinie 2 einsteigen. Am Museum steigen Sie dann aus.
TOURIST: Darf ich auch einen Stadtplan mitnehmen?
BEAMTIN: Selbstverständlich.
TOURIST: Vielen Dank für Ihre Hilfe.
BEAMTIN: Bitte sehr.

NOTE ON USAGE

Nicht dürfen

The equivalent for English *must not* is **nicht dürfen**.

Die Ausstellung dürfen Sie nicht verpassen.	*You mustn't (really shouldn't) miss the exhibit.*

Wortschatz 1

Verben

Angst haben vor (+ *dat.*) to be afraid of
auf·räumen to tidy up, straighten up
sich aus·kennen to know one's way around
Ich kenne mich hier nicht aus. I don't know my way around here.
bitten, bat, hat gebeten um to ask for, request
sich freuen auf (+ *acc.*) to look forward to
sich gewöhnen an (+ *acc.*) to get used to
hinein·gehen to go in
interessieren to interest
sich interessieren für to be interested in
klopfen (an + *acc.*) to knock (on)
sich kümmern um to look after, take care of; to deal with
sich lohnen to be worthwhile, worth the trouble
mit·nehmen (nimmt mit), nahm mit, hat mitgenommen to take along
Ski fahren (fährt Ski), fuhr Ski, ist Ski gefahren to ski
verpassen to miss (*an event, opportunity, train, etc.*)
sich vor·bereiten auf (+ *acc.*) to prepare for
vor·haben to plan, have in mind
warten auf (+ *acc.*) to wait for
zu·hören (+ *dat.*) to listen (to)
Hören Sie gut zu! Listen carefully.
Hör mir zu. Listen to me.

Substantive

der **Schalter, -** counter, window
das **Mittelalter** the Middle Ages
das **Wohnzimmer, -** living room
die **Auskunft** information
die **Haltestelle, -n** (streetcar or bus) stop
die **Hilfe** help
die **Linie, -n** (streetcar or bus) line
die **Straßenbahn, -en** streetcar

Adjektive und Adverbien

böse (+ *dat.*) angry, mad (at); bad, evil
Sei mir nicht böse. Don't be mad at me.
direkt direct(ly)
unordentlich disorderly, messy

Nützliche Ausdrücke

Herein! Come in! (*See pages 362–363.*)
Was gibt's Neues? What's new?
von jetzt an from now on
Es kommt darauf an. It depends.
Es kommt darauf an, was Sie sehen wollen. It depends on what you want to see.
Wie komme ich dahin? How do I get there?

Gegensätze

böse ≠ gut evil ≠ good
sich interessieren ≠ sich langweilen to be interested ≠ to be bored
unordentlich ≠ ordentlich disorderly, messy ≠ orderly, neat

Mit anderen Worten

baff sein (*colloq.*) = **sehr staunen, sprachlos sein**
unordentlich = **schlampig** (*colloq.*)

Das Historische Museum in Basel

Straßenbahnhaltestelle in Zürich

Variationen

A Persönliche Fragen

1. Brigitte freut sich auf die Semesterferien. Freuen Sie sich auf etwas?
2. Sie hat vor Ski zu fahren. Was haben Sie am Wochenende vor?
3. Fahren Sie in den Semesterferien irgendwohin?
4. Bei Nina sieht's schlampig aus. Wie sieht es bei Ihnen im Zimmer aus?
5. Die anderen in der WG sind Nina böse, weil sie nicht aufräumt. Wann werden Sie böse?
6. Der Tourist kennt sich in Basel nicht aus, aber zu Hause kennt er sich natürlich sehr gut aus. In welcher Stadt kennen Sie sich besonders gut aus?
7. Der Tourist interessiert sich für das Mittelalter. Wann war denn das Mittelalter?
8. Der Tourist will die Ausstellung nicht verpassen. Haben Sie je etwas Gutes verpasst? Was denn?
9. Was machen Sie, wenn Sie sich in einer fremden Stadt nicht auskennen?

B Übung: Wie sagt man das mit anderen Worten?

1. Wenn man sehr wenig Geld hat, ist man ________.
2. Wenn man zu viel von etwas gehabt hat, sagt man: „Ich habe ________ voll."
3. Jemand, der besonders müde ist, nennt man ________.
4. Wenn Sie sich bei einer Vorlesung sehr gelangweilt haben, dann haben Sie sie ________ gefunden.
5. Etwas, was sehr groß ist, kann man auch ________ nennen.
6. Ein anderes Wort für *dumm* ist ________.

C Übung: Es kommt darauf an. (*It depends.*) Ihr Professor spielt die Rolle eines Bekannten, dem Sie verschiedene Dinge empfehlen sollen. Sie sagen ihm jedes Mal, es kommt darauf an.

BEISPIEL: Können Sie mir etwas *in der Stadt* empfehlen?
Es kommt darauf an, *was Sie sehen wollen.*

1. etwas auf der Speisekarte
2. ein gutes Buch
3. eine neue CD
4. ein Reiseziel
5. ein ruhiges Hotel
6. einen guten Wein
7. einen guten Computer
8. einen neuen Beruf

D Rollenspiel: Am Informationsschalter. (*Gruppen von 3 Personen*) Zwei von Ihnen sind Touristen und kennen sich in dieser Stadt nicht aus. Der/Die Dritte arbeitet am Infoschalter und gibt Auskunft. Vergessen Sie nicht „Sie" zueinander zu sagen. Fangen Sie so an:

TOURISTEN: Entschuldigung, dürfen wir Sie um Auskunft bitten?
BEAMTER/BEAMTIN: Gerne. Wie kann ich Ihnen helfen?

LYRIK ZUM VORLESEN

In-Text Audio CD

Eugen Gomringer was born to Swiss parents in Bolivia. True to his typically polyglot Swiss background, he has written poems in German, Swiss-German dialect, French, English, and Spanish. Gomringer is a leading exponent of concrete poetry (**konkrete Poesie**), which rejects metaphor, radically simplifies syntax, and considers the printed page a visual as much as a linguistic experience. The following poem consists entirely of nouns followed by relative clauses in strict parallelism. Readers must work out the interrelationships for themselves. Pay particular attention to the verb tenses as you read this poem aloud.

Eugen Gomringer

nachwort°

das dorf°, das ich nachts hörte
der wald, in dem ich schlief

das land, das ich überflog°
die stadt, in der ich wohnte

das haus, das den freunden gehörte
die frau, die ich kannte

das bild, das mich wach hielt°
der klang°, der mir gefiel

das buch, in dem ich las
der stein, den ich fand

der mann, den ich verstand
das kind, das ich lehrte°

der baum, den ich blühen° sah
das tier, das ich fürchtete

die sprache, die ich spreche
die schrift°, die ich schreibe

Eugen Gomringer (geboren 1925)

afterword
village
flew across
kept awake
sound
taught
blooming
writing

GRAMMATIK

1. Verbs with prepositional complements

Many verbs expand or change their meaning by the addition of a prepositional phrase. Such a phrase is called a PREPOSITIONAL COMPLEMENT.

Ich spreche.	*I'm speaking.*
Ich spreche **mit ihm**.	*I'm speaking **with him**.*
Ich spreche **gegen ihn**.	*I'm speaking **against him**.*

In the examples above, English and German happen to use parallel prepositions. In many cases, however, they do not. For example:

Er wartet **auf** seinen Bruder.	He's waiting ***for*** *his brother.*
Sie bittet **um** Geld.	*She's asking* ***for*** *money.*

For this reason, you must learn the verb and the preposition used with it *together*. For instance, you should learn **bitten um**, *to ask* ***for***. Here is a list of the verbs with prepositional complements that have been introduced so far:

- **Angst haben vor** (+ *dat.*) *to be afraid of*

  Hast du Angst vorm Fliegen? — *Are you afraid of flying?*

- **bitten um** *to ask for, request*

  Sie bat mich um Geld. — *She asked me for money.*

- **erinnern an** (+ *acc.*) *to remind of*

  Das erinnert mich an etwas Wichtiges. — *That reminds me of something important.*

- **sich erinnern an** (+ *acc.*) *to remember*

  Sie hat sich an meinen Geburtstag erinnert. — *She remembered my birthday.*

- **sich freuen auf** (+ *acc.*) *to look forward to*

  Ich freue mich auf die Ferien! — *I'm looking forward to the vacation!*

- **sich gewöhnen an** (+ *acc.*) *to get used to*

  Sie konnte sich nicht an das kalte Wetter gewöhnen. — *She couldn't get used to the cold weather.*

- **sich interessieren für** *to be interested in*

  Interessieren Sie sich für moderne Kunst? — *Are you interested in modern art?*

- **sich kümmern um** *to look after, take care of; to deal with*

  Ich werde mich mehr um die Wohnung kümmern. — *I'll take more care of the apartment.*

- **sprechen (schreiben, lesen, lachen usw.) über** (+ *acc.*) *to talk (write, read, laugh, etc.) about*

  Er hat über seine Heimat gesprochen. *He talked about his home.*

- **sich verloben mit** *to get engaged to*

  Rita hat sich mit Rudi verlobt. *Rita got engaged to Rudi.*

Notice: Perfect tense of **sich vorbereiten** is **hat sich vorbereitet** (no **-ge-**).

- **sich vor·bereiten auf** (+ *acc.*) *to prepare for*

  Wir haben uns auf seinen Besuch gut vorbereitet. *We prepared well for his visit.*

- **warten auf** (+ *acc.*) *to wait for*

  Auf wen warten Sie denn? *Whom are you waiting for?*

Notes on verbs with prepositional complements

1. The prepositional phrase tends to come at the end of the sentence or clause.

   Sie **schrieb** mir letzte Woche **über ihre neue Stelle**. *She wrote me about her new job last week.*

2. When a two-way preposition is used with a verb, you must also learn the case it takes (dative or accusative). Don't just learn **warten auf** = *to wait for*, but rather **warten auf** + *accusative* = *to wait for*.

3. The two-way prepositions **auf** and **über** almost always take the accusative case when used in a nonspatial sense.

Spatial	**Nonspatial**
Er wartet auf **der** Straße. *He's waiting on the street.*	Er wartet auf **die** Lehrerin. *He's waiting for the teacher.*
Das Bild hängt über **meiner** Tür. *The picture hangs above my door.*	Ich sprach über **meine** Heimat. *I talked about my homeland.*

Erstbesteigung (*first ascent*) des Matterhorns (4.478 m) im Jahre 1865

4. Some verbs have both a direct object *and* a prepositional complement.

d.o. *prep. compl.*	
Darf ich **Sie um Auskunft** bitten?	*May I ask you for information?*

5. Be careful not to confuse prepositional complements (**erinnern *an***) and separable prefixes (***an*kommen**).

Prepositional complement	**Separable prefix**
Er erinnert mich **an meinen Bruder.**	Der Zug kommt um 9 Uhr **an.**

FRAGEWÖRTER

To ask a question using a verb with a prepositional complement, German forms a question word by attaching the prefix **wo-** to the preposition: **wo- + vor = wovor**. (If the preposition begins with a vowel, the prefix is **wor-**: **wor- + auf = worauf**.)

Wovor hast du Angst?	***What*** *are you afraid* ***of****?*
Worauf wartest du denn?	***What*** *are you waiting* ***for****?*
Wofür interessieren Sie sich?	***What*** *are you interested* ***in****?*

SAM **Lab Manual** Kap. 13, Var. zu Üb. 1–4, 7.

SAM **Workbook** Kap. 13, A, B.

1 Kettenreaktion: Wovor hast *du* denn Angst? Es gibt viele Sachen, vor denen man manchmal Angst haben kann. Sagen Sie, wovor Sie Angst haben, und fragen Sie dann weiter. Die Liste gibt Ihnen einige Beispiele, aber Sie können auch frei antworten.

BEISPIEL: A: Ich habe Angst vor großen Hunden. Wovor hast *du* denn Angst?
B: Ich habe Angst vor ...

große Hunde	komplizierte Technik
tiefes Wasser	Klausuren
ein Besuch beim Zahnarzt	das Leben in der Großstadt
das Fliegen	eine Umweltkatastrophe

2 Übung: Darf ich Sie um etwas bitten? Sie brauchen alle etwas. Bitten Sie die Professorin darum.

BEISPIEL: Darf ich Sie um Hilfe bitten?
Natürlich. Ich helfe Ihnen gerne.

3 Kettenreaktion: Worauf wartest *du* denn? Sie stehen an einer Straßenecke und warten auf etwas. Sagen Sie, worauf Sie warten, und dann fragen Sie weiter.

BEISPIEL: A: Ich warte auf die Staßenbahn, Linie 2. Worauf wartest *du* denn?
B: Ich warte auf ________.

4 Kettenreaktion: Worauf freust *du* dich? Sagen Sie, worauf Sie sich besonders freuen, und dann fragen Sie weiter.

BEISPIEL: A: Ich freue mich auf die Semesterferien. Worauf freust *du* dich?
B: Ich freue mich auf ________.

Der Rohnegletscher

5 Kettenreaktion: Wofür interessierst *du* dich? Nicht alle interessieren sich für die gleichen Dinge. Sagen Sie, wofür Sie sich besonders interessieren, und dann fragen Sie weiter.

BEISPIEL: A: Ich interessiere mich für das Mittelalter. Wofür interessierst *du* dich?
B: Ich interessiere mich für ______.

6 Gruppenarbeit: Woran konnten Sie sich nicht gewöhnen? Wenn man anfängt zu studieren, ist es manchmal schwer sich an das Neue zu gewöhnen. Sagen Sie, woran Sie sich am Anfang nicht so leicht gewöhnen konnten.

BEISPIEL: A: Woran konnten Sie sich nicht gewöhnen?
B: Ich konnte mich nicht an das Klima hier gewöhnen.

7 Partnerarbeit: Worauf wartest du denn? Stellen Sie einander Fragen mit diesen Verben.

BEISPIEL: A: Worauf wartest du denn?
B: Ich warte auf die Straßenbahn.

1. sich freuen auf
2. sich interessieren für
3. sich ärgern über
4. sich kümmern um
5. sich erinnern an
6. warten auf
7. Angst haben vor
8. sich vorbereiten (müssen) auf

2. Pronouns as objects of prepositions: *da*-compounds and *wo*-compounds

Da-compounds

When noun objects of prepositions are replaced by pronouns (e.g., **für meinen Freund → für ihn**), German distinguishes between people (*for me* = **für mich**) and things (*for it* = **dafür**).

- Nouns referring to people are replaced by personal pronouns, as in English.

A: Steht Christof hinter Gabriele?	*Is Christof standing behind Gabriele?*
B: Ja, er steht **hinter ihr**.	*Yes, he's standing* ***behind her****.*
A: Wartet ihr auf Manfred?	*Are you waiting for Manfred?*
B: Ja, wir warten **auf ihn**.	*Yes, we're waiting* ***for him****.*

Da-compounds simplify things; they do not show case, number, or gender of the nouns they replace.

- Nouns referring to things are replaced by a so-called **da**-compound: the prefix **da-** is attached to the preposition (**da- + mit = damit**). If the preposition begins with a vowel, the prefix is **dar-** (**dar- + auf = darauf**).

A: Steht dein Auto vor oder hinter dem Haus?	*Is your car in front of the house or behind it?*
B: Es steht **dahinter**.	*It's* ***behind it****.*
A: Wie lange warten Sie schon auf den Zug?	*How long have you been waiting for the train?*
B: Ich warte schon 10 Minuten **darauf**.	*I've been waiting* ***for it*** *for 10 minutes.*

Cellular phone = **das Handy**

Damit haben Sie
das ganze Büro
in der Hand

Lab Manual Kap. 13, Üb. 8, 9, and Var. zu Üb. 11.

Workbook Kap. 13, C–G.

8 Übung. Antworten Sie wie im Beispielsatz.

BEISPIEL: A: Stand er neben dem Fenster?
B: Ja, er stand daneben.

1. Interessieren Sie sich für Fremdsprachen?
2. Hast du nach dem Konzert gegessen?
3. Fangt ihr mit der Arbeit an?
4. Wartet ihr schon lange auf die Straßenbahn?

5. Hat sie sich an das Wetter gewöhnt?
6. Hat sie wieder um Geld gebeten?
7. Bereitest du dich auf die Deutschstunde vor?
8. Liegt meine Zeitung unter deinem Rucksack?
9. Erinnerst du dich an die Ferien?
10. Haben Sie vor der Bibliothek gewartet?

9 Partnerarbeit. In diesen Sätzen kommt es darauf an, ob das Objekt eine Person ist. Wenn nicht, dann müssen Sie mit **da-** antworten.

BEISPIELE: A: Steht Ingrid neben *Hans-Peter*?
B: Ja, sie steht *neben ihm*.

A: Steht Ingrid neben dem *Wagen*?
B: Ja, sie steht *daneben*.

1. Hast du dich an das Wetter gewöhnt?
2. Bist du mit Ursula gegangen?
3. Erinnerst du dich an deine Großeltern?
4. Können wir über dieses Problem sprechen?
5. Wohnst du bei Frau Lindner?
6. Demonstrierst du gegen diesen Politiker?
7. Demonstrierst du gegen seine Ideen?
8. Interessierst du dich für Sport?
9. Gehst du mit Karin essen?
10. Hat er dir für das Geschenk gedankt?

Wo-compounds

The distinction between people and things also applies to the so-called **wo**-compounds. These are used to ask questions about things (*with what?* = **womit**?).

Worauf warten Sie denn?	***What** are you waiting **for**?*
Womit spielt das Kind?	***What** is the child playing **with**?*

Use the preposition + **wen** or **wem** to ask questions about people (with whom? = **mit wem**?).

Auf wen warten Sie denn?	***Whom** are you waiting **for**?*
Mit wem spielen die Kinder?	***Whom** are the children playing **with**?*

10 Übung: Wie sagt man das auf Deutsch?

BEISPIEL: What are you reading about?
Worüber liest du denn?

1. What are you waiting for?
2. What are you interested in?
3. What is she asking for?
4. What can't you get used to?
5. What is he afraid of?

11 Übung. What questions elicit the following answers?

BEISPIELE: Sie wartet *auf einen Brief.*
Worauf wartet sie?
Sie wartet *auf Peter.*
Auf wen wartet sie?

1. Ich freue mich auf die Semesterferien.
2. Ich arbeite mit Professor Hauser.
3. Ich verlobe mich mit Rita (mit Rudi).
4. Ich kümmere mich um die Wohnung.
5. Ich interessiere mich für deutschen Wein.
6. Ich habe keine Angst vor Polizeibeamten.
7. Ich erinnere mich an meinen komischen Onkel.
8. Ich kann mich an dieses Wetter nicht gewöhnen.

3. Future tense (*das Futur*)

Formation: *werden* + infinitive

Talking about the future is a communicative goal.

The future is a compound tense. It uses an inflected form of the verb **werden** plus a dependent infinitive in final position.

ich	**werde schlafen**	*I shall sleep*	wir	**werden schlafen**	*we shall sleep*
du	**wirst schlafen**	*you will sleep*	ihr	**werdet schlafen**	*you will sleep*
sie	**wird schlafen**	*she will sleep*	sie, Sie	**werden schlafen**	*they, you will sleep*

NOTE: **Werden** as the auxiliary (helping) verb for future tense corresponds to *shall* or *will* in English. Do not confuse it with the modal verb **wollen**.

Ich **werde** schlafen. — *I **will** sleep.*
Ich **will** schlafen. — *I **want to** sleep.*

When a modal verb is in the future tense, the order of the modal and its dependent infinitive is the reverse of English.

Wir werden es **tun müssen**.

*We will **have to do** it.*

Use of future tense

As you already know, German usually uses *present tense* to express future meaning, especially when a time expression makes the future meaning clear.

Sie kommt morgen zurück. — *She's coming back tomorrow.*

Future tense makes the future meaning more explicit, especially in the absence of a time expression such as **morgen**.

Sie wird selbstverständlich **zurückkommen**. — *Of course she will come back.*

SAM **Lab Manual** Kap. 13, Var. zu Üb. 12.

SAM **Workbook** Kap. 13, H.

12 Partnerarbeit: Noch nicht, aber bald. Fragen Sie einander, ob etwas schon passiert ist. Antworten Sie, dass es bald passieren wird.

BEISPIEL: A: Hast du schon gegessen?
B: Noch nicht, aber ich werde bald essen.

1. Hat es schon geregnet?
2. Hast du schon aufgeräumt?
3. Bist du schon Ski gefahren?
4. Ist er schon aufgestanden?
5. Hast du dich schon vorbereitet?
6. Hast du das schon machen müssen?
7. Hat Susi schon angerufen?
8. Seid ihr schon essen gegangen?

13 Partnerarbeit: Wie wird es sein? Lesen Sie die Zukunft Ihres Partners oder Ihrer Partnerin aus der Hand. Diese Hand gibt Ihnen einige Ideen.

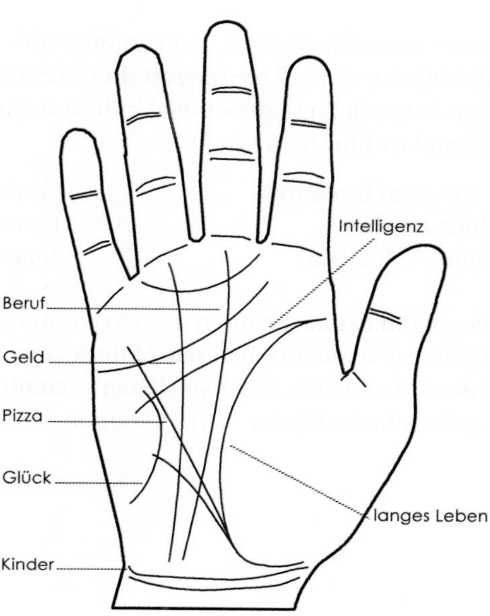

BEISPIEL: Du wirst ein langes Leben haben. Du wirst dich oft verloben und dreimal heiraten (*get married*). Du wirst ...

Schweizer Winterlandschaft: Dorf in Kanton Graubünden

4. Directional prefixes: *hin-* and *her-*

German has two separable prefixes that combine with verbs of motion to show whether that motion is *toward the speaker* (**her-**) or *away from the speaker* (**hin-**). You are already familiar with these directional indicators from the question words **woher**? (*from where?*) and **wohin**? (*to where?*).

Können wir nicht **hin**fahren?	*Can't we go **there**?*
Komm doch mal **her**.	*Come **here** a minute.*
Wie komme ich (da)**hin**?	*How do I get **there**?*

Look again at the stage direction in the second dialogue on p. 350: **Sie gehen hinein. ...** Notice that the preposition **in** becomes the prefix **ein**: **hineingehen** = *to go in.*

These directional indicators are often used in combination with other separable prefixes that indicate direction. Two sets of these are **auf und unter** (*up and down*) and **ein und aus** (*in and out*). The two elements combine to make one separable prefix that can be attached to any verb of motion.

hinausgehen

herauskommen

hereinkommen

hineingehen

heraufsteigen

hinuntergehen

In spoken German, both directional prefixes are often replaced by initial **r**: **Raus mit dir! Gehen wir rein/rauf/runter.** (Computersprache: **runterladen** = *to download.*)

The prefixes **hin-** and **her-** must be used when the sentence does not contain a directional phrase such as **in die Kirche** or **ins Haus**. It is *incorrect* to say ***Gehen wir ein.*** Correct is: **Gehen wir hinein.**[1]

Da ist eine gotische Kirche.	*There's a Gothic church.*
Gehen wir **hinein**.	*Let's go in.*
Draußen scheint die Sonne.	*The sun is shining outside.*
Gehen wir **hinaus**.	*Let's go out.*

NOTE: When someone knocks at the door, simply say:

Herein!	*Come in!*

[1] Even when a prepositional phrase is used, the directional prefixes are sometimes added.

Er ist **aus** dem Haus **heraus**gekommen.	*He came **out** of the house.*
Sie ging **in** die Kirche **hinein**.	*She went **into** the church.*

Workbook Kap. 13, I.

14 Gruppenarbeit: Gehen wir hinein! Complete these sentences by filling in the missing words.

You're standing *outside* the house.

1. Gehen wir ________. (*in*)
2. Karl, komm doch ________! (*out*)
3. Anna ist vor einer Minute ________. (*gone in*)
4. Bald kommen die Kinder aus dem Haus ________. (*out*)

You're standing *inside* the house.

5. Kommt Grete bald ________? (*in*)
6. Es ist so schön, ich möchte jetzt ________. (*go out*)
7. Wir sollten alle ________. (*go out*)
8. (*Es klingelt.*) ________! (*"Come in!"*)

You're standing *at the top* of the steps.

9. Warum kommt ihr nicht ________? (*up*)
10. Jörg ist gerade ________. (*gone down*)

You're standing *at the bottom* of the steps.

11. Susi, ich brauche Hilfe! Komm mal schnell ________! (*down here*)
12. Ich bin jetzt müde. Ich gehe ________ (*up*) und lege mich aufs Bett.

15 Partnerarbeit: Wo kommt sie her? Wo geht er hin? Beschreiben Sie, was diese Menschen machen.

5. Wanting *X* to do *Y*

Telling people you'd like them to do something is a communicative goal.

To express the idea that a person wants something to happen or be done, English uses a direct object and an infinitive phrase.

	d. o.	*infin. phrase*
She would like	***the music***	***to stop.***
I don't want	***him***	***to think that.***

German uses **wollen** or **möchten** followed by a **dass**-clause to express the same idea.

Sie möchte, **dass die Musik aufhört**.
Ich will nicht, **dass er das glaubt**.

Lab Manual Kap. 13, Var. zu Üb. 16, 17.

Workbook Kap. 13, J.

16 Übung: Ich möchte etwas ändern. Diese Situationen gefallen Ihnen nicht. Sagen Sie, wie Sie sie ändern möchten. Mehrere Antworten sind möglich.

BEISPIEL: Die Musik ist Ihnen zu laut.
Ich möchte, dass sie leiser wird.
… , dass sie aufhört.

1. Draußen regnet es.
2. Das Wetter ist Ihnen zu kalt.
3. Ihre Mitbewohner quatschen zu viel.
4. Ihr kleiner Bruder stört Sie bei der Arbeit.
5. Man verschwendet zu viel Glas und Papier.
6. Ihre Mitbewohner sind Ihnen zu schlampig.

17 Partnerarbeit: Ich will, dass du dich änderst. Sagen Sie Ihrem Partner, wie er sein Leben ändern soll. Dann antwortet er darauf. (Das ist nur ein Spiel. Nehmen Sie es also nicht zu ernst!)

BEISPIEL: A: Ich will, dass du früher aufstehst!
B: Warum denn? Ich schlafe doch gern. *Ich* möchte, dass *du* …

LESESTÜCK

Tipps zum Lesen und Lernen

Tipps zum Vokabelnlernen

***German equivalents for** only* When *only* is an adjective (meaning *sole* or *unique*), use **einzig-**. Otherwise use **nur**.

Er ist der **einzige** Mechaniker in der Gegend.	*He's the **only** mechanic in the area.*
Ich habe **nur** fünf Euro in der Tasche.	*I have **only** five euros in my pocket.*

Übung: Wie sagt man das auf Deutsch?

1. I have only one pencil.
2. My only pencil is yellow.
3. A cup of coffee costs only €1,00.
4. That was the only restaurant that was open.

Lab Manual Kap. 13, Üb. zur Betonung.

Leicht zu merken

die **Barriere, -n**	Barriere
(das) **Chinesisch**	
der **Dialekt, -e**	Dialekt
die **Globalisierung**	
konservativ	konservativ
kritisch	
neutral	neutral
offiziell	offiziell
romantisch	

Einstieg in den Text

In dem Lesestück auf Seite 368 sagt der Schweizer Dr. Anton Vischer, dass er sich manchmal über die Klischees ärgert, die er im Ausland über seine Heimat hört. Wenn man an die Schweiz denkt, denkt man z.B. automatisch an Schokolade, Schweizer Käse und gute Uhren. Diese Klischees sind Ihnen vielleicht auch bekannt. Aber interessanter ist sicher das Neue, was er über seine Heimat erzählt.

Nachdem Sie den Text gelesen haben, machen Sie sich eine Liste von wenigstens fünf neuen Dingen, die Sie über die Schweiz gelernt haben.

Konditorei (*pastry shop*) in Basel

Wortschatz 2

Verben

antworten auf (+ *acc.*) to answer (something); to respond to
sich ärgern (über + *acc.*) to get annoyed (at), be annoyed (about)
denken, dachte, hat gedacht to think
denken an (+ *acc.*) to think of
sich erholen (von) to recover (from); to get well; to have a rest
reagieren auf (+ *acc.*) to react to
sich etwas überlegen to consider, ponder, think something over
Das muss ich mir überlegen. I have to think it over.
vor·stellen to introduce; to present
Darf ich meine Tante vorstellen? May I introduce my aunt?
sich wundern (über + *acc.*) to be surprised, amazed (at)

Use **antworten** + *dat.* for answering people (**Antworten Sie mir.**). Use **antworten auf** for answering questions (**Antworten Sie auf meine Frage.**).

Substantive

der **Druck** pressure
der **Ort, -e** place; town
der **Rechtsanwalt, ¨-e** lawyer (*m.*)
der **Schweizer, -** Swiss (*m.*)
das **Gespräch, -e** conversation
das **Werk, -e** work (of art); musical composition
die **Rechtsanwältin, -nen** lawyer (*f.*)
die **Schweizerin, -nen** Swiss (*f.*)
die **Schwierigkeit, -en** difficulty
die **Vereinigung** unification

Adjektive und Adverbien

französisch French
froh happy
schweizerisch Swiss
stolz auf (+ *acc.*) proud of

Andere Vokabel

beides (*sing.*) both things

Nützliche Ausdrücke

eines Tages some day (*in the future*); one day (*in the past or future*)
in Zukunft in the future

Gegensatz

froh ≠ **traurig** happy ≠ sad

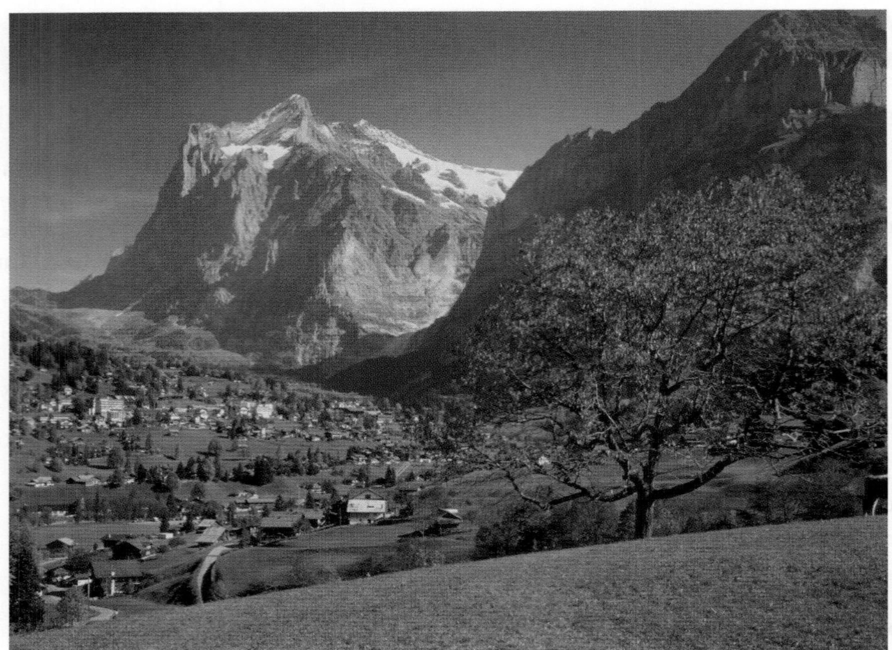

„In den Bergen kann man sich körperlich und seelisch erholen."

Zwei Schweizer stellen ihre Heimat vor

Dr. Anton Vischer (45 Jahre alt), Rechtsanwalt aus Basel[2]

„In meinem Beruf bin ich für die Investitionen° ausländischer Firmen verantwortlich und reise darum viel ins Ausland. Dort höre ich oft die alten Klischees über meine Heimat. Wenn man sagt, dass man aus der Schweiz kommt, denken viele Menschen automatisch an saubere Straßen, Schokolade, Uhren, Käse und an die Schweizer Garde[3] im Vatikan. Darüber ärgere ich mich immer ein bisschen. Ich möchte lieber, dass andere wissen, was für eine politische Ausnahme° die Schweiz in Europa bildet°. Ich werde versuchen Ihnen etwas davon zu beschreiben.

Schon seit dem 13. Jahrhundert hat die Schweiz eine demokratische Verfassung°.[4] Sie gehört also zu° den ältesten und stabilsten Demokratien der Welt. In beiden Weltkriegen ist die Schweiz neutral geblieben. Diese Tradition der stolzen schweizerischen Unabhängigkeit° beeinflusst° noch heute die politische Diskussion.

investments

Learning about the culture and history of Switzerland is the cultural goal of this chapter.

exception / constitutes

constitution

gehört ... = ist also eine von

independence / influences

[2] **Basel** (*French* Bâle): Swiss city on the Rhine.

[3] The Vatican's Swiss Guards, founded in 1505 by Pope Julius II, are the remnant of the Swiss mercenaries who served in foreign armies from the 15th century on. The Vatican guards are recruited from Switzerland's Catholic cantons.

[4] In 1991, Switzerland celebrated the 700th anniversary of the Oath of Rütli, the defense pact among the three original cantons against the Austrian Habsburgs. Wilhelm Tell is the legendary hero of this period of Swiss resistance to foreign power.

Wir sind erst seit 2002 in der UNO, aber weder in der NATO noch° in der EU.[5] Unter dem Druck der Globalisierung wird sich das vielleicht eines Tages ändern.

weder ... noch = *neither ... nor*

Einige werden unsere Gesellschaft wohl zu konservativ finden. Die Frauen, z. B., können erst seit 1971 wählen. Anderseits° hat eine Frau schon im Jahre 1867 an der Uni Zürich den Doktorgrad° bekommen – zum ersten Mal in Europa. Und man darf nicht vergessen, dass es in der Schweiz durchaus° auch einen Platz für kritische Stimmen gibt. Das zeigen die Werke unserer bekanntesten Schriftsteller wie Max Frisch und Friedrich Dürrenmatt.[6]

on the other hand
Ph.D.
definitely

Jemand fragte mich einmal, ob ich stolz bin, Schweizer zu sein. Darauf habe ich sofort mit Ja reagiert, aber in Zukunft werde ich mir die Antwort genauer überlegen. Ich werde einfach sagen, ich bin *froh* Schweizer zu sein, denn meine Heimat ist das schönste Land, das ich kenne. Da ich meine Freizeit immer auf Bergtouren verbringe, ist mein Leben mit der Alpenlandschaft eng verbunden°. Wenn ich von einer langen Bergwanderung wieder ins Tal herunterkomme, dann fühle ich mich körperlich und seelisch° erholt. Das klingt vielleicht romantisch, aber eigentlich bin ich ein ganz praktischer Mensch."

eng verbunden = *closely connected*
körperlich ... *physically and emotionally*

Nicole Wehrli (24 Jahre alt), Dolmetscherin° aus Biel

interpreter

„Ich bin in der zweisprachigen° Stadt Biel – auf Französisch Bienne – aufgewachsen, direkt an der Sprachgrenze zwischen der französischen und der deutschen Schweiz. Bei uns können Sie manchmal im Ort Gespräche hören, in denen die Menschen beides – Französisch *und* Deutsch – miteinander reden. In der Schule habe ich dann Latein°, Englisch und Italienisch gelernt. Sie werden sich also nicht wundern, dass ich mich für Fremdsprachen interessiere. Eines Tages möchte ich sogar Chinesisch lernen.

bilingual
Latin

Die Eidgenossenschaft[7] ist ein Unikum° in Europa, denn sie ist viersprachig. Die Sprachbarrieren waren lange Zeit ein großes Hindernis° für die politische Vereinigung der Kantone.[8] Heute gibt es keine großen Schwierigkeiten mehr, denn fast alle Schweizer können wenigstens zwei Landessprachen, und viele können auch

something unique
obstacle

Milch- und Käse- Spezialitäten
natürli
us de Region Zürcher Berggebiet

This ad contains Swiss dialect. Can you guess the standard German for **natürli** and **us de Region**?

[5] **Die UNO** = the *United Nations Organization;* **die NATO** = the *North Atlantic Treaty Organization*, a defensive alliance of the USA, Canada, Turkey, and certain western European nations which was formed after World War II; **die EU** = the **Europäische Union**.

[6] Max Frisch (1911–1991) and Friedrich Dürrenmatt (1921–1990) both wrote novels, essays, and plays.

[7] **Eidgenossenschaft** = Confederation. *Confoederatio Helvetica* is the official (Latin) name for modern Switzerland, hence CH on Swiss cars.

[8] Switzerland is composed of 23 confederated cantons, each with considerable autonomy.

Kinder mit Schlitten (*sleds*) in der Altstadt von Basel

Englisch. 64% der Bevölkerung° hat Deutsch als Muttersprache, 19% sprechen Französisch, 8% Italienisch und etwa° ein Prozent Rätoromanisch[9]. Unser „Schwyzerdütsch"[10] können die meisten Deutschen nicht verstehen. Da unsere Kinder Schriftdeutsch° erst in der Schule lernen müssen, ist es für sie oft so schwer wie eine Fremdsprache. Die geschriebene und offizielle Sprache in den Schulen bleibt Schriftdeutsch, aber nach dem Unterricht° reden Lehrer und Schüler Schwyzerdütsch miteinander."

population
approximately
standard written German
***nach ...** after class*

[9] **Rhaetoromansch**, or simply **Romansch**. It is a Romance language, a linguistic remnant of the original Roman occupation of the Alpine territories, spoken by about 40,000 rural Swiss in the canton of Grisons (**Graubünden**). Long under threat of extinction, it was declared one of the four national languages in 1938.

[10] **Schweizerdeutsch** = *Swiss-German dialect.* **Hochdeutsch** (*High German*) is the official, standardized language of German-speaking countries. It is the language of the media, the law, and education and is based on written German (**Schriftdeutsch**). Educated native speakers are bi-dialectal, knowing their local dialect and High German, which they may speak with a regional accent.

NACH DEM LESEN

Lab Manual Kap. 13, Diktat.

Workbook Kap. 13, K, L.

A Antworten Sie auf Deutsch.

1. Was ist Dr. Vischer von Beruf?
2. Welche Klischees hört er über die Schweiz, wenn er im Ausland ist?
3. Wie reagiert er darauf?
4. Seit wann hat die Schweiz eine demokratische Verfassung?
5. Was macht Herr Vischer in seiner Freizeit?
6. Warum ist die Stadt Biel, wo Nicole Wehrli aufgewachsen ist, besonders interessant?
7. Wie viele Schweizer sind deutschsprachig?
8. Warum haben manche Deutschen Schwierigkeiten die Schweizer zu verstehen?

B Schweizer Deutsch. In diesem Kapitel haben Sie über den Schweizer Dialekt – das Schwyzerdütsch – gelesen. Hier ist der Anfang eines Märchens auf Schwyzerdütsch mit einer Übersetzung ins Schriftdeutsche. Das Märchen kommt aus dem Kanton Aargau, westlich von Zürich. „Der Ma im Mond"[11] erzählt von einem Mann, der am Sonntag Holz (*wood*) stiehlt. Gott bestraft (*punishes*) ihn, indem er ihn zum Mann im Mond (*moon*) macht (*by making him . . .*).

---

[11] From: *Kinder- und Hausmärchen aus der Schweiz.* Collected and edited by Otto Sutermeister, with drawings by J. S. Weißbrod. Aarau: H. R. Sauerländer, 1873.

er Ma im Mond.

Der Ma im Mond

Weisch, wer dört oben im Mond lauft? Das isch emol en usöde Ma gsi, de het nid umegluegt ob's Sunntig oder Wärchtig gsi isch; goht einisch am ene heilige Sunntig is Holz und fangt a e Riswälle zsämestäle; und won er fertig gsi isch, und die Wälle bunde gha het, nimmt er si uf e Rügge und isch e heimlige Wäg us, won er gmeint het, das ihm kei Mönsch begägni. Aber wer em do begägnet, das isch der lieb Gott sälber gsi.

Lesen Sie jetzt eine Übersetzung ins Schriftdeutsche.

Der Mann im Mond

Weißt (du), wer dort oben° im Mond läuft? Das ist einmal ein böser Mann gewesen, der hat sich nicht umgesehen°, ob es Sonntag oder Werktag° gewesen ist; (er) geht einmal an einem heiligen° Sonntag ins Holz° und fängt an, ein Reisigbündel° zusammenzustehlen; und als er fertig gewesen ist und das Bündel gebunden hat°, nimmt er es auf den Rücken° und ist einen heimlichen Weg° hinausgegangen, wovon er gemeint hat, dass ihm kein Mensch begegnet°. Aber wer ihm dort begegnet, das ist der liebe Gott selber gewesen.

up there
sich ... *didn't pay attention / weekday*
holy / woods / bundle of sticks
tied up
back / secret path
begegnen *(+ dat.) = to encounter*

Vokabeln zum Thema

Wie stellt man sich vor?

Introducing yourself and others is a communicative goal.

Wie stellt man sich oder einen Bekannten auf Deutsch vor? Es kommt auf die Situation an. Unten sind vier verschiedene Situationen, aber zuerst ein paar Bemerkungen (*comments*).

Unter jungen Menschen ist es nicht so formell: Man sagt einfach seinen Namen und **Hallo** oder **Tag**, wie zum Beispiel in *Situation 1* (unten). Wie Sie schon wissen, sagen Studenten sofort **du** zueinander.

Wenn man ältere Menschen zum ersten Mal kennen lernt, ist es formeller (*Situationen 2* und *3*). Man sagt **angenehm** oder **freut mich** oder **sehr erfreut** (alle drei = *pleased to meet you*). Natürlich sagt man **Sie** statt **du**.

In allen Situationen ist es höflich einander die Hand zu geben (*shake hands*). Das machen die Europäer viel öfter als die Amerikaner.

1. Die Studentin Sonja stellt ihrem Freund Wolfgang ihre Freundin Margaret aus Amerika vor.

SONJA: Hallo Wolfgang! Darf ich vorstellen? Das ist meine Freundin Margaret aus Chicago.
WOLFGANG: (*gibt ihr die Hand*) Hallo Margaret!
MARGARET: Hallo Wolfgang.
WOLFGANG: Nett, dich kennen zu lernen.
MARGARET: Danke, gleichfalls.

2. Bernd, 20, stellt seiner Mutter einen Freund vor.

BERND: Mutti, ich möchte dir meinen Freund Theo vorstellen.
FRAU RINGSTEDT: Freut mich, Sie kennen zu lernen, Theo.
THEO: Angenehm, Frau Ringstedt. (*Sie geben sich die Hand.*)

3. Der amerikanische Austauschstudent Michael Hayward stellt sich einem Professor in der Sprechstunde (*office hour*) vor.

MICHAEL HAYWARD: Guten Tag, Professor Mohr. Darf ich mich vorstellen? Mein Name ist Hayward. (*Gibt ihm die Hand.*)
PROF. MOHR: Kommen Sie bitte herein, Herr Hayward. Nehmen Sie Platz.

4. Zwei Geschäftsleute treffen sich auf einer Konferenz.

FRAU MÜLLER: Guten Tag, mein Name ist Müller.
HERR BEHRENS: Freut mich, Frau Müller. Behrens.

C Rollenspiele. Spielen Sie diese Miniszenen mit anderen Studenten zusammen.

1. Darf ich mich vorstellen?
   Sie sind alle zusammen auf einer Studentenparty, wo Sie einander noch nicht kennen. Stehen Sie alle auf und stellen Sie sich einander vor.
2. Ich möchte euch meine Freunde vorstellen.
   Zwei Studenten spielen die Rollen der Eltern. Ein dritter Student bringt zwei Freunde mit nach Hause und stellt sie den Eltern vor.
3. Now pretend that you're all business people at a convention. Introduce yourselves to each other. (In this kind of situation, people usually give only their last names.)

Info-Austausch

Partner B's information can be found in Appendix 1.

D Hobbys. Arbeiten Sie mit einem Partner zusammen. Wofür interessieren sich diese Leute? Welche Hobbys haben sie?

BEISPIELE: A: Wofür interessierst sich Vladimir?
B: Er interessiert sich für Entomologie. Was sammelt er denn?
A: Er sammelt Schmetterlinge.
B: Nina spielt Trompete. Wofür interessiert sie sich?
A: Sie interessiert sich für Jazz.

Partner A:

Name	Interessiert sich für ...	Sammelt/Spielt/Macht ...
Vladimir		Schmetterlinge (*butterflies*)
Nina	Jazz	
Bobby		Schach (*chess*)
Steffi	Sport	
Lutz		Fotos
Claudio	klassische Musik	
Beate		Gymnastik
mein Partner		
ich		

SCHREIBTIPP

Formulating interview questions

- When you are interviewing someone to obtain information, it is important to formulate your questions in advance.
- In addition to the question words you have learned (e.g., **was, woher, warum, wie viele**), you can now ask a wider range of questions using **wo**-compounds (e.g., **Wofür interessierst du dich**?).

Schreiben wir mal. Arbeiten Sie mit einem Partner zusammen und interviewen Sie einander über Ihr Leben und Ihre Interessen. Schreiben Sie zuerst zehn Fragen, die Sie Ihrem Partner stellen wollen. Dann schreiben Sie einen Absatz (*paragraph*) über Ihren Partner.

E Wie sagt man das auf Deutsch?

1. Are you looking forward to the end of the semester?
2. Yes, I'm planning to go skiing in Switzerland.
3. That sounds good. Have a good trip.

4. What do you think of when people talk about Switzerland?
5. I remember my father's aunt who came from Switzerland.

6. Excuse me, do you know your way around in the library?
7. A bit. How can I help you?
8. I'm interested in books on Switzerland. Do you know where they are?
9. I'll have to think it over. Yes . . . Do you see the stairs over there? Go up there and you'll find them.

10. What are you so annoyed about?
11. My roommate asked me for money.
12. She wants me to give it to her soon.
13. Will you give it to her?
14. I don't think so.

ALMANACH

VIDEO

Zürich

Profile of Switzerland

Area: 41,288 square kilometers; 15,941 square miles (approximately the same area as the states of Massachusetts, Connecticut, and Rhode Island combined)

Population: 7,489,000; density 181 people per square kilometer (*470 per square mile)*

Currency: **Schweizer Franken** (*Swiss Franc*); 1 sfr = 100 **Rappen** or **Centimes**

Major Cities: Berne (**Bern**, capital, pop. 130,000), Zurich (**Zürich**, largest city, pop. 366,800), Basel, Geneva (**Genf**), Lausanne

Religions: 46% Roman Catholic, 40% Protestant, 14% other

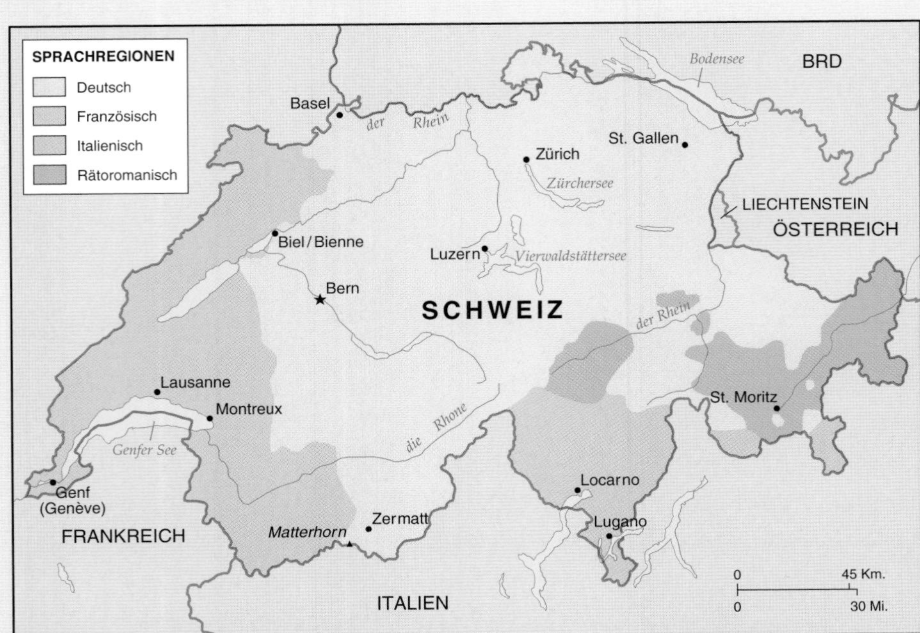

Switzerland has one of the highest per capita incomes in the world, as well as one of the highest standards of living. The literacy rate is 99.5%. The beauty of the Swiss Alps has made tourism Switzerland's main service industry; the alpine rivers provide inexpensive hydroelectric power.

Switzerland has not sent troops into foreign wars since 1515. It guards its neutrality even to the extent of staying out of the European Union. After having been a member of many UN agencies for years, Switzerland finally joined the UN in 2002. The second headquarters of the UN are in Geneva, which is also the seat of the International Red Cross and the World Council of Churches.

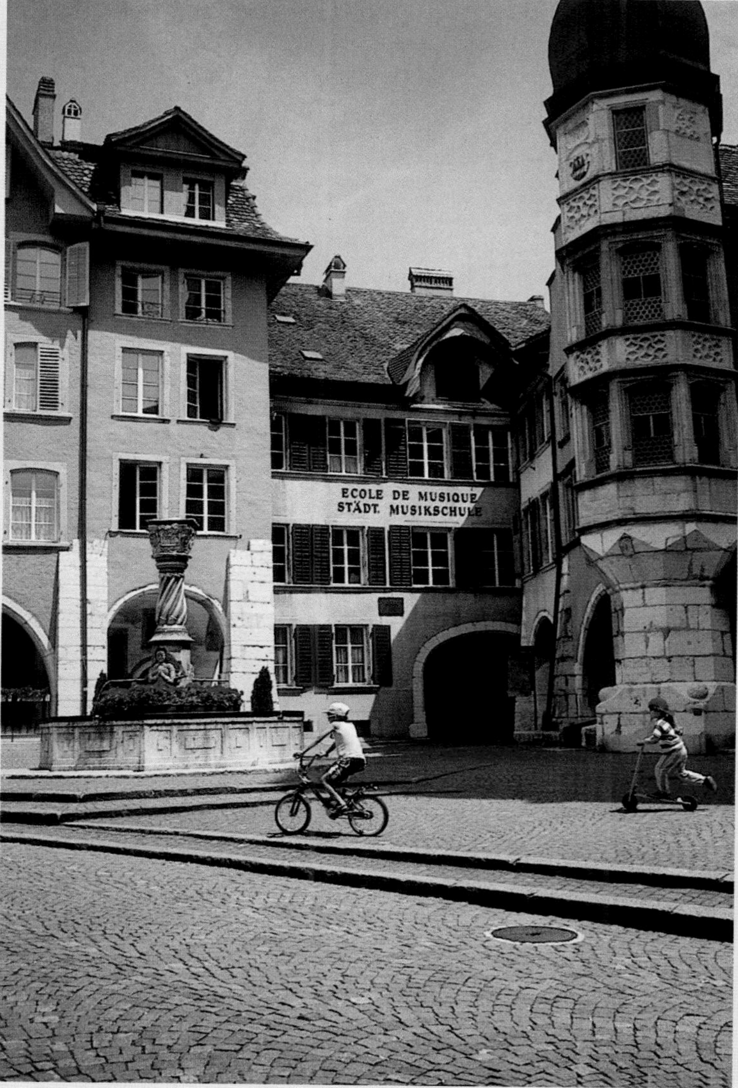

In der zweisprachigen Stadt Biel / Bienne

KAPITEL

14

Wien, U-Bahnstation Karlsplatz (1899); Architekt: Otto Wagner

Österreich

Kommunikation

- Expressing wishes contrary to fact
- Making suggestions
- Making polite requests
- Talking about contrary-to-fact situations
- Talking about hypothetical situations
- Reserving a hotel room

Kultur

- Austrian identity

In diesem Kapitel

- **Lyrik zum Vorlesen**
  Ernst Jandl, "ottos mops"
- **Grammatik**
  1. Subjunctive: Present tense
  2. Subjunctive: Past tense
  3. Subjunctive with **als ob**
- **Lesestück**
  Georg Kreisler, "Heimat"
- **Almanach**
  Profile of Austria

DIALOGE

Lab Manual Kap. 14, Dialoge, Fragen, Hören Sie gut zu!

Auf Urlaub in Salzburg

Das Ehepaar Burckhardt aus Bern hat heute Morgen in Salzburg viel unternommen. Jetzt haben sie Hunger und wollen etwas essen. Sie sehen einen Würstelstand.

Würstelstand: stand selling grilled or boiled sausages, snacks, cold drinks, and coffee.

HERR BURCKHARDT: Ursula, hast du irgendwo einen Bankautomaten gesehen?
FRAU BURCKHARDT: Nein, wieso? Hast du kein Bargeld mehr?
HERR BURCKHARDT: Leider alles ausgegeben. Wenn ich ein paar Euro übrig hätte, könnten wir drüben am Stand eine Wurst essen. Die nehmen sicher keine Kreditkarte.
FRAU BURCKHARDT: Kein Problem. Entweder finden wir in der Fußgängerzone einen Bankautomaten, oder wir können im Hotel Geld wechseln.

An der Rezeption

heute Nacht = *tonight*, but also *last night* if said early in morning.

Most hotels in Europe include breakfast in the room price.

TOURIST: Grüß Gott! Hätten Sie noch ein Zimmer frei für heute Nacht?
ANGESTELLTER: Wünschen Sie ein Einzelzimmer oder ein Doppelzimmer?
TOURIST: Am liebsten hätte ich ein Einzelzimmer mit Dusche.
ANGESTELLTER: Das hätte ich Ihnen vor zwei Stunden geben können, aber im Moment ist nur ein Doppelzimmer mit Bad frei.
TOURIST: Was würde das denn kosten?
ANGESTELLTER: 70 Euro mit Frühstück. Es ist ein ruhiges Zimmer und sehr gemütlich.
TOURIST: Dürfte ich mir das Zimmer ansehen?
ANGESTELLTER: Selbstverständlich. (*Gibt ihm den Schlüssel.*) Gehen Sie hier die Treppe hinauf, das wäre Zimmer Nummer 14 im ersten Stock.

NOTE: **im ersten Stock** is the equivalent of American *on the second floor*.

Ausflug zum Heurigen

Heurige are taverns in and around Vienna, each originally belonging to a vineyard and serving wine (called **Heuriger**) pressed from the current harvest (**heuer** = *this year*).

Grinzing, a suburb of Vienna, has many vineyards with **Heurige**.

ANDREAS: Hallo Helene! Du siehst aus, als ob du nicht viel geschlafen hättest.
HELENE: Ach, merkt man das? Ja, gestern war doch sehr stressig.
ANDREAS: Wenn du heute Abend nicht zu müde bist, dann könnten wir vielleicht nach Grinzing zum Heurigen fahren.
HELENE: Ja, höchste Zeit, dass wir den neuen Wein probieren! Und es wäre auch schön dort zu essen.
ANDREAS: Gute Idee! Bis dann hab' ich sicher einen Riesenhunger.
HELENE: Dann sollten wir gleich losfahren.

Bach-Hengl
SEIT 1685
WEINGUT
GRINZING
HEURIGER
GRINZING,
SANDGASSE 9,
TEL. 32 24 39
MUSIK
BUFFET
PRÄMIERTE
FLASCHENWEINE

Wortschatz 1

Auf der Bank

wechseln to exchange (money)
der **Bankautomat, -en, -en** cash machine, automatic teller machine
das **Bargeld** cash
die **Bank, -en** bank
die **Kasse, -n** cash register; cashier's office
die **Kreditkarte, -n** credit card

Im Hotel

das **Bad, ¨-er** bath; bathroom
ein Bad nehmen to take a bath
das **Badezimmer, -** bathroom
das **Doppelzimmer, -** double room
das **Einzelzimmer, -** single room
die **Dusche, -n** shower
die **Rezeption** reception desk

Verben

aus·gehen, ging aus, ist ausgegangen to go out
los·fahren (fährt los), fuhr los, ist losgefahren to depart; to start; to leave
merken to notice
probieren to sample, try

Substantive

der/die **Angestellte, -n** employee
der **Ausflug, ¨-e** outing, excursion
der **Fußgänger, -** pedestrian
der **Stock** floor (*of a building*)
der **erste Stock** the second floor
im ersten Stock on the second floor
das **Ehepaar, -e** married couple
das **Erdgeschoss** first floor, ground floor
die **Ehe, -n** marriage
die **Fußgängerzone, -n** pedestrian zone
die **Nummer, -n** number

Adjektive und Adverbien

gemütlich comfortable, cozy
österreichisch Austrian
übrig left over, remaining

Andere Vokabeln

als ob (*sub. conj.*) as if
entweder ... oder (*conj.*) either . . . or

Nützliche Ausdrücke

höchste Zeit high time
Das wäre schön! That would be nice!

Gegensätze

entweder ... oder ≠ weder ... noch either . . . or ≠ neither . . . nor
gemütlich ≠ ungemütlich comfortable ≠ uncomfortable

Mit anderen Worten

der Riesenhunger = sehr großer Hunger

Weinberge (*vineyards*) in Grinzing

Variationen

A Persönliche Fragen

1. Haben Sie je Geld wechseln müssen? Wo?
2. Zahlen Sie im Restaurant mit Kreditkarte oder Bargeld?
3. Haben Sie je in einem Hotel übernachtet? Wo war das?
4. Würden Sie lieber in Jugendherbergen oder in Hotels übernachten, wenn Sie nach Österreich reisen? Warum?
5. Haben Sie ein Doppel- oder ein Einzelzimmer im Studentenwohnheim?
6. Wenn Sie am Ende des Monats Geld übrig haben, was machen Sie damit, sparen oder ausgeben?
7. Grinzing ist ein Ausflugsort in der Nähe von Wien. Kennen Sie in Ihrer Gegend einen schönen Ausflugsort?

German dormitories have only singles and doubles. A triple would be called **ein Dreibettzimmer**.

B Übung: Was ist ein Riese? Ein berühmter Riese in der Bibel hieß Goliath. Sie kennen schon das Wort „riesengroß". So nennt man etwas sehr Großes. Jetzt wissen Sie auch, wenn man sehr hungrig ist, sagt man: „Ich habe Riesenhunger!" Also:

Pronounced with stress on the first syllable: **Go-liath**

1. Einen riesengroßen Hunger nennt man auch *einen Riesenhunger.*
2. Einen sehr sehr großen Koffer nennt man auch ________.
3. Eine ganz große Freude ist ________.
4. Wenn viele Menschen zusammen demonstrieren, dann hat man ________.
5. Wenn ein Supertanker einen Unfall hat und sein Öl ins Meer fließt, dann ist das ________.
6. Ein sehr großes Hotel kann man auch ________ nennen.

Das Wiener Riesenrad: The 67-meter-high Ferris wheel dates from 1897 and offers splendid views. It is the location of a famous scene in *The Third Man* (directed by Carol Reed, starring Orson Welles, 1949), a film that unforgettably evokes the divided city of Vienna in the post-war era.

C Partnerarbeit: Wie wäre das? (*How would that be?*) Ihr Partner schlägt Ihnen etwas vor. Reagieren Sie darauf mit Ihren eigenen Worten: **Das wäre ... !** (Switch roles for second column.)

BEISPIEL: A: Sollen wir einen Ausflug machen?
B: Ja, das wäre toll!

ins Kino gehen?	uns die Stadt ansehen?
zum Heurigen fahren?	zu Hause sitzen?
Freunde einladen?	das Zimmer aufräumen?
Ski fahren gehen?	im Restaurant essen?
Theaterkarten kaufen?	eine Radtour machen?

D Übung: entweder ... oder. Sagen Sie, Sie machen entweder **dies** oder **das**.

BEISPIEL: Was trinken Sie heute Abend?
Ich trinke entweder Tee oder Kaffee.

1. Wohin fahren Sie im Sommer?
2. Was möchten Sie gern essen?
3. Mit wem wollen Sie Tennis spielen?
4. Welche Fremdsprache werden Sie nächstes Jahr lernen?
5. Wer war denn das?
6. Wissen Sie, in welchem Stock Ihr Hotelzimmer ist?
7. Wie kann man im Hotel zahlen?
8. Wann wollen Sie das nächste Mal Ski fahren gehen?

Vokabeln zum Thema Hotel

Im Hotel

Auf Seite 383 sehen Sie die Rezeption in einem Hotel. Hier ist eine Liste von Vokabeln, die Ihnen zum größten Teil (*for the most part*) schon bekannt sind.

Die Hotelgäste

sich an·melden	*to register*
das **Gepäck**	
der **Koffer, -**	
der **Reisepass, -pässe**	*passport*
ein Zimmer reservieren	
ein Taxi bestellen	

An der Rezeption

der/die **Angestellte**	
die **Kasse**	
der **Zimmerschlüssel, -**	
der **Stadtplan, ⸚e**	
der **Stadtführer, -**	*city guidebook*
der **Speisesaal**	*dining room*
der **Lift**	*elevator*

Im Hotelzimmer

das **Bad**
die **Dusche**
das **Telefon (telefonieren)**
sich duschen — *to shower*
sich um·ziehen — *to change clothes*

E Rollenspiele. ***(Gruppen von 3 Personen)*** Spielen Sie diese Situationen zusammen. Improvisieren Sie.

Reserving a hotel room is a communicative goal.

An der Rezeption

Zwei Touristen kommen gerade vom Flughafen im Hotel an. Sie haben schon ein Zimmer reserviert. Sie melden sich an der Rezeption an und stellen Fragen über das Zimmer.

Eine Stunde später

Die Touristen haben sich geduscht und umgezogen. Jetzt wollen sie ausgehen und sich die Stadt ansehen. An der Rezeption bitten sie um Auskunft. Der Angestellte gibt ihnen viele Informationen über die Stadt, z. B. über das kulturelle Leben, Verkehrsmittel, Restaurants usw. Bei ihm bekommen sie auch Stadtführer, Stadtpläne und Broschüren (*brochures*). Sie müssen auch Geld wechseln.

The Austrian poet Ernst Jandl was born in Vienna. In the following poem, he shows that it is possible to tell a whole story using only one vowel. Reading it aloud will be a good review of the German long and short **o**! Like many other modern poets, Jandl does not capitalize nouns.

ottos mops°

pug (dog)

ottos mops trotzt° — *won't obey*
otto: fort° mops fort — *go away*
ottos mops hopst° fort — *hops*
otto: soso

otto holt koks° — *charcoal briquettes*
otto holt obst
otto horcht° — *listens*
otto: mops mops
otto hofft

ottos mops klopft° — *knocks*
otto: komm mops komm
ottos mops kommt
ottos mops kotzt° — *pukes*
otto: ogottogott

Ernst Jandl (1925–2000)

Karikatur von Wilhelm Busch (1832–1908). Busch war Zeichner und Dichter, der seine humoristischen Erzählungen mit seinen eigenen Zeichnungen illustrierte. Werke wie **Max und Moritz** (1865) waren die ersten modernen Comics. Diese Zeichnung ist aus dem Jahre 1870.

GRAMMATIK

1. Subjunctive: Present tense (*der Konjunktiv*)

Language presents information in various ways. It can present not only facts but also hypotheses, conjectures, and situations that are contrary to fact. Both German and English have two different sets of verb forms for these two possibilities, called the *indicative* and the *subjunctive.*

Up to now, you have been using the INDICATIVE (**der Indikativ**) to talk about what is definite, certain, and real.

Barbara **ist** nicht hier.	*Barbara **isn't** here.*
Ich **habe** Zeit.	*I **have** time.*
Helfen Sie mir später?	*Will you **help** me later?*

The SUBJUNCTIVE (**der Konjunktiv**), on the other hand, is used to talk about hypothetical, uncertain, or unreal situations, and also to make polite statements and requests.

Wenn Barbara nur hier **wäre**!	*If only Barbara **were** here!*
Wenn ich mehr Zeit **hätte** ...	*If I **had** more time . . .*
Würden Sie mir später helfen?	***Would** you help me later?*

A common subjunctive form in English is *were,* as in *if I were you*.

In English, *present* subjunctive uses what look like *past-tense* forms, or uses *would* + verb.

*If you **lived** nearby, we **would visit** you.*	(condition contrary to fact: You *don't* live nearby.)
*If only I **had** more time!*	(wish contrary to fact: I *don't* have more time.)
*I **would like** to have a room.*	(polite request in place of "I *want* a room.")

Note that the verbs *lived* and *had* in the examples above are identical to the past indicative in *form,* but have present-tense meaning.

*If you **lived** nearby . . .*	(right now, at the moment)
*If only I **had** more time!*	(right now, at the moment)

In Austria, **Servus** means both *hello* and *so long*. It originally meant "Your servant" in Latin. It is used only by speakers who say **du** to each other.

Subjunctive with *würden* + infinitive

By far the most frequent subjunctive construction is a form of **würden** (the subjunctive of **werden**) plus infinitive. You already learned this structure in **Kapitel 7** (see page 186) to express intentions, opinions, preferences, and polite requests.

1 Übung: Was würden Sie in diesen Situationen machen? Partner A beschreibt die Situation, Partner B sagt, was er/sie tun würde. Partner B beschreibt die nächste Situation, usw.

BEISPIEL:
A: Du bist auf der Autobahn.
B: Ich würde schnell fahren. Du hast 1.000 Euro.
A: Ich ...

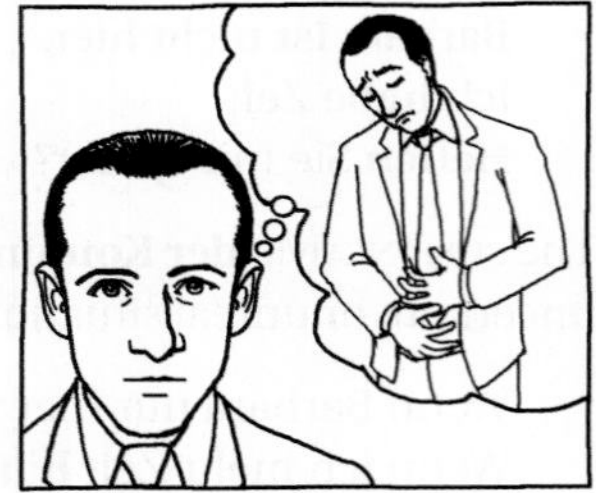

Subjunctive of modal verbs

Like **werden**, the modal verbs form their subjunctive by simply adding an umlaut to the past tense of the indicative:

Past indicative		Present subjunctive	
ich konnte	*I was able to*	ich **könnte**	*I could, would be able to*
ich mochte	*I liked*	ich **möchte**	*I would like to*
ich musste	*I had to*	ich **müsste**	*I would have to*

EXCEPTIONS: The present subjunctive of **sollen** and **wollen** is *not* umlauted, and so it looks just like the past indicative.

Note that **sollen** and **wollen** lack an umlaut in their infinitive as well.

ich sollte	*I was supposed to*	ich **sollte**	*I ought to*
ich wollte	*I wanted to*	ich **wollte**	*I would want to*

Lab Manual Kap. 14, Var. zu Üb. 1, 2.

2 Übung: Hören Sie gut zu! (*mit geschlossenen Büchern*) Listen to each pair of sentences, then say which one is past indicative and which present subjunctive. Then, with open books, repeat each sentence aloud and give the English equivalent.

1. Durfte sie das machen?
   Dürfte sie das machen?
2. Wir könnten ihn abholen.
   Wir konnten ihn abholen.
3. Sie müsste das wissen.
   Sie musste das wissen.
4. Mochte er das Frühstück?
   Möchte er das Frühstück?

Making suggestions is a communicative goal.

NOTE ON USAGE

Using the subjunctive to make suggestions

Wir **könnten** zusammen ausgehen. *We **could** go out together.*
Wir **sollten** eigentlich hier bleiben. *We really **ought** to stay here.*

3 Gruppenarbeit: Was könnten wir denn unternehmen? (*3 Personen*) Die folgende Seite aus dem Wiener Kulturprogramm zeigt drei berühmte kulturelle Attraktionen der Stadt: die Spanische Hofreitschule, die Wiener Sängerknaben und das Kunstmuseum im Oberen Belvedere. Besprechen Sie miteinander, was Sie unternehmen könnten.

BEISPIEL: A: Wir könnten ...
B: Ja, oder wir könnten ...

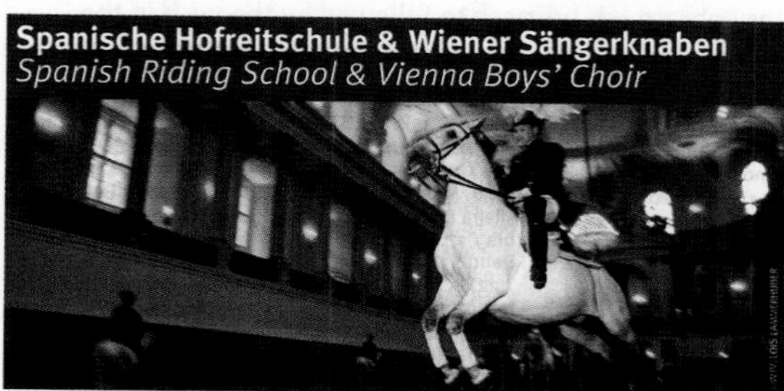

The **Spanische Hofreitschule** *(Spanish Riding School)* was founded in 1572 to cultivate the classic skills of horsemanship by breeding and training show horses originally from Spain. The breed is called **Lipizzaner** after the original stud farm at Lipizza in Slovenia. They are now bred in Piber near Graz. The art museum in the palace called **Oberes Belvedere** houses nineteenth- and twentieth-century paintings, including the famous painting shown on the program, *Der Kuss* (1907–1908) by Gustav Klimt.

Spanische Hofreitschule
Hofburg, 1., Michaelerplatz 1
Tel. 533 90 31, www.srs.at

Vorführung / Performance / Répresentation / Esibizione: **1. 7.** um 11 Uhr
Sitzplätze / Seats / Places assises / Posti a sedere: 45–110 €
Stehplätze / Standing places / Places debout / Posti in piedi: 22 €
Piber meets Vienna. Lipizzanergestüt Piber zu Gast in Wien / An Introduction to the Federal Stud Piber:
3.–7. & 10.–14. 7. von 11–12 Uhr
Sitzplätze: 13–26 €, Stehplätze: 9 €
Mutterstuten und Fohlen in der Sommerreitbahn / Mares and Foals in the Summer Riding School: 3.–8. & 10.–13. 7. von 17.30–19 Uhr (Tickets: 3 €)
Tickets: Spanische Hofreitschule, Hofburg, Michaelerplatz 1, 1010 Wien, Tel. 533 90 31, tickets@srs.at

Morgenarbeit der Lipizzaner / Morning Training / Entrainement / Allenamento mattutino: 21.–25. & 28.–31. 8. Tickets: 12 € (keine Reservierung / no reservation / pas de reséervations / non è possibile prenotare)

Führungen mit Besichtigung der Stallungen / Guided tours including Stables (D, E): Di–Sa um 14, 15 & 16 Uhr (ausser / except 15. 8.), So & 15. 8. um 10, 11, 13, 14 & 15 Uhr (ausser / except 5. 8.)
Anmeldung empfohlen / registration recommended: Tel. 533 90 31, office@srs.at

1. Wiener Klaviersommer
in der Spanischen Hofreitschule
siehe „Konzerte" Seite 31 / 1st Vienna Piano Festival at Spanish Riding School see „Concerts" page 31

* * *

Lipizzaner Museum
1., Reitschulgasse 2
täglich 9–18 Uhr
www.lipizzaner.at

Wiener Sängerknaben
Im Juli und August finden keine Messen oder Konzerte mit den Wiener Sängerknaben statt. / [E] During July and August there are no Masses or concerts with the Vienna Boys' Choir. / [F] Pendant les mois de juillet et août il n'y a ni messes ni concerts avec les Petits Chanteurs de Vienne. / [I] Durante i mesi di luglio e agosto non hanno luogo messe o concerti con i Piccoli Cantori di Vienna.
www.hofburgkapelle.at, www.wsk.at

4 Partnerarbeit: Was ich möchte und was ich sollte. Erzählen Sie einander, was Sie nächstes Wochenende am liebsten machen möchten und was Sie eigentlich machen sollten. Die Liste gibt Ihnen einige Möglichkeiten.

BEISPIEL: Ich möchte am liebsten Karten spielen, aber ich sollte eigentlich mein Zimmer aufräumen.

Ich möchte am liebsten ...	Ich sollte eigentlich ...
spazieren gehen	das Zimmer aufräumen
Karten spielen	Hausaufgaben machen
italienisch essen gehen	das Auto waschen
einen Ausflug machen	mich auf die Klausur vorbereiten
ins Konzert gehen	Lebensmittel einkaufen

NOTE ON USAGE

Wishes contrary to fact

A contrary-to-fact wish uses the introductory phrase **Ich wünschte** followed by the wish in the subjunctive mood. You can also use a **wenn**-clause (verb last!) with an added **nur**.

Ich wünschte, ich könnte fliegen.	*I wish I could fly.*
Wenn ich nur fliegen könnte.	*If only I could fly.*

5 Übung: Ich wünschte, es wäre anders! Ihre Professorin beschreibt eine Situation im Indikativ. Sie wünschen im Konjunktiv, dass es anders wäre.

BEISPIEL: Christine kann kein Englisch.
Ich wünschte, sie könnte Englisch.

1. Ich kann kein Französisch.
2. Du musst nach Hause.
3. Ich darf nicht länger bleiben.
4. Helene will nicht nach Grinzing mitkommen.
5. Wir können nicht mitfahren.
6. Du musst abfahren.
7. Ich darf nicht alles sagen.
8. Andreas will nicht helfen.

Subjunctive of irregular and strong verbs

Like **werden** and the modal verbs, **haben** and **wissen** also form their subjunctive by adding an umlaut to the simple past of the indicative.

Past indicative		Present subjunctive	
ich hatte	*I had*	ich **hätte**	*I would have*
ich wusste	*I knew*	ich **wüsste**	*I would know*

6 Kettenreaktion: Was hätten Sie gern? Sagen Sie, was Sie gern hätten.

BEISPIEL: A: Ich hätte gern ein frisches Brötchen. Und du?
B: Ich hätte gern ein-________.

7 Kettenreaktion: Was wüssten Sie gern? Sagen Sie, was Sie gern wüssten.

BEISPIEL: A: Ich wüsste gern, wo ich Geld verdienen könnte. Und du?
B: Ich wüsste gern, ________.

The present subjunctive of strong verbs is also based on their simple past indicative forms (see p. 266–267), but these forms are modified according to the following three-step procedure.

- *Step 1*: Take the simple past stem of the verb.

kommen → **kam-** gehen → **ging-** sein → **war-**

Remember that you can only add an umlaut to **a**, **o**, **u**, and **au**.

- *Step 2*: Add an umlaut to the stem vowel whenever possible.

käm- **ging-** **wär-**

- *Step 3*: Add the following personal endings.

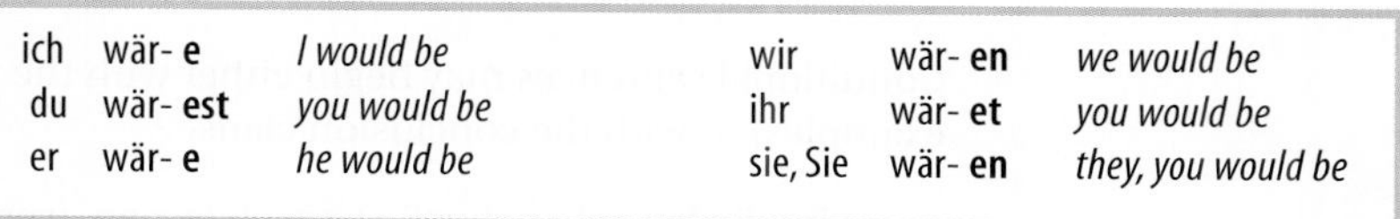

ich	wär- **e**	*I would be*	wir	wär- **en**	*we would be*
du	wär- **est**	*you would be*	ihr	wär- **et**	*you would be*
er	wär- **e**	*he would be*	sie, Sie	wär- **en**	*they, you would be*

Note the differences in the endings of the present subjunctive and the past indicative of a strong verb:

Present subjunctive *(would go)*		**Past indicative** *(went)*	
ich	ginge	ich	ging
du	ging**est**	du	ging**st**
sie	ginge	sie	ging
wir	ging**en**	wir	ging**en**
ihr	ging**et**	ihr	ging**t**
sie, Sie	ging**en**	sie, Sie	ging**en**

Only the **wir-** and the plural **sie**-endings are the same.

In contemporary spoken German, with the exception of **wäre**, most strong verbs use **würde** + *infinitive* instead of the one-word form; **Ich tränke Rotwein** is replaced by **Ich würde Rotwein trinken**.

Lab Manual Kap. 14, Var. zu Üb. 8.

Workbook Kap. 14 A, B, C.

8 Übung: Ich wünschte, es wäre anders! Jetzt hören Sie eine Situation im Indikativ. Sie wünschen im Konjunktiv, dass es anders wäre.

BEISPIEL: Meine Gäste gehen nicht nach Hause.
Ich wünschte, sie gingen nach Hause.

1. Gabi ist nicht mehr hier.
2. Robert kommt nicht um zwölf.
3. Karin geht nicht mit uns spazieren.
4. Wir sind nicht fit.
5. Die Uhr geht nicht richtig.
6. Ich habe keine Kreditkarte.
7. Er ist mir böse.
8. Ich habe keine Freunde in Salzburg.

Talking about contrary-to-fact situations is a communicative goal.

Conditions contrary to fact: "If *X* were true, then *Y* would be true."

In **Kapitel 8** you learned about conditional sentences containing a **wenn**-clause (see p. 208). When the conditional sentence is describing a situation that is contrary to fact, the verbs must be in the subjunctive.

A **wenn**-clause states the condition contrary to fact: "If X were true . . ."

Wenn wir jetzt in Deutschland wären ...	*If we were in Germany now . . .*
Wenn ich mehr Geld hätte ...	*If I had more money . . .*

The main clause (with an optional **dann** as the first word) draws the unreal conclusion: ". . . then Y would be true."

... (dann) würden wir sehr schnell Deutsch lernen.	. . . (*then*) *we would learn German very quickly.*
... (dann) müsste ich nicht so viel arbeiten.	. . . (*then*) *I wouldn't have to work so much.*

Putting them together:

Wenn wir jetzt in Deutschland wären, würden wir sehr schnell Deutsch lernen.
Wenn ich mehr Geld hätte, dann müsste ich nicht so viel arbeiten.

Conditional sentences may begin either with the **wenn**-clause (as in the two previous examples) *or* with the conclusion clause.[1]

Wir **würden** sehr schnell Deutsch lernen, wenn wir jetzt in Deutschland **wären**.
Ich **müsste** nicht so viel arbeiten, wenn ich mehr Geld **hätte**.

NOTE ON USAGE

One-word subjunctive of weak verbs

All weak verbs have a one-word present subjunctive form which is identical to the simple past indicative:

Past indicative		**Present subjunctive**	
ich wohnte	*I lived*	wenn ich wohnte	*if I lived*
du wohntest	*you lived*	wenn du wohntest	*if you lived*
usw.		usw.	

This form (instead of the present subjunctive with **würde** + infinitive) occurs most frequently in the **wenn**-clause of a conditional sentence.

Wenn ich in Wien **wohnte**, würde ich oft ins Kaffeehaus gehen.

[1] The **wenn** is sometimes omitted from the **wenn**-clause. Its verb is then placed at the *beginning* of the clause. Compare the similar structure in English that omits *if*:

Hätte er das Geld, (dann) würde er mehr kaufen.
Had *he the money, he would buy more.*

„Wenn ich in Wien wohnte, würde ich oft ins Kaffeehaus gehen." (Café Griensteidl, Wien)

SAM
Lab Manual

Lab Manual Kap. 14, Üb. 9.

SAM
Workbook

Workbook 14, D–H.

9 Übung: Aber wenn es anders wäre ... (*mit offenen Büchern*) Ihr Professor beschreibt eine Situation im Indikativ. Sie sagen im Konjunktiv, wie es wäre, wenn die Situation *anders* wäre. (Note that the logic of these sentences demands changing positive to negative and vice versa.)

BEISPIEL: Weil es so kalt ist, können wir nicht schwimmen.
Aber wenn es *nicht* so kalt *wäre, könnten* wir schwimmen.

1. Weil es so weit ist, können wir nicht zu Fuß gehen.
2. Weil ich kein Geld übrig habe, mache ich es nicht.
3. Weil dieses Buch langweilig ist, lesen wir es nicht.
4. Weil der Dom geschlossen ist, können Sie ihn nicht besuchen.
5. Weil ich keine Zeit habe, kann ich kein Bad nehmen.
6. Weil sie nicht in Wien wohnt, kennt sie Grinzing nicht.
7. Weil ich keinen Hunger habe, bestelle ich nichts.
8. Weil sie sich nicht für diesen Film interessiert, geht sie nicht mit.

10 Übung. (*mit offenen Büchern*) Wiederholen Sie, was Sie schon in **Übung 9** gemacht haben, aber diesmal beginnen Sie *nicht* mit **wenn**.

BEISPIEL: Wir kommen zu spät, weil du nicht schneller fährst.
Aber wir würden nicht zu spät kommen, wenn du schneller fahren würdest.

1. Wir bleiben hier, weil er uns braucht.
2. Ich muss jetzt wechseln, weil ich keine Euros habe.
3. Wir gehen nicht spazieren, weil es regnet.
4. Wir fahren mit dem Zug nach Italien, weil wir keinen Wagen haben.
5. Ich lese die Zeitung nicht, weil ich so müde bin.
6. Er kann mir nicht danken, weil er meinen Namen nicht weiß.
7. Wir sehen uns nicht, weil er nicht mehr vorbeikommt.

11 Gruppenarbeit: Ein Cartoon. The humor of this cartoon depends on the use of subjunctive in a hypothetical question and answer. Can you guess from context the meaning of **einsame Insel**?

Lab Manual Kap. 14, Var. zu Üb. 12.

12 Gruppenarbeit: Studentenreise nach Österreich. (*4–5 Personen*) Sie reisen nächstes Jahr mit einer Studentengruppe nach Österreich. Sie müssen sich jetzt darauf vorbereiten.

1. Was sollte man mitbringen?
2. Was für Bücher könnte man über Österreich lesen?
3. Was sollte man dort sehen? (Die Fotos in diesem Kapitel geben Ihnen vielleicht einige Ideen.)
4. Was würden Sie am liebsten in Österreich machen?

Polite requests

Note the difference in the tone of the following two requests:

Indicative		*Subjunctive*
Can *you do this for me?*	*vs.*	**Could** *you do this for me?*

In the second sentence, the subjunctive softens the request and makes it more polite. German uses the subjunctive in the same way as English to make polite requests. These are sometimes in the statement form you have already used.

Ich **hätte** gern eine Tasse Kaffee.	*I'd like to have a cup of coffee.*
Ich **wüsste** gern, wo der Bahnhof ist.	*I'd like to know where the train station is.*

Sometimes polite requests are questions.

Könnten Sie mir bitte helfen?	*Could you please help me?*
Würden Sie mir bitte den Koffer tragen?	*Would you please carry my suitcase?*
Dürfte ich eine Frage stellen?	*Might I ask a question?*

13 Übung: Könnten Sie das bitte machen? Benutzen Sie den Konjunktiv statt des Indikativs, um höflicher zu sein.

BEISPIEL: Können Sie mir bitte ein Einzelzimmer zeigen?
Könnten Sie mir bitte ein Einzelzimmer zeigen?

SAM Lab Manual
Lab Manual Kap. 14, Var. zu Üb. 14.

SAM Workbook
Workbook Kap. 14, I.

1. Können Sie mir bitte sagen, wann der Zug nach Berlin abfährt?
2. Haben Sie Zeit eine Tasse Kaffee mit mir zu trinken?
3. Darf ich mich hier setzen?
4. Tragen Sie mir bitte die Koffer?
5. Ist es möglich eine Zeitung zu kaufen?
6. Können Sie mir meinen Platz zeigen?
7. Haben Sie ein Einzelzimmer mit Dusche?
8. Wissen Sie, wo man Karten kaufen kann?

14 Partnerarbeit: Kellner und Gast im Lokal. Spielen Sie diese Situation zusammen. Seien Sie höflich und benutzen Sie den Konjunktiv! Der Kellner fragt den Gast, was er (oder sie) bestellen möchte. Der Gast fragt, ob man verschiedene Gerichte (*dishes*) hat, und bestellt dann ein großes Essen. (*You can use some food vocabulary from* ***Kapitel 8****, p. 220.*) Seien Sie bereit Ihren Dialog vor der Klasse zu spielen.

KELLNER/IN: Bitte sehr? Was hätten Sie gern?
GAST: Hätten Sie vielleicht ... ? Könnten Sie mir sagen ... ? Ich hätte gern ...

Talking about what could or might have happened in the past is a communicative goal.

2. Subjunctive: Past tense

Past subjunctive is used to talk about hypothetical or contrary-to-fact situations *in the past*, e.g., "*I would have waited* for you yesterday." Now that you have learned how to use present-tense subjunctive, PAST SUBJUNCTIVE will prove quite easy. Its form is similar to the *perfect tense* of the indicative. The only difference is that the auxiliary verb is in the *present subjunctive* (a form of **hätten** or **wären** instead of **haben** or **sein**).

Past subjunctive					
ich	**hätte** gewartet	*I would have waited*	ich	**wäre** gekommen	*I would have come*
du	**hättest** gewartet	*you would have waited*	du	**wärest** gekommen	*you would have come*
er	**hätte** gewartet	*he would have waited*	sie	**wäre** gekommen	*she would have come*
wir	**hätten** gewartet	*we would have waited*	wir	**wären** gekommen	*we would have come*
ihr	**hättet** gewartet	*you would have waited*	ihr	**wäret** gekommen	*you would have come*
sie, Sie	**hätten** gewartet	*they, you would have waited*	sie, Sie	**wären** gekommen	*they, you would have come*

CAUTION! Note that English uses the word *would* in both the present and past subjunctive, while German uses **würden** *only* in the present subjunctive, *not* in the past.

Present:	Er **würde** mitkommen.	*He **would** come along.*
Past:	Er **wäre** mitgekommen.	*He **would have** come along.*

Note also that the subjunctive mood has *only this one past tense*, unlike the indicative, which has three past tenses (simple past, perfect, past perfect).

Lab Manual Kap. 14, Var. zu Üb. 15, 16, 18, 19.

Workbook Kap. 14, J–M.

15 Übung: Aber *ich* hätte das gemacht. Ihre Professorin sagt Ihnen, was sie nicht gemacht hat. Sie sagen, dass *Sie* es gemacht hätten.

BEISPIEL: Ich habe keinen Ausflug gemacht.
Aber *ich* hätte einen Ausflug gemacht.

1. Ich habe nicht um Auskunft gebeten.
2. Ich habe Anna nicht geholfen.
3. Ich habe die Adresse nicht gewusst.
4. Ich bin nicht Ski gefahren.
5. Ich habe mir die Haare nicht gekämmt (*combed*).
6. Ich bin nicht lange geblieben.
7. Ich habe den Plan nicht verstanden.
8. Ich bin nicht tanzen gegangen.

16 Übung: Wie sagt man das auf Deutsch?

1. I would have hated that.
2. Bernd wouldn't have waited.
3. We would have bought a piano.
4. I would have gotten up earlier.
5. That would have lasted a long time.
6. That would have cost too much.
7. You wouldn't have been happy.
8. They would have stayed longer.

17 Gruppenarbeit: Was hätten Sie gemacht, wenn ... So ist es *nicht* gewesen, aber es hätte so sein können. Was hätten Sie gemacht ...

1. wenn Sie dieses Semester nicht studiert hätten?
2. wenn Sie letztes Jahr eine Million Euro bekommen hätten?
3. wenn Sie vor 100 Jahren gelebt hätten?
4. wenn Sie gestern einen Autounfall gehabt hätten?
5. wenn Ihr Professor sich gestern das Bein gebrochen hätte?

18 Gruppenarbeit: Ich wünschte, ich hätte das nicht gemacht. Als Kinder haben wir alle viel gemacht, was wir lieber nicht gemacht hätten. Sagen Sie, was Sie lieber gemacht oder nicht gemacht hätten.

BEISPIELE: Ich wünschte, ich hätte meine ältere Schwester nicht so oft geärgert.
Ich wünschte, ich hätte mehr Klavier geübt.
Ich wünschte, ich wäre ...

Past subjunctive of modal verbs

Review the double-infinitive construction in perfect indicative of modals, p. 158, and in the perfect tense of **lassen**, p. 338–339.

The past subjunctive of modal verbs is also similar to the perfect indicative tense. Because modal verbs always use **haben** as their auxiliary, their past subjunctive is formed with **hätten** plus the *double infinitive.*

Du **hättest** doch **anrufen können**.	*You could have called.*
Das **hätte** ich **machen sollen**.	*I should have done that.*

In English, the past subjunctive of modal verbs uses *would have, could have,* or *should have.* Notice how simple and consistent German modals are compared to English.

Ich **hätte** kommen **dürfen**.	*I **would have been allowed** to come.*
Ich **hätte** kommen **können**.	*I **could have** come.*
Ich **hätte** kommen **müssen**.	*I **would have had to** come.*
Ich **hätte** kommen **sollen**.	*I **should have** come.*
Ich **hätte** kommen **wollen**.	*I **would have wanted to** come.*

19 Übung: Das hätten Sie machen sollen. Ihr Professor hat vergessen viele wichtige Dinge zu machen. Sagen Sie ihm, er hätte sie machen sollen.

BEISPIEL: Ich habe vergessen meinen Regenschirm mitzubringen.
Sie hätten ihn doch mitbringen sollen.

1. Ich habe vergessen mein Bett zu machen.
2. Ich habe vergessen meine Bücher mitzubringen.
3. Ich habe vergessen meine Frau anzurufen.
4. Ich habe vergessen eine Zeitung zu kaufen.
5. Ich habe vergessen das Fenster zu schließen.
6. Ich habe vergessen den Witz zu erzählen.

20 Übung: Wie sagt man das auf Deutsch?

1. We could have flown.
2. We would have had to buy tickets.
3. Frank should have come along.
4. He wouldn't have wanted to come along.
5. He wouldn't have been allowed to come along.

3. Subjunctive with *als ob*

The subordinating conjunction **als ob**[2] (*as if, as though*) must be followed by a verb in the subjunctive. Clauses with **als ob** are preceded by introductory phrases such as the following (note the special meaning of **tun** in the first example).

Du tust (so), als ob ...	*You act as though . . .*
Du siehst aus, als ob ...	*You look as if . . .*
Es war, als ob ...	*It was as if . . .*
Es klingt, als ob ...	*It sounds as if . . .*
Er tut, **als ob** er nichts **wüsste**.	*He acts as if he didn't know anything.*
Du siehst aus, **als ob** du krank **wärest**.	*You look as though you're ill.*
Es war, **als ob** wir uns immer **gekannt hätten**.	*It was as if we had always known each other.*
Es klingt, **als ob** du viel zu tun **hättest**.	*It sounds as if you have a lot to do.*

21 Übung: Aber Sie tun doch, als ob Sie gesund wären! Ihr Professor erzählt Ihnen etwas über sich selbst. Sagen Sie ihm, er tut, als ob das Gegenteil stimmte.

SAM Lab Manual **Lab Manual** Kap. 14, Var. zu Üb. 21.

SAM Workbook **Workbook** Kap. 14, N.

BEISPIEL: Ich fühle mich heute krank.
Aber Sie tun doch, als ob Sie gesund wären.

1. Ich bin traurig.
2. Ich bin knapp bei Kasse.
3. Ich bin von Natur aus (*by nature*) faul.
4. Ich bin relativ altmodisch.
5. Ich bin eigentlich ein schlampiger Mensch.
6. Ich bin fast immer ernst.
7. Eigentlich bin ich dumm.

---

[2] Sometimes this conjunction is used in the abbreviated form of **als** alone (without **ob**). In this case, the verb immediately follows it rather than coming at the end of the clause: Du siehst aus, als **wärest** du krank.

22 Gruppenarbeit: Sie sehen aus, als ob ... Sehen Sie sich die Menschen auf diesen Fotos an. Wie sehen sie aus? (Gefühle, Berufe usw.)

BEISPIEL: Sie sieht aus, *als ob ...*

1. 

2. 

3. 

4. 

LESESTÜCK

Tipps zum Lesen und Lernen

Tipps zum Vokabelnlernen: Adverbs of time

***The suffix** -lang* To form the German equivalents of the English adverbial phrases *for days, for hours,* etc., add the suffix **-lang** to the plural of the noun.

Can you guess the meaning of **jahrzehntelang**?

Compare the **Note on Usage** on p. 276.

minuten**lang**	*for minutes*	monate**lang**	*for months*
stunden**lang**	*for hours*	jahre**lang**	*for years*
tage**lang**	*for days*	jahrhunderte**lang**	*for centuries*
wochen**lang**	*for weeks*		

23 Übung: Wie lange hat's gedauert? Ihre Professorin möchte wissen, ob etwas lange gedauert hat. Wählen Sie ein Zeitadverb mit **-lang** für Ihre Antwort.

BEISPIEL: Haben Sie lange im Zug von Paris nach Berlin gesessen?
Ja, *stundenlang.*

1. Hat das elegante Abendessen lange gedauert?
2. Haben Sie lange auf den Bus warten müssen?
3. War's letzten Sommer sehr heiß?
4. War der Chef lange am Telefon?
5. Waren die alten Römer lange Zeit in Nordeuropa?

Lab Manual Kap. 14, Üb. zur Betonung.

Leicht zu merken

die Ambivalenz	Ambivalenz
die Armee, -n	Armee
der Charakter, -e	Charakter
definieren	definieren
sich distanzieren von	distanzieren
der Essay, -s	
golden	
der Humor	Humor
sich identifizieren mit	identifizieren
die Illusion	Illusion
die Ironie	Ironie
die Karriere, -n	Karriere
logisch	
positiv	positiv
die Solidarität	Solidarität

Einstieg in den Text

In the following reading selection Georg Kreisler uses subjunctive mood for conjectural and hypothetical statements, as well as for a wish contrary to fact. Below is one example of each type. After reading through the text once, write down other examples of subjunctive mood used for these purposes; be sure you understand them and can give English equivalents.

Hypothetical statement: **Ich wäre bereit, Wien nicht nur mit Worten, sondern auch mit Taten zu verteidigen ...**

Conjecture: **Gäbe es die gute alte Zeit nicht, hätten wir überhaupt keine Heimat.**

Wish contrary to fact: **Wenn sie es nur merken würden!**

Wien: Karlskirche, erbaut 1716–1739 von Fischer von Erlach

Wortschatz 2

Verben

sich identifizieren mit to identify with
nach·denken, dachte nach, hat nachgedacht über (+ *acc.*) to think about, ponder
sich verlassen auf (+ *acc.*) to rely on, count on
sich wohl fühlen to feel well, feel good
verteidigen to defend

Substantive

der **Einfluss, ⸚e** influence
der **Inhalt, -e** contents
der **Witz, -e** joke; wit
das **Klavier, -e** piano
die **Laune, -n** mood
die **Tat, -en** deed
das **Herz, -en** heart
die **Donau** the Danube River
die **Einsamkeit** loneliness

Adjektive und Adverbien

einsam lonely
jahrelang for years
streng strict
täglich daily

Andere Vokabeln

damit (*sub. conj.*) so that
gegenüber (*prep. with dat.*) across from; with respect to

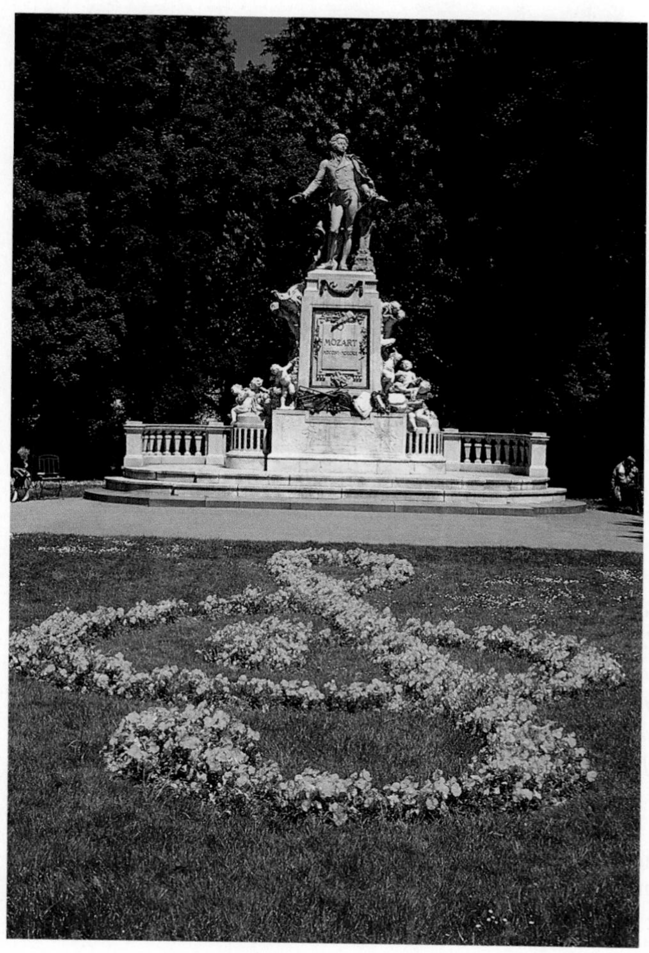

Mozartdenkmal im Burggarten, Wien (1896)

Georg Kreisler

Heimat

Der Sänger und Klavierspieler Georg Kreisler ist 1922 in Wien geboren. Weil seine Familie von den Nazis als jüdisch definiert wurde, wanderte er 1938 mit seinen Eltern in die USA aus. Dort lebte er jahrelang, wurde amerikanischer Staatsbürger und diente° während des Zweiten Weltkrieges in der US-Armee. Damals begann auch seine Karriere als Musiker. Er komponierte° musikalische Shows. 1955 ging er nach Wien zurück und trat mit witzigen Kabarettliedern auf.° Heute lebt er in Basel.

In dem folgenden kleinen Essay zeigt er eine typisch österreichische Ambivalenz seiner Heimatstadt gegenüber. Obwohl er sich mit Wien identifiziert, distanziert er sich durch Witz und Ironie von den Klischees der österreichischen Kultur: die schöne Donau, die große Vergangenheit des Habsburgerreiches,[3] das goldene Wiener Herz. Vielleicht ist es typisch für den österreichischen Humor, dass man über die eigene schlechte Laune Witze machen kann.

served
composed
trat ... auf = *performed*

[3] The Habsburgs ruled the Holy Roman Empire from 1278 to 1806, and Austria (later Austria-Hungary) until 1918. At one time or another the Habsburg empire included Germans, Dutch, Burgundians, Hungarians, Czechs, Poles, Italians, Romanians, and Ukranians. The Spanish branch of the family ruled Spain and its colonies in the New World.

Die Albertina, Wien

Meine Heimat ist Österreich. Natürlich nicht ganz Österreich, da gibt es ja entlegene° Täler im Vorarlberg[4], von denen ich keine Ahnung habe, wie die meisten Wiener, also sagen wir: Meine Heimat ist Wien.

Lissabon° hat ein angenehmeres Klima, aber meine Heimat ist Wien. Die Luft in Oslo ist gesünder, aber meine Heimat ist Wien. Das Essen in Paris ist interessanter, aber Wien ist meine Heimat. Die Menschen in Kopenhagen sind freundlicher, aber ich bin halt° Wiener. In Berlin kann ich problemloser° parken, aber Wien bleibt Wien.

Schließlich° bin ich in Wien geboren, wenn ich auch zugeben° muss, dass ich damals noch jung war und auf meinen Geburtsort keinen Einfluss hatte; trotzdem, meine ersten Eindrücke waren Wiener Eindrücke: Der strenge Vater, die eingeschüchterte° Mutter, die ungerechten° Lehrer, die boshaften Schulkollegen°, die Unsicherheit, die Prügel°, die Enttäuschungen – das alles habe ich Wien zu verdanken°. Es hat natürlich auch positive Eindrücke in meiner Kindheit gegeben – lassen Sie mich nachdenken ...

Warum ist Wien meine Heimat? Nun, ich identifiziere mich mit dem Wiener Charakter, der zwar nicht sehr positiv zu beurteilen° ist, aber dafür° kann ich mich auf seine negativen Aspekte verlassen. Jeder Wiener kennt den typischen Wiener Charakter, denn er kennt seinen eigenen. Schwamm drüber!° Wien ist eine schöne Stadt, vielleicht nicht ganz so schön wie Venedig oder Honolulu, aber trotzdem eine schöne Stadt, auf die ich stolz sein kann, so wie ein Frankfurter auf Frankfurt stolz ist, obwohl er dazu nicht die mindeste Ursache° hat. [...]

Eigentlich hat man eine Heimat nur deshalb, damit° man etwas zu verteidigen hat. Wer nichts zu verteidigen hat, ist heimatlos. Ich wäre bereit, Wien nicht nur mit Worten, sondern auch mit Taten zu verteidigen, allerdings° mit einigen Einschränkungen°. Ich würde, zum Beispiel, gerne den Inhalt der Albertina[5] verteidigen, aber nicht den Bunker in der Gumpendorferstraße.[6] Ich würde auch lieber Wien in der Biedermeierzeit[7] verteidigen als Wien in der Nazizeit, überhaupt° würde ich Wien lieber im vorigen° Jahrhundert verteidigen, denn was sollte ich jetzt verteidigen? Die U-Bahn? Das Hilton? Den ORF[8]? Vielleicht ist das unlogisch, denn man muss das Ganze verteidigen, nicht nur die bevorzugten° Teile des Ganzen. Heimat bleibt eben° Heimat, auch wenn man mit ihr geschlagen° ist. [...]

Gäbe es die gute alte Zeit nicht, hätten wir überhaupt° keine Heimat. Wir fühlen uns im modernen Wien wohl, weil wir die Tradition des alten Wiens pflegen°, das wir Gott sei Dank überwunden° haben. Wir haben keine Habsburger, kein Weltreich und keine gute Luft mehr. Wir haben uns eine neue Heimat geschaffen°, damit wir uns der alten Heimat verbunden° fühlen können. [...]

remote
Lisbon
***bin ...** happen to be* / **problemlos = ohne Problem**
after all / *admit*
intimidated / *unfair* / = **böse Mitschüler** / *beatings*
***habe ...** I owe to Vienna*
assess / ***zwar ... aber dafür** = it's true . . . but on the other hand* / ***Schwamm ...** Let's forget it!*
***mindeste ...** slightest reason*
nur deshalb ... *only so that*
to be sure
qualifications
in general
im vorigen = im letzten (19. Jahrhundert)
preferred
just / *afflicted; stuck*
überhaupt = gar
cultivate
overcome
created
connected to

---

[4] **Vorarlberg:** the westernmost Austrian **Bundesland**, see map, p. 407.
[5] **Albertina:** a famous collection of works of art on paper housed in museum of the same name.
[6] **Bunker in der Gumpendorferstraße:** one of six massive, concrete anti-aircraft towers built in 1942.
[7] **Biedermeierzeit:** the period between the end of the Napoleonic wars in 1815 and the revolution of 1848, in which the arts flourished under middle-class patronage.
[8] **ORF = Österreichischer Rundfunk** (Austrian Broadcasting Company)

Die Heimat der Wiener liegt in der Illusion. Ihre tägliche Zerstörung ist ein Teil unserer Heimatliebe. Daher° kann sich auch jeder Wiener seine geliebte Heimat so vorstellen wie er will. Einer° stellt sich unter Heimat die Donau vor, der zweite° den Grillparzer[9], der dritte den Grillparzer wie er in der Donau ertrinkt°. Wichtig ist nur, dass es damals besser war als heute.

In unserer Wiener Heimat gibt es keine Einsamkeit. In unserer Heimat wollen alle dasselbe°: die Heimat. In der Heimat liegt unsere Solidarität, die man sonst nicht merkt. Alle Wiener, die sich gnadenlos bekämpfen°, haben die selbe Heimat. In allen Wienern schlägt das gleiche° goldene Wiener Herz. Wenn sie es nur merken würden!

daher = darum
***einer = jemand / der zweite = eine andere Person** / drowns*

the same thing
***sich ...** fight with each other ruthlessly / same*

[9] **Franz Grillparzer (1791–1872):** the greatest Austrian dramatist of the nineteenth century, still widely performed and taught in schools.

NACH DEM LESEN

SAM **Lab Manual** Kap. 14, Diktat.

SAM **Workbook** 14, 0.

A Antworten Sie auf Deutsch.

1. Warum hat Georg Kreisler seine Karriere als Musiker in den USA und nicht in Österreich begonnen?
2. Warum sagt er, seine Heimat ist nicht ganz Österreich, sondern nur Wien?
3. Was ist in anderen europäischen Hauptstädten anders – oder sogar besser – als in Wien?
4. Er erzählt witzig-satirisch über seine Wiener Jugend. Was sagt er darüber?
5. Hat er auch positive Eindrücke aus seiner Kindheit?
6. Was sagt er über den Wiener Charakter?
7. Er schreibt, man hat eine Heimat, damit man etwas zu verteidigen hat. Was würde er an seiner Heimatstadt verteidigen? Was lieber nicht?
8. Was würden Sie an Ihrer Heimatstadt verteidigen? Was nicht?
9. Was meint er, wenn er sagt: „Die Heimat der Wiener liegt in der Illusion"?

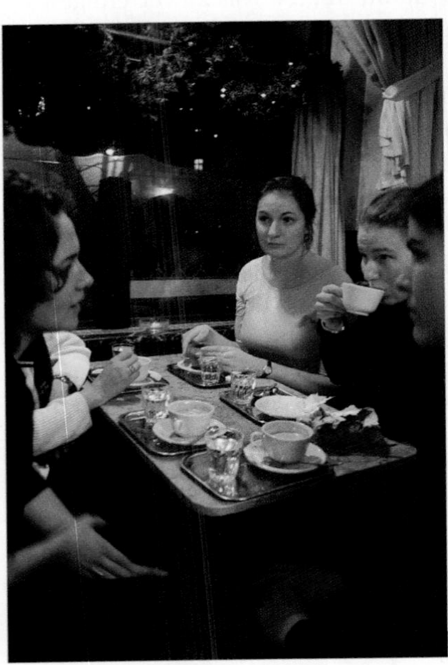

Wiener Kaffeehaus-Kultur (Café Tiroler Hof)

B **Gruppendiskussion: Wie könnten wir das ändern?** An Ihrer Uni gibt es sicher Sachen, die Sie gern ändern würden. Machen Sie eine Liste davon. Dann diskutieren Sie, wie man sie ändern oder anders machen könnte.

BEISPIEL: Die Bibliothek schließt zu früh. Das müsste man ändern. Sie sollte länger offen bleiben, besonders am Semesterende. Ja, das wäre viel besser. Dann hätte man mehr Zeit zu lernen. Aber natürlich würde das mehr kosten. Wer würde das bezahlen?

Prepare by reviewing "Specifying time" in the **Zusammenfassung und Wiederholung 3** in the Workbook section of your SAM.

C **Übung: Eine witzige Anekdote aus Österreich.** Provide the missing time word or phrase (in parentheses) in the following anecdote.

_______ (*Many years ago*), _______ (*when*) noch relativ wenige Touristen nach Österreich kamen, erzählte man eine Anekdote über eine reiche Amerikanerin, die _______ (*one month*) in den österreichischen Alpen verbrachte. Sie wohnte in einem gemütlichen Hotel in einem kleinen Dorf, wo die Menschen sie sehr interessant fanden. _______ (*Each morning*), _______ (*when*) sie Frühstück aß, bestellte sie nur wenig zu essen: ein weich gekochtes Ei [*soft-boiled egg*] und eine Tasse Kaffee. _______ (*Whenever*) das Wetter gut war, verbrachte sie _______ (*the whole day*) draußen und aß Brot und Käse aus ihrem Rucksack, _______ (*when*) sie Hunger hatte. _______ (*When*) die Dame endlich wieder nach Hause musste, sagte sie dem Wirt [*innkeeper*] _______ (*on Sunday*), sie würde _______ (*day after tomorrow*) abfahren. _______ (*On Tuesday*) bestellte sie nach dem Frühstück die Rechnung [*bill*]. Sie las die Rechnung und sagte _______ (*for a while*) nichts. Darauf stand „für 28 Eier: 300 Schilling". Es stimmte, sie hatte _______ (*for weeks*) _______ (*every morning*) ein weiches Ei gegessen, aber sie konnte sich nicht erinnern, _______ (*when*) sie je in ihrem Leben so teure Eier gegessen hatte. Sie ließ sofort den Wirt kommen und bat ihn um eine Erklärung. „_______ (*When*) ich _______ (*every morning*) mein Ei bestellte," sagte sie, „wusste ich nicht, dass sie bei Ihnen so selten [*rare*] sind." Der Wirt antwortete: „Ja, wissen Sie, gnädige Frau [*Madame*], die Eier sind bei uns *nicht* so selten, aber *Amerikanerinnen* sehr." Sie lachte, bezahlte die Rechnung und sagte, sie würde _______ (*next year*) wiederkommen. „Hoffentlich sind _______ (*then*) Amerikanerinnen _______ (*no longer*) so selten und die Eier weniger teuer!"

Austrian currency from 1925 until 2002 was the schilling. **100 Groschen = 1 Schilling**.

D **Übung: Partizipien und Adjektive.** For each pair of sentences below, fill in the past participle cued in English in the first sentence. In the second sentence, it is used as an attributive adjective. Don't forget the adjective ending!

1. Wer hat im Zimmer _______? (*straightened up*)
   Es ist schön in einem _______ Zimmer zu sitzen.
2. Letztes Jahr habe ich sehr viel Geld _______. (*saved*)
   Mit meinem _______ Geld will ich eine Reise ins Ausland machen.
3. Hat man dir den Rucksack _______? (*stolen*)
   Ja, und meine neue Kamera war leider im _______ Rucksack.
4. Ich habe meine Hemden _______. (*washed*)
   Die _______ Hemden hängen draußen hinter dem Haus.
5. Der Mann, mit dem sie sich verlobt hat, ist immer gut _______. (*dressed*)
   Sie geht nur mit gut _______ Männern aus.
6. Frau Schwarzer hat ihren Wagen selber _______. (*repaired*)
   Ihr _______ Wagen läuft jetzt gut.

E Gruppenarbeit: Buttje, Buttje, in der See. Es gibt ein bekanntes norddeutsches Märchen („Der Fischer und seine Frau"), in dem ein großer Butt (*flounder*) einem Fischer seine Wünsche erfüllt (*grants*). Der Fischer ruft ihn immer wieder aus der See mit den Worten: „Buttje, Buttje, in der See" und sagt ihm, was er sich wünscht. Jetzt sagen Sie einander, was Sie sich wünschen. Antworten Sie, ob Sie den Wunsch erfüllen können oder nicht.

BEISPIEL: A: Ich wünschte, ich könnte wie ein Vogel fliegen!
B: Das kann ich dir leider nicht erfüllen!

F Wenn ich ein Vöglein wär'. You have learned that the subjunctive is used to express wishes contrary to fact. As you might expect, this use of subjunctive occurs frequently in poems about love and longing. A well-known German folk song begins like this:

Wenn ich ein Vöglein wär'
Und auch zwei Flüglein° hätt' — *little wings*
Flög' ich zu dir.
Weil's aber nicht kann sein,
Bleib' ich allhier°. — = ***hier***

Try creating a short poem of your own (either rhymed or not) in which you express such an unfulfillable wish.

Wenn ich ...
...
Dann ...

Using the subjunctive to write a speculative essay

The essay topic asks you to speculate about what you *would* do *if* you had the power to rule the world. Because you will be writing about a situation contrary to fact, you must use the subjunctive mood. However, a series of sentences all beginning with „Ich würde ...“ would soon become boring. Here are two strategies for making your essay more interesting:

- Combine subjunctive and indicative clauses:

  Weil viele Menschen nicht genug zu essen **haben, würde** ich ...

- Use modal verbs to make your essay more varied:

  Wenn ich noch Zeit hätte, dann **könnte** (or **wollte**) ich ...

Schreiben wir mal: Wenn ich die Welt regieren könnte. Stellen Sie sich vor, Sie könnten eine Woche lang die Welt regieren. Was würden Sie für die Völker der Erde tun? Was würden Sie ändern? Schreiben Sie eine Seite darüber.

G Wie sagt man das auf Deutsch?

1. Would you like to go out with us tomorrow night?
2. That would be great, but unfortunately I don't feel very well.
3. That's a shame! Perhaps we could go on an outing together on Saturday.
4. Gladly, if I'm better! My old friend Rainer will be here, and maybe he could come along.

5. Max has been in Vienna for weeks.
6. It would be nice to write him a postcard.
7. If only I knew where he is living now.
8. He's either in the Hotel Europa or in a youth hostel.

9. Can't you study in your room?
10. No, Marie always disturbs me with her loud music.
11. If you didn't have a piano in your room, you wouldn't have a problem.
12. That's right, but then I would have to look for a new roommate.

Profile of Austria

Area: 83,858 square kilometers; 32,377 square miles (slightly smaller than the state of Maine)
Population: 8,193,000; density 98 people per square kilometer (253 people per square mile)
Currency: der Euro; 1 € = 100 Cent
Major Cities: Wien (English: Vienna; capital, pop. 1,700,000), Graz, Linz, Salzburg, Innsbruck
Religion: 73% Roman Catholic, 5% Protestant, 22% other

Austria consists of nine states (**Bundesländer**). It became a member of the European Union in 1995. In addition to basic industries such as machinery, iron and steel, textiles, and chemicals, tourism provides an important source of income. The literacy rate is 98%.

Austria plays a vital role in the United Nations, and Vienna is an important point of contact between eastern and western Europe. With the opening of the "UNO City" in 1979, Vienna became the third seat of the United Nations. It is also the headquarters for OPEC (the Organization of Petroleum Exporting Countries).

Innsbruck, Blick nach Norden auf die Nordkette

Das Palmenhaus im Schönbrunner Park, Wien; erbaut 1882

KAPITEL

15

Fußballfans während der Weltmeisterschaft 2006

Kulturelle Vielfalt

Kommunikation

- Talking about houses and apartments

Kultur

- Cultural diversity in the German-speaking countries

In diesem Kapitel

- **Lyrik zum Vorlesen**
  Vier Gedichte von Mascha Kaléko
- **Grammatik**
  1. Passive voice
  2. The present participle
- **Lesestück**
  Zafer Şenocak, "Ich bin das andere Kind"
- **Almanach**
  Foreigners Living and Working in Germany

DIALOGE

Lab Manual Kap. 15, Dialoge, Fragen, Hören Sie gut zu!

Ich bin *doch* hier geboren: See p. 261 for flavoring particle **doch**.

Wo liegt die Heimat?

Emine, Schülerin aus einer türkischen Familie in Berlin-Kreuzberg, wird für die Schülerzeitung interviewt.

INTERVIEWER: Emine, du kannst ja perfekt Deutsch. Was sprecht ihr denn zu Hause?

EMINE: Ja, ich bin doch hier geboren, und mit meinen Geschwistern spreche ich oft Deutsch. Aber wir sprechen mit den Eltern und Großeltern immer Türkisch.

INTERVIEWER: Wo fühlst du dich eigentlich zu Hause, in Deutschland oder in der Türkei?

EMINE: Das frag' ich mich auch. Hier in Berlin habe ich viele Freunde, aber in Istanbul auch viele liebe Kusinen. Eigentlich fühle ich mich in beiden Kulturen zu Hause.

verpasste: Notice the adjectival use of this past participle.

Die verpasste Geburtstagsfeier

LILLI: Bei Sonjas Geburtstagsfeier wurde bis drei Uhr früh getanzt. Wo warst denn du? Wurdest du nicht eingeladen?

FELIX: Doch, und ich wünschte, ich wäre dabei gewesen. Aber ich war auf Urlaub in Spanien.

LILLI: Du hättest wenigstens anrufen können, um ihr zu gratulieren.

FELIX: Da hast du Recht. Das hätte ich machen sollen.

Vor der Post

Vor der Hauptpost sehen Herr und Frau Becker einen Briefkasten.

drauf (*colloq.*) = **darauf**

FRAU BECKER: Da kannst du deinen Brief einwerfen.

HERR BECKER: Augenblick. Hab' ich genug Briefmarken drauf? Vielleicht sollte ich hineingehen und ihn wiegen lassen.

FRAU BECKER: Zeig mal her – aber Hartmanns sind doch umgezogen! Das ist ihre alte Adresse.

HERR BECKER: Verflixt nochmal! Das hätte ich nicht vergessen sollen.

FRAU BECKER: Ach, reg dich nicht auf! Wir kaufen schnell einen neuen Umschlag.

Hans Becker
Kieler Straße 314
22083 Hamburg

Frau
Annemarie Hartmann
Vogelsangstraße 17
60327 Frankfurt

Wortschatz 1

An der Post

ein·werfen (wirft ein), warf ein, hat eingeworfen to mail (a letter); (*literally*) to throw in
wiegen, wog, hat gewogen to weigh (*trans. and intrans.*)
der **Briefkasten, ¨** mailbox
der **Umschlag, ¨e** envelope
die **Adresse, -n** address
die **Briefmarke, -n** stamp
die **Post** post office; postal service; mail

Verben

sich auf·regen (**über** + *acc.*) to get upset (about), get excited (about)
dabei sein to be present, attend
sich fragen to wonder, ask oneself
Ich frage mich, ob ... I wonder if . . .
gratulieren (+ *dat.*) to congratulate
Ich gratuliere dir zum Geburtstag! Happy birthday!
tanzen to dance

Substantive

(das) **Spanien** Spain
die **Feier, -n** celebration, party
die Geburtstagsfeier birthday party
die **Vielfalt** variety, diversity

Nützlicher Ausdruck

Zeig mal her. Let's see. Show it to me.

Mit anderen Worten

Verflixt nochmal! (*colloq.*) = **So ein Mist!** (*Das sagt man, wenn man sich über etwas sehr ärgert.*)

Spanien: *adj.* **spanisch.** Idiom: **Das kommt mir spanisch vor** (*It's all Greek to me*). The expression recalls the elaborate customs introduced to the Habsburg court from Spain in the 16th century.

Variationen

A Persönliche Fragen

1. Emine weiß nicht genau, wo sie sich eigentlich zu Hause fühlt. Wo fühlen Sie sich zu Hause: wo Sie jetzt wohnen, wo Ihre Eltern wohnen oder wo Sie geboren sind?
2. Felix hat Sonjas Geburtstagsfeier verpasst. Haben Sie je etwas Wichtiges verpasst? Erzählen Sie davon.
3. Schreiben Sie oft Briefe? An wen? Telefonieren Sie lieber oder benutzen Sie E-Mail?
4. Wo ist hier der nächste Briefkasten?
5. Wann gehen Sie zur Post? Was lassen Sie dort machen?

Telefonieren = *to use the phone, talk on the phone* (intrans.): **Es ist billiger abends zu telefonieren.**

anrufen = *to call up, telephone* (trans.): **Rufe mich morgen vor zehn an.**

B Gruppenarbeit: Reg dich nicht auf! (*Take it easy!*) Manchmal regt man sich unnötig auf. In welchen Situationen regen Sie sich besonders auf? Wenn Sie etwas vergessen haben? Wenn Sie etwas Wichtiges vorhaben? Machen Sie zusammen eine Liste von solchen Situationen.

BEISPIEL: Ich rege mich auf, wenn ich ein Referat halten muss.

C Klassendiskussion: Geburtstagstraditionen Was macht man in Ihrer Familie, wenn jemand Geburtstag hat? Gibt es bestimmte Familientraditionen? Feiern Sie zu Hause oder im Restaurant? Lädt man viele Gäste ein oder gibt es nur eine kleine Feier? Darf sich das Geburtstagskind (die Person, die Geburtstag hat) sein Lieblingsessen bestellen?

LYRIK ZUM VORLESEN

Mascha Kaléko wurde 1907 als Tochter eines russischen Vaters und einer österreichischen Mutter geboren. Nach dem Ersten Weltkrieg zog die Familie nach Marburg. Kaléko studierte in Berlin, wo sie in den frühen 30er-Jahren begann, für führende Zeitungen zu schreiben. 1938 verließ sie Hitlers Drittes Reich und ging nach New York ins Exil. 1966 zog sie nach Israel, wo sie 1975 starb.

Kalékos Gedichte, die oft in der Alltagssprache der Großstadt geschrieben sind, zeigen Witz, Ironie und manchmal etwas Melancholie. Diese vier kurzen Gedichte erschienen (*appeared*) zuerst in der Sammlung *Kleines Lesebuch für Große* (1934).

Von Mensch zu Mensch

Nun, da du fort° bist, scheint mir alles trübe°.
Hätt' ich's geahnt°, ich ließe dich nicht gehn.
Was wir vermissen°, scheint uns immer schön.
Woran das liegen mag° –. Ist das nun Liebe?

= ***weg*** / = ***traurig***
foreseen
Was ... = ***Was uns fehlt***
Woran ... *I wonder why that is*

Von Elternhaus und Jugendzeit

Jetzt bin ich groß. Mir blüht kein Märchenbuch.°
Ich muss schon oft „Sie" zu mir selber sagen.
Nur manchmal noch, an jenen stillen° Tagen,
Kommt meine Kindheit heimlich ° zu Besuch.

Mir ... *Life's not going to be a fairy tale.*
jenen ... *those quiet*
in secret

Von den Jahreszeiten

Der Frühling fand diesmal im Saale statt.°
Der Sommer war lang und gesegnet°.
– Ja, sonst gab es Winter in dieser Stadt.
Und sonntags hat's meistens geregnet ...

fand ... *took place in a room*
blissful

Von Reise und Wanderung

Einmal sollte man seine Siebensachen°
Fortrollen aus diesen glatten Geleisen°.

Man sollte sich aus dem Staube machen°
Und früh am Morgen unbekannt verreisen°.

possessions
Fortrollen ... *roll off of these smooth tracks*
sich ... *hit the road*
= ***wegreisen***

Mascha Kaléko (1907–1975)

GRAMMATIK

1. Passive voice (*das Passiv*)

Compare the following sentence pairs:

Die meisten Studenten lesen diesen Roman.	*Most students read this novel.*
Dieser Roman wird von den meisten Studenten gelesen.	*This novel is read by most students.*

Both sentences essentially convey the same idea, but the first is in the ACTIVE VOICE while the second is in the PASSIVE VOICE. The passive voice emphasizes that something is *being done* (the *novel* is being *read*). The active voice emphasizes that someone is *doing* something (the *students* are reading it).

In active sentences, the grammatical subject is the *performer* of an action (called the *agent*).

Die Studenten *lesen.* *The students read.*

In passive sentences, the grammatical subject is the *object* of the action.

Der Roman *wird gelesen.* *The novel is being read.*

Since the passive voice emphasizes the thing acted upon, most passive sentences do not express the agent at all. For passive sentences with an agent, see p. 418.

Every passive sentence can be thought of as the transformation of an active sentence *with a transitive verb and a direct object*. The direct object (always in the *accusative*) of the active sentence becomes the *subject* (always in the *nominative*) of the passive sentence.

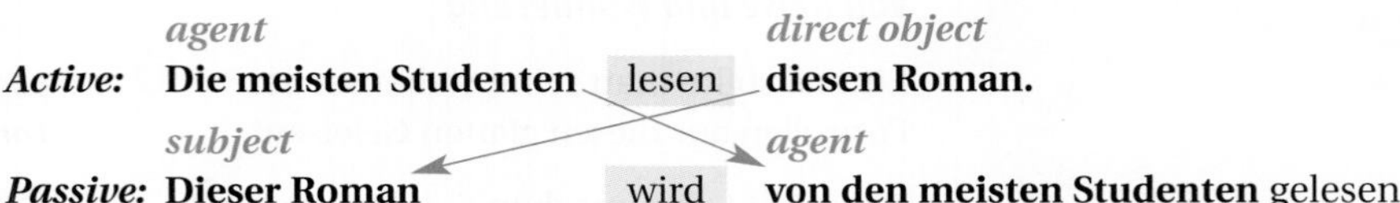
agent
direct object
Active: **Die meisten Studenten** lesen **diesen Roman.**
subject
agent
Passive: **Dieser Roman** wird **von den meisten Studenten** gelesen.

Formation of the German passive voice

The passive voice in English consists of the auxiliary verb *to be* plus a past participle.

Active voice	→	Passive voice			
			auxiliary		*participle*
They see him.	→	*He*	***is***		***seen.***
We never do that.	→	*That*	***is***	*never*	***done.***
They drank coffee.	→	*Coffee*	***was***		***drunk.***

The passive voice in German consists of the auxiliary verb **werden** plus a past participle.

Active voice	→	Passive voice			
			auxiliary		*participle*
Sie sehen ihn.	→	Er	**wird**		**gesehen.**
Wir machen das nie.	→	Das	**wird**	nie	**gemacht.**
Sie tranken Kaffee.	→	Kaffee	**wurde**		**getrunken.**

Lab Manual Kap. 15, Var. zu Üb. 1 und Üb. 3.

Workbook Kap. 15, A, B.

1 Übung: Was wird morgens gemacht, bevor Emine zur Schule geht? Jeden Morgen bevor Emine in die Schule geht, werden verschiedene Sachen gemacht. Sagen Sie, was gemacht wird.

Das Frühstück wird ...

Der Tee wird ...

Below is a table showing the formation of all tenses of **gesehen werden** (*to be seen*).

Passive voice				
passive infinitive: **gesehen werden** *to be seen*				
present	Sie **wird**	gesehen.	*She **is***	*seen.*
past	Sie **wurde**	gesehen.	*She **was***	*seen.*
future	Sie **wird**	gesehen **werden.**	*She **will be***	*seen.*
perfect	Sie **ist**	gesehen **worden.**	*She **has been***	*seen.*
			*(or: She **was***	*seen.)*
past perfect	Sie **war**	gesehen **worden.**	*She **had been***	*seen.*

Note the following:

Use Appendix 2, pp. 439–440, to review the past participles of strong transitive verbs.

- In both German and English passive, the past participle (**gesehen**/*seen*) appears in all tenses. The auxiliary verb (**werden** = *to be*) is conjugated.
- The normal past participle of **werden** (**geworden**) is contracted to **worden** in the perfect tenses of the passive voice.
- The German passive infinitive is in the reverse order of English:

NOTE ON USAGE

Summary of uses of *werden*

Be careful not to confuse the three uses of **werden**:

- as main verb = *become, get*

  Sie **wird** alt. — She's ***getting*** old.

- as auxiliary verb for future tense: **werden** + *infinitive*

  Sie **wird** mich sehen. — She ***will*** see me.

- as auxiliary verb for passive voice: **werden** + *past participle*

  Sie **wird** gesehen. — She ***is*** seen.

This advertisement contains two passive structures. Can you figure them out from context?

Lab Manual Kap. 15, Üb. 9, 14, and Var. zu Üb. 8, 12.

Workbook Kap. 15, E–G.

Übungen 2, 3, 6: Each of these sentences in the active voice has a personal pronoun or **man** as its subject. These pronoun subjects disappear in the passive voice. Do not try to express an agent in these passive sentences.

2 Übung. Change the sentences from the active to the passive. Be careful to keep the same tense as in the active sentence.

Present tense

1. Man liest diese Romane oft.
2. Morgens kaufen wir die Zeitung.
3. Bei uns sieht man nicht viele Deutsche.
4. Ich rufe meine Eltern jedes Wochenende an.
5. Man versteht mich nicht!
6. Wir feiern morgen deinen Geburtstag.
7. Wir räumen die Schlafzimmer jeden Samstag auf.
8. Ich schicke dieses Paket nach Australien.

Simple past tense

9. Im 18. Jahrhundert schrieb man viele Briefe.
10. In der ganzen Welt las man seinen ersten Roman.
11. Man zeigte den Film in jedem Kino.
12. Man erzählte viele Witze.

Future tense

13. Was wird man sagen?
14. Man wird dieses Wahlplakat nicht sehen.
15. Man wird neue Wohnungen für die Armen bauen.
16. Man wird dieses Thema besprechen.

Perfect tense

17. Man hat die alte Wohnung verkauft.
18. Man hat die Briefe eingeworfen.
19. Man hat den jungen Künstler eingeladen.
20. Man hat unsere Umwelt verschmutzt.

Das neue Museum heißt Deutsches Auswandererhaus und dokumentiert die deutsche Auswanderung im 19. Jahrhundert. (You can find its website by entering "deutsches auswandererhaus" in your search engine.)

Fachwerkhaus (*half-timbered house*) und modernes Museumsgebäude (Bremerhaven). Welches wurde früher gebaut?

3 Übung: Das wird sofort gemacht! Sie sind alle Hotelangestellte. Ihre Professorin ist Gast im Hotel und bittet Sie etwas für sie zu machen. Sie sagen, alles wird sofort gemacht.

BEISPIEL: Können Sie mir bitte diese Uhr reparieren?
Ja, sie wird sofort repariert!

1. Können Sie mir bitte einen Brief einwerfen?
2. Können Sie mir bitte einen Tisch reservieren?
3. Können Sie mir bitte das Zimmer aufräumen?
4. Können Sie mir bitte meine Kleider aufhängen?
5. Können Sie mir bitte das Bett machen?
6. Können Sie mir bitte ein Taxi bestellen?

4 Übung. Erzählen Sie die „Lebensgeschichten" der folgenden Dinge im Passiv. Das wird so gemacht:

You can connect your sentences with **dann: Die Zeitung wird zuerst von Journalisten geschrieben, *dann* wird sie ...**

BEISPIEL: Zeitung: Journalisten / schreiben
Die Zeitung wird zuerst von Journalisten geschrieben. (usw.)

1. die Zeitung: Journalisten / schreiben
am Morgen auf der Straße / kaufen
zwischen sieben und halb acht / lesen
im Zug / vergessen
alter Mann / finden und lesen
2. der Roman: Schriftsteller / schreiben
in der Buchhandlung / kaufen
zu Hause / lesen
einem Freund / leihen
vom Freund / verlieren
3. die Wurst: Metzger (*butcher*) / machen
Restaurant / kaufen
in Wasser / kochen
zum Mittagessen / servieren

4. die Postkarte: in Italien / kaufen
Barbara / schreiben
zur Post / bringen
in den Briefkasten / einwerfen
Familie / lesen

Erzählen Sie weiter von den folgenden Gegenständen (*objects*): das Buch, das Auto, das Brötchen, die Weinflasche, das Foto.

5 Gruppenarbeit: Trivial Pursuit. (*2 Mannschaften*) Jetzt spielen Sie ein bisschen „Trivial Pursuit". Jede Mannschaft stellt der anderen Fragen über Geschichte, berühmte Personen, Kunst, Literatur usw. Benutzen Sie das Passiv.

BEISPIEL: Von wem wurde *Faust* geschrieben?
Wo wurde Jazz zuerst gespielt?

Passive voice with a modal verb

It is often necessary to say that something *must* be done, *should* be done, *can* be done, or *may* be done. In such cases, use the modal verb with a passive infinitive.

Active:	Er muss es	**tun.**	*He has **to do** it.*
Passive:	Es muss	**getan werden.**	*It has **to be done**.*

This table shows the formation of all tenses of a modal verb with the passive voice. In this chapter, you will only be required to use present and past tenses actively.

Passive with a modal verb		
present	Das **muss** getan werden.	*That **has** to be done.*
past	Das **musste** getan werden.	*That **had** to be done.*
future	Das **wird** getan werden **müssen**.	*That **will have** to be done.*
perfect	Das **hat** getan werden **müssen**.	*That **had** to be done.*
past perfect	Das **hatte** getan werden **müssen**.	*That **had had** to be done.*

NOTE: The dependent infinitive is the two-word *passive infinitive* (e.g., **getan werden**) rather than the one-word active infinitive (**tun**). The modal is the inflected verb. The passive infinitive remains unchanged throughout all tenses.

Lab Manual Kap. 15, Var. zu Üb. 6.

Workbook Kap. 15, C.

6 Übung. Change the sentences from active to passive voice. Be sure to use the same tense as in the active sentence.

Present

1. Wir müssen die Wohnung aufräumen.
2. Wir müssen noch den Wein kaufen.
3. Du darfst deine Freunde einladen.
4. Ich muss Oma nach Hause bringen.
5. Ich soll diese Briefe wiegen.

Past

6. Man musste die Fenster schließen.
7. Man musste die Kinder abholen.
8. Man konnte das Mädchen nicht interviewen.
9. Man durfte nichts kochen.
10. Ich durfte diesen Witz nicht erzählen.

7 Übung: Was muss nachmittags gemacht werden, wenn Emine nach Hause kommt? Nach der Schule muss vieles gemacht werden. Sagen Sie, was alles noch gemacht werden muss.

Das Gemüse muss ...

Briefmarken müssen ...

Ein Brief muss ...

8 Gruppenarbeit: Was kann gemacht werden? (*mit offenen Büchern*) Diskutieren Sie, was gemacht werden kann, um die Umwelt zu retten. Unten sind einige Möglichkeiten zum Kombinieren; Sie können auch Ihre eigenen Ideen benutzen.

BEISPIEL: Der Müll kann zum Recycling gebracht werden.

der Müll	schließen
das Altglas	finden
Alternativen	organisieren
Atomkraftwerke	zum Recycling bringen
Demonstrationen	ändern
unser Denken	bauen
umweltfreundliche Autos	sammeln

Passive voice with an agent

Most passive sentences do not mention the agent performing the action.

Diese Häuser wurden sehr schnell gebaut.	*These houses were built very quickly.*
Das wird oft gesagt.	*That is often said.*

When the person performing the action *is* mentioned, **von** + *dative* is used.

Ich wurde **von Sonja** eingeladen.	*I was invited by Sonja.*
Dieses Haus wurde **von meinen Großeltern** gebaut.	*This house was built by my grandparents.*

Lab Manual Kap. 15, Üb. 9.

9 Übung. Restate the following sentences in the passive. Use the same tense as in the active sentence.

BEISPIEL: Meine Freundin liest jetzt den Roman.
Der Roman wird jetzt von meiner Freundin gelesen.

1. Fast alle Physikstudenten belegen dieses Seminar.
2. Viele deutsche Schüler tragen gern Turnschuhe.
3. Unser Professor empfahl dieses Buch.
4. Alle Schüler in der Schweiz müssen Fremdsprachen lernen.
5. Michael hat mich eingeladen.
6. Die Gruppe hat das Referat besprochen.
7. Mein Freund hat die Gäste abgeholt.
8. Die Kinder singen immer dieses Lied.
9. Der Gepäckträger (*porter*) schleppte den Koffer zum Taxi.
10. Die ganze Familie feiert Omas Geburtstag.

Info-Austausch

Partner B's information can be found in Appendix 1.

10 Von wem? Jeder Partner bekommt zwei Listen mit den Titeln **Was?** und **Von wem?** Stellen Sie einander Fragen im Passiv, um Ihre Listen zu ergänzen (*complete*).

BEISPIEL:

Was?	Von wem?
Don Giovanni komponieren	Bäcker
Brot backen	Mozart

A: Von wem wird Brot gebacken? B: Vom Bäcker.
B: Von wem wurde *Don Giovanni* komponiert? A: Von Mozart.

Partner A:

Was?	Von wem?
Hamlet schreiben	Automechaniker
Vorlesungen an der Uni halten	Schriftsteller
die 9. Symphonie komponieren	Goethe
Zeitungsartikel schreiben	Kellner
die Relativitätstheorie formulieren	Sigmund Freud

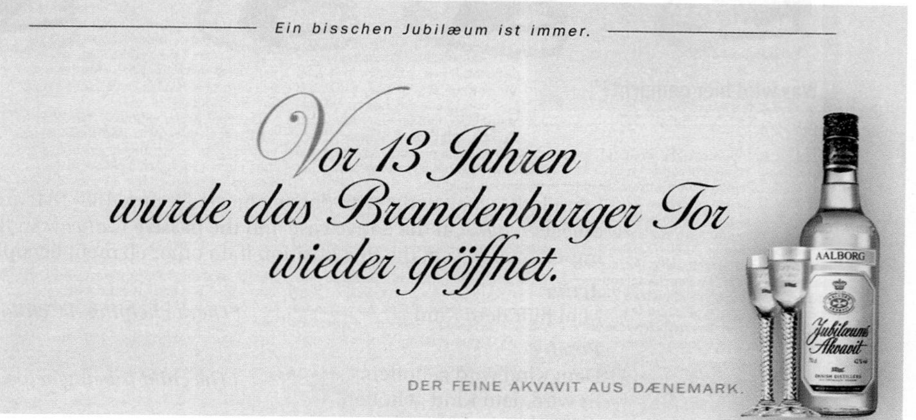

Note that impersonal passive is only passive in *structure*, not in *meaning*. The verb does not need to be transitive, but must designate a human activity. Impossible: ***Hier wird geregnet*** (not a human activity).

Impersonal passive

One use of the German passive voice has no precise English equivalent. It is used to say that some human activity is going on, without mentioning who performs it. No subject is expressed at all, and the verb is *always* in the third-person singular.

Bis halb vier **wurde gefeiert**.	*The party went on until 3:30.*
Hier **wird** bis zwei Uhr morgens **getanzt und gesungen**.	*There's dancing and singing here until 2:00 AM.*

If no other element occupies first position in the sentence, an impersonal **es** is used to fill it. This **es** is not a real subject and disappears if any other element occupies first position.[1]

Es wurde bis halb vier gefeiert.
Es wird hier bis zwei Uhr morgens getanzt.

SAM Workbook — **Workbook** Kap. 15, D–F, G–I.

11 Übung: Anders gesagt. Diese Sätze mit **man** kann man auch als unpersönliche Passivsätze formulieren.

BEISPIEL: Heute isst man um neun Uhr.
Heute wird um neun Uhr gegessen.

1. Hier singt man zu laut.
2. Beim Bäcker fängt man früh an.
3. In Leipzig demonstrierte man.
4. Damals arbeitete man schwer.
5. Morgen liest und schreibt man viel.
6. Jetzt kauft man ein.
7. Gestern tanzte man bis zwei Uhr.
8. In unserer Stadt baut man immer mehr.

„Was wird hier gemacht?"

---

[1] Similarly, when verbs with dative objects (see pp. 183–184) are used in the passive voice, their objects *remain* in the dative case and the passive is *always* in the third-person singular. An impersonal **es** is in the first position if no other element occupies it.

Active
Man hilft dem Kind. — *(They're helping the child.)*

Passive
Dem Kind wird geholfen. / Es wird dem Kind geholfen. — *(The child is being helped.)*

Refer to p. 149 for furniture vocabulary.

This vocabulary focuses on an everyday topic or situation. Your instructor may assign some supplementary vocabulary for active mastery.

Vokabeln zum Thema Haus und Wohnung

Hier ist der Grundriss (*floorplan*) vom Erdgeschoss einer typischen deutschen Wohnung. Wahrscheinlich gibt es auch noch einen ersten Stock mit mehr Schlafzimmern. Wie ist diese deutsche Wohnung anders als eine amerikanische? In Deutschland gibt es zum Beispiel keine eingebauten Schränke (*built-in closets*) wie in Amerika, sondern man hat einen großen Kleiderschrank (*wardrobe*) im Schlafzimmer. Merken Sie andere Unterschiede?

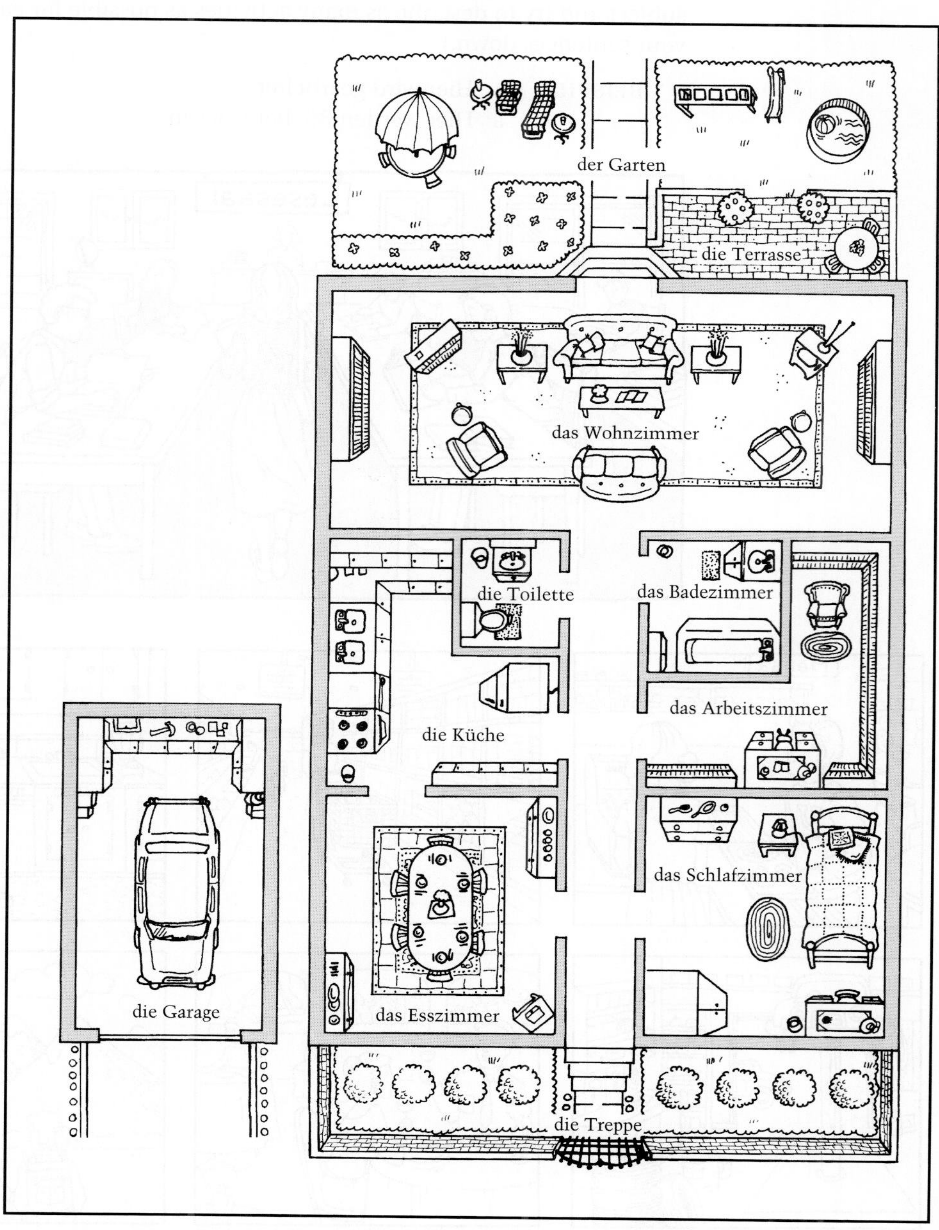

12 Übung: Was wird wo gemacht?

Um diese Übung zu machen müssen Sie zuerst die Namen der Zimmer wissen.

1. Wo wird das Essen gekocht?
2. Wo wird das Auto geparkt?
3. Wo werden Referate, Briefe usw. geschrieben?
4. Wo wird ferngesehen?
5. Was wird in der Küche gemacht?
6. Was wird im Garten gemacht?
7. Wo wird geschlafen?
8. Wo wird gebadet?
9. Wo wird gegessen?

13 Partnerarbeit: Was wird hier gemacht? Arbeiten Sie zusammen. Sagen Sie einander, was auf jedem Bild gemacht wird. (Use passive sentences with or without a subject and try to describe as many activities as possible for each picture. Then write your sentences down.)

BEISPIEL: A: Hier wird gearbeitet.
B: Hier werden Bücher gelesen.

2. The present participle (*das Partizip Präsens*)

To form the present participle (English: *sleeping*, *reading*, etc.) of a German verb, simply add **-d** to the infinitive.

schlafend	*sleeping*	**denkend**	*thinking*
folgend	*following*	**lesend**	*reading*

The present participle is used:

Remember that past participles can also be used as adjectives. See p. 308.

- as an attributive adjective with the standard adjective endings:

Wir wollen das **schlafende** Kind nicht stören.	*We don't want to disturb the sleeping child.*
Lesen Sie die **folgenden** Seiten.	*Read the following pages.*

- occasionally as an adverb:

Das Kind lief **weinend** ins Zimmer.	*The child ran into the room crying.*

The German present participle is *not* used as a verbal noun. German uses the infinitive for this purpose: *No Parking* = **Parken verboten** (see p. 191).

Schlafende Hunde beißen nicht.

SAM Lab Manual **Lab Manual** Kap. 15, Üb. 14.

14 Übung. Use the present participle of the cued verb as an adjective.

BEISPIEL: Wir können die Preise nicht mehr zahlen. (steigen)
Wir können die steigenden Preise nicht mehr zahlen.

1. Jeder Mensch weiß das. (denken)
2. Was meinen die Politiker? (führen)
3. Die Arbeitslosigkeit ist ein Problem. (wachsen)
4. Sie hörte die Kinder. (lachen)
5. Bitte stören Sie meinen Mitbewohner nicht. (schlafen)

Tschechische Studentenkneipe in Jena

LESESTÜCK

Tipps zum Lesen und Lernen

Tipps zum Vokabelnlernen

***German equivalents for** to think* The English verb *to think* has several meanings, for which German has various verbs (rather than just one). You have already learned most of these verbs as separate vocabulary items.

- When *to think* = *to have an opinion*, use **glauben**, **meinen**, or **finden**.

Ich **finde** das toll.	*I think that's great.*
Ich **meine**, das stimmt nicht.	*I think that's incorrect.*
Ich **glaube** schon.	*I think so.*
Ich **glaube** nicht.	*I don't think so.*

In contemporary colloquial usage, **denken** is frequently used as a synonym for **meinen**.

- When *to think* = *to think of, keep in mind*, use **denken an**.

Er **dachte an** seine Jugend.	*He was thinking of his youth.*
Denken Sie **an** die anderen.	*Think of the others.*

Synonyms for **halten für**: **Ich *finde* das zu schwer. Ich *meine*, das ist zu schwer.**

- When *to think* = *to think X is . . ., to take X for . . .*, use **halten für**.

Ich **hielt** sie **für** eine Deutsche.	*I thought she was a German.*
Ich **halte** das **für** zu schwer.	*I think that's too difficult.*

- When *to think* = *to think about, ponder*, use **sich etwas überlegen**.

Das muss ich mir **überlegen**.	*I have to think about that.*
Ich werde mir die Alternativen **überlegen**.	*I'll think about the alternatives.*

Übung: Wie sagt man das auf Deutsch?

1. I often think of you.
2. I think she's a good doctor.
3. What do *you* think?
4. I have to think about the answer.
5. I think that's a great idea!
6. Do you think I'm crazy?
7. I don't think so.

SAM **Workbook** Kap. 15, J, K.

SAM **Lab Manual** Kap. 15, Var. zu Üb. 6.

Leicht zu merken

der **Autor, -en**	
emigrieren	emigrieren
der **Essay, -s**	
die **Identität, -en**	Identität
interkulturell	interkulturell
konfrontieren	konfrontieren
die **Nationalität, -en**	Nationalität

Ausländische Studentinnen bereiten sich auf eine Klausur vor.

Einstieg in den Text

Recognizing the passive voice in context The following text contains four passive constructions. You will recognize them by the fact that they all have some form of **werden** plus a past participle. Here is the first occurrence of passive voice (l. 5):

> *... seine Gedichte, Essays, Artikel und Erzählungen sind in viele Sprachen übersetzt worden.*

As you encounter the others, jot them down and make sure you understand them. Other passive constructions in lines 9–10, 15–16, and 22.

Wortschatz 2

Verben

aus·sprechen (spricht aus), sprach aus, hat ausgesprochen to pronounce
erkennen, erkannte, hat erkannt to recognize
schütteln to shake
den Kopf schütteln to shake one's head
trennen to separate
übersetzen to translate

Substantive

der **Ausländer, -** foreigner (*m.*)
der / die **Erwachsene, -n** (*adj. noun*) adult, grown-up
der **Sinn** sense
Das hat keinen Sinn. That makes no sense. It's pointless.
der **Streit** argument, conflict
der **Türke, -n, -n** Turk (*m.*)
das **Thema,** *pl.* **Themen** topic, subject, theme
(das) **Türkisch** Turkish (language)
die **Ausländerin, -nen** foreigner (*f.*)
die **Kindheit, -en** childhood
die **Rede, -n** talk; speech
die Rede ist von ... They're talking about . . .
die **Ruhe** rest, quiet, peace
jemand in Ruhe lassen to leave someone in peace, leave alone
die **Seele, -n** soul
die **Türkin, -nen** Turk (*f.*)

Adjektive

brav well-behaved, good
erwachsen adult, grown-up
unschuldig innocent

Andere Vokabeln

vieles (*sing. pron.*) many things

Gegensätze

den Kopf schütteln ≠ nicken shake one's head (meaning no) ≠ nod (meaning yes)
unschuldig ≠ schuldig innocent ≠ guilty

Ich bin das andere Kind

Zafer Şenocak

Zafer Şenocak ist 1961 in Ankara (Türkei) geboren. 1970 emigrierte seine Familie nach München, wo er auch das Gymnasium besuchte. Also wuchs er nicht nur in der Türkei, sondern nach dem neunten Lebensjahr auch in Deutschland auf, wo er später Germanistik, Politik und Philosophie studierte.

Heute schreibt er auf Deutsch, und seine Gedichte, Essays, Artikel und Erzählungen sind in viele Sprachen übersetzt worden.

Die Hauptthemen dieses Autors sind die deutsch-türkische Literatur und die Probleme der interkulturellen Integration in Europa. Besonders wichtig sind ihm Momente des menschlichen Kontakts zwischen den Kulturen, denn erst dort werden wichtige Fragen zur Definition der eigenen Nationalität gestellt.

Im folgenden Ausschnitt denkt Kamile, eine junge türkisch-deutsche Frau, an ihre Kindheit und stellt sich Fragen zur eigenen Identität. Was wird aus einem Menschen, der seine ersten Jahre in der türkischen Kultur verbringt, aber später in die deutsche Sprache und Kultur hineinwächst°? Er ist mit dem Problem konfrontiert, wie sich seine Identität ändert, wenn seine Muttersprache Türkisch, allmählich° durch Deutsch ersetzt° wird.

grows into
gradually
replaced

Ich war zweimal Kind. Einmal auf türkisch, einmal auf deutsch. Als türkisches Kind konnte ich noch kein Deutsch, als deutsches Kind schon Türkisch. So lernte das türkische Kind Deutsch. Das deutsche Kind aber hat nie Türkisch lernen müssen.

Wenn von meiner Kindheit die Rede ist, weiß ich niemals° genau, welche gemeint ist, die türkische oder die deutsche. Wenn ich ein Wort geschrieben sehe wie „ruh", muss ich erst hören, wie es ausgesprochen wird, um zu verstehen, was damit gemeint ist. Das türkische Kind übersetzt es dem deutschen als „ruch", „Seele", das deutsche Kind aber schüttelt den Kopf, es weiß genau, was mit „ruh" gemeint ist. Es heißt doch nur ruhig sein, Ruhe haben, gib endlich Ruh'.

*= **nie***

Ich will in den Streit der beiden nicht eingreifen°. Es hätte keinen Sinn. Ein jedes soll glauben, was es will, verstehen, was es will, erzählen, was es will. Ein jedes° in seiner Sprache.

intervene
*= **Ein jedes Kind***

Das türkische Kind ist verschüchtert°. Es ist vielen Fremden begegnet°. Es wurde nie erwachsen. Es lebt. Das deutsche Kind aber musste denken und sterben, um groß zu werden. So bin ich jetzt Kind auf türkisch und erwachsen auf deutsch. Ich kann reden, was ich will, schreiben, was ich will, in welcher Sprache auch immer°, jedes meiner Worte hat eine türkische Kindheit. Wenn die Deutsche vergisst, erinnert sich das türkische Kind. Wenn das türkische Kind nicht versteht, erklärt die Deutsche. Ob das gut geht?°

intimidated / encountered
***in...** in whichever language*
***Ob...** I wonder if that will work out?*

„Die Deutschen sind Fremde", sagt mein Vater. „Wir verstehen sie nicht", sagt meine Mutter. „Vieles trennt uns." Sie hegen und pflegen° das türkische Kind, sorgen dafür°, dass es niemals groß wird. Es soll immer so bleiben, wie sie es sich vorstellen, brav, unschuldig, schüchtern.° Vor der Deutschen haben sie Angst. Sie ist ihnen fremd. Als Kind haben sie sie nicht weiter beachtet°. Sie waren sich unsicher, ob sie ihr eigenes Kind war.

***hegen...** lavish love upon*
***sorgen...** make sure*
shy
*= **gesehen***

„Ich bin es“, sage ich immer, wenn ich sie besuche. Als genügte ihnen nicht meine Erscheinung,° um mich zu erkennen. Ja, ich bin es noch. „Wir haben dich nicht verloren, Mädchen, du bist zurück“, ruft meine Mutter. Mein Vater singt. Ich könnte alles verstehen, das Gefühl haben, zu Hause zu sein. Aber ich nicke nur flüchtig°, wie eine, die andeuten° will, dass sie wenig Zeit hat und nicht bleiben kann.

Ich möchte meine Eltern über meine deutsche Kindheit ausfragen°. Sie aber erinnern sich nur an das türkische Kind. In ihren Augen bin ich nur das eine Kind. Mein deutsches Ich° reagiert gelassen°. Es lässt das türkische Kind in Ruhe. Das türkische Kind wurde sieben Jahre alt. Dann wurde es unsterblich.° Es führt Selbstgespäche°. Manchmal schreibt es auch Briefe an alte Bekannte. Briefe, die es nicht abschicken kann, weil es nicht weiß, wo jene abgeblieben sind°.

***Als...** As if my physical presence weren't enough for them*

= ***kurz und schnell** / convey*

ask about, quiz

ego, identity / calmly

immortal

= ***Monologe***

wo... was aus ihnen geworden ist

Autoaufkleber in Berlin

NACH DEM LESEN

Lab Manual Kap. 15, Diktat.

Workbook Kap. 15, L, M.

A Antworten Sie auf Deutsch.

1. Was meint die Frau, wenn sie sagt: „Ich war zweimal Kind“?
2. Was ist ihre Muttersprache und was ist ihre Zweitsprache?
3. Warum musste das deutsche Kind in ihr „sterben“, obwohl das türkische Kind „unsterblich“ ist?
4. In welcher Sprache ist sie eine Erwachsene?
5. Wie wird sie von ihren Eltern angesehen?
6. Sind ihre Eltern in die deutsche Gesellschaft integriert?
7. Wenn sie ihre Eltern besucht, sagt sie immer: „Ich bin es.“ Warum ist das problematisch?
8. Leben Sie jetzt in einer anderen Kultur als die Kultur Ihrer Kindheit?
9. Wie stark ist Ihre kindliche Identität noch?

B Übung: Wie wird das im Passiv gesagt? Rewrite these sentences in passive voice. Keep the same tense.

1. Man akzeptiert mich fast überall.
2. Robert interviewt eine italienische Schülerin.
3. Man warf den Brief in den Briefkasten ein.
4. Die Studenten haben eine Europareise geplant.
5. Hat jemand die Wohnung im ersten Stock schon gekauft?
6. Dort sprach man nur Türkisch.
7. Man muss dieses Problem verstehen.
8. Die Gäste haben meine Großmutter überrascht.
9. Der Beamte muss das Gepäck kontrollieren.
10. Am Montag soll man dieses Thema diskutieren.

C Gruppenarbeit: Zur Diskussion

Talking about houses and apartments is a communicative goal.

1. Wie wohnen Sie zu Hause? Beschreiben Sie das Haus oder die Wohnung Ihrer Familie.
2. Wie würde Ihr Traumhaus aussehen? Beschreiben Sie es.

SCHREIBTIPP

Choosing between the subjunctive and the indicative

Look at the three topics given below.

- *Topic 1* asks you to reflect upon a real situation. Use present indicative here.
- *Topic 2* asks you to speculate about the present. You thus need to use the present subjunctive.
- *Topic 3* asks you to speculate about the past (e.g., how *would* you have lived if you *had been* . . .). Use past subjunctive here.

Schreiben wir mal.

1. Kommen Sie aus einem anderen Land oder haben Sie Bekannte, die aus dem Ausland kommen? Welche kulturellen Unterschiede erkennen Sie?
2. Was für Schwierigkeiten hätten Sie in einem Land, wo Sie die Landessprache nicht verstehen? Beschreiben Sie einige typische Situationen.
3. Wählen Sie eine historische Person und stellen Sie sich vor, Sie wären dieser Mensch gewesen. Wie hätten Sie gelebt? Hätten Sie etwas anders gemacht?

BEISPIEL: Wenn ich Einstein gewesen wäre ...

Albert Einstein (1879–1955)

D Wie sagt man das auf Deutsch?

1. Would you like to have lived in the nineteenth century?
2. I have to think about that.
3. How would life have been different back then?
4. You would not have been able to work with a computer.

5. My paper has to be written soon.
6. When are you going to start? (*Use future tense.*)
7. Either today or the day after tomorrow.
8. What are you writing about?
9. About foreigners in the EU.
10. That's a current topic that interests me too.

11. There is the post office. Didn't you want to mail your letter?
12. Yes, let's go in. I could also buy some stamps.

With this chapter you have completed the last third of ***Neue Horizonte***. For a concise review of the grammar and idiomatic phrases in chapters 11–15, you may consult the **Zusammenfassung und Wiederholung 3** (*Summary and Review 3*) in the Workbook section of the SAM. The review is followed by a self-correcting test.

VIDEO

Foreigners Living and Working in Germany

Since the early 1960s, Germany has attracted large numbers of people from other countries. In 2005, 7.3 million foreigners were living in Germany, comprising about 9 percent of the total population.

In the economic recovery following World War II, manpower shortages existed in the industrialized countries of northern Europe. From the 1960s to the early 1970s, workers from Turkey, Yugoslavia, Italy, Greece, Spain, and Portugal were brought to West Germany. Many of these workers and their families have lived in Germany for years and recent changes in the law make it easier for them to become citizens.

Another large class of foreigners in Germany are those seeking asylum from political persecution in their native countries. The German Basic Law (**Grundgesetz**) of 1949 stated that "those being persecuted politically have a right to asylum." But by the early 1990s, the densely populated country was finding it increasingly difficult to support large numbers of political refugees (438,000 in 1992). In 1993 the Basic Law was amended to make the requirements for asylum seekers much more restrictive. In 2005, some 29,000 individuals applied for asylum.

The liberalization of Eastern Europe and the opening of what used to be called the Iron Curtain in the late 1980s and early 1990s led to an influx into the Federal Republic of ethnic Germans (the so-called **Aussiedler**) from Poland, the Soviet Union, and Romania. Under the German constitution, they are entitled to citizenship.

The "graying" of German society and the extremely low birth rate in the Federal Republic have led to an increasingly urgent debate about how best to attract to Germany young, educated immigrants with advanced education and skills.

The result of all these trends has been to make German society increasingly diverse in its ethnic and racial makeup.

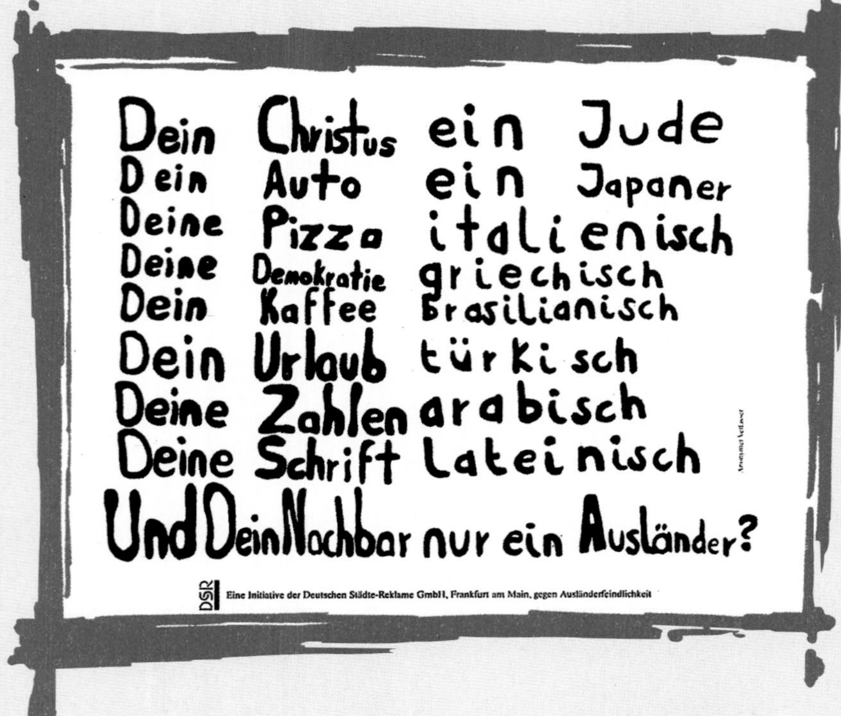

Reference Section

Throughout ***Neue Horizonte*** there are activities entitled **Info-Austausch** in which you will exchange information with a partner. Partner A uses the version of the activity shown in the chapter. Partner B uses the version of the activity given here in Appendix 1.

Info-Austausch Activities: Part B

Kapitel 1 *(Exercise 17, p. 33)*

Was machen die Kinder heute? Work together to say what people are doing today.

BEISPIEL: A: Was machen die Kinder heute?
B: Sie spielen draußen. Was macht Karin heute?
A: Sie ________.

Partner B:

	spielen draußen
Karin	
	arbeitet nicht viel im Moment
Herr Lehmann	
	fliegt nach Wien
Hans	

Kapitel 3 *(Exercise F, p. 87)*

F Was trägst du in diesen Situationen? Work with a partner to say what you would wear in the following situations. The drawing on page 86 will help you with clothing vocabulary.

BEISPIEL: A: Es regnet. Was trägst du?
B: Ich trage einen Regenmantel oder einen Regenschirm.
Es schneit. Was trägst du?
A: Ich trage ________.

Partner B:

Situation	Kleider
	einen Regenmantel oder einen Regenschirm
Es schneit.	
	eine Jacke und eine Mütze
Die Sonne scheint und es ist sehr warm.	
	(für Männer): einen Anzug und eine Krawatte (für Frauen): einen Rock und eine Bluse
Wir machen heute Abend eine Party.	

Kapitel 4 *(Exercise 31, p. 108)*

31 Dann sollst du schlafen gehen! Work with a partner. One partner states a desire or need. The other says what to do about it.

BEISPIEL: A: Ich bin so müde!
B: Dann sollst du schlafen gehen. Ich bin so hungrig.
A: Dann sollst du...

Partner B:

	schlafen gehen
Ich bin so hungrig.	
	schwimmen gehen
Ich brauche Geld.	

Kapitel 5 *(Exercise C, p. 139)*

C Wer macht was? Work together to assign an occupation and a job description to each person in the chart. Partner A assigns an occupation to the first person from the information given below. Partner B chooses the appropriate job description for that person. Partner B then chooses an occupation for the next person and Partner A gives the appropriate job description.

BEISPIEL: A: Jörg Krolow ist Fabrikarbeiter. Was macht er?
B: Er arbeitet in einer Fabrik. Klaus Ostendorff ist Journalist. Was macht er?
A: Er...

Name	Was ist er/sie von Beruf?	Was macht er/sie?
Jörg Krolow		
Klaus Ostendorff		
Marina Spira		
Pawel Kempowski		
Christine Sauermann		
Vanessa Johnson		
Hasan Turunç		
Antje Hakenkamp		
Melanie von Schmolke		

Partner B:

Berufe
Verkäufer / Verkäuferin
Journalist / Journalistin
Professor / Professorin
Buchhändler / Buchhändlerin

Berufsbeschreibungen
bäckt Brote und Brötchen
macht Bilder und Zeichnungen (*drawings*)
macht die Hausarbeit und betreut (*takes care of*) die Kinder
arbeitet in einer Fabrik
unterrichtet (*teaches*) an einer Schule

C Welches Fach ist das? Arbeiten Sie mit Ihrem Partner zusammen. Finden Sie die richtige Beschreibung (*description*) von jedem Hauptfach.

BEISPIEL: A: Man studiert Philosophie. Was macht man an der Uni?
B: Man studiert und analysiert große Denker wie Kant und Wittgenstein.
B: Man studiert Organismen: Tiere (*animals*) und Pflanzen (*plants*). Welches (*which*) Fach ist das?
A: Das ist Biologie.

Partner B:

Im Hauptfach studiert man...	Das macht man an der Uni.
Politikwissenschaft	Man lernt über Sprache, Literatur, Geschichte und Kultur in den deutschsprachigen Ländern.
Pädagogik	Man studiert Organismen: Tiere (*animals*) und Pflanzen (*plants*).
Geschichte	Man studiert und analysiert große Denker wie Kant und Wittgenstein.
Physik	Man schreibt Programme und entwickelt (*develops*) Software für Computer.

17 Wann kommt der Zug an? Arbeiten Sie mit einem Partner zusammen und ergänzen Sie (*complete*) die Informationen in dem Zugfahrplan am Hauptbahnhof Mannheim.

BEISPIEL: A: Wann kommt der Zug Nummer 6342 in Mannheim an?
B: Um 14.22 Uhr. Wann fährt der Zug Nummer 2203 nach Innsbruck in Mannheim ab?

Partner B:

Ankunft (*arrivals*) **und Abfahrt** (*departures*)					
Zug-Nr.	**ab**[1]	**an**[1]	**Zug-Nr.**	**ab**	**an**
6342	Hamburg	Mannheim	1338	Mannheim	Zürich
		14.22 Uhr		5.20 Uhr	
7422	München	Mannheim	2472	Mannheim	Nürnberg
	10.03 Uhr			6.06 Uhr	
1387	Frankfurt/Main	Mannheim	6606	Mannheim	Straßburg
		12.01 Uhr			8.40 Uhr
7703	Wien	Mannheim	2203	Mannheim	Innsbruck
		17.56 Uhr			15.46 Uhr
9311	Berlin	Mannheim	3679	Mannheim	Prag
	11.05 Uhr				20.09 Uhr

[1]**ab** = time and place of departure; **an** = time and place of arrival.

Kapitel 11 *(Exercise 20, p. 304)*

20 Weihnachtsgeschenke (*Christmas presents*). Sie und Ihr Partner schenken einander viele Sachen zu Weihnachten. Fragen Sie, was Sie einander schenken.

BEISPIEL: A: Schenkst du mir etwas Neues?
B: Ja, ich schenke dir eine tolle neue CD. Schenkst du mir etwas Warmes?
A: Ja, ich schenke dir einen neuen Pulli.

Partner B:

lecker	
	ein Fahrrad
klein	
	eine Armbanduhr aus Gold
groß	
	eine Pflanze
warm	
	eine tolle neue CD

Kapitel 12 *(Exercise 27, p. 339)*

27 Du kannst das selber machen. Arbeiten Sie mit einem Partner/einer Partnerin zusammen. Sagen Sie, er/sie soll etwas machen lassen, oder sagen Sie, er/sie soll es selber tun.

BEISPIEL: A: Mein Handy ist kaputt.
B: Du sollst es reparieren lassen. Ich möchte Kaffee trinken.
A: Du kannst ihn selber kochen.

Partner B:

	reparieren lassen
Ich möchte Kaffee trinken.	
	schneiden lassen
Ich habe Hunger.	
	tippen lassen
Ich brauche Lebensmittel.	
	waschen lassen

Kapitel 13 *(Exercise D, p. 374)*

D Hobbys. Arbeiten Sie mit einem Partner zusammen. Wofür interessieren sich diese Leute? Welche Hobbys haben sie?

BEISPIEL: A: Wofür interessiert sich Vladimir?
B: Er interessiert sich für Entomologie. Was sammelt er denn?
A: Er sammelt Schmetterlinge.
B: Nina spielt Trompete. Wofür interessiert sie sich?
A: Sie interessiert sich für Jazz.

Partner B:

Name	Interessiert sich für...	Sammelt, spielt, macht...
Vladimir	Entomologie	
Nina		Trompete
Bobby	Strategie	
Steffi		Tennis
Lutz	Kunst und Technik	
Claudio		Klavier
Beate	Tanz (*dance*) und Sport	
mein Partner		
ich		

Kapitel 15 *(Exercise 10, p. 419)*

10 Von wem? Jeder Partner bekommt zwei Listen mit den Titeln **Was**? und **Von wem?** Stellen Sie einander Fragen im Passiv, um Ihre Listen zu ergänzen (*complete*).

BEISPIEL:

Was?	**Von wem?**
Don Giovanni komponieren	Bäcker
Brot backen	Mozart

A: Von wem wird Brot gebacken? B: Vom Bäcker.
B: Von wem wurde *Don Giovanni* komponiert? A: Von Mozart.

Partner B:

Was?	Von wem?
Faust schreiben	Journalisten
das Essen im Restaurant bringen	Beethoven
Romane schreiben	Professoren
die Psychoanalyse gründen	Shakespeare
Autos reparieren	Einstein

Principal Parts of Strong and Irregular Verbs

The following table contains the principal parts of all the strong, mixed, and irregular verbs in ***Neue Horizonte***. With a few exceptions, only the basic stem verbs are listed, e.g., **gehen**, **bringen**, and **kommen**. Verbs formed by adding a prefix—e.g., **weggehen**, **verbringen**, and **ankommen**—change their stems in the same way as the basic verb.

Infinitive	Third-person sing. present	Simple past	Perfect	English
anfangen	fängt an	fing an	hat angefangen	*begin*
beginnen		begann	hat begonnen	*begin*
bitten		bat	hat gebeten	*ask for, request*
bleiben		blieb	ist geblieben	*stay*
brechen	bricht	brach	hat gebrochen	*break*
bringen		brachte	hat gebracht	*bring*
denken		dachte	hat gedacht	*think*
dürfen	darf	durfte	hat gedurft	*may, be allowed to*
einladen	lädt ein	lud ein	hat eingeladen	*invite*
empfehlen	empfiehlt	empfahl	hat empfohlen	*recommend*
entscheiden		entschied	hat entschieden	*decide*
essen	isst	aß	hat gegessen	*eat*
fahren	fährt	fuhr	ist gefahren	*drive*
fallen	fällt	fiel	ist gefallen	*fall*
finden		fand	hat gefunden	*find*
fliegen		flog	ist geflogen	*fly*
fließen		floss	ist geflossen	*flow*
geben	gibt	gab	hat gegeben	*give*
gehen		ging	ist gegangen	*go*
genießen		genoss	hat genossen	*enjoy*
haben	hat	hatte	hat gehabt	*have*
halten	hält	hielt	hat gehalten	*hold, stop*
hängen[1]		hing	hat gehangen	*be hanging*
heißen		hieß	hat geheißen	*be called*
helfen	hilft	half	hat geholfen	*help*
kennen		kannte	hat gekannt	*know, be acquainted with*
klingen		klang	hat geklungen	*sound*
kommen		kam	ist gekommen	*come*
können	kann	konnte	hat gekonnt	*can, be able to*
lassen	lässt	ließ	hat gelassen	*leave; let; allow to; cause to be done*

[1] When it is transitive, **hängen** is weak: **hängte**, **hat gehängt**.

Infinitive	Third-person sing. present	Simple past	Perfect	English
laufen	läuft	lief	ist gelaufen	*run*
leihen		lieh	hat geliehen	*lend*
lesen	liest	las	hat gelesen	*read*
liegen		lag	hat gelegen	*lie*
mögen	mag	mochte	hat gemocht	*like*
müssen	muss	musste	hat gemusst	*must, have to*
nehmen	nimmt	nahm	hat genommen	*take*
nennen		nannte	hat genannt	*name, call*
raten	rät	riet	hat geraten	*guess*
rufen		rief	hat gerufen	*call, shout*
scheinen		schien	hat geschienen	*shine, seem*
schlafen	schläft	schlief	hat geschlafen	*sleep*
schließen		schloss	hat geschlossen	*close*
schneiden		schnitt	hat geschnitten	*cut*
schreiben		schrieb	hat geschrieben	*write*
schweigen		schwieg	hat geschwiegen	*be silent*
schwimmen		schwamm	ist geschwommen	*swim*
sehen	sieht	sah	hat gesehen	*see*
sein	ist	war	ist gewesen	*be*
singen		sang	hat gesungen	*sing*
sitzen		saß	hat gesessen	*sit*
sollen	soll	sollte	hat gesollt	*should*
sprechen	spricht	sprach	hat gesprochen	*speak*
stehen		stand	hat gestanden	*stand*
stehlen	stiehlt	stahl	hat gestohlen	*steal*
steigen		stieg	ist gestiegen	*climb*
sterben	stirbt	starb	ist gestorben	*die*
tragen	trägt	trug	hat getragen	*carry, wear*
treffen	trifft	traf	hat getroffen	*meet*
treiben		trieb	hat getrieben	*drive, propel*
trinken		trank	hat getrunken	*drink*
tun		tat	hat getan	*do*
vergessen	vergisst	vergaß	hat vergessen	*forget*
vergleichen		verglich	hat verglichen	*compare*
verlassen	verlässt	verließ	hat verlassen	*leave*
verlieren		verlor	hat verloren	*lose*
verschwinden		verschwand	ist verschwunden	*disappear*
wachsen	wächst	wuchs	ist gewachsen	*grow*
waschen	wäscht	wusch	hat gewaschen	*wash*
werden	wird	wurde	ist geworden	*become*
werfen	wirft	warf	hat geworfen	*throw*
wiegen		wog	hat gewogen	*weigh*
wissen	weiß	wusste	hat gewusst	*know (a fact)*
wollen	will	wollte	hat gewollt	*want to*
ziehen		zog	hat gezogen	*pull*

Special Subjunctive and Extended Modifiers

A. Special Subjunctive (*Konjunktiv I*) for Indirect Quotation

Speech is often reported using indirect rather than direct quotation. Compare the following sentences:

> *John said, "I'm tired."* (direct quotation)
> *John said he was tired.* (indirect quotation)

In formal written and spoken German (as in a term paper, newspaper article, or television news report), indirect quotation of spoken or written material is expressed with a special subjunctive form of the verb. This special subjunctive occurs predominantly in the third person singular, where it is formed by adding the ending **-e** to the unchanged infinitive stem of any verb except **sein,** which lacks the ending.

The following examples contain special subjunctive as you might encounter it in the media. Note the elegant simplicity of using this form to indicate that someone is being quoted indirectly. English needs verbs like "*he continued*" and "*she said*" to make the same thing clear.

> Bei seinem Besuch in Rostock sagte der Bundeskanzler, er **wisse** noch nicht, wie man dieses Problem lösen **werde**, aber er **glaube**, dass etwas bald entschieden werden **müsse**. Man **habe** nicht mehr viel Zeit.
>
> *On his visit to Rostock, the Chancellor said he didn't know yet how they would solve this problem, but he believed that something had to be decided soon. (He continued that) there wasn't much time left.*
>
> In einem exklusiven Interview mit unserem Reporter sagte der junge Tennisstar, sie **hoffe** noch eine lange Karriere vor sich zu haben. Sie **sei** noch jung und **fühle** sich sehr fit, besonders seit sie sich von einer schlimmen Erkältung erholt **habe**.
>
> *In an exclusive interview with our reporter, the young tennis star said that she hoped to have a long career still ahead of her. (She said) she was still young and felt very fit, especially since recovering from a bad cold.*

Special subjunctive is also sometimes used instead of regular subjunctive in an **als ob** clause: **Sie sah aus, als ob sie krank sei.**

B. Extended Modifiers

Both German and English can extend noun phrases by inserting a series of adjectives and adverbs between a limiting word (**diese**) and its noun (**Schriftstellerin**). In German, however, such a series can be continued much further than in English. English tends to use a relative clause for such extended modifiers.

diese *deutsche* Schriftstellerin	*this **German** writer*
diese *bekannte deutsche* Schriftstellerin	*this **well-known German** writer*
diese *sehr bekannte deutsche* Schriftstellerin	*this **very well-known German** writer*

diese *unter jungen Lesern sehr bekannte deutsche* Schriftstellerin	*this* ***German*** *writer* ***who is very well known among young readers***
diese *unter jungen Lesern in Europa sehr bekannte deutsche* Schriftstellerin	*this* ***German*** *writer* ***who is very well known among young readers in*** *Europe*
diese *heute unter jungen Lesern in Europa sehr bekannte* deutsche Schriftstellerin	*this* ***German*** *writer* ***who is very well known among young readers in Europe today***

Such extended modifiers are encountered primarily in written German, and their use or avoidance is a matter of stylistic preference. The extended modifier is a substitute for a relative clause.

diese **unter Studenten bekannte** Schriftstellerin =
diese Schriftstellerin, **die unter Studenten bekannt ist**

Extended modifiers often contain a present or past participle functioning as an attributive adjective. This participle would be the conjugated verb in the corresponding relative clause:

Die Schüler freuen sich auf **die in zwei Tagen *beginnenden* Ferien.** =
Die Schüler freuen sich auf die Ferien, **die in zwei Tagen *beginnen*.**

Eine so gut *bezahlte* Stelle ist schwer zu finden. =
Eine Stelle, **die so gut *bezahlt wird***, ist schwer zu finden.

English Equivalents of the *Dialoge*

Note that English translations are idiomatic, not always word-for-word.

Kapitel 1 (p. 18)

In a Hurry

MR. L: Good morning, Mrs. Hauser.
MRS. H: Morning, Mr. Lehmann. Forgive me, but I'm in a hurry. I'm flying to Vienna at eleven.
MR. L: When are you coming back?
MRS. H: I'll be back in the office on Wednesday. Well then, good-bye.
MR. L: Bye! Have a good trip!

The University Cafeteria

KARIN: Hi, Michael!
MICHAEL: Hello, Karin! How's the soup today?
KARIN: It's pretty good. By the way, are you working a lot at the moment?
MICHAEL: No, not very much. Why do you ask?
KARIN: I'm going to Horst's tonight. You too?
MICHAEL: Yes, of course.
KARIN: Great! Well, so long, until then.

Typical for September

MRS. B: Hello, Mrs. Kuhn. How are you today?
MRS. K: Hi, Mrs. Bachmann. Very well, thanks, and you?
MRS. B: Thanks, I'm fine too. What are the kids doing today?
MRS. K: They're playing outside—the weather is so nice.
MRS. B: Yes, the sun is finally shining. But maybe it will rain again tomorrow.
MRS. K: That is typical for September.

Kapitel 2 (p. 43)

Who's Reading the Newspaper?

FATHER: Kurt, I'm looking for my newspaper. Do you know where it is?
SON: Your newspaper? Sorry, but I'm reading it at the moment.
FATHER: That's okay. What are you reading?
SON: I'm reading an article about our school.

I've Got a Question

ANNETTE: Katrin, I've got a question. Do you know that man over there?
KATRIN: Whom do you mean?
ANNETTE: He's talking with Stefan. I see he knows you.
KATRIN: Of course I know him—that's my brother Max!
ANNETTE: Oh right, you have a brother too! I only know your sister.

Georg Is Looking for a Room

GEORG: Do you know many people in Munich?
STEFAN: Yes, my family lives there. Why?
GEORG: I'm studying there next semester and need a room.
STEFAN: Our house is pretty big. I'm sure my parents have a room free.
GEORG: Fantastic! Thanks a lot!
STEFAN: You're welcome. Don't mention it.

Kapitel 3 (p. 65)

You've Got It Made!

Renate is visiting her friend Monika in Hinterwalden.

MONIKA: You've got it made in Frankfurt, Renate.
RENATE: What do you mean?
MONIKA: It's always really boring here in Hinterwalden.
RENATE: Then you have to visit me soon. Or don't you want to?
MONIKA: Sure I do. I would really like to go to Frankfurt, but unfortunately I don't have any money.
RENATE: I certainly understand that, but surely you can earn enough by June.

A Break

Kurt and Stefan are driving to Innsbruck.

STEFAN: How long do we still have to drive?
KURT: Just one more hour to Innsbruck.
STEFAN: Can we take a break now? I'd like to walk a bit.
KURT: Me too. We can stop over there, can't we?
STEFAN: Yes. (*They stop.*) Man, the mountain is really steep!
KURT: What's the matter? Aren't you in shape?
STEFAN: Sure! I can manage that easily.

There's No Chemistry Class Today

ANJA: Hey, Klaus, have you heard already?
KLAUS: What's up?
ANJA: There's no chemistry class today!
KLAUS: How come?
ANJA: Frau Helmholtz has a cold.
KLAUS: Great! Then we don't have to take the test!
ANJA: Right! Want to have coffee?
KLAUS: Sure. Then we can go home early.

Kapitel 4 (p. 92)

At the Lake

MRS. M: Do you want to go swimming again, Mrs. Brinkmann?
MRS. B: No, I'd rather not. I'm a little tired. And the water is awfully cold this summer. You go without me.
MRS. M: Maybe you'd rather play cards?
MRS. B: Yes, gladly!

Winter Vacation

RICHARD: This year would you like to go to Austria in the winter?
EVA: Great! Let's go to Kitzbühel in January!
RICHARD: I hope we can still get a hotel room.
EVA: I don't think it's too late yet.

Nine-Thirty in the Morning

ANITA: So long then. I've got to go now.
BEATE: Wait a second! Not without breakfast! At least eat a roll.
ANITA: Unfortunately I'm out of time. Every Monday I have my seminar. It begins at ten, and today I have to buy a notebook beforehand.
BEATE: Take the roll along. Later you're sure to get hungry.
ANITA: You're right. Well, see you later!

Kapitel 5 (p. 119)

The New Baker's Apprentice

Six AM. Georg is opening the bakery.

MARTIN: Morning. My name is Martin Holst. I'm starting here today.
GEORG: Pleased to meet you. My name is Georg. You'll meet the boss soon.
MARTIN: Okay. How long have you been working here?
GEORG: Only for a year. Now come with me and I'll show you the shop.

At the Baker's

CLERK: May I help you?
CUSTOMER: Give me six rolls and one loaf of dark bread, please.
CLERK: (*She gives him the bread.*) There you are. Anything else?
CUSTOMER: Are these pretzels fresh?
CLERK: Yes, from this morning.
CUSTOMER: Then give me six of those. How much is that, please?
CLERK: Together that comes to three euros and seventy-five cents.
CUSTOMER: Thank you. Good-bye.
CLERK: Bye.

School or Profession?

FATHER: Why do you want to leave school now? Your grades are pretty good and you've only got one more year.
KURT: But I don't need the *Abitur*. I want to be an auto mechanic.
FATHER: Don't be so dumb. You won't earn much as an apprentice.
KURT: But I'm fed up. I'd rather work with my hands.
FATHER: Nonsense! You pass your *Abitur* and I'll give you a motorcycle. Is it a deal?
KURT: Hmmm.

Kapitel 6 (p. 146)

Karin Is Looking for a Room

STEFAN: Have you finally found a room?
KARIN: Nope, I'm still looking. Unfortunately I didn't get a place in the dorm.
STEFAN: Hey! Yesterday Helga moved out of our living group. So now there's a room free and we're looking for a roommate. Do you want to move in with us?
KARIN: Terrific! Do you think it's possible?
STEFAN: Of course, no problem!

At the Beginning of the Semester

CLARA: Where were you for so long?
EVA: In the library and later at the bookstore.
CLARA: Did you bring me a course catalogue?
EVA: Yes, I put it on the desk.
CLARA: Oh yeah, it's lying under the newspaper. How much did it cost?
EVA: Three euros, but I'll give it to you for free.
CLARA: That's really nice of you! Thanks a lot.
EVA: Don't mention it.

At the University in Tübingen

PETRA: Have you met Peter yet?
KLAUS: Is that the exchange student from Canada?
PETRA: Yes. He speaks fantastic German, doesn't he?
KLAUS: I think he's already studied two semesters in Konstanz.
PETRA: So that's why!

Kapitel 7 (p. 175)

At the Train Station

A student sees an elderly lady with a lot of luggage and wants to help her.

STUDENT: May I help you?
TOURIST: Yes, please. Would you carry my suitcase?
STUDENT: Gladly. Where do you have to go?
TOURIST: Track thirteen. My train leaves at 11:27.

Before the Trip

MARION: Are you looking for the thermos bottle?
THORSTEN: No, not the thermos, but the road atlas. I think I put it on the table.
MARION: Yes, here it is, under my jacket.
THORSTEN: Hang up the jacket, then we'll have more room. We've got to plan our trip to Venice.
MARION: Let's not forget, our tickets are in the pocket.

On the Telephone

Marion and Thorsten have been on the road with their car for three weeks. Now they're back home, and Marion calls her father in the afternoon. It rings for a long time, but finally Mr. Krogmann comes to the phone.

MR. K: Krogmann.
MARION: Hello, Dad. This is Marion. Why didn't you answer right away?
MR. K: Oh, Marion, are you back? I was lying on the sofa and fell asleep.
MARION: Oh, sorry, Dad. I woke you up.
MR. K: Doesn't matter. I wanted to get up anyway. How was your trip?
MARION: Everything was wonderful.

Kapitel 8 (p. 202)

In a Restaurant: Check Please!

PATRON: Check please!
WAITRESS: Just a moment. . . (*She comes to the table.*) How was everything?
PATRON: Excellent!
WAITRESS: Would you like to order anything else?
PATRON: No thanks. I'd like the check, please.
WAITRESS: You had a cutlet, French fries, a salad, and a beer, right?
PATRON: Yes, and also a cup of coffee.
WAITRESS: All together that comes to €13.50 please.
PATRON: (*Gives her 20 euros*) 14 euros.
WAITRESS: Thank you, and six euros change.

What Else Do We Need?

DORA: This morning I invited Max to supper. Do you know if he's coming?
FRANZ: Yes, but he told me that he couldn't come until 6:30. What time is it now?
DORA: 5:30. So I need to run around the corner to buy a few things. What else do we need?
FRANZ: A kilo of potatoes, 200 grams of liverwurst, cheese, a bottle of red wine, and fruit for dessert.
DORA: Is that all?
FRANZ: I think so.

A Stroll Through Town

Marianne is visiting her friend Helmut in Cologne. He hasn't shown her around the center of town yet because it's been raining.

HELMUT: Hey look, the rain's finally stopped! Would you like to do something?
MARIANNE: Sure. Now we can take our walk through town, but can we eat something first? I'm really hungry!
HELMUT: Of course. Near the cathedral there's a place where we can eat Greek food.

MARIANNE: Hmm, that sounds delicious!
HELMUT: Then we can visit the cathedral afterwards, and from there it's not far to the art museum.

Kapitel 9 (p. 233)

Recycling in Our Apartment Building

Ms. Berg meets Mr. Reh on the stairs.

MS. B: Oh my gosh! Where to with that huge sack?
MS. R: To the cellar. The new trash containers are here. Now we can collect (old) glass and waste paper here in the building.
MS. B: At last! Now I don't have to haul my trash to the recycling center anymore.
MS. R: Fortunately that's no longer necessary. If we all participate, then that's great progress.

An Ecological Birthday Present

DANIEL: Hi, Frank! What a beautiful bicycle! Where'd you get it?
FRANK: Marianne gave it to me for my birthday because we've sold our second car.
DANIEL: How come?
FRANK: It was kaput anyway, and since we've moved to the city, I can ride my bike to work.
DANIEL: Then you're saving a lot of money.
FRANK: Yes, and it also feels good to be doing something about air pollution.

Do You Like to Play Sports?

BOY: Hey, do you like to play sports?
GIRL: Sure. I spend all weekend on the tennis court. Do you play tennis too?
BOY: Yes, that's my favorite sport, but I'm not a good player.
GIRL: Then I can recommend a wonderful tennis instructor to you.

Kapitel 10 (p. 261)

Back Then

Two senior citizens are sitting on a bench in the afternoon.

MR. Z: How long have you lived here, Mrs. Planck?
MR. P: Since last year. Before that, I lived in Mainz.
MR. Z: Really? I didn't know that. When I was a child, I always spent the whole summer there with my grandparents.
MR. P: Yes, of course, back then before the war, the city was very different.

That Annoys Me!

JÜRGEN: Heinz, what's wrong? You look so worried.
HEINZ: Oh, Barbara loaned me her new iPod two weeks ago. . .
JÜRGEN: So? You haven't lost it, have you?
HEINZ: No idea. I had it in my backpack, but then ten minutes ago I suddenly couldn't find it.
JÜRGEN: What a drag! You think somebody ripped it off?
HEINZ: No, I don't think so, because my wallet's not missing. . . Man, that annoys me.

Tough Times

As a homework assignment, Steffi (age 14) has to interview her grandmother.

STEFFI: Grandma, for school we're supposed to interview our grandparents about the war years.
OMA: Well, what do you want to know, Steffi?
STEFFI: Let's see . . . when were you born, anyway?
OMA: In 1935. When the war began I was still a little girl.
STEFFI: Please tell me what it was like for you back then.
OMA: Thank goodness we lived in the country, and at first things were relatively good although we weren't rich.
STEFFI: What happened then?
OMA: That lasted only until 1943. Then my brother was killed in action in Russia and a year later my mother died.

Kapitel 11 (p. 289)

At the Brandenburg Gate

Helen from the USA was in Berlin in 1989. Now she's there again to visit her friend Anke. They're standing together at the Brandenburg Gate.

ANKE: Do you remember what it looked like here at the Wall on November 9, 1989?
HELEN: When the GDR opened the border? I'll never forget it!
ANKE: People were so happy, even the police officers were friendly.
HELEN: Yes, the difference is unbelievable! Today you see nothing but new architecture and nothing at all of the Wall anymore.
ANKE: Yes you do: a piece of the Wall still exists as a memorial. But just imagine, for school children today that's all just history now.
HELEN: Yes, in the meantime, Berlin has become a great European capital again.

An Accident: Stefan Breaks His Leg

11:00 PM. Stefan's father is already in bed. His mother is talking on the telephone. Suddenly she runs into the bedroom.

MOTHER: Markus, get dressed quickly and come along! Something bad has happened.
FATHER: What's wrong?
MOTHER: Stefan hurt himself riding his bike! I'm afraid he's broken his leg.
FATHER: For heaven's sake! Let's hurry!

Anna Visits Stefan in the Hospital

ANNA: How are you, you poor fellow?
STEFAN: Hi, Anna! Nice of you to come.
ANNA: Do you feel better today or does your leg still hurt?
STEFAN: Oh, fortunately it's not so bad. I can already wash myself, but they won't let me get up yet.
ANNA: Too bad. Look, I've brought you chocolate and flowers.
STEFAN: Oh, those are pretty. Thanks, that's really nice of you!
ANNA: Don't mention it. Get well soon!

Kapitel 12 (p. 319)

Idiot-proof

H-P: Karin, do you have the book with you that I lent you?
KARIN: Oh, sorry. I left it at home again. I'm still working on my paper.
H-P: Doesn't matter. Go ahead and keep it. Do you still have a lot to do?
KARIN: No, I'm almost done. I'm using my new laptop for the first time. The software is really idiot-proof.

Gossip

PETRA: Who was the guy Rita left with yesterday?
LUKAS: The man who was dressed so funny?
PETRA: Exactly. He's the one I mean.
LUKAS: That was Rudi. Just imagine, she's gotten engaged to him!
PETRA: At least he looked more intelligent than her last boyfriend.

At the Front Door

Ms. Schwarzer, who has recently moved into the building, is talking after work to her neighbor, Mr. Beck.

MS. S: Oh, Mr. Beck, I wanted to ask you something. Where can I get my VW repaired around here?
MR. B: I recommend Mr. Haslinger in the next cross street. He's the best mechanic here but unfortunately not the cheapest.
MS. S: Hmm. . . At the moment I'm somewhat short of cash. I think I'll do it myself this time.
MR. B: Well, have fun. . . Then I'll wish you a good evening.
MS. S: Thanks, you too.

Kapitel 13 (p. 350)

Skiing in Switzerland

Shortly before the end of the semester, two students are talking about their vacation plans.

BRIGITTE: I'm really looking forward to semester break!
JOHANNA: Do you plan to go skiing again?
BRIGITTE: Yes, I'll spend two weeks in Switzerland. Tomorrow morning I fly to Zürich.
JOHANNA: Really? I'm flabbergasted! Before, you were always afraid of flying!
BRIGITTE: True, but I've simply gotten used to it.

Problems in the Group Apartment: The Living Room Is Messy

Nina is reading in her room. Ute and Lutz knock on her door.

NINA: Come in! (*They go in.*) Morning! What's new?
LUTZ: Hi, Nina. Can we have a quick word with you about something?
NINA: Sure. What is it?
UTE: Listen. Will you finally straighten up your things in the living room?
NINA: Oh, sorry! I'll do it right away. Don't be mad at me—I was in a big rush this morning.
LUTZ: Yeah, you always say that. Now we're really fed up.
UTE: Everybody in the apartment has to pitch in.
NINA: You're right. From now on I'll take better care of it.

At the Information Window in Basel

TOURIST: Excuse me. May I ask you for information?
CLERK: Sure. How can I help you?
TOURIST: I'm in Basel for only a day, and I don't know my way around here. What can you recommend (to me)?
CLERK: It depends on what you want to see. The Historical Museum is especially worthwhile. If you're interested in the Middle Ages, you mustn't miss the new exhibit.
TOURIST: That interests me a lot. How do I get there?
CLERK: Go out here, and right in front of the train station is the streetcar stop. You need to get on the number 2 streetcar. Then get off at the museum.
TOURIST: May I take a city map too?
CLERK: Of course.
TOURIST: Many thanks for your help.
CLERK: You're welcome.

Kapitel 14 (p. 379)

On Vacation in Salzburg

Mr. and Mrs. Burckhardt from Bern have done a lot in Salzburg this morning. Now they're hungry and want to have a bite to eat. They see a sausage stand.

MR. B: Ursula, have you seen an ATM anywhere?
MRS. B: No, why? Don't you have any more cash?
MR. B: All spent, I'm afraid. If I had a few euros left, we could eat a sausage at that stand over there. I'm sure they don't take credit cards.
MRS. B: No problem. Either we'll find an ATM in the pedestrian zone, or we can change money in the hotel.

At the Reception Desk

TOURIST: Hello, would you still have a room free for tonight?
CLERK: Do you want a single or a double room?
TOURIST: I'd prefer a single room with a shower.
CLERK: I could have given you one two hours ago, but at the moment there is only a double room with bath available.
TOURIST: What would that cost?
CLERK: 70 euros with breakfast. It's a quiet room and very comfortable.
TOURIST: May I please have a look at the room?
CLERK: Of course. (*Hands him the key.*) Go up the stairs here. That would be room number 14 on the second floor.

Outing to a *Heuriger*

ANDREAS: Hi, Helene! You look as if you hadn't slept much.
HELENE: Oh, is it obvious? Yes, yesterday was pretty stressful.
ANDREAS: If you aren't too tired tonight, then maybe we could go to a *Heuriger* in Grinzing.
HELENE: Yes, high time that we try the new wine! And it would be nice to eat there too.
ANDREAS: Good idea! By then I'm sure I'll be famished.
HELENE: Then we ought to leave right away.

Kapitel 15 (p. 409)

Where Is Home?

Emine, a student from a Turkish family in Berlin-Kreuzberg, is being interviewed for the school newspaper.

INTERVIEWER: Emine, you really do speak perfect German. What do you and your family speak at home?
EMINE: Well, I was born in Berlin and I usually speak German with my brothers and sisters. But we always speak Turkish with my parents and grandparents.
INTERVIEWER: Where do you actually feel at home, in Germany or Turkey?
EMINE: I ask myself that as well. I have a lot of friends here in Berlin, but also many nice cousins in Istanbul. Actually, I feel at home in both cultures.

The Missed Birthday Party

LILLI: At Sonja's birthday party people were dancing until 3:00 AM. Where were you? Didn't you get invited?
FELIX: Yes I was, and I'd really like to have been there, but I was on vacation in Spain.
LILLI: You should have at least called and congratulated her.
FELIX: You're right. I should have done that.

In Front of the Post Office

Mr. and Mrs. Becker see a mailbox in front of the main post office.

MRS. B: You can mail your letter there.
MR. B: Just a second. Do I have enough stamps on it? Maybe I should go in and have it weighed.
MRS. B: Let me see—but the Hartmanns have moved! That's their old address.
MR. B: Darn it! I shouldn't have forgotten that.
MRS. B: Oh, don't get upset! We'll just buy a new envelope.

German-English Vocabulary

The following list contains all the words introduced in ***Neue Horizonte*** except for definite and indefinite articles, personal and relative pronouns, possessive adjectives, cardinal and ordinal numbers, and words glossed in the margins of the **Lesestücke.** The code at the end of each entry shows where the word or phrase is introduced in the text:

12-1	Kapitel 12, Wortschatz 1
9-2	Kapitel 9, Wortschatz 2
Einf.	Einführung (Introductory Chapter)
2-G	Kapitel 2, Grammatik
5-TLL	Kapitel 5, Tipps zum Lesen und Lernen (*in the section* Leicht zu merken)
10-VzT	Kapitel 10, Vokabeln zum Thema

Strong and irregular verbs are listed with their principal parts: **nehmen (nimmt), nahm, hat genommen.** Weak verbs using **sein** as their auxiliary are shown by inclusion of the perfect: **reisen, ist gereist.**

Separable prefixes are indicated by a raised dot between prefix and verb stem: **ab·fahren.** This dot is *not* used in German spelling.

When a verb has a prepositional complement, the preposition follows all the principal parts. If it is a two-way preposition, the case it takes with this verb is indicated in parentheses: **teil·nehmen (nimmt teil), nahm teil, hat teilgenommen *an*** (+ *dat.*).

Adjectival nouns are indicated thus: der/die **Verwandte, -n.**

Masculine N-nouns like **der Student** and irregular nouns like **der Name** are followed by both the genitive singular and the plural endings: der **Student, *-en,* -en**; der **Name, *-ns,* -n.**

Adjectives followed by a hyphen may only be used attributively: **eigen-.**

If an adjective or adverb requires an umlaut in the comparative and superlative degrees, or if these forms are irregular, this is indicated in parentheses: **arm (ärmer)**; **gern (lieber, am liebsten).**

The following abbreviations are used here and throughout ***Neue Horizonte.***

acc.	accusative	*intrans.*	intransitive
adj.	adjective	*m.*	masculine
adj. noun	adjectival noun	*neut.*	neuter
adv.	adverb	*pers.*	person
colloq.	colloquial	*pl.*	plural
conj.	conjunction	*prep.*	preposition
coor. conj.	coordinating conjunction	*sing.*	singular
dat.	dative	*sub. conj.*	subordinating conjunction
f.	feminine	*trans.*	transitive
gen.	genitive	*usw.*	(= **und so weiter**) etc.

A

der **Abend, -e** evening, 1-1, 8-1
am Abend in the evening, 8-1
gestern Abend yesterday evening, 12-G
Guten Abend! Good evening, *Einf.*
heute Abend this evening, tonight, 1-1
das **Abendessen, -** supper, evening meal, 8-1
zum Abendessen for supper, 8-1
abends (in the) evenings, every evening, 5-2
aber (1) but (*coor. conj.*), 1-1; (2) (*flavoring particle*), 9-1
ab·fahren (fährt ab), fuhr ab, ist abgefahren to depart, leave (by vehicle), 7-1
ab·holen to pick up, fetch, get, 5-2
das **Abi** (*slang*) = **Abitur,** 5-1
das **Abitur** final secondary school examination, 5-1
ach oh, ah, 2-1
das **Adjektiv, -e** adjective
die **Adjektivendung, -en** adjective ending, 9-G
der **Adler, -** eagle, 10-VzT
die **Adresse, -n** address, 15-1
das **Adverb, -ien** adverb
ähnlich (+ *dat.*) similar (to), 3-2
Sie ist ihrer Mutter ähnlich. She's like her mother.
die **Ahnung** notion, inkling, hunch
(Ich habe) keine Ahnung. (I have) no idea. 10-1
der **Akkusativ** accusative case, 2-G
aktiv active, 9-TLL
aktuell current, topical, 5-2
akut acute, 9-TLL
alle (*pl.*) all; everybody, 2-2
allein alone, 1-2
alles everything, 6-2
der **Alltag** everyday life, 8-2
der **Almanach, -e** almanac
die **Alpen** (*pl.*) the Alps, 4-TLL
als (1) when (*sub. conj.*), 10-1; (2) as a, 5-1; (3) than (*with comparative degree*), 12-1
als ob (+ *subjunctive*) as if, as though, 14-1
also (1) well . . . 1-1; (2) thus, 3-2
alt (älter) old, 2-2
die **Alternative, -n** alternative, 2-TLL
altmodisch old-fashioned, 4-2
die **Altstadt, ⸚e** old city center, 5-2
die **Ambivalenz** ambivalence, 14-TLL
(das) **Amerika** America, 3-2
der **Amerikaner, -** American (*m.*), 1-2
die **Amerikanerin, -nen** American (*f.*), 1-2
amerikanisch American, 3-2
an (*prep.* + *acc.* or *dat.*) to, toward; at, alongside of, 6-1
ander- other, different, 11-1
ändern to change (*trans.*), 11-2
sich ändern to change (*intrans.*), 11-2
anders different, 2-2
der **Anfang, ⸚e** beginning, 6-1
am Anfang at the beginning, 6-1
an·fangen (fängt an), fing an, hat angefangen to begin, start, 5-1
der **Anfänger, -** beginner, 5-TLL
angenehm pleasant; pleasure to meet you, 13-VzT
der/die **Angestellte, -n** (*adj. noun*) employee, 14-1
die **Anglistik** English studies, 6-VzT
die **Angst, ⸚e** fear, 3-2
Angst haben to be afraid, 3-2
Angst haben vor (+ *dat.*) to be afraid of, 13-1
an·kommen, kam an, ist angekommen to arrive, 5-1, 7-1
an·kommen auf (+ *acc.*) to depend on, be contingent on
Es kommt darauf an. It depends. 13-1
sich an·melden to register (at a hotel, at the university, etc.), 14-VzT
an·rufen, rief an, hat angerufen to call up, 5-1
ansehen: sich etwas an·sehen (sieht an), sah an, hat angesehen to take a look at something, 11-1
anstatt (*prep.* + *gen.*) instead of, 8-G
die **Antwort, -en** answer, 2-1
antworten (+ *dat.*) to answer (a person), 1-1
antworten auf (+ *acc.*) to answer (something), respond to, 13-2
an·ziehen, zog an, hat angezogen to dress
sich anziehen to get dressed, 11-1
sich etwas anziehen to put something on, 11-G
der **Anzug, ⸚e** suit, 3-VzT
die **Apotheke, -n** pharmacy, 8-VzT
der **Appetit** appetite
Guten Appetit! *Bon appétit!* Enjoy your meal! 8-1
(der) **April** April, *Einf.*
die **Arbeit** work, 2-2
arbeiten to work, 1-1
der **Arbeiter, -** worker (*m.*), 5-2
die **Arbeiterin, -nen** worker (*f.*), 5-2
arbeitslos unemployed, 8-2
die **Arbeitslosigkeit** unemployment, 8-2
das **Arbeitszimmer, -** study, 15-VzT
der **Architekt, -en, -en** architect (*m.*), 8-TLL
die **Architektin, -nen** architect (*f.*), 8-TLL
ärgern to annoy; offend, 10-1
sich ärgern (**über** + *acc.*) to get annoyed (at), be annoyed (about), 13-2
arm (ärmer) poor, 10-1
der **Arm, -e** arm, 10-2
die **Armbanduhr, -en** wristwatch, 3-VzT
die **Armee, -n** army, 14-TLL
der **Artikel, -** article, 2-1
der **Arzt, ⸚e** doctor (*m.*), 5-VzT; 11-1
die **Ärztin, -nen** doctor (*f.*), 5-VzT; 11-1
der **Aspekt, -e** aspect, 8-TLL
das **Atom, -e** atom, 9-TLL
das **Atomkraftwerk, -e** atomic power plant, 9-2
auch also, too, 1-1
auf (*prep.* + *acc.* or *dat.*) onto; on, upon, on top of, 6-1
die **Aufgabe, -n** task, assignment, 8-2
auf·geben (gibt auf), gab auf, hat aufgegeben (*trans. & intrans.*) to give up, quit, 11-2
auf·hängen to hang up, 7-1
auf·hören (mit etwas) to cease, stop (doing something), 5-1
auf·machen to open, 5-1
auf·räumen to tidy up, straighten up, 13-1
sich auf·regen (**über** + *acc.*) to get upset (about), get excited (about), 15-1
der **Aufsatz, ⸚e** essay
das **Aufsatzthema, -themen** essay topic
der **Aufschnitt** (*no pl.*) cold cuts, 4-VzT
auf·stehen, stand auf, ist aufgestanden (1) to stand up; to get up; (2) to get out of bed, 5-1
auf·wachen, ist aufgewacht to wake up (*intrans.*), 7-1
auf·wachsen (wächst auf), wuchs auf, ist aufgewachsen to grow up, 8-2
das **Auge, -n** eye, 11-1
der **Augenblick, -e** moment, 8-1
(Einen) Augenblick, bitte. Just a moment, please. 8-1
im Augenblick at the moment, 12-1
(der) **August** August, *Einf.*
aus (*prep.* + *dat.*) out of; from, 5-1
aus·brechen (bricht aus), brach aus, ist ausgebrochen to break out
der **Ausdruck, ⸚e** expression
der **Ausflug, ⸚e** outing, excursion, 14-1
aus·geben (gibt aus), gab aus, hat ausgegeben to spend (money), 6-2
aus·gehen, ging aus, ist ausgegangen to go out, 14-1
ausgezeichnet excellent, 8-1
sich aus·kennen, kannte aus, hat ausgekannt to know one's way around, 13-1
die **Auskunft** information, 13-1
das **Ausland** (*sing.*) foreign countries, 7-2
im Ausland abroad (*location*), 7-2
ins Ausland abroad (*destination*), 7-2
der **Ausländer, -** foreigner (*m.*), 15-2

die **Ausländerin, -nen** foreigner (*f.*), 15-2
ausländisch foreign, 10-2
aus·sehen (sieht aus), sah aus, hat ausgesehen to appear, look (like), 5-2
außer (*prep. + dat.*) except for; besides; in addition to, 5-1
aus·sprechen (spricht aus), sprach aus, hat ausgesprochen to pronounce, 15-2
aus·steigen, stieg aus, ist ausgestiegen to get out (of a vehicle), 7-2
die **Ausstellung, -en** exhibition, 10-2
der **Austauschstudent, -en, -en** exchange student (*m.*), 6-1
die **Austauschstudentin, -nen** exchange student (*f.*), 6-1
aus·wandern, ist ausgewandert to emigrate, 11-2
der **Ausweis, -e** I.D. card, 6-2
aus·ziehen, zog aus, ist ausgezogen to move out, 6-1
sich ausziehen to get undressed, 11-1
das **Auto, -s** car, 2-2
die **Autobahn, -en** expressway, high-speed highway, 7-2
automatisch automatic, 6-TLL
der **Automechaniker, -** auto mechanic (*m.*), 5-1
die **Automechanikerin, -nen** auto mechanic (*f.*), 5-1
der **Autor, -en** author, 15-TLL

B

der **Bäcker, -** baker (*m.*), 5-1
die **Bäckerei, -en** bakery, 5-1
die **Bäckerin, -nen** baker (*f.*), 5-1
das **Bad, ¨-er** bath, 14-1
ein Bad nehmen to take a bath, 14-1
sich baden to take a bath, 11-G
das **Badezimmer, -** bathroom, 14-1, 15-VzT
baff sein (*colloq.*) to be flabbergasted, speechless, 13-1
die **Bahn** railroad, railway system, 7-2
der **Bahnhof, ¨-e** train station, 7-1
bald soon, 1-2
die **Bank, ¨-e** bench, 10-1
die **Bank, -en** bank, 14-1
der **Bankautomat, -en** automatic teller machine, 14-1
der **Bär, -en, -en** bear, 10-VzT
barbarisch barbaric, 4-TLL
das **Bargeld** cash, 14-1
die **Barriere, -n** barrier, 13-TLL
die **Basis** basis, 9-TLL
bauen to build, 8-2
der **Bauer, -n, -n** farmer (*m.*), 5-1
die **Bäuerin, -nen** farmer (*f.*), 5-1
das **Bauernbrot** dark bread, 5-1
der **Baum, ¨-e** tree, 4-2
der **Beamte, -n** (*adj. noun*) official, civil servant (*m.*), 11-1
die **Beamtin, -nen** official, civil servant (*f.*), 11-1
beantworten to answer (a question or letter), 6-2
bedeuten to mean, signify, 2-2
die **Bedeutung, -en** meaning, significance, 10-2
sich beeilen to hurry, 11-1
die **Begeisterung** enthusiasm, 11-1
beginnen, begann, hat begonnen to begin, 4-1
behalten (behält), behielt, hat behalten to keep, retain, 12-1
bei (*prep. + dat.*) (1) at the home of; near; at, 5-1; (2) during, while -ing, 11-G
beid- (*adj.*) both, 11-2
beide (*pl. pronoun*) both (people)
beides (*sing. pronoun*) both things, 13-2
das **Bein, -e** leg, 11-1
das **Beispiel, -e** example, 9-2
zum Beispiel for example, 1-2
bekannt known; well known, 7-2
der/die **Bekannte, -n** (*adj. noun*) acquaintance, friend, 11-1
bekommen, bekam, hat bekommen to receive, get, 4-1
belegen to take (a university course), 6-2
benutzen to use, 9-2
das **Benzin** gasoline, 7-2
bequem comfortable, 7-2
bereit prepared, ready, 9-2
der **Berg, -e** mountain, 3-1
bergig mountainous, 4-VzT
berichten to report, 5-2
der **Beruf, -e** profession, vocation, 2-2
Was sind Sie von Beruf? What is your profession? 5-VzT
berufstätig employed, 2-2
berühmt famous, 11-2
beschreiben, beschrieb, hat beschrieben to describe, 4-2
besitzen, besaß, hat besessen to own, 2-2
besonders especially, 5-2
besorgt worried, concerned, 10-1
besprechen (bespricht), besprach, hat besprochen to discuss, 3-2
besser better, 12-G
die **Besserung: Gute Besserung!** Get well soon! 11-1
best- best, 12-G
bestellen to order, 8-1
der **Besuch, -e** visit, 12-1
besuchen to visit, 3-1
die **Betriebswirtschaft** management, business, 6-VzT
das **Bett, -en** bed, 6-1
ins Bett gehen to go to bed, 7-1
bevor (*sub. conj.*) before, 10-2
bezahlen to pay, 6-2
die **Bibliothek, -en** library, 6-1
das **Bier, -e** beer, 4-2
das **Bild, -er** picture; image, 5-2
billig inexpensive, cheap, 6-2
die **Biologie** biology, 6-VzT
bis (*prep. + acc.*) until, *Einf.*; by, 1-1
bis dann until then, 1-1
Bis morgen. Until tomorrow, *Einf.*
Bis nachher! See you later!, 4-1
ein bisschen a little; a little bit; a little while, 3-1
bitte (sehr) (1) you're welcome, 2-1; (2) please, 1-2; (3) here it is, there you are, 5-1
bitten, bat, hat gebeten um to ask for, request, 13-1
Er bittet mich um das Geld. He's asking me for the money.
blau blue, 3-2
bleiben, blieb, ist geblieben to stay, remain, 2-2
der **Bleistift, -e** pencil, *Einf.*
blitzschnell quick as lightning, 3-2
blöd dumb, stupid, 5-1
die **Blume, -n** flower, 11-1
die **Bluse, -n** blouse, 3-VzT
der **Boden, ¨-** floor, 6-VzT
böse (+ *dat.*) angry, mad (at); bad, evil, 13-1
die **Boutique, -n** boutique, 5-TLL
brauchen to need, 2-1
braun brown, 3-2
brav well-behaved, good, 15-2
die **BRD** (= **Bundesrepublik Deutschland**) the FRG (= the Federal Republic of Germany), 2-2
brechen (bricht), brach, hat gebrochen to break, 11-1
die **Brezel, -n** soft pretzel, 5-1
der **Brief, -e** letter, 6-2
der **Briefkasten, ¨-** mailbox, 15-1
die **Briefmarke, -n** postage stamp, 15-1
der **Briefträger, -** letter carrier, mailman, 5-TLL
die **Briefträgerin, -nen** letter carrier (*f.*)
die **Brille** (*sing.*) (eye)glasses, 3-VzT
bringen, brachte, hat gebracht to bring, 6-1
das **Brot, -e** bread, 5-1
das **Brötchen, -** roll, 4-1
die **Brücke, -n** bridge, 8-2
der **Bruder, ¨-** brother, 2-1
das **Buch, ¨-er** book, *Einf.*
das **Bücherregal, -e** bookcase, 6-VzT
der **Buchhändler, -** bookseller (*m.*), 5-2
die **Buchhändlerin, -nen** bookseller (*f.*), 5-2
die **Buchhandlung, -en** bookstore, 5-2
die **Bude, -n** (*colloq.*) (rented) student room, 6-2
der **Bummel, -** stroll, walk, 8-1
einen Stadtbummel machen to take a stroll through town, 8-1
die **Bundesrepublik Deutschland** the Federal Republic of Germany, 2-2
bunt colorful, multicolored, 3-2

das **Büro, -s** office, 1-1
der **Bus, -se** bus, 7-VzT
die **Butter** (*no pl.*) butter, 4-VzT

C

das **Café, -s** café, 5-TLL; 8-VzT
campen to camp, 5-TLL
die **CD, -s** CD (compact disk), 6-VzT
der **CD-Spieler** CD player, 6-VzT
die **Chance, -n** chance, 9-2
der **Charakter, -e** character, 14-TLL
der **Chef, -s** boss (*m.*), 5-1
die **Chefin, -nen** boss (*f.*), 5-1
die **Chemie** chemistry, 6-VzT
die **Chemiestunde** chemistry class, 3-1
(das) **China** China, 11-TLL
der **Chinese, -n, -n** Chinese (*m.*), 11-TLL
die **Chinesin, -nen** Chinese (*f.*), 11-TLL
chinesisch Chinese (*adj.*), 11-TLL
(das) **Chinesisch** Chinese (language), 13-TLL
der **Computer, -** computer, 5-TLL
der **Container, -** large trash container, 9-1
der **Cousin, -s** cousin (*m.*), 2-2
die **Cousine, -n** cousin (*f.*), 2-2

D

da (1) there, 1-1; (2) then, in that case, 9-1; (3) since (*sub. conj., causal*), 8-G
da drüben over there, 2-1
dabei sein to be present, be there, 15-1
dahin: Wie komme ich dahin? How do I get there? 13-1
damals at that time, back then, 10-1
die **Dame, -n** lady, 10-2
damit (*sub. conj.*) so that, 14-2
der **Dank** thanks
Vielen Dank! Many thanks! Thanks a lot, 2-1
danke thanks, thank you, *Einf.*; 1-1
Danke, gleichfalls. You too. Same to you. *Einf.*; 12-1
danken (+ *dat.*) to thank, 7-1
Nichts zu danken! Don't mention it! 2-1
dann then, 1-1
darf (*see* **dürfen**)
darum therefore, for that reason, 3-2
das sind (*pl. of* **das ist**) those are, 2-2
dass that (*sub. conj.*), 8-1
der **Dativ** dative case, 5-G
das **Datum,** *pl.* **Daten** date, 9-G
dauern to last; to take (time), 10-1
die **DDR (= Deutsche Demokratische Republik)** the GDR (= the German Democratic Republic), 11-1
die **Decke, -n** ceiling, 6-VzT
definieren to define 14-TLL
die **Demokratie, -n** democracy, 10-TLL
demokratisch democratic, 10-TLL
die **Demokratisierung** democratization, 11-TLL
die **Demonstration, -en** demonstration, 11-TLL
denken, dachte, hat gedacht to think, 13-2
denken an (+ *acc.*) to think of, 13-2
das **Denkmal, ⸚er** monument, memorial 11-1
denn (1) (*flavoring particle in questions*), 2-1; (2) (*coor. conj.*) for, because, 7-G
deutlich clear
deutsch (*adj.*) German, 2-2
(das) **Deutsch** German language, 3-2
auf Deutsch in German, 1-2
der/die **Deutsche, -n** (*adj. noun*) German (person), 1-2
die **Deutsche Demokratische Republik** German Democratic Republic (GDR), 11-1
(das) **Deutschland** Germany, 1-2
deutschsprachig German-speaking
die **Deutschstunde, -n** German class, 3-1
(der) **Dezember** December, *Einf.*
d.h. (= das heißt) i.e. (= that is), 6-2
der **Dialekt, -e** dialect, 13-TLL
der **Dialog, -e** dialogue
der **Dichter, -** poet
(der) **Dienstag** Tuesday, *Einf.*
dies- this, these, 4-1
diesmal this time, 12-1
das **Ding, -e** thing, 7-2
direkt direct(ly), 13-1
der **Direktor, -en** director, 10-TLL
die **Diskussion, -en** discussion, 2-2
sich distanzieren von to distance oneself from, 14-TLL
doch (1) (*stressed, contradictory*) yes I do, yes I am, yes he is, etc., 3-1; (2) (*unstressed flavoring particle with commands*), 4-1; (3) (*unstressed flavoring particle with statements*), 10-1
der **Dom, -e** cathedral, 8-1
die **Donau** Danube River, 14-2
(der) **Donnerstag** Thursday, *Einf.*
das **Doppelzimmer, -** double room, 14-1
das **Dorf, ⸚er** village, 5-2
dort there, 2-1
die **Dose, -n** (tin) can, 9-2
draußen outside, 1-1
dreckig (*colloq.*) dirty, 9-1
dritt- third, 9-G
drüben over there, 2-1
der **Druck** pressure, 13-2
dumm (dümmer) dumb, 5-1
dunkel dark, 3-2
durch (*prep.* + *acc.*) through, 4-1
dürfen (darf), durfte, hat gedurft may, to be allowed to, 3-1
Was darf es sein? What'll it be? May I help you? 5-1
der **Durst** thirst, 8-1
Durst haben to be thirsty, 8-1
die **Dusche, -n** shower, 14-1
sich duschen to take a shower, 11-G; 14-VzT
duzen *to address someone with* **du,** 1-2
die **Dynastie, -n** dynasty, 8-TLL

E

echt real, genuine (*colloq.*), 3-2
die **Ecke, -n** corner, 8-1
an der Ecke at the corner, 8-1
um die Ecke around the corner, 8-1
egal: Das ist (mir) egal. It doesn't matter (to me). I don't care. 7-1
die **Ehe, -n** marriage, 14-1
das **Ehepaar, -e** married couple, 14-1
ehrlich honest, 3-2
das **Ei, -er** egg, 4-VzT
eigen- own, 9-2
eigentlich actually, in fact, 3-2
die **Eile** hurry
in Eile in a hurry, 1-1
einander (*pronoun*) each other, 1-2
der **Eindruck, ⸚e** impression, 8-2
einfach simple, easy, 5-1
der **Einfluss, ⸚e** influence, 14-2
einige some, 6-2
ein·kaufen to shop for; to go shopping, 5-2
ein·laden (lädt ein), lud ein, hat eingeladen to invite, 8-1
einmal once, 4-1
noch einmal once again, once more, 4-1
ein paar a couple (of), a few, 5-2
eins one, *Einf.*
einsam lonely, 14-2
die **Einsamkeit** loneliness, 14-2
ein·schlafen (schläft ein), schlief ein, ist eingeschlafen to fall asleep, 7-1
ein·steigen, stieg ein, ist eingestiegen to get in (a vehicle), 7-2
der **Einstieg, -e** entrance, way in
einverstanden Agreed. It's a deal. O.K. Okay. 5-1
ein·wandern, ist eingewandert to immigrate, 11-2
ein·werfen (wirft ein), warf ein, hat eingeworfen to throw in; to mail (a letter), 15-1
das **Einzelzimmer, -** single room, 14-1
ein·ziehen, zog ein, ist eingezogen to move in, 6-1
einzig- single, only, 12-2
das **Eis** (1) ice; (2) ice cream, 8-VzT
das **Eishockey** ice hockey, 9-VzT
der **Elefant, -en, -en** elephant, 10-VzT
die **Elektrizität** electricity, 9-TLL
die **Elektrotechnik** electrical engineering, 6-VzT
der **Elektrotechniker, -** electrical engineer (*m.*), 5-VzT

die **Elektrotechnikerin, -nen** electrical engineer (*f.*), 5-VzT
die **Eltern** (*pl.*) parents, 2-1
die **E-Mail, -s** e-mail, 1-TLL
emigrieren to emigrate, 15-TLL
empfehlen (empfiehlt), empfahl, hat empfohlen to recommend, 9-1
das **Ende, -n** end, 6-2
am Ende at the end, 6-1
Ende Februar at the end of February
zu Ende sein to end, be finished, be over, 10-2
endlich finally, 1-1
die **Energie, -n** energy, 9-TLL
der **Engländer, -** Englishman, 11-TLL
die **Engländerin, -nen** Englishwoman, 11-TLL
englisch English, 11-TLL
(das) **Englisch** English language, 3-2
der **Enkel, -** grandson, 2-1
die **Enkelin, -nen** granddaughter, 2-1
die **Enkelkinder** grandchildren, 2-1
enorm enormous, 9-TLL
entscheiden, entschied, hat entschieden to decide, 3-2
Entschuldigung! Pardon me! Excuse me! 1-1
enttäuschen to disappoint, 6-2
entweder ... oder either . . . or, 14-1
die **Epoche, -n** epoch, 10-TLL
die **Erde** earth, 12-2
das **Erdgeschoss** ground floor, first floor, 14-1 (*see* **Stock**)
erfinden, erfand, hat erfunden to invent
sich erholen (von) (1) to recover (from), get well; (2) to have a rest, 13-2
erinnern an (+ *acc.*) to remind of, 12-1
sich erinnern an (+ *acc.*) to remember, 12-1
die **Erinnerung, -en** memory, 12-1
erkältet sein to have a cold, 3-1
sich erkälten to catch a cold, 11-1
erkennen, erkannte, hat erkannt to recognize, 15-2
erklären to explain, 10-2
ernst serious, 9-2
etwas ernst nehmen to take something seriously, 14-2
erst (*adv.*) not until; only, 5-1
erst- (*adj.*) first, 9-G
erstaunlich astounding, 9-2
erwachsen adult, grown-up, 15-2
der / die **Erwachsene, -n** (*adj. noun*) adult, grown-up, 15-2
erzählen to tell, recount, 6-2
die **Erzählung, -en** story, narrative, 12-2
der **Esel, -** donkey, 10-VzT
der **Essay, -s** essay, 14-TLL, 15-TLL
essen (isst), aß, hat gegessen to eat, 2-1
das **Essen** food; meal, 2-1

das **Esszimmer, -** dining room, 15-VzT
etwas (1) (*pronoun*) something, 3-1; (2) (*adj. & adv.*) some, a little; somewhat, 12-1
der **Euro, -s** euro (€), 5-1
(das) **Europa** Europe, 3-2
der **Europäer, -** European (*m.*), 3-2
die **Europäerin, -nen** European (*f.*), 3-2
europäisch European, 11-1
die **Europäische Union (EU)** European Union, 11-TLL
existieren to exist, 11-1
extrem extreme, 10-TLL

F

die **Fabrik, -en** factory, 8-2
das **Fach, ¨-er** area of study; subject, 6-VzT
fahren (fährt), fuhr, ist gefahren to drive, go (by vehicle), 3-1
die **Fahrkarte, -n** ticket (for bus, train, streetcar, etc.), 7-2
das **Fahrrad, ¨-er** bicycle, 7-2
der Fall fall, 11-TLL
fallen (fällt), fiel, ist gefallen (1) to fall; (2) to die in battle, 10-1
falsch false, incorrect, wrong, *Einf.*; 3-1
die **Familie, -n** family, 2-1
fantastisch fantastic, 2-1
die **Farbe, -n** color, 3-2
fast almost, 2-2
faul lazy, 5-2
(der) **Februar** February, *Einf.*
fehlen to be missing; to be absent, 10-1
die **Feier, -n** celebration, party, 15-1
feiern to celebrate, party 6-2
das **Fenster, -** window, *Einf.*
die **Ferien** (*pl.*) (university and school) vacation, 6-2
fern distant, far away, 12-2
fern·sehen (sieht fern), sah fern, hat ferngesehen to watch TV, 5-2
der **Fernseher, -** television set, 2-2
fertig (mit) (1) done, finished (with); (2) ready, 5-1
der **Film, -e** film, movie, 6-TLL
finanzieren to finance, 6-TLL
finden, fand, hat gefunden to find, 2-2
Das finde ich auch. I think so, too. 3-2
der **Finger, -** finger, 11-1
die **Firma,** *pl.* **Firmen** firm, company, 5-2
der **Fisch, -e** fish, 9-2
fit in shape, 3-1
flach flat, 4-2
die **Flasche, -n** bottle, 7-1
das **Fleisch** meat, 2-1
fleißig industrious, hard-working, 5-2
fliegen, flog, ist geflogen to fly, 1-1
fließen, floss, ist geflossen to flow, 4-2
der **Flughafen, ¨-** airport, 7-VzT
das **Flugzeug, -e** airplane, 7-2

der **Fluss, ¨-e** river, 4-2
folgen, ist gefolgt (+ *dat.*) to follow, 8-2
die **Form, -en** form, 10-TLL
formell formal, 1-TLL
formulieren to formulate
der **Fortschritt, -e** progress, 9-1
das **Foto, -s** photograph, 6-TLL; 7-2
ein Foto machen to take a picture, 7-2
die **Frage, -n** question, 2-1
eine Frage stellen to ask a question, 10-2
der **Fragebogen** questionnaire
fragen to ask, 1-1
sich fragen to wonder, ask oneself, 15-1
(das) **Frankreich** France, 7-2, 11-TLL
der **Franzose, -n, -n** Frenchman, 11-TLL
die **Französin, -nen** Frenchwoman, 11-TLL
französisch French, 11-TLL; 13-2
die **Frau, -en** woman; wife, 1-1, 2-1
Frau Kuhn Mrs./Ms. Kuhn, *Einf.*
das **Fräulein, -** young (unmarried) woman
frei free; unoccupied, 2-1
die **Freiheit, -en** freedom, 7-2
(der) **Freitag** Friday, *Einf.*
die **Freizeit** free time, leisure time, 5-2
fremd (1) strange; (2) foreign, 3-2
die **Fremdsprache, -n** foreign language, 3-2
die **Freude, -n** joy, 12-2
freuen
Das freut mich. I'm glad. *Einf.*
(Es) freut mich. Pleased to meet you. 5-1
sich freuen to be happy, 11-1
sich freuen auf (+ *acc.*) to look forward to, 13-1
der **Freund, -e** friend (*m.*), 2-1
die **Freundin, -nen** friend (*f.*), 3-1
freundlich friendly, 1-2
der **Frieden** peace, 6-2
frisch fresh, 5-1
froh happy, glad, 13-2
früh early, 3-1
der **Frühling** spring, 4-1
das **Frühstück** breakfast, 4-1
zum Frühstück for breakfast, 4-1
frühstücken to eat breakfast, 4-1
der **Fuchs, ¨-e** fox, 10-VzT
sich fühlen to feel (*intrans.*), 11-1
sich wohl fühlen to feel well, 14-2
führen to lead, 8-2
der **Führerschein** driver's license, 7-2
den Führerschein machen to get a driver's license, 7-2
für (*prep.* + *acc.*) for, 1-1, 4-1
furchtbar terrible, *Einf.*
fürchten to fear, 11-1

der **Fuß, ¨-e** foot, 4-2
zu Fuß on foot, 4-2
der **Fußball** soccer; soccer ball, 5-2
Fußball spielen to play soccer, 9-VzT
der **Fußballspieler, -** soccer player (*m.*), 9-VzT
die **Fußballspielerin, -nen** soccer player (*f.*), 9-VzT
der **Fußgänger, -** pedestrian, 14-1
die **Fußgängerzone, -n** pedestrian zone, 8-VzT; 14-1
das **Futur** future tense, 13-G

G

die **Gabel, -n** fork, 8-VzT
ganz entire, whole, 9-1
ganz gut pretty good, 1-1
das ganze Wochenende all weekend, the whole weekend 9-1
den ganzen Sommer (Tag, Nachmittag usw.) all summer (day, afternoon, etc.), 10-1
gar
gar nicht not at all, 3-2
gar kein no . . . at all, not a . . . at all, 11-1
die **Garage, -n** garage, 15-VzT
der **Garten, ¨** garden, 15-VzT
der **Gast, ¨-e** guest; patron, 8-1
das **Gebäude, -** building, 8-1
geben (gibt), gab, hat gegeben to give, 2-2
es gibt (+ *acc.*) there is, there are, 2-2
Was gibt's Neues? What's new? 13-1
das **Gebirge, -** mountain range, 4-TLL
geboren born
Wann bist du/sind Sie geboren? When were you born? 10-1
der **Geburtstag, -e** birthday, 7-2
Ich gratuliere dir zum Geburtstag! Happy birthday! 15-1
Wann hast du Geburtstag? When is your birthday? 7-2
zum Geburtstag for (one's) birthday, 9-1
die **Geburtstagsfeier, -n** birthday party, 15-1
der **Gedanke, -ns, -n** thought
das **Gedicht, -e** poem
die **Gefahr, -en** danger, 9-2
gefährlich dangerous, 9-2
gefallen (gefällt), gefiel, hat gefallen (+ *dat. of person*) to please, appeal to, 7-1
das **Gefühl, -e** feeling, 9-1
gegen (*prep. + acc.*) (1) against, (2) around, about (*with time*), 4-1
die **Gegend, -en** area, region, 12-1
der **Gegensatz, ¨-e** opposite
das **Gegenteil: im Gegenteil** on the contrary, 8-2
gegenüber (*prep. + dat.*) across from; with respect to, 14-2
gehen, ging, ist gegangen (1) to go; (2) to walk, 1-1
Es geht. It's all right. 4-1
Es geht nicht. Nothing doing. It can't be done. 4-1
Wie geht es Ihnen/dir? How are you? *Einf.*, 1-1
gehören (+ *dat. of person*) to belong to (a person), 7-1
gelaunt
gut gelaunt in a good mood, 7-2
schlecht gelaunt in a bad mood, 7-2
gelb yellow, 3-2
das **Geld** money, 2-2
der **Geldbeutel, -** wallet, change purse, 10-1
die **Gelegenheit, -en** opportunity, chance, 8-2
das **Gemüse** vegetables, 2-1
gemütlich cozy, comfortable; quiet, relaxed, 14-1
genau exact, precise, 11-1
genauso ... wie just as . . . as, 12-G
genießen, genoss, genossen to enjoy, 7-2
der **Genitiv** genitive case, 8-G
genug enough, 3-1
die **Geographie** geography, 4-TLL
geographisch geographical, 4-TLL
das **Gepäck** luggage, 7-1
gerade just, at this moment, 6-2
geradeaus straight ahead, 8-2
die **Germanistik** German studies, 6-VzT
gern(e) (lieber, am liebsten) gladly, with pleasure, 3-1
verb + **gern** to like to do something, 4-G
verb + **lieber** prefer to, would rather, 4-1
Lieber nicht. I'd rather not. No thanks. Let's not. 4-1
das **Geschäft, -e** business; store, 5-2
die **Geschäftsfrau, -en** businesswoman, 5-VzT
der **Geschäftsmann,** *pl.* **Geschäftsleute** businessman, 5-VzT
das **Geschenk, -e** present (*gift*), 9-1
die **Geschichte, -n** (1) story; (2) history, 6-2, 6-VzT
geschlossen closed (*see* **schließen**), 11-2
die **Geschwister** (*pl.*) siblings, brothers and sisters, 2-2
die **Gesellschaft, -en** society, 9-2
das **Gesicht, -er** face, 11-1
das **Gespräch, -e** conversation, 13-2
gestern yesterday, 6-1
gestern Abend yesterday evening, 12-G
gestern früh yesterday morning, 12-G
gesund healthy, 9-2
die **Gesundheit** health, 9-2
sich gewöhnen an (+ *acc.*) to get used to, 13-1
das **Glas, ¨-er** glass, 8-1
glauben (+ *dat. of person*) (1) to believe; (2) to think, 4-1
Ich glaube nicht. I don't think so. 8-1
Ich glaube schon. I think so. 8-1
gleich right away, immediately, 5-1
das **Gleis, -e** track, 7-1
die **Globalisierung** globalization, 13-TLL
das **Glück** (1) happiness; (2) luck, 6-2
Glück haben to be lucky, 6-2
glücklich happy, 4-1
glücklicherweise fortunately, 9-1
golden golden, 14-TLL
der **Gott, ¨-er** god
Gott sei Dank thank goodness, 4-1
Grüß Gott hello (in southern Germany and Austria), *Einf.*
Um Gottes Willen! For heaven's sake! Oh my gosh! 9-1
das **Gramm** gram, 8-1
die **Grammatik** grammar
der **Graphiker, -** graphic artist (*m.*), 5-2
die **Graphikerin, -nen** graphic artist (*f.*), 5-2
gratulieren (+ *dat. of person*) to congratulate, 15-1
Ich gratuliere (dir) congratulations, 15-1
grau gray, 3-2
grausam terrible, gruesome; cruel, 12-2
die **Grenze, -n** border, 11-1
(das) **Griechenland** Greece
griechisch (*adj.*) Greek, 8-1
groß (größer, am größten) big, tall, 2-1
(das) **Großbritannien** Great Britain, 8-TLL
die **Größe, -n** size; greatness, 12-1
die **Großeltern** (*pl.*) grandparents, 2-2
die **Großmutter, ¨** grandmother, 2-2
die **Großstadt, ¨-e** large city (*over 500,000 inhabitants*), 8-2
der **Großvater, ¨** grandfather, 2-2
grün green, 3-2
der **Grund, ¨-e** reason
die **Gruppe, -n** group, 2-2
grüßen to greet, say hello, 1-2
Grüß dich! Hello! (*informal,* in southern Germany and Austria), 1-2
Grüß Gott hello (in southern Germany and Austria), *Einf.*
gut (besser, am besten) good, well, *Einf.*; 1-1
ganz gut pretty good, 1-1
Guten Abend! Good evening! *Einf.*
Guten Morgen! Good morning! *Einf.*
Gute Reise! Have a good trip! 1-1

Guten Tag! Hello! *Einf.*
Ist gut. (*colloq.*) O.K. Fine by me. 5-1
Schon gut Fine. It's okay. No problem 2-1
das **Gymnasium,** *pl.* **Gymnasien** secondary school (prepares pupils for university), 3-2

H

das **Haar, -e** hair, 6-2
sich die Haare kämmen to comb one's hair, 11-G
haben (hat), hatte, hat gehabt to have, *Einf.*; 2-1
der **Hafen, ¨** port, harbor, 8-2
halb (*adv.*) half
halb acht seven-thirty, *Einf.*
Hallo! Hello! *Einf.*
halten (hält), hielt, hat gehalten (1) to stop (*intrans.*); (2) to hold, 3-1
die **Haltestelle, -n** (streetcar or bus) stop, 8-VzT; 13-1
die **Hand, ¨e** hand, 5-1
der **Handschuh, -e** glove, 3-VzT
das **Handy, -s** cell phone; mobile phone, 6-VzT
hängen (*trans.*) to hang, 7-1
hängen, hing, hat gehangen (*intrans.*) to be hanging, 7-1
hart (härter) hard; tough; harsh, 10-2
der **Hass** hatred, 11-2
hassen to hate, 3-2
hässlich ugly, 1-1
Haupt- (*noun prefix*) main, chief, primary, most important, 4-TLL
das **Hauptfach, ¨er** major field (of study), 6-2
die **Hauptstadt, ¨e** capital city, 4-TLL; 11-1
das **Haus, ¨er** house; building, 2-1
nach Hause home (*as destination of motion*), 3-1
zu Hause at home, 2-2
die **Hausarbeit** housework, 2-TLL
die **Hausaufgabe, -n** homework assignment, 3-2
die **Hausfrau, -en** housewife, 2-2
der **Hausmann, ¨er** househusband, 5-VzT
das **Heft, -e** notebook, *Einf.*
die **Heimat** native place or country, homeland, 11-2
die **Heimatstadt** hometown, 8-2
heiß hot, *Einf.*
heißen, hieß, hat geheißen to be called, *Einf.*
das heißt that means, in other words, 6-2
Ich heiße ... My name is . . . *Einf.*
Wie heißen Sie?/Wie heißt du? What's your name? *Einf.*
hektisch hectic, 8-TLL
helfen (hilft), half, hat geholfen (+ *dat.*) to help, 7-1
hell bright, light, 3-2
das **Hemd, -en** shirt, 3-2
her- (*prefix*) *indicates motion toward the speaker,* 15-G
der **Herbst** fall, autumn, 4-1
Herein! Come in! 13-1
der **Herr, -n, -en** man, gentleman, 1-1
Herr Lehmann Mr. Lehmann, *Einf.*
herrlich great, terrific, marvelous, 7-2
das **Herz, -en** heart, 14-2
Herzlich willkommen! Welcome! Nice to see you! 6-2
heute today, *Einf.*
heute Abend this evening, tonight, 1-1
heute Morgen this morning, 5-1
heute Nachmittag this afternoon, 12-G
heutig today's, of today, 11-2
hier here, 1-1
die **Hilfe** help, aid, 13-1
hin- (*prefix*) *indicates motion away from speaker,* 15-G
hinein- (*prefix*) in, into, 15-1
hinein·gehen, ging ... hinein, ist hineingegangen to go in, 13-1
hinter (*prep.* + *acc.* or *dat.*) behind, 6-1
historisch historic, 8-TLL
hoch (*predicate adj.*), **hoh-** (*attributive adj.*) **(höher, am höchsten)** high, 4-2
höchste Zeit high time, 14-1
das **Hochland** highlands, 4-TLL
Hockey spielen to play hockey, 9-VzT
der **Hockeyspieler, -** hockey player (*m.*), 9-VzT
die **Hockeyspielerin, -nen** hockey player (*f.*), 9-VzT
hoffen to hope, 7-2
hoffentlich (*adv.*) I hope, 4-1
höflich polite, 1-2
hoh-, höher (*see* **hoch**)
holen to fetch, get, 12-2
der **Honig** (*no pl.*) honey, 4-VzT
hören to hear; to listen, 1-2
der **Horizont, -e** horizon, 7-TLL
die **Hose, -n** trousers, pants, 3-2
das **Hotel, -s** hotel, 4-1
hübsch pretty, handsome, 11-1
der **Hügel, -** hill, 4-2
hügelig hilly, 4-VzT
der **Humor** humor, 14-TLL
der **Hund, -e** dog, 11-G
hundert hundred, 2-G
der **Hunger** hunger, 8-1
Hunger haben to be hungry, 8-1
hungrig hungry, 4-1
der **Hut, ¨e** hat, 3-VzT

I

die **Idee, -n** idea, 10-2
sich identifizieren mit to identify with, 14-2, 14-TLL
die **Identität, -en** identity, 15-TLL
ideologisch ideological, 10-TLL
idiotensicher foolproof, 12-1
illegal illegal, 10-TLL
die **Illusion, -en** illusion, 14-TLL
immer always, 3-1
immer größer bigger and bigger, 12-G
immer noch still, 4-2
der **Imperativ** imperative mood, 4-G
das **Imperfekt** simple past tense, 6-G
in (*prep.* + *acc.* or *dat.*) in, into, 1-1, 6-1
der **Indikativ** indicative, 14-G
die **Industrie, -n** industry, 9-TLL
der **Infinitiv** infinitive, 1-G
der **Infinitivsatz** infinitive phrase, 8-G
die **Inflation** inflation, 10-TLL
die **Informatik** computer science, 6-VzT
der **Ingenieur, -e** engineer (*m.*), 5-VzT
die **Ingenieurin, -nen** engineer (*f.*), 5-VzT
der **Inhalt** contents, 14-2
die **Insel, -n** island, 4-TLL
das **Instrument, -e** instrument, 7-TLL
die **Integration** integration, 11-TLL
intelligent intelligent, 12-1
interessant interesting, 3-1
interessieren to interest, 13-1
sich interessieren für (+ *acc.*) to be interested in, 13-1
interkulturell intercultural, 15-TLL
international international, 3-TLL
interviewen to interview, 10-1
investieren to invest, 11-TLL
inzwischen meanwhile, in the meantime, 11-1
der **iPod, -s** iPod, 10-1
irgend- (*prefix*)
irgendwann sometime or other, 12-TLL
irgendwie somehow or other, 12-TLL
irgendwo somewhere or other, 12-TLL
die **Ironie** irony, 14-TLL
(das) **Italien** Italy, 4-2
der **Italiener, -** Italian (*m.*), 11-TLL
die **Italienerin, -nen** Italian (*f.*), 11-TLL
italienisch (*adj.*) Italian, 7-2

J

ja (1) yes; (2) (*unstressed flavoring particle*), 1-1
die **Jacke, -n** jacket, 3-2, 3-VzT
das **Jahr, -e** year, 4-1
im Jahr(e) 1996 in 1996, 8-2
jahrelang (*adv.*) for years, 14-TLL
die **Jahreszeit, -en** season, 4-1
das **Jahrhundert, -e** century, 8-2
jahrhundertelang (*adv.*) for centuries, 14-TLL
jährlich annually, 9-2
(der) **Januar** January, *Einf.*
je ever, 6-2
die **Jeans** (*pl.*) jeans, 3-TLL

jed- each, every, 4-1
jeder (*pronoun*) everyone
jemand somebody, someone, 2-2
jetzt now, 3-1
von jetzt an from now on, 13-1
der **Job, -s** job 2-2
der **Joghurt, -s** yogurt, 4-VzT
der **Journalist, -en, -en** journalist (*m.*), 5-TLL
die **Journalistin, -nen** journalist (*f.*), 5-VzT
jüdisch Jewish, 12-2
die **Jugend** (*sing.*) youth; young people, 9-2
die **Jugendherberge, -n** youth hostel, 7-2
(der) **Juli** July, *Einf.*
jung (jünger) young, 2-2
der **Junge, -n, -n** boy, 9-1
(der) **Juni** June, *Einf.*
Jura (study of) law, 6-VzT

K

der **Kaffee** coffee, 3-1
kalt (kälter) cold, *Einf.*
die **Kamera, -s** camera, 7-TLL
kämmen to comb
sich die Haare kämmen to comb one's hair, 11-G
(das) **Kanada** Canada, 5-TLL; 6-1
der **Kanadier, -** Canadian (*m.*), 11-TLL
die **Kanadierin, -nen** Canadian (*f.*), 11-TLL
kanadisch (*adj.*) Canadian, 11-TLL
das **Kännchen, -** small (coffee or tea) pot, 8-VzT
der **Kapitalismus** capitalism, 11-TLL
das **Kapitel, -** chapter
kaputt (*colloq.*) (1) broken, kaput; (2) exhausted, 9-1
kaputt·machen to break, 12-1
die **Karriere, -n** career, 14-TLL
die **Karte, -n** (1) card; (2) ticket; (3) map, 4-1
die **Kartoffel, -n** potato, 8-1
der **Käse** cheese, 2-1
die **Kasse, -n** cash register; cashier's office, 14-1
katastrophal catastrophic, 10-TLL
die **Katastrophe, -n** catastrophe, 6-2
die **Katze, -n** cat, 11-G
kaufen to buy, 4-1
das **Kaufhaus, ¨-er** department store, 8-VzT
kein not a, not any, no, 3-1
kein ... mehr no more . . .; not a . . . any longer, 4-G
der **Keller, -** cellar, basement, 9-1
der **Kellner, -** waiter, 5-VzT; 8-1
die **Kellnerin, -nen** waitress, 5-VzT; 8-1
kennen, kannte, hat gekannt to know, be acquainted with, 2-1
kennen lernen to get to know; to meet, 5-1
die **Kette, -n** chain
die **Kettenreaktion, -en** chain reaction
das **Kilo** (*short for* **das Kilogramm**), 8-1
das **Kilogramm** kilogram, 8-1
der **Kilometer, -** kilometer
das **Kind, -er** child, 1-1
die **Kindheit** childhood, 9-TLL, 15-2
das **Kino, -s** movie theater, 6-2
die **Kirche, -n** church, 8-2
klar (1) clear; (2) (*colloq.*) sure, of course, 9-1
die **Klasse, -n** class; grade, 3-1
klasse (*colloq.*) great, terrific, wonderful, 6-2
die **Klassenarbeit** written test, in-class examination, 3-1
der **Klatsch** gossip, 12-1
klauen (*colloq.*) to rip off, steal, 10-1
die **Klausur, -en** written test (university), 6-2
das **Klavier, -e** piano, 14-2
das **Kleid, -er** dress (*pl.* = dresses *or* clothes), 3-2, 3-VzT
der **Kleiderschrank, ¨-e** clothes cupboard, wardrobe, 6-VzT
die **Kleidung** clothing, 3-2
klein little, small; short, 2-1
die **Kleinstadt, ¨-e** town (5,000 to 20,000 inhabitants), 8-2
das **Klima** climate, 4-2
klingeln to ring, 7-1
klingen, klang, hat geklungen to sound, 8-1
das **Klischee, -s** cliché, 2-2
klopfen (an + *acc.*) to knock (on), 13-1
klug (klüger) smart, bright, 5-1
knapp scarce, in short supply, 12-1
knapp bei Kasse short of cash, 12-1
die **Kneipe, -n** tavern, bar, 6-2
kochen to cook, 2-2
der **Koffer, -** suitcase, 7-1
der **Kollege, -n, -n** colleague (*m.*), 5-2
die **Kollegin, -nen** colleague (*f.*), 5-2
(das) **Köln** Cologne, 8-1
die **Kolonie, -n** colony, 4-TLL
komisch peculiar, odd; funny, 12-1
kommen, kam, ist gekommen to come, *Einf.*; 1-1
kommen aus to come from, *Einf.*
der **Kommunismus** Communism, 11-TLL
der **Komparativ** comparative degree, 12-G
die **Konditorei, -en** pastry café, 8-VzT
der **Konflikt, -e** conflict, 2-TLL
konfrontieren to confront, 15-TLL
die **Konjunktion, -en** conjunction, 7-G
die **koordinierende Konjunktion** coordinating conjunction, 7-G
die **subordinierende Konjunktion** subordinating conjunction, 8-G
der **Konjunktiv** subjunctive mood, 14-G
können (kann), konnte, hat gekonnt can, be able to, 3-1
Ich kann Deutsch. I can speak German. 3-G
die **Konsequenz, -en** consequence, 9-TLL
konservativ conservative, 13-TLL
der **Kontakt, -e** contact, 7-TLL
der **Kontrast, -e** contrast, 4-TLL
das **Konzert, -e** concert, 6-TLL
der **Kopf, ¨-e** head, 11-1
Das geht mir nicht aus dem Kopf. I can't forget that. 12-2
der **Korrespondent, -en, -en** correspondent, 5-TLL
(das) **Korsika** Corsica
kosten to cost, 5-1
Wie viel kostet das bitte? How much does that cost, please?
kostenlos free of charge, 6-2
die **Kraft, ¨-e** power; strength, 9-2
das **Kraftwerk, -e** power plant, 9-2
der **Kram** (*colloq.*) stuff; things, 8-1
krank (kränker) sick, 3-1.
das **Krankenhaus, ¨-er** hospital, 11-1
der **Krankenpfleger, -** nurse (*m.*), 5-VzT
die **Krankenschwester, -n** nurse (*f.*), 5-VzT
die **Krankheit, -en** sickness, 9-2
die **Krawatte, -n** tie, 3-VzT
die **Kreditkarte, -n** credit card, 14-1
die **Kreide** chalk, *Einf.*
(das) **Kreta** Crete
das **Kreuz, -e** cross, 8-2
der **Krieg, -e** war, 6-2
kritisch critical, 13-TLL
die **Küche, -n** kitchen, 15-VzT
der **Kuchen, -** cake, 8-VzT
der **Kugelschreiber, -** ballpoint pen, *Einf.*
kühl cool, *Einf.*
die **Kultur, -en** culture, 4-TLL
das **Kulturzentrum** cultural center, 8-TLL
sich kümmern um (+ *acc.*) to look after, take care of, deal with, 13-1
der **Kunde, -n, -n** customer (*m.*), 5-1
die **Kundin, -nen** customer (*f.*), 5-1
die **Kunst, ¨-e** art, 8-1
die **Kunstgeschichte** art history, 6-VzT
der **Künstler, -** artist (*m.*), 5-VzT; 8-2
die **Künstlerin, -nen** artist (*f.*), 5-VzT; 8-2
kurz (kürzer) short; for a short time, 4-1
die **Küste, -n** coast, 4-TLL

L

das **Labor, -s** laboratory, 6-VzT
lachen to laugh, 3-2
der **Laden, ¨** shop, store, 5-1
die **Lampe, -n** lamp, 6-VzT
das **Land, ¨-er** country, 4-2
auf dem Land in the country, 8-2
aufs Land to the country, 8-2
die **Landkarte, -n** map, *Einf.*

die **Landschaft, -en** landscape, 4-2
die **Landsleute** (*pl.*) compatriots
der **Landwirt, -e** farmer (*m.*), 5-VzT
die **Landwirtin, -nen** farmer (*f.*), 5-VzT
lang(e) (länger) long; for a long time, 4-1
langsam slow, *Einf.*, 3-2
sich langweilen to be bored, 13-1
langweilig boring, 3-1
der **Laptop, -s** laptop computer, 12-1
lassen (lässt), ließ, hat gelassen (1) to leave (something or someone); to leave behind; (2) to let, allow; (3) to cause to be done, 12-1
laufen (läuft), lief, ist gelaufen (1) to run; (2) (*colloq.*) to go on foot, walk, 3-1, 9-VzT
der **Läufer, -** runner (*m.*), 9-VzT
die **Läuferin, -nen** (*f.*), 9, VzT
die **Laune, -n** mood, 14-2
laut loud, *Einf.*
leben to live, be alive, 2-2
das **Leben** life, 4-2, 11-2
die **Lebensmittel** (*pl.*) groceries, 5-2
der **Lebensstandard** standard of living, 9-TLL
die **Leberwurst, ¨-e** liverwurst, 8-1
lecker tasty, delicious, 8-1
leer empty, 5-1
legen to lay, put down, 6-1
der **Lehrer, -** teacher (*m.*), *Einf.*
die **Lehrerin, -nen** teacher (*f.*), *Einf.*
der **Lehrling, -e** apprentice, 5-1
leicht (1) light (in weight); (2) easy, 3-1
das **Leid** sorrow
Es tut mir Leid. I'm sorry. 7-1
leider unfortunately, 3-1
leihen, lieh, hat geliehen (1) to lend, loan; (2) to borrow, 10-1
leise quiet, soft, *Einf.*
leisten: sich etwas leisten können to be able to afford something, 11-1
die **Leitfrage, -n** guiding question
lernen to learn, 3-2
lesen (liest), las, hat gelesen to read, 2-1
lesen über (+ *acc.*) to read about, 2-1
das **Lesestück, -e** reading selection
letzt- last, 10-1
letzte Woche last week, 6-2
die **Leute** (*pl.*) people, 2-1
lieb dear; nice, sweet, 6-2
Das ist lieb von dir! That's sweet of you! 6-2
Lieber Fritz! Dear Fritz, (salutation in letter), 6-TLL
die **Liebe** love, 11-2
lieben to love, 3-2
lieber (*verb* +) preferably, would rather (*see* **gern**), 4-1
Lieber nicht. I'd rather not. No thanks. Let's not. 4-1
Lieblings- (*noun prefix*) favorite, 9-1
der **Lieblingssport** favorite sport, 9-1
liebsten: am liebsten most like to, like best of all to (*see* **gern**), 12-G
das **Lied, -er** song, 4-2
liegen, lag, hat gelegen to lie; to be situated, 4-2
der **Lift, -s** elevator, 14-VzT
lila violet, lavender, 3-VzT
die **Limnologie** limnology
die **Linguistik** linguistics, 6-VzT
die **Linie, -n** (streetcar or bus) line, 13-1
links to the left; on the left, 8-2
die **Liste, -n** list
der **Liter** liter, 8-1
der **Löffel, -** spoon, 8-VzT
logisch logical, 14-TLL
sich lohnen to be worthwhile, worth the trouble, 13-1
das **Lokal, -e** neighborhood restaurant or tavern, 8-1
los: Was ist los? (1) What's the matter? (2) What's going on? 3-1
lösen to solve, 9-2
los·fahren (fährt los), fuhr los, ist losgefahren to depart; to start; to leave, 14-1
die **Lösung, -en** solution, 9-2
der **Löwe, -n, -n** lion, 10-VzT
die **Luft** air, 4-VzT; 9-1
die **Luftverschmutzung** air pollution, 9-1
die **Lust** desire
Ich habe keine Lust. I don't want to. 3-1
Lust haben (etwas zu tun) to want to do (something), 8-1
lustig fun; humorous, 3-2
die **Lyrik** poetry

M

machen (1) to make; (2) to do, 1-1
Das macht (mir) Spaß. That is fun (for me). 7-1
Das macht nichts. That doesn't matter. 7-1
Das macht zusammen ... All together that comes to . . . 5-1
die **Macht, ¨-e** power, might, 11-2
das **Mädchen, -** girl, 9-1
mag (*see* **mögen**)
(der) **Mai** May, *Einf.*
mal (*flavoring particle with commands, see* p. 100), 4-1
das **Mal, -e** time (in the sense of occurrence), 12-1
das nächste Mal (the) next time, 12-G
jedes Mal every time, 12-1
zum ersten Mal for the first time, 12-G
man one (*indefinite pronoun*), 1-2, 3-G
der **Manager, -** manager, 11-TLL
mancher, -es, -e many a, 9-2
manche (*pl.*) some, 9-2
manchmal sometimes, 2-2
manipulieren to manipulate, 10-TLL
der **Mann, ¨-er** (1) man; (2) husband, 2-1
der **Mantel, ¨** coat, 3-2
das **Märchen, -** fairy tale, 4-2
das **Marketing** marketing, 5-TLL
die **Marmelade** jam, 4-VzT
(das) **Marokko** Morocco
(der) **März** March, *Einf.*
der **Maschinenbau** mechanical engineering, 6-VzT
die **Mathematik** mathematics, 6-VzT
die **Mauer, -n** (freestanding or exterior) wall, 11-1
der **Mechaniker, -** mechanic (*m.*)
die **Mechanikerin, -nen** mechanic (*f.*)
die **Medizin** (field of) medicine, 6-VzT
das **Meer, -e** ocean, 4-2
mehr more, 2-2
nicht mehr no longer, not any more, 2-2
mehrere several, a few, 11-1
meinen (1) to be of the opinion, think, 1-2; (2) to mean, 2-1
die **Meinung, -en** opinion
meist- most (*see* **viel**)
meistens mostly, usually, 5-2
die **Menge, -n** quantity; crowd
eine Menge a lot, lots of, 6-2
die **Mensa** university cafeteria, 1-1
der **Mensch, -en, -en** person, human being, 6-1
Mensch! Man! Wow! 3-1
die **Menschheit** mankind, human race, 9-2
menschlich human, 15-2
merken to notice, 14-1
leicht zu merken easy to remember
das **Messer, -** knife, 8-VzT
die **Methode, -n** method, 10-TLL
die **Milch** milk, 8-VzT; 12-2
mild mild, 4-TLL
die **Million, -en** million, 11-TLL
die **Minute, -n** minute, 3-1
minutenlang (*adv.*) for minutes, 14-TLL
Mist: So ein Mist! (*crude & colloq.*) (1) What a drag. (2) What a lot of bull. 10-1
mit (*prep.* + *dat.*) with, 2-1; (*adv.*) along with, 4-1
der **Mitbewohner, -** fellow occupant, roommate, housemate (*m.*), 6-1
die **Mitbewohnerin, -nen** fellow occupant, roommate, housemate (*f.*), 6-1
mit·bringen, brachte mit, hat mitgebracht to bring along, take along, 6-1
miteinander with each other, together, 1-2

das **Mitglied, -er** member, 11-2
mit·kommen, kam mit, ist mitgekommen to come along, 5-1
mit·machen to participate, cooperate, pitch in, 9-1
mit·nehmen (nimmt mit), nahm mit, hat mitgenommen to take along, 13-1
das **Mittagessen** midday meal, lunch, 5-2
das **Mittelalter** the Middle Ages, 13-1
(der) **Mittwoch** Wednesday, *Einf.*
die **Möbel** (*pl.*) furniture, 6-VzT
möbliert furnished, 6-VzT
das **Modalverb, -en** modal verb, 3-G
modern modern, 4-2
modernisieren to modernize, 11-TLL
mögen (mag), mochte, hat gemocht to like, 4-1
möchten would like to, 3-1
möglich possible, 6-1
der **Moment, -e** moment
im Moment at the moment, 1-1
die **Monarchie, -n** monarchy, 10-TLL
der **Monat, -e** month, 10-1
monatelang (*adv.*) for months, 14-TLL
(der) **Montag** Monday, *Einf.*
morgen tomorrow, *Einf.*
morgen Abend tomorrow evening, 12-G
morgen früh tomorrow morning, 12-G
morgen Nachmittag tomorrow afternoon, 12-G
der **Morgen, -** morning, 1-1
Guten Morgen! Good morning! *Einf.*
morgens (*adv.*) in the morning(s), every morning, 4-1; 5-TLL
das **Motorrad, ¨-er** motorcycle, 5-1
müde tired, weary, 1-2
das **Müesli** (*no pl.*) cereal, 4-VzT
der **Müll** trash, refuse, 9-1
(das) **München** Munich, 7-2
der **Mund, ¨-er** mouth, 11-1
das **Museum,** *pl.* **Museen** museum, 8-1
die **Musik** music, 3-2
die **Musikwissenschaft** musicology, 6-VzT
müssen (muss), musste, hat gemusst must, to have to, 3-1
die **Mutter, ¨** mother, 2-1
die **Muttersprache, -n** native language, 5-2
die **Mutti, -s** mama, mom, 2-2
die **Mütze, -n** cap, 3-VzT

N

na well . . . 12-1
Na endlich! At last! High time! 9-1
Na und? And so? So what? 10-1
nach (*prep. + dat.*) (1) after, 5-1; (2) to (with cities and countries), 1-1
nach Hause home (as destination of motion), 3-1
der **Nachbar, -n, -n** neighbor (*m.*), 11-2
die **Nachbarin, -nen** neighbor (*f.*), 11-2
nachdem (*sub. conj.*) after, 10-1
nach·denken, dachte nach, hat nachgedacht über + *acc.* to think about, ponder, 14-2
nachher (*adv.*) later on, after that, 4-1
der **Nachmittag, -e** afternoon, 7-1
am Nachmittag in the afternoon, 7-1
nachmittags (in the) afternoons, every afternoon, 5-TLL
nächst- next; nearest, 12-1
nächstes Semester next semester, 2-1
die **Nacht, ¨-e** night, 1-1, 12-1
Gute Nacht. Good night. 12-1
in der Nacht in the night, at night, 12-1
der **Nachtisch, -e** dessert, 8-1
zum Nachtisch for dessert, 8-1
nachts at night, every night, 5-TLL
nagelneu brand-new, 3-2
nah(e) (näher, am nächsten) near, 8-1
die **Nähe** nearness; vicinity
in der Nähe (von or + *gen.*) near, nearby, 8-1
der **Name, -ns, -n** name, 5-1
die **Nase, -n** nose, 5-1
Ich habe die Nase voll. I'm fed up. I've had it up to here. 5-1
nass wet, damp, 4-2
die **Nationalität, -en** nationality, 15-TLL
die **Natur** nature, 9-TLL
natürlich natural, naturally; of course, 1-1
der **Nebel** fog, mist, 4-VzT
neben (*prep. + acc.* or *dat.*) beside, next to, 6-1
das **Nebenfach, ¨-er** minor field (of study), 6-2
der **Nebensatz, ¨-e** subordinate clause, 8-G
neblig foggy, misty, *Einf.*
nee (*colloq.*) no, 6-1
nehmen (nimmt), nahm, hat genommen to take, 2-1
nein no, *Einf.*; 1-1
nennen, nannte, hat genannt to name, call, 8-2
nerven (*colloq.*) to annoy, 10-1
nett nice, 6-1
neu new, 3-2
neulich recently, 12-1
neutral neutral, 13-TLL
nicht not, *Einf.*; 1-1
gar nicht not at all, 3-2
nicht mehr no longer, not any more, 2-2, 4-1
nicht nur ... sondern auch not only . . . but also, 7-2
nicht wahr? isn't it? can't you? doesn't she? etc., 3-1
nichts nothing, 3-1
Nichts zu danken! Don't mention it! 2-1
Das macht nichts. It doesn't matter. 7-1
nicken to nod, 15-2
nie never, 3-1
niedrig low, 9-2
niemand nobody, no one, 2-2
noch still, 1-2
noch ein another, an additional, 2-2
noch einmal once again, once more, 4-1
noch etwas something else, anything more, 8-1
noch immer still, 4-2
noch jemand someone else
noch kein- not a . . . yet, not any . . . yet, 4-G
noch nicht not yet, 4-1
der **Nominativ** nominative case, 1-G
(das) **Nordamerika** North America, 2-TLL
der **Norden** the north, 4-2
normal normal, 2-TLL
die **Note, -n** grade, 5-1
nötig necessary, 9-1
(der) **November** November, *Einf.*
die **Nummer, -n** number, *Einf.*, 14-1
nun (1) now; (2) well . . . , well now, 10-1
nur only, 2-1
nützlich useful

O

ob (*sub. conj.*) if, whether, 8-1
oben (*adv.*) above; on top
das **Objekt** object
das **direkte Objekt** direct object, 2-G
das **indirekte Objekt** indirect object, 5-G
das **Obst** fruit, 2-1
der **Obstsalat, -e** fruit salad, 4-VzT
obwohl (*sub. conj.*) although, 9-2
oder (*coor. conj.*) or, 1-2
offen open, 11-2
offiziell official, 13-TLL
öffnen to open, 11-1
oft (öfter) often, 1-2
ohne (*prep. + acc.*) without, 4-1
ohne ... zu without . . . -ing, 8-G
das **Ohr, -en** ear, 11-1
ökonomisch economic, 8-TLL
das **Ökosystem, -e** ecosystem, 9-TLL
(der) **Oktober** October, *Einf.*
das **Öl** oil, 9-2
die **Oma, -s** grandma, 2-2
der **Onkel, -** uncle, 2-2
der **Opa, -s** grandpa, 2-2
die **Opposition, -en** opposition, 10-TLL
optimistisch optimistic, 3-TLL

orange (*adj.*) orange, 3-VzT
der **Orangensaft, ⸚e** orange juice, 4-VzT
ordentlich tidy, orderly, 13-1
die **Ordinalzahl, -en** ordinal number, 9-G
der **Ort, -e** (1) place; (2) town, 13-2
der **Osten** the east, 4-2
(das) **Österreich** Austria, 4-1
der **Österreicher, -** Austrian (*m.*), 11-TLL
die **Österreicherin, -nen** Austrian (*f.*), 11-TLL
österreichisch Austrian, 11-TLL, 14-1
(das) **Osteuropa** Eastern Europe, 11-TLL

P

paar: ein paar a couple (of), a few, 5-2
packen to pack, 7-TLL
die **Pädagogik** (field of) education, 6-VzT
das **Papier, -e** paper, *Einf.*, 9-1
die **Partei, -en** political party, 9-2
das **Partizip** participle
das **Partizip Präsens** present participle, 15-G
der **Partner, -** partner, 5-TLL
die **Party, -s** party, 6-TLL
passieren, ist passiert to happen, 10-1
das **Passiv** passive voice, 15-G
die **Pause, -n** break; intermission, 3-1
eine Pause machen to take a break, 3-1
Pech haben to have bad luck, be unlucky, 6-2
perfekt perfect, 5-TLL
das **Perfekt** perfect tense, 6-G
die **Person, -en** person
das **Personalpronomen, -** personal pronoun, 1-G
persönlich personal
pessimistisch pessimistic, 3-TLL
der **Pfeffer, -** pepper, 8-VzT
die **Pflanze, -n** plant, 9-2
die **Philosophie** philosophy, 6-TLL; 6-VzT
die **Physik** physics, 6-VzT
das **Plakat, -e** (political) poster, 10-2
planen to plan, 7-1
das **Plastik** plastic, 9-TLL
der **Platz, ⸚e** (1) place; (2) space; (3) city square, 6-1; (4) seat, 7-2
plötzlich suddenly, 10-1
der **Plural** plural, 1-G
das **Plusquamperfekt** past perfect tense, 10-G
die **Politik** (1) politics; (2) policy, 9-2
der **Politiker, -** politician (*m.*), 5-VzT; 9-2
die **Politikerin, -nen** politician (*f.*), 5-VzT; 9-2
die **Politikwissenschaft** political science, 6-VzT
politisch political, 9-TLL
die **Polizei** (*sing. only*) the police, 11-1
die **Pommes frites** (*pl.*) French fries, 3-2
die **Portion, -en** order, helping (of food), 8-VzT
positiv positive, 14-TLL
die **Post** (1) post office; postal service; (2) mail, 8-VzT; 15-1
das **Poster, -** poster, *Einf.*
die **Postkarte, -n** postcard, 5-2
das **Prädikat** predicate, 3-G
praktisch practical, 6-TLL
die **Präposition, -en** preposition, 4-G
das **Präsens** present tense, 1-G
das **Präteritum** simple past tense, 10-G
der **Preis, -e** price, 9-2
prima terrific, great, *Einf.*, 1-1
privat private, 6-TLL
probieren to sample, try, 14-1
das **Problem, -e** problem, 2-2
produzieren to produce, 9-TLL
der **Professor, -en** professor (*m.*), *Einf.*
die **Professorin, -nen** professor (*f.*), *Einf.*
das **Programm, -e** program, 6-TLL
der **Protest, -e** protest, 6-TLL
das **Prozent** percent, 9-TLL
die **Prüfung, -en** examination
die **Psychoanalyse** psychoanalysis, 14-TLL
die **Psychologie** psychology, 6-VzT
der **Pulli, -s** (*slang*) = **Pullover,** 3-2
der **Pullover, -** pullover, sweater, 3-2
pünktlich punctual, on time, 7-2
putzen to clean, 11-G

Q

Quatsch! Nonsense! 5-1
quatschen (*colloq.*) (1) to talk nonsense; (2) to chat, 7-2
die **Querstraße, -n** cross street, 12-1

R

das **Rad, ⸚er** (1) wheel; (2) bicycle, 7-2
Rad fahren (fährt Rad), ist Rad gefahren to bicycle, 7-2, 9-VzT
der **Radfahrer, -** bicyclist (*m.*), 9-VzT
die **Radfahrerin, -nen** bicyclist (*f.*), 9-VzT
der **Radiergummi** eraser, *Einf.*
radikal radical, 9-TLL
das **Radio, -s** radio, 6-VzT
sich rasieren to shave, 11-G
raten (rät), riet, hat geraten to guess
Raten Sie mal! Take a guess!
das **Rathaus, ⸚er** town hall, 8-VzT
reagieren auf (+ *acc.*) to react to, 13-2
die **Reaktion, -en** reaction
realistisch realistic, 5-TLL
Recht: Recht haben (hat Recht), hatte Recht, hat Recht gehabt to be right, 4-1
Du hast Recht. You're right. 4-1
rechts (*adv.*) to the right; on the right, 8-2
der **Rechtsanwalt, ⸚e** lawyer (*m.*), 5-VzT; 13-2
die **Rechtsanwältin, -nen** lawyer (*f.*), 5-VzT; 13-2
das **Recycling** recycling; recycling center, 9-1
reden to talk, speak, 12-1
die **Rede, -n** talk; speech, 15-2
die Rede ist von ... They're talking about . . .
das **Referat, -e** (1) oral report; (2) written research paper, 6-2
ein Referat halten to give a report, 6-VzT
ein Referat schreiben to write a paper, 6-VzT
das **Reflexivpronomen** reflexive pronoun, 11-G
das **Reflexivverb** reflexive verb, 11-G
die **Reform, -en** reform, 11-TLL
reformieren to reform, 11-TLL
das **Regal** shelf
der **Regen** rain, 4-VzT; 8-1
der **Regenschirm, -e** umbrella, 3-VzT
die **Regierung, -en** government in power, administration (U.S.), 10-VzT; 11-2
die **Region, -en** region, 4-TLL
regnen to rain, 1-1
Es regnet. It's raining. *Einf.*
regnerisch rainy, 4-VzT
reich rich, 10-1
das **Reich, -e** empire; realm, 10-2
die **Reise, -n** trip, journey, 1-2
eine Reise machen to take a trip, 1-2
Gute Reise! Have a good trip! 1-1
der **Reiseführer, -** (travel) guidebook, 5-2
reisen, ist gereist to travel, 5-2
der **Reisepass, ⸚e** passport, 14-VzT
relativ (*adj. and adv.*) relative, 2-TLL
das **Relativpronomen** relative pronoun, 12-G
der **Relativsatz** relative clause, 12-G
reparieren to repair, 12-1
repressiv repressive, 11-TLL
die **Republik, -en** republic, 10-TLL
reservieren to reserve, 7-1
die **Residenz** (1) residence; (2) royal seat or capital, 8-TLL
das **Restaurant, -s** restaurant, 8-1
die **Restauration, -en** restoration, 8-TLL
retten to save, rescue, 9-2
die **Revolution, -en** revolution, 11-TLL
die **Rezeption** hotel reception desk, 14-1
der **Rhein** the Rhine River, 4-TLL
richtig right, correct, 3-1

der **Riese, -n, -n** giant
riesen- (*noun and adj. prefix*) gigantic
riesengroß huge, gigantic, 8-2
Ich habe Riesenhunger. I'm famished (*or*) hungry as a bear. 14-1
der **Rock, ¨-e** skirt, 3-VzT
die **Rolle, -n** role, 2-2
der **Roman, -e** novel, 5-2
romantisch romantic, 13-TLL
rosa pink, 3-VzT
rot (röter) red, 3-2
der **Rucksack, ¨-e** rucksack, backpack, 7-2
rufen, rief, hat gerufen to call, shout, 11-2
die **Ruhe** rest, quiet, peace, 15-2
jemand in Ruhe lassen to leave someone in peace, leave alone, 15-2
ruhig (1) calm, peaceful, 10-2; (2) (*as sentence adverb*) "feel free to . . ." or "go ahead and . . ." 12-1
die **Ruine, -n** ruin, 8-TLL
(das) **Rumänien** Romania, 11-TLL
der **Russe, -n, -n** Russian (*m.*), 11-TLL
die **Russin, -nen** Russian (*f.*), 11-TLL
russisch Russian, 11-TLL
(das) **Russland** Russia, 11-TLL

S

die **Sache, -n** (1) thing; item, 8-1; (2) matter, affair
(das) **Sachsen** Saxony, 8-2
der **Sack, ¨-e** sack, 9-1
der **Saft, ¨-e** juice, 8-VzT
sagen to say; to tell, 1-2
Sag mal, ... Tell me, . . .
die **Sahne** cream, 8-VzT
der **Salat, -e** (1) salad; (2) lettuce, 8-1
das **Salz, -e** salt, 8-VzT
sammeln to collect, 9-1
(der) **Samstag** Saturday, *Einf.*
der **Satz, ¨-e** sentence; clause, 1-G
sauber clean, 9-1
sauer (*colloq.*) (1) ticked off, annoyed, 4-1; (2) sour, acidic, 9-2
schade too bad, 11-1
Das ist schade! That's a shame! What a pity! 11-1
schaffen to handle, manage, get done, 3-1
der **Schalter, -** counter, window, 13-1
schauen to look, 11-1
Schau mal. Look. Look here. 11-1
das **Schaufenster, -** store window, 5-2
der **Scheck, -s** check, 14-1
scheinen, schien, hat geschienen (1) to shine; (2) to seem, 1-1
schenken to give (as a gift), 5-1
schicken to send, 6-2
das **Schiff, -e** ship, 12-2
der **Schinken** ham, 8-VzT
schlafen (schläft), schlief, hat geschlafen to sleep, 3-1
das **Schlafzimmer, -** bedroom, 11-1; 15-VzT
schlampig (*colloq.*) messy, disorderly, 13-1
die **Schlange, -n** snake, 10-VzT
schlecht bad, *Einf.*; 1-1
schleppen (*colloq.*) to drag, lug (along), haul, 9-1
schließen, schloss, hat geschlossen to close, 5-2
schlimm bad, 6-2
das **Schloss, ¨-er** palace, 8-2
der **Schlüssel, -** key, 6-VzT; 11-2
schmecken (1) to taste (*trans. and intrans.*); (2) to taste good, 8-1
sich schminken to put on make-up, 11-G
schmutzig dirty, 9-1
der **Schnee** snow, 4-2
schneiden, schnitt, hat geschnitten to cut, 11-1
schneien to snow, 1-2
Es schneit. It's snowing. *Einf.*
schnell fast, *Einf.*, 3-2
schnell machen (*colloq.*) to hurry, 11-1
das **Schnitzel, -** cutlet, chop, 8-1
die **Schokolade** chocolate, 11-1
schon (1) already, yet, 1-2; (2) (*flavoring particle; see p. 65*)
schon lange for a long time, 10-G
schön beautiful, 1-1
schrecklich terrible, 4-2
schreiben, schrieb, hat geschrieben to write, 1-2
Wie schreibt man das? How do you write (spell) that? *Einf.*
der **Schreibtisch, -e** desk, 6-1
der **Schriftsteller, -** writer (*m.*), 5-VzT; 10-2
die **Schriftstellerin, -nen** writer (*f.*), 5-VzT; 10-2
der **Schuh, -e** shoe, 3-2
schuldig guilty, 15-2
die **Schule, -n** school, 1-2
der **Schüler, -** grade school pupil or secondary school student (*m.*), *Einf.*, 1-1
die **Schülerin, -nen** grade school pupil or secondary school student (*f.*), *Einf.*, 1-1
das **Schulsystem, -e** school system, 3-TLL
schütteln to shake, 15-2
schwach (schwächer) weak, 8-2
schwarz (schwärzer) black, 3-2
schweigen, schwieg, hat geschwiegen to be silent, 12-1
die **Schweiz** Switzerland, 4-2
der **Schweizer, -** Swiss (*m.*), 11-TLL; 13-2
die **Schweizerin, -nen** Swiss (*f.*), 11-TLL; 13-2
schweizerisch Swiss, 11-TLL; 13-2
schwer (1) heavy; (2) hard, difficult, 3-1
die **Schwester, -n** sister, 2-1
schwierig difficult, 5-1
die **Schwierigkeit, -en** difficulty, 13-2
das **Schwimmbad, ¨-er** swimming pool, 8-VzT
schwimmen, schwamm, ist geschwommen to swim, 4-1, 9-VzT
der **Schwimmer, -** swimmer (*m.*), 9-VzT
die **Schwimmerin, -nen** (*f.*), 9-VzT
der **See, -n** lake, 4-1
am See at the lake, 4-1
die **Seele, -n** soul, 15-2
sehen (sieht), sah, hat gesehen to see, 2-1
die **Sehenswürdigkeit, -en** sight, attraction, place of interest, 8-2
sehr very, 1-1
sein (ist), war, ist gewesen to be, *Einf.*; 1-1
dabei sein to be present, attend, 15-1
seit (*prep. + dat., sub. conj.*) since, 5-1
seit einem Jahr for the past year, 5-1
seit langem for a long time, 10-G
die **Seite, -n** page; side
selber (*or*) **selbst** (*adv.*) by oneself (myself, yourself, ourselves, etc.), 6-2
selbstverständlich It goes without saying that . . .; of course, 4-1
selten seldom, 1-2
das **Semester, -** semester, 2-1
nächstes Semester next semester, 2-1
die **Semesterferien** (*pl.*) semester break, 6-2
das **Seminar, -e** (university) seminar, 4-1
der **Senior, -en, -en** senior citizen, 10-1
separat separate, 11-TLL
(der) **September** September, *Einf.*
die **Serviette, -n** napkin, 8-VzT
setzen to set (down), put, 7-1
sich setzen to sit down, 11-1
sich (*3rd person reflexive pronoun*) himself, herself, themselves; (*formal 2nd person*) yourself, yourselves, 11-1
sicher certain(ly), sure(ly), 2-1
die **Sicherheit** security, safety; certainty, 9-TLL
siebt- seventh, 9-G
siezen to address someone with **Sie,** 1-2
singen, sang, hat gesungen to sing, 3-2
der **Sinn** sense, 15-2
Das hat keinen Sinn. That makes no sense. It's pointless. 15-2
die **Situation, -en** situation, 10-TLL
sitzen, saß, hat gesessen to sit, 5-2
(das) **Skandinavien** Scandinavia
Ski fahren (fährt Ski), ist Ski gefahren (*pronounced* "Schifahren") to ski, 9-VzT; 13-1
der **Skifahrer, -** skier (*m.*), 9-VzT
die **Skifahrerin, -nen,** skier (*f.*), 9-VzT

so (1) like this, 3-2; (2) so, 7-2
so lange (*adv.*) for such a long time, 6-1
sofort immediately, right away, 6-2
die **Software** software, 12-1
sogar even, in fact, 2-2
der **Sohn, ⸚e** son, 2-1
solcher, -es, -e such, such a, 9-2
die **Solidarität** solidarity, 14-TLL
sollen (soll), sollte, hat gesollt should, be supposed to, 3-1
der **Sommer** summer, 4-1
im Sommer in the summer, 4-1
das **Sommersemester** spring term (usually May–July), 6-VzT
sondern (*coor. conj.*) but rather, instead, 7-1
nicht nur ... sondern auch not only . . . but also, 7-2
(der) **Sonnabend** Saturday, *Einf.*
die **Sonne** sun, 1-1
sonnig sunny, *Einf.*
(der) **Sonntag** Sunday, *Einf.*
sonst (*adv.*) otherwise, apart from that, 6-2
Sonst noch etwas? Will there be anything else? 5-1
sortieren to sort, 9-TLL
sowieso anyway, 7-1
sowjetisch Soviet, 9-TLL
die **Sowjetunion** Soviet Union, 11-TLL
sozial social, 2-TLL
der **Sozialarbeiter, -** social worker (*m.*), 8-TLL
die **Sozialarbeiterin, -nen** social worker (*f.*), 8-TLL
die **Soziologie** sociology, 6-VzT
(das) **Spanien** Spain, 15-1
sparen to save (money *or* time), 7-2
der **Spaß** fun
Das macht (mir) Spaß. That is fun (for me). 7-1
Viel Spaß. Have fun. 12-1
spät late, 3-1
Wie spät ist es? What time is it? *Einf.*
später later, 4-1
spazieren gehen, ging spazieren, ist spazieren gegangen to go for a walk, 5-2
die **Speise, -n** food, dish (menu item)
die **Speisekarte, -n** menu, 8-VzT
der **Speisesaal** (hotel) dining room, 14-VzT
der **Spiegel, -** mirror, 6-VzT; 11-2
spielen to play, 1-1
spontan spontaneous, 7-TLL
der **Sport** sport, 3-TLL; 9-1
Sport treiben to play sports, 9-1
sportlich athletic, 9-1
die **Sprache, -n** language, 3-2
sprechen (spricht), sprach, hat gesprochen to speak, talk, 1-2
sprechen über (+ *acc.*) to talk about, 2-1
der **Staat, -en** state, 10-2
der **Staatsbürger, -** citizen, 6-2
stabil stable, 11-TLL
die **Stadt, ⸚e** city, 4-2
der **Stadtbummel, -** stroll through town, 8-1
der **Stadtführer, -** city guidebook, 14-VzT
der **Stadtplan, ⸚** city map, 5-2, 14-VzT
das **Stadtzentrum** city center, 8-1
die **Stammform, -en** principal part of a verb, 10-G
stark (stärker) strong, 8-2
statt (*prep. + gen.*) instead of, 8-G
staunen to be amazed, surprised, 6-2
stecken to put (into), insert; to be (inside of), 7-1
stehen, stand, hat gestanden to stand, 5-1
stehlen (stiehlt), stahl, hat gestohlen to steal, 10-1
steigen, stieg, ist gestiegen to climb, 10-2
steil steep, 3-1
der **Stein, -e** stone, 12-2
die **Stelle, -n** job, position, 2-2
stellen to put, place, 7-1
eine Frage stellen to ask a question, 10-2
sterben (stirbt), starb, ist gestorben to die, 5-2
die **Stimme, -n** voice, 2-2
stimmen to be right (*impersonal only*)
das stimmt that's right, that's true, 1-2
Stimmt nicht. That's wrong. 3-2
Stimmt schon. That's right. 3-2
stinklangweilig (*colloq.*) extremely boring, 3-1
das **Stipendium,** *pl.* **Stipendien** scholarship, stipend, 6-2
der **Stock** floor (of a building), 14-1
der erste Stock the second floor, 14-1 (*see* **Erdgeschoss**)
im ersten Stock on the second floor, 14-1
stolz auf (+ *acc.*) proud of, 13-2
stören to disturb, 10-2
die **Straße, -n** street; road, 1-1
der **Straßenatlas** road atlas, 7-1
die **Straßenbahn, -en** streetcar, 8-VzT; 13-1
der **Streit** argument, conflict, 15-2
streng strict, 14-2
der **Stress** stress, 5-2
stressig stressful, 5-2
das **Stück, -e** piece, 5-1
ein Stück Kuchen a piece of cake, 8-G
sechs Stück six (of the same item), 5-1
der **Student, -en, -en** university student (*m.*), *Einf.*; 1-2
der **Studentenausweis, -e** student I.D., 6-2
das **Studentenwohnheim, -e** student dormitory, 6-1
die **Studentin, -nen** university student (*f.*), *Einf.*, 1-2
studieren to attend a university; to study (a subject); to major in, 1-2
studieren an (+ *dat.*) to study at, 6-VzT
das **Studium** university studies, 6-2
der **Stuhl, ⸚e** chair, *Einf.*
die **Stunde, -n** (1) hour; (2) class hour, 3-1
stundenlang (*adv.*) for hours, 14-TLL
das **Substantiv, -e** noun
suchen to look for, seek, 2-1
der **Süden** the south, 4-2
super super, great, terrific, 4-1
der **Superlativ** superlative degree, 12-G
der **Supermarkt, ⸚e** supermarket, 5-TLL
der **Supertanker, -** super tanker, 9-TLL
die **Suppe, -n** soup, 1-1
süß sweet, 9-2
das **Symbol, -e** symbol, 11-TLL
symbolisch symbolic, 8-TLL
sympathisch friendly; congenial, likeable, 7-2
das **System, -e** system, 3-TLL

T

die **Tafel, -n** blackboard, *Einf.*
der **Tag, -e** day, 1-1, 12-1
eines Tages some day (in the future); one day (in the past or future), 13-2
Guten Tag! Hello! *Einf.*
jeden Tag every day, 4-G
Tag! Hi! Hello! *Einf.*
tagelang (*adv.*) for days, 14-TLL
täglich daily, 14-2
das **Tal, ⸚er** valley, 4-2
die **Tante, -n** aunt, 2-2
tanzen to dance, 15-1
die **Tasche, -n** (1) pocket, (2) hand or shoulder bag, 3-VzT; 7-2
die **Tasse, -n** cup, 8-1
die **Tat, -en** deed, 14-2
tatsächlich actually, really, 10-1
die **Taube, -n** dove, pigeon, 10-VzT
tausend thousand, 2-G
das **Taxi, -s** taxicab, 8-VzT
die **Technik** technology, 9-2
der **Tee** tea, 4-VzT
der **Teil, -e** part, 11-2
das **Telefon, -e** telephone, 6-VzT; 7-1
telefonieren to telephone, make a phone call, 14-VzT
telefonisch (*adv.*) on the telephone, 15-1
die **Telefonnummer, -n** telephone number, *Einf.*
der **Teller, -** plate, 8-VzT
das **Tempo** pace, tempo, 6-2
das **Tennis** tennis, 9-1
der **Tennisplatz, ⸚e** tennis court, 9-1
der **Teppich, -e** rug, 6-VzT

der **Termin, -e** appointment, 6-2
die **Terrasse, -n** terrace, 15-VzT
terroristisch terrorist (*adj.*), 10-TLL
teuer expensive, 6-2
der **Text, -e** text
das **Theater, -** theater, 3-TLL
das **Thema,** *pl.* **Themen** topic, subject, theme, 15-2
die **Thermosflasche, -n** thermos bottle, 7-1
das **Ticket, -s** ticket, 7-VzT
tief deep, 11-2
das **Tiefland** lowlands, 4-TLL
das **Tier, -e** animal, 9-2
der **Tipp, -s** tip, hint, suggestion
der **Tisch, -e** table, *Einf.*
die **Tochter, ¨** daughter, 2-1
der **Tod** death, 11-2
todmüde (*colloq.*) dead tired, 4-1
die **Toilette, -n** lavatory, 15-VzT
toll (*colloq.*) great, terrific, 3-1
das **Tor, -e** gate, 11-1
tot dead, 11-2
die **Tour, -en** tour, 7-TLL
der **Tourist, -en, -en** tourist (*m.*), 1-2
die **Touristin, -nen** tourist (*f.*), 1-2
die **Tradition, -en** tradition, 8-TLL
traditionell traditional, 2-TLL
tragen (trägt), trug, hat getragen (1) to carry; (2) to wear, 3-1
traurig sad, 13-2
treffen (trifft), traf, hat getroffen to meet, 9-1
treiben, trieb, hat getrieben to drive, force, propel, 9-1
Sport treiben to play sports, 9-1
trennen to separate, 15-2
die **Treppe** staircase, stairs, 9-1; 15-VzT
auf der Treppe on the stairs, 9-1
trinken, trank, hat getrunken to drink, 3-1
trocken dry, 4-2
trotz (*prep. + gen.*) in spite of, despite, 8-G
trotzdem (*adv.*) in spite of that, nevertheless, 8-2
Tschüss! So long! *Einf.*
das **T-Shirt, -s** T-shirt, 3-VzT
tun, tat, hat getan to do, 7-1
Das tut mir weh. That hurts (me). 11-1
Er tut, als ob . . . (+ *subjunctive*) He acts as if . . . 14-G
Es tut mir Leid. I'm sorry (about that). 7-1
die **Tür, -en** door, *Einf.*
der **Türke, -n, -n** Turk (*m.*), 15-2
die **Türkei** Turkey, 5-2
die **Türkin, -nen** Turk (*f.*), 15-2
türkisch Turkish, 5-2
(das) **Türkisch** Turkish (language), 15-2
der **Turnschuh, -e** sneaker, gym shoe, 3-2
der **Typ, -en** (1) type; (2) (*slang*) guy, 12-1
typisch typical, 1-1

U

die **U-Bahn** (= **Untergrundbahn**) subway train, 8-VzT
üben to practice, *Einf.*
über (1) (*prep. + acc.*) about, 2-1; (2) (+ *acc.* or *dat.*) over, across; above, 6-1
überall everywhere, 2-2
sich etwas überlegen to consider, ponder, think something over, 13-2
übermorgen the day after tomorrow, 12-1
übernachten to spend the night, 7-2
übersetzen to translate, *Einf.*, 15-2
übrig left over, remaining, 14-1
übrigens by the way, 1-1
die **Übung, -en** exercise
die **Uhr, -en** clock; watch, *Einf.*
9 Uhr 9 o'clock, *Einf.*
Wie viel Uhr ist es? What time is it? 7-1
um (1) at (with times), 1-1; (2) around (the outside of), 4-1
um ... zu in order to..., 8-1
der **Umschlag, ¨e** envelope, 15-1
um·steigen, stieg um, ist umgestiegen to transfer, change (trains, buses, etc.), 7-VzT
die **Umwelt** environment, 3-2
umweltfreundlich environmentally safe, nonpolluting, 9-1
um·ziehen, zog um, ist umgezogen to move, change residence, 9-1
sich um·ziehen, hat sich umgezogen to change clothes, 14-VzT
unbekannt unknown, 7-2
unbequem uncomfortable, 7-2
unbesorgt unconcerned, carefree, 10-1
und (*coor. conj.*) and, 1-1
der **Unfall, ¨e** accident, 9-2
ungefähr approximately, 9-2
ungemütlich unpleasant, not cozy, 14-1
unglaublich unbelievable, 11-1
unglücklich unhappy, 4-1
die **Uni, -s** (*colloq.*) = **Universität,** 6-1
die **Universität, -en** university, 1-TLL; 6-1
an der Universität/Uni at the university, 6-1
unmenschlich inhuman, 15-2
unmöglich impossible, 6-1
unnötig unnecessary, 9-1
unordentlich messy, disorderly, 13-1
unruhig restless, troubled, 10-2
unschuldig innocent, 15-2
unsympathisch unlikable; unfriendly, 7-2
unten (*adv.*) below, on the bottom
unter (+ *acc.* or *dat.*) (1) under, beneath; (2) among, 6-1
unterbrechen (unterbricht), unterbrach, hat unterbrochen to interrupt, 10-2
unternehmen (unternimmt), unternahm, hat unternommen to do, start (an activity), undertake, 8-1
Hast du Lust etwas zu unternehmen? Do you want to do something?, 8-1
der **Unterschied, -e** difference, 11-1
unterwegs on the way, en route; on the go, 7-1
unwichtig unimportant, 2-2
uralt ancient, 3-2
der **Urlaub, -e** vacation (from a job), 4-1
Urlaub machen to take a vacation
auf (*or*) **im Urlaub sein** to be on vacation
in Urlaub gehen (*or*) **fahren** to go on vacation
die **USA** (*pl.*) the USA, 5-TLL
usw. (= **und so weiter**) etc. (= and so forth), 1-1

V

die **Variation, -en** variation
der **Vater, ¨** father, 2-1
der **Vati, -s** papa, dad, 2-2
(das) **Venedig** Venice (Italy), 7-1
verantwortlich für responsible for, 6-2
das **Verb, -en** verb, 1-G
verboten forbidden, prohibited
verbringen, verbrachte, hat verbracht to spend (time), 7-2
verdienen to earn, 2-2
vereinen to unite, 11-2
die **Vereinigung** unification, 13-2
Verflixt nochmal! (*colloq.*) Darn it all! 15-1
die **Vergangenheit** past (time), 11-2
vergessen (vergisst), vergaß, hat vergessen to forget, 5-2
vergleichen, verglich, hat verglichen to compare, 12-2
verkaufen to sell, 4-1
der **Verkäufer, -** salesman, 5-1
die **Verkäuferin, -nen** saleswoman, 5-1
der **Verkehr** traffic, 7-VzT
das **Verkehrsmittel, -** means of transportation, 8-VzT
verlassen (verlässt), verließ, hat verlassen to leave (a person or place), 5-1
sich verlassen auf + *acc.* to rely on, count on, 14-2
sich verletzen to injure oneself, get hurt, 11-1
verliebt in (+ *acc.*) in love with, 7-2

verlieren, verlor, hat verloren to lose, 5-2
sich verloben mit (+ *dat.*) to become engaged to, 12-1
verpassen to miss (an event, opportunity, train, etc.), 13-1
verrückt crazy, insane, 7-2
verschieden different, various, 11-2
verschmutzen to pollute; to dirty, 9-2
die **Verschmutzung** pollution, 9-1
verschwenden to waste, 9-2
verschwinden, verschwand, ist verschwunden to disappear, 11-2
sich verspäten to be late, 11-1
verstehen, verstand, hat verstanden to understand, 3-1
versuchen to try, attempt, 10-2
verteidigen to defend, 14-2
der/die **Verwandte, -n** (*adj. noun*) relative, 11-1
viel (mehr, am meisten) much, a lot, 1-1
viele many, 1-2; (*pronoun*) many people, 7-2
vielen Dank many thanks, 2-1
vieles (*sing. pron.*) many things, 15-2
die **Vielfalt** variety, diversity, 15-1
vielleicht maybe, perhaps, 1-1
das **Viertel** quarter
Viertel vor/nach sieben quarter to/past seven, *Einf.*
der **Vogel, ̈-** bird, 9-2
die **Vokabel, -n** word
das **Volk, ̈-er** people, nation, folk, 10-2
das **Volkslied, -er** folk song, 4-2
voll full, 5-1
der **Volleyball** volleyball, 9-VzT
der **Volleyballspieler, -** volleyball player (*m.*), 9-VzT
die **Volleyballspielerin, -nen** volleyball player (*f.*), 9-VzT
von (*prep. + dat.*) from, 4-2; of; by, 5-1
vor (*prep. + acc.* or *dat.*) in front of, 6-1
vor einem Jahr a year ago, 10-G
vorbei·kommen, kam vorbei, ist vorbeigekommen to come by, drop by, 5-2
vor·bereiten to prepare
sich vor·bereiten auf (+ *acc.*) to prepare for, 13-1
vorgestern the day before yesterday, 12-1
vor·haben (hat vor), hatte vor, hat vorgehabt to plan, have in mind, 13-1
vorher (*adv.*) before that, previously, 4-1
vor·lesen (liest vor), las vor, hat vorgelesen to read aloud
die **Vorlesung, -en** university lecture, 6-1
das **Vorlesungsverzeichnis, -se** university course catalogue, 6-1
der **Vorschlag, ̈-e** suggestion
vor·stellen to introduce, present, 13-2
sich vor·stellen to introduce oneself
sich etwas vor·stellen to imagine something, 11-1
das **Vorurteil, -e** prejudice, 13-VzT

W

wachsen (wächst), wuchs, ist gewachsen to grow, 10-2
der **Wagen, -** car, 7-1
die **Wahl, -en** (1) choice; (2) election, 10-2
wählen (1) to choose; (2) to vote; to elect, 10-2
der **Wähler, -** voter, 10-2
wahnsinnig (*adv. colloq.*) extremely, incredibly, 3-1
wahr true, 3-1
nicht wahr? isn't it? can't you? doesn't she? etc., 3-1
während (*prep. + gen.*) during, 8-G
wahrscheinlich probably, 1-2
der **Wald, ̈-er** forest, 4-2
die **Wand, ̈-e** (interior) wall, *Einf.*
die **Wanderlust** wanderlust, 7-TLL
wandern, ist gewandert to hike, wander, 4-2
die **Wanderung, -en** hike, 5-2
wann? when? *Einf.*, 1-1; 10-G
die **Ware, -n** product, 9-2
warm (wärmer) warm, *Einf.*
warten to wait, 4-1
warten auf (+ *acc.*) to wait for, 13-1
Warte mal! Wait a second! Hang on! 4-1
warum? why? 1-1
was? what? *Einf.*
was für? what kind of? 9-1
Was ist los? What's the matter? What's going on? 3-1
waschen (wäscht), wusch, hat gewaschen to wash, 11-1
das **Wasser** water, 4-1
wechseln to change (money), 14-1
wecken to wake up (*trans.*), 7-1
der **Wecker, -** alarm clock, 6-VzT
weder ... noch neither . . . nor, 14-1
weg (*adv.*) away, gone, 4-1
wegen (*prep. + gen.*) because of, on account of, 8-G
weg·gehen, ging weg, ist weggegangen to go away, leave, 12-1
weg·werfen (wirft weg), warf weg, hat weggeworfen to throw away, 9-2
weh·tun, tat weh, hat wehgetan (+ *dat. of person*) to hurt, 11-1
weil (*sub. conj.*) because, 8-G
der **Wein, -e** wine, 4-2
weinen to cry, 3-2
weiß white, 3-2
weit far, far away, 8-1
weiter·gehen, ging weiter, ist weitergegangen to go on, continue
welcher, -es, -e which, 7-1
die **Welt, -en** world, 3-2
wem? (*dat.*) to whom? for whom? 5-1
wen? (*acc.*) whom? 2-1
wenig little bit, not much, 1-1
wenige few, 11-1
wenigstens at least, 2-2
wenn (*sub. conj.*) (1) if, 8-G; (2) when, whenever, 10-G
wer? (*nom.*) who? *Einf.*
werden (wird), wurde, ist geworden to become, get (*in the sense of* become), 4-1
werden aus to become of, 12-2
Was ist aus ihnen geworden? What became of them? 12-2
werfen (wirft), warf, hat geworfen to throw, 9-2
das **Werk, -e** work (of art), musical composition, 13-2
wessen? whose? 2-1
der **Westen** the west, 4-2
das **Wetter** weather, *Einf.*; 1-1
die **WG, -s** (= **Wohngemeinschaft**) communal living group, shared apartment, 6-1
wichtig important, 2-2
wie (1) how, *Einf.*; (2) like, as, 1-1
Wie bitte? I beg your pardon? What did you say? *Einf.*
wie lange? how long? 3-1
Und wie! And how! 15-1
wieder again, 1-1
wiederholen to repeat, *Einf.*
die **Wiederholung, -en** repetition; review
wieder·sehen (sieht wieder), sah wieder, hat wieder gesehen to see again, meet again, 12-2
Auf Wiedersehen! Good-bye! *Einf.*
wiegen, wog, hat gewogen (*trans. and intrans.*) to weigh, 15-1
(das) **Wien** Vienna, 1-1
wieso? How come? How's that?; What do you mean? 3-1
wie viel? how much? 5-1
Wie viel Uhr ist es? What time is it? 7-1
wie viele? how many? *Einf.*
Wievielt-: Den Wievielten haben wir heute?/Der Wievielte ist heute? What's the date today? 9-G
wild wild, 4-TLL
Willen: Um Gottes Willen! For heaven's sake! Oh my gosh! 9-1
willkommen welcome
Herzlich willkommen! Welcome! Nice to see you!, 6-2
der **Wind** wind, 4-VzT
windig windy, *Einf.*

der **Winter, -** winter, 4-1
im Winter in the winter, 4-1
das **Wintersemester** fall term (usually Oct.–Feb.), 6-VzT
wirklich real, 6-1
die **Wirtschaft** economy, 11-2
wirtschaftlich economic, 11-2
die **Wirtschaftswissenschaft** economics, 6-VzT
der **Wischer, -** (blackboard) eraser, *Einf.*
wissen (weiß), wusste, hat gewusst to know (a fact), 2-1
Weißt du noch? Do you remember? 11-1
die **Wissenschaft, -en** (1) science; (2) scholarship; field of knowledge, 6-VzT
der **Witz, -e** (1) joke; (2) wit, 14-2
witzig witty, amusing, 5-2
wo? where? *Einf.*
die **Woche, -n** week, 1-2
das **Wochenende, -n** weekend, 5-2
am Wochenende on the weekend, 5-2
Schönes Wochenende! (Have a) nice weekend! *Einf.*
wochenlang (*adv.*) for weeks, 14-TLL
woher? from where? *Einf.*
wohin? to where? 3-1
wohl probably, 6-2
sich wohl fühlen to feel well, 14-2
wohnen to live, dwell, 1-1
die **Wohngemeinschaft, -en** communal living group, shared apartment, 6-1
das **Wohnhaus, ¨-er** apartment building, 9-1
die **Wohnung, -en** apartment, 6-2
das **Wohnzimmer, -** living room, 13-1, 15-VzT
die **Wolke, -n** cloud, 4-VzT
wolkig cloudy, *Einf.*
wollen (will), wollte, hat gewollt to want to, intend to, 3-1
worden (*special form of the past participle of* **werden** *used in the perfect tenses of the passive voice*), 15-G
das **Wort** word (*2 plural forms:* **die Worte** = words in context; **die Wörter** = words in a list, as in a dictionary), 5-2
das **Wörterbuch, ¨-er** dictionary, 5-2
der **Wortschatz** vocabulary
die **Wortstellung** word order, 1-G
das **Wunder, -** miracle
wunderbar wonderful, 7-1
sich wundern (über + *acc.*) to be surprised, amazed (at), 13-1
wunderschön very beautiful, 1-1
wünschen to wish, 12-1
die **Wurst, ¨-e** sausage, 8-1
Das ist mir Wurst (*or* **Wurscht**). I don't give a darn. 7-1

Z

die **Zahl, -en** number, *Einf.*
zahlen to pay, 8-1
Zahlen bitte! Check please! 8-1
zählen to count, 10-2
der **Zahn, ¨-e** tooth, 11-1
sich die Zähne putzen to brush one's teeth, 11-G
zeigen to show, 5-1
Zeig mal her. Let's see. Show it to me. 15-1
die **Zeile, -n** line (of text)
die **Zeit, -en** time, 3-2
höchste Zeit high time, 14-1
die **Zeitschrift, -en** magazine, 5-2
die **Zeitung, -en** newspaper, 2-1
zentral central, 11-TLL
zerstören to destroy, 8-2
die **Zerstörung** destruction
ziehen, zog, hat gezogen to pull, 6-1
das **Ziel, -e** goal, 11-2
ziemlich fairly, quite, 1-2
zigmal (*adv.*) umpteen times, 12-G
das **Zimmer, -** room, 2-1
der **Zimmerschlüssel, -** room key, 14-VzT
zirka circa, 4-TLL
die **Zone, -n** zone, 11-TLL
zu to; too, 1-1; (*prep.* + *dat.*) to, 5-1
zu Fuß on foot, 4-2
zu Hause at home, 2-2
zueinander to each other, 1-2
zuerst first, at first, 8-1
zufrieden satisfied, 5-2
der **Zug, ¨-e** train, 7-1
zu·hören (+ *dat.*) to listen (to), 13-1
die **Zukunft** future, 9-2, 11-2
in Zukunft in the future, 13-2
zuletzt last of all, finally, 8-1
zu·machen to close, 5-1
zurück back, 1-1
zurück·bringen, brachte zurück, hat zurückgebracht to bring back
zurück·kommen, kam zurück, ist zurückgekommen to come back
zusammen together, 1-2
die **Zusammenfassung** summary
zweimal twice, 12-G
zweit- second, 9-1
der **Zweitwagen, -** second car, 9-1
zwischen (*prep.* + *acc.* or *dat.*) between, 2-2, 6-1

English-German Vocabulary

Strong and irregular verbs are marked by an asterisk: ***brechen**, ***können**, ***bringen.** Their principal parts can be found in Appendix 2.

A

able: be able to *können
about über (*prep. + acc.*)
about (with time) gegen (*prep. + acc.*)
above oben (*adv.*); über (*prep. + dat.* or *acc.*)
abroad im Ausland (*location*); ins Ausland (*destination*)
absent: be absent fehlen
accident der Unfall, ¨-e
account: on account of wegen (+ *gen.*)
accusative case der Akkusative
acidic sauer
acid rain der saure Regen
acquaintance der/die Bekannte, -n (*adj. noun*)
acquainted: be acquainted with *kennen
across über (*prep. + dat.* or *acc.*)
across from (*prep. + dat.*) gegenüber
act: He acts as if . . . Er tut, als ob ...
active aktiv
actually eigentlich, tatsächlich
acute akut
address die Adresse, -n
address with *du* duzen
address with *Sie* siezen
adjective das Adjektiv, -e
adjective ending die Adjektivendung, -en
administration, government in power die Regierung, -en
adult erwachsen (*adj.*); der / die Erwachsene, -n (*adj. noun*)
adverb das Adverb, -ien
affair (matter) die Sache, -n
afford: be able to afford something sich etwas leisten können
afraid: be afraid (of) Angst haben (vor + *dat.*)
after nach (*prep. + dat.*); nachdem (*sub. conj.*)
afternoon der Nachmittag, -e
every afternoon jeden Nachmittag
in the afternoon am Nachmittag
(in the) afternoons nachmittags
this afternoon heute Nachmittag (*adv.*)
afterwards, after that nachher (*adv.*)
again wieder
against gegen (*prep. + acc.*)
ago vor (+ *dat.*)
a year ago vor einem Jahr
agreed einverstanden
ah ach
aid die Hilfe
air die Luft
air pollution die Luftverschmutzung
airplane das Flugzeug, -e
airport der Flughafen, ¨-
alarm clock der Wecker, -
alive: be alive leben
all alle (*pl.*)
all summer (day, afternoon, etc.) den ganzen Sommer (Tag, Nachmittag usw.)
allow *lassen
allowed: be allowed to *dürfen
almanac der Almanach, -e
almost fast
alone allein
leave alone in Ruhe lassen
along with mit (*adv.*)
alongside of an (*prep. + acc.* or *dat.*)
a lot viel (mehr, am meisten); eine Menge
Alps die Alpen (*pl.*)
already schon
also auch
alternative die Alternative, -n
although obwohl (*sub. conj.*)
always immer
amazed: be amazed staunen; **be amazed (at)** sich wundern (über + *acc.*)
ambivalence die Ambivalenz
America (das) Amerika
American amerikanisch (*adj.*); der Amerikaner, -; die Amerikanerin, -nen
among unter (*prep. + acc.* or *dat.*)
amusing witzig
ancient uralt
and und (*coor. conj.*)
angry (at) böse (+ *dat.*)
animal das Tier, -e
annoy ärgern; nerven (*colloq.*)
be annoyed sauer sein
get annoyed sich ärgern (über)
annually jährlich
another (an additional) noch ein
answer die Antwort, -en
answer (a person) antworten (+ *dat.*)
answer (something) antworten auf (+ *acc.*)
anything
Anything more/else? (Sonst) noch etwas?
Will there be anything else? Sonst noch etwas?
anyway sowieso
apart from that sonst
apartment die Wohnung, -en
apartment building das Wohnhaus, ¨-er
appeal to *gefallen
appear *aus·sehen
appetite der Appetit
appointment der Termin, -e
apprentice der Lehrling, -e
approximately ungefähr
April (der) April
architect der Architekt, -en, -en; die Architektin, -nen
area die Gegend, -en
argument (conflict) der Streit
arm der Arm, -e
army die Armee, -n
around (with time) gegen (*prep. + acc.*)
around (the outside of) um (*prep. + acc.*)
arrive *an·kommen
art die Kunst, ¨-e
art history die Kunstgeschichte
article der Artikel, -
artist der Künstler, -; die Künstlerin, -nen
as wie
as a als
as if, as though als ob (+ *subjunctive*)
ask fragen; **ask oneself** sich fragen
ask a question eine Frage stellen
ask for *bitten um
aspect der Aspekt, -e
assignment die Aufgabe, -n
astounding erstaunlich
at bei (*prep. + dat.*); an (*prep. + acc.* or *dat.*); (*with times*) um (*prep. + acc.*)

At last! Na endlich!
at least wenigstens
athletic sportlich
atom das Atom, -e
atomic power plant das Atomkraftwerk, -e
attempt versuchen
attend (be present) dabei *sein
attraction (place of interest) die Sehenswürdigkeit, -en
August (der) August
aunt die Tante, -n
Austria (das) Österreich
Austrian österreichisch (*adj.*); der Österreicher, -; die Österreicherin, -nen
author der Autor, -en; die Autorin, -nen
automatic automatisch
automatic teller machine (ATM) der Bankautomat, -en
auto mechanic der Automechaniker, -; die Automechanikerin, -nen
automobile das Auto, -s; der Wagen, -
autumn der Herbst
away weg (*adv.*)

B

back zurück (*adv.*)
backpack der Rucksack, ⸚e
bad schlecht; schlimm; böse (*evil*)
bag die Tüte, -n
baker der Bäcker, -; die Bäckerin, -nen
bakery die Bäckerei, -en
ballpoint pen der Kugelschreiber, -
bank die Bank, -en
bar (tavern) die Kneipe, -n
barbaric barbarisch
barrier die Barriere, -n
basement der Keller, -
basis die Basis
bath das Bad, ⸚er
  take a bath ein Bad *nehmen
bathroom das Badezimmer, -
be *sein
be (inside of) stecken
bear der Bär, -en, -en
beautiful schön
  very beautiful wunderschön
because weil (*sub. conj.*)
  because, for denn (*coor. conj.*)
  because of wegen (+ *gen.*)
become, get *werden
bed das Bett, -en
  get out of bed *auf·stehen
  go to bed ins Bett *gehen
bedroom das Schlafzimmer, -
beer das Bier, -e
before bevor (*sub. conj.*)
before that vorher (*adv.*)
begin *an·fangen; *beginnen
beginner der Anfänger, -
beginning der Anfang, ⸚e
  at/in the beginning am Anfang
behind hinter (*prep.* + *acc.* or *dat.*)
believe glauben (+ *dat. of person*)
belong to (a person) gehören (+ *dat.*)
below unten (*adv.*); unter (*prep.* + *acc.* or *dat.*)
bench die Bank, ⸚e
beneath unter (*prep.* + *acc.* or *dat.*)
beside neben (*prep.* + *acc.* or *dat.*)
besides (in addition) außer (+ *dat.*)
best best-
like best of all to am liebsten (+ *verb*)
better besser
between zwischen (*prep.* + *acc.* or *dat.*)
bicycle das Fahrrad, ⸚er; das Rad, ⸚er (*colloq.*)
  ride a bicycle Rad *fahren
bicyclist der Radfahrer, -; die Radfahrerin, -nen
big groß (größer, größt-)
  bigger and bigger immer größer
biology die Biologie
bird der Vogel, ⸚
birthday der Geburtstag, -e
  birthday party die Geburtstagsfeier, -n
  for one's birthday zum Geburtstag
  Happy birthday! Ich gratuliere dir zum Geburtstag!
  When is your birthday? Wann hast du Geburtstag?
black schwarz (schwärzer)
blackboard die Tafel, -n
blouse die Bluse, -n
blue blau
book das Buch, ⸚er
bookcase das Bücherregal, -e
bookseller der Buchhändler, -; die Buchhändlerin, -nen
bookstore die Buchhandlung, -en
border die Grenze, -n
bored: be bored sich langweilen
boring langweilig
  extremely boring stinklangweilig (*colloq.*)
born geboren
borrow *leihen
boss der Chef, -s; die Chefin, -nen
both beid-
  both (people) beide (*pl. pronoun*)
  both (things) beides (*sing. pronoun*)
bottle die Flasche, -n
bottom: at the bottom unten (*adv.*)
boutique die Boutique, -n
boy der Junge, -n, -n
brand-new nagelneu
bread das Brot, -e
  dark bread das Bauernbrot
break, intermission die Pause, -n
  take a break eine Pause machen
break *brechen; kaputt·machen
  break out *aus·brechen
breakfast das Frühstück, -e
  eat breakfast frühstücken
  for breakfast zum Frühstück
bridge die Brücke, -n
bright (light) hell
bright (intelligent) klug (klüger)
bring *bringen
bring along *mit·bringen
bring back *zurück·bringen
broken kaputt (*colloq.*)
brother der Bruder, ⸚
brown braun
brush one's teeth sich die Zähne putzen
build bauen
building das Gebäude, -; das Haus, ⸚er
bus der Bus, -se
business das Geschäft, -e
business (field of study) die Betriebswirtschaft
business people die Geschäftsleute
businessman der Geschäftsmann
businesswoman die Geschäftsfrau, -en
but aber (*coor. conj.*)
but rather sondern (*coor. conj.*)
butter die Butter
buy kaufen
by
  by (a certain time) bis (*prep.* + *acc.*)
  by oneself (myself, yourself, etc.) selbst *or* selber (*adv.*)
  by the way übrigens

C

café das Café, -s
  pastry café die Konditorei, -en
cafeteria (at the university) die Mensa
cake der Kuchen, -
call *rufen; nennen
  be called *heißen
  call up *an·rufen
  What do you call that? Wie nennt man das?
calm, peaceful ruhig
camera die Kamera, -s
camp campen
can die Dose, -n
can, be able to *können
Canada (das) Kanada
Canadian kanadisch (*adj.*); der Kanadier, -; die Kanadierin, -nen
cap die Mütze, -n
capitalism der Kapitalismus
car das Auto, -s; der Wagen, -
card die Karte, -n
care: I don't care. Das ist mir egal.
  take care of sich kümmern um
career die Karriere, -n
carefree unbesorgt

carry *tragen
cash das Bargeld
cash register die Kasse, -n
cashier's office die Kasse, -n
cat die Katze, -n
catalogue (university) das Vorlesungsverzeichnis, -se
catastrophe die Katastrophe, -n
catastrophic katastrophal
cathedral der Dom, -e
cause to be done *lassen (+ *infinitive*)
CD (compact disc) die CD, -s
CD player der CD-Spieler, -
cease auf·hören (mit etwas)
ceiling die Decke, -n
celebrate feiern
celebration die Feier, -n
cellular phone das Handy
cellar der Keller, -
central zentral
century das Jahrhundert, -e
for centuries jahrhundertelang
cereal das Müesli (*no pl.*)
certain, sure sicher
certainty die Sicherheit
chain die Kette, -n
chain reaction die Kettenreaktion, -en
chair der Stuhl, ¨-e
chalk die Kreide
chance die Gelegenheit, -en; die Chance, -n
change ändern (*trans.*); sich ändern (*intrans.*)
change (clothes) sich *um·ziehen
change (money) wechseln
change (trains, buses, etc.) *um·steigen
change purse der Geldbeutel, -
chapter das Kapitel, -
character der Charakter, -e
chat quatschen (*colloq.*)
cheap (inexpensive) billig
check der Scheck, -s; die Rechnung, -en (*restaurant bill*)
Check please! Zahlen bitte!
check kontrollieren
cheerful munter
cheese der Käse
chemistry die Chemie
chemistry class die Chemiestunde
chief Haupt- (*noun prefix*)
child das Kind, -er
childhood die Kindheit
China (das) China
Chinese (das) Chinesisch (*language*); chinesisch (*adj.*); der Chinese, -n, -n; die Chinesin, -nen
chocolate die Schokolade
choice die Wahl, -en
choose wählen
chop, cutlet das Schnitzel, -
church die Kirche, -n
circa zirka
citizen der Staatsbürger, -
city die Stadt, ¨-e
capital city die Hauptstadt, ¨-e
city center das Stadtzentrum
city guidebook der Stadtführer, -
city map der Stadtplan, ¨-e
city square der Platz, ¨-e
large city (*population over 500,000*) die Großstadt, ¨-e
old city center die Altstadt, ¨-e
small city (*population 5,000 to 20,000*) die Kleinstadt, ¨-e
civil servant der Beamte (*adj. noun, m.*); die Beamtin, -nen (*f.*)
claim to *wollen
class die Klasse, -n
class hour die Stunde, -n
clean sauber (*adj.*); putzen (*verb*)
clear klar; deutlich
clerk der Verkäufer, -; die Verkäuferin, -nen
cliché das Klischee, -s
climate das Klima
climb *steigen
clock die Uhr, -en
close *schließen, zu·machen
closed geschlossen
cloth das Tuch
clothes die Kleider (*pl.*)
clothes cupboard der Kleiderschrank, ¨-e
clothing die Kleidung
cloud die Wolke, -n
cloudy wolkig
coast die Küste, -en
coat der Mantel, ¨-
coffee der Kaffee
cold kalt (kälter)
catch a cold sich erkälten
have a cold erkältet sein
cold cuts der Aufschnitt (*no pl.*)
colleague der Kollege, -n, -n; die Kollegin, -nen
collect sammeln
Cologne (das) Köln
colony die Kolonie, -n
color die Farbe, -n
colorful bunt
comb kämmen
comb one's hair sich die Haare kämmen
come *kommen
All together that comes to ... Das macht zusammen ...
come along *mit·kommen
come back *zurück·kommen
Come in! Herein!
come by *vorbei·kommen
I come from ... Ich komme aus ...
Where do you come from? Woher kommst du?
comfortable bequem; gemütlich
communal living group die Wohngemeinschaft, -en; die WG, -s
Communism der Kommunismus
company die Firma, (*pl.*) Firmen
comparative degree der Komparativ
compare *vergleichen
compatriots die Landsleute (*pl.*)
computer der Computer, -
laptop computer der Laptop, -s
computer science die Informatik
concentrate on sich konzentrieren auf (+ *acc.*)
concerned besorgt
concert das Konzert, -e
conclusion der Schluss, ¨-e
in conclusion zum Schluss
conflict der Konflikt, -e, der Streit
confront konfrontieren
congenial sympathisch
congratulate gratulieren (+ *dat. of person*)
Congratulations. Ich gratuliere (dir/Ihnen).
conjunction die Konjunktion, -en
consequence die Konsequenz, -en
conservative konservativ
consider something sich etwas überlegen
contact der Kontakt, -e
contents der Inhalt
contingent: be contingent on (depend on) *an·kommen auf (+ *acc.*)
contrary: on the contrary im Gegenteil
contrast der Kontrast, -e
conversation das Gespräch, -e
converse with sich *unterhalten mit
cook kochen
cool kühl
cooperate mit·machen
corner die Ecke, -n
around the corner um die Ecke
at/on the corner an der Ecke
correct richtig
correspondent der Korrespondent, -en, -en
Corsica (das) Korsika
cost kosten
How much does that cost, please? Wie viel kostet das bitte?
count zählen
count on sich verlassen auf (+ *acc.*)
counter, window der Schalter, -
country das Land, ¨-er
in the country auf dem Land
to the country aufs Land
couple
a couple (of) ein paar
married couple das Ehepaar, -e
course: of course selbstverständlich
cousin der Cousin, -s; die Cousine, -n
cozy, relaxed gemütlich
crazy verrückt
cream die Sahne
creative kreativ
credit card die Kreditkarte, -n
Crete (das) Kreta
critical kritisch
cross das Kreuz, -e
cross street die Querstraße, -n

crowd die Menge, -n
cruel grausam
cry weinen
cultural center das Kulturzentrum
culture die Kultur, -en
cup die Tasse, -n
current aktuell (*adj.*)
customer der Kunde, -n, -n; die Kundin, -nen
cut *schneiden
cutlet das Schnitzel, -

D

dad (der) Vati, -s
daily täglich
damp nass
dance tanzen
danger die Gefahr, -en
dangerous gefährlich
Danube River die Donau
dark dunkel
darn
  Darn it! Verflixt nochmal!
  I don't give a darn. Das ist mir Wurst (*or* Wurscht).
date das Datum, *pl.* Daten
  What's the date today? Der Wievielte ist heute? Den Wievielten haben wir heute?
dative case der Dativ
daughter die Tochter, ¨
day der Tag, -e
  day after tomorrow übermorgen
  day before yesterday vorgestern
  for days tagelang
  in those days damals
  one day (in the past or future) eines Tages
  some day (in the future) eines Tages
dead tot
deal with sich kümmern um
dear lieb
death der Tod
December (der) Dezember
decide *entscheiden
deed die Tat, -en
deep tief
defend verteidigen
define definieren
delicious lecker
democracy die Demokratie, -n
democratic demokratisch
democratization die Demokratisierung
demonstration die Demonstration, -en
depart *ab·fahren; *los·fahren
department store das Kaufhaus, ¨er
depend on *an·kommen auf (+ *acc.*)
describe *beschreiben
desire die Lust
desk der Schreibtisch, -e
despite trotz (+ *gen.*)
dessert der Nachtisch, -e
  for dessert zum Nachtisch
destroy zerstören
destruction die Zerstörung
dialect der Dialekt, -e
dialogue der Dialog, -e
dictionary das Wörterbuch, ¨er
die *sterben
  die in battle *fallen
difference der Unterschied, -e
different (other) ander- (*attributive adj.*); anders (*predicate adj.*)
different (various) verschieden
difficult schwer; schwierig
difficulty die Schwierigkeit, -en
dining room das Esszimmer, -; der Speisesaal, (*pl.*) Speisesäle
direct(ly) direkt
director der Direktor, -en
dirty schmutzig; dreckig (*colloq.*)
disappear *verschwinden
disappoint enttäuschen
discuss *besprechen
discussion die Diskussion, -en
dish (menu item) die Speise, -n
disorderly schlampig (*colloq.*); unordentlich
distance oneself from sich distanzieren von
distant fern
disturb stören
diversity die Vielfalt
divide teilen
do machen; *tun; *unternehmen
doctor der Arzt, ¨e; die Ärztin, -nen
dog der Hund, -e
done fertig
  get done schaffen (*colloq.*)
donkey der Esel, -
door die Tür, -en
dove die Taube, -n
drag schleppen
dress das Kleid, -er
dress: get dressed sich *an·ziehen
drink *trinken
drive (a vehicle) *fahren
drive (force) *treiben
driver's license der Führerschein, -e
drop by *vorbei·kommen
dry trocken
dumb (stupid) dumm (dümmer); blöd
during während (+ *gen.*)
during . . . (while . . . -ing) bei ...
dwell wohnen
dynasty die Dynastie, -n

E

each jed-
  each other einander
eagle der Adler, -
ear das Ohr, -en
early früh
earn verdienen
earth die Erde
east der Osten
Eastern Europe (das) Osteuropa
easy (simple) einfach; leicht
eat *essen
economic wirtschaftlich; ökonomisch
economics die Wirtschaftswissenschaft
economy die Wirtschaft
ecosystem das Ökosystem, -e
educated gebildet
education (as field of study) die Pädagogik
egg das Ei, -er
either . . . or entweder ... oder
elect wählen
election die Wahl, -en
electrical engineer der Elektrotechniker, -; die Elektrotechnikerin, -nen
electrical engineering die Elektrotechnik
electrician der Elektrotechniker, -; die Elektrotechnikerin, -nen
electricity die Elektrizität
elephant der Elefant, -en, -en
elevator der Lift, -s
e-mail die E-Mail, -s
emigrate aus·wandern, emigrieren
empire das Reich, -e
employed berufstätig
employee der/die Angestellte, -n (*adj. noun*)
empty leer
end das Ende, -n; der Schluss, ¨e
  at the end am Ende
  at the end of February Ende Februar
  end (be finished) zu Ende *sein
energy die Energie
engaged: become engaged to sich verloben mit
engineer der Ingenieur, -e; die Ingenieurin, -nen
English (*adj.*) englisch
  English (language) (das) Englisch
  English studies die Anglistik
Englishman der Engländer, -
Englishwoman die Engländerin, -nen
enjoy *genießen
enormous enorm
enough genug
en route unterwegs
enthusiasm die Begeisterung
entire ganz
entrance, way in der Einstieg, -e
envelope der Umschlag, ¨e
environment die Umwelt
environmentally safe umweltfreundlich
epoch die Epoche, -n
eraser der Radiergummi (*pencil*); der Wischer, - (*blackboard*)
especially besonders
essay der Aufsatz, ¨e; der Essay, -s
  essay topic das Aufsatzthema, *pl.* -themen
etc. usw. (= und so weiter)
euro der Euro, -s

Europe (das) Europa
Eastern Europe (das) Osteuropa
European europäisch (*adj.*); der Europäer, -; die Europäerin, -nen
European Union die Europäische Union
even (in fact) sogar
evening der Abend, -e
  evening meal das Abendessen
  every evening jeden Abend
  good evening guten Abend
  in the evening am Abend
  (in the) evenings abends
  this evening heute Abend
  yesterday evening gestern Abend
ever je
every jed-
  every time jedes Mal (*adv.*)
everybody alle (*pl. pron.*)
everyday life der Alltag
everyone jeder (*sing. pron.*)
everything alles
everywhere überall
evil böse (*adj.*)
exact genau
examination die Prüfung, -en; das Abitur (*final secondary school exam*); das Abi (*slang*)
  in-class examination die Klassenarbeit, -en, die Klausur, -en
example das Beispiel, -e
  for example zum Beispiel
excellent ausgezeichnet
except for außer (+ *dat.*)
exchange student der Austauschstudent, -en, -en; die Austauschstudentin, -nen
excursion der Ausflug, ⸚e
Excuse me. Entschuldigung.
exercise die Übung, -en
exhausted kaputt (*colloq.*)
exhibition die Ausstellung, -en
exist existieren
expect erwarten
expensive teuer
experience die Erfahrung, -en
explain erklären
expression der Ausdruck, ⸚e
expressway die Autobahn, -en
extreme extrem
extremely wahnsinnig (*colloq. adv.*)
eye das Auge, -n
eyeglasses die Brille (*sing.*)

F

face das Gesicht, -er
fact: in fact eigentlich; **in fact (even)** sogar
factory die Fabrik, -en
fairly ziemlich
fairy tale das Märchen, -
fall (*season*) der Herbst
fall term das Wintersemester
fall der Fall; *fallen
  fall asleep *ein·schlafen
false (incorrect) falsch
family die Familie, -n
famous berühmt
fantastic fantastisch
far, far away weit; fern
farmer der Bauer, -n, -n; die Bäuerin, -nen; der Landwirt, -e; die Landwirtin, -nen
fast schnell
father der Vater, ⸚
favorite Lieblings- (*noun prefix*)
  favorite sport der Lieblingssport
fear die Angst, ⸚e; Angst haben (vor + *dat.*); fürchten
February (der) Februar
Federal Republic of Germany (FRG) die Bundesrepublik Deutschland (BRD)
fed up: I'm fed up. Ich habe die Nase voll.
feel sich fühlen (*intrans.*)
  to feel well sich wohl fühlen
feeling das Gefühl, -e
fetch holen
fetch, pick up ab·holen
few wenige
  a few ein paar, mehrere
film der Film, -e
finally endlich; zum Schluss; zuletzt
finance finanzieren
find *finden
Fine by me. Ist gut. (*colloq.*)
finger der Finger, -
finish: finished with fertig mit; **be finished** zu Ende *sein
firm (company) die Firma, *pl.* Firmen
first erst- (*adj.*); zuerst (*adv.*)
  at first zuerst
  first (of all) zunächst
fish der Fisch, -e
flabbergasted baff (*colloq.*)
flat flach
floor (of a building) der Stock
  ground floor (= first floor) das Erdgeschoss
  on the second floor im ersten Stock
  second floor der erste Stock
floor (of a room) der Boden, ⸚
flow *fließen
flower die Blume, -n
fly *fliegen
fog der Nebel
foggy neblig
folk das Volk, ⸚er
folk song das Volkslied, -er
follow folgen, ist gefolgt (+ *dat.*)
food das Essen
foolproof idiotensicher
foot der Fuß, ⸚e
  on foot zu Fuß
for für (*prep.* + *acc.*)
  for (because) denn (*coor. conj.*)
  for a long time lange; seit langem; schon lange
  for years seit Jahren
forbidden verboten
force (propel) *treiben
foreign ausländisch
  foreign, strange fremd
  foreign countries das Ausland (*sing.*)
  foreign language die Fremdsprache, -n
foreigner der Ausländer, -; die Ausländerin, -nen
forest der Wald, ⸚er
forget *vergessen
  I can't forget that. Das geht mir nicht aus dem Kopf.
fork die Gabel, -n
form die Form, -en
formal formell
formulate formulieren
fortunately glücklicherweise
fox der Fuchs, ⸚e
France (das) Frankreich
free
  free, unoccupied frei
  free of charge kostenlos
  free time die Freizeit
freedom die Freiheit, -en
French (*adj.*) französisch
French fries die Pommes frites (*pl.*)
Frenchman der Franzose, -n, -n
Frenchwoman die Französin, -nen
fresh frisch
Friday (der) Freitag
friend der Freund, -e; die Freundin, -nen; der/die Bekannte, -n (*adj. noun*)
friendly freundlich; sympathisch
from aus (+ *dat.*); von (+ *dat.*)
front: in front of vor (*prep.* + *dat.* or *acc.*)
fruit das Obst
  fruit salad der Obstsalat, -e
full voll
fun der Spaß; lustig (*adj.*)
  Have fun. Viel Spaß.
  make fun of sich lustig machen über (+ *acc.*)
  That is fun (for me). Das macht (mir) Spaß.
funny (peculiar) komisch
furnished möbliert
furniture die Möbel (*pl.*)
future die Zukunft
  in the future in Zukunft
future tense das Futur

G

garage die Garage, -n
garden der Garten, ⸚
gasoline das Benzin
gate das Tor, -e
genitive case der Genitiv
gentleman der Herr, -n, -en
genuine echt
geographical geographisch
geography die Geographie

German deutsch (*adj.*); der/die Deutsche, -n (*adj. noun*)
German class die Deutschstunde, -n
German Democratic Republic (GDR) die Deutsche Demokratische Republik (DDR)
German (language) (das) Deutsch
German studies die Germanistik
in German auf Deutsch
German-speaking deutschsprachig
Germany (das) Deutschland
get (receive) *bekommen
get (become) *werden
get (fetch) holen
get (pick up) ab·holen
get in (a vehicle) *ein·steigen
get done schaffen
get out (of a vehicle) *aus·steigen
get there: How do I get there? Wie komme ich dahin?
get up (get out of bed) *auf·stehen
giant der Riese, -n, -n
gigantic riesengroß; riesen- (*noun and adj. prefix*)
girl das Mädchen, -
give *geben
give (as a gift) schenken
give up *auf·geben
glad froh
I'm glad. Das freut mich.
gladly, with pleasure gern(e) (*adv.*)
glass das Glas, ¨er
glasses die Brille (*sing.*)
globalization die Globalisierung
glove der Handschuh, -e
go *gehen
go (by vehicle) *fahren
go away *weg·gehen
go in *hinein·gehen
go on foot laufen
go out *aus·gehen
on the go unterwegs
goal das Ziel, -e
god der Gott, ¨er
golden golden
gone weg
good gut (besser, best-); brav (= **well-behaved**)
Good-bye! Auf Wiedersehen!
Good evening! Guten Abend!
Good morning! Guten Morgen!
Have a good trip! Gute Reise!
pretty good ganz gut
gossip der Klatsch
government in power die Regierung, -en
grade, class die Klasse, -n
grade (on a test, paper, etc.) die Note, -n
gram das Gramm
grammar die Grammatik
grandchildren die Enkelkinder
granddaughter die Enkelin, -nen
grandfather der Großvater, ¨
grandma die Oma, -s
grandmother die Großmutter, ¨
grandpa der Opa, -s
grandparents die Großeltern (*pl.*)
grandson der Enkel, -
graphic artist der Graphiker, -; die Graphikerin, -nen
gray grau
great (terrific) herrlich; prima, toll, klasse (*colloq.*)
Great Britain (das) Großbritannien
greatness die Größe
Greece (das) Griechenland
Greek griechisch (*adj.*)
green grün
greet grüßen
groceries die Lebensmittel (*pl.*)
group die Gruppe, -n
grow *wachsen
grow up *auf·wachsen
grown up erwachsen (*adj.*); der/die Erwachsene, -n (*adj. noun*)
gruesome grausam
guess *raten
Take a guess! Raten Sie mal!
guest der Gast, ¨e
guidebook der Reiseführer, -
guilty schuldig
guy der Typ, -en (*slang*)
gym shoe der Turnschuh, -e

H

hair das Haar, -e
half halb (*adv.*)
ham der Schinken
hand die Hand, ¨e
handle (manage, get done) schaffen (*colloq.*)
handsome hübsch
hang hängen (*trans.*); *hängen (*intrans.*)
hang up auf·hängen
happen passieren, ist passiert
happiness das Glück
happy glücklich, froh
be happy sich freuen
Happy birthday. Ich gratuliere dir zum Geburtstag.
harbor der Hafen, ¨
hard hart (härter)
hard, difficult schwer
hard-working fleißig
harsh hart (härter)
hat der Hut, ¨e
hate hassen
hatred der Hass
haul schleppen
have *haben
have in mind *vor·haben
have to (must) *müssen
head der Kopf, ¨e
health die Gesundheit
healthy gesund (gesünder)
hear hören
heart das Herz, -en
heaven: For heaven's sake! Um Gottes Willen!
heavy schwer
hectic hektisch
hello Grüß Gott! Grüß dich! (*in southern Germany and Austria*); Guten Tag! Hallo!
say hello to grüßen
help die Hilfe; *helfen (+ *dat.*)
helping (portion) die Portion, -en
here hier (*location*); her (*destination*)
Here it is. Bitte.
Hi! Tag!
high hoch (*pred. adj.*), hoh- (*attributive adj.*) (höher, höchst-)
High time! Höchste Zeit! Na endlich!
highway die Autobahn, -en
hike die Wanderung, -en; wandern
hill der Hügel, -
hilly hügelig
hint der Tipp, -s
historic historisch
history die Geschichte, -n
hockey das Hockey
hold *halten
home (as destination of motion) nach Hause
at home zu Hause
in/at the home of bei (+ *dat.*)
homeland die Heimat
homesickness das Heimweh
hometown die Heimatstadt
homework assignment die Hausaufgabe, -n
honest ehrlich
honey der Honig (*no pl.*)
hope hoffen
I hope hoffentlich (*adv.*)
horizon der Horizont, -e
hospital das Krankenhaus, ¨er
hot heiß
hotel das Hotel, -s
hour die Stunde, -n
for hours stundenlang
house das Haus, ¨er
househusband der Hausmann, ¨er
housemate der Mitbewohner, -; die Mitbewohnerin, -nen
housewife die Hausfrau, -en
housework die Hausarbeit
how? wie?
How come? Wieso?
how long? wie lange?
how many? wie viele?
how much? wie viel?
And how! Und wie!
however aber
huge, gigantic riesengroß
human (*adj.*) menschlich
human being der Mensch, -en, -en
human race die Menschheit
humor der Humor
humorous lustig

hunch die Ahnung, -en
hundred hundert
hunger der Hunger
hungry hungrig
  be hungry Hunger haben
hurry die Eile; sich beeilen, schnell machen (*colloq.*)
  in a hurry in Eile
hurt *weh·tun (+ *dat. of person*)
  get hurt sich verletzen
  That hurts (me). Das tut (mir) weh.
husband der Mann, ¨er; der Ehemann, ¨er

I

ice das Eis
ice cream das Eis
ice hockey das Eishockey
idea die Idee, -n
  (I have) no idea. (Ich habe) keine Ahnung.
I.D. card der Ausweis, -e
to identify with sich identifizieren mit
identity die Identität, -en
ideological ideologisch
idiot-proof idiotensicher
i.e. (= that is) d.h. (= das heißt)
if wenn (*sub. conj.*)
if (= whether) ob (*sub. conj.*)
illegal illegal
illusion die Illusion, -en
image das Bild, -er
imagine something sich etwas vor·stellen
immediately gleich; sofort
immigrate ein·wandern
imperative mood der Imperativ
important wichtig
  most important Haupt- (*noun prefix*)
impossible unmöglich
impression der Eindruck, ¨e
in (= into) in (*prep. + acc.* or *dat.*); hinein- (*prefix*)
incorrect (false) falsch
incredibly wahnsinnig (*colloq. adv.*)
indicative der Indikativ
industrious fleißig
industry die Industrie, -n
inexpensive billig
infinitive der Infinitiv
  infinitive phrase der Infinitivsatz, ¨e
inflation die Inflation
influence der Einfluss, ¨e
information die Auskunft
inhuman unmenschlich
injure oneself sich verletzen
inkling die Ahnung, -en
innocent unschuldig
insane verrückt
insert stecken
instead sondern (*coor. conj.*)
  instead of anstatt (+ *gen.*); statt (+ *gen.*)
instrument das Instrument, -e
integration die Integration
intelligent intelligent
intend to *wollen
intercultural interkulturell
interest interessieren
be interested in sich interessieren für
interesting interessant
intermission die Pause, -n
international international
interrupt *unterbrechen
interview interviewen
into in (*prep. + acc.*); hinein- (*prefix*)
introduce vor·stellen
introduce oneself sich vor·stellen
invent *erfinden
invest investieren
invite *ein·laden
iPod der iPod, -s
irony die Ironie
island die Insel, -n
Italian italienisch (*adj.*); der Italiener, -; die Italienerin, -nen
Italy (das) Italien

J

jacket die Jacke, -n
jam die Marmelade
January (der) Januar
jeans die Jeans (*pl.*)
Jewish jüdisch
job, position der Job, -s; die Stelle, -n
joke der Witz, -e
journalist der Journalist, -en, -en; die Journalistin, -nen
journey die Reise, -n
joy die Freude, -n
juice der Saft, ¨e
  orange juice der Orangensaft, ¨e
July (der) Juli
June (der) Juni
just, at the moment gerade
just as . . . as genauso ... wie

K

kaput kaputt (*colloq.*)
keep *behalten
key der Schlüssel, -
kilogram das Kilogramm; das Kilo (*colloq.*)
kilometer der Kilometer, -
kitchen die Küche, -n
knife das Messer, -
knock (on) klopfen (an + *acc.*)
know (a fact) *wissen
  get to know kennen lernen
  know (= be acquainted with) *kennen
  know one's way around sich *aus·kennen
known bekannt

L

lab(oratory) das Labor, -s
lady die Dame, -n
lake der See, -n
at the lake am See
lamp die Lampe, -n
landscape die Landschaft, -en
language die Sprache, -n
laptop der Laptop, -s
last letzt-
  last of all zuletzt
  last, take time dauern
late spät
  be late sich verspäten
  I'm late. Ich bin spät dran.
  later on nachher (*adv.*)
laugh lachen
lavatory die Toilette, -n
lavender lila
law (study of) Jura
lawyer der Rechtsanwalt, ¨e; die Rechtsanwältin, -nen
lay (put down) legen
lazy faul
lead führen
learn lernen
leave (something, someone) *lassen
  leave behind *lassen
  leave (a person or place) *verlassen
  leave (by vehicle) *ab·fahren; *los·fahren
  leave (go away) *weg·gehen
lecture (university) die Vorlesung, -en
left: to the left links (*adv.*) **on the left** links (*adv.*)
left over (remaining) übrig
leg das Bein, -e
leisure time die Freizeit
lend *leihen
let *lassen
letter der Brief, -e
  letter carrier der Briefträger, -; die Briefträgerin, -nen
lettuce der Salat, -e
library die Bibliothek, -en
lie, be situated *liegen
life das Leben
light (in color) hell
light (in weight) leicht
like *mögen; wie (*conj.*)
  I like that. Das gefällt mir.
  like something etwas gern haben; etwas mögen
  like this so
  like to (do something) gern (+ *verb*)
  would like to möchten
likeable sympathisch
limnology die Limnologie
line (of text) die Zeile, -n
line (streetcar, bus) die Linie, -n
linguistics die Linguistik
lion der Löwe, -n, -n
list die Liste, -n

listen (*to people*) zu·hören (+ *dat.*); (*to music*) hören
liter der Liter
literary literarisch
little klein (*adj.*); wenig (*pronoun*)
  a little etwas
  a little; a little bit; a little while ein bisschen
live leben
live (dwell) wohnen
lively munter
liverwurst die Leberwurst, ¨-e
loan *leihen
logical logisch
loneliness die Einsamkeit
lonely einsam
long lang(e) (länger)
  for a long time lange; (*stretch of time continuing in the present*) schon lange, seit langem
  for such a long time so lange
  no longer nicht mehr
look schauen
  look after sich kümmern um
  look (appear) *aus·sehen
  look for (seek) suchen
  look forward to sich freuen auf (+ *acc.*)
  Look here. Schau mal.
  take a look at something sich etwas *an·sehen
lose *verlieren
lots of eine Menge; viel
loud laut
love die Liebe; lieben
  in love with verliebt in (+ *acc.*)
low niedrig
luck das Glück
  be lucky Glück haben
  be unlucky (have bad luck) Pech haben
lug (along) schleppen (*colloq.*)
luggage das Gepäck
lunch, midday meal das Mittagessen

M

mad (at) böse (+ *dat.*)
magazine die Zeitschrift, -en
mail die Post
mail (a letter) *ein·werfen
mailbox der Briefkasten, ¨-
mailman der Briefträger, -
main Haupt- (*noun prefix*)
major field (of study) das Hauptfach, ¨-er
major in (a subject) studieren
make machen
make-up: put on make-up sich schminken
mama (die) Mutti, -s
man der Mann, ¨-er
Man! Mensch!
manage schaffen (*colloq.*)
management (field of study) die Betriebswirtschaft
manager der Manager, -
manipulate manipulieren
mankind die Menschheit
many viele (*adj.*)
  many a manch-
  many people viele (*pl. pron.*)
  many things vieles (*sing. pron.*)
map die Karte, -n; die Landkarte, -n
March (der) März
marketing das Marketing
marmalade die Marmelade
marriage die Ehe, -n
married man der Ehemann, ¨-er
married woman die Ehefrau, -en
marvelous herrlich
mathematics die Mathematik (*sing.*)
matter (affair) die Sache, -n
matter
  It doesn't matter. Es macht nichts.
  It doesn't matter (to me). Das ist (mir) egal. I don't care.
  That doesn't matter. Das macht nichts
  What's the matter? Was ist los?
May (der) Mai
may, be allowed to *dürfen
maybe vielleicht
meal das Essen
mean, signify bedeuten
mean (think) meinen
  that means, in other words das heißt
  What do you mean? Wieso?
meaning die Bedeutung, -en
meanwhile, in the meantime inzwischen
meat das Fleisch
mechanic der Mechaniker, -; die Mechanikerin, -nen
mechanical engineering der Maschinenbau
medicine die Medizin
meet (for the first time) kennen lernen
  meet again wieder *sehen
  meet (by appointment) *treffen
melancholy die Melancholie
member das Mitglied, -er
memorial das Denkmal, ¨-e
memory die Erinnerung, -en
mention: Don't mention it. Nichts zu danken.
menu die Speisekarte, -n
messy schlampig (*colloq.*); unordentlich
method die Methode, -n
Middle Ages das Mittelalter (*sing.*)
might die Macht
mild mild
milk die Milch
million die Million, -en
minor field (of study) das Nebenfach, ¨-er
minute die Minute, -n
  for minutes minutenlang
miracle das Wunder, -
mirror der Spiegel, -
Miss Fräulein
miss (an event, opportunity, train, etc.) verpassen
missing: be missing fehlen
mist der Nebel
misty neblig
mobile phone das Handy
modal verb das Modalverb, -en
modern modern
modernize modernisieren
mom die Mutti, -s
moment der Augenblick, -e; der Moment, -e
  at the moment im Augenblick; im Moment
  at the moment, just gerade
  Just a moment, please. (Einen) Augenblick, bitte.
monarchy die Monarchie, -n
Monday (der) Montag
money das Geld
month der Monat, -e
  for months monatelang
monument das Denkmal, ¨-er
mood die Laune, -n
  in a good/bad mood gut/schlecht gelaunt
more mehr
not any more nicht mehr
morning der Morgen, -
  Good morning! Guten Morgen!
  in the morning(s) morgens (*adv.*)
  this morning heute Morgen
Morocco (das) Marokko
most meist-
  most like to am liebsten (+ *verb*)
mostly meistens
mother die Mutter, ¨-
motorcycle das Motorrad, ¨-er
mountain der Berg, -e
  mountain range das Gebirge, -
mountainous bergig
mouth der Mund, ¨-er
move, change residence *um·ziehen
  move in *ein·ziehen
  move out *aus·ziehen
movie der Film, -e
movie theater das Kino, -s
Mr. Herr
Mrs. Frau
Ms. Frau
much viel (mehr, meist-)
  not much wenig
Munich (das) München
museum das Museum, *pl.* Museen
music die Musik
musicology die Musikwissenschaft
must *müssen

N

name der Name, -ns, -n; *nennen
  My name is . . . Ich heiße ...
  What's your name? Wie heißen Sie?/Wie heißt du?
napkin die Serviette, -n
narrative die Erzählung, -en

nation (folk) das Volk, ¨-er
nationality die Nationalität, -en
native
native language die Muttersprache, -n
native place or country die Heimat
natural natürlich
nature die Natur
near nah (näher, nächst-)
near(by) in der Nähe (von, *or* + *gen.*)
nearness die Nähe
necessary nötig
need brauchen
neighbor der Nachbar, -n, -n; die Nachbarin, -nen
neither . . . nor weder ... noch
neutral neutral
never nie
nevertheless trotzdem
new neu
brand-new nagelneu
newspaper die Zeitung, -en
next nächst-
next to neben
nice nett; lieb
night die Nacht, ¨-e
every night, nights nachts
Good night. Gute Nacht.
in the night, at night in der Nacht; nachts
no nein; nee (*colloq.*)
no, not a kein (*negative article*)
no more . . . kein ... mehr
no one niemand
nobody niemand
nod nicken
nominative case der Nominativ
nonpolluting umweltfreundlich
Nonsense! Quatsch!
normal normal
north der Norden
North America (das) Nordamerika
nose die Nase, -n
not nicht
not a kein (*negative article*)
not a . . . at all gar kein
not a . . . any longer kein ... mehr
not any kein
not any more, no longer nicht mehr
not any . . . yet noch kein ...
not at all gar nicht
not much wenig
not only . . . but also nicht nur ... sondern auch
not until only, erst
not yet noch nicht
notebook das Heft, -e
nothing nichts
notice merken
notion die Ahnung
noun das Substantiv, -e
novel der Roman, -e
November (der) November
now jetzt; nun
from now on von jetzt an
number die Nummer, -n; die Zahl, -en
nurse der Krankenpfleger, - (*m.*); die Krankenschwester, -n (*f.*)

O

object, thing die Sache, -n; Objekt, -e
objective objektiv
ocean der Ozean, -e
o'clock Uhr (3 o'clock = 3 Uhr)
October (der) Oktober
odd komisch
of von (*prep.* + *dat.*)
of course natürlich
of course, sure klar (*colloq.*)
offend ärgern
office das Büro, -s
official offiziell (*adj.*); der Beamte (*adj. noun, m.*); die Beamtin, -nen (*f.*)
often oft (öfter)
oh ach
oil das Öl
O.K. Ist gut; einverstanden; okay (*colloq.*)
old alt (älter)
old-fashioned altmodisch
on auf (*prep.* + *acc.* or *dat.*)
once einmal
once again (once more) noch einmal
one eins
one (*indefinite pronoun*) man
oneself: by oneself (myself, yourself, etc.) selber, selbst
only nur (*adv.*)
only, single einzig- (*adj.*)
onto auf (*prep.* + *acc.* or *dat.*)
open offen (*adj.*); auf·machen, öffnen (*verb*)
opinion die Meinung, -en
be of the opinion (think) meinen
opportunity die Gelegenheit, -en
opposite der Gegensatz, ¨-e
opposition die Opposition, -en
optimistic optimistisch
or oder (*coor. conj.*)
orange orange (*adj.*)
orange juice der Orangensaft
order die Portion, -en (*of food*); bestellen
in order to um ... zu
orderly ordentlich
other ander-
otherwise sonst
outing der Ausflug, ¨-e
out of aus (*prep.* + *dat.*)
outside draußen (*adv.*)
over über (*prep.* + *dat.* or *acc.*)
over there drüben; da drüben
over: be over zu Ende *sein
own eigen- (*adj.*); *besitzen

P

pace das Tempo
pack packen
page die Seite, -n
palace das Schloss, ¨-er; die Residenz
pants die Hose, -n
papa der Vati, -s
paper das Papier, -e
write a paper ein Referat schreiben
written research paper das Referat
Pardon me. Entschuldigung.
I beg your pardon? Wie bitte?
parents die Eltern (*pl.*)
part der Teil, -e
take part in *teil·nehmen an (+ *dat.*)
participate mit·machen
participle das Partizip
partner der Partner, -
party die Party, -s
party (political) die Partei, -en
passive voice das Passiv
passport der Reisepass, ¨-e
past (time) die Vergangenheit
past perfect tense das Plusquamperfekt
patient der Patient, -en, -en
patron der Gast, ¨-e
pay bezahlen; zahlen
peace der Frieden; die Ruhe
leave someone in peace jemand in Ruhe lassen
peaceful (calm) ruhig
peculiar komisch
pedestrian der Fußgänger, -
pedestrian zone die Fußgängerzone, -n
pen (ballpoint) der Kugelschreiber, -
pencil der Bleistift, -e
people die Leute (*pl.*)
people (nation, folk) das Volk, ¨-er
pepper der Pfeffer, -
percent das Prozent
perfect perfekt
perfect tense das Perfekt
perhaps vielleicht
person der Mensch, -en, -en; die Person, -en
personal persönlich
personal pronoun das Personalpronomen
pessimistic pessimistisch
pharmacy die Apotheke, -n
philosophy die Philosophie
photograph das Foto, -s
physics die Physik (*sing.*)
piano das Klavier, -e
pick up ab·holen
picture das Bild, -er
take a picture ein Foto machen
piece das Stück, -e
pigeon die Taube, -n
pink rosa
pitch in mit·machen
pity: What a pity! Das ist schade!
place der Ort, -e; der Platz, ¨-e
place (put) stellen
plan *vor·haben
plan, make plans planen
plant die Pflanze, -n
plastic das Plastik

plate der Teller, -
play spielen
play sports Sport *treiben
pleasant angenehm
please bitte
please, appeal to *gefallen (+ *dat.*)
Pleased to meet you. Sehr erfreut. *or* Es freut mich.
Pleasure to meet you. Angenehm.
pocket die Tasche, -n
poem das Gedicht, -e
poet der Dichter, -; die Dichterin, -nen
poetry die Lyrik
police die Polizei (*sing. only*)
policy die Politik
polite höflich
political politisch
political science die Politikwissenschaft
politician der Politiker, -; die Politikerin, -nen
politics die Politik
pollute verschmutzen
non-polluting, ecologically beneficial umweltfreundlich
pollution die Verschmutzung
ponder something sich etwas überlegen
poor arm (ärmer)
port der Hafen, ¨
portion die Portion, -en
position, job die Stelle, -n
positive positiv
possible möglich
postage stamp die Briefmarke, -n
postal service die Post
postcard die Postkarte, -n
poster das Poster, -
poster (political) das Plakat, -e
post office die Post
pot: small (coffee or tea) pot das Kännchen, -
potato die Kartoffel, -n
power die Kraft, ¨e; die Macht, ¨e
power plant das Kraftwerk, -e
practical praktisch
practice üben
precise genau
prefer (to do something) lieber (+ *verb*)
preferably lieber
prejudice das Vorurteil, -e
prepared, ready bereit
prepare for sich vor·bereiten auf (+ *acc.*)
present (gift) das Geschenk, -e
be present, be there dabei *sein
pressure der Druck
pretty hübsch
pretzel die Brezel, -n
previously vorher
price der Preis, -e
primary Haupt- (*noun prefix*)
private privat
probably wahrscheinlich; wohl
problem das Problem, -e
produce produzieren
product, ware die Ware, -n
profession der Beruf, -e
What is your profession? Was sind Sie von Beruf?
professor der Professor, -en; die Professorin, -nen
program das Programm, -e
progress der Fortschritt, -e
prohibited verboten
pronounce *aus·sprechen
propel *treiben
protest der Protest, -e
proud of stolz auf (+ *acc.*)
psychoanalysis die Psychoanalyse
psychology die Psychologie
pull *ziehen
pullover der Pullover, -; der Pulli, -s (*colloq.*)
punctual pünktlich
pupil der Schüler, -; die Schülerin, -nen
put stellen
put down (lay) legen
put down (set) setzen
put (into) stecken

Q

quantity die Menge, -n
quarter das Viertel, -
quarter to/past Viertel vor/nach
question die Frage, -n
ask a question eine Frage stellen
guiding question die Leitfrage, -n
questionnaire der Fragebogen
quick as lightning blitzschnell
quiet (rest, peace) die Ruhe
quiet (*adj.*) leise
quit, to give up *auf·geben
quite ziemlich

R

radical radikal
radio das Radio, -s
railroad (railroad system) die Bahn
rain der Regen; regnen
rainy regnerisch
rather
I'd rather not. No thanks. Let's not. Lieber nicht.
would rather (do something) lieber (+ *verb*)
reaction die Reaktion, -en
react to reagieren auf (+ *acc.*)
read *lesen
read about lesen über
read aloud *vor·lesen
reading selection das Lesestück, -e
ready (= finished) fertig
ready (= prepared) bereit
real wirklich, echt
realistic realistisch
really tatsächlich, echt (*colloq.*)
really fun(ny) echt lustig
realm das Reich, -e
reason der Grund, ¨e
receive *bekommen
recently neulich
reception desk die Rezeption
recognize * erkennen
recommend *empfehlen
recover (from) sich erholen von
recycling (recycling center) das Recycling
red rot (röter)
reform die Reform, -en; reformieren
refuse (trash) der Müll
regard as *halten für
regime das Regime
region die Gegend, -en; die Region, -en
register (at a hotel, the university, etc.) sich an·melden
register for, take (a university course) belegen
relative relativ (*adj.* and *adv.*); der/die Verwandte, -n (*adj. noun*)
relaxed gemütlich
rely on sich verlassen auf + *acc.*
remain *bleiben
remaining (left over) übrig
remember sich erinnern an (+ *acc.*)
Do you remember? Weißt du noch?
remind of erinnern an (+ *acc.*)
repair reparieren
repeat wiederholen
repetition die Wiederholung, -en
report berichten
give a report ein Referat *halten
oral report das Referat, -e
repressive repressiv
republic die Republik, -en
request *bitten um
rescue retten
reserve reservieren
residence, seat of a court die Residenz
respond to antworten auf (+ *acc.*)
responsible for verantwortlich für
rest (quiet, peace) die Ruhe
have a rest sich erholen
restaurant das Restaurant, -s; das Lokal, -e
restless unruhig
restoration die Restauration, -en
retain *behalten
review die Wiederholung
revolution die Revolution, -en
Rhine River der Rhein
rich reich
right (correct) richtig
be right Recht *haben (*with person as subject*); stimmen (*impersonal only*)
right away sofort; gleich
That's right. Das stimmt. Stimmt schon.

to the right, on the right rechts (*adv.*)
You're right. Sie haben Recht.
ring klingeln
rip off (steal) klauen (*colloq.*)
river der Fluss, ¨-e
road die Straße, -n
road atlas der Straßenatlas
role die Rolle, -n
roll das Brötchen, -
Romania (das) Rumänien
romantic romantisch
room das Zimmer, -
dining room das Esszimmer, -; der Speisesaal, (*pl.*) Speisesäle
double room das Doppelzimmer, -
living room das Wohnzimmer, -
rented student room die Bude, -n (*colloq.*)
single room das Einzelzimmer, -
roommate der Mitbewohner, -; die Mitbewohnerin, -nen
rubble die Trümmer (*pl.*)
rucksack der Rucksack, ¨-e
rug der Teppich, -e
ruin die Ruine, -n
run *laufen
Russia (das) Russland
Russian russisch (*adj.*); der Russe, -n, -n; die Russin, -nen

S

sack der Sack, ¨-e
sad traurig
safety die Sicherheit
salad der Salat, -e
salesman der Verkäufer, -
saleswoman die Verkäuferin, -nen
salt das Salz, -e
sample probieren
satisfied zufrieden
Saturday (der) Samstag, (der) Sonnabend
sausage die Wurst, ¨-e
save (rescue) retten
save (money, time) sparen
Saxony (das) Sachsen
say sagen
What did you say? Wie bitte?
saying: It goes without saying that . . . selbstverständlich
Scandinavia (das) Skandinavien
scarce, in short supply knapp
scarf das Tuch, ¨-er
scholarship die Wissenschaft
scholarship (stipend) das Stipendium, *pl.* Stipendien
school die Schule, -n; das Gymnasium, *pl.* Gymnasien (*prepares pupils for university*)
elementary school pupil or secondary school student der Schüler, -; die Schülerin, -nen
school system das Schulsystem, -e
science die Wissenschaft, -en
sea das Meer, -e
season die Jahreszeit, -en
seat der Platz, ¨-e
second zweit-
second car der Zweitwagen, -
security die Sicherheit
see *sehen
Let's see. Zeig mal her.
see again wieder *sehen
See you later! Bis nachher!
seek (look for) suchen
seem *scheinen
seldom selten
self: by oneself (myself, yourself, etc.) selbst *or* selber (*adv.*)
sell verkaufen
semester das Semester, -
semester break die Semesterferien (*pl.*)
seminar das Seminar, -e
send schicken
senior citizen der Senior, -en, -en
sense der Sinn
That makes no sense. Das hat keinen Sinn.
sentence der Satz, ¨-e
separate (*verb*) trennen
separate (*adj.*) separat
September (der) September
serious ernst
take something seriously etwas ernst *nehmen
set (down) setzen
seventh siebt-
several mehrere, einige
shake schütteln
shame: That's a shame! Das ist schade!
shape: in shape fit
shared apartment die Wohngemeinschaft, -en; die WG, -s
shave sich rasieren
shelf das Regal, -e
shine *scheinen
ship das Schiff, -e
shirt das Hemd, -en
shoe der Schuh, -e
shop, store der Laden, ¨
shop: go shopping ein·kaufen
short kurz (kürzer); klein (*short in height*)
short of cash knapp bei Kasse
should *sollen
shoulder bag die Tasche, -n
show zeigen
Show it to me. Zeig mal her.
shower die Dusche, -n
take a shower sich duschen
siblings die Geschwister (*pl.*)
sick krank (kränker)
sickness die Krankheit, -en
side die Seite. -n
sight, place of interest die Sehenswürdigkeit, -en
significance die Bedeutung, -en
silent: be silent *schweigen
similar (to) ähnlich (+ *dat.*)
simple (easy) einfach; leicht
since (causal) da (*sub. conj.*)
since (temporal) seit (*prep. + dat. & sub. conj.*)
sing *singen
single, only einzig- (*adj.*)
sister die Schwester, -n
sit *sitzen
sit down sich setzen
Sit down! Setz dich! Setzen Sie sich!
situated: be situated *liegen
situation die Situation, -en
size die Größe, -n
ski Ski *fahren
skirt der Rock, ¨-e
sleep *schlafen
slow langsam
small klein
smart klug (klüger)
snake die Schlange, -n
sneaker der Turnschuh, -e
snow der Schnee; schneien
so so
solidarity die Solidarität
So long! Tschüss!
so that damit (*sub. conj.*)
So what? Na und?
soccer (der) Fußball
soccer ball der Fußball, ¨-e
social sozial
social worker der Sozialarbeiter, -; die Sozialarbeiterin, -nen
society die Gesellschaft, -en
sociology die Soziologie
soft (quiet) leise
software die Software
solidarity die Solidarität
solution die Lösung, -en
solve lösen
some etwas (*sing.*); einige (*pl.*); manche (*pl.*)
somebody jemand
somehow or other irgendwie
someone jemand
something etwas
sometime or other irgendwann
sometimes manchmal
somewhat etwas
somewhere or other irgendwo
son der Sohn, ¨-e
song das Lied, -er
soon bald
sore (ticked off) sauer (*colloq.*)
sorry I'm sorry about that. Das tut mir Leid.
I'm sorry. Es tut mir Leid.
sort sortieren
soul die Seele, -n
sound *klingen
soup die Suppe, -n
sour (acidic) sauer
south der Süden

Soviet sowjetisch (*adj.*)
Soviet Union die Sowjetunion
space der Platz, ¨-e
Spain (das) Spanien
speak reden; *sprechen
I can speak German. Ich kann Deutsch.
speech die Rede, -n
speechless baff (*colloq.*)
speed das Tempo
spell: How do you spell that? Wie schreibt man das?
spend (money) *aus·geben
spend (time) *verbringen
spend the night übernachten
spite in spite of trotz (+ *gen.*)
in spite of that (nevertheless) trotzdem (*adv.*)
spontaneous spontan
spoon der Löffel, -
sport der Sport
play sports Sport *treiben
spouse die Ehefrau, -en (*f.*); der Ehemann, ¨-er (*m.*)
spring der Frühling
spring term das Sommersemester
square: city square der Platz, ¨-e
stable (*adj.*) stabil
staircase die Treppe, -n
stairs die Treppe, -n
stamp die Briefmarke, -n
stand *stehen
stand up *auf·stehen
standard of living der Lebensstandard
start *an·fangen
start, depart (by vehicle) *los·fahren
state der Staat, -en
stay *bleiben
steal stehlen
steal, rip off klauen (*colloq.*)
steep steil
still (*adv.*) noch; noch immer; immer noch
stipend das Stipendium, *pl.* Stipendien
stone der Stein, -e
stop (for streetcar or bus) die Haltestelle, -n
stop *halten (*intrans.*)
stop (doing something) auf·hören (mit etwas)
store das Geschäft, -e
store, shop der Laden, ¨
story die Geschichte, -n
story (narrative) die Erzählung, -en
straight ahead geradeaus
straighten up auf·räumen
strange (foreign) fremd
street die Straße, -n
streetcar die Straßenbahn, -en
strength die Kraft, ¨-e
stress der Stress
stressful stressig
strict streng
stroll der Bummel, -
stroll through town der Stadtbummel, -
take a stroll einen Bummel machen
strong stark (stärker)
student (at university) der Student, -en, -en; die Studentin, -nen
student dormitory das Studentenwohnheim, -e
student I.D. der Studentenausweis, -e
studies (at university) das Studium
study das Arbeitszimmer, -
study (a subject), major in studieren
study at studieren an (+ *dat.*)
stuff der Kram (*colloq.*)
stupid blöd; dumm
subject, (area of study) das Fach, ¨-er
subject (topic) das Thema, *pl.* Themen
subjective subjektiv
subjunctive mood der Konjunktiv
subway train die Untergrundbahn; die U-Bahn
success der Erfolg, -e
such solcher, -es, -e
suddenly plötzlich
suggestion der Vorschlag, ¨-e; der Tipp, -s
suit der Anzug, ¨-e
suitcase der Koffer, -
summary die Zusammenfassung, -en
summer der Sommer
in the summer im Sommer
sun die Sonne
Sunday (der) Sonntag
sunny sonnig
super super
super tanker der Supertanker, -
supermarket der Supermarkt, ¨-e
supper das Abendessen
for supper zum Abendessen
supposed: be supposed to *sollen
sure (certain) sicher
sure, of course klar (*colloq.*)
be surprised staunen
be surprised (about) sich wundern (über + *acc.*)
sweater der Pullover, -; der Pulli, -s (*colloq.*)
sweet süß, lieb
That's sweet of you! Das ist lieb von dir!
swim *schwimmen
swimming pool das Schwimmbad, ¨-er
Swiss schweizerisch (*adj.*); der Schweizer, -; die Schweizerin, -nen
Switzerland die Schweiz
symbol das Symbol, -e
symbolic symbolisch
system das System, -e

T

T-shirt das T-Shirt, -s
table der Tisch, -e
take *nehmen
take along *mit·bringen; *mit·nehmen
take (a university course) belegen
take for *halten für
talk die Rede, -n
talk reden; *sprechen
talk about sprechen über (+ *acc.*)
talk nonsense quatschen (*colloq.*)
tall groß; (**building**) hoch (höher, höchst-)
task die Aufgabe, -n
taste; taste good schmecken
tasty lecker
tavern die Kneipe, -n; das Lokal, -e
taxicab das Taxi, -s
tea der Tee
teacher der Lehrer, -; die Lehrerin, -nen
technology die Technik
telephone das Telefon, -e; telefonieren
on the telephone telefonisch (*adv.*)
television set der Fernseher, -
watch television *fern·sehen
tell sagen
tell, recount erzählen
tell me sag mal
tempo das Tempo
tennis das Tennis
tennis court der Tennisplatz, ¨-e
terrace die Terrasse, -n
terrible furchtbar; grausam; schrecklich
terrific herrlich; prima; toll, klasse (*colloq.*)
terrorist terroristisch (*adj.*)
test die Prüfung, -en
written test die Klausur, -en; die Klassenarbeit, -en
text der Text, -e
than (*with comparative degree*) als
thank danken (+ *dat.*)
thank goodness Gott sei Dank
thanks der Dank
thanks (thank you) danke
thanks a lot (many thanks) vielen Dank
that dass (*sub. conj.*)
theater das Theater, -
theme das Thema, *pl.* Themen
then dann
then (in that case) da (*adv.*)
there da, dort
How do I get there? Wie komme ich dahin?
there is, there are es gibt (+ *acc.*)
There/here you are. Bitte (sehr)
therefore darum
thermos bottle die Thermosflasche, -n
thing das Ding, -e
thing, item die Sache, -n

things der Kram (*colloq.*)
think *denken; meinen, glauben
***nach·denken über** + *acc.* to think about, ponder
I don't think so. Ich glaube nicht.
I think so. Ich glaube schon.
I think so too. Das finde ich auch.
think of *denken an (+ *acc.*)
think something over sich etwas überlegen
third dritt-
thirst der Durst
thirsty Durst haben
this, these dies-
thought der Gedanke, -ns, -n
through durch (*prep.* + *acc.*)
throw *werfen
throw in *ein·werfen
throw away *weg·werfen
Thursday (der) Donnerstag
thus also
ticked off (sore) sauer (*colloq.*)
ticket die Karte, -n; die Fahrkarte, -n (*bus, train, streetcar, etc.*)
tidy ordentlich
tidy up auf·räumen
tie die Krawatte, -n
time die Zeit, -en
for a long time (schon) lange
for a short time, briefly kurz
for such a long time so lange
high time höchste Zeit
on time, punctual pünktlich
take time, last dauern
What time is it? Wie spät ist es? *or* Wie viel Uhr ist es?
time (in the sense of "occurrence") das Mal, -e
at that time, back then damals
for the first time zum ersten Mal
the next time das nächste Mal
this time diesmal (*adv.*)
umpteen times zigmal
tin can die Dose, -n
tip der Tipp, -s
tired, weary müde
dead tired todmüde
to (*prep.*) an (*prep.* + *acc.* or *dat.*); nach (+ *dat., with cities and countries*); zu (+ *dat., with people and some places*)
to each other zueinander
today heute
today's, of today heutig (*adj.*)
together zusammen; miteinander
tomorrow morgen
tomorrow afternoon morgen Nachmittag
tomorrow evening morgen Abend
tomorrow morning morgen früh
tonight heute Abend
too auch; zu
too bad schade
tooth der Zahn, ⁻̈e
top: on top oben (*adv.*)
topic das Thema, *pl.* Themen
topical aktuell
tough hart (härter)
tour die Tour, -en
tourist der Tourist, -en, -en; die Touristin, -nen
toward an (*prep.* + *acc.* or *dat.*)
town (*population 5,000–20,000*) die Kleinstadt, ⁻̈e
small town der Ort, -e
town hall das Rathaus, ⁻̈er
track das Gleis, -e
tradition die Tradition, -en
traditional traditionell
traffic der Verkehr
train der Zug, ⁻̈e
train station der Bahnhof, ⁻̈e
transfer (trains, buses) *um·steigen
translate übersetzen
trash der Müll
trash container der Container, -
travel reisen
travel agency das Reisebüro, -s
tree der Baum, ⁻̈e
trip die Reise, -n
Have a good trip! Gute Reise!
take a trip eine Reise machen
trousers die Hose, -n
true wahr
try versuchen (*attempt*); probieren (*sample*)
Tuesday (der) Dienstag
Turk der Türke, -n, -n; die Türkin, -nen
Turkey die Türkei
Turkish türkisch
twice zweimal
type der Typ, -en
typical typisch

U

ugly hässlich
umbrella der Regenschirm, -e
unbelievable unglaublich
uncle der Onkel, -
uncomfortable unbequem
unconcerned unbesorgt
under unter (*prep.* + *acc.* or *dat.*)
understand *verstehen
undertake *unternehmen
undress: get undressed sich *aus·ziehen
unemployed arbeitslos
unemployment die Arbeitslosigkeit
unfortunately leider
unfriendly unsympathisch
unification die Vereinigung
unimportant unwichtig
unite vereinen
university die Universität, -en; die Uni, -s (*colloq.*)
attend a university studieren
at the university an der Uni(versität)
university studies das Studium
unknown unbekannt
unlikable unsympathisch
unnecessary unnötig
unoccupied frei
unpleasant ungemütlich
until bis
Until tomorrow. Bis morgen.
not until erst
upon auf (*prep.* + *acc.* or *dat.*)
upset: get upset (about) sich auf·regen (über + *acc.*)
USA die USA (*pl.*)
use benutzen
used to: get used to sich gewöhnen an (+ *acc.*)
useful nützlich
usually meistens

V

vacation (from university or school) die Ferien (*pl.*)
be on vacation auf (*or*) im Urlaub sein
go on vacation in Urlaub gehen/fahren
take a vacation Urlaub machen
vacation (from a job) der Urlaub, -e
valley das Tal, ⁻̈er
variation die Variation, -en
variety die Vielfalt
various verschieden
vegetables das Gemüse (*sing.*)
Venice (Italy) (das) Venedig
verb das Verb, -en
very sehr
vicinity die Nähe
Vienna (das) Wien
village das Dorf, ⁻̈er
violet lila
visit der Besuch, -e; besuchen
vocabulary der Wortschatz
voice die Stimme, -n
volleyball der Volleyball
vote wählen
voter der Wähler, -

W

wait (for) warten (auf + *acc.*)
Wait a second! Hang on! Warte mal!
waiter der Kellner, -
waitress die Kellnerin, -nen
wake up wecken (*trans.*); auf·wachen (*intrans.*)
walk der Bummel, -; *gehen; *laufen (*colloq.*)
go for a walk spazieren *gehen
wall (freestanding or exterior) die Mauer, -n
wall (interior) die Wand, ⁻̈e

wallet der Geldbeutel, -
wander wandern
wanderlust die Wanderlust
want to *wollen
I don't want to. Ich habe keine Lust.
want to do something Lust haben, etwas zu tun
war der Krieg, -e
wardrobe der Kleiderschrank, ¨-e
warm warm (wärmer)
wash *waschen
waste verschwenden
watch die Uhr, -en
wristwatch die Armbanduhr, -en
watch zu·schauen (+ *dat.*)
watch television *fern·sehen
water das Wasser
way: on the way unterwegs
weak schwach (schwächer)
wear *tragen
weary (tired) müde
weather das Wetter
Wednesday (der) Mittwoch
week die Woche, -n
for weeks wochenlang (*adv.*)
weekend das Wochenende, -n
on the weekend am Wochenende
weigh *wiegen
welcome willkommen (*adj.*)
Welcome! Nice to see you! Herzlich willkommen!
You're welcome. Bitte (sehr).
well . . . also . . . ; na ... ; nun ...
well (*adv.*) gut
get well sich erholen von
Get well soon. Gute Besserung.
well-behaved brav
well known bekannt
west der Westen

wet nass
what? was?
what kind of? was für?
What's new? Was gibt's Neues?
wheel das Rad, ¨-er
when als (*sub. conj.*); wann (*question word*); wenn (*sub. conj.*)
whenever wenn (*sub. conj.*)
where? wo?
from where? woher?
to where? wohin?
whether, if ob (*sub. conj.*)
which? welch-?
while während (*sub. conj.*)
for a while eine Zeit lang
while . . . -ing bei ...
white weiß
who? wer?
whole ganz
whose? wessen?
why? warum?
wild wild
wind der Wind
window das Fenster, -
store window das Schaufenster, -
window, counter der Schalter, -
windy windig
wine der Wein, -e
winter (der) Winter
in the winter im Winter
wish wünschen
wit der Witz, -e
with mit
with each other miteinander
without ohne
without . . . -ing ohne ... zu
witty witzig
woman die Frau, -en
young unmarried woman das Fräulein, -

wonder, ask oneself sich fragen
wonderful wunderbar, klasse (*colloq.*)
word das Wort; *two plural forms:* die Worte (*in context*), die Wörter (*unconnected*); die Vokabel, -n
work die Arbeit
work (of art) das Werk, -e
work arbeiten
worker der Arbeiter, -; die Arbeiterin, -nen
world die Welt, -en
worried besorgt
worthwhile: be worthwhile, worth the trouble sich lohnen
Wow! Mensch!
write *schreiben
writer der Schriftsteller, -; die Schriftstellerin, -nen
wrong falsch
That's wrong. Das stimmt nicht.

Y

year das Jahr, -e
for years jahrelang
yell *schreien
yellow gelb
yes ja
yes I do, yes I am, etc. doch
yesterday gestern
yesterday evening gestern Abend
yesterday morning gestern früh
yogurt der Joghurt, -s
young jung (jünger)
young people die Jugend (*sing.*)
youth die Jugend
youth hostel die Jugendherberge, -n

Z

zone die Zone, -n

Text

Page 46: Hermann Hesse, “Liebeslied” in *Die Gedichte* © Suhrkamp Verlag, Frankfurt am Main 1977; **264:** Bertolt Brecht, “Mein junger Sohn fragt mich” in *Gesammelte Werke,* Vol. 9, Suhrkamp Verlag, Frankfurt am Main, 1967. © 1964 by Stefan S. Brecht; **353:** “nachwort” by Eugen Gomringer from *The Book of Hours/Stundenbuch.* Reprinted by permission of Eugen Gomringer; **384:** “ottos mops” by Ernst Jandl from *Der künstliche Baum,* 1970. Reprinted by permission of Luchterhand Literaturverlag GmbH.; **401:** Kreisler, Georg, “Heimat” from *Ist Wien überflüssig?* © 1987 by Verlag Carl Ueberreuter, Wien. Reprinted with permission; **411:** From Mascha Kaléko, *Das Lyrische Stenogrammheft.* © 1956. Reprinted by permission of Rowohlt Verlag GmbH; **426:** Zafer Şenocak, “Ich bin das andere Kind” from *Gefährliche Verwandtschaft.* Babel Verlag, Bülent Tulay, München, 1998. Reprinted by permission of the author.

Illustrations

Mark Heng/Uli Gersiek: **Pages 11** (bottom right); **46**; **51** (page bottom, top row, left-most); **51** (page bottom, top row right); **51** (page bottom, bottom row, left-most); **76** (bottom left); **149**; **170**; **188** (bottom row, left); **188** (bottom row, right); **212**; **325**; **330**; **386**; **413**; **418**;
Ruth J. Flanigan: All other line art

Maps

Patti Isaacs/Parrot Graphics

Photographs

Page 1: Thomas Hansen; **5:** Richard T. Nowitz/Corbis; **10** (left): Kevin Galvin/Stock Boston; **10** (right): Beryl Goldberg; **11:** Thomas Hansen; **12:** Brilliant Pictures, Inc.; **13:** Thomas Hansen; **16:** ullstein bild/Granger Collection, NY; **17:** Javan Makhmali; **18:** Beryl Goldberg; **21** (top): Lawrence Manning/Corbis; **21** (center left): ullstein bild/Granger Collection, NY; **21** (center right): Thomas Hansen; **21** (bottom): ullstein bild/Granger Collection, NY; **23:** Ulrike Welsch; **28:** Thomas Hansen; **31:** Susanne Even; **35** (left): Granitsas/Image Bank; **35** (right): Beryl Goldberg; **38:** David R. Frazier Photolibrary; **40:** David Dollenmayer; **42:** Kurt Fendt; **45:** Kees Van Den Berg/Photo Researchers; **46:** Gret Widmann; **54:** Walter Smith/Corbis; **56:** Judy Poe; **59** (top): Bob Krist; **59** (bottom): Ulrike Welsch; **60:** Beryl Goldberg; **62:** Nathan Benn/Corbis; **64:** ullstein bild/Granger Collection, NY; **74** (a): Nik Wheeler/Corbis; **74** (b): David Reed/Corbis; **74** (c): Roger Wood/Corbis; **74** (d): Linda Pape; **74** (e): Thomas Hansen; **82:** Susanne Even; **84:** ullstein bild/Granger Collection, NY; **91:** Wolfgang Kaehler; **92:** Tony Freeman; **96:** Thomas Hansen; **103:** Mike Mazzaschi/Stock Boston; **107:** Thomas Hansen; **111:** Vandystadt/Photo Researchers; **112:** Karl-Heinz Haenel/Corbis; **114** (left): Judy Poe; **114** (center): Thomas Hansen; **114** (right): Wolfgang Kaehler; **116:** Bettmann/Corbis; **118**: ullstein bild/Granger Collection, NY; **119**: Thomas Hansen; **123**: Brilliant Pictures, Inc.; **135**: Beryl Goldberg; **141** (top): German School, Washington, D.C.; **141** (left): Beryl Goldberg; **141** (right): Thomas Hansen; **145**: ullstein bild/Granger Collection, NY; **164**: ullstein bild/Granger Collection, NY; **167** (top): Kevin Galvin; **167** (bottom): Thomas Hansen; **171**: ullstein bild/Granger Collection, NY; **172**: dpa Picture Alliance GmbH; **174**: Farrell Grehan/Photo Researchers; **175**: ullstein bild/Granger Collection, NY; **177**: Thomas Hansen; **182**: Susanne Even; **184**: Thomas Hansen; **189**: Thomas Hansen; **190**: Judith Bach; **192**: Thomas Hansen; **193**: Ellen Crocker; **195**: Ulrike Welsch; **198**: Judith Bach; **201**: ullstein bild/Granger Collection, NY; **209**: Susanne Even; **211**: Thomas Hansen; **214**: Kurt Fendt; **216**: Thomas Hansen; **220**: Thomas Hansen; **224**: David Dollenmayer: **225**: Bettmann/Corbis; **232**: Susanne Even; **236** (top): Ellen Crocker; **236** (bottom): Interfoto; **240**: Thomas Hansen; **245**: Helga Lade Fotoagentur; **254**: Thomas Hansen; **255**: W. Geiersperger/Interfoto; **259** (top): Thomas Hansen; **259** (bottom): Susanne Even; **260**: Owen Franken/Stock Boston; **268**: Thomas Hansen; **278**: Thomas Hansen; **287**: Beryl Goldberg; **288**: David Tumley/Corbis; **303**: Judith Bach; **310**: ullstein bild/Granger Collection, NY; **311**: Margot Granitsas/The Image Works **315**: Corbis; **316** (top): Keystone Photo/The Image Works; **316** (center): Keystone Photo/The Image Works; **316** (bottom): Bettmann/Corbis; **317**: Bettmann/Corbis; **318**: Mike Mazzaschi/Stock Boston; **321**, **324**, **334**, **340**, **344**: Thomas Hansen; **345**: ullstein bild/Granger Collection, NY; **348** (top left): David Barnes/Tony Stone/Getty Images; **348** (top right): Swiss Tourist Bureau; **348** (bottom left): Kurt Fendt; **349**, **351**, **352**: Arthur Jaffe; **353**: ullstein bild/Granger Collection, NY; **357**: Kurt Fendt; **362**, **366**: Arthur Jaffe; **368**: Premium Stock/Corbis; **370**: Ulrike Welsch; **376**: Nowitz/Corbis; **377**: Judy & Thierry Lenzin; **378**, **380**: Thomas Hansen; **381**: ullstein bild/Granger Collection, NY; **391**, **393**: Thomas Hansen; **397** (top left): Kevin Galvin; **397** (top right): Helga Lade Fotoagentur; **397** (bottom left): Stuart

Cohen; **397** (bottom right): Helen Marcus/Photo Researchers; **400**: EMI Music Austria; **401:** Alexander Šimec; **402**, **406**, **407**: Thomas Hansen; **408:** ullstein bild/Granger Collection, NY; **423:** David Dollenmayer; **415** (bottom left): David Dollenmayer; **415** (bottom right): Susanne Even; **416:** Thomas Hansen; **414:** Kurt Fendt; ullstein bild/Granger Collection, NY; **425:** ullstein bild/Granger Collection, NY; **427:** Thomas Hansen

Realia

Page 12: Ristorante Vivarium, Darmstadt, Schloß Schwetzingen, ArchiMeDes Gbr, Berlin, Berufskleidung Marx, Wetzlar; Hotel & Restaurant Zum Ritter, Fulda; **49:** © Marie Marcks, Heidelberg, Germany; **52:** Spiegel Verlag, Hamburg; **61:** Photo: Karl-Heinz Raach, Freiburg; **70:** © Marie Marcks, Heidelberg, Germany; **109:** Samuel Dollenmayer; **116:** From: Lothar Bohnert, ed. "Ausflüge in die Römerzeit," 4th edition, Bad Krözingen, 1989, p. 55; **122:** (woodcut) Fritz Kredel; **126:** (Merian magazine cover): Jahreszeiten Verlag GmbH, Hamburg; **129**: BMW NA; **130:** Matthew W. Hansen; **131** (top): Deutsche Telekom; **136**: Libri.de, Hamburg; **140**: Deutsche Schule Washington, Washington, D.C.; **143:** © Marie Marcks, Heidelberg, Germany; **150**: Freies Deutsches Hochstift – Frankfurter Goethemuseum; **152** (right): L'Oréal Paris, Marketingleitung, Düsseldorf; **173**: UNICUM Oktober 2006; **180**: Deutsche Bundesbahn; **186**: Thüringer Tourismus GmbH; **189**: ÖBB Personenverkehr AG; **197:** From: Discovering Germany by bike 2001/02 www.germany-tourism.de/e/biking.html **200**: DJH Service GmbH; **202**: Photocase; **203**: Goldener Adler; **216**: Friedrich-Schiller Universität Jena; **227**: Fuchs-Verlag; **234**: E.ON AG, Düsseldorf; **242**: Berliner Kindl Brauerei; **243**: Deutscher Taschenbuch Verlag; **244**: Accor/Suitehotel Berlin; **247**: Rundfunk-Sinfonieorchester Berlin; **249**: TIP; **257**: Die Grünen; **263** (top): Dr. Ziegler Naturkaufhaus; **263** (bottom): www.berlin-tourist-information.de; **291**: Nationalgalerie Berlin; **329**: HanseNet Telekommunikation GmbH; **336**: Langnese/Iglo; **337**: Frankfurter Allgemeine; **346**: Gutenberg Museum; **384**: Wilhelm Busch; **392**: Beck, Berlin; **404**: From: *The Complete Grimm's Fairy Tales* by Jakob Ludwig Karl Grimm and Wilhelm Karl Grimm. Copyright © 1944 by Pantheon Books and renewed 1972 by Random House, Inc. of Pantheon Books, a division of Random House, Inc.; **419:** V & S Distillers, Copenhagen, Denmark; **429**: Deutsche Post AG

Table of Equivalent Weights and Measures

Weight

1 Gramm = 0.03 ounces
1 Pfund (500 Gramm) = 1.1 pounds
1 Kilogramm *oder* Kilo (1 000 Gramm) = 2.2 pounds

1 ounce = 28 Gramm
1 pound = 0,45 Kilo
1 U.S. ton (2,000 lbs) = 900 Kilo

Liquid Measure

1/4 Liter = 0.53 pints
1/2 Liter = 1.06 pints
1 Liter = 1.06 quarts

1 pint = 0,47 Liter
1 quart = 0,95 Liter
1 gallon = 3,8 Liter

Distance

1 Zentimeter (10 Millimeter) = 0.4 inches
1 Meter (100 Zentimeter) = 39.5 inches *or* 1.1 yards
1 Kilometer (1 000 Meter) = 0.62 miles

1 inch = 2,5 Zentimeter
1 foot = 0,3 Meter
1 yard = 0,9 Meter
1 mile = 1,6 Kilometer

Temperature

0° Celsius (centigrade) = 32° Fahrenheit
100° Celsius = 212° Fahrenheit

$$°C = \frac{10\,(°F - 32)}{18}$$

$$°F = \frac{18 \times °C}{10} + 32$$